I0797930

The Broadside Ballad in Early Modern England

MATERIAL TEXTS

The Broadside Ballad in Early Modern England

Moving Media, Tactical Publics

Patricia Fumerton

University of Pennsylvania Press

Philadelphia

Published by
University of Pennsylvania Press
Philadelphia, Pennsylvania 19104-4112
www.upenn.edu/pennpress

Printed in the United States of America on acid-free paper
10 9 8 7 6 5 4 3 2 1

Library of Congress Cataloging-in-Publication Data

Names: Fumerton, Patricia, author.
Title: The broadside ballad in early modern England : moving media, tactical publics / Patricia Fumerton.
Other titles: Material texts.
Description: 1st edition. | Philadelphia : University of Pennsylvania Press, [2020] | Series: Material texts | Includes bibliographical references and index.
Identifiers: LCCN 2020004311 | ISBN 978-0-8122-5231-6 (hardcover)
Subjects: LCSH: Broadsides—England—History. | Ballads, English—Great Britain—History and criticism.
Classification: LCC PR976 .F86 2020 | DDC 821/.04409942—dc23
LC record available at https://lccn.loc.gov/2020004311

For Lian

Contents

Note on Audio Tracks and Citation Conventions

Audio Tracks: The Companion Website

Audio tracks 1–48 cited in the book can be accessed through the Audio Companion website hosted by the University of Pennsylvania Library in collaboration with the University of Pennsylvania Press, at https://repository.upenn.edu/fumerton_broadside-ballad/.

Catalog Information for Ballads

The bibliography provides a list of selected ballads (by title)—those ballads most discussed in the book—as a subsection of Primary Texts. For all ballads referenced from the English Broadside Ballad Archive (EBBA), ebba.english.ucsb.edu, including those not listed under Selected Ballads, full bibliographic information—including author (if any), library holding, shelfmark, imprint, and first lines—can be accessed by going to the EBBA website and typing the cited EBBA number in the archive's search bar. This number alone (without the word "EBBA" preceding it) is the equivalent for the database of a ballad's title.

Spelling

Throughout the book I transcribe all early modern texts according to the following rules of modernization employed by EBBA: "u" is transcribed as a "v" when a modern would expect a "v" in the spelling (for instance, "loue" is written "love"); "i" is transcribed as a "j" when a modern would expect a "j" in the spelling (for instance, "iustice" is written "justice"); and the long "s"—

which looks something like an "f"—is rendered as a modern "s." However, I provide the original spelling of titles of all works in the bibliography, for ease of searching across databases, including library catalogs (the EBBA website provides both modernized and original spelling of titles).

Capitalization

Unlike EBBA, when words in early modern ballad titles appear in all caps, I render only the first letter as a capital; the rest of the word is lowercased (this rule also applies to sequences of words that are capitalized).

Fonts

Whereas EBBA distinguishes between black-letter (Gothic) and white-letter (roman) fonts, I do not attempt to make such distinctions. However, when the original is in italics, I duplicate the italic font. Other italics inserted in the text that reflect my emphases will be so indicated. Music transcriptions of recordings, or "Music Notations," follow a different set of font rules to indicate strong and less strong musical metric emphasis (bold italics and italics, respectively).

Citing Ballad Texts

Ballad texts are cited by stanza, if the stanzas are easily countable. Sometimes, however, after the first two columns of verse, which typically appear below a large woodcut, there follows a very long, third column of many stanzas, followed by yet two more columns of verse. In such instances, citing the stanzas by consecutive numbers becomes too cumbersome. In these cases, I cite the stanzas in consecutive order up to the end of the second column of verse; I subsequently provide the column number of the verse, followed by stanza number within that column (counting down from the first full stanza, e.g., col. 3, st. 4).

Introduction

On a March afternoon in 2015, I felt the frisson of being touched by the hand of time. Seated with a colleague inside Manchester Central Library in England, having tracked to that unlikely locale two slim volumes of early modern broadside ballads (135 in total, most of them unique), and wondering how the heck they ended up in a public library in the mid-North of England, I was struck, as if physically, by a handprint some 400 years old. Small in size—only about 3″ at the widest part of the palm's darkest impression and 6″ to the height of the middle finger—the seventeenth-century hand could have belonged to a female helpmate or to a young male apprentice.[1] The inked hand is caught in motion: as it was being laid down with a slight rolling of the fingers from left to right (you can see a partial thumbprint just above and to the right of the blackest part of the hand's palm-mark); then again as a part of the hand was placed on the sheet a second and maybe even a third time. The inky hand now touches the paper more lightly and only partially imprints itself, leaving just traces of the right edge of the palm, with more thumbprints, and smudges of possibly the index and bent middle fingers (Figure 1).

Then what? We don't know for sure, of course; I don't even know for sure whether the sequence of hand actions I have described so far is accurate. But to paint a larger imaginary scenario: Perhaps the perpetrator had distractedly (or tiredly) placed his—let's go with the best guess and say *his*—inky hand on a pile of printed ballad sheets, quickly lifted his hand on realizing his error, then tried, and ultimately succeeded, to lightly pick up the marred top sheet with as little touching as possible. Let's further suppose that, alarmed at leaving his inky marks on the paper, the apprentice surreptitiously slipped the sheet deeper into the stack of broadsides, where it would not be seen by his master, or at least not right away. In this admittedly imaginative re-creation, the broadside ballad then ended up being distributed to a publisher or directly to a consumer at the printer's shop, who thought it worth buying the imper-

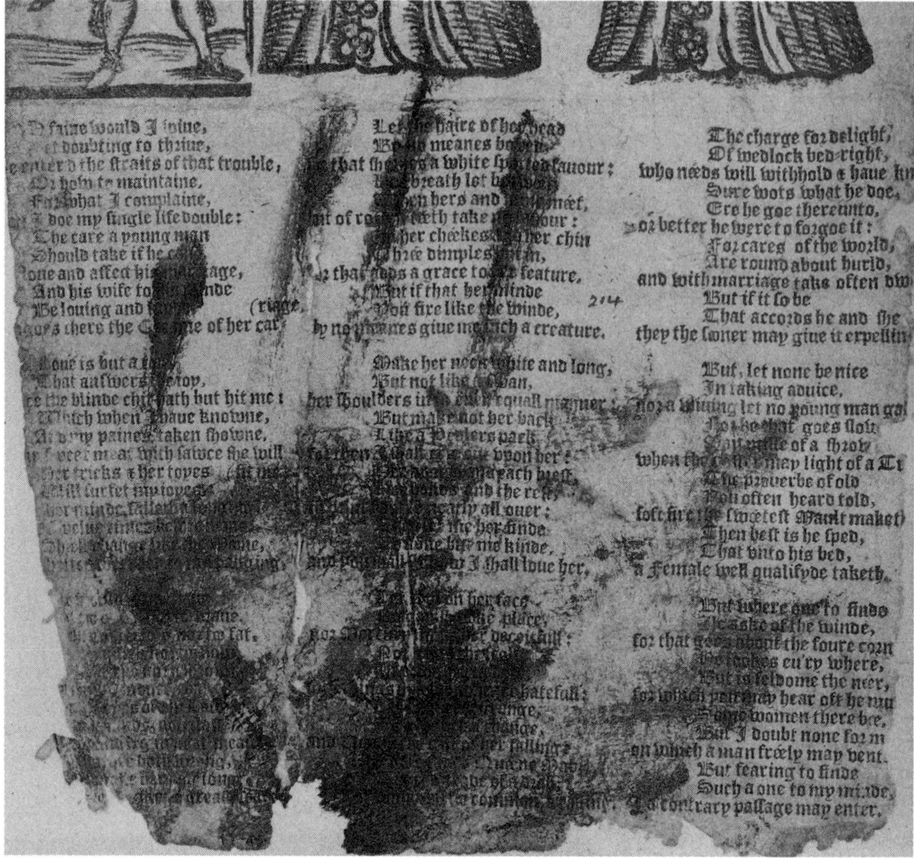

Figure 1. Closeup of handprint on "Oh faine would I marry Yet divers occasions a while make me tarry, Before he will wedd he is thrifty to see, And set downe with *Items* what charge It will be" (c. 1635), EBBA 36094. Manchester Central Library, Blackletter Ballads, 2.47, BR f 821.04 B49. By permission of the Henry Watson Music Library, Courtesy of Manchester Libraries, Information and Archives, Manchester City Council.

fect, multiply imprinted ballad for the going rate of a pence or halfpence, or perhaps—if both distributor and consumer acknowledged its imperfection—accepting it for free. The new owner repeatedly folded, unfolded, and refolded the sheet, probably carrying it on his or her person to show off to friends in passing, as evidenced by the much-torn vertical crease running through the palm and second finger of the handprint and the less damaging horizontal crease running just below the woodcut illustrations.

Then more hands—whose hands?—at some point cut the whole sheet in half, and the second half (the better half?) subsequently disappeared. What remains of the original whole sheet—or what our archival searching hands have so far uncovered—is just the first half of the ballad, with handprint,

Figure 2. Album facsimile, Left: "[Accommodation of peace,]" (c. 1642), EBBA 36411; right: "Oh faine would I marry Yet divers occasions a while make me tarry, Before he will wedd he is thrifty to see, And set downe with *Items* what charge It will be" (c. 1635), EBBA 36094. Manchester Central Library, Blackletter Ballads, 2.47, BR f 821.04 B49. By permission of the Henry Watson Music Library, Courtesy of Manchester Libraries, Information and Archives, Manchester City Council.

pasted in what looks like an act of handy restoration onto a single piece of backing paper beside the second half of another cut-apart ballad sheet. It is as if the collector were attempting not only to preserve these individual bedraggled ballad parts but, in placing the halves side by side, to restore the look of a whole ballad (although the sheet fragments are unrelated and have not been pasted onto the album page in the typical first-part/second-part order). The half sheet on the left, facing our half sheet with the handprint on the right, has been boldly numbered in ink from a previous assemblage (as was probably the case of the now-disappeared second half of our marred ballad). Perhaps at the same time that the fragments were restored into the likeness of a coherent whole, or perhaps later, they were pasted together with their restorative backing paper onto their current album page (the watermark on the album pages shows the date 1883). And at some point subsequently, they were bound together with other album pages sporting ballad sheets—some, but not all, of the sheets also with inked numbers on their second halves—into two volumes. The books were fashioned at the hands of the late nineteenth-century bookbinder Charles Winstanley (1851–1934), whose shop was located, not surprisingly, in Manchester (Figure 2).

Manchester Central Library—freely serving the general public of Manchester—opened in 1934, and the binding was likely commissioned by the library around that time. Soon after the library's acquisition of the volumes, a small seven-page printed pamphlet, authored by Robert Langton, Fellow of the Royal Historical Society, was inserted at the front of the first volume; it mostly focuses on a sampling of ballad woodcuts and the dates of some of the ballads in the volumes. Probably around this same time a librarian also added, in faint pencil, a number in the upper right-hand corner of each album page that has a ballad sheet pasted onto it (the numbers count the pages sequentially within each volume but not consecutively between the two volumes). Yet another librarian has written, more assertively in ink, though in a small hand, numerals that run consecutively between both volumes. While such multiple numbering by collectors and curators is by no means uncommon,[2] this last additional set of numbers on the assembled ballads stands out as quite odd. They are written between one of the columns of verse printed on each half sheet (regardless of whether the sheet's two halves are cut apart and whether they belong to the same ballad) and thus record the total count of ballad *halves* in the volumes, running in sequence from 1 to 190. It is as if the librarian had become so unsure of which halves belonged to which ballad wholes that she or he determinedly recorded all halves of the ballad sheets as independent units. Finally, the same or yet another librarian pasted onto a blank album page at the front of each volume hand-mimeographed sheets with yet a different numerical system. Under each number is detailed the first lines of both ballad halves appearing on an album page, even when those halves are mismatched; the lists are numbered 1 through 56 for the first volume and 1 through 57 for the second.

So many hands in motion over so many hundreds of years, leaving so many marks; so many differently assembled, disassembled, and reassembled ballad parts! And we have yet even to consider closely the constituent printed pieces that made up the broadside ballads themselves as aesthetic, multimedia, and cultural artifacts. We have yet to study the extant fragment of black-letter text in the ballad half that carries our handprint, wherein the speaker expresses desire for, but more worry about, taking a wife ("Oh faine would I marry," EBBA

36094). Coincidentally, such anxiety is physically represented in the youth's inked hand blackening out much of the text's imprinted desire. We have also yet to consider the woodcut impressions, in which the arm of a "man's man"—a man in full late Tudor armor (despite the *English Short Title Catalogue*'s, or ESTC's, dating of the ballad to c. 1635, the Caroline era)—gripping a staff of support and weaponry while at the same time extending that arm toward not just one but two look-alike "sisters"—interchangeable potential wives?—also wearing Elizabethan-period style dress. Our doubled ladies derive from a popular set of woodcuts used well into the seventeenth century; they appear more than fifty times in the Samuel Pepys ballad collection of more than 1,800 ballads alone, sometimes simply reused, and sometimes entirely recut. The wear and tear on these woodblocks in their many journeys through the press is evident in the impressions they made on the sheet: the woman in the first is missing her left eye; in the second, she's lost her signature fan (Palmer, "Cutting Through the Wormhole").[3] The middle finger of our inked handprint points to the first lady; the armed man looks and gestures to her as well, but his gaze also takes in her look-alike sister, and the fact that the woman's role is doubled by the two look-alike impressions apparently raises no concern for him, as if all potential wives are the same—in a word, interchangeable. Nor—and here we witness firsthand the need to inhabit ballad aesthetics and culture—does their interchangeability apparently raise concern for the audience/viewers. Or perhaps, given the popularity of the cuts, their recurrence provoked double the delight. At the same time, the well-worn woodcuts connect this ballad to a long tradition of printed ballad reassemblage that makes the pieces seem ever more promiscuous. Such loose arrangements (whether ironically unintentional or deliberate) further illustrate the speaker's anxious dilemma: I fain would marry, he tells us, but for the fear that, in marriage, "I doe my *single* life *double*: / The care of a young man" (st. 1; my emphases).

In fact, we might entertain a *tripling* of this young man's doubt, by way of the tune named on the ballad sheet. The tune title is prominently announced on its own line near the top of the page: "*To the tune of Drive the cold Winter away*."[4] This melody, over the course of the early modern period, undergoes numerous rearrangings, reassociations, and renamings. Though the tune is in the minor mode, its renamings alone suggest a similar upbeat optimism to our sheet's version of the title. Not only can the tune, we've comfortingly heard, "Drive the cold Winter away"; its alternate namings suggest the melody can also capture an idyllic time "*When Phoebus did rest*" (EBBA 30024), greet the glorious past with the exuberant "*All Hail to the dayes*" (EBBA 33327), and capture the momentous moment when "*General* Monk *had advanc'd himself since he came from the* Tower" (EBBA 31860). Perhaps this sense of optimism associated with the tune's titlings contributed to its notable popularity, for it is cited on twelve extant broadside ballads.[5] Of these twelve, an impressive seven specifically celebrate male good fellowship in the form of men assembled together in alehouses. Textual assertions of masculine fellowship are further witnessed by the visual dominance in these ballads of men depicted gathered around tables drinking. Such ballads would probably have been sung in a hearty, stein-swinging vein, as heard in the recording of our hand-marred ballad on **Track 1** of the online Audio Companion to this book.[6]

Is homosocial good cheer, suggested by such alehouse ballads associated with "Drive the Cold Winter Away," what our conflicted would-be lover in fact chooses over marriage by the end of this ballad? Would he have solved his indecision by forgoing the hand of marriage altogether, and blissfully hanging out with the guys at the alehouse instead, joining with them in a comfortable because noncommittal union of drink and song? The ballad, sadly, is unique, so we will never know its outcome for sure. But the tune's minor mode in voicing the cheerful words heard on **Track 1** might come into play here, inviting inquiry about the sincerity of friendships that begin and end at the tavern door. Conflicted desire expressed by tune and text are multiplied by the puzzling role played by the twin-like potential wives depicted in the woodcut illustrations. Yes, the look-alike ladies would probably have been fondly familiar to consumers; but in the context of our wooer's expression of anxious uncertainty over marriage, does their duplication make them equally acceptable—or equally *un*acceptable? We have inherited something of a media conundrum, made all the more puzzling for early moderns and moderns alike by the ballad's unsettled history of production and transmission. Marred, cut apart, preserved paradoxically as a "whole" fragment, and subject to continual re-sortings, the ballad sheet itself undertakes the role of dividedness, conflict, and uncertainty.

How, then, can we keep track of all these diverse moving parts and yet retain some grasp of the broadside ballad's conceptual unity? How can we attend at once to the extant ballad artifacts cut apart and reassembled by consumers and curators over time, as well as to the multimedia bits and pieces that originally made up those artifacts (text, woodcuts, tunes, etc.)? The latter piecemeal making, arranged and rearranged by its producers, critically occurs at the very moment of the ballad's inception. Where can we turn to get a handle on such motley bricolage-like singularity that spontaneously mixes the attuned and dissonant, the physical and metaphorical (part as thing, part as role), as well as the historical and transhistorical (then, later, now)?

To the "New Textualism," one might well answer. Certainly, my own scholarship has been solidly situated within this field of bibliographic studies since its emergence some two decades ago out of a formalism focused on the meaning-filled "law" of the "word" (to reference the adoption of the phrase in jurisprudence to indicate "literalism" versus "intent"). The formalism of the New Textualism embraces a broader and more contextualized materiality than that alone bodied forth within a refined meaning of words. It extends to include study of the formal features of the material artifacts that situate and "contain" textuality, as well as their practical making. In the spirit of this methodology, my 2008 article (reprinted in 2010), "Remembering by Dismembering," pursues the intriguing similarities in the production, dissemination, and use of databases and book-based collections. What emerges, we see, is a complicated and reverberative webwork that bridges centuries. Scholars working within the New Textualism have most recently recovered the book and other "published" material objects as precisely subject to collage-like remaking, especially by collectors and readers. Such early modern re-creative practices are beautifully generated in *Renaissance Collage* (2015) by Juliet Fleming, her coeditors, and her contributors.[7]

But despite all the exciting discoveries within this new wave of bibliographical studies, the movement cannot fully address our pressing queries. It fails on three fronts key to this study: (1) New Textualism's emphasis has been almost exclusively on the book or the compiled manuscript, to the neglect of the single printed sheet—especially if that sheet was printed for a popular, mass market. Yet broadside ballads were, after official proclamations, the most disseminated form of print in early modern England. In Tessa Watt's estimation, they were likely issued, as early as the late sixteenth century, in the millions (*Cheap Print*, 11)—only to soar in greater numbers by the early seventeenth century, prompting the attempted monopolizing of the market by the Ballad Partners (1624). (2) Though expanding significantly our understanding of reading into a "grammar" or "writing" of making, New Textual materialism typically includes only one other medium in addition to the textual: the visual. Broadside ballads, understood fully as multimedia, underscore the glaring absence in this approach: orality. (3) Finally, New Textual materialism has focused on consumers at one remove—usually individuals or governed groups—who act as collage-like readers or remakers of published "whole" texts. But broadside ballads, as we have seen, from the moment of their production in the print shop (and perhaps even prior, in authorship), were conceived, constituted, and passed on as assemblages of independent and continually rearrangeable fragments. They invited both physical and interpretative remakings at all procedural and temporal stages of their handling, even if those appropriating them might have their own private or public agendas, or both. Such expansive tactical making and remaking, which often continues into curation, goes far beyond the bibliographic focus of New Textualism.

Once we have expanded our understanding of piecemeal ballad fashioning to include the many contextualized stages or phases of participants in the practice, we might further turn for a methodological helping hand to "historical phenomenology." This approach—brilliantly espoused by Bruce R. Smith in *Phenomenal Shakespeare*—foregrounds human subjects in all their plurality as agents. But they are also understood to be experiential extensions of their material and cultural surroundings. Seen through the lens of historical phenomenology and looking beyond the dramatic stage, we recognize that the human hand, like the self-conscious human subject of which it is an extension, is willy-nilly a part of broadside ballad collage work. Smith thus aptly offers as frontispiece to his book the picture of a person touching a hand as if it were an object at one remove and yet their own (the hand playfully stamped with yet another objectified image: Shakespeare's Folio portrait; Figure 3).

This frontispiece is Smith's launching point into an argument substantiating our ability to feel emotions akin to those performed by early modern actors on the stage and, furthermore—though denuded of the enlivened

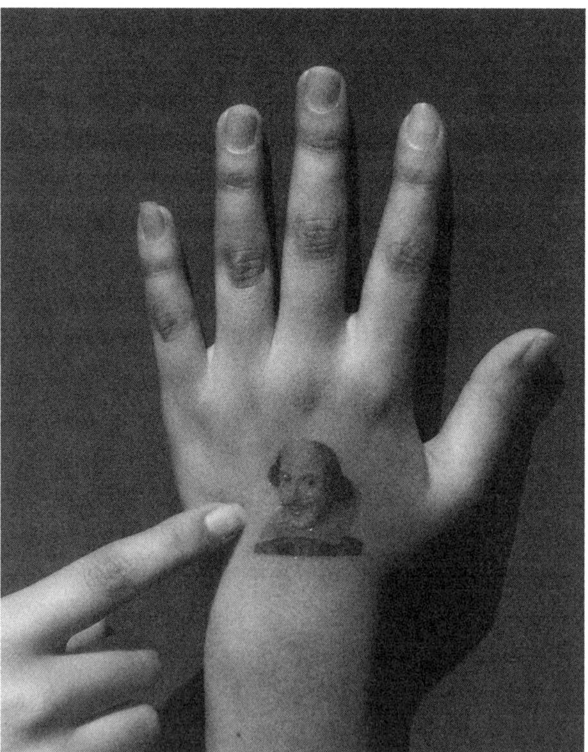

Figure 3. Shakespeare tattoo. Photograph courtesy of Bruce R. Smith, *Phenomenal Shakespeare* (Malden, MA, Oxford, UK, and Chichester, West Sussex, UK: Wiley-Blackwell, 2010), p. v. © Bruce R. Smith.

Figure 4. Jean-Baptiste-Siméon Chardin (1699–1779), *L'enfant au toton (Portrait de Auguste Gabriel Godefroy)* (1738). Oil on canvas. Musée du Louvre, Paris. Courtesy of Wikimedia Commons, https://commons.wikimedia.org. Public domain.

affect of performance—as narratively expressed through meaning-filled words printed on Shakespeare's folio pages. As much a historicized cognitive-science approach as a historical phenomenology (but who would change such a wonderfully evocative title as *Phenomenal Shakespeare*?), Smith's book often gestures to cognitive studies. In a recent article on ballads and dance ("'Ball'"), he further references Guillemette Bolens's *The Style of Gestures: Embodiment and Cognition in Literary Narrative*. Bolens opens this book with a discussion of another work of visual art, which calls attention to the human hand: Jean-Baptiste-Siméon Chardin's oil painting of *L'enfant au toton: August Gabriel Godefroy* (1738; Figure 4). This arrestingly charming portrait features an aristocratic boy with right hand poised as he intently concentrates on his spinning toy top. Though the boy stands at a writing table, he has apparently pushed the scholarly books and writing implements off to the side to clear space for play with his toy (so much for Sir Philip Sidney's maxim to teach *and* delight).

We see the boy's hand positioned on the table in the afterlife grip of a motion to initiate the spinning; we also see the top twirling away, though on a bit of a tilt, suggesting it might soon need another spin. The gesture of the boy's poised hand captures simultaneously his having spun and being ready to re-spin the top. Like an oil-painting snapshot of the boy's interaction with his environment, the picture movingly captures the essence of historical phenomenology at play, which involves an interaction of the whole person. With slightly upturned lips—the hint of a smile—and eyes fixed on the spinning top, the boy appears both cognitively and affectively fully engaged with his toy. His poised hand especially catches our eye, and, like a manicule, points to the painting's pervasive sense of ready-to-act fixation. In this seized-upon moment, the hand and the subject that it encapsulates are simultaneously active upon and reactive to an object (the toy top). As viewers, we engage with the painting in a similar way. We look upon an objectified moment of "forever" stasis that is at the same time cognitively and emotively charged as a stasis-in-action. The painting works upon us as if we were ourselves reactive objects, spinning us into a delightful anticipation sympathetic with that of the boy pictured. In Bolens's words, we experience a "type of perceptual, sensorial, and narratorial participation"—"a kinesic intelligence" (4; see also Banks, *Kinesic Intelligence*).

Great advances have been made recently in cognitive science to "get in touch" not only with the subject (as cognitive, affective, and reflexive individual) and with inter-subjects (selves necessarily interacting with other selves) but also with inter-subjects-objects (selves as influencing but also influenced by their material surroundings, including embodied things). Such multiple modes of being and action are quintessentially applied in the recent work of "distributed cognition," a field expertly historicized by Evelyn B. Tribble in her *Cognition in the Globe*. Making related strides are practitioners of affect theory, such as Melissa Gregg and Gregory J. Seigworth (*Affect Theory Reader*) as well as Patricia Ticineto Clough and Jean Halley (*Affective Turn*). Together, such studies from the wide (and, as Tribble underscores, by no means homogeneous) field of cognition offer opportune helping hands for those of us trying to understand what we feelingly see when we look at a 400-year-old handprint caught in motion on a printed page—a hand that was in motion before making the impression, at the time of making it, and transhistorically afterward, when it became an inorganic part of a continually moving assemblage and reassemblage of aesthetic material media and cultural exchanges, even after reaching its last collected resting state in a library's bound album.

While both textual materialism and historical phenomenology offer handy tools in advancing this study, neither fully equips me to tackle the complex matrix of queries I've posed. Neither quite meets this book's imperative that we stand back and take a larger survey of the cultural aesthetics involved in the practice of making and consuming broadside ballads. I want to touch the living *printing* hand, yes, as well as those other hands in motion which appropriated and reappropriated broadside ballads for their own purposes. But I also want to touch the *printed* hand and the other assembled aesthetic handiworks made, evoked, and used in the production and dissemination of broadside ballads. Or, to put it another way, I am especially invested in the historical and cultural aesthetics of the ballad-as-experience. Experiential ballad aesthetics includes appreciation of the made objects as well as of the set of processes involved in their making (pressed sheets of paper, voiced narratives and dialogues, carved woodblocks of scenes and portraits, fictional identities, and collective memories, to name only a few). An experiential ballad aesthetic also requires understanding the multimodal group of individual and collaborative roles involved in such makings (author, printer, hawker, singer, auditor, reader, collector). Experiential ballad aesthetics is, furthermore, generative and protean, capable of seemingly endless shifts and renewals. Constantly moving with the political and social times, it thrives and can be appreciated today much as in early modern England: as text, song, art, and cultural record.

The ambitious transhistorical goals of this book are, of course, doomed to failure. How can we fully inhabit the early modern felt experience of the printed hand (or the other media assembled on and invoked by the broadside ballad sheet)? How can we capture from 400 years of distance the processes of early modern printing or making hands, or the tactics of assembled publics that produced and consumed such artifacts, reshaping them, however on the fly, to their own ends? For that matter, how can we see or sing through early modern eyes and voices? We can't. But we might well capture something of those lived experiences at one remove. We might in a multimedia, close-up, and hands-on way bring the facets of ballad culture alive to the modern scholar, student, and general public. Such felt liveliness lies at the heart of appreciating the early modern broadside ballad experience. What I am suggesting, then, is something along the lines of Smith's notion of sympathetic "analogy" with the past. As Smith conceives this term, we cannot and should not attempt to capture an experience of "is" or "was" but rather an approximation or "like" experience with the past (*Phenomenal Shakespeare*, 170–71). With such cautionary caveats in hand, this book, like Menelaus, wrestles with the Protean early modern English broadside ballad in order to achieve a cultural appreciation that speaks a truth, if not *the* truth. What we discover in such intimate grappling with early modern ballads is multidimensional artifacts that convey multifarious possibilities for assemblage and reassemblage, including improvisational, tactical purposing and repurposing toward momentary publics as part of the early modern and modern lived ballad experience.

In making this statement, I gesture toward the need for a capacious enough theory, or, rather, a complement of theories, which will allow maneuverability along a spectrum of the micro- to the macro-, thing to person, individual to collective, subject to public, tactical to strategic, making to made. Only by moving between these scales, forms, and practices can we begin to fathom the curious mobility of the ballad and its parts, across its early modern contexts and across time.

The Play of Lego Blocks and Ballad Bits Ahead

I shall address in more depth in Chapter 1 the theoretical aids I prominently draw upon, beyond textual materialism and historical phenomenology, to pursue this goal. What I offer here is meant as an outline of the component bits and pieces of those theories and of the individual chapters that make up this book.

After discussing the critical history of broadside ballads and the multiple key ways in which they are "moving," I will turn first for assistance in advancing my study of broadside ballads to assemblage theory as articulated in Manuel DeLanda's *A New Philosophy of Society: Assemblage Theory and Social Complexity*. The concept of "assemblage," versus "assimilation" or "integration," as articulated by DeLanda, will be instrumental to our understanding of the nature of ballad parts. DeLanda's term, of course, is itself an appropriation and reassemblage of Gilles Deleuze and Félix Guattari's theory by the same name, articulated foremost in *A Thousand Plateaus*, wherein wholes are characterized by what DeLanda emphatically summarizes as "*relations of exteriority*" (10). By this phrase, DeLanda captures in a nutshell the philosophers' vision that things (a category that, for both them and DeLanda, also includes persons) are not innately related in a fixed or determined way—that is, they are not connected through what DeLanda refers to, with much more negative emphasis, as "*relations of interiority*" (9). Objects and living things, Deleuze and Guattari insist, are independent; they retain their singularity even when extracted from one whole and plugged into another. DeLanda's systematic theory of assemblage (which I will qualify with the view to achieving a more enlivened and thus necessarily more messy psychological, social, and historical contextualization) will be especially helpful as we begin this study. It will give us a stable framework for reevaluating the moving roles played by the, perhaps paradoxically, independent and at the same time interconnected media in broadside artifacts, as well as by the various subjects intermingled in their assembled production and consumption.

Assemblage theory, incisive as it is, however, can tend toward the taxonomic. Thus, we will also need to add a complementary approach, one that will allow us to think more flexibly about the experiential practice of ephemera. We need a mobile and adaptable theory of on-the-fly use, and for that I unabashedly appropriate and redirect to my own ends the theory of "tactical media," first advocated by David Garcia and Geert Lovink in 1996 ("ABC of Tactical Media"). I perversely invoke tactical media to talk not so much about media, which I have already dubbed multiply moving, but about tactics. In doing so, I draw on the same core of inspiration as the activists of tactical media; that is, Michel de Certeau's theory of improvisational maneuvers (as opposed to predetermined strategies), which he sees playing out within the context of lived everyday experiences and conventions (*Practice of Everyday Life*). The idea of "tactics" as quintessentially extemporaneous and mobile presents us with a crafty inroad to understanding occasional, provisional publics, which both produce and consume the broadside ballad's moving multimedia.

To this cause of impromptu making (at both the production and consumption ends, in small and large public contexts, and arising from historically specific as well as transhistorical cultures), I bring my knowledge of the project "Making Publics: Media, Markets, and Association in Early Modern Europe," a multiyear collaboration based at McGill University under the direction of Paul Yachnin (2005–10). The Making Publics (MaPs) team over this time engaged in bouts of lively contestation, to be sure. As in playing with Lego blocks, each of us sought to put together individual but variously interconnecting pieces of early modern culture to make something we individually imagined as a whole thing—the concept of "publics"; but each of us, we discovered, had a different mental picture of what the final conceptual product should or would look like. We also continually faced the reality that some pieces in our game of concept building seemed to fit together perfectly, but others stubbornly resisted that satisfactory "snap" of coming together, forcing us to reject that assemblage and to alter the shape of our imagined "whole." Still, we collaboratively produced some hard-won consensus that allowed us to fit enough pieces together confidently to identify an idea (if not the only idea) of "plural publics." Such publics, as we imagined them to be constructed, are more capacious in structure and function than DeLanda's schematic and materialist notion of assemblages-within-assemblages. By MaPs's collective definition, publics are plural, open, and fluid. Importantly, they are also always tactical. That is, in forming publics, early moderns assembled in loose, improvisational, and temporary associations *to a particular end or goal*. A final essential feature:

because they are necessarily plural (unlike the famed Habermasian "public" or the familiar "American public" or even "general public"), early modern public*s* are continually in the making (and, furthermore, in the *un*making). To pursue our Lego-block metaphor full circle: a completely constructed Object (read also Concept or Idea) can be easily disassembled or can simply fall apart.

Drawing on all the theoretical helping hands delineated above, then, we will set out in this book to catch something of the multifaceted, aesthetically rich lived experience—if only ever experienced partially, then and now—of a contemporary's imagined "whole" in the formation of early modern ballad publics. "Imagined," I argue, reads as true for contemporaries of the past as of today. Early moderns, like we modern critics who seek to understand them and their culture, were engaged in a cultural practice analogous to Lego-block play when it came to encountering and making sense of the bits and pieces of ballad media. From extemporaneously picked-up blocks of texts, illustrations, and tunes—as independent in their exchangeability or incompatibility as Lego blocks—early moderns sought to give form to their imagined whole (call it their personal understanding of the ballad experience or, more broadly, of ballad culture or of ballad publics). As with the members of the MaPs group, they particularly would have sought out those ballad parts that seemed most compatible—that is, the best fit—toward building their individual ideation. But regardless of whether the ballad media parts accommodated each other, by virtue of their uniqueness or ill-fittedness in the play of combining them, they would have caused deviations in a player's preconceived end product or form. Form, we discovered, is a process; it is not an end. Putting ballad parts together created (and still creates today) new possibilities, orientations, and imaginations. Any piece that snaps satisfyingly into another piece (or not) triggers improvisational alterations and reconceptualizations to the player's guiding imagined whole. Assembling ballad parts, like playing with Lego blocks, is full of satisfaction, frustration, and surprises.

Finally, foundational to this study or, rather, to its Spenserian Garden of Adonis—the verdantly generative matrix of my book's material—is the NEH-funded online English Broadside Ballad Archive (EBBA), cited above, which I founded in 2003 at the University of California, Santa Barbara (UCSB) and still direct. I am especially indebted to EBBA's music tool, informally named "Minstrel," developed by Erik Bell and showcased in the subsequent chapters of this book in its beta version. Minstrel functions as a kind of translation or bridge between the different demands of two modes of emphasis at play in any song; that is, poetic stress and musical stress. Minstrel bridges these modes by providing a note-to-text transcription of each ballad's sung lyrics, which unfolds on the tracks of the Audio Companion to this book. Through Minstrel, users can at once hear the musical stresses on the text and also see how the sung words are being matched to the tune, syllable by syllable. Minstrel also provides a purely instrumental, electronic track for each ballad (again, with underlaid and stressed words) through its fiddle audio component. This added feature slows the tempo of the sung lyrics for closer study. Minstrel, then, facilitates our movement beyond broad and relatively abstract discussions of a tune's notation, or themes associated with it, or the general affect of its soundscape toward a detailed critical appreciation of the often complex interchange between poetry and melody. Here again we encounter something of a Lego-block experience at play. Any generalized tune or notation at first separated from a particular poetic text, but now named as the tune of a specific ballad, necessitates that the singer try to fit the blocks of notes and distinctive text together. At the same time, the Lego-block practice of assembling tune and text into a unity necessarily morphs, in surprising and often pleasing ways, from any fixed ideation of the tune the singer might hold. And we cannot forget the eye-catching blocks of illustrations and ornament. Images as well as text and tune(s) are prominently displayed together on the early modern ballad sheet, demanding to be treated—that is, meaningfully assembled—on an equal playing field.

Minstrel is but one (perhaps one of the most important) tools that EBBA offers this project, allowing us to grapple with the protean multimedia broadside ballad as a playfully lived aesthetic experience. In fact, though, the archive's mark can be seen everywhere in this book. It is indelible, so I naturally begin and end Part I with a discussion of digital archives and their interrelation with rare books (or, in our case, sheets of broadside ballads). We find that a well-built digital archive can offer not only necessary access to but also multiple viewings and hearings of printed ballads. Furthermore, it can do so in such a way that allows a user to approximate something of the experience of average early moderns in their everyday encounters with these artifacts. We can approach the past's ballad culture as an improvisational whole made of assemblages of mobile component blocks, both intentionally and fortuitously constructed by producer and consumer alike. However, despite all that we can gain through the compendium of early modern ballad material compiled in the EBBA archive, fortified with an expansive, multimedia methodology of putting together mobile blocks of textual, visual, and oral units, my foundational thesis in this book is that a whole early modern ballad experience—both then and now—can be achieved only in the making or only *partially*.

The Broadside Ballad in Early Modern England, putting this theory into practice, is itself organized as an assemblage of case studies. Its units are as follows: first, an in-depth introduction to set in play the book's complex of mobile ideas and critical background; then, four parts in which the book's ideas are variously assembled and reassembled many times, creating a reading practice akin to searching the web and gathering together associated results, or what we often call (in resonantly metaphorical language) "hits." Within each of the reassemblable bits that make up the parts of this book, we will hear some of these hits resound again and again; even so, my selections are intended to function more like a customizable playlist than like a radio station you might surf. I have drawn an arc through an arrangement of songs, but it is by no means the only arc, and these are by no means the only available tracks. Listen to the whole lineup, if you like—or skip through; read and remake the assemblage in proportion to your own associational authority.

To delineate how the early modern experience of the broadside ballad (and modern access to it) would have been a mobile and only partial whole, I begin Part I, in Chapter 2, tracking the fragmentary assembling and disassembling of two unique but not atypical extant editions (published relatively close together) of one broadside ballad, "Mock-Beggar Hall." As we encounter Lego-like pieces of texts, illustrations, and tunes, in moving from one edition of the ballad to the next, possible meanings multiply and fracture. Chapter 3 includes, in addition, potential associative hits that contemporaries could easily and extemporaneously have made with "like" ballads to these two editions of the "same" ballad. As we will discover, such potential hits are abundant because of the impromptu, patchwork, and mobile nature of ballad production, dissemination, and reception.

In Part II, I turn to the collectors of such moving artifacts. I open Chapter 4 with a discussion of collectors' varying attitudes and practices toward collecting in the early modern period. Then, I focus on what DeLanda would call the "loose assemblage" or "network" of ballad collectors: persons of around the same generation in the seventeenth century who sought out specifically black-letter broadside ballads. What, one wonders, motivated their collecting practices? To what extent did this group, whose members knew each other and formed networks of connectedness (almost, but not quite, we shall see, actual publics), advance a specific "cause"? We find that these particular ballad gatherers shared what appears to be an intentional but also what one might dub a subliminal or visceral attraction to the visual features of the printed ballad—especially to its ornamental woodcuts and decorative black-letter typeface. At the same time, as we witness in Chapter 5, they saw themselves as embarked on an intellectual mission to record the history of calligraphy and its fraught intersection with print, especially with black-letter typeface. Our broadside ballad collectors formed a network in the service of an emotive, intellectual, and historical cause of preserving black letter (in script and in print) even as that deep-rooted and much-cherished typeface receded and transformed before their very eyes into another creature entirely: white-letter or roman type (and its kin, italic script and type).

Part III focuses on one black-letter broadside ballad collector, Samuel Pepys, who stands out because he not only assembled the largest collection of pre-1701 black-letter broadside ballads but also determinedly moved beyond circles of collecting networks in an impulsive and at times Machiavellian determination to participate in and create ballad publics. Pepys, indeed, was in many ways the epitome of the tactical consumers who surrounded him, as we shall see through his *Diary* (1660–69) and collecting practices. Of course, for Pepys, his two main foci in his *Diary* were gender and politics; they were the end goals to which most of his Lego-block assemblage of ballad parts was directed. Following his line of thinking, then, Chapters 6 and 7 view his engagement with and making of ballad publics specifically through the lenses of gender and politics, respectively.

Part IV, the final part of this study, offers—in Chapter 8—what we have been missing so far: an extensive and expansive study of one ballad as its assemblable parts build toward versions of an objectionable story, which nevertheless (or because of its horror) gripped audiences across genders and classes in its own time and for at least another 150 years afterward. The ballad, which I cite for brevity as "The Lady and the Blackamoor," was extremely popular and sensational—with no fewer than thirty-seven extant editions up to 1701 alone. By narrowing in on this plethora of variant singularity, I hope to show the ballad genre's ability to multiply move audiences both diachronically within a complex society and synchronically (across large expanses of time and space). In support of the latter point, the chapter opens with a 1789 *Georgia Gazette* news story of a massacre of a landowner's family by his black slave. What we uncover, however, is that this eighteenth-century New World newspaper report is in fact a retelling or recollection of a sixteenth-century ballad, licensed in 1569–70 in the Stationers' Register in London. This ballad, in its early evolution, tells a nearly identical story to that in the *Georgia Gazette* but to very different audiences and ends.

In the Conclusion, I open our perspective wider in a different way to look, in a variation on *Star Trek* language, where no woman has gone. That is, I consider another kind of "trans" movement, this time across genres, with a specific focus on the stage, and call into question a long-standing assumption made by modern critics: that broadside ballads are performative in the same way as (but always somehow "lesser" than) plays. Not quite, I argue. The broadside ballad, in all its multiply moving facets, offered the potential for more intensive, expansive, *and* inclusive performative interactions with publics—and indeed more unpredictable and tactical interactions with publics—than did sited stage drama. Nearly every play of the period quotes snatches of ballads; likewise, plays usually closed with a dialogue ballad, perhaps accompanied by instrumentalists and engaging the much-loved kinesic medium of dance—that is, a jig. It is thus not surprising that *The Winter's Tale*—one of Shakespeare's last plays and one of his greatest experiments in the nature of drama—almost obsessively foregrounds broadside ballads. Not only does this play feature the rogue/hawker/ballad seller, Autolycus, it fills act 4 in Bohemia with an expansive social and multimedia ballad-like experience of festivity; furthermore, even when the play returns us to the moribund court of Sicilia, it incessantly evokes scattered fragments of the earlier fully felt broadside ballad experience. Text, illustration, and tune are all as omnipresent in these last scenes as they were early on, but they are so disconnected and parceled off as to endanger the play's success. In some circles, it is anathema to surmise that even one of Shakespeare's plays "failed," even if we posit that the playwright deliberately set the play on an impossible course; to call the broadside ballad experience a roaring success (especially by comparison with the entire staged drama) would be almost unspeakable. But of such I speak.

So, like a ballad returning again and again to a familiar refrain, I end my study where I began, gesturing toward the sort of intersubjective frisson that is felt when we, unexpectedly, find some imaginative "imagined product." In support of my admittedly ambitious, expansive, and at times even spiritedly conjectural study, I can only appropriate the words of Paulina in *The Winter's Tale* and ask that "You do awake your faith." I ask not for a divinely inspired faith in my ability to bring one static medium, such as a statue, to life, but for a more human and humane faith in our shared capabilities (experiential and critical) to enliven. In these pages, I offer one collection of reassemblable ballad and drama Lego blocks, complete with my own carefully drawn instructions for what might be built, which are themselves based on my step-by-step study of what early moderns seem to have made of these many multimedia pieces as they associated and reassociated tunes, texts, and images. I hold out, in sum, the possibility that we can indeed experience something of the broadside ballads' almost infinite tactical capacity to "move," both in whole and in part.

CHAPTER 1 ❧

The Critical and Theoretical Parts

Moving, Assemblage, Publics, and Tactics

The intent of this chapter is to track the critical history that has inspired *The Broadside Ballad in Early Modern England* and to define the key theoretical terms—their geneses, interconnections, and even contradictions—upon which I draw in my declared effort to approximate something of the lived aesthetics and mobile makings of early modern English broadside ballad culture.

A Multimedia Artifact

In a necessary first step, we must fully acknowledge the key features of broadside ballads as experienced during their heyday, which is the focus of this book. By "heyday," I refer to the remarkable period in the late sixteenth century through much of the seventeenth (until the 1690s) when the appeal of decorative black-letter print on broadside ballads was bolstered by a demand for additional media that had previously only occurred sporadically on ballad sheets: specifically, woodcut illustrations and ornaments as well as melodies (conveyed through printed tune titles). Even the space that temporarily grounds these media—the sheet—expanded in the early heyday period, as folio sizes for broadside ballads grew in width and nearly doubled in length (Nebeker, "Ballad Sheet Sizes"). New aesthetics emerged with such media innovations: sheets were commonly rotated to landscape mode to better accommodate the multiplication of illustrations (often now four or more running across the top of the sheet); with this abundance of page-space, texts also became longer and more complicated (and were often now divided into two parts). One way of grasping this new heyday aesthetic is in terms of what

Jay David Bolter and Richard Grusin call "hypermedia"; that is, the coexistence—and, indeed, amplification—of familiar media formats during periods of media innovation. Such commingling of the known and the novel, Bolter and Grusin argue, has the paradoxical effect of both enhancing and fracturing a consumer's experience of "immediacy." That is, hypermedia encourages unselfconscious immersion in an enhanced aesthetic moment. At the same time, however, the phenomenon disrupts a full sense of immediacy precisely because of its hyperness. It easily triggers a consumer's self-conscious awareness of just how much artistic craft is needed to produce the illusion of the immersion (*Remediation*). Heyday broadside ballads, as we shall see, encourage such hypermedia experiences. Producers of heyday ballads immersed audiences in a multisensory imaginary at the same time as they exposed, through their tactical craft, the artifice of such immediacy. Taking the idea of hypermedia one step further, producers and disseminators of heyday ballads urged active consumer participation in the paradoxical moment of crafted immediacy. Much more so than in film, upon which Bolter and Grusin focus, heyday ballads encouraged early modern consumers to join disseminators and other consumers in reading, viewing, hearing, and/or singing these ballads. In this way, consumers themselves became wielders of ballad artifice. Heyday ballads thus functioned recursively. This fact, we will find, is critical to my study. Of course, to the extent that the ballad's multimedia are physically sited as if a family on a home-sheet (though they often move in, relate to, and jostle with other media on other sheets), one might also be tempted to dub heyday ballad media "intermedia," following Daniel Fischlin's 2014 use of the term, in the introduction to his *OuterSpeares* (3–4).[1]

Both "intermedia" and "hypermedia" aid our understanding of the intensification and multiplication of media that appeared on heyday broadside ballads. But for historical and genre reasons, which will become more transparent in the course of this chapter, I emphasize the *plurality* of heyday ballad media as our starting point, even as I embrace the interconnection of such multifold media and, for that matter, their "hyper" mode. In the heyday ballad genre, such plurality spreads from multiplication of media to the veritable smorgasbord of enticing subjects and, in fact, even to subject *positions* that the media communicate. Themes range from antique stories of tragic love and miraculous heroes to include, among many others, topical subjects of religion, politics, marriage, and sex, as well as more occasional events like the latest wonder, monstrous birth, or other in-the-news happening.

Such hyper-plurality—in which multimedia begets multiplicity of many kinds—was, of course, a marketing ploy. Innovations were introduced by producers and disseminators in an effort to expand further the broadside ballads' already considerable commercial reach. To enable such an expansive reception, however, printers and publishers had to maintain their product's affordability. Printers cut costs by using low-grade paper and ink, recycled type and woodcuts, and on-the-fly production—even at the cost of letting typographical errors or smeared print slip by. By reducing expenditure on production, the makers of broadside ballads could boast the cheapest form of literature (or art or music or culture; printed ballads were all these things). Indeed, heyday broadside ballads were typically sold for just a penny, the cost of (or less than) the price of a pint of ale or a loaf of bread. Toward the end of the seventeenth century, the price dropped even further—to half a penny. They were affordable to all but the poorest of the poor. Their catchy tunes and appealing visuals would have especially attracted the lower-order passersby who might be illiterate or semiliterate. Indeed, the textually challenged would likely have considered the ballad's swirling black-letter typeface, or what we today call "Gothic" print, to be as ornamental as the ballad's eye-catching woodcut illustrations and other decorations. Similarly, though tune titles were now being printed at the tops of the sheets, almost as an extension of a ballad's title, the increasing embeddedness of ballads in daily life meant that their presence alone could carry a message to potential consumers: no worries if you cannot read! Both ballad title and tune title—even snippets of the ballad text—would have been called out or sung by hawkers peddling their ballad wares. The tune titles, furthermore, typically referenced recognizable or easy-to-learn melodies, even though they were often dubbed "new," so that all prospective members of the audience, however musically literate, would either already know, or be able quickly to learn, the ballad's melody (or at least the peddler's version of it).

This summary of the component parts, and, for that matter, the sheer multiplicity of the heyday broadside ballad will likely come as no surprise to a scholar of the genre. But to date there has been little detailed effort to study ballad texts, illustrations, and tunes *simultaneously* and *interactively* in conversation with each other. Deserving of more attention as well is how these multimedia prompt active engagement with other related media, such as dance. As we shall see, however, it is only through concerted multi-, hyper-, and intermedia study that we can begin to track the ways in which broadside ballad artifacts moved their early modern contemporaries at so many levels: mentally, physically, and practically, as well as individually and collectively. The printed ballad tradition is animated by this inherently generative potential; the endless variety of configurations into which a plurality of media parts can be combined and recombined has always been part of their allure.

A Critical History

Until relatively recently, early broadside ballads, to the extent they have received scholarly attention at all, have primarily been studied in the cause of textuality. Moreover, critics have in large part focused on broadside ballads as a *literary* genre, which traditionalists have imagined to be a poor cousin to the more esteemed oral or folk ballad. Helpful genre studies, including those that center on literacy and the oral–print debate, include those by David Atkinson (*Traditional Ballad*; and his more recent *Ballad and Its Pasts*), David Buchan (*Ballad and Folk*), Adam Fox (*Oral and Literate Culture*), Leslie Shepard (*Broadside Ballad*), and Albert B. Friedman (*Ballad Revival*). Waving the flag of what might be called, in an allusion to the generic labels so widely applied to music today, "alternative ballads"—political ballads in white-letter (or roman) typeface—is Angela McShane's impressive annotated bibliography (*Political Broadside Ballads*). More recently, thinkers in the field of genre studies have begun to situate the printed ballad within a larger, more complicated literary history; such critics include Paula McDowell ("'Art of Printing Was Fatal'"), Steve Newman (*Ballad Collection, Lyric, and the Canon*), and Eric Nebeker ("Broadside Ballad and English Literary History").

On the oral/print debate front, Francis James Child, folklorist of the late nineteenth century, takes the pro-orality prize for most famously denouncing the two largest collections of seventeenth-century printed ballads, those of Pepys and Roxburghe, as "veritable dung-hills" (cited by Brown, "Child's Ballads," 67). Child's enormous influence set back the study of broadside ballads for more than a century. At the very same time that Child promulgated the imaginary of a purely oral folk (whose songs could only be captured, if at a remove, by transcriptions or field recordings made in remote areas, such as the Scottish Highlands or American Appalachians), other antiquarians of his generation and subsequent to him nevertheless doggedly published editions of extant broadside ballads, especially of named collections, such as the *Pepys* (Hyder E. Rollins, ed.), *Roxburghe* (William Chappell and Joseph Woodfall Ebsworth, eds.) and *Bagford Ballads* (Ebsworth, ed.). But these published collections—I suspect because they mainly offered modernizations of the texts without their accompanying images or tunes (with the odd exception of the images Ebsworth himself carved in imitation of the original woodcuts and then scattered throughout volumes 3–9, which he edited for the *Roxburghe* collection)—could not win out against the dominant appeal of the mythology of the "folk" and its "pure" orality.

In the subsequent slow period of scholarly recovery of ballads as published artifacts, there has arisen some attention not only to their genre but to their print history. Most notable are Cyprian Blagden's influential article, "Notes on the Ballad Market"; Rollins's publication of the ballad entries from the Stationers' Registers, 1557–1709 (*Analytical Index*); Robert S. Thomson's unpublished dissertation ("Broadside Ballad Trade"); and Tessa Watt's extensive treatment of the "ballad partners," a collective of licensed printers and publishers working in the seventeenth century (*Cheap Print*). Writing about the same time as Watt, in the 1990s, Natascha Würzbach (*Rise of the English Street Ballad*) introduced a kind of performance-cum-reader-response approach in her consideration of the oral communication and reception of this printed genre. The same decade saw an important shift from the oral/print debate to thematic and cultural studies of broadside ballads, interestingly often focused particularly on women. The turn (anticipated by Dianne M. Dugaw's 1989 *Warrior Women*) is evident in Joy Wiltenburg's *Disorderly Women* and Deborah A. Symonds's study of women and infanticide (*Weep Not for Me*). Continuing this trend into the twenty-first century are Mark Hailwood's chapter on women in lower-order drinking holes (in *Alehouses and Sociability*) and Sarah F. Williams's study of witches and affiliated dangerous women (*Damnable Practises*).

Significant consideration of media on the printed sheet other than the text of the broadside ballad has lagged considerably behind such textual studies, even when they are deeply historicized (as, for example, is Hailwood's book). But there has been a discernible new wave of interest in the last fifteen years in broadside ballad woodcuts and even more recently in their tunes. Typically ahead of the curve, Watt stands out for her early and extensive discussion of ballad illustrations in the context of traditional religious iconography. Subsequent important contributions to this new focus on the visual include two articles in the last decade by Alexandra Franklin ("Art of Illustration" and "Broadside Ballad Illustrations"). Following Watt, Franklin has focused on what she terms an "iconography" of ballad images; like Watt, Franklin emphasizes how stable meanings can emerge across a genre as ephemeral as broadside ballads. Equally important is James A. Knapp's "The Bastard Art" (2005), which ingeniously addresses both ballad illustrations and black-letter typeface. Knapp reminds us that woodcuts were from the beginning designed to be reused, originally in the making of patterns on textiles and then on playing cards, before they reached other popular forms such as broadside ballads.

Perhaps one of the most fascinating studies of woodcut reuse in printed ballads focuses on banderoles, or "speech bubbles," which might appear blank or variously filled in at the printer's discretion (or available time). Written by Kevin D. Murphy and Sally O'Driscoll, this study forms the introduction to their 2013 collection of essays, *Studies in Ephemera*, in which Franklin's most recent article also appears. Attention to the visual component of broadside ballads flourishes in two other articles within this edition (Burk, "Visuality of Execution," and Barrow, "Repeated Woodcut"). Importantly, also advancing the culture of ballad visual media are articles by Megan E. Palmer ("Picturing Song Across Species"), Christopher Marsh ("Woodcut and Its Wanderings"), and—considered from the digital and modern perspective—Carl G. Stahmer ("Digital Analytical Bibliography"), all published in the 2016 special issue I edited for *Huntington Library Quarterly* (*HLQ*), titled "Living English Broadside Ballads, 1550–1750: Song, Art, Dance, Culture" (221–78). Palmer and I further excitedly discovered two extant sister woodcuts hidden away at the Huntington Library, which we tracked to their larger family of woodcut impressions and their ongoing engagement in seventeenth-century topics of politics and taste, in our 2017 "Lasting Impressions of the Common Woodcut." More recently, drawing on this earlier work and EBBA's April 2018 launch of its woodcut association tool, Katie Sisneros offers shrewd observations about the similarity between woodcut reuse in seventeenth-century broadside ballads and modern memes ("Early Modern Memes").

I organized the *HLQ* special issue referenced above to foreground the broadside ballad as a multimedia experience, grouping the essays according to the three key media that constituted the ballad artifact: text, illustration, and tune. In addition to themes and images, the issue includes a section titled "Song and Performance" (279–339), featuring essays by Una McIlvenna ("The Rich Merchant"), Roger Clegg ("'Pleasant Newe Jigge,'"), and Bruce R. Smith ("'Ball'"). Like Clegg, Smith investigates the ballad as dramatic dialogue-song performed in after-play jigs, but he also returns us to the jig's more basic meaning as a high-stepping dance—we shall call upon both notions of the jig in this book's Conclusion—which can be kinesically invoked by the ballad song and lies rooted in the ballad's origins in the Old French *baler*, to dance (323).

But detailed and finely tuned attention to the melody as a crucial making part of the ballad's *poetic* assemblage—the two media of tune and text always in an active meaning-filled interchange—still lags. Chapters of two excellent books, which focus on ballad sounds (in the first instance) and tunes (in the second), demand recognition for calling more attention to the oral media of broadside ballads: Smith's *Acoustic World* and Marsh's *Music and Society*. Jenni Hyde's 2018 book on mid-Tudor ballads admirably cultivates new ground not only by looking further back historically but also by including in her early scope Tudor manuscripts as well as printed ballads and by contextualizing both, especially on the subject of news, through attention to surviving court records (*Singing the News*). Hyde also provides many music notations of tunes with text underlay and analysis of some notable features of the melody. However, she surprisingly keeps the two media of text and tune mostly separate, never grappling with the experientially charged moment of the *two-way* encounter between intermedial text and sung tune (each with its own metric demands) or highlighting ways music's meter and phenomenal accents change or charge poetic meaning. My coedited e-book, with Andrew Griffin and Carl Stahmer, *Making of a Broadside Ballad*, attempts to forge more progress toward investigating the cooperation and contestation between text and tune (in which tune was adjusted to text but also, and likely more often, text to tune). The entire study is a hands-on, experiential, and experimental inquiry into the processes of assembling, from the ground up, the component pieces of a seventeenth-century broadside ballad. As such, section 5, "Finding and Singing Tunes," attends to the many negotiations necessary to verse-writing practices.

Making of a Broadside Ballad, then, investigates theoretical issues through appreciation of the material practicalities that face (and have always faced) ballad makers in the experiential processes of composing and, for that matter, singing broadside ballads. This practical focus differs from Marsh's book, in large part followed by Hyde's, to the extent that Marsh adopts primarily a thematic approach to ballad tunes. His methodology tends to produce something of an iconographical reading of music (rather like Franklin's work on woodcut illustrations). In the last section of his chapter on melodies, "Meaning by Associations," for example, Marsh posits consistent responsive codes that are communicated through specific tunes—they are lascivious or villainous or lamentable or godly, for example. This is how he sees the melodies variously understood as well as adapted or even parodied by producers and consumers of their time. My focus in *Making* on the practical experience of making broadside ballads not only allows for some stable thematic cross-ballading of tunes but also exposes the instability of any ballad experience effected by the convergence of text and tune, especially as the ballad evolves—that's one reason the tunes kept being renamed, after all. Also, notably untouched in Marsh's and Hyde's books is the wide array of ways in which tunes might be sung in interplay with the other media that comprise the ballad artifact, most importantly the visual; taken together, the interaction of text, tune, and illustration allows for a wide range of tactical resources at the disposal of producer and consumer.

As a correction to all previous unifocal or bifocal studies, *I seek to explore the multifold ways the media of broadside ballad artifacts interact with each other within and between ballads, as well as within and between audience members as they respond in the form of a plural collectivity or publics to a multimedia cultural experience.*[2]

Admittedly, in calling for *fully* acknowledging broadside ballads as multimedia artifacts, I am demanding that scholars juggle many balls at once, some of which lie outside our disciplinary comfort zones. Deft handling of so many moving parts also inevitably leads to a lengthy, indeed, potentially unending investigation. But if we don't at least attempt such an expansive analysis, as in the many case studies I offer here, we lose the significant plurality of meanings these cheap but media-filled and interactive artifacts could have conveyed to the vast sector of early moderns. For that matter, we lose the enlivening "connect" for many moderns, whether scholars, students, or the general public, who all enjoy broadside ballads, I would argue, precisely for their engaging multimedia appeal.

Much of the work that precedes this study has been invaluable in paving the way, even in prompting and providing a sense of urgency for my own work, *The Broadside Ballad in Early Modern England*. Thanks to my predecessors, we are well poised to jump-start a broadside ballad revolution.

The "stuff" of such a revolution derives in large part from major digital advances that have recently made artifacts that were previously hidden away and even, as Smith remarks, "largely forgotten" ("Shakespeare's Residuals," 206) now publicly available. A trailblazer in this cause—appearing on the Internet as early as 1999 in its first-generation interface—is the Bodleian Ballads Online (BBO, http://ballads.bodleian.ox.ac.uk/). The BBO contains basic cataloging and images digitized from microfilm of the library's own holdings of approximately 1,600 early broadside ballads (with many more from later periods). The site also offers some 300 sample color images. But its mostly black-and-white images, digitized quick-and-dirty, diminish full user appreciation of the visual appeal of heyday broadside ballads. The website also lacks the important media component of tune recordings. Another digital resource well-known to scholars, Early English Books Online (EEBO, proquest.com/go/eebo), has its own drawbacks. Although the database is extremely large—EEBO aims to provide digitized microfilm images of all works printed in England before 1701, regardless of genre and even language—its resources are not freely available to the public; indeed, access to the website is expensive even for libraries to purchase. Furthermore, while it offers a sophisticated variant spelling search, EEBO's cataloging is rudimentary at best. It is also missing 50–60 percent of extant early English broadside ballads. Most egregious of all—at least from the perspective of capturing each printed item as a unique instance of the assemblage of component parts drawn from multiple kinds of media—EEBO typically collapses all "editions" of a given ballad (versions of which can be wildly variant) into a single entry and image. Like the BBO, it further lacks recordings of the ballad tunes, thus once again significantly diminishing a user's ability to approach anything like a full-bodied broadside ballad experience.

It is to rectify these deficits in digital access to early printed ballads that in 2003 I founded and have since directed the English Broadside Ballad Archive (EBBA, http://ebba.english.ucsb.edu). Housed in the English Department of the University of California, Santa Barbara, and generously funded by the National Endowment for the Humanities since 2006, EBBA will, by about 2023–24, provide open access to all the estimated 12,000 extant instances of pre-1701 English broadside ballads. In building this digital archive, I have benefited over the course of seventeen years from hands-on access to every broadside ballad the website makes available. I have also gained much insight from lively interactions with the EBBA team and enlightening, if also sometimes frustrating, behind-the-scenes makings and remakings of the site's offerings (which require continual rethinking of "What *is* a broadside ballad?"). Importantly for this book project and scholarly work generally, the EBBA website, unlike the others cited above, emphasizes and provides access to all the media that contribute to a full-bodied heyday broadside ballad experience. In fact, the site offers a three-pronged approach that simultaneously privileges text, illustration, and tune. In terms of visual media, EBBA uniquely renders facsimiles from high-resolution TIFF color images, allowing users to discern fine details in paper, text, and woodcut impressions—the woodcut images now searchable through our digital impressions recognition tool, Arch-V. The difficult-to-read black-letter text is also transcribed but not as a separate medium. Rather, the transcribed poetry is inserted via Photoshop into the facsimile sheet image of each ballad to create what we dub a "Facsimile Transcription." This viewing of the text not only allows modern users easy readability—of the kind enjoyed by the literate in the ballad's time—but does so without losing sight of the ballad's equally important visually compelling features. Users might also read and view the ballad while listening to it being sung, thus entertaining all three component heyday ballad media at once. Crucial for research that embraces the plurality of broadside ballads, as we shall discuss further in Chapter 2, EBBA's advanced search tool is extremely nuanced. It offers users not one—because there cannot be just one—but a wide range of pathways "where to begin" (Smith, "Shakespeare's Residuals," 216).

In the spirit of *The Broadside Ballad in Early Modern England*, EBBA attempts to capture not only all extant editions of broadside ballads pre-1701 but also something of the multifaceted early modern ballad experience, including many ways of reading as well as viewing and hearing broadside ballads. But EBBA cannot do what this book's theoretical and critical exploratory project attempts to offer; the website is more a tool or an aid for broadside ballad research and appreciation, as it was intended to be, functioning something like a fertile ground as well as a maze of pathways that scholars might independently and critically follow, and from which they might glean means for more penetrating multimedia inquiries.

One of EBBA's latest methodological tools, Minstrel, makes its beta debut in this book. A new critical resource for understanding the music dimension of broadside ballads, Minstrel was developed at the inspiration of EBBA's music specialist, Erik Bell. This resource provides modern notational transcriptions of the recordings of ballad tunes as they were adapted by a particular singer to a specific ballad text (and vice versa). The text is underlaid to the notation so that the poetic syllables or words line up visually with the notes to which they are sung. In addition, the underlaid text is innovatively rendered so as to indicate where the musical-metric, as opposed to the poetic-metric, stresses lie on the sung words (with ***bold italic*** indicating a strong music emphasis and *italic* indicating a less strong one).[3] Revealing how the tune emphasizes words and syllables is critical for those of us trained in poetic scansion but not in musical meter. What Minstrel shows, we see, is that the poetry and tune often metrically complement each other but at other times just as tellingly reveal a tension or pull against each other, complicating meaning. For the purposes of the present volume, I provide a separate online Audio Companion to my printed analyses, available at https://repository.upenn.edu/fumerton_broadside-ballad/. This website consolidates all sung recordings discussed in this book that are derived from EBBA and other sources, as well as the many variations upon those recordings which I introduce to open critical analyses of tunes, texts, and, yes, even illustrations, since these media interact dynamically with each other. The Companion furthermore offers slowed-down audio files of the music transcriptions of the recordings (Minstrel's next instantiation will render these transcriptions as MIDI files in MEI/XML notations), so readers and listeners can follow easily and carefully along. The audio files of the transcriptions play to an electronically generated sound of a fiddle—the early modern instrument most associated with the lowly and, indeed, the one most likely taken up to accompany the singing of a popular ballad when instrumentation was near at hand (the major exception occurring in more elaborate post-Restoration theatrical productions and in the homes of the higher sorts).

Minstrel's music transcriptions made from actual recordings of the ballads, it is important to note, are often very different from the music transcriptions provided by Claude M. Simpson (*British Broadside Ballad and Its Music*). Simpson is the recognized authority on seventeenth-century broadside ballad melodies. At the same time, though, Simpson's notations are printed without any accompanying text. Often, he has adopted them from one of the many editions of *The Dancing Master*, a work of extraordinary popularity that was published in many editions by John Playford and his successors, from 1651 until c. 1728. Simpson also draws on other book and manuscript sources of the seventeenth century and earlier. The majority of these were written down for more cultivated or musically literate contemporaries, who favored the lute, cittern, or virginal as accompaniment over the lowly fiddle. But most people at this time could not read music. Thus, popular ballad songs, although often derived from dance tunes, and often even originating in foreign and native court culture before their widespread dissemination, tended to be passed on orally to the masses.

If popular culture was primarily an oral culture, as the folklorists would certainly argue, why, you might ask, draw on any of the notational sources of this early period at all, as do Simpson and EBBA? Why refer to the recordings as "popular" broadside ballads, given that most of their extant sources were clearly made for the more elite (and often specifically notated for instrumentation favored by the upper sorts, such as the lute)? How reflective can they be of popular oral tunes, especially when such are sung a cappella, as would typically have been the case of broadside ballads sung on the streets or even in the workplaces of early modern London (whether such workplaces are public or, as in the labor of spinning, domestic—which, like many work activities, required both hands)? Posing as a kind of devil's advocate, Christopher Marsh has raised variations of these queries in an email exchange with me. He also noted that a musical instrument, like the cittern, can attain with more ease a wide variation and range of notes than can the average human voice. Again, then, one might ask, can we really assume that notation for such an instrument reflects popular song? This critique, though indeed devilish, is certainly valid. But some of the notated tunes for instrumentation, such as "Rogero," also include underlaid text, indicating that the music notation was meant for singing as well as for playing. In addition, pre-1701 music notation associated with ballads is notably less florid than that of later centuries. The simpler rendering of such early popular melodies suggests that such tunes could well have derived from heard songs, the melodies of which were copied down for instrumental or dance use, as opposed to the other way around.

Certainly, most of the ballad notations Simpson discovered—and those EBBA has unearthed that Simpson missed—lie well within an octave or twelfth range, which would be comfortable for the average singer, even if vocally untrained. When there appears a challenging complication in the written notation, furthermore—such as a sudden series of variations in the notes or a leap to a difficult high note—that does not necessarily exclude the music's origin in and adoption from popular song. People of the earlier periods—for whom live singing, whether solo or communal, was an ever-present feature of both the home and the workplace—could well have taken up the challenge of singing tricky melodies. As in our singing along (or not) to the usually a cappella rendered "Star-Spangled Banner," with its frequent leaps in notes, especially between phrases, there would have been always the choice whether to take up the challenge.

The element of choice involved in the lived, experiential singing of broadside ballads is why transcriptions of the sung versions are so important to this study; they illustrate at least one singer's decisions, even if she or he is not 400 years old, in adapting tune to text and text to tune. As an example, we might return briefly to our hand-marred ballad discussed in the Introduction, and its tune, "Drive the Cold Winter Away." I provide below the notation for the melody from Playford's *Dancing Master*:

In his modernization of Playford's music (198), as of other early modern tunes, Simpson adds bars to indicate measures and separates the long line of music notes into several divided lines of grouped measures. He roughly divides up the notation to fit imagined lines of poetry to which the tune might be sung (four measures—a measure defined by the notes between vertical lines—approximately being equal to two lines of poetry). But Simpson has no specific poetic text in mind.

Bell, adopting strategies similar to Simpson's but taking them several steps further, attends to the lyrics of individual ballads while also showing how the music can be understood in modern notational terms. Employing Minstrel, Bell transcribes a recording of the melody as sung to a designated poetic text—in this case, to our hand-marred ballad's first stanza—which can be heard on **Track 2** of the Audio Companion. The notation thus reflects the choices the singer made in necessarily bringing to a kind of harmony tune and text. The poetic text is, furthermore, carefully underlaid to the music notation and signposted to indicate where the musical stresses lie. A fiddle audio file of the transcribed recording is also provided (for the transcription below, available on **Track 3**):

Bell's transcription of his recording of our hand-marred ballad stands out immediately as different from Playford's. I refer to other than the obvious change in pitch that he makes in order to fit the tune to his baritone voice, shifting the key from D minor to C♯ minor (which brings the melody down a half step).[4] The striking difference lies in Bell's transcription of the twelfth measure which concludes line 6 of the eight-line stanza (the end of the third line of music notation above), where Bell sang "his marriage." Playford at this point in his abstracted tune notates a large leap of a minor tenth, from D4 (on the word "his") to F5 (on both syllables of "***mar**-riage*"). But Bell altered this big leap to a more modest one, from C♯4 to E4. He did so because, as a singer, he found the minor tenth leap to be both difficult and awkward to sing at the end of the musical phrase. His change in singing the notation was both a practical and an aesthetic choice: The note leap is not out of Bell's vocal reach and, indeed, you can hear him singing that high leap, from a C♯4 to a E5, in accord with Playford's notation, on **Track 4** of the Audio Companion (fiddle audio, **Track 5**). Most fascinating from the perspective of the ballad's text is the fact that the high note falls on the first syllable and extends to the second syllable of—within the context of the narrative of the ballad—the most important word in the song, and certainly in the stanza, "mar-riage." Both the poetic meter and the musical meter strongly stress the first syllable of this word, underscoring the would-be lover's consternation over whether to choose marriage. The music's meter drives his (di)stress phenomenally home by repeating the high note and doing so on a less stressed syllable, "riage," which, because of the repetition in notes and its placement at the end of a measure/line, actually gains power: "***mar**-riage*" is heard more like "***mar-riage***." In sum, the high leap as notated in Playford, when sung within the context of our hand-marred ballad and the singer's choosing whether to "go for it," could be most telling of the choice facing and even made by the narrator. Within the context of the metrical, poetic, and phenomenal stresses, the singer's/narrator's choice extends well beyond simply practical or aesthetic preference.

Should the singer embrace the high note, or reject it? Should the narrator marry, or not? Is the choice arbitrary, like the doubling of the ladies in the woodcut impressions (look-alike variations upon the same woodcut)? One can imagine a fellowship of men in an alehouse, perhaps by this point a little tipsy, having great fun trying to hit the high note, and even yelling it out, as Kenneth Slovik suggests the boozing Anacreonic club would have done in singing the high notes of the eighteenth-century English original of our national anthem, then titled "To Anacreon in Heav'n" (cited in Macko-Hardy, "Why Is the National Anthem so Hard to Sing?"). In sum, the choice of how to sing the music notation at this point in the tune source for our hand-marred ballad, considering the word voiced on the high note—"marriage"—speaks volumes.

This one instance—and there is much more going on in the interaction of text with tune in this ballad—is why my providing notations of the recordings with music stresses of at least parts of ballad texts as sung is so important to our understanding the possible tactics adopted by early modern hawkers and consumers of broadside ballads. The source notation, with no text underlay of any kind, as adapted by Simpson into "standard" notation, simply cannot capture the necessary decisions and adjustments that must have been made by early modern and modern singers, and even, if instrumentation happened to be on hand, by the accompanying musicians. Even if the sung version is a rendering of a melody orally passed along, as opposed to a reading of its notation (which requires musical literacy), the dilemma would be handed down as well. Singers of the ballad "Oh faine would I marry" are faced, as is every American encountering the leaps of notes in our national anthem, with a critical choice, and the options vary according to the singing of a specific ballad's verses, not some extracted notation of the tune. When the illustrations on the broadside ballad sheets are taken into account as well, potential meanings and associations for readers/viewers/singers/listeners proliferate nearly endlessly.

The aim of this study is foremost to make use of all newly available resources, whether secondary or primary, and whether—in the latter case—handwritten, printed, or online, in order to gain a more meaningful encounter with representative multimedia broadside ballads, which were also *the* most printed and widely disseminated artifacts of their time. In so doing, I offer the first book-length work that devotes extended critical analysis, within modern publishing limits, of the key interactive media (text, art, and song) that make up ballad aesthetics and their everyday production and cultural reception. I also seek to expand our understanding of printed ballads temporally and geographically as they shape-shift their way over hundreds of years (well beyond the scope of EBBA) across classes, genders, collectors, continents, and genres.

Multiply Moving

To understand the complex aesthetics and experience of the broadside ballad is not only to recognize the artifact as a single sheet assembled of individual and interactive multimedia, which calls for an engaged and perhaps differently approached interchange of human subjects, as suggested above, but also to acknowledge that the component media sung were continually *moving*.

After much deliberation, I have chosen this term—*moving*—as being most accurate in describing the material and cultural features of the broadside ballad genre. In my 2002 article, "Not Home," which took shape as I was also working on my book on the mobile poor, *Unsettled* (and with the idea for this book bubbling in the back of my brain), I described the migratory and patchwork character of the broadside ballad as what I there termed "an aesthetics of displacement" (504). By the publication of *Unsettled* in 2006, as if in sympathy with the early modern mobile poor (who extended across a large swath of the middling to low population), my terminology had morphed into "an aesthetics of unsettledness" (146).

Today, after an intensive dozen more years immersed in the features and culture of broadside ballads, I have reinvented my terminology yet again and dub the phenomenon "an aesthetics of *moving media*." But whatever one's descriptor of preference (or priorities for choosing it),[5] the important point is to recognize, as I shall further detail here, that the early modern broadside ballad, more than any cultural artifact of the early modern period, can only be understood as *moving*, in parts and in wholes. Of course, all writing and all printing (and, as Walter J. Ong argues in *Orality and Literacy*, all recitation as well) are to some extent fragmentary and unstable. As I note in the Introduction, the New Textualism has become particularly attuned to the collage-like nature of books made not only by printers and publishers but also by readers, in their engaged cut-and-paste practices that extend well beyond the much-studied commonplace books and miscellanies of the period. In Fleming's words, "Early modern readers cut as they read, and read by cutting, printed books" (*Renaissance Collage*, 445–46; see also Knight, *Bound to Read*; and, thinking more expansively, but still along the cutting line, Smith, *Shakespeare|Cut*). Note here, however, as I point out in the Introduction, Fleming's focus is on the book, even if manuscript pieces or printed slips might contribute to making that book.

We fascinatingly find flashes of scholarly attention beyond the compiled or printed book (however cut-and-pasted) in some manuscript studies. As early as 1981, Paul Zumthor coined the term "*mouvance*" (or movement) to describe the high level of textual variation or "essential instability"—rearrangings, replacements, and modifications—typically found in medieval manuscripts, especially in anonymous texts before the end of the fifteenth century, as they mutated in the course of scribal and oral transmission ("Intertextualité et mouvance," 160).

But we encounter a category unique unto itself in the moving multimedia of the broadside ballad, which is something of an everywhere protean creature, seemingly impossible to pin down because its making is always in process, its component fragments always interchangeable, and the resultant product always multifariously on the move. We shall pursue such moving aesthetics here. To do so, we must not give up the Menelean effort to pin down as an interpretable identity such shape shifting; however, at the same time, we must admit that the Menelean cause can succeed only momentarily, perhaps producing but a glimpse or trace of a meaningful or interpretable whole, given all the cultural and affective moving parts of broadside ballads with which we must grapple.

Before proceeding to wrestle with our broadside ballad Proteus, though, I must acknowledge a possible unintended misdirection in my terminology. In describing broadside ballads in their multimedia as constantly "moving," I draw on a term closely associated with modern film and animation studies. In this field, the idea of moving specifically refers back to the term "*motion* picture"; that is, it denotes an art composed of moving frames of images experienced by the viewer as *action*. But if "moving" has been revived for the purposes of present-day media critique, the term is nevertheless of value for our investigation of early modern popular print culture because it connotes many fundamental features that help identify the broadside ballad's identity, as we shall see. First, we must address the ballad genre's "moving" elements, which are indeed multiple—including material, aesthetic, cognitive, and emotive as well as spatial and temporal forms of movement. With a fuller idea of such media as moving, we will be better positioned to pose theoretical approaches that will further advance the goals of this book and, if only momentarily, pin them down.

(1) At the level of assembled parts on the sheet, "moving media" connotes the sense that text, illustration, and tune title, as well as other features of the broadside ballad, such as its title and imprint, are gathered together only tem-

porarily for a one-time job. Like the media appearing on the ballad fragment with a handprint on it, which we have already encountered, the component media of a printed ballad are assembled on the sheet in a bricolage, makeshift fashion. They should thus be understood as potentially rearrangeable parts that could at any moment, as if individuals, go their separate ways from their coworkers (other component ballad parts), even in the process of a single or, more often, subsequent print run. These singular entities, furthermore, acquire "roles" that in miniature epitomize and make more material the roles of individual human contributors invested in bookmaking, as envisaged by Adrian Johns: They are like the many distinct persons active in the printing process who, despite the ideal of collaboratively working together, in fact are subject to the destabilizing contingencies of the printing process (*Nature of the Book*, 3). Indeed, far more than the pages of science books for the highly educated that are Johns's focus, the pieces of cheap broadside ballads produced for and disseminated to the masses were assembled and pressed out in extreme haste, corrected and altered hurriedly on the fly, and continually disassembled and reassembled to keep production costs low and the "newness" of the wares alive.

It's hard to know to what extent the human collaborators—author, publisher, or printer (or woodcut carver, compositor, or apprentice)—had a hand in putting together the movable fragmentary parts that made up any one broadside ballad. But likely all of these persons (and even more) were to some extent engaged, and just as likely the scope of involvement varied from ballad to ballad. The extent of participation would also have depended on the nature of the relationship between the individual "makers." Perhaps sometimes a publisher gave the printer a manuscript copy of a ballad text, including tune title, and told him what woodcuts to commission or use. More likely, the printer would have chosen the cuts himself from his available stock. And, at other times, the publisher might have simply handed the printer a copy of an already circulating ballad and have instructed him to repackage it and make it look "new."

(2) "Moving media" also refers to the fact that producers of broadside ballads continually changed the artifact's aesthetic features and subject matter over time, even during its pre-1701 heyday. This constant aesthetic remaking can create extreme difficulty for modern scholars wanting to differentiate firmly between broadside ballads and other single-sheet verses or poems that increasingly proliferated in this period, some of them deliberately constructed as ballad look-alikes (with the intent of capitalizing on the broadside ballad's popularity). Based on selections made by seventeenth- to nineteenth-century contemporaries for their self-titled "ballad" collections, it would appear that most of these antiquarians were themselves flummoxed by the same problem:

What is a broadside ballad? (Fumerton, "Digging into 'Veritable Dunghills'"). Collectors of black-letter broadside ballads in the seventeenth century (Samuel Pepys, Robert Harley, John Bagford, Anthony Wood, and others) were acutely aware, even as they made their collections, that they were grappling to pin down an artifact "on the move," changing its aesthetic form before their very eyes. Moreover, they were highly attuned to a larger movement in process wherein print—especially black-letter print—and handwritten script were continually intersecting and diverging (a topic I address more fully in Chapters 4 and 5). It wasn't only the aesthetics of broadside ballads that were on the move, however; so was the targeted audience. As McShane has shown (*Political Broadside Ballads*), white-letter ballads tended to speak to more socially and politically erudite groups. Especially in the Restoration, we also find courtiers who took up the fad of writing in, and even parodying, ballad formats (like the Earl of Rochester, as we shall see in Chapter 7). The history of broadside ballads is the history of a hydra whose many aesthetic heads and body parts are always in motion.

(3) "Moving media," in addition, means that broadside ballads were not simply sold in printers' and publishers' shops or in their book stalls (though they *were* sold there), but that they were also disseminated on the streets of London by apprentices and hawkers, as well as far into the countryside by chapmen, who carried them in their packs along with other trifles, including little chap (or cheap) books. Watt estimates that broadside ballads were, as of the late sixteenth century, likely circulated in the millions (*Cheap Print*, 11). That is, they were prolific and everywhere both on view and heard.

A person could not walk from point A to point B in London without seeing ballads pasted or pinned up on posts or on walls of public buildings, peddled outside as well as inside public theaters (as Edward Filmer complains as late as 1698, 32), or displayed in other commercial spaces such as alehouses. They also occupied more liminal public/private spaces, such as workplaces; they even moved into the interior spaces of the middling and poor, where they might be proudly displayed as art—the poor man's oil painting, if you will. You would furthermore have heard them almost anywhere being sung. Reinforcing their eye-catching postings, hawkers singing broadside ballads belted them out to compete on public streets with criers of other marketable stuff or in more targeted public spaces where people typically gathered, such as the marketplace or scaffold. Craftsmen, such as shoemakers, blacksmiths, and weavers, readily sung them to mark the rhythm of their repetitive work as well as to pleasingly pass the time. Women sang ballads to the same ends when milking cows or scrubbing clothes at the local washing hole. Just as broadside ballads decorated domestic spaces, so they were heard there too; again, like their more publicly placed male counterparts working in shops to ballad rhythms, maids and wives in the home sang as they spun their wheels. But broadside ballads could also have been heard voiced anywhere in the home by any and all members of the household—servants, children, parents, and other relatives—for the sheer pleasure of singing a familiar or tantalizing new tune.

In their multifaceted everywhereness, broadside ballads became a lived part of day-to-day experiences and movements. Aiding their infiltration into all facets of daily life was their sheer affordability, as we have seen. Being so low-priced, they traveled the uncertain course of cheap ephemera. While many printed ballads were cherished and preserved, their status as ephemera subjected most broadside ballads to a short life, like the mayfly or 24-hour fever cited as the earliest usages of "ephemera" (*OED*). They were here, there, and then gone in a flash. They were subject to deterioration more than other printed artifacts, such as books, due precisely to their being made from the cheapest and flimsiest paper. They could fall apart through their much handling—not only being carried and passed around but, in the process, repeatedly folded and unfolded—and though perhaps finding a resting place in being pasted up on walls, they might later be ripped down or whitewashed over. Finally, as a major part of the mobile daily activities of early moderns, these cheap ephemera were much recycled. Sometimes printers themselves recycled them by issuing new ballads on the versos of foul sheets or on the backs of ballads deemed out-of-fashion. But consumers in their own ways freely transmuted or repurposed broadside ballads on a daily basis. Old or sufficiently consumed ballad sheets were recycled into pie or bird-cage lining, kindling, or even toilet paper. Given their immense reusability and disposability, it is remarkable that as many as 12,000 broadside ballads have survived from the period!

Their infiltration into people's day-to-day lives—whether through on-the-spot multimedia consumption or repurposing; through intimate handling/voicing/display or more public forms of dissemination—made broadside ballads "everywhere" artifacts in yet one further way. They were known to everyone of all social sorts. Though targeting the middling to low, they clearly also appealed to the very literary and social elite who showed their cards by readily reciting the broadside ballads they often openly disparaged. Not coincidentally, then, it was well-educated antiquarians from the middling to higher sorts who were most responsible for preserving by collecting broadside ballads. Even Sir John Cornwallis, who tells the story of wiping his bum with torn-off halves of lewd ballad sheets, notably mentions reading them first (Marsh,

Music and Society, 233, 263).[6] Such multifaced exposure to broadside ballads also made them pliant to "remakings" within social contexts, as we shall explore in Chapters 6 and 7.

(4) "Moving media" also refers to the way in which, at the level of the individual sheet, the interchangeable aesthetic parts that constituted a broadside ballad were additionally moving in being subjected to further physical fragmentation and mutability once they left the shop. Ballads would often be promoted publicly in pieces. As Rollins explains, eye-catching parts of the ballads—titles and fragments of the whole sheet—would be placed "in cleft sticks erected for the purpose [that is, for advertising] in prominent places," or they would be pasted "on public posts, walls, or church doors." Otherwise, he notes, the seller risked the danger of the whole ballad being "read and memorized or even stolen" ("Black-Letter Broadside Ballad," 325). Alternatively, ballad sheets might be waved up high by hawkers on the streets or within public places, in a full-sight blur for the passersby to view only partially, as the sellers attempted to draw attention to their wares. In belting out the tune, the predominant strategy for hawkers was also piecemeal. They might only sing the first half of the ballad, in the case of two-part ballads, or just call out the title and stanza-length subtitle of verse below the title, when it became the fashion to format ballads that way (from about 1625 to the end of the century, excluding the nostalgic return to two-part ballads from the 1670s through the 1680s). These tactics impelled people to pay in order to get, and be able themselves to sing, the remaining part or "whole" ballad ("Black-Letter Broadside Ballad," 316). The inverse of the fragmentary posting and singing of ballad sheets was the selling of them in bulk, by the bundle—for example, "a groat's worth of ballads" (a groat being four pence)—the purchaser not knowing exactly what might be included in his or her retrieved ballad bunch (Chettle, *Kind-Heartes Dreame*, 19).

(5) "Moving media" further describes how such mobile fragmentation of ballad parts also happened in a more personal and occasional way, as broadside ballads circulated from hand to hand, eye to eye, voice to voice, and collector to collector. Walking the streets of London, viewers or listeners necessarily saw or heard ballads in a hit-or-miss and piecemeal fashion, as noted above. But what needs to be stressed is how such encounters took the form of unexpected and partial convergences. For instance, one's coming upon a specific broadside ballad depended on where one happened to be walking or standing—the book stall, the marketplace, the alehouse, the theater, or the scaffold, among other places. Different kinds of ballads would have been favored for peddling at those different places (themes, illustrations, and tunes often fitting the site). Ballads celebrating community and homosocial pleasures would

be more saleable at the alehouse, as would likely be our hand-marred ballad. There were popular alehouse tunes aplenty. “Good night ballads,” in which a criminal being executed supposedly laments his or her crime *on the scaffold*, would be favorites at executions (Chess, “‘And I my vowe did keepe’”; Dolan, “Petty Traitor”; Wiltenburg, “Emotional Life of Crime”).

Even when a ballad was offered as a whole artifact—held up as an intact single sheet for full view, or pasted up for all customers to see on an alehouse wall, for example, or handed around proudly by its buyer, or even sung in total by a less-than-canny or desperate-to-sell hawker showing off his wares—potential customers might well have accessed it fragmentarily. They might have focused on and made their choice of what to hear, read, look at, or buy based on a particularly alluring feature of its many aesthetics as well as its topic. They might have been attracted by one or more of the ballad’s intriguing woodcut illustrations and/or its curling black-letter typeface, its catchy tune, its promise of “news” or other intriguing topic, its resemblance to another ballad illustration/text/tune/story, or some other notable feature.

(6) “Moving media” captures, as well, the way broadside ballads invited people physically to approach the performer or hawker and form a crowd around him (usually “him” pre-Restoration). This was one facet of the street ballad that particularly worried authorities. In gathering people together, officials feared, hawkers of ballads might incite a riot. This fear explains the arrest in 1654 of Methusalah Flower in Bristol for the “singing of ballads, thereby contracting people together in a tumultuous manner” (Beier, *Masterless Men*, 98). But despite the authorities’ anxiety of their instigating public disturbances, broadside ballads tended to engage their audiences in less riotous, though potentially insidious, ways. They invited them to envision, read, or voice all subject positions represented in the ballads, or, as I have alternatively termed the experience in *Unsettled*, to engage in “multifarious role speculation.” Not only listening to but also often joining in, the audience either sings in the first person(s) or adopts that persona’s voice through the narrator—termed at the time the “relator,” as Frances E. Dolan observes (*True Relations*; “Mopsa’s Method”). Even in the act of relating events, the narrator usually gives first-person voice to the characters in his or her sung story; the audience members who sang along would as well. In fact, as I have previously argued, ballads “written from the perspective of the many for the many, project a myriad of different roles or identities that may be promiscuously picked up and discarded by their audiences upon hearing or viewing them, quite literally with a mere turn of the head.” I thus concluded, “In effect, a mobile ‘freedom’ and ‘variety’ of identity is what broadside ballads marketed. Whether the audiences paid for the ballads or not, the songs made available to consumers a plethora of

subjectivities on a psychologically 'no-cost,' provisional basis. A new role lay just around the corner, on the very next broadside ballad sheet, and often even between the lines of the same page" (Fumerton, *Unsettled*, 146; see also Smith, *Acoustic World*, esp. 190–201). I explore this complex phenomenon more fully in Chapter 8 of this book through an in-depth examination of multiple possible subject positions offered by a very popular and long-surviving broadside ballad—so popular it crosses the Atlantic as a news story—which tells of a gruesome murder of a wife and children by their lord's blackamoor slave.

(7) "Moving media" pertains, too, to the motion of human bodies not only physically but also affectively and viscerally. As part of their invitation to engage in ballad singing and adopt sung roles, broadside ballads stir their audiences' five senses, and more. In the words of Melissa Gregg and Gregory J. Seigworth, they incite ways that "the 'outside' realms of the pre-/extra-/paralinguistic intersect with the 'lower' or proximal senses," which include not only sight and sound but also "touch, taste, smell, rhythm and motion-sense, or, alternatively/ultimately, the autonomic nervous system" (*Affect Theory Reader*, 8). Smith explores this affective phenomenon specifically in terms of emotion or "passion" ("Shakespeare's Residuals," 215) and the triggering of the kinesics of dance ("'Ball'"). Such a barrage of affective processes produces what Brian Massumi describes as unpredictable feedback loops, constitutive, he argues, of a "chaos" that is the condition of the possibility of the social (*Parables for the Virtual*, 9). This unpredictability of affective response plays a critical role in my discussions in Chapters 6 through 8. It is also one of the reasons I argue in my Conclusion, focused as exemplum on Shakespeare's *The Winter's Tale*, that—and I say this even in the near-daunting face of Smith's brilliant advocacy for the sensory immediacy of the dramatic stage—early modern theater often loses in competition with the multimedia, more participatory, and more mobile popular ballad experience. Furthermore, I argue, Shakespeare, for one, knew it.

(8) "Moving media," finally, opens our discussion to allow us to embrace the idea of a "multividual collective" affected by ballads. This point deserves a section of its own.

The Multividual Collective

So far in my discussion, the individual "I" has been my focus. But, in fact, it takes a collaborating creative group (author included, if an actual author, in the traditional sense of the term, is even involved) to bring together as one the separable aesthetic parts that uneasily reside together on a ballad sheet. It also requires a collective of printers, publishers, hawkers, and chapmen to effect the sheet's dissemination. Further bringing alive the moving broadside ballad necessitates an audience. This audience could be singular, if also, in being variously moved, multiple; by "multiple," I refer to a subject who, despite his or her individuality, adopts many voices or roles in singing or experiencing a ballad. But the ballad audience is foremost constituted of a "we": a gathering of persons coming together as one or more public assemblages in a moment of a shared encounter.

I here embark on what is, for me, new and shifting ground—well beyond my lifetime scholarly preoccupation with the individual subject, which admittedly appears almost obsessively throughout all my published books. The trajectory of my investigations into subjectivity, which led me finally to broadside ballads, is worth tracking because it almost inevitably leads from the notion of a stable "I" to an unsettled plural "I" to mobile assemblages of multividuals in communal, if also potentially plural, ballad publics.

Such a claim might seem more transparent when considered in terms of the low, who are especially targeted by broadside ballads in the artifacts' expansive embrace. As I argue in *Unsettled*, "home" not simply for the vagrant but for the poor (who constituted as much as 50 percent of the early modern population) was an unstable space, characterized by economic, psychological, and even physical displacement. Impoverished householders and their spouses held a variety of jobs or by-employments, or moved from job to job, or even from place to place in an effort to "get by" (130–52). Such an unsettled audience of the printed street ballad, I noted in a later article ("Mocking Aristocratic Place"), shared a kinship with broadside ballad sheets themselves, which were often hawked by the very transient. These itinerant and unemployed subjects, though seeking temporary work selling broadside ballads, were by virtue of their mobility deemed by authorities to be as socially disposable as a ballad sheet.

But what I underscore in the introduction to a subsequent (2010) collection of essays (*Ballads and Broadsides in Britain*) is that this fact of unsettledness does not mean that only the lowest of a ballad's targeted audience was represented by its moving aesthetics and practices of production, dissemination, and use, or that only the low experienced themselves as unsettled (or even that all of them did all of the time). Middling sorts were also subject to occasional and "life cycle" instability and poverty. This includes many middling-to-low printers and publishers of broadside ballads. For that matter, even the socially higher sorts, who pretended disdain for ballads, were themselves vulnerable to social and economic instability—as were many erudite hobbyist ballad collectors like Anthony Wood, who teetered most of his adult life on poverty.

To the extent that the higher sorts actively engaged with broadside ballads in everyday encounters, they had at least partly to enter the unstable, unsettled, one might say even "vagrant" worldview of the artifacts' moving media.

It is thus not coincidental that aristocratic figures who took pride, ironically, in being idle, in the sense of not working with their hands, are commonly pictured on broadside ballads alongside images of the middling and low. In fact, their images far outnumber those of the poorer sorts. Though clearly aristocratic impressions on the sheets enhanced or elevated the prettiness of ballad artifacts as *art*—at least from the perspective of those lowly for whom fancy dress was otherwise unimaginably attainable—they also imply some shared sensibility. Indeed, in *Cultural Aesthetics*, I argue that any notion of an attained or singular aristocratic "I" in the period is illusional; the upper sorts are caught up in a perpetual fracturing, deferral, and unattainability or unknowability of self. The precarious identity experienced by the lower-class subject might thus be understood as an alter-mapping of an aristocratic interiority endlessly deferred. In other words, though the unsettled aesthetics of broadside ballads would likely have best spoken to and represented the unstable poor, who often found themselves literally displaced, the possibility for ballad aesthetics to represent fragmentation and displacement metaphorically or at one remove extended well beyond that low social group. Broadside ballads reached from earth to (idealistically speaking) heaven; they were simultaneously marketed to the poor, the middling, and even the upper sorts.

The reason for this rather long self-fragmenting, retrospective digression into my scholarly career is to provoke an act of recognition and re-cognition (as if looking at the trajectory of my research in Zumthor's fragments of a mirror; 160) that, as with Richard II's mirror scene, signals new thoughts of self and community. When we talk about mass-marketed artifacts like broadside ballads, we must recognize that we have to move beyond the individual "I," even when it is imagined, as I have previously (and rather awkwardly) termed it, a "'multividual' subjectivity," and embrace groups of such "I's" at all levels of society. That is, ballad audiences need not follow social fault lines. Indeed, at one level, the ballad artifacts refuse to allow such demarcations. Not only do they mix social orders in their woodcut impressions as well as in commonly known texts and tunes, but they conflate social orders through the very lived act of being experienced collectively. High and low rub elbows on the streets. Thus, the collective experience produced by an enticing broadside ballad would not have been predictable. After all, broadside ballads were meant to be sung, often through a spontaneous happening in space and time, with *someone*, but the someone(s) cannot be predetermined. In the impromptu public moment, they would have created a gathering of diverse voices, ears, and eyes, during which the sense of class distinction might well have melted away. In sum, the unpredictable group experience of the ballad's on-the-fly and moving multimedia would have not only contributed to Massumi's cognitive "chaos" constitutive of the possibility of the social but also unexpectedly brought together very unusual multividual groupings, or "assemblages," to return to Manuel DeLanda's theory.

Assemblage Theory

DeLanda's concept of societal assemblages nicely enlivens the Lego-block analogy of the Introduction as well as expands my discussion earlier in this chapter about nonhuman as well as human entities that are "moving" (and "moved") component parts, which together form a whole ballad experience. For DeLanda, an assemblage is a material and social combination of singular units, both inanimate and animate, which maintain their integrity within a whole and thus might be switched out with other units without suffering a loss of identity, though their role within the whole might change. The multiple media that reside on a ballad sheet, viewed as heterogeneous components in an assemblage, function precisely in DeLanda's sense of autonomous parts, which he compares to individuals. They are defined by "relations of exteriority" rather than by "relations of interiority" (the latter considered negatively by DeLanda as fully integrated into—indeed, inextricable from—a seamless whole).

In the reusable collage-like assemblage of the ballad's multimedia parts, we can now see more clearly how, Lego-like, "a component part of an assemblage may be detached from it and plugged into a different assemblage in which its interactions are different" (DeLanda, *A New Philosophy of Society*, 10–22; Deleuze and Guattari, *A Thousand Plateaus*). When, for instance, a woodcut illustration is detached from one ballad sheet and plugged into a new assemblage of cuts, text, and tune on another ballad sheet, that illustration retains its autonomy though its role changes (sometimes quite surprisingly). The same can be said of every media component of the broadside ballad, indeed of every element sited on the ballad page, as we shall more fully examine in Chapters 2 and 3.

But we need to pull back for a moment to consider how we might understand larger, *social* ballad groupings using DeLanda's ontology. As we zoom out to envision the collective "we" in the assemblage that constitutes a ballad audience, DeLanda would say, we simply encounter yet again the individual, whether thing or living being: "The ontological status of any assemblage, inorganic, organic or social, is that of a unique, singular, historically contingent individual" (40). Individuals that are able to function as both component parts and assemblages or sub-assemblages of larger assemblages would, in this thinking, include material illustrations, texts, tunes, sheets of paper, handprints, printers, publishers, hawkers, and—extending our gaze to larger societal assemblages—networks, communities, organizations, and even city- or nation-states (10, 11). What I find especially intriguing and useful about this analysis is DeLanda's insistence not only on the individuality of things as well as humans (what Jane Bennett, in *Vibrant Matter*, envisions as a sociopolitical ecosystem) but also on the individuality of the social collective. If we conceive of a ballad audience itself as a "unique, singular, historically contingent individual," we can better talk about that collective's distinct character, role, and responsiveness. And, since assemblages are constituted of sub-assemblages, the collective ballad audience "individual" is itself potentially composed of smaller groups of persons who also together function like individuals, with like facets of singular identity. Furthermore, DeLanda does not think of the assemblage that is an individual or of its component parts that are autonomous as entirely unreflexive or unmoving. Each, he says, is "historically contingent," influenced, for instance, by its locale (94–95). In fact, while adamantly resisting the term "organic," which Bennett favors, DeLanda recognizes that component parts of an assemblage—like ballad texts, illustrations, and tunes—not only change as a function of their relationships with each other but can accumulate other layers of meaning or personality as they connect with larger assemblages: "As larger assemblages emerge from the interactions of component parts, the identity of the parts may acquire new layers, as the emergent whole reacts back and affects them" (25). This concept of influential interactions between autonomous component parts and wholes is as important for our understanding of a collective ballad "we" as of the collection of multimedia assembled on a ballad sheet.

Still, there is a hint of an infinite regression or proliferation of component parts and "individuals" in DeLanda's theory. This derives from his determined materialism and antagonism to both postmodern linguistics, in which language dominates societal systems, and what he calls "taxonomic essentialism" (like the ideology of the Great Chain of Being), wherein all things are defined by their internal relation to an organic whole. If the Chain of Being posits a hierarchy of entities defined as interconnected links within a larger chain, DeLanda's ontology of assemblages is, in his word, "flat." As he explains, "it contains nothing but differently scaled "*individual singularities* (or *hacceitis*)" (28; emphasis DeLanda). While "flat" here may connote stasis, DeLanda's notion of individual singularities evolves upward through a hierarchy of assemblages-

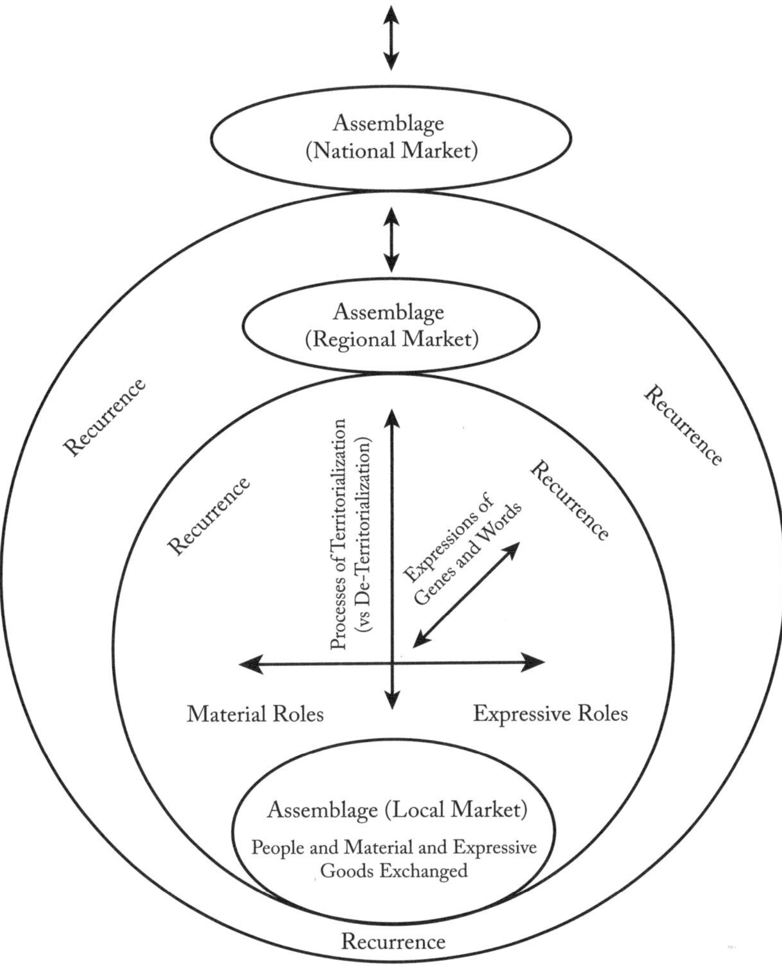

Figure 5. Assemblage Theory Model, from Manuel DeLanda, *A New Philosophy of Society: Assemblage Theory and Social Complexity* (London: Continuum, 2006).

within-assemblages. These are affected by key facets or axes, which, he posits, form the backbone of an assemblage: the influence of locale, such as in his notion of towns clustered around a market; the role of component parts, ranging from the material to the expressive (including human relationships); the complementary expressive component of genetic coding and words; and, most importantly, the synthetic processes of repetition and territorialization—the latter always threatened by the potential for deterritorialization (both spatially and nonspatially conceived). I have tried to capture some of this dynamism in a diagram of DeLanda's new ontology, expanding upon his example of a market; the sketch is admittedly limited both by my abilities and by DeLanda's loosely defined concepts (Figure 5).

But, even forgiving a certain conceptual looseness to his theory, I keep returning with unease to DeLanda's insistence on a "flat" ontology. In many ways, this "flatness" fits with the moving Lego-block way things and people interrelate in the ballad experience, from the micro- to the macro-level of production and consumption. But the notion of flatness is a problem on two important fronts: (1) Despite being dynamic, DeLanda's ontology, in which all things and beings are simultaneously both components of assemblages and individuals, tends toward a dehumanizing of both the assemblage and the individual. Of course, the same might be said of Deleuze and Guattari's vision of assemblages, upon which DeLanda draws, but the dynamism with which his source-philosophers imagine relationships between component parts energizes, enlivens, and—sometimes frustratingly so—resists systematization. DeLanda's worldview is much more static and schematic, as suggested by my use of the term "ontology." Within DeLanda's worldview, I often feel like I would be an interchangeable piece of machinery on an assembly line, or—as in the picture on the cover of the 2006 paperback edition of his book—like just one more worker bee in a hive, rather than a unique human subject (even though DeLanda would reject that idea; he'd say I always retain my "irreducible properties" [10], whatever they might be). At times, DeLanda's assemblage theory threatens to veer more toward emergence theory as in cellular automata phenomena—wherein "*discrete, abstract computational systems*" allow one "to study pattern formation and complexity in a pure, abstract setting"—such as in the Game of Life.[7] (2) His theory also faces the ever-looming threat of turning into an infinite regression of assemblage-individuals or an ever-widening accumulation of assemblages-within-assemblages so that his terms can, as noted above and rather ironically (given his materialist agenda), lose concrete and specific meaning.

DeLanda himself is aware of this potential critique of his ontology, though the descriptor he uses is more visually containing: "a Russian doll or set of Chinese boxes." In his self-defense, he points out that there are heterogeneous ways of participating in and across assemblages and "*a wide range of scales*" (33; emphasis DeLanda). Despite this qualification, however, it is hard to imagine as essentially the same or as born of the same principles, on the one hand, a spontaneous gathering of subjects "assembled" as if forming one individual entity around a ballad singer, and, say, on the other hand, an established corporation of elected officials protected by the law as if a single person, such as the still extant 500-year-old United Kingdom's Clothworkers' Company.[8] Though DeLanda would insist that these examples reflect the same essential processes, he would also likely qualify the former instance, the ballad assemblage, as an example of what he terms "ephemeral assemblages." But his example of such is a conversation between two persons, not a group gathering. He furthermore quickly moves up through his imagined scale of assemblages by adding more persons to such encounters, which, within three pages of his book, become dubbed "interpersonal networks," and, within another page, a "community" (56–57). If there is an "I" here, among all of DeLanda's individual assemblages, he or she seems personally irrelevant or truly "flat," as does the collective "we" made up of "I's" according to DeLanda's rules of assemblage.

DeLanda's assemblage theory remains excitingly thought provoking and helpful to our thinking about the ways heterogeneous multimedia parts of ballads, both as produced and as consumed, might momentarily be experienced in the form of a unified or individual whole. His notion of informal assemblages between people as "networks" is also most useful for thinking about relations between seventeenth-century collectors of black-letter broadside ballads, which I address in Chapter 4. But if we are to approximate more nuanced relations between collective "we's" as assemblages of historical and potentially multividual "I's," we need more conceptual options. I propose that we complement and complicate DeLanda's assemblage theory with a methodology that embraces the processes of making plural loosely formed associations or "publics" and also add into the conceptual mix the theory of situation-specific "tactics." Both concepts, as we shall see, disrupt the static and mechanic valences of a flat DeLandian system.

Making Publics

I turn at this point for further assistance, especially in Chapters 4 through 7, to an important new movement within public sphere studies, which has been especially nourished by the project Making Publics: Media, Markets, and Association in Early Modern Europe, 1500–1700, directed by Paul Yachnin, 2005–2010, http://makingpublics.mcgill.ca/, in which I had the privilege of participating. The MaPs project, named after its two focal points—plural *publics* always in the *making*—has been the springboard of much later important work by scholars involved in the project and those influenced by its widely disseminated, international reach.

The critical sights of the MaPs project, it should be noted, were not set primarily in opposition to reified ontologies or linguistic dominance, as are DeLanda's. Rather, MaPs was reacting against the idea of a singular, post-1701 "public" or "public sphere." Articulated by Jürgen Habermas in his 1962 book, written in German, the theory of the public sphere gained immense global traction on the book's being published in English in 1989 (*Structural*

Transformation of the Public Sphere). Habermas here argues that the public sphere began its rise in the mid-1690s, reached maturity in the eighteenth century, and was a function of the ripening of three historical factors: market capitalism, the press, and an educated bourgeois class. The market-invested bourgeoisie, he argues, gathered in public places, especially coffee houses, and capitalized on the dissemination of information, especially the newspaper, to engage in rational political and intellectual discourse that challenged aristocratic state power. In this narrative of social history, furthermore, private householders emerge as a public against the state (or, in DeLandian terms, as an established assemblage against a larger, more authoritarian assemblage): "The bourgeois public sphere may be conceived above all as the sphere of private people come together as a public . . . against the public authorities themselves" (Habermas, 27).

As its starting point, MaPs queried Habermas's story line of a smooth historical transition into a seemingly homogeneous public sphere. The project on this front benefited from a number of earlier historians, theorists, and cultural critics, represented well in Craig Calhoun's 1993 collection of essays, *Habermas and the Public Sphere*. Even early scholars who accepted the basic through-line and end-point of the Habermasian model often resisted its homogeneity, especially pointing to its gender exclusivity (e.g., Fraser, "Rethinking the Public Sphere"). Increasingly as well, critics have wanted to push back Habermas's public sphere to a (variously specified) earlier period. Especially favored has been the seventeenth century; Raymond Joad, for instance, argues that seventeenth-century newspapers contributed to a political culture of debate more than a half century before Habermas's posited public sphere ("Newspaper," 128). Accompanying this thrust backward in time and promoting both class and media diversity, Alexandra Halasz (*Marketplace of Print*) points to a seventeenth-century populist and market-driven pamphlet public; and Michelle O'Callaghan ("Textual Gatherings") shows how sixteenth-century elite communities consolidated their private, sociopolitical alliances by commandeering the marketplace of print to publish themselves in elegiac anthologies—even as their printed anthologies increasingly reached out to embrace a larger commercial public desirous of scandal and news.[9]

The MaPs group quickly turned its collective energies to investigating what would have preceded any established idea of "the"—that is, of a singular—public sphere. Together, we concluded that the pre-life of such a notion of empowering singularity would by definition have consisted of partial, ad hoc, unofficial, informal, and open associations of people brought together toward some collective cause or moment (whether such a shared agenda need be political was much contested and never agreed upon).[10] In advocating that publics in the plural were makeshift and open formations, the project excluded all government-sanctioned, rule-based, and exclusive organizations, such as guilds. Furthermore, publics, as plural and transient entities, we argued, were always in the process of being made. That is, they organically grew and died (not necessarily living a full "life cycle")—hence, "*Making* Publics."

Advancing a version of MaPs's idea of early modern publics as plural, ad hoc, and intermittent, Peter Lake and Steven Pincus, in "Rethinking the Public Sphere" (2007), argue for a post-Reformation "episodic" series of sociopolitical publics. Publics, conceived by these critics, emerge only occasionally and sequentially, in response to specific historical controversies or crises. More recently, Lake, in his monumental 2017 *How Shakespeare Put Politics on the Stage*, microscopically magnifies (in 666 pages) one such episodic moment. He focuses on the instabilities and anxieties of the late 1580s and the 1590s—specifically, over the succession crisis—arguing that such disturbance was instrumental in shaping Shakespeare's history plays. Though Lake maddeningly conflates readers of printed plays and audiences of performances, and frustratingly flattens the history plays into only vehicles of politics (ignoring other pressing cultural factors), he nevertheless offers insightful readings of a playwright who engagingly conversed and even debated with his audience, if only in the playgoers' minds.

Steven Mullaney's recent (2015) *Reformation of Emotions in the Age of Shakespeare* also concentrates on how the theater of Shakespeare and his contemporaries reflected "a culture in crisis" (47) marked by "uncertainty and indetermination" (36). The two authors strike the same note of cultural angst. But whereas Lake looks to the 1580s and 1590s and to politics, Mullaney broods over the "affective" influence of the religious Reformation and what he describes as a resulting self- and collective-identity crisis. Mullaney is more keenly aware of the sitedness of the stage than is Lake, thus dodging a conflation of reader and audience; and, indeed, both authors, in the spirit of MaPs, nicely explore the possibilities of the stage not simply to perform but also, dialectically and often through indirection, momentarily to elicit contradiction, disruption, and even alliances within and between its playgoing and reading audiences—to be, in Mullaney's words, "refractive, unsettling, and creative or world-making" (47).

We will return, in the Conclusion, to the possibilities and limitations of making publics through stage drama. For the moment, though, I want to remind my readers of the other genres I have mentioned in passing, which thrived outside the theaters—genres that had a spacious as well as an influential and multiply moving reach, if always in an ad hoc manner: newspapers, pamphlets, and elegies, as well as, of course, broadside ballads. We might, in this context, recall an early assertion made by MaPs director Paul Yachnin: "The emergence of publics in early modernity amounted to an overall expansion of forms of public expression, feeling, identity, self-representation, influence, and action *for people usually excluded from public life*" (my emphasis).[11] Those most "excluded from public life," the sociopolitically marginalized, consisted of the poorest sorts. Many had little or no formal education; they could only afford the nothingness it cost to hear and see the mass-marketed fragments of broadside ballads and other street literature that roamed London's public and in-between spaces, and far beyond. Not only would the low jostle with the high in being situated side by side in woodcut impressions on broadside ballad sheets but also, occasionally, they would be brought together into rare public assemblages on the open streets.

You might at this point cry out "That's not a public!"; to that, my answer would be: that's because you are thinking like Habermas, in terms of a larger intellectually informed bourgeoisie or, like Lake and Mullaney, in terms of a larger sociopolitical dramatization. Not incidentally, both ways of thinking envisage publics as fully contained or sited, the one in the coffee house, the other in the theater. They do not extend outward to include on-the-fly, makeshift happenings across space and time. In this book, I draw on the originating spirit of MaPs, which posited an early modern culture constituted of messy and plural assemblages that cannot easily be plugged into a stable site any more than they can be fitted into DeLanda's ever-enlarging hierarchy of assemblages within assemblages. To understand the extent to which consumers "on the move" not only made up the broadside ballad market but also were actively involved in the making of experiential and imaginary collectivities (regardless of whether they were officially sanctioned), we might additionally ruminate on the role in ballad publics of "tactics."

Tactics

By "tactics," I refer to the opposite of "strategies" (a distinction made by de Certeau, *Practice of Everyday Life*). I reference spontaneous, makeshift, and—to the extent they reuse and remake available public media and conventions—potentially subversive or, at least, manipulative practices. By "tactical publics," I mean to capture together two dynamically interrelated actors: those publics that are movingly fashioned (however phantasmically) by the printer's and his collaborators' tactics (their effort to discover, generate, and/or shape consumers) and those consuming publics, of varying size and character, who performatively redeploy such making processes to realize their own collective ambitions or desires (which may or may not intersect with any printer's or publisher's intentions). Both publics drew on and affected the multivalent mobility of the broadside ballad I've detailed above. As we shall see in Chapter 7, for instance, a printer/publisher in 1666 could, to political ends, refashion an age-old ballad imaginary about St. George and the Dragon, with its familiar array of texts, tunes, and woodcuts, into a still recognizable but tactically reconfigured broadside designed to celebrate the (questionable) nautical victories and national supremacy of George, Duke of Albemarle, in the wars with the Dutch. That is how we can begin to understand the recursivity within the "system" of broadside balladry, wherein printers/publishers and their co-producers survived (or thrived) by responding to consumer publics both imagined and real.[12]

My focus is especially on consumers as tactical makers of plural publics, though the processes of production and consumption, making and remaking, necessarily fold in upon themselves in the recursive performativity of broadside ballad culture. Bear with me through this relatively brief discussion of one last theoretical angle, which might help us grab hold of the protean moving media of broadside ballads, and we shall end on an illuminating case study: a reading of a rare printed ballad survivor from the early 1640s that demonstrates an imaginary of possible consumer tactics in action, "Alas poore Trades-Men what shall we do?"

To clarify more fully what printers and publishers effected in their ballad assemblages: they anticipated mobile makings not only within their shops but also in the public life of the birthed ballad as it was performatively disseminated. Evidence strongly suggests that printers and publishers tried to anticipate their publics but that they also—or perhaps more accurately—deliberately created many loose and ephemeral assemblages and sub-assemblages of the ballads' media and personae in order to capture the widest market and allow consumers to exploit tactically the ballad experience to their own ends. Such remakings on reception might have occurred within a united large group or within a more fractured subgroup(s), or even simply within the sole imaginary of the multividual "I." The possibility for diverse tactical employment of ballad assemblages ironically lay in the printers'/publishers' and audiences' shared understanding of ballad aesthetics and practices. Such knowledge did not derive from the education of a bourgeois civil society but from everyday experiences; it consisted of a broad notion of cultural "literacy" (Cressy, "Literacy in Context," 309–15). Whatever their many differences (in personality, status, up-rearing, belief, and so forth), early modern subjects of all sorts, like contemporary subjects today, were raised within broadly shared cultural expectations about behavior and social interaction, as well as about popular literary genres and meaning making. But what is different from today is the extraordinary *everywhereness* of broadside ballads (though we certainly have our own embracive media). Printed ballads read, seen, and sung everywhere established a common experiential foundation upon which both producers and consumers could capitalize. All kinds of people on a daily basis were experientially immersed in the ballad culture that surrounded them, regardless of whether they wanted to be. Precisely that common experience, in turn, allowed for assemblages of shared interests and expectations, though such gatherings were not always of a unifying kind, and in some cases were quite insidious. A united assemblage of collective "I's" could have potentially gathered in common experience of a ballad, sharing the moment as if one individual; but, so too, the very multivalent inflection of the media-filled artifact and its cultural moment of dissemination could have opened the possibility for rogue, singular reactions as well as for formations of sub-assemblages or, to use Michael Warner's term, "counterpublics" (*Publics and Counterpublics*)—a concept to which we shall return in Chapters 6 and 7.

To describe these latter kinds of publics as "tactical" might seem anachronistic. Today the word *tactical* is most often associated in critical circles with modern activism, as in the "tactical media" movement, with its focus on spontaneous subversion from within the dominant system, which often occurs at moments of "crisis." But both broadside ballads and tactical media, we find, are modes of mass communication that can be characterized as ephemeral, fragmentary, mobile, and improvisational. At least in the original conception of tactical media, as articulated in 1997 by David Garcia and Geert Lovink ("ABC of Tactical Media"), both modes are further marked by "cheap 'do it yourself' media." In the case of tactical media, this originally meant, and in large part still means, easy access to the new global explosion of low-cost communication technology, like cell phones and the Internet. Such cheap technology was widely used to spread news of the 2010 Arab Spring protests, for instance.[13] In the case of early modern broadside ballads, tactical media were also constituted of mass-marketed and low-cost modes of communication: specifically, single sheets of cheap paper printed with recycled woodcut impressions, tune titles, and song texts. Ballad sheets could be quickly printed in great numbers and speedily circulated widely. Importantly, the other medium of hastily printable and disseminated black-letter sheets of the period were government proclamations, the printed voice of authority. By virtue of their formal aesthetics and distribution, black-letter ballads from their inception made an intervention in official propaganda. It should not be surprising, then, that early modern printers of ballads occupied the social margins of "acceptable" print society (though one group did manage to pool its resources to form the powerful Ballad Partners of the 1620s); they also practiced what Garcia and Lovink term "a quick and dirty aesthetic" that, like tactical media, could make hit-and-run insertions into the print market under the establishment radar. Despite the 1557 law requiring that all works be authorized for publication by the Stationers' Company, for instance, Rollins estimates that of the surviving ballads only about 50 percent were ever registered in the Company's books.[14] Half of the producers of broadside ballads thus escaped simultaneously the six-pence registration fee per ballad, copyright rules, and official monitoring ("Black-Letter Broadside Ballad," 281).

Where modern "tactical media" and tactical ballad publics most productively converge, however, is in one of tactical media's less strident, if still foundational, inspirations, where the stress is more on "tactics" than media: Michel de Certeau's *The Practice of Everyday Life*. In this influential work—also, significantly, an inspiration for Deleuze and Guattari as well as DeLanda—de Certeau allows us to think more embracingly about the way consumers, surrounded by all the elements of their social "languages," can choose, in his words, the "'phrasing' produced by the bricolage (the artisan-like inventiveness) and the discursiveness that combine these elements, which are all in general circulation" (xviii). De Certeau certainly shares with proponents of tactical media their opposition to those in control of production or, in his metaphor quoted above, of dominant "language." But his vision is flexible and expansive enough to include a tactic as simple as jaywalking. It is thus open to more individual and less politicized (with a capital *P*)—or, should we say, to more *everyday*—ideas of redirecting or redeploying production and consumption. As such, de Certeau's approach to tactics is especially useful for thinking about the black-letter broadside ballad. This genre typically worked subtly from within the dominant system, drawing on common, everyday conventions and language to create alternative readings without ever being overtly (or admittedly) subversive. Maneuvering within the everydayness and the everywhereness of the broadside ballad's "moving media," producers as well as consumers could participate in the making of momentary tactical publics. This is where I diverge from de Certeau. Not all producers are wielders of dominant "strategy," as he imagines in his social model, especially not the producers of broadside ballads, whose personal and especially commercial interests would not be served by wholeheartedly embracing and parroting the powers that be.

Snapshot: "Alas Poore Trades-Men What Shall We Do?"

Looking forward to the chapters ahead, I conclude this so far rather abstract critical and theoretical chapter with a brief concrete snapshot of how moving and tactical media might work within a single ballad.

In addition to our ballad smudged with a handprint, Manchester Central Library holds many rare and unique survivals from the turbulent 1640s, most of which were not entered by the Stationers' Company in its Register and thus not legally printed. As is the case of all authoritarian regimes, the emerging new establishment of the time had a vested interest in controlling the information available to the public. The revolutionary parliamentarians (soon to represent the Commonwealth led by the New Model Army under Oliver Cromwell), instituted on June 14, 1643, a draconian Licensing Order governing the publication of all printed materials (Acts and Ordinances). The act was an apparatus of state censorship designed to oversee the printing industry and specifically to suppress oppositional voices, especially Royalist propaganda. In the black-letter broadside ballads that were printed and disseminated during this time that are held at Manchester Central Library, we can see how producers of the artifacts' mobile and makeshift aesthetics tactically used everyday ballad conventions in ways that permitted consumers to provisionally assemble into publics of various sizes and kinds, some of which could have been slyly subversive of governing policy without specifically naming names or political positions.

Let us take as an example the broadside ballad, the title of which, significantly, is not a statement but a question: "Alas poore Trades-Men what shall we do?" (c. 1646); EBBA 36028. The ballad's narrator, or "relator" (Dolan, *True Relations*), directly addresses, and in doing so calls for a public gathering of, poor tradesmen to answer this query. The refrain for each stanza of the ballad is the same as the ballad's questioning title (with only a variant spelling of "do"): "Alas poore Trades-men / what shall we doe?" Through such insistent interrogation at the end of each stanza, demanding (to the extent of almost begging for) an answer, the narrator insinuates himself into our thoughts regardless of whether we are poor tradesmen (Figure 6).

The ballad's subtitle? "Londons Complaint through badnesse of Trading, / For work being scant, their substance is fadeing." The relator here momentarily shifts roles and puts himself in the persona of his workplace, a lamenting London. But this is only a momentary subject position. Indeed, if one were to

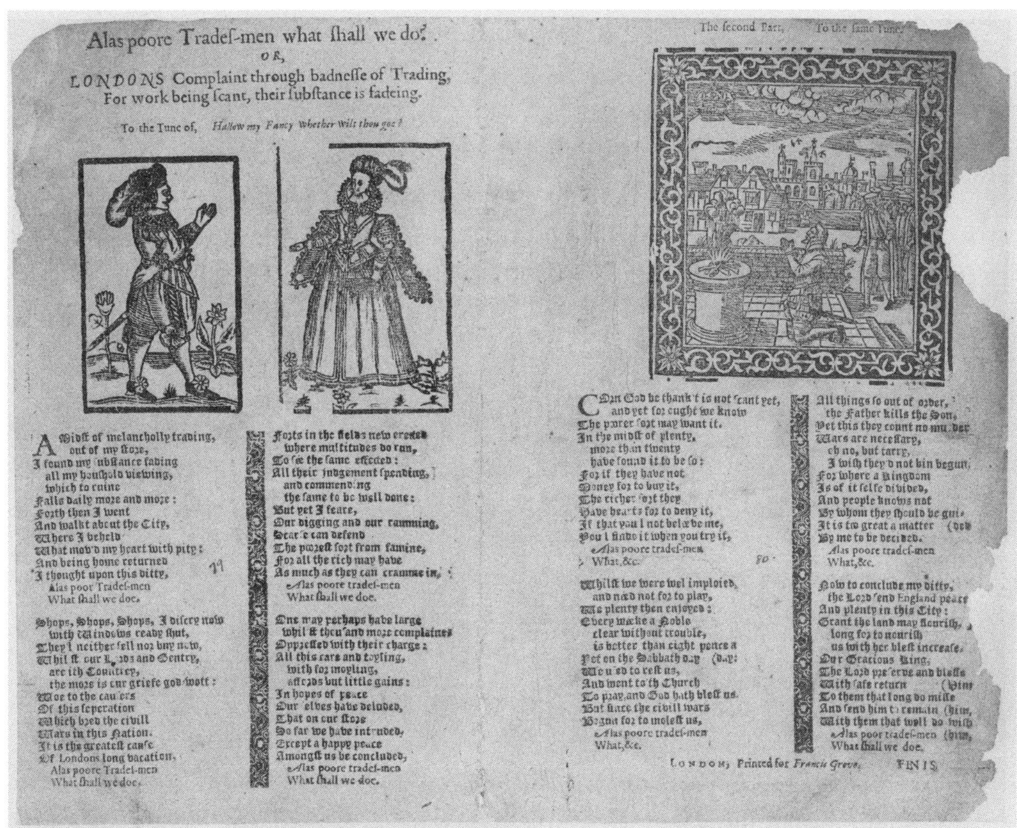

Alas poore Tradeſ-men what ſhall we do?

OR,

LONDONS Complaint through badneſſe of Trading,
For work being ſcant, their ſubſtance is fadeing.

To the Tune of, *Hallow my Fancy Whether Wilt thou goe?*

The ſecond Part, To the ſame Tune.

Amidst of melancholly trading,
out of my store,
I found my substance fading
all my houshold viewing,
which to ruine
Falls daily more and more:
Forth then I went
And walkt about the City,
Where I beheld
What mov'd my heart with pity:
And being home returned
I thought upon this ditty,
Alas poor Trades-men
What shall we doe.

Shops, Shops, Shops, I discry now
with Windows ready shut,
They'l neither sell nor buy now,
Whilst our Lords and Gentry,
are ith Countrey,
the more is our griefe god wott:
Woe to the causers
Of this seperation
Which bred the civill
Wars in this Nation.
It is the greatest cause
Of Londons long vacation,
Alas poore Trades-men
What shall we doe.

Forts in the fields new erected
where multitudes do run,
To see the same effected:
All their judgement spending,
and commending
the same to be well done:
But yet I feare,
Our digging and our ramming,
Scarse can defend
The poorest sort from famine,
For all the rich may have
As much as they can cramme in,
Alas poore trades-men
What shall we doe.

One may perhaps have large
whilst thousand more complaines
Oppressed with their charge:
All this care and toyling,
with for moyling,
affords but little gains:
In hopes of peace
Our selves have deluded,
That on our store
So far we have intruded,
Except a happy peace
Amongst us be concluded,
Alas poore trades-men
What shall we doe.

Corn God be thank't is not scant yet,
and yet for ought we know
The poorer sort may want it.
In the midst of plenty,
more than twenty
have found it to be so:
For if they have not
Money for to buy it,
The richer sort they
Have hearts for to deny it,
If that you'l not beleeve me,
You'l finde it when you try it,
Alas poore trades-men
What, &c.

Whilst we were wel imploied,
and need not for to play,
We plenty then enjoyed:
Every weeke a Noble
clear without trouble,
is better than eight pence a (day:
Yet on the Sabbath day
We used to rest us,
And went to th Church
To pray, and God hath blest us.
But since the civill wars
Begun for to molest us,
Alas poore trades-men
What, &c.

All things so out of order,
the Father kills the Son,
Yet this they count no murder
Wars are necessary,
oh no, but tarry,
I wish they'd not bin begun,
For where a Kingdom
Is of it selfe divided,
And people knows not
By whom they should be gui-
It is too great a matter (ded
By me to be decided.
Alas poore trades-men
What, &c.

Now to conclude my ditty,
the Lord send England peace
And plenty in this City:
Grant the land may flourish,
long for to nourish
us with her blest increase.
Our Gracious King,
The Lord preserve and blesse
With safe return (him
To them that long do misse
And send him to remain (him,
With them that well do wish
Alas poor trades-men (him,
What shall we doe.

LONDON, Printed for *Francis Grove*. FINIS.

Figure 6. Ballad sheet facsimile, "Alas poore Trades-men what shall we do? *Or, Londons* Complaint through badnesse of Trading, For work being scant, their substance is fadeing" (c. 1646), EBBA 36028. Manchester Central Library, Blackletter Ballads, 1.38, BR f 821.04 B49. By permission of the Henry Watson Music Library, Courtesy of Manchester Libraries, Information and Archives, Manchester City Council.

encounter the broadside ballad on the streets of London, or for that matter in the city of Manchester, perhaps pasted on a wall or cried out by a hawker, one might ascribe the relator's complaint not to a tradesman or to a personified London but to a forsaken lover. "Complaint" in the subtitle is a common signifier for a tale told about tragic love. Though complaints can be about other matters, the designated tune for the ballad (now no longer extant) reinforces the connection to love. The melody is titled *"Hallow my Fancy Whether Wilt thou goe?"* As if figuring forth riven desire, the woodcut impressions printed below the tune title are of a dashing gentleman (albeit crudely drawn, with seemingly disjointed armpits) reaching out, as if longingly, to a "fancy" lady—

a descriptor for this apparent addressee suggested by the tune title itself, "Hallow *my Fancy*." The lady is also dressed, as if reciprocally to the gentleman, in fashionable early seventeenth-century clothing. Each courtly looking figure reaches out to the other (both have often appeared on other printed ballads, so their assemblage here would be simultaneously familiar and, in this placement, new to the viewer). The abrupt shift in persona to London in the subtitle and the more subtle evocations of the relator's identity to include romantic love through the evocative subtitle's "Complaint," the tune title's questioning of a departed "Fancy," and the woodcut images of paired but severed upper-class sorts would seem to function as decoys put "out there" in the hopes of attracting a larger audience for the ballad than just poor tradesmen. Or perhaps they serve to empower economic with romantic desire, or at least with intimate affect. The tradesman's heart, like that of a lover, we would find out, if we were to pause and be drawn in to read or hear more of the song text of the ballad, is "mov'd" "with pity" if not romantically, then socioeconomically.

On finding his "substance is fadeing," as the narrator relates at the beginning of what he terms his "ditty" (humbly playing down the weightiness of his song, as befits his lowly social status), the poor tradesman decides to walk the streets of London. He thus follows a common ballad trope that begins with a relator walking out and seeing or hearing something. What our relator sees is that *all* the shops, like his, are closed tight. He cries out, as if momentarily personifying the shops, as he did earlier the city of London: "Shops, Shops, Shops, I discry now / with Windows ready shut." The cause? Not the withdrawal of a lady-love but of "our Lords and Gentry," who, he relates, "are ith Country, / the more is our griefe god-wotte" (st. 2). The tradesman in more detail then attributes this desertion of London to "Forts in the [rural] fields new erected / where multitudes do run." There, way out in the countryside, far from the city of London, "multitudes" (whoever they are) go "To see the same [forts] effected: / All their judgement spending, / and commending / the same to be well done" (st. 3). The many people who follow the "Lords and Gentry" out of London into the countryside are spending their judgment, not their money—a subtle, metaphorical critique.

But the relator refrains from naming names, instead crying out generally, "Woe to the causers / Of this seperation / Which bred the civill / Wars in this Nation" (st. 2). Nevertheless, he twice takes a quick jab at the unspecified "richer sort": they "may have," he complains, "As much as they can cramme in" while "the poorest sort" are left to "famine" (st. 3); in addition, they "Have hearts for to deny" grain to the "poorer sort" who "may want it" (st. 5). Clearly, most if not all the hapless poor left in London, still a hotbed of unrest at the time, would rally around this relator/singer as the ballad was being performed; they would in the process join his fellow lowly tradesmen abandoned in their desperate economic want. How radical such a rallying was meant to be, however, and who else would muster in support of it, is part of the question, "Alas poore Trades-men what shall we do?" which the relator asks over and over again in the ballad's refrain. His two critiques of the "rich" would seem to us moderns to be aimed at the House of Lords, which mostly supported the king. Charles I was himself at this time in the countryside desperately trying to rally support for his now pretty clearly lost cause (this explains the estimated date of printing, since Charles was captured in 1646). The cavalier dress of our aristocratic-looking man would suggest such royal allegiance. But then again, from the perspective of the "poorer sort," both "Lords and Gentry" were rich, as were many of the middling sorts, and indeed individuals of high social status took both sides in the power struggle between king and Parliament. The well-off landed gentry, it should be further noted, were those who put forward candidates for election to the House of Commons; and their land holdings lay outside London, to which "outside" the multitudes run. Nevertheless, since no sides are named or blamed, either party's members could self-assuredly nod in assent with this ballad's singer/relator as he multimodally performs the terrible loss of London's ruined economy resulting from the fact that the kingdom has come to civil war. Each political party would also likely think that the other side was at fault.

In typically evasive hit-and-run fashion, despite his implied critiques of both "Lords and Gentry," the relator also invokes for possible blame those unnamed multitudes who follow the upper sorts into the countryside. His attacks or "hits" are always passing, tactical strikes. "All things [are] so out of order," he cries, and then, as if quoting someone else, he adds, "Wars are necessary"—but then he again catches himself: "oh no, but tarry, / I wish they'd not bin begun." He explains his "wish" further while protesting that he himself cannot judge, unlike Habermas's reasoning educated elite:

> For where a Kingdom
> Is of itselfe divided,
> And people knows [sic] not
> By whom they should be guided
> It is too great a matter
> By me to be decided. (st. 7)

Here the poor tradesman's constant questioning takes the form of removing himself (safely) from any declared opinion. He tactically hides his twice-made critique of the "rich"—including in this category perhaps many of the multitudes who "spend" in running after the rich, even if they only spend their judgment—behind a claimed and conventional ignorance born of his lowly status.

The relator's inability or refusal to name names and cite specific causes (other than most broadly condemning "civill wars"), and his only in passing laying blame on the "rich" and the "multitudes" able to spend, is a deliberate refusal of decision-making or openly taking sides. Such evasiveness is beguiling, since it is voiced from the self-described lowly position of a "poor ignorant," with whom his fellow tradesmen would likely identify. You can lose your head in these troubled times if you too overtly express your judgment. It's both the "Lords and Gentry" who are at fault, and neither the "Lords" nor "Gentry" who are at fault, just to muddle the blame. The abstracted "multitudes" are included, too—those who have faultily deserted the city following these rich "to see" and "judgement spending, / and commending / the same to be well done." It's all beyond *me*, he on the surface seems to say. And yet, especially the "richer sort," including "Lords and Gentry," by comparison with the relator/singer and those who would assemble around him, are the twice jabbed-at "richer sort."

Surprisingly, what emerges most strongly in the second half of the ballad, however, is another, more interventionist tactical allegiance specifically aligned with the Royalist cause (which at this historical point was the cause *losing* authority). Again, the relator/singer in the second half of the ballad adopts a position only metaphorically, and thus at one remove; he says that in the good ole days, tradesmen easily "*enjoyed*: / Every weeke a *Noble* [a gold coin worth six shillings, eight pence] / clear without trouble" (st. 6; my emphases). "Noble," especially aligned with "enjoyed" (versus the more literal economic designation of "made" or "earned"), metaphorically invokes the House of Lords again but now more sympathetically—it is "enjoyed." The relator takes another temporary hit at the Lords' opponents—the rising parliamentarians—through the use of ballad convention. After his nonspecific, almost commonplace lament on things being "so out of order," he follows the convention of many broadside ballads by concluding with a prayer for the health of the ruler. At this moment in time, such a prayer could be seen as still nothing but patriotic given that "The Protestation Act," requiring that all adults sign an oath of allegiance to the monarch, was still in effect.[15] We might, however, by now make an association between the twice-invoked godly "Lord" prayed to in the concluding stanza of the ballad and the House of *Lords* (reminding us again of the wanted "Noble" referenced above), as well as between the same Lord God and the king as divinely sanctioned. We now clearly, if only momentarily, hear a most moving plea for the restoration of the king to his center of power, London. Turning from his fellow poor tradesmen's lost economy to recall their lost "Gracious King," the relator wishes that "The Lord preserve and blesse Him / with safe return / To them that long do miss him, / And send him to remain / With them that well do wish him" (st. 8)—a prayer that places new, unsettling reverberations on the restated refrain that immediately follows, "Alas poor trades-men / What shall we doe?" The relator knows what he *wants* to do: he wishes to put the king back on the throne at the site of his seat of power, London. But he has no power to do so.

This protestatory ballad, in the form of insistent questioning, asks us to review the seemingly obvious meaning of the tune title and the illustrated cavalier-looking man and the fancy lady, who face and gesture to each other, as if in separated longing. The tune title underscores a sense of lamentable sundering: "*Hallow my Fancy whether wilt thou goe?*" The audience could now choose to hear the expression of love and the asking "whether wilt thou goe?" in the context of sociopolitical movements, both pro-parliamentarian and pro-Royalist. We also now might hear it multiply reverberating in our thoughts as we turn to more closely study the third woodcut impression above the second half of the ballad. The illustration represents a late Tudor-looking lord or gentleman—it's unclear by his garb of his exact status—seemingly making a sacrifice and kneeling in prayer. Aggressively approaching him is a crowd of what look like Tudor middling sorts (again their garb is unclear regarding their social placement, but the flat hat each wears was a Tudor fashion and the lack of evident fur lining to their robes makes them more middling than well-to-do). The image appears just above the tradesman's lament in the last column of text, "All things so out of order," to which he adds, "the Father kills the Son" (st. 7). Stated as if caption to the impression, with its sacrificial-like pyre and praying gentleman, one cannot help but think of the sacrifice of Isaac by Abraham in the Bible. Maybe suddenly, maybe earlier or later, one further catches a glimpse of the almost out-of-the-picture, royal crown floating above the pyre and seemingly dispersing the clouds, in the top left of the image. Within the context of the ballad, the crown clearly represents the king, Charles I, who appears through the diadem like a shining sun/Christ-like son in the heavens. The analogy is reinforced by the allusion to Abraham sacrificing his son. Together, sun of the heavens, son of god, son by divine right—the king—and son of Abraham become the subjects and objects of sacrificial prayer. Supporting this reading is another, likely earlier broadside ballad with the same illustration on it. The ballad laments a lost love who is twice referred to as "Queen" (in "*A well wishing to a place of pleasure*," c. 1629, sts. 6–8; EBBA 30305). The allusion in this ballad is to the Tudor queen Elizabeth I, who was especially associated with the sun. In the Armada portrait, for instance, Elizabeth's face is as bright as the sun shining down and shedding God's grace on her ships, which sail out to engage the Spanish Armada; the enemies of Elizabeth/God, in turn, only encounter a dark and deadly storm. Elizabeth's reign, in the middle of the turbulent times of insurrection against Charles I, was fondly and nostalgically remembered.

The invitation for a pro-Royalist public position, as tactically offered by the moving media of this ballad, is strong—not overt, not declared or named, but strong. Three possible social assemblages might coalesce around the singer through his on-the-fly jabs at the rich, combined with his inventive use of ballad conventions and of everyday language (following de Certeau's notion of tactical "phrasing," 229) together with the other mobile assemblages and remakings of ballad aesthetics (art and song). One possible singular assemblage would be a collectivity or public of poor city tradesmen, perhaps extending to embrace all poor sorts, in lament over the economic and social damage done to them by those richer than they are, especially the "Lords and Gentry" and their "multitudes" of followers. Another singular assemblage is of those same poorer sorts but further united with the governing gentry, nodding along to the song in agreement that the rich, twisted cavaliers and lords are at fault (such a Parliament-aligned assemblage might even see the city crowd in the third illustration as not angrily threatening but heatedly backing up a gentrified member of Parliament willing to sacrifice the king not to sacrifice *for* the king). The third singular assemblage might be of Royalists rallying around the poor tradesmen in sympathetic prayer for the restoration of a God-given (and sociopolitically lords-given) order ruled by King Charles. All such possible assemblages, even the last, which I have most prominently foregrounded, are possible ephemeral publics. Indeed, the ballad ends on a question, not an answering, of: what to do? With whom should we ally? The mobile multimedia of this broadside ballad makes all three moving tactical publics momentarily possible but ultimately also impossible. The disseminated, performed, and entertained (in many senses of the word) broadside ballad artifact makes possible publics only to unmake them at the same time, knowing it cannot definitely *do* anything.

This broadside ballad is not an instance elucidating the concepts of assemblage theory, of making publics, or of tactical media. As in selecting Lego-block pieces from different piles for creating some "new" imagined thing, the ballad combines facets of all three theories toward a novel end. Like snapping together familiar Lego-block shapes, it employs the simple aesthetics and established vocabulary of culturally specific but common ballad experience—akin to what de Certeau dubs "the everyday." The ballad deploys its constituent moving media into a tactical production and consumption of several possible ephemeral assemblages or, more accurately, many provisional publics. None is solely family or guild or class based (all of these categories DeLanda would include on his sliding scale of assemblages). Most important, more than one assemblage of publics is tactically offered by those on the production end of this broadside ballad—those printing licentiously (since unlicensed) at this historical moment—but no one position or group, other than that voiced by the marginalized poor tradesman, who reaches out in his questioning to embrace an abstracted collective *more*, is sanctioned. Whom the viewer, reader, or listener attempts to tactically gather round in common cause is left deliberately open-ended, despite subtle insinuations—not actively advocated for—of an answer to the title's question, "Alas poore Trades-men what shall we do?" and to the tune's backup question, "*Hallow my Fancy whether wilt thou goe?*" Indeed, the tune's question is not *whither* but *whether*, and the answer seems to be, sadly, nowhere.

This is just one moving example, rare in its political interventions (however tactically guarded), as opposed to other ways of extemporaneously making publics, which we will also pursue in this book, drawing upon the methodological matrix of assemblage theory, making publics, and tactics. This close-reading snapshot of the multimedia of one lone surviving edition of a broadside ballad, otherwise lost forever, like its unrecoverable melody, suggests why broadside ballads were so popular in their own time, gaining more popularity with accessibility today, and in need of the kind of multipronged study I here offer in the following pages, images, and audio tracks of *The Broadside Ballad in Early Modern England.*

Part I

Assembling by Disassembling

Archives, Databases, and Ballad Bits

CHAPTER 2

Accessing the Artifact, Now and Then

Large databases such as EEBO, ECCO (Eighteenth Century Collections Online), and EEBO-TCP (EEBO Text Creation Partnership) have opened up early modern scholarship. Despite their high subscription fees, these digital archives allow almost immediate access to facsimiles and even, in the case of the TCP, to diplomatic transcriptions of rare texts that could formerly have been viewed only on difficult-to-retrieve microfilm (itself costly) or through long and expensive travel to visit "the real thing."[1] Nearly as important to advancing scholarship, because they offer free access, are the online projects inspired by such databases as UC Santa Barbara's English Broadside Ballad Archive (EBBA, ebba.english.ucsb.edu), which is the primary resource for this book. But it is not just facsimiles we can now access online. Digital methods of data mining (algorithmically processing large amounts of information) and visualization tools (for querying TEI/XML-encoded text), often made freely available, have even further opened our access to early modern works. Michael Witmore, for instance, describes experiments in the lemmatizing of texts algorithmically so that they can be searched by forms of grammatical address; this is one goal of the Working Group for Digital Inquiry at the University of Wisconsin–Madison, which to this end has incorporated 1,000 TCP items printed in Britain and North America from 1630 through 1809. Through such large digital analyses, texts become, in Witmore's words, "*massively addressable*" ("Text: A Massively Addressable Object"; emphasis Witmore's). But have digital archives and computational methods and analytics done more than widen the doors to early modern scholarship? Have their modus operandi also changed the way we actually perceive, understand, or "remember" the early modern past? This question is especially relevant to my present inquiry, not least because I draw extensively on the EBBA website. I thus rely heavily on its granular citations and advanced search options—

including its evolving digital tools, such as computational analytics—designed to make fully available the archive's multiple facsimile viewings, image associations, and recordings.

In some ways, one might argue, capacious databases and digital analyses don't reflect a dramatic change or new way of thinking from old methods of searching and gathering materials of the early modern corpus. There is nothing much new in the drive to assemble and categorize different kinds of information on a grand scale. The digital archiving that is now proceeding fast apace and on a global scale expresses an age-old "human obsession," as Kevin Curran observes. Providing some historical perspective, Curran points out that "the relentless endeavor to gather information (on just about anything) and to store it, has been going on since antiquity" ("Virtual Scholarship"; see also Luciana Duranti, "Archives as a Place"). For Matthew Steggle, collecting impulses have especially deep roots in the history of early modern scholarship. An example he cites, among many such ambitious projects, is the *Short-Title Catalogue of Books Printed in England . . . 1475–1640 (STC)*, edited by A. W. Pollard and G. R. Redgrave, and its continuation, covering 1641–1700, compiled by Donald Goddard Wing (now online and updated as a single resource, the ESTC). Steggle argues that "the digital 'revolution' is made possible and shaped by, and must be considered in relation to, the major scholarly compendiums of the pre-digital age at which early modernists have long excelled" ("'Knowledge will be multiplied'"). Witmore would add that "physical texts [of all eras] were already massively addressable before they were ever digitized, and this variation in address was and is registered at the level of the page, chapter, the binding of quires, and the like." By "address," Witmore would seem to indicate some kind of physical or mental interaction or engagement by the reader with the work. For example, he offers "an index or marginal note in a text" ("Text: A Massively Addressable Object").

Still, one might counter-respond that something very new is afoot via the expansive circuits of the Internet in the ways we collect and think about the past. This is the position of Roger Chartier, who argues that what categorizes the new is, in a word, fragmentation:

> Reading in front of the computer screen is generally a discontinuous reading process that seeks, using keywords or thematic headings, the fragment that the reader wishes to find: an article in an electronic periodical, a passage in a book, or some information in a website. This is done without the identity or coherence of the entire text from which the fragment is extracted necessarily being known. In a certain sense, one might say that in the digital world all textual entities are like

> databases that offer fragments, the reading of which in no way implies a perception of the work or the body of works from which they come. ("Languages, Books, and Reading," 142)

In large part, I agree with Chartier's rendering of the web experience of accessing and reading texts. But along the lines of historical "continuum theories," such as those proposed by Curran, Steggle, and Witmore, one wonders: is the modern felt experience of a received fragmentariness really something radically new? Or does such fragmentariness, rupture, or what one might call the *dis*assembling of digital delivery also characterize the methods of traditional scholarship of the early modern period and, perhaps even more fundamentally, the ways early moderns themselves experienced their print culture? My answer, of course, is "yes" (as we shall see especially here and through Chapter 5). In both the early modern period—through experiences of what I call the moving or *passing present*—and in today's modern times—through searches to access the removed or "distant past"—early modern print culture was experienced as *re*collected early modern print culture. That is, there has always been an ongoing process, then and now, of assembling by disassembling in which fragmentation plays a key role. This is especially the case with early modern street literature like broadside ballads.

I do not, I want to emphasize, imply any notion of the privative in my use of "fragmentation" and "fragment." These terms, as I employ them, do not signify a lack. To think in this negative way is to embrace a holistic ontology of the kind defined and opposed by DeLanda, as we saw in Chapter 1. A holistic ontology, to reiterate DeLanda's position, is built upon "relations of interiority" in which the fragment or part is seen to be integrated into a seamless or organic whole—derogatorily labeled by DeLanda as "taxonomic essentialism" (28). In breaking away from such a role-determining whole, the part becomes an undirected and incomplete fragment. Such a privative notion of the part gains momentum with Romanticism and explains the movement's fashion for writing unfinished verse. The verse fragment here represents deficiency; in Romantic reasoning, it points to an ideal but unattainable end product or design. Calling attention to the unattainable whole, Romantics often included "Fragment" in the titles of their works. Such thinking further led to a process of "ceaseless revision" by Shelley and other Romantics, and hence to many unpublished, because unfinished, pieces of poetry.[2] However, as early as the sixteenth century, according to the *Oxford English Dictionary* (*OED*), "fragment" could also mean an autonomous part of something that is simply "detached from a whole." Consider, for instance, Claudius Hollyband's

1583 statement: "They promised to bring me . . . some of the leavinges, or fragmentes [of the feast]" (cited in *OED*, "Fragment," 1). A fragment of the feast—a leaving—retains its independent autonomy. It is not limited by "relations of interiority." That is, by virtue of its independence, a fragment can be extracted from a whole without its suffering a loss of individual identity and, like a Lego block, can be plugged into another whole. In the process, it maintains its enduring self but acquires different kinds of relations and thus significances. Such an autonomous but newly interactive fragment should be understood, as we have seen, in terms of DeLanda's "relations of exteriority." That is, to return to the example of Hollybrand's "leavings" from the feast, the extracted edible fragments could have been mixed together without loss of their singular properties; but newly mingled, they would have produced a fresh assemblage that likely would have acquired, in the aggregate, novel tastes, textures, and even smells. Furthermore, to extend DeLanda's logic, any assemblage thus formed out of reassembled independent parts can itself become a part of a larger assemblage. DeLanda's theory, in sum, leads to an ontology of "assemblages-within-assemblages." Whatever the roles of the parts within the newly assembled wholes, "relations of exteriority" continue to define the resultant aggregates. In such continual reassembling processes, the consumer would not sense what Chartier understands as the necessary result of fragmentation—"rupture."

For Chartier, the "rupture" created by what he sees negatively as the fragmenting web comes largely from the missing physical book (the "whole" that can be held in one's hands and in its entirety stored with others of its ilk in a sited library). We might thus begin our investigation into the ramifications of new digital archives and data analytics of textual artifacts by taking one step back to the moment before the reading of a text even begins, and consider the process of finding books, then and now. Looking back roughly to the pre-1990s, compare searching for texts via card catalogs in an "old-style" research library, on the one hand, and via computers in modernized libraries, on the other. In some ways, there *was* more predictability and "wholeness" to the former process. Everyone necessarily proceeded through stable subject categories (prescribed by the Library of Congress), or by author or title, and when one searched by subject, the title card would be embedded alphabetically amid a multitude of other cards on the same topic among which one might further browse. In the subsequent old-style method of physically searching for the actual book on the shelf, which continues today (though card catalogs have mostly become things of the past or, as in the remodeled Yale Sterling Library, mere decoration), books are similarly gathered with many others of like sort, allowing again for a kind of overview or "whole" vision.

In the searching of databases, however, the Library of Congress subject categories tend to be inconsistently applied by catalogers working with programmers, or they tend to produce too huge a return. One frequently resorts to the option of querying by nonstandardized keywords or phrases, which can produce a helter-skelter array of "hits." For example, a keyword search for "blackamoor" in EEBO turns up a long and motley list of plays, romances, sermons, ballads, and pamphlets, some of which contain a casual metaphorical use of the term, some of which discuss actual blackamoors, and most of which apparently have little to do with each other. The results of such a search in our electronic age, especially for those of us who remember using the old card catalogs, can indeed appear sometimes overwhelmingly fragmentary, in the privative sense, and hopelessly haphazard. The sense of a bewildering randomness can intensify with new analytics like the potential algorithmic lemmatization imagined by Witmore, in which, for any one text or set of texts, "we could talk about individual lines of print, all the nouns in every line, every third character in every third line," and so on ("Text: A Massively Addressable Object").

But this is not to say that the old method of research was not also prone to confusion (especially when one was unsure of the Library of Congress subject category or the exact title of a work or the exact spelling of an author's name) and—often more fortuitously—subject to accidental "hits." We sometimes forget how the haphazard was actually a key part of old-style library research, both in searching through a card catalog and in roaming the physical shelves. Looking for a sonnet sequence for my first book in the stacks of the University of Wisconsin–Madison, for instance, I remember finding shelves of other sonnet sequences, but also, right below them, two shelves of miscellanies (little books containing short poems much like sonnet sequences). I ended up writing a chapter that addressed both kinds of small lyric assemblages as linked cultural phenomena, a combined study that I might never have imagined without being physically in the shelves and by happenstance seeing the material connections, and which I probably never would have encountered through a database search. At the same time, in the physical stacks my eye would often skip over shelves, scanning them for similar titles, if not systematically looking at every third shelf or third book, and make some other "happy"-stance connections.

So, in a key way, the new electronic database age is no different from the old card catalog and shelf-searching age. There has always been a haphazard or an accidental or a partial means of accessing the extant repositories of the early modern period. There has never been a system of accessing a "whole" vision of the past, only dismembered or piecemeal glimpses of it. Any apparently achieved whole story, as Frances E. Dolan observes in her essay "Tracking the Petty Traitor," is in fact a composite narrative constructed by researchers from historical fragments and, as such, is fictional: "a deceptively coherent tale" (164). Even the Library of Congress subject categories provide only partial windows onto the total repository of books, and they function to separate them out as much as to gather them together.

The difference between old and new is really more one of degree, due to the magnitude of the many modern databases and the almost infinite piecemeal analytics and assemblages their searches make possible.[3]

But two additional—and admittedly paradoxical—points need to be stressed about the resulting intensified digital worldview of early modern print culture, parts of which I have passingly addressed in the Introduction and Chapter 1:

1. The accelerated or intensive fragmentation of vision made available via large databases such as EEBO and ECCO, and especially by more focused as well as more multimedia and multiply searchable databases such as EBBA, allows us to create a more nearly whole vision of the past than was previously available through traditional research avenues precisely because it offers us manifold and mobile fragmentary "views."

2. Such reassembling through countless disassemblings or fragmentations approximates the early modern period's own access to its printed materials—at both the macro and micro levels—which could never have been stable and "whole." As a corollary to this point, I posit that early moderns likely did not equate such fragmentation of access with faulty incompletion or a mangling of texts but rather with a perceived routine or everyday experience of partial encounters with textual artifacts.

As with my first point, I have already gestured to my second point in Chapter 1, in surveying the multifarious ways broadside ballads were "moving." But a further fleshing out of the piecemeal practices of putting together the ballad's component parts, both in the shop (on the artifact's production) and in public and/or domestic spaces (on its dissemination), will better allow us to discern more precisely how the ballad's "whole" protean identity was always only partially graspable. I offer as exempla two variant editions, each extant in one unique copy, of a topical ballad—more topical than might at first appear, as we shall see. I've standardized the ballads' titles (which also sport some differences) for ease of reference as "Mock-Beggar Hall." Moving between these two ballad editions well illustrates the extraordinary extent to which publishers and printers at both micro and macro levels tactically rearranged a ballad's component bits and pieces—of words, illustrations, and tune(s)—into an apparent whole entity. In Chapter 3, focusing on the first of these "Mock-Beggar Hall" ballads, I offer a sampling of possible "hits" or associations a contemporary might have made to this ballad, either in whole or in part(s). Such hits would not have occurred in an ethereal cyberspace search, of course, but in the everyday act of geographically, temporally, cognitively, and affectively traversing early modern London and its environs (as well as far into the countryside and beyond). In their routine daily lives, contemporaries had many random encounters with other broadside ballads that might well have provoked ties with either of our two in-the-news ballads or with one or more of their component parts. Associational hits accumulate, creating further links to other ballad artifacts or to just one or more of *their* component parts as well as to other bricolage-like fragments of related street ephemera. At the end of Chapter 3, I will return to the problematics of digital access and more fully address my first point above, revisiting how modern databases, such as EBBA, can re-create something of the production, dissemination, and consumption of the haphazard and fragmentary hits an early modern might make on a daily basis.

Micro Stirring Bits and Pieces: The One/Two Ballad(s) of "Mock-Beggar Hall"

Let us first turn then to my representative case of tactical piecemeal making: the fascinating reassemblages made to the ballad "Mock-Beggar Hall" upon its being reissued in a second edition. As was not uncommon practice, neither edition of "Mock-Beggar Hall" was registered, as required by law, with the Stationers' Company. Both ran under the official radar. The ballads have also endured only in one broadside ballad collection: the immense four-volume (five-book) Roxburghe collection, begun in the seventeenth century by Robert Harley and now held at the British Library. By the nineteenth century, the assemblage of ballads had passed through many antiquarians' hands, and each collector added to what became known as the Roxburghe Ballads, named after its fourth owner, John Ker, third Duke of Roxburghe (1740–1804). The volumes eventually expanded to include some 1,428 mostly pre-1701 broadside

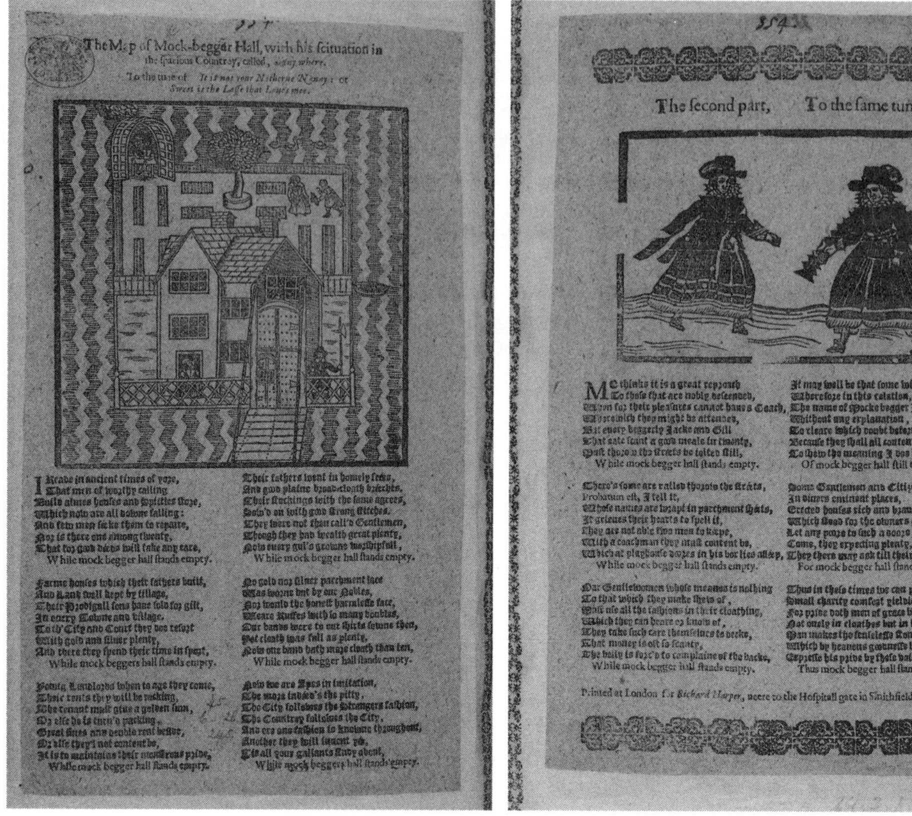

Figure 7. Album facsimile (closeup), "The Map of Mock-begger Hall, with his scituation in the spacious Countrey, called, *Anywhere*" (c. 1633–35), EBBA 30174. Post-photographic processing by EBBA. British Library, Roxburghe 1.252–253, C.20.f.7.252–253. © The British Library Board.

ballads. Our two "Mock-Beggar Hall" editions are Roxburghe 1.252–253 and 3.218–219 (EBBA 30174 and 30866). They are datable, I shall argue more fully in the next chapter, based on their topicality, to c. 1633–35 and c. 1639–40, respectively.[4] I cite them for further ease of reference as the first and second "Mock-Beggar Hall" ballads (Figures 7 and 8).

In anticipation of the possible objection to my using just two surviving editions, or copies, of a broadside ballad as "representative" of ballad piecemeal assemblage and reassemblage, I want to underscore that only half of extant ballads are listed by the Stationers' Company in its Register (Rollins, "Black-Letter Broadside Ballad," 281). Broadside ballads were thus often issued without legal approval, either to escape the sixpence fee or to evade sanction. Furthermore, as the saying goes, love kills. Specifically, some of

Mock-Beggers Hall, with his scituation in the spacious Country, called, Any where.
To the Tune of It is not your Northern Nanny; or Sweet is the Lass that loves me.

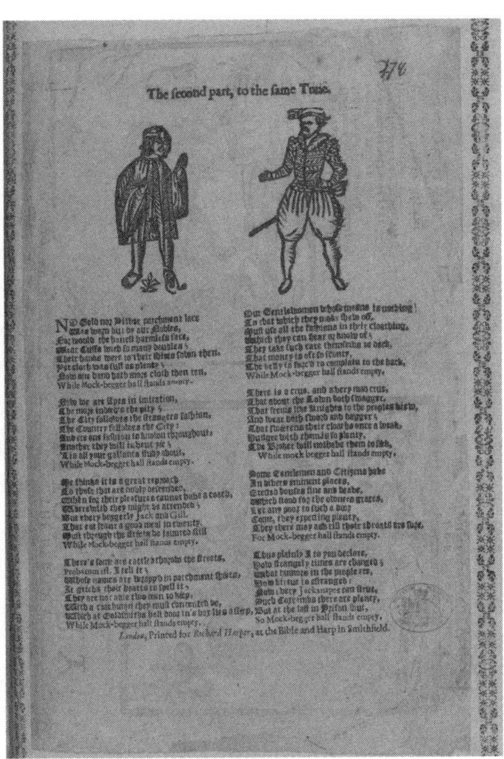

The second part, to the same Tune.

London, Printed for Richard Harper, at the Bible and Harp in Smithfield.

Figure 8. Album facsimile (closeup), "*Mock-Beggers Hall, with his scituation in the spacious Country, called,* Any where" (c. 1639–40), EBBA 30866. Post-photographic processing by EBBA. British Library, Roxburghe 3.218–219, C.20.f.9.218–219. © The British Library Board.

the most popular early modern broadside ballads, of which we hear frequent snatches in the literature of the period, don't survive because they were so savored that they got "used up"—overhandled, to the extent of being folded and refolded into pieces, or proudly displayed on walls that were later whitewashed over. In addition, though occasional ballads were much cherished at the moment of their topicality, once no longer fashionable or in the news, they were frequently discarded or recycled.

Consider, for instance, "Anne Wallens Lamentation" (Pepys Ballads 1.124–125, c. 1616; EBBA 20053). This sole-surviving ballad powerfully tells the story of a real-life husband murderer, Anne Wallen. The ballad visually, orally, and textually depicts her most moving story, voiced in the first person, as she stands bound to the stake about to be burned alive for her crime—the fire apparently engulfing her as she pronounces her final stanza! The gruesome punishment enacted in life and in the ballad was the penalty for petty treason whereby a wife murdered her husband (servants sentenced for petty treason, for killing their masters, on the other hand, were simply hanged). The sensational show put on by the execution of a woman for husband murder naturally drew a crowd. As told by John Chamberlain, the burning alive of Anne, furthermore, seems to have violently affected at least one of the many bystanders: a woman, on her way home after witnessing Anne's fiery fate for husband murder, Chamberlain recounts, ruthlessly murdered her own child (reported in Dolan, "Petty Traitor," 159–60). Adding fuel to such a strong emotive response to the real-life execution, the broadside ballad not only capitalizes on Anne's spectacular crime and punishment by rendering her story in her own voice but also was likely hawked at the very scene of her execution. Given the large gathering and stirring news value of the event being witnessed, one would think that the broadside ballad would have been in much demand as a memento by the onlookers and by later readers/viewers/listeners of Anne's stirring story. And, yet once again, we note, only one copy survives. It was preserved by the avid ballad-lover and collector Samuel Pepys. The many other disseminated copies of the ballad likely suffered consumption not through fire, like Anne, but rather through popularity. Such could also well have been the fate of what must have been thousands of copies of our two "Mock-Beggar Hall" editions (certainly, as we shall see in the next chapter, the two ballads captured imaginations, as evidenced in the renaming of later tunes after the ballads' insistent, if slightly variant, refrain, "While mock begger hall stands empty"; for example, EBBA 35353, 33670, 31959, 30825, and 31954).

The two "Mock-Beggar Hall" ballads that *do* survive offer layers of topicality, as we shall see in this chapter and the next. At the most elemental level, they provide variant commentaries upon the same bottom line and familiar complaint of the time: that the landed wealthy, who have estates in the countryside, have been lured by the delights of London to sell off their rural properties, head for London, spend their wealth on city and court fashions, and thus leave their country halls inhospitably empty. In the ballads' joint frontal attack on the period's perceived decline in country hospitality, they might not—at least not at first glance to the modern reader—seem to offer much in the way of "news" or to be that different from each other. Nor would they seem to employ particularly evasive "tactics," as we have discussed such maneuvers in de Certeau's sense of the word in Chapter 1 and seen them at work in the c. 1646 ballad, "Alas poore Trades-men what shall we do?" De Certeauian tactics, we recall, involve spontaneous, on-the-fly redirections and remakings of conventional (read "status quo," even "authoritarian") tools and practices. But appearances, as de Certeau pointedly observes—and especially the surface conventions of broadside ballads, as we shall repeatedly witness in this study—can be deceiving on many fronts.

Telltale signs of more subtle tactics at work are evident in both ballads' repeating over and over at the end of each of their stanzas the refrain "While mock begger hall stands empty." The relator of the first ballad fears (somewhat disingenuously, I suspect) that the refrain, specifically the phrase "mock begger," might cause confusion: "It may well be that some will muse, / Wherefore in this relation, / The name of Mocke begger I doe use," he says. He thus offers an explanation to "cleare which doubt before I end" (st. 10). This stated need to clarify or "cleare" the meaning of "Mocke begger" is notably absent from the second ballad. Such is the case, I suspect, because by the time the second edition is issued, the relator's mockery has greatly expanded; it ranges so broadly now that it cannot be pinned down to a single explanation (as we also occasionally find in the first edition). Still, while only the first ballad explicitly recognizes the need for clarification, the stanza containing the offered explanation reappears and remains roughly the same in both editions:

> Some Gentlemen and Citizens have
> In divers eminent places,
> Erected houses rich and brave,
> Which stood for the owners graces,
> Let any poore to such a doore
> Come, they expecting plenty,
> They there may ask till their throats are sore,
> For mock begger hall stands empty. (st. 11)

As an empty hall—empty both of its owners and their "graces"—the "rich and brave" country estate, this explanatory stanza implies, is now but a mockery of beggars. The "poore" are left outside the estate's doors, empty-stomached and hoarse of throat; though by tradition they would have been relieved with "plenty," such ancient customs now ring hollow in the empty hall.

But how "cleare" is my rendering of the relator's "explanation" of "Mocke begger"? Who even is doing the mocking, as described in the stanza, if anyone? Despite the initial "hit"—by which I mean both strike at and association with—"Gentlemen and Citizens," the very powerful and rich nobles are not named, only metaphorically alluded to. They are just hinted at in the sly reference to "owners *graces*." As he does throughout both ballads, the relator dodges the danger of striking the very high, even though nobles were most guilty of abandoning their "eminent places" in the country for the delights and selfish opportunities offered by city and court. The proposed clarification of the phrase "Mocke begger" further dodges outright clarity as it returns, like the repressed, in the echoing final line of the stanza. Instead of employing a verb form of "mock"—e.g., "mocked"—and thus exposing a condemnable act of insult done to the poor by the high, the relator returns by the end of the stanza to the more passive adjectival form of "mock." The verb becomes the descriptor of the poor. It is as if the beggar is inherently, that is, by nature, not by any direct action of the high, a "mock begger." Such a subtle slide away from directly accusing the rich and powerful elite of mocking beggars (which slippage occurs at the end of every stanza of both ballads and thus insinuates itself into our thinking), leaves open some wiggle room—an "out" equally available for the potentially offending relator and the potentially offended higher sort of consumer. Both ballads thus employ a hit-and-run approach typical of tactical strikes. After all, to provide a "cleare" and sustained attack upon the powerful aristocracy could lead to its powerfully striking back.

The two "Mock-Beggar Hall" ballads, then, share a tactical critique of the wealthy upper sorts for neglecting rural hospitality, impelled by their greed for city and court fashions. But from this shared point of contact, they in other ways significantly diverge. Indeed, the producers of the second ballad have radically plucked out, reordered, and supplemented bits and pieces as well as large chunks of the first ballad, remodeling it into something of a different tactical order of beast.

Textually, what is perhaps at first glance most striking are the variations between the ballads at the most micro level of orthography, punctuation, and formatting. The full title to the first (earlier) ballad is "The Map of Mockbegger Hall, with his scituation in / the spacious Countrey, called, *Anywhere*"; the second (later) ballad is titled "*Mock-Beggers Hall, with his scituation in the spacious / Country, called,* Any where." The printing of the ballads' tune titles—and, as if deliberately making the job of pinning down these protean ballad creatures more difficult, we are offered not one but two possible tunes to which they might be sung—undergo similar micro piecemeal takings apart and putting back together. The following indicates alterations made to the first ballad's printed tune titles by the second, shown in square brackets: "*It is not your Northerne* [*Northern*] *Nanny:* [Nanny;] or <new line in first edition; no new line in second> *Sweet is the Lasse* [*Lass*] *that Loues* [*loves*] *mee* [*me*]." Such micro moving around of textual bits occurs throughout the second ballad.

Exemplifying assemblage theory, as we have seen it advanced most notably by DeLanda, the living persons who cooperate to make ballads as well as to manipulate their component inanimate pieces are also mobile, independent units subject to reassemblage. Thus, though the publisher of the ballads identified on the ballad sheets seems at first a stable identity linking the two artifacts—with a consistent typeface and spelling of his name—he too plays a movable part. The ballads' imprints imply he has shifted his place of sale, or at least its naming, between printings. The first imprint, which the British Book Trade Index (BBTI, www.bbti.bham.ac.uk/), dates as in use from 1634 through 1637, reads "Printed at London for Richard Harper, *neere to the Hospitall gate* in Smithfield" (the hospital here is St. Bartholomew's). But the second imprint, dated by the BBTI to 1639–40, declares "London, Printed for Richard Harper, *at the Bible and Harp* in Smithfield" (my emphases). Though only the accomplished fact of the ballads' printing and no particular printer, nor place of printing, is named, in all likelihood the printer too has been switched out along with the publisher's shifting places of sale. It is as if the printer, like the Lego-block pieces that made up ballads, were himself but an interchangeable component of the ballads' production. The strong suggestion of different printers at work in the different ballads is especially flagged by the changes made to the second ballad in the families of typeface used as well as in the text's grammar and orthography (printers tended to favor their own mental style sheet).[5]

But why, one might still ask, would Harper change printers when the first printer's product was popular enough to encourage Harper's investment in a reissue of it? The reason could be attributed to practicality: perhaps the second printer was simply closer to Harper's new place of business. But London was at the time a small city, easy to traverse, and publishers often favored certain printers whom they used over and over again even if they switched locales. Most likely, I posit, Harper's goal was precisely to introduce the many micro changes into the first ballad that he knew would ensue on changing printers, given their individual printing styles. The end product would be both familiar enough to evoke an "ah, yes!" consumer sense of comfortable continuity and new enough to create the "oh, now what?" of consumer curiosity.

From Micro to Macro Stirrings of Multimedia

As we have seen, the second printing of our two "Mock-Beggar Hall" ballads engages in micro piecemeal textual moving about, in terms of pulling out and plugging in, individual letters, bits of punctuation, and—what can only be perceived by the viewer as altered empty space—moving around bits of spacing material (quads, thins, leading, furniture, etc.). But to ensure an eye-

and ear-catching new continuous experience, the reissue also produces more macro changes to all the ballad's component media.

The macro textual alterations to the first edition would have been obvious on reading or hearing the two ballads together or even after a lapse in time. In effect, the author, printer, and/or publisher, working either individually or as an assembled team, created something of an optical illusion to make it seem like major textual changes have been made. But the tactic employed is relatively simple. Two stanzas from the first edition have been dropped (including the key one discussed above, stating the need for an "explanation" of the insistent use of "Mocke begger"). In addition, five new stanzas are inserted. New are the first three stanzas as well as the third-to-last and the final stanza. The new stanzas are thus placed so as to create a fresh introduction and conclusion to the first edition. The alteration of just these few stanzaic parts does not just add extra pieces to the first ballad's patchwork (so that, for instance, the earlier version's eleventh—and penultimate—stanza appears, in the later ballad, as the thirteenth stanza, and though retaining its penultimate status, is now sandwiched, one might even say "crowded out," by two new stanzas, which expand and dominate the conclusion). These few alterations also change the alignment of stanzas on the page so that the visual effect, on glancing at the text, is of an (almost) entirely new ballad.

Even more slyly on the producer(s)' part, though the three initial stanzas of the first ballad are now completely switched out, starting us out on a new textual note, retained is a near-repetition of the lead-in phrase of the first ballad's opening line, "I Reade in ancient times of yore." But now that recognizable phrase is plugged into a different section of the text. Especially mobile, the phrase turns up slightly altered, and like a faint echo of its first positioning, a full twenty-five lines later, rendered as "I read in ancient times of *poor*" (st. 4; my emphasis). By cutting, moving around, and adding whole stanzas, as well as moving and altering micro bits of text, the second "Mock-Beggar Hall" becomes a newly fashioned fifteen-stanza ballad versus the original twelve-stanza one. In the final analysis, though, two-thirds of the text of the first ballad is retained in the second. It just feels like much more of the poetry has been altered because of the adding of macro parts of text; the rearranging of the individual stanzas; and, of course, the micro switching out of letters, words, phrases, and punctuation—again as if every bit and piece of the whole was an autonomous and thus freely movable part.

The new text of the second ballad introduces from the very beginning more strongly than the first edition the absence of country hospitality in present times; most striking, in a dramatic extension of this point, it depicts the grimy descent into urban greed of all the city's orders. Everyone, it would now seem, not just the well to do who have abandoned their country estates, has succumbed to a prideful lust for money and city fashions—to the extent that social aspirants engage in criminal behavior to achieve them. The first stanza of the second edition strikes the new grungy note, stressing "stealing" and "false knaves" (st. 1), as opposed to ancient "plain dealing." The second and third stanzas evoke aggression and criminality as well, picturing the rather ludicrous image of a fashionable hangman—"The hangman now the fashion keeps, / And swaggers like our gal[l]ants"—as well as violent men who "flout" "Prodigals" (st. 2), and, in another rather ridiculous image, whores who aggressively seek uppity styles. The cited example, in stanza 3, is "Joan Du[s]t," who "hath bought a smock of Lawn. / And now begins to quarrell." The new thirteenth stanza reinforces the initial quarrelsome and swaggering attitudes in describing "a very mad crue, / That about the Town doth swagger, / That seems like Knights to the peoples view / And wear both sword and dagger" (st. 13). And in the new final stanza, we hear that "now [e]very *Jackanapes* [trained monkeys or ridiculous upstarts] can strut, / Such Coxcombs [foolish, conceited, showy persons] there are plenty, / But at the last in Prison shut, / So Mock-begger hall stands empty" (st. 15).[6] By the final lines of the second ballad's disillusioned story of London greed and social decay, not only does the "eminent" country hall remain empty, but the corrupt city's prisons are fast filling up.

Reinforcing the sheer craziness of this "now" low-life urbanity, in which all classes take part, are the illustrations to the second ballad, which have bumped those of the first edition and would have been the most eye-catching difference between the two ballads. As we shall see more fully, they are idealized images and relics of a different age. When viewed within the context of the text that they supposedly illustrate, they can thus be only understood as ironic, even satiric. The first ballad's illustrations are more consonant with its more focused narrative complaint of abandoned country hospitality by the wealthy in greedy pursuit of money and city fashion—but also with a twist.

Yes, the prominent initial woodcut impression on our first "Mock-Beggar Hall" ballad pictures a large country estate—the kind of "eminent" place, we are told, that the wealthy landed "Gentlemen and Citizens" built and then abandoned. But the woodcut also distorts the ballad's insistent refrain, "While mock begger hall stands empty," because, well, the hall is far from empty. In fact, it is a picture of contradictory repulsion and occupation. The hall is surrounded by a seemingly forbidding moat. However, the drawbridge is down, providing easy crossing. Then again, the heavy iron-studded and window-barred door to the hall is firmly shut, and beside that impenetrable door stands a guard on alert, with pike in hand, as if to protect the entrance against all unwelcome guests. A woman (perhaps the owner or his wife?) stands with hands planted firmly on her hips, facing out at us through another window uninvitingly, conveying a passive aggression. But, then, curiously—participating in the odd population of this supposedly "empty" estate—at the backside, within the hall's fenced inner garden, a prospective male lover appears to have surreptitiously gotten access to the hall's grounds by means of a bauble of a boat, and we see him temporally and visually twice within the garden: on the right, in mid-wooing of a lady, and, in the far left back corner, nestled with the lady in an intimate banqueting arbor, apparently having succeeded in his courtship. In other words, select persons *can* gain access to this pictured hall. The occupants simply seem in no mood to "grace" unwelcome visitors—that is, the poor. Furthermore, in a deviation from the ballad's narrative, the image (and the hall?) caters to another desire that trumps greed or fashion: lust.

The second illustration to the first "Mock-Beggar Hall" ballad is of a very different sort. It mostly holds to the narrative thrust of the ballad, though it also tactically, through topical allusion, adds to the ballad's critique of the wealthy. The woodcut from which the impression was made has clearly been much reused and has consequently suffered from the repeated force of the press: we detect worn-off areas to the black border and to part of the decorative band hanging from the top back shoulder of the woman on the left as well as loss of detail in both women's dresses. The woodcut has also been attacked by the insatiable worms which eventually ate into all the woodcuts of the time (to the perverse good fortune of helping modern scholars date the cuts). The worms leave circular holes, which can clearly be seen in the three prominent circles in the left woman's dress and the two at the bottom right of the black border. Still, one can make out the impression of two women with feathered hats and short hair aggressively facing each other. Though now mostly cut out of the woodblock, traces of a sword held in the right hand of the woman on the left can be detected (you can see it crossing her left arm). All of the sword but the part that crosses her arm has been at some point removed from the block, likely for use of the woodblock on an earlier ballad or pamphlet for which the sword was ill-suited to its theme. That said, the woman on the right still holds a dagger in her left hand and what looks like a money bag in her right hand. How odd! The long bands that hang from both their backs like extra sleeves were a Jacobean fashion,[7] and they are specifically complained about in both ballads as an excess not only of the use of cloth but—in anticipation of the concluding stanza to the first ballad—of newfangled "pride," unlike the old days, we are told early on, when "Our bands were to our shirts sowne then, / Yet cloath was full as plenty." In a show of pride, the narrator laments, "Now one band hath more cloath than ten" (st. 5). Also relevant to the narrative of the both ballads is the apparent money bag that the lady on the right grasps. As noted above, both ballads, and especially the first "Mock-Beggar Hall" ballad, repeatedly complain about those well-to-do who hold country property but sell off their lands. Their goal?: to get "gold and silver plenty" (st. 2)—to fill their purses—so they can spend their money on such city fashions as these ladies sport, odd though they might look to us moderns.

The ladies' feathered hats, short hair, and aggressive stances in this first ballad are not directly commented upon in the text. But such features *are* the focus of other texts of the period and attributed to a new peculiar fashion adopted particularly by urban gentlewomen. They mark these women precisely with the kind of mannishness complained about in the antifeminist debate pamphlets, which peak in the 1610s and 1620s (though they continue into the mid-century).[8] After much searching through these pamphlets, I have yet to locate this particular cut. Nevertheless, the association with these pamphlets is unavoidably strong—especially for contemporaries who would have been visually literate in the fashions of their times. As we shall see, the associative hits this ballad might evoke with just such pamphlets and like-minded broadside ballads, which we will explore more fully in the next chapter, could very powerfully strike home. Even viewed as only component parts of our first "Mock-Beggar Hall" ballad, our two illustrations, considered in relation to the more tactically cautious text of the ballad, function to more vividly fill out its narrative critique of "citified" male and female wealthy sorts. They picture yet more deviant desires and fashions—to the point of making us question who or what is actually being mocked. To this question we shall return in expanding our vision of this ballad through associations with other broadside ballads, as well as with other cheap print of the time.

In the subsequent "Mock-Beggar Hall" ballad, issued some five years later, both of the first ballad's illustrations are not only removed but also replaced by three "new" ones. The replacement images, like those of the first set, are recycled woodcuts. The first picture now represents the "ancient times of yore" that both ballads textually extol. More accurately, the elite appear here prominently as they are imaginatively and idealistically recalled. The woodcut impression shows a lady with one hand resting on a scabbard from which a knight draws his sword, as if he were in the act of manly chivalry, and these two apparent lovers stand in front of an "eminent" estate-cum-castle, which the image implies is their residence. In sum, the elite in this illustration are very much present—indeed, foregrounded—as occupying their country hall, and presumably also supplying traditional hospitality. The entire woodcut looks downright ancient or medieval, and, indeed, it is. The impression derives from a woodcut that is over 100 years old. It was used by Wynkyn de Worde for his printing of the book-length edition of *Le Morte d'Arthur* and was likely custom cut for that publication.[9]

The third image, on the far right, is also a throwback, in this case to a time closer to the printing of the ballad but still an earlier, more fondly remembered, era from the perspective of many Jacobeans. Here we see a Tudor gentleman who is fashionably but not excessively well dressed. In the middle cut on the ballad appears a person very plainly clothed, who seems almost like a pauper. The gentleman and apparent pauper face each other and even reach out to each other, as if in rapport.

So, even though all of the second "Mock-Beggar Hall" ballad's illustrations have replaced those of the first—switching them out as if they were autonomous, interchangeable parts—the second ballad's pictures relate to both ballads in calling up the ideal "ancient times" referenced in their texts, and even, in its second and third illustrations, makes a gesture of actually acknowledging—to the extent of visually representing—the needy poor, who might well come to the occupied hall of the castle for relief, *and receive it.* These idealized illustrations bespeak a nostalgia for a lost past of "plain dealing" versus fashion, chivalry versus pride, and hospitality versus greed.

But—and this point would be perceived as either hilariously funny or bitterly sad—the idealized illustrations of an ancient past in the second "Mock-Beggar Hall" ballad have been tactically turned into a mockery of the text's newly issued depiction of widespread urban degeneration (or perhaps the new grimy urban reality, evoked so vividly in the text, mocks the imaginative nostalgia of the illustrations). In the second ballad's textual world, we have seen that violent, knavish, and self-promoting fashion rules, not the gentile and gentle rural hospitality of ancient times. In just the approximately five years between the printings of the two ballads, the already unsettled world of the text of the first "Mock-Beggar Hall" has fully fallen apart, making the "new" images ironic to the point of satiric. The seeds of such a radical decline and visual-textual clash—like all the aggressive, swaggering clashing of social sorts that now occupy London's city streets—were only germinating in the first ballad. They appear in passing references to "Apes in imitation" (st. 6) and "every beggarly Jacke and Gill [who] . . . Must thorow the streets be jolted still" (st. 7), and—as we will see when we look to other associative hits in the next chapter—in yet other evocative ways as well. But in the second ballad, the text, depicting widespread and violently knavish fashions, jostles in a most unsettling way with the idealized images supposedly illustrating it (and vice versa). Driving this perplexing critique home, the second edition of "Mock-Beggar Hall" retains a version of the second-to-last stanza of the first edition, describing "Gentlemen and Citizens" who "have / In divers eminent places,

/ Erected houses fine and brave, / Which stood for the owners graces." But most of the ballad's severely critical text, which jars with its romantic illustrations, proves that such estates in fact no longer stand "for the owners graces" of relieving the poor. Thus the second ballad retains (if even on this point constantly unsettling, through its variation), the derogatory refrain, which concludes the ballad: "So Mock-begger hall stand empty."

The tactical hit made by the clash of the illustrations with this penultimate stanza of one-time wealthy "Gentlemen and Citizens," however, is textually less upfront in the second ballad than in the first. Or, rather, it is more buried among a generalized satire in the narrative of all aspiring urban social sorts. The satire spreads across classes as well as genders, making the ballad text more widely mocking of London life in general. Tactically, the textual foregrounding of the decline of *all* society is politically safer than the much more evasive hits made in the first "Mock-Beggar Hall" ballad. That is, almost everyone—not any specific social sort—is now greedy, knavish, and fashion mad. The second ballad's target is so broad, even at points outlandish, that any individual consumer, especially one of the upper sorts, could have laughed at it without considering him- or herself personally indicted.

Micro and Macro Parts Voiced: Multiplying Tunes

Further complicating the textual and visual dissonances within and between the two sister ballads is the multiplication of tunes offered. In each case, the ballad sheet prints not one but two tune titles. The challenges of capturing even a "like" experience of the early modern singing and reception of ballad tunes, as we have discussed, here pose special obstacles. With the printing of two suggested tunes for each ballad, efforts at any recovery have been made doubly problematic. One seller, or one participatory audience assembled around the seller, might have chosen the first tune listed on the sheet by which to sing the text. But another such gathered group, especially if situated in an entirely different physical and social setting, might have chosen the second tune. Hearing one ballad sung to one tune and the same or its sister ballad sung to the other tune, a contemporary passing by—already bombarded by a plethora of aural stimuli from traversing the bustling streets of London—might have experienced a strong sense of disjointed familiarity; or, busily hustling along, he or she might not have made any connection at all!

The tunes, furthermore, are separable in more than two ways. Hawkers and/or consumers typically had their own personal singing styles, as singers do today, and also exercised their own personal tactics for adjusting a tune to make it fit the varying lines of a text, and vice versa, as Bell points out in his essay, "Fitting Texts to Tunes." Choices about which tune to sing to the text(s) of our ballad(s), and how to sing them, could have varied not only because of personal preferences and on-the-fly decisions about making the necessary adaptations between the score of music and the lines of poetry but also because singers likely also made choices on the basis of their own vocal skills. Indeed, the second listed tune on the ballad sheets, as we shall discuss more fully below, is considerably more difficult to sing than the first. For all these reasons, as discussed in Chapter 1, every tune I analyze in this book is accompanied by a modern musical transcription of a recording of the tune as it was sung by an individual, with a text underlay that both aligns the units of text to the notes sung and also indicates where the singer has placed the musical metrical (as opposed to the poetic metrical) stresses. This is why I also supplement the notational transcriptions from each recording with a slowed-down fiddle audio of the notes played; the listener—especially those not trained in music—can thus more easily both see and hear the musical and textual choices the singer has made. Of course, the individual singer is not, alas, an early modern, miraculously revived after 400 or more years. In addition, we must rely on early modern printed and manuscript music notations for our sources, when popular singers and audiences of the time may well have been musically illiterate (though by no means therefore unattuned to subtle and even sophisticated notation as orally passed on and heard). That said, it is worth noting that many tunes written down and published in the period were transcribed from oral tradition; that is, the notably plainer notations found in pre-1701 manuscript and print likely reflect a close correlation to lived song. Most important for the purposes of this book, our goal is to attain a "like" early modern singing experience, not to achieve "the" experience—some singular, Platonic peak. If we don't work with the evidence we have in hand, we are left not dumb-founded but deaf-founded.

Complicating any attempt to critically appreciate the ballads' tunes is the fact that music theory was in great flux on the continent and in England during the seventeenth century. This was a period of musical transition, where we might hear discussion of some twelve modes of music, as in Thomas Morley's *Plaine and Easie Introduction to Practicall Musicke* (1597), or just five, as in Charles Butler's *Principals of Musik* (1626). There is also evidence that the whole idea of modes was gradually giving way during the seventeenth century in favor of what would become today's major-minor tonality.[10] Furthermore, theory is just that: theory. It took music theory considerable time to catch up to changes that had already been made in music composition and practice at the time. And rarely did theory align with the customs of everyday singing—

particularly customs of singing popular melodies, with which music theory was little concerned. Butler, for instance, only briefly mentions ballads in his treatise and simplifies the genre. He characterizes what he calls the Ionian mode (comparable to today's major mode) as typical of "the infinite multitude of Balads" of his day; it was a fitting mode, he thought, for what he interpreted as ballads' upbeat or "pleasant and delightful" tunes. By contrast, he says, the Dorian—somewhat similar to the Aeolian or today's minor mode—fits the psalms in meter and "all grave," "honest," and "sober" songs.[11] But Butler's description of ballads as mostly cheery leaves out a large percentage of the genre, from the bitingly satiric to the painfully doleful—as well as the many ballads that, in one singing, traversed a wide range of affects—and his "rules" about modes and the emotions they conveyed were by no means hard and fast or universally held (as we shall especially see with the case of "Greensleeves" in Chapter 7). Music theorists themselves varied widely in their assessments of the emotive meanings of modes, tones, and even keys, as Dietrich Bartel points out (*Musica Poetica*, 40–46). In attributing meaning and emotional resonances to tunes, we must necessarily rely to some extent on our modern ear while giving attention to the music's meter and phenomenal accent. This approach privileges each specific tune in its own right over general concepts associated by music theorists with modes. To do so is not at all anachronistic. Jeremy Barlow sums up what we shall often find in our analyses in his introduction to his collected edition of Playford's country dance tunes. With something of an understatement, Barlow declares, "A flexible attitude existed towards the modality of popular tunes in the 17th century" (*Complete Country Dance Tunes*, 10).[12]

Here, it is useful to revisit the assertion I made in Chapter 1 about music's metrical stress in the broadside ballad genre. The meter of the tunes in our versions of "Mock-Beggar Hall"—as, indeed, of ballads cited throughout this book—is chiefly constituted of four stresses (which alternate strong and less strong). The four musical stresses roughly accommodate a single line of ballad verse (consisting of four or three or sometimes even five poetic stresses). This general pattern of intertwined musical and poetic metric stress provides a baseline for scansion of ballad as song. Singers and listeners interpret and adjust this baseline according to potential phenomenal stresses in the notation as well as a keen recognition that both kinds of metrical stress are in "conversation with" each other. The first tune named on the "Mock-Beggar Hall" ballads, standardized in spelling to "*It is not your Northern Nanny*," or simply, "Northern Nanny," is a good illustration of this process. Though no tune to this exact title has yet been found, a very close extant variant—"Northern Nancy"—fits our ballads as well as later ballads whose tune is named after variant spellings of their shared refrain (Simpson, *British Broadside Ballad and Its Music*, 517–18). In fact, "Northern Nancy" could well be a contraction and mutation into "Northern Nanny," the latter possibly resulting from the common error in composing type of mistakenly substituting one letter for another ("Nan**ny**" thus becoming "Nan**cy**").

In privileging "Northern Nancy" for the "Northern Nanny" melody, Simpson considers whether possible tunes fit what he calls "the eight-line tetrameter stanza of the ballads" of "Mock-Beggar Hall." But when scanned poetically, the "Mock-Beggar Hall" ballads more closely approach alternating tetrameter and trimeter, rather than simply repeating tetrameter lines. And herein lies an example of the musical/poetic metrical rub. Simpson is referring to the four *musical* stresses of the tune, called for across every two measures of notes that roughly make up a poetic line (a measure consisting of the notes between bars). Below you can see Playford's notation of the "Northern Nancy" tune in *The Dancing Master*'s fourth through sixth editions (1670–79), split into two musical lines in Bell's modernized transcription (as it is in Simpson's, 518), thus indicating how the notes approximately align with the text of the lyrics. Since there are four measures per musical line, two lines of poetry are sung to each of line of music.[13]

Though the alignment of notes above allows a reader to better imagine a fit between the music notation and a given poetic text—that is, between musical meter and poetic meter—texts that are in 4-3 ballad measure, as are the "Mock-Beggar Hall" ballads, do not fully align with the music's metrical stresses. Not only do the tune's four musical stresses alternate between strong and weak ones—a conventional system of meter foreign to traditional poetic scansion—but also four stresses of any kind would only fit the poetic scansion of the odd lines of the "Mock-Beggar Hall" stanzas (1, 3, 5, and 7). The even lines (2, 4, 6, and 8), as noted above, poetically scan as trimeter lines, consisting of three stresses. The vocalist adhering to the music scansion of an alternation of four stresses per line—***strong***, weak, *less strong*, weak, ***strong***, weak, *less strong*, weak—must thus make adjustments to his or her singing of these lines to accommodate two different claims to stress: the poetic, on the one hand, and the musical, on the other. In favoring the music's metrical emphasis in singing the poetry, as would most singers, the last poetic syllable in the stanza's evenly numbered lines—typically a poetically unstressed feminine ending falling outside the iambic feet of the lines—must be lightly stressed by the singer to render the poetic meter into something approaching musical tetrameter. Consider st. 1, l. 2 of our first "Mock-Beggar Hall" ballad, for example, first poetically and then musically scanned:

Poetic Scansion:	That **men** | of **wor**-| -thy **call**-ing
Musical Scansion:	That ***men*** | of *wor-* | -thy ***call-ing***

"Calling," in meeting the musical metrical (versus poetic) demands for some stress on "ing," accentuates not only the duty or the "calling" of worthy men but also the ballad's *recalling* nostalgically a time long gone when such men made hospitality their calling. At the same time, poetically speaking (and reading), not singing, "wor" in "worthy" demands a strong, not just a weak stress (as required by the music's meter), and, in doing so, foregrounds more strongly the virtue or worthiness now lost temporally as it is lost in the music's lesser emphasis. Both demands of stress, though different, work together in these lines to drive home the sense of the ballad. But when differences arise between musical and poetic metrical stress, they can also call attention to a certain pull or tension, even conflict, in the ballad, as we shall see on closer inspection.

In the modern transcription of Playford's "Northern Nancy," above, which, like the original, is in G major, the first line of the music notation covers not just the first two but the first four poetic lines of each eight-line stanza of "Mock-Beggar Hall." That is, the repeat signs (comprised of two dots preceding double bars), combined with the two different endings (marked, above the relevant measures, with volta brackets and small numbers) indicate that each line of music represents a pair of poetic lines, which are then repeated and differ on the repeat only in the second pair's ending. That is, the third and fourth poetic lines are sung to the first line of music using the second ending instead of the first; the same rule applies for the seventh and eighth poetic lines that are sung to the second line of music. A quick glance at the notation also reveals a doubling up of the first note in the first measure (aligning with the beginning of poetic lines 1 and 3). This repetition gives the tune an initial bounciness, like a dancer whose stride springs into a jump. The melody then mostly smooths out into a stepwise motion, containing only a single leap from the high D down to an F-sharp (F♯), over the telling syllables or words—if we take the first stanza of the first "Mock-Beggar Hall" ballad as an example—on "of ***wor***-" (in "of worthy") and on "are ***all***." Here the syllables already stressed by the music's meter gain further phenomenal accent in the form of the fall in notes: the music itself enacts the decline of "***all wor***thy."[14]

The second half of the tune, indicated by the second line of the music score as printed above, contains more variation. Playford's natural symbol (♮) above the F (the fourth note) indicates that, in the fifth and seventh lines of every stanza, the tune momentarily veers out of pure major. This creates what could be referred to as a "Mixolydian" effect.[15] You can hear Bell singing the first of the "Mock-Beggar Hall" ballads to this music notation on **Track 6** of the Audio Companion (rendered transcribed in part below in G major—in an other instance given in G minor—to create consistency of comparison of the transcribed notations in this and the next chapter no matter what key they are sung in). Do you hear the outsider note, the F natural (F♮), in the recording, in the second word to the fifth and seventh lines of each stanza? Often this "off" note in "Northern Nancy" not only jars with the otherwise smooth and upbeat rhythm of the melody but, in doing so, places emphasis on important words.

The tendency of this musical framework to stress keywords in the odd-numbered lines as well as to create tension between poetic and musical scansion in the even-numbered lines becomes clearer when we consider the second half of the melody in Bell's modern transcription of his recording. I have chosen as an example the second half of stanza 2 from the first "Mock-Beggar Hall" ballad (pointed to by additional indentation below) because it is here that the ballad's relator turns from a general introduction of the ballad's theme to specifics about the problem he's addressing:

Farme houses which their fathers built,
And Land well kept by tillage,
Their Prodigall sons have sold for gilt,
    In every Towne and Village.
    To th' City and Court they doe resort
    With gold and silver plenty,
    And there they spend their time in sport,
    While mock beggers hall stands empty.

You can hear just the indented lines sung by Bell on **Track 7**. Below is the music transcription of the indented lines as sung, with text underlay:

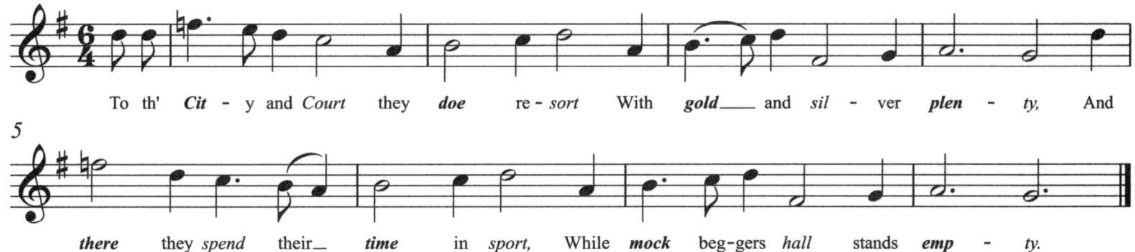

You can listen to a slowed-down version of these notated four lines of the sung text played, for following along, on the fiddle audio on **Track 8**. Notice how the F-natural note (F♮) combines with other features of the melody and text to create a phenomenal accent on the first syllable of the word "***Cit***-y." "To the ***Cit***-y and *Court*" begins with a skip upward from D, which had been until now our highest note, to the F♮ (that calls even more attention to the first syllable of "***Cit***-y."[16]

At hypermetric, phenomenal levels, the first syllable in "***Cit***-y" is the most important syllable within the fifth line of this stanza, if not within the entire last half of the stanza.[17] Only vying with it textually for place of emphasis, but otherwise repeating the same phenomenal value, is the word "***there***" in the seventh line. Not coincidentally, this word references the very same place it echoes in its notation, the ***Cit***-y. By adding these phenomenal accents to what is already a strong beat/syllable pairing, the tune works with the text to situate "***Cit***-y" negatively—as, indeed, is also the case with "*Court*." As if an afterthought, the phrase "and *Court*" is marked by a declension or fall in notes, implying also a social decline in locale. Furthermore though "*Court*" is technically owed less stress by the music's meter, the word receives a boost downward through its falling on a half note, rather than (more typical for this tune) a dotted quarter note. In a notable decline of worth, the wealthy have absconded from country to both city and court, leaving far behind "***Farme*** hous-es" "well *kept*" and "***Land***" made fruitful, as emphasized by the music's metrical scansion, with "***til-****age*." The melody also uses two notes to draw out its metrical emphasis on "***gold***," and though the notes rise expectantly to the high D of "and," the stock of riches plunges to a low F#—elongated to a half note—falling on "*Sil*"-ver. Thus, the drive for wealth, the metrical and phenomenal accents of the melody underscore, is not as successful as these greedy sorts would like. Their purses only slightly begin to fill up but then decrease, as the rise to the dotted half A note on "***plen-***" is completed by the less emphasized, lower pitch of G on "*ty*." At the same time, however, "beggers," nowhere visible in the illustrations to the first "Mock-Beggar Hall" ballad, reach up for attention in the rising notes of measure 7; but they receive no musical metrical stress whatsoever, and they suffer a swift and deep dive from a high D to a low F♯ on "*hall*." And what does the music notation, overriding the poetic scansion (but not rhyme scheme), say about that country hall? It is echoingly "***emp***-*ty*." Indeed, the rhyme scheme of lines 6 and 8 of the stanza draws attention to the melodic and textual sympathy between the echoing melodically drawn-out words, "***plen***-*ty*" and "***emp***-*ty*." The drive for plenty, it would seem, when gold and silver are at stake—both tune and poetry reinforce—ironically leads to empty-ness. It is an emptiness of hall, of worth, of grace, and even ultimately, of wealth.

The tune thus mostly echoes the narrative and poetic stresses of the ballad—with one major exception. Scanning the lines poetically, one would naturally place an emphasis on "beg" in "**beg**-gers." Indeed, given the guttural stop created by the doubled "g" in the word, it is nearly impossible to avoid stressing "beg." But the music's metrical emphasis asks us to do just that. It gives the strong stress, instead, to the adjective "***mock***" that describes the multiply weak "beg-gers." As with the difference between alternating tetrameter-trimeter poetic scansion and the consistently tetrameter music scansion, text and tune here are not in accord but at odds with each other. There seems almost a pull in the ballad between the desire for poetic emphasis on "**beg**-gers"—nowhere to be visually seen in the first "Mock-Beggar Hall" ballad—and the melodic emphasis on "***mock***." It is as if the poetic scansion of the song wants the ballad to be a lament precisely for the beggars abandoned outside empty country estates or halls because of the selfish pride of the landed rich who have exchanged eminent places for urban spaces, country for city, plain dealing for monstrous fashion, and charity for gold and silver. But the melody of "Northern Nancy" favors jovial, stein-swinging, all-in-good-fun mockery of such ill practices. Sung in the major mode, with the uplifting bounce at the beginning of lines 1, 3, 5, and 7, followed by a mostly stepwise dance-like motion, in a rousing rhythm, "Northern Nancy" asks us musically to be upbeat. There are only occasional tactical hints, through phenomenal accents, of an unsettled, ill feeling, mostly when the melody gets more complicated in the second half of the stanzas, as in that repeated "off" note (the F♮), the fall in notes from "and *sil*-" and—after the deceptive one-note rise in "beg-gers"—the same fall to "*hall*." This hall, through the melodically long and low notes of the tune, is phenomenally accented as especially, indeed, echoingly "***emp***-*ty*." Here lie openings for a heartfelt lament, or perhaps, within the overall upbeat melody and illustrative critical pictures, for a more jabbing mockery not of the low, who through the tension between musical and poetic metric scansion, are even more puzzlingly "mock beggers," but of the high.

Still, "Northern Nancy" overall is without doubt a jovial tune. It is also fairly easy to sing, especially in the first four lines of poetic text. It here ranges from F♯4 to F5, which is slightly less than an octave (an octave being a range of eight notes). Both this relatively small reach and the stepwise texture of "Northern Nancy" would make it more singable for the masses, including those who need not be skilled in reading or singing music to hear the nuances in the melody's notes orally communicated. Simply in ease of singing, this tune might be more attractive as the song of choice between the two offered tunes printed on the ballad sheet, for both hawkers and consumers. This may also explain why it is listed first among the two tunes printed on the ballad sheet. Presumably those of the low-middling to lower sorts would have also felt some comfort in the mostly upbeat movement of the tune, despite or even because, in embracing such joviality, one must repress the reality of beggary. The lower sorts could have, further, still well appreciated the textual hits at aspiring landed wealthy farmers and rack-renting "Young landlords." They might have found downright pleasure in hearing that the former are the real beggars of the ballad, in expending all their land-grabbing wealth on city fashions to the extent of impoverishing themselves so that, we are told, "every beggerly Jacke and Gill / That eate scant a good meale in twenty / Must thorow the streets be jolted still / While mock begger hall stands empty" (st. 7). Not only do these lines transfer the nature of beggarly-ness to social aspirants, but also their musical metrical emphasis underscores the main point of the text's narrative, falling on the first syllable "*beg*" in "*beg*-ger-ly." This melodic accent is bolstered by a phenomenal accent in the downward movement of the syllables of the word "*beg*-ger-ly" from C to B to A, with a further emphasis in the dotted quarter note that draws out the already metrically accentuated "*beg*."

Those of the poorer sorts, always on the verge of having to resort to begging, might find even more comfort toward the end of the ballad, in the tactical jab specifically aimed at the established wealthy (the "Gentlemen and Citizens") who actually own the kind of "eminent" estates in the country that were by tradition expected to provide for the begging poor. The lower orders thus might warm to the buoyant rhythm. But the upper sorts suffer only glancing strikes, as we have seen, and the nobles throughout escape outright censure. This first "Mock-Beggar Hall" ballad is much more focused, at least in its first half, on the less recognizable (and less able to strike back) "upper sorts" in the sense of relatively wealthy farmers, young landlords, and social upstarts—"every beggarly Jacke and Gill." The ballad offers the truly high orders an out. They are allowed, should they choose, to read and see and hear the ballad as tactically targeting those much lower down the social spectrum than the class space they occupy—despite the three hits they take toward the end of the ballads. They are also allowed in a most jovial mood to "***mock***" the notably absent and mostly unstressed "beg-ger" if they emphasize the musical metrical (as opposed to poetic) stresses of the ballad, as the tune "Northern Nancy" encourages.

The second named tune, standardized in spelling to "*Sweet is the Lass that Loves me*," offers further complications and options. Musically, it presents something of a melodic challenge even for a trained singer. Its range is much wider than that of "Northern Nancy," from B3 to G5 according to Simpson (a minor thirteenth versus just an octave), and it includes leaps much more often than does "Northern Nancy," some of them as large as an octave. As Marsh has well substantiated, many early modern ballad hawkers likely possessed strong musical skills; he has shown, too, that consumers of the time must have been on the whole fairly talented as well. Even so, he notes, the typical range of a ballad is rarely much wider than an octave; he finds only two among his list of most popular tunes that are a perfect twelfth. "*Sweet is the Lass that Loves me*" stretches that twelfth to a minor thirteenth. It is not for the faint of voice, though it might be easily within the range of many of the more musically talented consumers.[18]

The tune can be confidently traced to the standard tune title "Damask Rose."[19] It could be considered as in the Aeolian or perhaps Dorian mode,[20] which was evolving by the early seventeenth century into today's minor. As such, the tune occupies a more diverse range of emotions on the affect spectrum from, most simply put, sad to happy, as such feelings were understood from the late Renaissance onward. Again, however, we must be careful in making generalized emotive claims based merely on mode or tone; analysis of metrical and phenomenal accent is our most reliable guide to a detailed understanding of any individual ballad. For comparison with "Northern Nancy," you can hear Bell singing the first "Mock-Beggar Hall" ballad to "Damask Rose" on **Track 9** of the Audio Companion. Notice that the melody of "Damask Rose" is much livelier than that of "Northern Nancy" because it requires the voice not to bounce in place by singing two notes on a single pitch, as in the opening to "Northern Nancy," but to skip and leap acrobatically from low to high and back again, especially in the second half of each stanza. Playford's notation modernized, and unrelated to any specific text, as in the source, the Skene MS, is given below:

The above modern transcription of "Damask Rose" follows our practice throughout this book of roughly aligning one music line of four measures to fit two lines of poetry. But note that the transcription of "Damask Rose" requires three lines of music notation for an eight-line stanza, as opposed to just the two lines for "Northern Nancy." The need for an additional line in "Damask Rose" arises because only the first two lines of its music repeat (which would constitute together approximately the first four lines of the song). Then the tune takes off, with no repetition of melodic material at all for the last four lines of stanzaic verse.[21]

Bell's recording of just the last four lines of stanza 2 of the first "Mock-Beggar Hall" ballad to "Damask Rose" can be heard on **Track 10**. His transcription of the recording is provided below.[22] Again, to allow easy comparison with "Northern Nancy," I show the transcribed music notation, with text underlay and musical metrical stresses, of the last four lines of the second stanza. The fiddle audio can be heard on **Track 11**.

As we can now see (and hear) more easily, not only is there no melodic repetition within each of the stanza's last four lines, but also the melody's range is even broader in the second than in the first half of the tune. Whereas the first half of "Damask Rose" mostly occupies the octave between G4 and G5, the second half stretches the scale more widely and also rests in a higher range. However, befitting the uniqueness of the individual lines of this melody, the highest note occurs only once, in the second half of the stanza, in the culmination of a rise in notes that reaches the already metrically emphasized—yes, again—"To th' ***Cit***-y." Other metrically accented syllables are also made more phenomenally emphatic, although by different melodic means and to different ends than in "Northern Nancy." In the sixth line, "With ***gold*** and *sil*-ver ***plen-ty***," the melody begins the dive for money sooner, not in the notational drop from "and" to the less metrically stressed "*sil*-"(ver), but from "With" to the strongly stressed "***gold***," a drop of a minor seventh (almost a full octave). The effect is to phenomenally increase the emphatic drop in "***gold***." The tune makes an effort at recouping the grab for money by giving another, less striking but still meaningful leap up in the second note devoted to "***gold***," effectively extending the greed for gilt and adding to this movement a climb upward, with musical and poetic stress as well as denotation merging in a further stepping up on "*sil*-ver ***plen***-ty." But such fullness in the ever-rising and elongated notes on "***plen-ty***" is illusory. Again, poetic and musical scansion align with poetic and musical phenomenal meaning in the first syllable of the final word that ends every stanza, and which here ironically aligns, through rhyme, with "***plen-ty***"—"***emp-ty***." The final word and musical stress of line 6 on "***plen-ty***," carried as it is over two notes in the sung melody, and both fully occupying and extending beyond a full measure—imitating both visually and orally the "spilling over" of "***plen-ty***"—vividly captures the haunting sound of an echoing empty hall even more than does "Northern Nancy."

Musical and poetic metrical stress are not always in such sympathetic accord, however, as discussed briefly above. An example of significant tension along these lines falls on the most important word in the title and refrain of both ballads—"mock." This derogatory adjective receives even more musical metrical stress in "Damask Rose" than it does in "Northern Nancy." Indeed, the former tune gives extra emphasis to "***mock***" in its E-natural (E♮) to F motion over "While," which leads up to "***mock***" on a high G.[23] But though "beg-gers" are again neglected by the music's metrical accent, its phenomenal accent joins forces with our poetic inclination vocally to stress the first syllable, "beg." Rather than a token rise in the notes on "beg-gers" as we see in "Northern Nancy," "Damask Rose" assigns to "beg" the same eminence—a high G—as it does to "***mock***." It further audibly enacts the ballad's lament over the neglect of beggars in the subsequent major drop from that high G to the low "G" of the word's completion in "gers"—a dive of a full octave. Despite efforts after such a swift vocal descent to then climb back up the musical scale, the tune continues to hover in the low range, especially on the final, emphatically echoing hollow word, "***emp-ty***."

Considering its melodic and phenomenal movement, as well as its alignment of melodic stress with poetic denotation, if not always with poetic metrical stress, "Damask Rose" leaves a wide opening for out-and-out irony and even satire in the way the ballad's lament might be sung. With all its skipping around and drawn-out syllables, which can create many dramatic emphases, as we've seen, the tune could certainly have been employed to convey a very broad range of emotions: from joyful delight, to heartfelt earnestness, to doleful lament, to distressed agitation, to sour bitterness, and even to indignant anger. One can hear the potential for sorrow even in the relatively neutral singing of the first ballad to "Damask Rose" by Bell. This potential is more fully realized in the recording by Leeza Bautista, in this case to the second "Mock-Beggar Hall" ballad, on **Track 12**. Bautista's rendering of the melody feels almost eerily doleful because her female, crystalline voice sings in a high register and draws out the many notes per syllable or word as well as the ups and downs of the melody. One hears poignantly, even sweetly, a nostalgic lament for a lost past and the forgotten needs of the poor. The differences between Bell's rendition of "Damask Rose" and Bautista's, though they both sing in the Dorian mode, show just how much a singer can make a song *mean* not only in tune choice but in the way he or she chooses to sing that tune, whether it is in the Ionian mode (today's major), Aeolian mode (today's minor), or Dorian mode (similar to the minor).

Still, within the context of the demands of the poetic narrative as well as the melodic and phenomenal stresses, a singer might well follow the lead of the emphatic "Mock-Beggar" refrain, which reveals a certain openness to conveying a bitter and even biting (if at the same time sorrowful) ***mock***-ery. Such would seem to be especially appropriate to the second "Mock-Beggar Hall" ballad. In this second version, as we have seen, we encounter an almost parodic disconnect between the idyllic illustrations on the sheet and the text of the ballad, where selfish greed, mean-spirited knavery, and prideful fashion have run rampant through the entire social spectrum of London (with the exception, tactfully/tactically on the relator's part, of the nobles). Bell offers another recording of the second "Mock-Beggar" Hall ballad (here just of the first three stanzas) on **Track 13** to show just how easily the tune of "Damask Rose" can be turned from Bautista's doleful lament to biting mockery. That said (or that sung), so widespread and ridiculous is the lamentable state of urban affairs in the second "Mock-Beggar Hall" ballad—a fashionable hangman and whore?—that everyone and thus no one in particular, in this rendering of the text with tune (as in the text with illustrations discussed above), seems in the end to be mocked. In something of a paradox, everyone is mocked and thus no one in particular is mocked.

In the final analysis, the multifarious options for creating affect and interpretation made available by the two tunes of the "Mock-Beggar Hall" ballads, especially when considered in conjunction with their accompanying texts and illustrations, epitomize the way ballads are at every level constituted of an enormous number of meaning-making relational bits and pieces, like individual notes. In every part, from word to image to melody, they are subject to being assembled, disassembled, and reassembled both by their producers and—regardless of whether intended by the producers—by their consumers. Rather than locking down any individual or collective meaning, such a multitude of mobile fragmentary pieces throws wide open the intermedial doors of interpretation. In sum, and as we shall now pursue in depth, any encountered ballad—its own mobile components coming together momentarily into a meaningful (if provisional) whole—might have been disassembled and reassembled by a consumer making associational hits between that ballad's parts and those of "Mock-Beggar Hall," as the consumer draws on his or her mental corpus of street ephemera.

CHAPTER 3 ❧

Random Tactical Hits

Now that we have spent some time playing with the multimedia fragments that make up the two extant versions of the "Mock-Beggar Hall" ballad, we can begin to widen our search for additional connections: for relationally aesthetic parts and fragmentarily constructed wholes that a contemporary might "hit" upon as part of early modern pop culture (the sort of cultural experience that particularly saturated daily urban life for the middling to low). Only by expanding the parameters of our scholarly inquiry in this way will we begin to see the enormous scope of what I have called the hyper-plurality of broadside ballads. In this chapter, we will consider ballad multimedia within the larger popular culture of repeatedly circulating and recirculating provisional wholes and pieces of texts, illustrations, and tunes of their times, drawing not only from other broadside ballads (artifacts which, we should recall, early modern Londoners probably encountered in the hundreds, and even thousands, annually) but also from other familiar sources of cheap print, such as pamphlets. Widening our search in this way will also allow us as moderns to think transhistorically, reconsidering both how early modern contemporaries assembled and accessed personal mental archives in a world brimming with printed ephemera and how we moderns do so today in our own digitally saturated culture.

Huge data sets of possible conceptual assemblages were potentially available to an early modern contemporary. But, of course, they were not retrieved from a virtual and impersonal vastness of cyberspace. They were personally and interpersonally accessed by physically traversing the diverse geographical and temporal expanses that connected ballad producers, disseminators, and consumers in early modern England. As multisensory artifacts, broadside ballads and their tunes extended over sometimes very short and other times very long historical periods. They also traveled across sometimes close and sometimes wide geographical areas, crossing the streets of London, public spaces, workplaces, domestic homes, and—further into the outer reaches of the countryside—trekking as far as Newcastle and Scotland (where many English broadside ballads and songs were imitated by the up-and-coming Edinburgh and Glasgow printers and publishers).[1] As we shall see in Chapter 8, they even set sail in the long journey across the Atlantic. By taking such expansive fragmentary connectedness into account, we modern scholars can begin to get a glimpse of the extensive and variable possible mental hits an early modern consumer might have made upon encountering the moving ballad parts, which often connected with other popular print that she or he might have happened upon in the haphazard course of lived experience.

Complicating the picture of the available associative mental cache that anyone might have gathered, we must remember, is the fact that distinct relatable parts of a broadside ballad, when reassembled into another provisional whole, accumulated new relationships. As we have observed, Manuel DeLanda helpfully uses the terms of assemblage theory for this phenomenon. He affirms, "As larger assemblages emerge from the interactions of component parts, the identity of the parts may acquire new layers, as the emergent whole reacts back and affects them" (25). The array of possible associational meaning-makings arising from hits that a contemporary might randomly form are consequently enormous; indeed, they are probably beyond our ability even approximately to predict. This chapter thus cannot be holistic. Nor is that my goal. Rather, I invite you to join me on an often surprising adventure into the world of early modern broadside ballad culture characterized by spontaneous, chance, and partial encounters. I invite you to join me not in wrapping up an argument but in opening one up. I seek to cultivate our awareness of the immense availability within ballad culture of rhizomatic associations between fragmentary parts and wholes, both those of ballads and those of other popular print forms. A modern digital term that captures something of the unpredictable, hit-and-miss nature of this broadside ballad experience is that of "retrieved hits." This term could be used for everything that an early modern might have experienced on encountering one or both of our "Mock-Beggar Hall" ballads (by intent or by chance) within the larger search that was synonymous with the act of everyday living.

In what follows, we shall also see an upsetting of what Christopher Marsh has described as "binary divisions" in ballads. After a rare intermedial analysis of one particular ballad's illustrations, lyrics, and words from which it derives its tune title, Marsh expands upon this observation in declaring that the ballad is "an instrument of negotiation" between binaries.[2] My intent in this chapter is to complicate the notion of binaries in heyday ballads (Chapter 8 does similar work). Oppositions, we find, fragment and split off and move from one ballad to another so that the terms of any seemingly simple debate often shift and accumulate meaning depending on the associations being made at any time by the audience. Such associations can be shared between listeners forming transitory publics who are not in a negotiating mood at all. Positions of all sorts are given a momentary voice, allowing listeners collectively to inhabit a cause—however mixed or inflected this cause might be by any individual's cache of associations. In sum, binaries do not hold, either within or between, ballads. They atomize into multiple meanings more reflective of the complexities of everyday life. To see this fragmentation clearly, we might best begin (perverse as it seems) by considering ballads in exactly oppositional terms. For the sake of manageability (and sanity), however, we must prune back the multitudinous possible examples available for study; in this chapter, I will thus mostly focus on the earlier, or, as I have styled it, the first, of our two "Mock-Beggar Hall" ballads (published c. 1633–35).

Some Assemblage Hits: Mock-Gender

Contemporaries thinking associatively about broadside ballads they had recently encountered on the street, in the alehouse, and other places, might have noticed that the second woodcut (the one on the right) of our first "Mock-Beggar Hall" ballad, shown close-up in Figure 9, had appeared on a number of other ballads; this might spur the making of connections. For instance, the two women aggressively facing off in this illustration appear within conceivable recent memory of someone living in the mid-1630s, on a popular broadside ballad published about a sailor and his love. To date, I have located five copies of this ballad, two of them from the 1620s or 1630s. The copy likely closest in time to our first "Mock-Beggar Hall" ballad, and possibly circulating along with it on the same streets, was collected by Pepys (1.422–423, EBBA 20198). Titled "A pleasant new Song, betwixt *The Saylor and his Love*" (hereafter cited simply as "The Sailor and his Love"), the ballad is dated by the English Short Title Catalogue (ESTC) as c. 1625. It was printed for John Grismond, who published between 1616 and 1638 and was one of the original "ballad partners" (co-aligned in 1624, in an effort to create a broadside ballad monopoly).[3] Likely the ESTC's dating of Pepys's edition is based on the fact that the ballad partners registered (in many cases re-registered) with the Stationers' Company a large batch of ballads in 1624. But ballads were not always published right after licensing (indeed, some were never published at all after licensing, so far as we can ascertain; the licensing appears sometimes to have just staked a claim). Thus, the c. 1625 dating is very conjectural. The

Figure 9. Close-up of second woodcut impression on "The Map of Mock-Begger Hall, with his scituation in the spacious Countrey, called, *Anywhere*" (c. 1633–35), EBBA 30174. British Library, Roxburghe 1.252–253, C.20.f.7.252–253. © The British Library Board.

woodcut illustration that the ballad shares with "Mock-Beggar Hall" is far less deteriorated on Grismond's "The Sailor and his Love," which at the very least confirms that the "Sailor" ballad was printed earlier, but given Grismond's wide range of printing—1616–38—we cannot ascertain how much earlier. A clear sign of age, the impression made on the "Mock-Beggar Hall" ballad reveals many wormholes, as we have seen. In addition, we also noticed that parts of the cut have been worn or broken off (evident in the left figure's sleeves and parts of the border); such wear was usually the result of much use, an indication of how popular this eye-catching image must have been. It would thus be more prone to be stored in a viewer's mental cache of images, which might well include its more ship-shape, but not much earlier, showing on "The Sailor and his Love" (Figure 10).

Though clearly this woodcut was often used and popular, we should resist the knee-jerk and long-standing assumption that its appearance on ballads was thus random and not deserving of interpretative study (Fumerton and Palmer, "Lasting Impressions," 386). The new wave of critical attention to woodcut impressions has put that dismissive impulse to rest. Still, to the modern viewer seeing the illustration without context, it might look quite odd and

A pleaſant new Song, betwixt
The Saylor and his Loue.
to the tune of Dulcina.

VVhat doth aile my Loue, ſo ſadly
in ſuch heauy dumps to ſtand;
Doth ſhe grieue or take vnkindly,
that I am ſo neere at hand?
Or doth ſhe vow,
She will not know,
Nor ſpeake to me when I doe come:
If that be ſo,
Away Ile goe,
firſt kiſſe and bid me welcome home.

Had I euer thee forſaken,
putting thee out of my minde,
Thou then mighſt haue iuſtly ſpoken
that I was to thee vnkind.
Or ſhould I take
Some other make,
Then mighſt thou haue iuſt cauſe to (mourne
But let me die
Before that I,
doe ſo: then bid me welcome home.

Sooner ſhall the graſſe leaue growing,
from the hare the hound ſhall run,
Husbandmen ſhall leaue their ſowing,
flouds ſhall run the land vpon,
The fiſh ſhall flye,
The Sea run dry,
The birds no more ſhall ſing but mourne
Ere I of thee
Unmindfull be,
then kiſſe and bid me welcome home.

Smile on me, be not offended,
pardon grant for my amiſſe:
Let thy fauour ſo befriend me,
as to ſeale it with a kiſſe:
To me, I ſweare,
Thou art ſo deare,
That for thy ſake Ile fancy none,
Then doe not frowne,
But ſit thee downe,
Sweet, kiſſe and bid me welcome home.

If thou haſt proued chaſt Diana,
ſince from thee I did depart.
I as conſtant haue béene to thee,
for on thee ſixt was my heart:
No not for ſhe
Iupiter ſée,
Dinae in her tower alone.
Should me intice,
No Ile be nice,
then kiſſe and bid me welcome home.

No nor Venus Cupids mother,
nor the fairest wife of Ioue,
Should Lucretia or ſome other,
ſéeke by gifts to win my loue,
Should Hellen faire,
To me repaire,
And vnto me for loue make mone,
Yet none of theſe
My minde ſhall pleaſe,
then kiſſe, and bid me welcome home

The ſecond part. To the ſame tune.

From thy ſight though I was baniſht
yet I alwayes was to thee,
Far more kinde then was Vlyſſes,
to his chaſte Penelope:
For why away
He once did ſtay
Ten yeares, and left her all alone.
But I from thee,
Haue not béene thrée,
Sweet kiſſe and bid me welcome him.

Come ſwéet heart come ſit downe by me,
and let thy lap my pillow me.
While ſwéet ſléepe my minde beguileth,
all my dreams ſhall be on thee.
I pray thee ſtay,
Steale not away,
Let lullaby be all my ſong:
With kiſſes ſwéet,
Lull mee aſleepe, (home,
and ſay ſweet heart thou'rt welcome

The womans anſwer.

I Haue beene ſad to ſée how from me,
thou ſo long away didſt ſtay,
Yet now I more reioyce to ſee thee,
happily ariu'd this day.
Than from our ſhore
Shalt goe no more,
To wander thus abroad alone:
But thou ſhalt ſtay
With me alway, (home.
for here's my hand, thou'rt welcome

I haue prou'd Diana to thee,
ſince from me thou wentſt away,
I haue had ſuters well-nigh twenty,
and much adoe had for to ſtay:
But I denyed,
When they reply'd,
And ſent them all away in ſcorne:
For I had ſworne,
To liue forlorne,
vntill that I ſee thee come home.

Seeing thou art home arriued,
thou ſhalt not goe away in haſte,
But louingly come ſit downe by me,
let thine armes embrace my waſt:
Farewell annoy,
Welcome my ioy,
Now lullaby is all my ſong,
For now my heart,
Sings loath to part, (home
then kiſſe, ſweet-heart, thou'rt welcome

Since ſweet heart thou doſt befriend me
thus to take me to thy loue,
Neuer more will I offend thee,
but will euer conſtant proue.
Thou haſt my heart,
Not to depart,
But euer conſtant to remaine:
And thou haſt mine,
And I haue thine,
then let vs kiſſe and welcome home.

FINIS.

Printed at London for *Iohn Griſmond.*

Figure 10. Ballad sheet facsimile, "A pleasant new Song, betwixt *The Saylor and his Loue*" (c. 1624), EBBA 20198. Post-photographic processing by EBBA. Magdalene College, Cambridge, Pepys Library, Pepys Ballads 1.422–423. By permission of the Pepys Library, Magdalene College, Cambridge.

therefore capricious, not only for the "Mock-Beggar Hall" ballad but also for "The Sailor and his Love." The woodcut *is* odd—but its placement as illustration of these ballads' particular texts is more telling than we might first think. As noted in Chapter 2, the ladies' feathered hats, short hair, and aggressive stances mark them with the kind of mannishness complained about and defended in the anti- and pro-feminist debate tracts, respectively, of the early seventeenth century. The debate peaked with the call-and-response pamphlets *Hic Mulier* and *Haec-Vir* in 1620.[4] Yes, a re-carver or handy printer at some point in the cut's history has toned down the testosterone-laced look of the women facing off combatively against each other by removing obvious signs of weaponry that women in debate tracts were described as bearing. As pointed out in the previous chapter, the passed-down cut has had erased from it most of the sword the woman on the left originally held (you can only see traces of it crossing her extended arm). But, though cutting out most of that weapon, the carver left untouched the dagger held in the hand of the confrontational woman on the right, perhaps because it blends in with her costume and would not have been as immediately evident as would the large sword. Despite these small efforts at some point in the woodcut's history to tone down the aggressiveness of the women represented (likely to suit the narrative of a ballad that no longer survives), the links with the male-like guises that women were accused of assuming in the tracts remain very strong.

Most important, since their mannish style of dress was identified by the anti-feminists as specifically an upper-class fashion, the cut especially fits the complaint in the one stanza of both "Mock-Beggar Hall" ballads about "Gentlewomen" who "Must use all the fashions in their cloathing, / Which they can hear or know of" (st. 9). Like the fashion-mongering men, the gentlewomen are perversely "Apes in imitation" (st. 6). Nor is the apparent money bag the woman on the right grasps in her right hand dissonant for the "Mock-Beggar Hall" ballad—focused most on the rich selling off their country estates for "gold and silver," as we have seen. A money bag is also fitting for "The Sailor and his Love." Sailors often brought home spoils won in combat at sea, or at least picked up on their return large sums of accumulated wages, if having been away on long sea voyages, especially if working for the East India Company (though the money was often spent in binges once back home).[5]

If a contemporary remembered the other woodcuts from "The Sailor and his Love" shown in Figure 10, especially in considering the cuts on our first "Mock-Beggar Hall" ballad, the plot thickens. The first woodcut visible (viewing from left to right) would have again reminded one of the gender perversions specifically associated with city (and court) fashions. Apparently an image of our sailor, it presents quite an effeminate-looking young gallant, also with feathered hat, like the two ladies on the far right. A bit of a dandy, he further sports fashionable bows at the tops of his stockings and a neatly trimmed and pointed beard. His right arm seems daintily, not imposingly, placed on his hip, as if he is posing. In addition, the sword he bears—fitting a fighting, not simply a sailing, profession—is an item that could only legally be carried by the gentry and above, suggesting social aspiration. It hangs inactively behind him, just as the staff the sailor holds in his left hand seems more ornamental than instrumental. Overall, the image creates an equivalence, traditionally speaking, between the man as effeminate on the left and the women as mannish on the far right of the ballad (despite the one lady being stripped of her sword). Tactically, the two balanced images might make us ask: who is

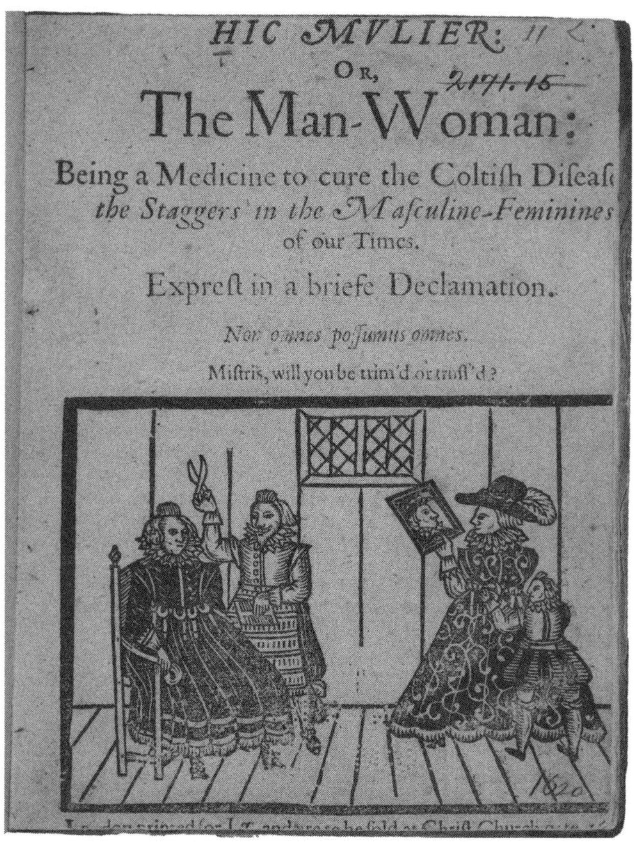
HIC MVLIER:
OR,
The Man-Woman:
Being a Medicine to cure the Coltiſh Diſeaſ
the Staggers in the Maſculine-Feminines
of our Times.
Expreſt in a briefe Declamation.
Non omnes poſſumus omnes.
Miſtris, will you be trim'd or truſs'd?

Figure 11. Frontispiece to *Hic Mvlier: Or, The Man-Woman: Being a Medicine to cure the Coltish Disease of the Staggers in the Masculine-Feminine, of our Times. Exprest in a briefe Declamation.* London[:] printed for I.T. [John Trundle] and are to be sold at Christ Church gate. 1620. LUNA: Folger Digital Image Collection, Folger Shakespeare Library, source call number STC 13374. https://luna.folger.edu. Public domain.

more masculine? And who is more feminine? Such invited questionings may well provoke further queries over the very nature of gender relations.

Yet another tactical association—and the most subversive one in "The Sailor and his Love"—is a more direct link to the anti-feminist debate tracts, likely viewed explicitly as such by contemporaries. This link is communicated by the ballad's middle woodcut. Anyone following the hot gender disputations of the times would have immediately recognized this cut as the right half—now but a fragment—of a woodcut that in its entirety appeared on the title page to the anti-feminist tract *Hic Mulier: Or, The Man-Woman* (London, 1620) (Figure 11).[6] Either the block was starting to split apart or, more likely, the woodcarver or printer decided to divide the block into two pieces to get double the cut for the price of one at a time when that woodblock was making

A most delicate, pleasant, amorous, new Song, made by a Gentleman that enioyes his Loue, shewing the worth and happinesse of Content, and the effects of loue, called, *All Louers Ioy*.
To the tune of *New Paradise*.

The Second Part. To the same Tune.

Printed at London for H. G.

Figure 12. Ballad sheet facsimile, "A most delicate, pleasant, amorous, new Song, made by a Gentleman that enioyes his Loue, shewing the worth and happi-nesse of Content, and the effects of loue, called, *All Louers Ioy*" (c. 1625), EBBA 20117. Post-photographic processing by EBBA. Magdalene College, Cambridge, Pepys Library, Pepys Ballads 1.254–255. By permission of the Pepys Library, Magdalene College, Cambridge.

news (and thus money). This isn't the only time ballads have capitalized in a tactical way—extemporaneously and subversively—on the in-the-news feminist debates. Another ballad, with the long, rambling title "A most delicate, pleasant, amorous, new Song, made by a Gentleman that enjoyes his Love, shewing the worth and happinesse of Content, and the effects of love, called *All Lovers Joy*. To the Tune of *New Paradise*," published by Henry Gosson around 1625, is a case in point (Figure 12; EBBA 20117). In this ballad, a gentleman sings the praises of his lady as surpassing all beauteous women (Cynthia, Helen of Troy, etc.): "My sweet Ladies glistering rayes, / now approve that Ages errour. / Hellen far her selfe's above, / Never liv'd a fairer Love" (st. 4). The woodcuts on the right, below "The Second Part. To the same Tune" of this ballad, are of an aristocratic man and our well-known lady with a fan.

Figure 13. Left: Close-up of "A most delicate, pleasant, amorous, new Song, made by a Gentleman that enioyes his Loue, shewing the worth and happi-nesse of Content, and the effects of loue, called, *All Louers Ioy*" (c. 1625), EBBA 20117. Magdalene College, Cambridge, Pepys Library, Pepys Ballads 1.254–255. By permission of the Pepys Library, Magdalene College, Cambridge. *Right:* Title page to *Haec-Vir: Or The Womanish-Man: Being an Answere to a late Booke intituled "Hic-Mulier."*. . . London[:] printed for I.T. [John Trundle] and are to be sold at Christ Church gate. 1620. The Huntington Library, call number 61257.

He is a manly man whose wide-cut garments emphasize strong shoulders and muscularity, an image completed by his prominent sword; she is a courtly lady in costly, well-ornamented garb. Thus they would appear to fit the ballad's theme (although we will have to qualify the presence of the lady with fan).

But there is one big, hilarious tactical upset in this otherwise pretty conventional, ho-hum ballad of a gentleman idealizing his lady love. The large first woodcut is taken wholly from the title page to the *Haec-Vir* pro-feminist debate tract (Figure 13, right).[7] In this woodcut, we see not a classic beauty surpassing Helen of Troy but a grimacing woman with the signature mannish fashion of feather in cap and short haircut. If that weren't enough, she holds a pistol in her right hand and sword in her left. By contrast, her head-over-heels "lover," the speaker of the ballad, stands beside her and looks like an effeminate dandy. In more ways than one, he is no match for her. His starched collar—excessively large and amusingly pointed—emphasizes the narrow slope of his shoulders; the tendrils of hair peeking out from under his soft-brimmed hat seem, like his mustache, carefully styled (especially when they are compared to, for example, the unruly carelessness of the hair and beard of the man who appears in the woodcut to his right, as seen in Figure 12). His trousers, though fastened near the knee like those of the more sober man beside him, are festooned all about with impractical, dangling ribbons. He holds—of all things—a badminton racket in his right hand and three birdies in his left, ready to play a set of a lightweight game, not engage in macho battle. Considering this woodcut, the ballad sung to the now-seen-to-be-ironically named tune "*New Paradise*," could hardly be understood *but* as a very funny tactical attack by printer and publisher on men who have become pathetically delusional and emasculated by love (of women and of feminine fashion). It is not difficult to picture the grand time to be had by women singing this ballad—perhaps joined by men mocking their fashion-mongering mates!

We seem, however, to have digressed from our analysis of "The Sailor and his Love"—or have we? The above discussion, after all, could well reflect the mental path of associated hits an early modern viewer might have made upon seeing the second woodcut of the aggressive mannish women in the first "Mock-Beggar Hall" ballad, especially someone intently following the much-talked-about and much-read feminist debate tracts. So, let's jump back to "The Sailor and his Love" (see Figure 10), now with this wider and more informed contemporary vision. In using not one but two woodcuts on the sailor ballad that are clearly linked to *both* sides of the popular pro- and anti-feminist debate tracts, the producers have made a very cagey tactical move. They allow a space for consumers, depending on their cache of associations and on their inclinations, to assemble around a subversive mockery either for or against the feminist stance that the sailor's lady can easily be seen to adopt in the ballad. Or not. Any of the varied gender alignments promoted by this possibly 1625 ballad and the tracts of the 1620s associated with it could most certainly have changed the ways an early modern viewer, who made such connections, assembled the different Lego-like pieces that also impart tactical gender mockery in the first and, by association, second "Mock-Beggar Hall" ballads.

"The Sailor and his Love" ballad bolsters potential for mixed mockery over gender relations through the very fact that the conflicting visual media co-inhabit the same sheet. The ballad's text seems on the surface to fall into the conventional genre about a soldier returning home from war and who is either embraced or temporarily rebuffed by his left-behind lady-love. In this case, he is at first firmly rebuffed and, for eight stanzas, speaking in the first person, he is on the defensive, protesting his constancy in love while he has been away for three years at sea, and pleading with his lady for acceptance, in variations on the refrain to each stanza, "then kisse and bid me welcome home." Finally, in the last four stanzas of the ballad, the woman, who has refused to acknowledge him, answers. She states that she is now satisfied that he has in fact been honest while away, and she welcomes him home, as if he has passed a test. She tells him how she herself has all this time rebuffed suitors in faithfulness to him. But, for all her now-welcoming words, there are insinuations of an ongoing aggressiveness on her part, which the illustrations to the ballad, now understood in their charged cultural gender context, encourage us to see. In the first stanza where she finally speaks, she informs him,

> Thou from our shore
> Shalt goe no more,
> To wander thus abroad alone:
> But thou shalt stay,
> With me alway,
> *for here's my hand, thou'rt welcome home.* (st. 9)

To sea, he "*shalt* goe no more"; he "*shalt* stay." These are not requests but commands.

Again, the lady takes the ruling hand in the third stanza of her response, with another "shalt": "Seeing thou art home arived, / thou *shalt* not goe away in haste" she asserts (st. 11; my emphasis). She concludes the ballad as commandingly, promising that "thou hast my heart, / Not to depart. / But ever constant to remain"—not that she ever went anywhere to begin with; he did. There's an added catch to this promise of her heart; again, spoken more by telling than asking: "And thou hast mine, / *And I have thine*, / *then let us kisse and welcome home*" (st. 12; my emphasis on second cited line). What, in many ballads, are conventional pleas by the lady that the sailor stay home with her upon his return from his sea voyages, here slyly take the form of imperious assertions on the part of a rather virile woman, made more manly by the images that illustrate the ballad. She has the upper hand from the very beginning of the ballad. She knows how to withhold in order to get what she wants. And when she gives, she does so in brief—occupying half the text the sailor wallows through. Though she may not literally wear the pants in their future union, she certainly rules—and sets the rules for—their relationship. Compared to the effeminately featured gentleman soldier/sailor, posing with feathered hat and bows at his knees, she is much more like the aggressive mannish women who dominate the visuals to the ballad (pictured in the second and third woodcuts—the image of the women in fighting stance literally above, or should we say, "on the side of," the woman's commanding response). Indeed, belligerent women are seemingly the only imaginable kind in the world of this ballad sheet. The tactically strong mockery of the male gender does not, of course, entirely preclude alternate readings (a point to which we shall return). Still, the very presence of these pro-feminist woodcuts draws the ballad irresistibly into the orbit of contemporary arguments about gender.

The text of the ballad, in the context of the woodcut illustrations, thus becomes an ironic version of the stereotypical or everyday "Sailor and his Love" ballad. By association, the first "Mock-Beggar Hall" ballad turns into an even more cutting (if still covert) jab at the landed aristocracy, this time targeting the aristocrats' inadequate gender performance rather than their inhospitality. Recollection of "The Sailor and his Love"—or even of just one or both of its aggressive mannish-women woodcuts (including the one-half of the cut from the title page of the anti-feminist tract *Hic Mulier*)—clarifies any questioning confusion a viewer of the first edition of "Mock-Beggar Hall" might have had over the woodcut impression on the right side of its sheet. That cut would now more likely be seen as a definitive strike against the citified upper sorts. *Hic Mulier*, in fact, particularly targets "great Ones" (women of high estate who affect mannish fashion), thus insinuating that even nobles, not just gentlemen or gentlewomen, are at fault for gender deviance. Furthermore, the pamphlet repeatedly calls such strange fashion-mongering, as in "Mock-Beggar Hall," "monstrous."[8] Reflection on the feminist debate tracts generally also encourages us to rethink the male-female relations being portrayed in the first woodcut image of the "Mock-Beggar Hall" ballad. Though a man appears in two conventional stages of romancing a woman (first, wooing her, leaning forward as if pleading, with hat in hand, and secondly, enjoying the fruits of his courtship, cozied up with her in a private garden arbor), this illustration smacks of sleazy, unmanly tactics on the wooer's part to fulfill his desire—sneaking via a bauble of a boat to make a secretive sexual assignation in the hall's back gardens. At the same time, in another gender reversal, the woman at the front of the house stands boldly in a window, adopting a manly stance that mirrors her male sentry; like his one arm, both her arms are staunchly planted on her waist and, like him, she seems aggressively on the lookout. When we add these elements of the cut's narrative to our growing data set of associations, the ballad's involvement with larger cultural issues becomes even clearer: it would seem that both aristocratic men and women who gave up their country estates for the city were not exactly above board in their gendered behavior to begin with, and such behavior has descended further into a perversion not only of their hospitality but of any "proper" gender roles.

This tactical critical stance does not allow opting in or out quite so easily as "The Sailor and his Love," which offers illustrations from *both* pro- and anti-feminist debate tracts, inviting alignment with or against the feminist position of the sailor's "love." As we have noted, the image of the two mannish women, which also appears on the earlier version of "Mock-Beggar Hall," is closely connected to the visual language—and illustrations, as seen in the title-page woodcuts for *Hic Mulier and Haec-Vir*—of contemporary feminist debates (making it all the more unfortunate that no early impression from the woodcut, before it acquired the damage visible on the ballad, seems to have survived time's ravages). In the context of the first woodcut and the text of the lyrics, this cut of the first "Mock-Beggar Hall" ballad increasingly seems to be putting a thumb on the scale of the gender debate, to the advantage of the anti-feminist position. It exemplifies the perversion of the wealthy upper sorts—already on a downward moral descent in the first cut—who have abandoned their responsibilities in selling off their lands and then buying into all the strange fashions of the city, to the extent of perverting their very gender identities. Two well-dressed, clearly well-to-do mannish women, seemingly attacking each other over a purse of "gold" or "silver," bring to the fore other phrases in the ballad, such as "monstrous pride" (st. 3) and "we are Apes in imitation" (st. 6) —wording that hits, if ironically, on *Hic Mulier*, which defends aristocratic women's adoption of monstrous male fashion as arising from their need to differentiate themselves from inferior (in class) "Apes" through such new styles of dress.[9]

In the same vein, in the line "It is to maintaine their monstrous pride" (st. 3), the melodies of both "Northern Nancy" and "Damask Rose" in their different ways especially emphasize "***mon***-strous" and give next emphases to "*pride*" (and, later on, to "*Apes*"). In "Northern Nancy," the "off" note of the F♮ (F natural) falls on the affirmative "is": "It ***is*** to main-*taine* their ***mon***-strous *pride*." That absolute "***is***" receives further emphasis by its length (being an eighth-note longer than the note preceding it) and because it is the highest note in the tune—the climax of an upward skipping motion.[10] "Damask Rose" uses different tactics to similar effects, perhaps the most notable example being that "mon" in "***mon***-strous" initiates an extended downward movement (from D to B to G), which both enacts and draws out the lamented decline of humanity into the "monstrous." Each tune imparts its own subtle flavor: "Northern Nancy" smacks of an agreeable piquancy, especially with its zesty phenomenal accent on "***is***" that drives home, without wallowing in, the pronounced but otherwise deemed distasteful urban decline into inhumanity—

the "monstrous"; "Damask Rose," however, tastes more distressfully sweet-and-sour, with the touch of an acidic smack capable of dominating, as we've seen, in the tune's extended reenactment, note by note, precisely of that "monstrous" decline.

The reader or listener might now become more attuned to the stanza that underscores a gendered symptom of unsavory monstrosity. I refer to the "apish" look of "Gentlewomen" in the "Mock-Beggar Hall" ballads. The figure these women of the upper sorts cut is far from palatable (especially to those familiar with the anti-feminist track record of images like the one printed on the first edition of the ballad, depicting ladies fashionably dressed as men and apparently fighting over a money bag). Such manly gentlewomen might well take up arms over money because they have spent all their means on the very latest style: "Our Gentlewomen whose meanes is nothing / To that which they make shew of, / Must use all the fashions in their cloathing, / Which they can heare or know of" (st. 9). This before unheard-of fashion, the ballad implies, echoing the anti-feminist debate tracts, is a violence against gender; the earlier words "monstrous" and "Apes" declare it to be downright unnatural, even inhuman. But the stanza further stands out in that it does not reference gentlewomen *aspirants*, like the aspiring farmers and landlords at the beginning of the first "Mock-Beggar Hall" ballad, but rather *actual* gentlewomen. Indeed, the stanza not only focuses on the perversions of fashion-crazed gentlewomen but also prompts the relator's stated desire in the first ballad to clarify what he means by "Mocke begger" and his subsequent direct finger-pointing at wealthy "Gentlemen and Citizens" (st. 11). In this instance, the textual context, even more than the musical metric and phenomenal accents established by the tune (no matter which tune has been chosen), bolsters the visual attack on the upper sort of women in the first "Mock-Beggar Hall." Verbal and visual critique could well have been further reinforced by the occurrence of the mannish-women image on the slightly earlier ballad "The Sailor and his Love." Of course, any such associational negativity might reverberate not only forward but also backward onto and within the earlier, more gender-complicated "The Sailor and his Love," tilting the expression and reception of the to-and-fro nature of this dialogue ballad more definitively against women.

Tactically, if also playfully, a significant aspect of the tune for "The Sailor and his Love" supports such a repositioning of our interpretation—in a way that would further recuperate the traditional, "natural" order of male dominance.

The tune named on the sheet to "The Sailor and his Love" is "Dulcina," modernized from a 1615 manuscript as follows:[11]

The "Dulcina" ballads, after which this tune was named, open with a sad shepherdess, Dulcina, lamenting the absence of her true love, Corydon. She is at last comforted by his return (the plot line fitting well with the conventional nautical version of the story wherein a lass bemoans the absence of her sailor-love but is in the end solaced by his homecoming). The tune is sung in the Ionian mode (equivalent to the modern major), as is "Northern Nancy." Recall that, according to Charles Butler, in his *Principles of Musik* (1626), the Ionian mode is typical of "the infinite multitude of Balads" of his time and their upbeat or "pleasant and delightful" tunes.[12] Of course, the storylines of the original "Dulcina" ballad, after which the tune is named, and the subsequent "Sailor and his Love," and, for that matter, "Mock-Beggar Hall," are for the most part *not* upbeat. But it's not uncommon for a tune to provide counterpoint to, and even relief from, extensive accounts of sad events, given that ballad songs can go on for some six to twelve to fifteen to even twenty or more minutes—far longer than today's typical three-minute song.[13] The recording of "The Sailor and his Love" in EBBA runs close to seven minutes; **Track 14** in the Audio Companion.

Still, the modern ear can hear a distinct difference between major and minor along the lines described by Butler's difference between Ionian and Aeolian. The major mode in which these songs are sung particularly fits the "turn" in the events from somber to happy in the "Dulcina" and "The Sailor and his Love" ballads, though, in the latter case, with a twist, as we have seen. "The Sailor and his Love" tactically and humorously turns around the gender roles of the ballad "Dulcina." In the "Sailor" ballad, it is the returned seaman who is complaining, not the lass. The problem is that he is *not* being welcomed home. The song opens with his surprised complaint, "What doth aile my Love, so sadly / in such heavy dumps to stand: / Doth she grieve or take unkindly, / that I am so neere at hand?" (st. 1). Listening to the ballad sung, we hear a charged resentment in the speaker's voice, insistently conveyed through the relatively simple rhythm by which he sings it, at least in the first four lines of the eight-line stanza. The tune then opens up to more variation and range, creating an almost swinging feeling. This turn in the melody foreshadows the turnaround in sentiment the ballad will enact at the level of plot, when the lady finally answers and (if most assertively) embraces the sailor.

"Dulcina" is fairly easy to sing, with a total range of a major tenth, just a couple of steps more than an octave, which is an average range for a ballad. And though the second part skips around more, it doesn't do so in a difficult but rather in a fun way. But there are two places in the melody of real complexity added by the conjoining of two note pairs (indicated by the curved line crossing the measure bar in lines 3 and 4 of the score). This "tie" indicates that the singer should combine the two shorter notes into one long note. The result is a forced pause on a word, producing a jolting rhythmic feel in lines 7 and 10 of each stanza of the ballad, disrupting what would otherwise be simple iambic rhythms.[14] And at precisely these moments of melodic jolts, the sailor often both melodically and textually wrests momentary gender dominance. That is, the rhythmic jolt in each stanza emphasizes the recurrent personal pronouns referring to *him*—the *sailor's* incessant request (demand?) in the first half of the ballad, "*first kisse and bid* ***me*** *welcome home*" and its variant in his final sung stanza, "*and say sweet heart* ***thou'rt*** *welcome home*" (sts. 1, 8; my bold emphases). Even in the lady's abbreviated response (four as opposed to his eight stanzas), where she sings her own version of the refrain, the personal pronoun referencing the sailor dominates in the rhythmic jolt: "*for here's my hand* ***thou'rt*** *welcome home*" (st. 9; my bold emphasis).

There's a lot of ego tied up in this ballad and, to a certain extent, a battle of wills as well as genders. The melody, when fit to the text, forces that point home. Furthermore, the tune's phenomenal emphasis in the final lines (on the male referents, "thou" and "thine") implies that the man, not the woman, wins. These lines complicate any inclination to privilege the woman as gaining the upper hand as visualized in the woodcuts of the ballad. The stress on the male possessives opens further the question of whose side the consumer would align with. Such a complication could carry over to the "Mock-Beggar Hall" ballads (directly, for the first; by association, for the second), where the selfish aristocratic fashion-mongers, male and female alike, privilege their own egos over those of the poor (do the poor even have egos, in the minds of the wealthy?), while still underscoring gender jostling for dominance. "The Sailor and his Love" melody, when adjusted to the text but also to the woodcut illustrations, allows audience members to inhabit more fully whatever choice of stance (or non-stance) they favor for singing, reading, or viewing the mostly merry tune, exploiting the either/or of the "he said/she said" nature of the dialogue format of the text. An associational hit to the melody of "The Sailor and his Love," or even to some of the multimedia fragments assembled as part of this provisional whole ballad, might especially entice the early modern to sing the "Mock-Beggar Hall" ballads to the more piquant, upbeat, if also mocking, "Northern Nancy," though the option to take the more sweetly lamentable-turned-sour satirical route of "Damask Rose" remains wide open.

The printers/publishers are here tactically offering their consumers an ever-widening interlocking range of Lego-block pieces of illustrations, texts, and tunes that might have been fit together in the mind of an early modern through further triggered associations on making initially just one hit from one woodcut on the first "Mock-Beggar Hall" ballad to its sister impression on another ballad. Such multiply generative interlocking links dismantle and, at the same time, accumulate "binary divisions" (as Marsh calls them) in ballads, allowing for more complicated, if sometimes puzzling, perspectives on any one ballad experience. Just how gender-focused would have become the mockery of our first "Mock-Beggar Hall" ballad in the mind of a consumer, thinking back, in associating the mannish women woodcut to "The Sailor and his Love"? And just how problematized would such a remembered hit, and its subsequent generative associations, make the already tense gender relations in that earlier ballad? Having put the Lego blocks together, whose voiced gender would the consumer have favored in the dialogue of "The Sailor and his Love"? How would the consumer's position have changed with the separation and moving about of its constitutive bits, especially as they fit into the pieces of another, later ballad, such as "Mock-Beggar Hall"? We are so far making just a few tentative steps along one pathway of random hits. A single association of one ballad fragment—a woodcut illustration—has opened a rhizomatic assemblage of results especially associated with the feminist debate tracts. How much of that route (or serendipitous encounters) any one early modern would have traversed in assembling her or his mental cache of broadside ballads—how many kinds of hits she or he would have assembled in the course of lived experience—is not fully fathomable.

Mock-Country and Mock-Class

You're probably thinking right now: "She's relying far too much on just one possible connection an early modern *might* have made between one woodcut on two ballads—which a contemporary might never even have seen or noticed—and then taken a sea voyage from there to the connecting ballads' texts and "Dulcina" tune as well as to other ballads and woodcuts, some of which aren't even on ballads, that just associatively come to mind!" That's true. And that's partly my point about how occasional and piecemeal ballad hits could have worked in the early modern period. But, to ease some readers' concerns or, for others, to add insult to injury, let's take another, different associative pathway a contemporary might have followed from that same second woodcut in the earliest "Mock-Beggar Hall" ballad that we've focused on. This divergent path leads to musing upon gender as well: this time, however, through a more self-conscious and complicated reflection upon the apparently clear-cut oppositions of country versus city and low (or poor) versus high (or wealthy). Through intermedial associations of component ballad parts, as in the mental links from the "Mock-Beggar Hall" ballads to the media bits that make up "The Sailor and his Love," such connections could also have influenced which tune would have been chosen for singing those ballads and the tone in which it would have been sung.

Let us posit, then, that the viewer of the first "Mock-Beggar Hall" ballad made a passing link from its second woodcut not to "The Sailor and his Love" but to a ballad titled, in the original spelling, "The Countrey Lasse" (hereafter modernized to "The Country Lass"). EBBA contains several ballads to "The Country Lass" tune, but only two whose main title is by the same name. Both were printed close to the same time, although with different woodcut illustrations. The one that might well have triggered an associational hit with our first "Mock-Beggar Hall" ballad is Pepys 1.268–269 (EBBA 20124; Figure 14). Of the three impressions on this ballad, the aggressive mannish women appear third, and yet again, as in all other instances where they've turned up, prominently on the far right of the sheet, below the title "The second part. To the same Tune."[15] This ballad was published roughly around 1628, very close to the 1633–35 date range that has been given for our first "Mock-Beggar Hall" ballad. "The Country Lass" ballad has another claim to an early modern's attention other than its timely sporting of our now familiar woodcut: it is authored by the prolific and highly popular ballad writer Martin Parker, who was active around 1623 to 1656—so notable that he was one of the rare ballad

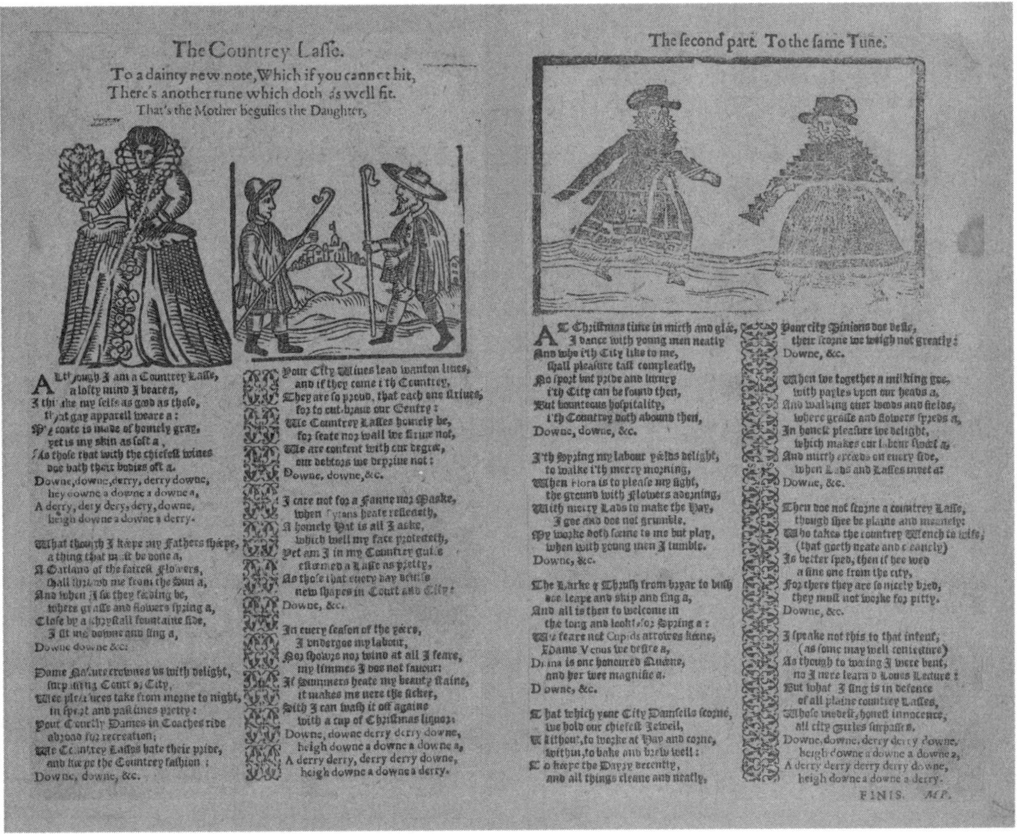
The Countrey Lasse.
To a dainty new note, Which if you cannot hit,
There's another tune which doth as well fit.
That's the Mother beguiles the Daughter.

The second part. To the same Tune.

FINIS. M.P.

Figure 14. Ballad sheet facsimile, "The Countrey Lasse. To a dainty new note, Which if you cannot hit, There's another tune which doth as well fit" (c. 1628), EBBA 20124. Post-photographic processing by EBBA. Magdalene College, Cambridge, Pepys Library, Pepys Ballads 1.268–269. By permission of the Pepys Library, Magdalene College, Cambridge.

authors who actually signposted his name on the ballad sheet (usually in the form of his initials, "M.P.").[16]

Parker's "The Country Lass" has obvious associations with the first "Mock-Beggar Hall" ballad beyond the notable intermedial link to the mannish women woodcut. In the "Mock-Beggar Hall" ballads, as we know, the landed wealthy are described as having deserted their country life for the lures of the newfangled fashions of the city. The country lass, however, speaking in her own voice, spends thirteen 12-line stanzas of text and over eight minutes of enthusiastic song, praising the simple delights of the country over the city and the superiority of country lasses over court and city ladies.[17] Despite her focus on women, gender is not this rural woman's only or even primary concern: the lass is most intent on privileging rural life over that of the court/city, and the homely "low" over the prideful "high."

As if setting a counter-precedent for the "Mock-Beggar Hall" ballads, she repeatedly condemns the pride of "Courtly Dames" and "City Wives" (sts. 3–5). Country lasses, by contrast, she repeatedly explains, are plain, hard-working, honest, but fun-loving maids. In all their "modest" "innocence" (st. 13), they enjoy a healthy sexuality as well, combining work with sexual play: she delights, she says, "With merry Lads to make the Hay . . . / when with young men I tumble" (st. 8). She also definitively speaks out *against* the monstrous fashions of city folk—"those that every day devise / new shapes in Court and City" (st. 5)—which would seem exemplified in the illustration of the third woodcut of the mannish women sporting just such strange "new shapes" of the latest adopted urban style. If the country poor are abandoned in the "Mock-Beggar Hall" ballads, especially in the first one, which keeps a clearer division of high (or wealthy) and low—who might readily sing that ballad in a tone of lament or bitter mockery—the left-behind humble sorts in "The Country Lass" happily celebrate their status back in the country as "homely" (st. 1) and "plaine" (sts. 12, 13). Indeed, the two ballads linked together might well have provoked the disjunctive thought that the same textual adjectives—"homely" and "plaine"—used to praise the poor in "The Country Lass" could also describe those whom the "Mock-Beggar Hall" ballads extol as "men of worthy calling" from seemingly lost "ancient times" (st. 1): wealthy men who did not indulge in but abstained from the so-called fashionable dress of urbanized (and "monstrous") "new shapes." "The Country Lass" reveals just how superior or inwardly "high" are not only the wealthy of olden times but also the lowly country folks of the present when compared to their self-exalted, monied, and prideful contemporaries in court and city. We also hear in "The Country Lass" a barely covert, tactical jab directed specifically at the citified wealthy in the "Mock-Beggar Hall" ballads who have abandoned their responsibility to offer "grace" or hospitality to the rural poor. The country lass pointedly states, "No sport but pride and luxury / i'th City can be found then, / *But bounteous hospitality, / i'th Countrey doth abound then*" (st. 7; my emphasis). That's a palpable hit.

Identification with the position of the country lass would likely have been very strong among the lower sorts in London, many of whom would have relatively recent and fond memories of country life. After all, much of the city's replenished and burgeoning population (especially base-born apprentices, servants, and unsettled poor) immigrated to London from the countryside to take up or seek work (not fashion) in the city, in the face of little livelihood—and no relief from the landed wealthy—back home.[18]

There's just one big complication, which breeds notice of several more, with this seemingly easy reading of "The Country Lass," especially when thought of in contrast to the "Mock-Beggar Hall" ballads that lament prideful court and city fashions. The most obvious problem is that the ballad's first woodcut illustration, which a viewer would naturally think represents the female speaker, since it is the first image on the sheet, and the only one of a single woman, in fact illustrates an aristocratic lady wearing courtly Tudor fashion, *not* a country lass. The image was made from one of the popular lady-with-fan woodcuts, versions of which we have already repeatedly seen impressed on ballads. This particular woman also made an appearance in the second part of the "All Lover's Joy" ballad, discussed above, which mocked the effeminacy of the male gender in the face of a mannish woman whom the male lover declares (at length) he adores (see Figure 12). To make matters more vexing, the last illustration on "All Lover's Joy" sports one of the many copies of this popular lady-with-fan, which supposedly also represents the country lass. On "All Lover's Joy," the lady is carved into a variant woodblock (her skirt is black, not white), which impression also appears on an early *anti*-feminist debate tract of 1615.[19] Despite, or perhaps *because* of, the appeal of this lady, who morphs but at the same time stays the same in her many recuttings for ballads and other street literature, the printer/publisher of "The Country Lass" may have tactically placed her image on the ballad to align her with the also now familiar image of the virile aristocratic women in the ballad's third woodcut. Certainly, her visual representation as a courtly lady (regardless of whether aggressively so) undermines her claim to homely country simplicity. This would have been a most cutting blow to all simple country folk who might have made the negative intermedial links noted above but who also wanted to seize upon the country lass's song as a proud celebration of the rural poor's superiority over the "high" in their collective plainness.

Without doubt, the country lass has a haughty attitude that, in a more sympathetic reading, might justify her elevated courtly garb as an allegorical reference to her inner moral worth. In her opening lines, she declares, "Although I am a Countrey Lasse, / *a lofty mind* I bear a, / I thinke my selfe as good as those, / that gay apparell weare a" (st. 1; my emphasis). But she then goes on to contradict our first visual impression of her, describing her plain country clothing and insisting, "We Countrey Lasses hate their [courtly and city women's] pride, / and keepe the Countrey fashion" (st. 3). So, what would the contemporary viewer have made of this introductory illustration of a country-cum-courtly lady fully decked out in a (nostalgic?) throwback to high Tudor fashion? Would the viewer in fact have seen the illustration as a metaphoric image of what the country lass's elevated virtuous inside, *not* outside, looks like? Or as an undermining not only of those whom she critiques but also of herself? Or—and here's where things get tricky—as an image of what she really wants to look like? Or even of what the author/printer/publisher thought consumers wanted her to look like? Note that both "Mock-Beggar Hall" ballads bitingly observe that "The City followes the Strangers fashion, / *The Countrey followes the City*" (st. 6; my emphasis). Is that what we are seeing at work in "The Country Lass"? Is the author/printer/publisher making a tactical maneuver by means of the first woodcut impression to show that, for all her talk, this rural woman and her neighbors in fact envy and want to imitate city fashions? And, in an even more cutting jab at rustics, is the illustration implying that, as a plain rustic, the country lass is fantasizing? She *wouldn't* and *couldn't* look like the decked-out lady with fan, who is far more aesthetically fetching than the unadorned simplicity the lass describes, and thus her illustration of "lofty" dress is a tactical undermining by the ballad's producers of everything she says.

The citified well-to-do, I suspect, would strongly have favored this last interpretation, which is there for the making, especially as a retaliation provoked by recalling this ballad in the course of mental hits made in viewing, reading, or hearing the mocking jabs they sustained in the "Mock-Beggar Hall" ballads. More determinedly imagining the illustration metaphorically, the lower sorts could have chosen the first option and seen the "raised" fashionable status of the country lass as simply imaging her self-described "lofty *mind*" and high inner value. Or they could have opted for the second option and, taking the image at face value, chosen to see it as illustrating precisely the overly ornate court and city fashion, which could even betray their own nostalgia for the days of Queen Elizabeth. This last interpretation exposes the opposition of the lower sorts to the newfangled city fashions the country lass says she rejects—just as, the same simple folk might have continued to say, the third image of the urbane mannish well-to-do women exemplifies the kind of strange "new shapes" the prideful wealthy "devise" "in Court and City." What makes this latter reading a potentially knotty one, though, is that consumers generally, of all social sorts, *did* enjoy seeing images of the fashionable upper sorts on ballads; socially high figures, decked out in full ornamental style, dominate the illustrations that appear on ballad sheets. It would seem that such well-dressed highborn were seen by all social sorts as, quite simply, pretty to look at, with all their fashionable adornments. But the problem is that such fashionable displays can complicate and even undermine the text and/or tune of a ballad and, in the case of "The Country Lass," they particularly open up that opportunity.[20] We should be especially on high alert with ballads authored by Martin Parker, as is "The Country Lass." Parker is typically most tricky. Working likely together with his printer and publisher, he as a rule complicated the relational component parts of his ballads so as to tactically embed multiple visions on topics (with the intent to sell more ballads)—just as he often wrote response ballads that would out-and-out counter an earlier voiced position that he also authored on another ballad!

It is not only the first woodcut of "The Country Lass" that proves tactically devious. The middle cut is also not as straightforward as it might at first appear: an image of two shepherds meeting in the countryside. The trouble lies in the fact that, while the one figure on the left does look like a country shepherd—plain-clothed, with hook in hand—the figure he faces, though also holding a shepherd's hook, otherwise resembles more an urbane well-groomed gentleman than a country fellow, with his stylish hat, cloak, and beard. Is this another case of the lowly sorts only seeming to enjoy their homely life, but in fact showing off their citified aspirations, as the first and even third images could have been interpreted, most likely by the upper sorts? Or are we seeing someone from the court or city just out and about enjoying the country life? But then why the look-alike costume? It's as if we are viewing King Polixenes disguised as a countryman at the sheepshearing feast in act 4 of *The Winter's Tale*. Is that what contemporaries in fact saw (or thought they saw) in this woodcut: an aristocrat just playing at being a shepherd? Further puzzling our interpretative stances is the passing jab in the text of the ballad made by the country lass at the city sorts who come into the country and try to "out-brave" the well-to-do country folk: if "City Wives . . . come i'th Countrey, / They are so proud, that each one strives, / for to out-brave our Gentry" (st. 4). Is that what the illustrations were meant to convey? that, despite the country lass's privileging of the homely country life over the city, she and her fellow lowly sorts are outbraved on their own turf? To add to the interpretative possibilities the viewer faces, these two imaged "shepherds" repeat in their face-to-face stance the two aggressive, citified, and upper-class mannish women in the far-right illustration on the same ballad sheet. This country setting can be seen as getting a tad overpopulated with well-to-do, urban upper sorts.

The text of the ballad, particularly when sung to the accompanying tune, "That's the Mother beguiles the Daughter" (later most known as, yes, "The Countrey Lasse"—hereafter in our discussion modernized, as I have the ballad's title after which the tune is renamed, to "The Country Lass"), further complicates the possible fragmentary assemblages or hits an early modern might have made, especially from the first "Mock-Beggar Hall" to this ballad. The simplest and earliest notation of "The Country Lass" tune resides in John Playford's *A booke of New Lessons*, 1652:[21]

The tune is notated in C major, with the range of a major ninth. With the exception of the octave leap in the first measure, which is repeated in singing lines 3, 5, and 7 of each of the twelve-line stanzas, and the same octave leap at the end of the tune's refrain for each stanza, it is not too difficult a tune to sing. But it does require some vocal agility. Indeed, a beginning musician or an untalented singer might find it challenging. The producers of the ballad apparently recognized such potential difficulty for consumers: they explicitly encourage free choice on the part of singers whether to "go for it" in singing this tune, as we discussed with the average person today deciding whether to sing the difficult leaps in "The Star-Spangled Banner." The c. 1628 edition of "The Country Lass" (Pepys Ballads 1.268–269; EBBA 20124), which we have cited throughout our discussion, explicitly states on the sheet that the tune is "To a dainty new note, / *which if you cannot hit, / There's another tune which doth as well fit*" (my emphasis). Underscored here is that, as in the "Mock-Beggar Hall" ballads, more than one tune might fit a ballad. As important, in their seeking the largest market, the producers offer options.

In reading the notated music from the sourcebook of the period, or even in simply having heard it orally sung to another ballad, a musician or potential singer might be further challenged in applying it to our specific text. The tune is notated for an eight-line poetic stanza, whereas "The Country Lass" stanzas consist of twelve lines, as evident in the first stanza below:

> Although I am a Countrey Lasse,
>   a lofty mind I beare a,

I thinke my selfe as good as those,
  that gay apparell weare a:
My coate is made of homely gray,
  yet is my skin as soft a,
As those that with the chiefest wines
  doe bath their bodies oft a.
Downe, downe, derry, derry downe,
  hey downe a downe a downe a,
A derry, dery dery, dery, downe,
  heigh downe a downe a derry. (st. 1)

Faced with this superabundance of poetic lines, two experienced broadside ballad singers I heard tackle this song independently came up with the same solution: they each repeated the first line of notation (roughly equivalent to two lines of poetry, we recall), not just once—as the two dotted bars at the end of that first line instruct—but *three* times. In addition, they saved the variation indicated by the "2." in the notation for the end only of the eighth poetic line (falling on "oft a" in the stanza above). They thus created a simple unity to the body of each stanza while at the same time marking its transition into the stanza's nonsense refrain, which consists of the second and third lines of music notated above. You can hear the ballad sung in this fashion by Rachel Short on **Track 15** of the Audio Companion.

Necessary modifications would have been less difficult to make in singing the tune to the body of the stanzas of the "The Country Lass" than to its refrain. The repeated first line of music notation for singing the first eight poetic lines consists of relatively easy to sing, mostly sidewise steps of notes. Once we reach the refrain, though, we encounter a noticeable difference. We've seen this happen before, in the "Mock-Beggar Hall" tune of "Damask Rose" and especially in "Dulcina." The singer voicing the text of "The Country Lass" at this point faces the first real challenge in adjusting tune to text, and vice versa: the first poetic line of the refrain (and all the subsequent lines except line 11) is a syllable short from those in the body of the stanza, consisting of seven syllables, not eight. There are thus more notes in the melody for the refrain than words to fit them. Listening again to the song as sung by Short, now focusing just on her rendition of the refrain, in **Track 16**, we can hear how she has adjusted for this problem in a canny way that emphasizes, rather than detracts from, the text's meaning (or at least, one meaning). Consider her delivery of the very first word of the refrain, "Downe," as seen in the following transcription:

"***Downe***," as we here see, is not only stressed by the poetic meter and by its privileged position initiating the refrain; it is also musically the metrically strongest stressed word of the line. Short hammers this emphasis further "down." She draws out the word over two quarter notes which add further phenomenal stress to "***Downe***" by conveying an oral and aural, and in the transcription, a visual plunge—the singer enacting for the listener and viewer a downward leap from A to D.

This simple but brilliant declension sung by Short on "***Downe***" occurs twice in the four-line refrain: in its first and second lines (lines 9 and 10 of the poetic stanza). In the second instance, it is as if the strong musical emphasis on "***downe***" actually prompts the enacted fall in notes from A to D over "***downe*** a." You can hear the fall more clearly in the slowed-down fiddle audio of the refrain on **Track 17**. Notice as well that the strongest emphases in the entire refrain lie mostly on "***downe***" and "***der***" in "***der***-ry" (also spelled "***der***-y"), but only once on "***heigh***."

Downward and upward. It is as if this seemingly nonsense refrain both enacts and playfully puzzles the key issues posed in the body of the ballad's stanzas (as well as accompanying illustrations). The musical metrical and phenomenal accents on "***downe***" and "***heigh***" expose class oppositions (low versus high) but also oppositions of monetary value and inner worth, emphasized through the onomatopoeic associations of "***der***-ry" with the lowly "dairy" of country life and also with "merry," or happiness, not sadness ("With *merry* Lads to make the Hay," exults the lass, we recall; st. 8, my emphasis). So too even "***heigh***" evokes many thoughts and feelings of the socially high up but also the happily high—as in "heigh ho!"—and the highness of satisfying values, which can be (best?) exhibited in those socially "***downe***." Nonsense has become meaning-filled play. It's as if we're on a whirligig ride or skipping around and occasionally falling down in fun, while dancing around a maypole—recall the country lass also affirming, "My worke doth seeme to me but play, / when with young men I tumble" (st. 8). All the downs and derrys and contortions throughout to get text to match the tune—let's just throw in an "a" here to make the meter work!—might feel a bit freewheeling. But this carefree up-and-down ride also suits the subject of rustic country life. Understood as meaningful play within the larger context and multimedia of the ballad, as well as at play with potential consumers of the ballad, such appropriateness of the nonsense refrain to the rustic could still potentially, though with much destabilization of positioning, have offered up alternative assemblages of publics.

Many a lowly and middling consumer would have likely collectively read or heard the ballad's oversimplified language, which careens into nonsense, as conveying precisely that the fun-loving country lass, along with her fellow country folk, rejects highfalutin language. That is, her speech imitates the delight in the homely and plain that rejects all things citified and "cultured." Understood in this light, any apparently conflicted aspiration by the maid to "high" dress, as seen in the first woodcut, or to a "lofty" mind, as heard in her expression, "a lofty mind I bear a"—which undercuts its very claim to high thinking in her unlofty-like grabbing for an extra "a" to make metrical sense of her song—is *deliberately* ironic. In undercutting her words, the country lass proves her point; she invokes to reject elitism. Identifying with such simple poetic and musical tactics, which naturally lead into what could now be understood as a deliberately nonsensical refrain, would have bolstered the interpretation that the first image of the lass in refined clothing reflects her inner high worth, not her desire to dress—any more than to speak—in lofty fashion. Anyone delighting in singing along to her nonsensical refrain—and who could not but enjoy singing such tongue-twisting and carefree wordplay?—would consciously or not be drawn into her consumer assemblage. Such a gathering would have recognized the fashionable dress in the woodcut illustrations (even when revealed in disguise) as decorative, certainly, like the stylish dress appearing on so many broadside ballads, but in "The Country Lass," to those drawn into the fun-loving tactics of simplicity, they also would have served as proof positive that the plain country life is better—so much so that the wealthy urban elite rush in to occupy it, like our urbane shepherd in the second woodcut illustration. From the lowly perspective, the wealthy elite are in fact overpopulating their countryside even though—looking forward or back especially from the first "Mock-Beggar Hall" ballad—the landed wealthy can't seem to manage to occupy their own country estates to extend hospitality to the poor. Indeed, if an early modern were to have made a "hit" from a fragment of the first "Mock-Beggar Hall" ballad to "The Country Lass," the most obvious tactical assemblage would seem to be around a mockery of the fantasies of the well-to-do, not of the low. The high and wealthy, the text and illustrations and tune of "The Country Lass" expose, could never be fully at home in the country—not necessarily in a scathing but in a playfully biting way—balanced by the true play of singing the silly (as in innocent) lass's nonsense refrain going up and down, with an almost unfocused emphasis on "*mock*."

The wit of the low could be turned against them, of course. The ballad also offered assembled consumers the opportunity to embrace, or at least aspire to, the "lofty" thinking of upper sorts, from whose position the nonsense refrain, while certainly fun to sing, would have been considered just that: unrefined nonsense. Despite the country lass's declared superiority, she would have been perceived by such an assemblage of consumers as an ignorant "silly" maid who is in effect the creation, toy, and mockery of the urbane poet and very courtly and city sorts she critiques. If the first image suggests, in their minds, that she secretly aspires to their status, her inadequate language, which keeps falling "***Downe/downe***" into the inarticulate, betrays her (adding a sharp edge to the fun of imitation in singing along with her). Rather than desiring to live in the lass's imagined simple world, such consumers could well have seen the country life simply as the playground of the very courtly and city folks the lass criticizes, as the illustrations, they might well have thought, testify. In this spirit, the aspiring middling and upper sorts that occupied the court and city would have delighted in viewing, reading, hearing, and singing the ballad (as much as would, for the entirely different reasons cited above, the simple country sorts themselves). This second tactical assemblage around the ballad's interrelated multimedia would explain why "The Country Lass" birthed an outright parody of rural commoners in 1727:[22] a mocking of country folk—wherein the lass's contradictory statement, "a lofty mind I beare a," would have been understood to be the ironic humor of the producers shaping her voice—has been tactically made available lurking in this ballad all along, for those who chose to seize it. As far as the well-to-do and their co-aspirants are concerned, "The Country Lass" could have further confirmed their confidence that all geographic spaces, both urban and country, are theirs to be occupied at will to satisfy their pleasures and fantasies. What a welcome relief, they might well have sighed, in making an associative hit to this ballad from the critiques of the "Mock-Beggar Hall" ballads—especially that very annoying first one, which more uncomfortably strikes home.

Any leaning to an assemblage adopted by consumers of this ballad, however, would have been constantly questioned and destabilized in the lived experience of its multiple and multiply moving media. Martin Parker and his printer and publisher were most canny in producing "The Country Lass." They have allowed the ballad's illustrations, text, and tune to work together to tactically turn the tables of mockery around and around, and in the process, have covered all their social bases. A single hit from the first "Mock-Beggar Hall" ballad's woodcut of aggressive manly women dressed in the strange fashion of urban upper sorts might well have provoked a mental association to "The Country Lass," which could have further sparked a fireworks of possible, if always moving, meaning-making interrelations of component fragments across ballads, any of which might have been momentarily accepted, dismissed, or mentally remade to suit the pleasures and fantasies of more than one public.

Hitting the Mock-Motherlode: *Holland's Leaguer*

Up to now we have seen that when a ballad, or one of its component parts, triggers an associative hit to another ballad or ballads, or to one or more of its or their component parts, many relational meaning-making fragments are set in motion. Typically, by virtue of the huge number of moving bits and pieces, any one ballad, especially when situated relationally with others, will offer multifarious possible viewings, readings, or singings that will potentially draw together different, even sometimes opposing, publics. The printers and publishers, occasionally in cahoots with an author, tactically assembled ballad fragments with preconceived intents for meaning-making that would attract the largest number of consumers and, in that spirit, recognized, even encouraged, their consumers to themselves tactically reassemble in their minds and at their will ballad hits. Ballads are, after all, bottom-line, mass-marketed goods. That said, there are times when only one response renders itself available or at least dominates, due to a powerful position a single ballad will take, with all (or at least most) of its component parts aligning in kind, or due to an especially strong associational hit it might make with potential consuming publics.

Such is the case of our final example. I here offer you what would have been the supreme tactical hit that might have been scored by Harper's first "Mock-Beggar Hall" ballad, which would undoubtedly have provoked hilarious mockery not only of "gentlemen" but of the court and even higher-up aristocrats. The trigger is the first impression so prominently displayed just below the title of the ballad and its offered tunes. This same illustration had recently made an appearance as the frontispiece to a pamphlet titled *Hollands Leaguer* (hereafter cited as *Holland's Leaguer*), printed by A[ugustine] M[athewes] for Richard Barnes in 1632 (Figure 15). The two impressions appear to have come from the same woodcut, suggesting that Mathewes printed *Holland's Leaguer* as well the first "Mock-Beggar Hall" ballad, though ballad woodcuts were shared and also sold between printers (as well as inherited when a printing operation was handed down within a family).[23]

HOLLANDS
LEAGVER:
OR,
AN HISTORICAL
DISCOVRSE OF THE
Life and Actions of Dona Britanica Hollandia the Arch-Mistris of the wicked women of EVTOPIA.
Wherein is detected the notorious Sinne of Panderisme, and the Execrable Life of the luxurious Impudent.

LONDON,
Printed by A.M. for Richard Barnes.
1632.

Figure 15. Frontispiece to *Hollands Leagver: Or, An Historical Discovrse of the Life and Actions of Dona Britanica Hollandia the Arch-Mistris of the wicked women of Evtopia*. . . . London, Printed by A.M. [Augustine Mathewes] for Richard Barnes. 1632. Courtesy of Wikimedia Commons. https://commons.wikimedia.org. Public domain.

With this association in mind, any imagined covert mockery of the landed wealthy in our first ballad intensifies into hilarity or even scathing bite because Holland's Leaguer was a famous London whorehouse, located in the south bankside liberty of Paris Garden. It is clearly evident on Aldwell's survey of Paris Garden in 1627, shown as situated close to the Swan theater, and, in more detail, on the Agas map of 1561, digitized and enhanced by the online Map of Early Modern London, or MoEML (Figure 16).[24] To add to the merriment of the first "Mock-Beggar Hall" ballad, the brothel originated as an aristocratic manor house owned by Queen Elizabeth's own cousin, Henry Carey, 1st Baron Hunsdon (1526–96). Passed from Hunsdon through several hands, by the 1630s the manor house had become infamous as the whorehouse leased and managed by Elizabeth Holland. It was all the news between January and May of 1632, during which time, fortified on one side by the Thames and on the other sides by water- and sewage-filled ditches (evident most clearly in the MoEML Agas map close-up), the manor was under siege by the authorities

Figure 16. Brothel of Holland's Leaguer, identified as the Paris Garden Manor House on the Agas map. Close-up of Agas map from The Map of Early Modern London (MoMEL), https://mapoflondon.uvic.ca/agas.htm. Reproduced with permission of the London Metropolitan Archives, City of London (COLLAGE: the London Picture Archive, ref 34373).

and tenaciously defended by its mostly female inhabitants, who refused eviction. The belligerent prostitutes could have been imagined by those making the connection to Holland's Leaguer as like to the aggressive mannish women in the facing woodcut illustration to the first "Mock-Beggar Hall" ballad.

Feeding demand for accounts of the onslaught by the authorities, no less than three texts—all titled "Holland's Leaguer"—were entered into the Stationers' Register in 1632: a play by Shakerley Marmion, another ballad by Lawrence Price, and the pamphlet by Nicholas Goodman, for which the hall pictured in our first "Mock-Beggar Hall" ballad serves as frontispiece. "Each of these texts," Natasha Korda notes, "is structured by a narrative of penetration that describes, with sexualized urgency, the storming of Holland's fortress-like brothel." It is precisely such urgency that leads me to believe that Harper published his first "Mock-Beggar Hall" ballad on the early side of the dates conjectured by modern scholars (the British Book Trade Index, BBTI, gives a possible range of 1634–37; ESTC estimates 1635). Or, as the evidence of the Holland controversy suggests, it might have been published even earlier, closer to 1633. Harper had completed his apprenticeship on May 6, 1633, when the battle over Elizabeth Holland's brothel would still be a very fresh memory for many, given how much notoriety it received just a year earlier. Thus, the woodcut used for the frontispiece to *Holland's Leaguer* would be especially eye-catching and marketable around this time. Lawrence Price, another well-known ballad writer unusual for identifying himself on his ballads (typically, as with Martin Parker, through his initials—"L.P."), got a piece of the demand for news about the brothel. His broadside ballad "Newes from *Hollands* Leager: / Or, / *Hollands* Leager is lately up broken, / This for certaine is spoken" (Pepys Ballads, 1.98–99, EBBA 20283), rightly dated by the ESTC as c. 1632, after the battle for the manor was resolved, is written to the telling tune title, "*Cannons are roaring*." The ballad is illustrated with two images, both figuring forth the main thrust of the tune's title. The first impression is of a large cannon being fired at a city that foregrounds what looks more like an estate; the second impression is of a city shown moated and walled all round and, encircling those barriers, a multitude of canons firing away . The mockery here lies in the overkill of weaponry used to seize what was just a brothel.

Recognition of the illustration of Holland's Leaguer on the first "Mock-Beggar Hall" ballad would likely have provoked a different kind of hilarity than the playful mockery potentially pointing at the fantasies and limitations of both country and city in "The Country Lass." To those in the know, what might have seemed a perplexing habitation of the illustrated country estate or hall in the first "Mock-Beggar Hall" ballad—a hall which the refrain of the ballad tells us over and over again is "empty"—suddenly becomes clear. Situated within the visually occupied hall, certainly recognized by consumers at the time to reside in the outlying suburbs of Paris Garden, not way out in the countryside, the authoritative-looking woman gazing out from the window in the foreground, as if defiantly staring us down and along with her mirroring guard defending her entrance, is now identifiable as Elizabeth Holland. Meanwhile, business goes on as usual in the background—the well-to-do indulging in spending their gilt in the city, or, actually, in the city's sleazy suburbs. The "lady" wooed in the background is now recognized as no lady but a prostitute. Even when occupying supposed "country" estates, the image says, gentlemen—or those who aspire to be such—are only interested in feeding their selfish desires, to the extent of sneaking through a back entrance of a whorehouse hall. Nor would participation in such solicitation be such a surprise, given that the landed wealthy in the ballad are emphatically described as selling off their properties, as in a kind of prostitution of self, to flaunt themselves on the streets of London, like our two "monstrous" mannish gentlewomen, fighting for gold, silver, and glamour.

For those aware of the location of the whorehouse of Holland's leaguer—not only south of the Thames but also close to the Swan theater—another reference in the first "Mock-Beggar Hall" ballad becomes revelatory and comic: that the landed wealthy are selling off their lands to acquire not only "monstrous" city fashions but also such uppity city goods as a coach and a driver, who "at playhouse doors in his box lies asleep" (in the second ballad, without the Holland's Leaguer woodcut, the coachman lies asleep at "Goldsmiths hall door," st. 11). Were the male members of the landed wealthy, who are now themselves "beggarly," slipping out of shows at the Swan playhouse to attend, instead, the sexual shows offered by Elizabeth Holland, where they could have played at wooing a lady? The upbeat tune of "Northern Nancy" allows the passerby or consumer to vocalize hearty recognition of the ridiculousness of it all, not only with its swinging rhythm but also its emphasis on "*beg*" in "*beg*-ger-ly" (st. 7, 1st "Mock-Beggar Hall) and its "Mixolydian" edge. "Damask Rose" could have been adopted vocally to express the same high humor through its skipping and leaping around, but given its minor mode, likely more bitingly, as sung by Bell on **Track 13**, conveying justifiable indignation and anger at the shame of it all, which the lowly poor of the city, including actual beggars, might well have felt. Of course, the possibility remains that, in the face of such unrightable and blatant injustice, the singer of "Damask Rose" might have turned its ups-and-down into something like the breathing in and sighing of grief, conveying a darker mood of helpless distress, as when sung by Bautista on **Track 12**. But even the poor could well have given over to expressing delight in the prominent display of a noble-estate-turned-notorious-whorehouse as representative of the kind of so-called eminent property sold off by the wealthy to indulge their lust for the fashionable delights of the city. Our first "Mock-Beggar Hall" ballad (and, by association, its second edition) thereby becomes a hall of mockery *by*, not *of*, beggars. None of the landed wealthy could escape tactical derision in this connection, not even the "noble" sorts otherwise seemingly escaping scot free.

In the later version of the two "Mock-Beggar Hall" ballads (published c. 1639–40), Harper and his new printer, perhaps with the help of an author, tried to make their assemblage of the first ballad look new, as we have seen, by changing the phrasing and fonts of the title, rearranging the stanzas and even words in lines, and taking out and adding new stanzas, at the beginning and toward the end of the ballad. They also switched out the first ballad's illustrations, dropping the pointedly mocking image of Holland's Leaguer, likely because it had by now lost its immediate recognizability as the aristocratic manor-turned-brothel-hall that had been all the news back in 1632. But, as if in recollection of the first ballad's then-newsworthy illustration, the producers added two references in the second and third stanzas to prostitutes which weren't in the first "Mock-Beggar Hall" ballad. Why must whores be textually represented in that first ballad, after all, when the image of Holland's Leaguer visually said it all? Apparently, they didn't. But they did in the second ballad, now without the image of the infamous hall. In the second stanza of the reassembled second edition of the ballad, the relator laments "To see them [gallants] waste their Talents; / Spend all their store upon a whore" (st. 2)—with a pun on talents as skills and money. In the third stanza, he not only calls up whores again but also depicts them as quarrelsome women, fighting for fashion: "Joan Du[s]t hath bought a smock of Lawn, / And now begins to quarrell, / She thinks her self poor silly elfe, / To be the best of twenty, / And yet the whore is wondrous poor" (st. 3). So, although the pictures of the brothel "hall" (occupied, itself, by monstrously aggressive women) and of the aggressive, manly women of newfangled fashion no longer appear in the illustrations on this second ballad sheet, they have been reincarnated in the ballad's text.

Thinking back to "The Country Lass," should a contemporary have made such a hit to that ballad, it's telling that not only the rich but also the poor—persons of "questionable character" with names like "Joan Du[s]t"—in this second printing are now getting into the act of buying into city fashions, which is slyly equated with prostituting oneself. One might also be reminded of the reverse phenomenon in the woodcut impressions of "The Country Lass"—or at least one interpretation of them—where the country folk seem dressed up like city folk, and vice versa, as if both were vying for the same space of privilege or recognition across city- and country-scapes. If the well-to-do similarly get to join in the fun of the second "Mock-Beggar Hall" ballad because it disperses its attack across the entire class spectrum of London, however, they could nevertheless not have escaped being tactically targeted in the first ballad's newsworthy illustration of a brothel as country estate.

Yet one more tactic is worth mentioning, though it looks forward to our next chapter about collectors. Intriguingly, Leba M. Goldstein (who made a handwritten catalog of the Pepys ballads at Magdalene College, Cambridge) argues that, in organizing the first volume of his five-volume ballad collection—including his oldest ballads, mostly acquired by an earlier collector,

John Selden—Pepys made his own "bitter joke" in ordering the ballads under his category of "History." He placed at the beginning of the "History" section, Goldstein points out, ballads on the Nine Worthies and other heroes from romances and English history and, at the conclusion of the series, Lawrence Price's "Newes from Hollands Leager." She posits that since Pepys was rearranging his collection as late as the 1690s, he took the opportunity here to make a covert jab at William of Orange, whose ascendancy to the throne as William III cost Pepys his job as Secretary of the Navy. In placing "Newes from Hollands Leager" last in the "History" series, she argues, Pepys was attacking the decline in history—everything, including himself, going "***downe***"—by the "***heigh***" ascent of William. The attack takes the form of an assault on William's nation of origin, Holland. One might add to Goldstein's argument a further hit that a later viewer of the volume might see: mockery made of William's perceived deficient masculinity (commonly believed by his opponents in England at the time of his ascendancy), visually represented by the overcompensation, or super-abundance, of cannons firing at a mere brothel. The potential for tactical mockery of the kind especially in the first "Mock-Beggar Hall" ballad has a long life, extending even to scholars of today. With that in mind, we might conclude our discussion of the random hits both "Mock-Beggar Hall" ballads might have made for an early modern contemporary with a final turn to their tunes, and especially think about their afterlife, where—in tribute to the ballads' popularity—we encounter a popular later ballad "To the Tune of, Mock-Beggers Hall stands empty."

The Forward Hits of "Mock-Beggar Hall" Tune(s)

Of course, the texts, illustrations, *and* tunes of the "Mock-Beggar Hall" ballads had not only a "during" but a "pre-" and—of particular interest for this section—an "afterlife," well beyond the publication of our two ballads, in the continual reassemblages of their Lego-block bits and pieces. Of special note is the afterlife of the tunes, which reflect back on the influence of all aspects of the ballads, since other ballads get named after a ballad's tune when the ballad as a whole or a striking relational part of that whole, not just its tune, had an impact.

The "Mock-Beggar Hall" ballads became popular enough that five later ballads in the EBBA archive are specifically named on their sheets to be sung "To the Tune of, Mock-Beggers Hall stands empty." Of course, the reference, as is common in renaming tunes, is to the earlier ballads' shared refrain. But to which of the two tunes offered by the "Mock-Beggar" ballads is this singularly titled tune alluding? All five ballads to which it is to be sung are named "The Ruined Lovers" (there's a sixth by that title as well but with no tune title printed on the sheet). They are printed between 1663 and 1692. The plot of this seemingly popular ballad is very conventional: a maid scorns a lover, who dies of grief, and then she, in repentance, dies as well. Which tune? Given what we know of the two listed tunes on the "Mock-Beggar Hall" ballads, as we have so far discussed them, it might seem that, if the singer had the vocal range and agility, she or he would just have to go with "Damask Rose," given its greater ability, being in the Dorian or minor mode, to convey doleful lament than "Northern Nancy" in the major mode. But there is one more option. In the seventh printing of *The Dancing Master* (1686), approximately two years after John Playford's son, Henry, had taken over the business with Robert Carr, "Northern Nancy" is printed in the minor, not the major:

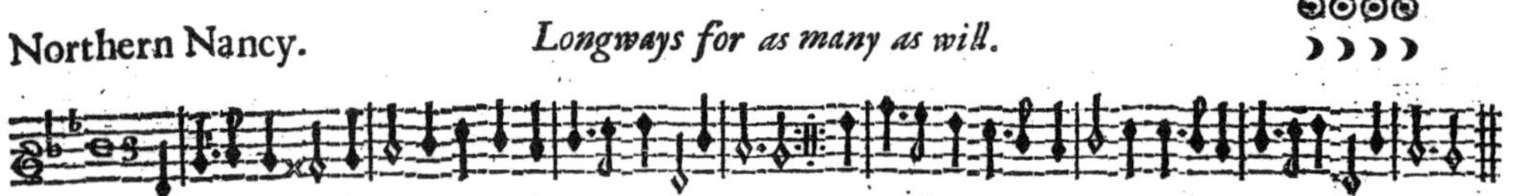

The changes made to "Northern Nancy" in the major, in order to turn it into the minor, involve repeated notational declensions: lowering every B to B-flat (B♭), every E to E♭, and some F-sharps (F♯) to F. The decline to B♭ imparts to "Northern Nancy" in G minor most of its sad or negative affect to our modern ears. But how was such a falling minor air heard by early moderns? There might well have been a degree of "like" or continuity with us moderns in their auditory and affective reception. As Bartel notes, we know some music theorists as early as the late sixteenth century interpreted the minor tune's notational descents as communicative of loss or sorrow. Since theory typically followed practice, the man or woman singing by ear on the streets might well have experienced the same affect, even if that person couldn't put his or her feelings into notated words.

To capture the full effect of altering major to minor, I invite you to compare the upbeat singing of our first "Mock-Beggar Hall" ballad to "Northern Nancy" major with its being sung to the same tune turned minor (see **Track 6** and **Track 18**, respectively, in the Audio Companion). For further ease of comparison, we might just focus, as we did in Chapter 2, on stanza 2, lines 5–8, of the same ballad and tune, first in major and then in minor (see **Track**

7 and **Track 19**, respectively). A transcription of the latter recording in minor can be seen below (again, you can follow the notation aurally to a slowed-down fiddle audio of this transcription on **Track 20)**:

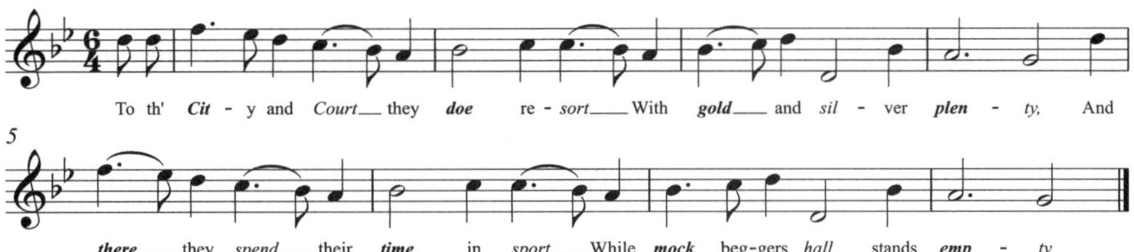

We might pause for a moment to discuss the first half of the ballad's stanzas as sung in minor. Following the music notation in Playford (see Music Notation p. 132), we notice that the second note sung in the first and third lines differs in minor from that in major (see p. 86). When notated and sung in minor, rather than being directly repeated, the first note is momentarily left and returned to via an upper neighboring note. This intervening higher note lessens the "bounce" that the direct repetition of notes gives to the major version. The effect in the minor is far smoother but also, as a consequence, far flatter or sadder than either "Northern Nancy" in the major or "Damask Rose" in Dorian. If we now focus on the second half of the stanza (again, of stanza 2, notated above), we hear and see that it actually starts out much the same way in the minor as it does in its major counterpart: with an upward motion from D to F. However, there is no "off" note in the minor—the F-natural (F♮) note experienced in the major mode. Furthermore, the F is left by a downward stepwise motion, making for an all-around smoother, but also, one might say, more depressed feel to the tune. There is another significant difference from the more upbeat major version of "Northern Nancy." As most easily seen in their respective transcriptions (on pp. 89 and above), the major variant ascends by steps to a D in the text, "they ***doe*** re-*sort*" (line 5) and "their ***time*** in *sport*" (line 7), adding both a high-note and long-note emphasis to the strong syllables at the ends of those two lines, "sort" and "sport." But the minor variant is denied an arrival upon D; instead, we are given a somewhat anticlimactic repetition of a C, and the beginning of a plodding downward motion. It's downright depressing.

Why did Henry Playford—at least it appears it was Henry's decision—change "Northern Nancy" from the major mode, which is how the tune had been printed in the first six editions of *The Dancing Master*, to the minor mode in subsequent editions, and why so long after our "Mock-Beggar Hall" ballads were published? The modern editor, Jeremy Barlow, who has collated Playford's many editions, suggests, rather vaguely, that the reason for such later changes lay in editorial taste or possibly the correction of perceived mistakes. But there are many other possible reasons for converting major to minor in the case of the tune of the "Mock-Beggar Hall" ballads, including the following: (1) "Northern Nancy" in the minor allowed the singer an easier way of expressing lament and depression over the inhospitable times than did "Damask Rose." That is, the singer could convey such affect without having to navigate the many difficult-to-sing skips and leaps of "Damask Rose," through which Bautista so beautifully expressed the sense of bereavement, on **Track 12**, and without alternatively resorting to biting mockery, to which Bell turned the tune, on **Track 13**—as if the singer's focus truly was now on the neglected destitute "beggers" of the ballads' refrain (certainly by the time of the earliest minor version of the ballad in 1686, the woodcut connection of the first ballad's "hall" to the brothel Holland's Leaguer, which might have previously sparked satire, or even simply hilarity, would have been long forgotten). (2) The more lamentable version of "Mock-Beggar Hall" had caught on, and resorting to an easier version of the offered tunes, singers had on their own initiative been rendering "Northern Nancy" major in a more minor mode (by this logic, Henry Playford was responding to consumer, rather than to editorial, taste). (3) The sorrowful "Ruined Lovers" ballad was becoming all the rage, so Henry changed the mode of "Northern Nancy" to make it better fit with the doleful theme of that ballad, again, without resorting to the more difficult-to-sing "Damask Rose." (4) "The Ruined Lovers" was actually often sung in the Dorian mode, akin to minor, of "Damask Rose," despite the tune's challenges, and, furthermore, often rendered dolefully, despite the tune's ability to convey a range of affect (as in Bautista's mournful rendering of the tune on **Track 12**); thus Henry's changing of "Northern Nancy" from the major to the minor mode simply allowed that melody, if chosen, to be sung more in line with the often-taken lamenting path of "Damask Rose." Any of these reasons, or a combination of them, could explain Henry Playford's rationale for altering "Northern Nancy" from the major to the minor. The possibilities that point to a closing of the gap between the two tunes offered by the "Mock-Beggar Hall" ballads, so that they converge in a minor affect (still potentially expressive of a range of emotions, including sorrow, anger, and bitterness), best explain why the tune title to "The Ruined Lovers"—"Mock-Beggers Hall stands empty"—is singular, not one of alternative tunes to which the ballad could be sung.

"Damask Rose" has a pre-life or simultaneous life to the "Mock-Beggar Hall" ballads that further could have influenced a contemporary's choice of tune and made possible a more complicated interpretative hit from the "Mock-Beggar Hall" ballads to "The Ruined Lovers." The original for the tune derived from a ballad authored by Martin Parker and licensed in 1632, titled "Loves Solace," in Roxburghe 1.202–203, EBBA 30139 (Simpson, 153), hereafter cited as "Love's Solace." The licensing date for "Love's Solace," if the ballad was in fact published around this time, places it squarely in the middle of the Holland's Leaguer controversy. But Parker's "Love's Solace" is the most extraordinarily idealistic dialogue between a lover and his love that one could imagine. You can hear the ballad sung by Erik Bell and Helena Harlow on **Track 21** of the Audio Companion. This ballad is everything the other conflicted media hits we have made from the "Mock-Beggar Hall" ballads are not. The illustrations and text to its Dorian tune are wholeheartedly united in a perfect vision of love (barring, perhaps, the now equivocal presence of our lady-with-fan as one of the ballad's illustrations, since she appeared on an anti-feminist debate tract; but her woodcut was *so* popular in the period that it was turned to multitudinous ends, which boggle any definitive lines of influence). More notable in "Love's Solace" than the familiar lady-with-fan is the unified woodcut visions of idealized aristocratic pairs of male and female, on one side of the ballad, and then, in balanced reflection, female and male figures, on the other. The dialogue in the text, split equally between its two parts, is also idealized in balancing the male and female expressions of love. First the man and then the woman sings extreme praise of, and pledges complete subservience to, the other. Each goes so far as to echo the other in echoing him- or herself. Both repeat their own phrasings—he restates "so chast" and "rare" (sts. 6, 7) in describing her; she repeats, "I will not change like to the wind" in answering him (sts. 8, 14). They even rephrase each other's words. He says he must leave her for a time "for so it doth behove me" (st. 8); she responds that though she has been wooed by many she will remain kind to him "as it doth best behove me" (st. 11), and later, more exactly mimics his wording, "for so it doth behove me" (sts. 14, 16). In fact, their relationship is such an interchange and intermixing of souls/pledges/minds/selves that personal pronouns also intertwine and reflect back on each other within the song. She affirms, for example, "And I my selfe still will be she / that shall with joyes unite thee" (st. 12), and again, concluding the penultimate stanza (st. 15)—which you may listen to specifically on **Track 22**, slowed down on the audio fiddle version on **Track 23**, and see transcribed below—she begins, "Although we part I leave my heart, / with him that dearely loves me" (st. 15), when, paradoxically, *he's* departing, not she.

In poetic line 6, as voiced above by the woman, she gives strong musical metrical stress to "***him***" and a weaker stress to the concluding self-referencing word of the line, "*me*"; mirroring that manner of emphasis, in poetic line 8, she devotes a strong musical metrical stress to "***I***" and a lesser stress to the concluding word referencing her lover, "*thee.*" The two lovers are is if interchangeable, poetically, musically, and, not to be forgotten, visually.

If listeners to either of the "Mock-Beggar Hall" ballads made a hit to "Love's Solace" through hearing them sung to "Damask Rose," such an association could well have provoked even more lament or bitterness at the impossibility of such perfect complementarity, whether in selves, gender, or class in the "Mock-Beggar Hall" ballads. But because the vision of love in "Love's Solace" is *so* perfect, even in the face of a lamentable parting, the ballad might also have suffered some backlash from the "Mock-Beggar Hall" ballads in the same way that the idealized illustrations of the second "Mock-Beggar Hall" ballad are undercut by the text of its song. Indeed, within some thirty years, such a perfectly depicted love-in-parting, as sung through "Damask Rose" (and as viewed or read), becomes the subject of back-and-forth parody, even satire, between the genders. These later ballads, also sung to "Damask Rose," make a mockery of ideal love as expressed through mirroring unity. They mock first one and then the other gender's trustworthiness in love, as if answering not so much themselves as Parker's "Love's Solace." Such later parodies well demonstrate how "Damask Rose" in the Dorian mode could, indeed, be turned to diverse affect, even so far as to express hearty and satirical laughter (a possibility now seen as more viable for an early modern adopting this tune to sing our "Mock-Beggar Hall" ballads).

Taken together, my analyses up to this point may, perhaps frustratingly for some readers, open up more questions than answers. We have only partially experienced the many possible meaning-making associations that could have been triggered in early modern England by the autonomous but potentially relational fragments of illustrations, texts, and tunes on and between ballad sheets and, for that matter, on and between other street ephemera. I have pursued just a few of the possible assemblages a contemporary might have made in the course of her or his daily on-the-fly and unpredictable encounters with the potentially infinitely moving media of broadside ballads, beginning with just two editions of the "same" ballad, and then focusing on the first to explore how associational hits might have been generated. In the process, I have also attempted to convey something of the thickness, or what Clifford Geertz would call the "deep play" (in his now famous article by that name), of possible interactions between component ballad parts, which participated in ever-expanding intermedial assemblages in the minds of audiences and consumers. Such organically growing, and thus also dying off (or forgotten) accumulations of associational meaning making—cognitively, affectively, and socially—strongly resists, even as it encourages, oppositional binaries. It also denies the possibility of any stable or all-encompassing whole. No contemporary could have possibly achieved a complete mental picture of the near infinitely moving mass-marketed street print that surrounded them.

In conclusion to this chapter, and to the first part of this book, we need, with this very point in mind, to return to the problematic that Roger Chartier raised about the role of the Internet in our own meaning making as scholars of early modern broadside ballads.

Digital Archives Revisited: Toward Reexperiencing a Fragmentary Past

Chartier's complaint about the Internet, we recall, is that search tools such as "keyword" or "subject" deliver "the fragment that the reader wishes to find . . . without the identity or coherence of the entire text from which the fragment is extracted necessarily being known." He concludes, "In a certain sense, one might say that in the digital world all textual entities are like databases that offer fragments, the reading of which in no way implies a perception of the work or body of works from which they come." As I hope I have demonstrated, such was as true of the early modern experience as it is of the modern experience. That is, the early modern contemporary encountered, likely on a daily basis, what we might think of as random and fragmentary results, or hits, retrieved from the vast consumer base (a sort of precursor to our computational database) of mass-produced, disseminated, and received moving ballad bits and pieces. Retrieved matches a contemporary might have made and "stored" would have been as random as those we "save" through our own hit-or-miss cyberspace searches. My offerings so far of possible ballad associations—or, to continue the analogy, of possible search results—have been themselves necessarily partial in a similar way, both because of the uneven survival rates of these ephemeral artifacts and because of my own choices about which of the brightest (of many bright) ballad jewels to pluck for our admiration. But my selections are not entirely arbitrary, as I hope the evidence I have offered of possible hits and their meaning-makings has shown. These partial associations offer a glimpse into what we as moderns can never hope to experience fully: the mental world of early modern ballad culture. They also offer a glimpse into what both now and in the past was the never-to-be-experienced entirety of the corpus, or the full vitality, of early modern ballad culture.

We are now well positioned to revisit the first qualification I had made of Chartier's critique that modern databases return only "fragments" of early modern texts in a modern context of the Internet. What we can now more clearly see is that when we encounter a massive database like EEBO, which aspires to collect the entire repository of extant early modern printed materials pre-1701 and, regardless of whether it is intentional, to make them infinitely disassembleable and reassembleable as a corpus, depending on how we define our search for the available data, we are working in something of an early modern mindset, not simply a modern or a postmodern one.

Of course, there is also the potential for a database to offer the fragmentary in a negative sense. Its methodologies for collecting and working with data on the developer-facing side of a project as well as its particular affordances for end users might not have been well thought out. At the same time, however, such practices might seem idiosyncratic or arbitrary until a user has spent time with the supporting documentation about the site's scholarly and technical praxis. Or the archive could simply be misleadingly incomplete. Until recently, for example, an image of only the first "Mock-Beggar Hall" ballad was included in EEBO. Indeed, when EEBO came on the Internet scene in 1998 (five years before EBBA was launched), ballads were hugely underrepresented in its database. That neglect has since been considerably compensated for through the inclusion of a much larger sampling of extant broadside ballads. But the inclusion of pre-1701 printed ballads in England is far from complete (consisting of only roughly 60 percent of extant copies). Furthermore, the methods of inclusion have been so haphazard as often to be downright confusing to users. For example, a search in EEBO under the keyword "Mock-Beggar" produces four apparent results. In actuality, however, only our two extant editions are "returned"; the first edition is simply displayed three times, misleadingly creating the impression that it exists in three copies. This is often the case in EEBO, even if we are most liberal with our definition of edition to include every single sheet that came off the press. More egregious, EEBO often provides only one result for many extant items, or only one facsimile image to represent many results.[25] The solution to this problem is simple, if labor-intensive: mount *all* facsimiles of all extant broadside ballads. Furthermore, make those images not from microfilm but from high-resolution color TIFFS so fine distinctions between versions can be discerned, and catalog not only the entire ballad sheet as an item but also every autonomous part that constitutes it (illustration, text, tune, and their key component features). At EBBA, we take the accessibility to ballad facsimiles even further by offering multiple viewings of each ballad: as an "album facsimile," that is, as manipulated by a collector or collectors (not only in tightly trimming the ballad sheets—nearly universally done by collectors—but also in frequently cutting the ballad sheet into two parts and pasting them on facing album pages or placing one half of the ballad above the other on the same album page (as variously seen in the Pepys, Roxburghe, and Bagford collections) or simply mounting the ballad sheet, usually framed by a hand-drawn black border, on stiff backing paper (typical, for instance, of the Crawford and Euing collections); as a "ballad sheet facsimile," that is, as a restoration of the whole ballad, including putting cut-apart halves back together and adding cutaway surrounding edging, in an approximation of the sheet as it came off the press; as a "facsimile transcription," that is, as a modern rendering of the early modern, often difficult-to-read black-letter typeface into Times New Roman while at the same time preserving all of the sheet's other features, including ornament, illustrations, and formatting, thus providing easy readability for the modern reader as the text would have been for an early modern literate contemporary (the original text, in creating this facsimile viewing, is first double-key transcribed and then Photoshop is used to insert the transcription into a grey-scaled "ballad sheet facsimile"); as TEI-XML encoded "Text Transcription," thus allowing fast downloading and reading of just the transcribed text as well as searchability and access across platforms; and as "Music," that is, as recorded songs (when the tune is extant).

Such a multipronged mode of address, though it is necessarily always "partial" for some records—ballads without illustrations, for example, or without printed tune titles or imprints—allows for a near-countless enormity of fragmentary hits by users. But when, to the best of our ability, we embrace the cyber spirit of such mass propagation and dispersal in our creating a digital archive, we open up the possibility of making a *more* whole (if never singular) vision of the past that actually captures something of the early modern experience of broadside ballads—precisely because such multifarious approaches offer us *multiple* fragmentary access to textual artifacts and, in the case of broadside ballads, to their multimedia, as was regularly encountered in everyday life by the early modern contemporary. Without doubt, the digital archive on which I most rely in this study, EBBA, cannot re-create the early modern phenomenal experience to the full, such as remembering a tune from childhood and all the associations that memory might have evoked for any individual, past or present. Nor can such a multipronged database re-create fully the polydimensional experience of personally encountering a broadside ballad in whole or in part "back then" on the streets of early modern London. But a database like EBBA *can* provide a virtual approximation through high-resolution images retrieved from many viewing points, including the oral and aural, offering something of a prismatic access to ballad texts, illustrations, and songs. We might thus approach something of a "like" experience of reading, seeing, and hearing an early modern broadside ballad in our moment, if not in an irrecoverable provisional "then."

In making such intensely fragmentary and contingent visions available, modern databases such as EBBA, or even the flawed but still immensely important because expansive archives of EEBO, ECCO, and EEBO-TCP, can bring the modern user closer to the full early modern experience in all its multifarious (if only momentarily) integrated and disassembled/reassembled fragmentariness. They can give us the tactics to remember the early modern period as it encountered itself: by and through extemporaneous dismembering.

In Part II, we will focus specifically on early modern ballad collectors who have significantly shaped our reception of broadside ballads (through what they chose to collect and how they collected them). Of most importance are the collectors' goals, strategically and tactically, in collecting these artifacts. The collectors deserve an entire section of this book to themselves because without them very few broadside ballads would have survived into the twenty-first century. Furthermore, collectors do not stand apart from their times: rather, in their own ways, even keeping their individual intentions in mind, they participated in the early modern culture of provisional and fragmentary aesthetics. What especially linked the seventeenth-century collectors of black-letter broadside ballads as a group, we shall see, is not an interest in the ballads' tunes but in their piecemeal visual components, including images and text. Their fascination with the visual is intimately linked to a shared concern for the preservation of black letter as it ties into the history of both calligraphy and print. Toward these larger historical goals, black-letter broadside ballad collectors formed a network, if perhaps not a full-fledged public, as I have defined such in this book. The one exception—as usual—is Samuel Pepys, who not only was a participant in the network of black-letter ballad collecting and its intersection with handwriting and the history of print but also was actively and tactically using broadside ballads on a daily basis to create temporary publics expressive of his personal, social, and sometimes political goals.

Part II ❧

Remembering by Dismembering

Black Letter, Calligraphy, and Print History

CHAPTER 4 ❧

The Network of Black-Letter Broadside Ballad Collectors

In Part I, "Assembling by Disassembling," we tackled the accusation that the Internet delivers texts only fragmentarily so that in accessing a digital archive, typically through the use of keywords, users lose any sense of "the whole": a complete corpus of works or an entire textual artifact. In addressing this perceived vexation, we undertook something of a thought experiment following Bruce Smith's principle of analogy—of "like," not "is"—regarding our ability to connect with the past (*Phenomenal Shakespeare*, 170–71). We sought to inhabit the early modern broadside ballad experience, yes; but we did so in order to approximate that experience in a lively, relatable way, not to nail it down as a coffined Truth. Engaging dynamically with how early modern contemporaries would have encountered, on a daily basis, ballad artifacts and their component multimedia, we found that the ballad "whole" was assembled and reassembled fragmentarily not only by printers in their shops but also by hawkers and consumers on the streets and elsewhere. Such moving media might well have triggered in passersby associational mental hits to other mobile ballad wholes and parts.

I have further posited that early moderns would likely have accepted such experiences as a matter of course: the norm. They might not have consciously pondered the haphazard and piecemeal production and dissemination of the ephemeral ballad media they witnessed on a daily basis. But, as we have seen, hyper-plural media forms, such as heyday broadside ballads, play along a different level of cognitive awareness. They simultaneously suppress and invite recognition of their "artifice"—just as, in the terms of Bolter and Grusin, hypermediacy creates the illusion of immediacy while still revealing the machine behind the wizard's curtain (*Remediation*). On this more playful, abstract level, heyday ballad culture also had a penchant for obliquely pointing out its own economic interests. It enticed consumers to see the marketing of ballad parts as something akin to playing a Lego-block game of diversely fitting those parts together and in such a way that catered consciously to multifarious consumer publics of which each player was a potential constituent. At varying degrees of conscious awareness, the person on the street understood that the partial, provisional production and on-the-fly dissemination of broadside ballad media bits—in which they themselves were a part—allowed them, willy-nilly, to make their own impromptu reassemblages.

In concluding Part I, we revisited digital archives, such as EBBA, to see how they might be constructed precisely to capitalize on Internet fragmentation to approximate something "like" the early modern lived ballad experience. By offering modern-day users a multiplicity of partial readings, viewings, and hearings of any one broadside ballad, such archives enact and make accessible the lively ways ballad media move (follow a tune through its permutations if you wish, or trace the use and reuse of a popular woodcut). We can see for ourselves how hits might be made to other broadside ballads and, in turn, to their Lego-like constituent parts. For these reasons, digital archives could even be said to effect in us an experience of ballads that is *more*, not less, of a felt whole because it is more partially, more dynamically, and more fragmentarily cached.

But our discussion to date has not given one subset of early modern consumers due recognition. In thinking through digitally built links between the "then" and the "now"—including the *now* of original artifacts in libraries or museums and the *now* of their re-presentations through digital facsimiles—we must pay special attention to those early modern contemporaries (and near contemporaries) who, with varying degrees of self-consciousness, acted as virtual emissaries across time and space. It is they who saved the *then* so that we have access to it *now*. Without the collectors who preserved the physical artifacts of broadside ballads, we would only be able to see through a glass darkly into the moving material and popular ballad culture of the past. These indispensable consumers as collectors pose something of a puzzle themselves. What, one wonders, impelled them—often persons of the middling to higher social sorts—to hold onto the ephemera that others were reusing or disposing of by the millions? And in what way(s) did they preserve these objects? The latter question is crucial since the answer casts yet more light on their contemporaries' attitudes to broadside ballads and significantly influences how we today encounter or receive them, whether in a physical site where the originals are held or in cyberspace where facsimiles of them are digitally displayed. Early modern ballad collectors are thus the focus of this chapter and the next, which together make up Part II. Collecting, we must stress, does not necessarily exclude participating in or manipulating public practices. Thus, in Part III, we will turn specifically to the greatest single collector of broadside ballads during their English seventeenth-century heyday—Samuel Pepys—as both collector and tactical consumer. Pepys, as we shall see, delighted in extemporaneously, craftily, and even often subversively manipulating the conventions of the multifaceted broadside ballad artifact to create momentary assemblages of political, social, and even private publics.

In this chapter, to provide some larger context for understanding early modern methods of collecting broadside ballads, we need first a brief overview of collecting practices of ballad artifacts from the sixteenth century to today. Of particular concern, given the focus of this book on the heyday of the seventeenth century—when text, illustration, and tune were most foregrounded on the printed ballad sheet—will be the collectors of black-letter ornamental ballads with printed tune titles. We will focus especially on those accumulators of heyday ballads who were alive when this genre flourished.

We shall see that these particular ballad hunter-gatherers reflected in their collecting practices a liberal awareness that ballads in their own time were constituted of autonomous parts that could be assembled and disassembled. The idea of the ontological "whole" was not preserved by them so much as were the autonomous fragments of the ballads' constituent parts. Moreover, a number of these collectors, or their assistants—it is not always clear whose hands were at work—evinced a sense of themselves as makers akin to producers of provisional ballad wholes, reassembling them at their will, sometimes with impressive re-creative whimsy. They were also acutely aware of themselves as preserving specifically physical, not oral, artifacts. It is as if orality—the ballad as song—existed for them mostly in the surrounding soundscape, which might have a history of its own but did not fall within their preservationist domain. These collectors, furthermore, had a keen sense of the ballad as ephemeral artifact and as caught up in a turbulent process of transition—what I call in the next chapter a "passing present." It is as if they were consciously stepping into the swift-moving river of time to snatch up a cupful or bucketful of history flowing by, to catch at least some small measure of what was only ever partially graspable, something that might otherwise be lost to the sea of time. In that interventionist moment, these collectors were especially attuned to the fleeting ballad artifacts they preserved as compellingly visual: constructed not only of attractive woodcut illustrations (which were temporarily transitioning out of use on ballad sheets at the end of the seventeenth century) but also of eye-catching ornamental black-letter typeface (increasingly and more definitively, by the end of the century, replaced on ballads, especially on political ballads, by the white-letter typeface that is today often called roman). The turn to roman type had already happened in most every other print form by the late sixteenth century. Exceptions include official legal and church documents, proclamations, some romances, and cheap fare. But black letter held on longest in broadside ballads—up to the end of the seventeenth century in England. As we shall see in Chapter 5, the collectors who were especially focused on black-letter ballads were fascinated with the typeface not only because of its visual impact but also because of its relation to the history of calligraphy and print more generally; indeed, these collectors were highly alert to ongoing (and sometimes unsettling) transitions within both manuscript media and print media, as well as to a competition between them. Black letter played a major role in the unfolding of these transitions.

A Short Overview of Broadside Ballad Collecting

To situate more accurately this project, it is important to contextualize black-letter ballad collectors, such as Pepys, within changing generations of collectors as well as alterations in ballad production, which largely influenced what was "out there" to be acquired. Sixteenth-century collectors, such as Captain Cox and William Fitch (the latter of whose collection was subsequently divided into the Huth ballads held at the British Library and the Britwell ballads at the Huntington Library),[1] were necessarily limited in their assemblages to comparatively simple artifacts. The broadside ballads of their time were typically printed on one side of a relatively small folio sheet of paper in black letter (what we know today as "Gothic" or "Old English" type). These sheets sported little, if any, ornamentation, named only occasionally a tune title, and addressed a modest range of topics—favoring religion, elegies/epitaphs, flytings (political-turned-personal debates/attacks), and strange wonders. The generation that lived through, or close to, the seventeenth-century heyday of the broadside ballad (c. 1600–1650; with a revival c. 1670–90) had the opportunity to collect a very different kind of ballad. During this period, the ballad's multidimensional and multimedia potential blossomed, as did its physical size. We find much larger folio sheets across which, in landscape fashion, texts, tune titles, and illustrations were liberally spread. Given their increased size, allowing for enhanced textual and visual media, they were usually divided into two "Parts." Sometimes multiple tune titles were printed on the sheet, as we have seen with the "Mock-Beggar Hall" ballads, offering consumers different options for singing the ballad. But aesthetics ruled. Abundant decorative black-letter text was accompanied typically by four (though sometimes two, and sometimes many more) woodcut impressions. Ornamental dividing lines and borders, as well as elaborate woodcut headers and footers, proliferated. Finally, the ballads offered a dizzying variety of topics—ranging from religion, elegies/epitaphs, and wonders, as they did before, to familiar "historical" stories, such as those of Chevy Chase and Robin Hood, to romantic love or marriage or sex, to murders or other timely news, to alehouse good fellowship, to politics, and so on (see, for example, Figures 2, 6–8, 10, 12, and 14). There was no topic or stance that heyday broadside ballads could not address. Notably, however, ballads of this period no longer included political and religious personal flytings; argumentation tended to embrace broader, more secular topics, such as the question of gender superiority. Ballads issued by the same author or printer/publisher often presented within single artifacts a dialogue debating two sides of an issue; we as often find issued by the same producers an entire ballad that promoted one stance followed swiftly by another ballad that adopted the opposite position (a tactic we have seen practiced by Martin Parker). The idea was to market something for everyone; producers aimed their wares at the widest mass of consumers, especially the large new market base of the middling to low—at least, to those who could afford to pay a penny or halfpenny or perhaps a pint of ale for a ballad, and who could appreciate its catchy tune, alluring illustrations, and decorative typeface (even if they could not always, or fully, have read the printed text).

While most other types of printed literature in England transitioned from black letter to white letter or roman font by the early seventeenth century, as noted above, the broadside ballad held onto its black-letter roots as well as its multimedia up to the end of the seventeenth century, even as the size of the sheets on which they were printed diminished (to more often a half-folio). In what appears a cultural nostalgia, furthermore, the ballad heyday's two-part format, for a time not printed on these smaller sheets, soon made a comeback, as can be seen in many ballad productions of the 1670s–90s. Collectors who lived through or close to the extended ballad heyday of the seventeenth century had the most access to ornamental black-letter ballads. They include John Selden (1584–1654), George Thomason (c. 1602–66), Elias Ashmole (1617–92), Anthony Wood (1632–95), Samuel Pepys (1633–1703), John Bagford (1650–1716), Narcissus Luttrell (1657–1732), and Robert Harley (1661–1724), among others. Though all their collections show some mix of black- and white-letter ballads, one can say generally that among these collectors, those who favored black-letter ornamental ballads were Selden, Wood, Pepys, Bagford, and Harley. That is, heyday ballads constituted the majority of, or at least had a prominent place in, their collections. Thomason, Ashmole, and Luttrell, however, privileged the newly emerging white-letter or roman-type ballad, which came eventually to dominate the late ballad scene.[2] In the seventeenth century, white-letter ballads, like black-letter ballads later in the second half of the period, were usually printed on smaller sheets. But, unlike their black-letter cousins, they featured less ornamentation—sometimes little more than a plain line that divided columns of stanzas or text from title—and, though they could embrace various topics, politics ruled. Political white-letter broadside ballads exploded at especially turbulent times (for example, in the 1640s—though few ballads survive from this tumultuous period—and among extant ballads, especially in the 1660s and 1680s). It is telling that collectors of these ballads often assembled political pamphlets as well.[3] Along with the typographical shift to white letter and its accompanying aesthetic and topical changes, furthermore, we find fewer and fewer tune titles printed on ballad sheets of the late seventeenth century and into the early eighteenth century. Fascinatingly, though, we also see some later ballads of the seventeenth century printed with musical notation on the sheet, even if the music is often declared by musicologists to be, in Simpson's word, "meaningless" (xii). This can be attributed to the popularization of songbooks around this time as well as to the rise of Restoration musical theater.

By the eighteenth century, ballads were most commonly distributed on mere slips of paper (with little, if any, ornamentation and usually no tune title) called, appropriately, "slip songs." Notable exceptions, or, more accurately, additions, were productions by the printers/publishers John White of Newcastle (1689–1769) and William and Cluer Dicey (c. 1707–56 and 1714/15–75, respectively), who issued broadside ballads in a range of white-letter ballad formats, often reintroducing woodcut illustrations and even copying earlier woodcuts, though typically updating their figures' fashions. But the slip song ruled—with as many as eight printed on a single sheet. Individual songs were cut out by the seller into separate "slips," when selected by a consumer for purchase. The 1754 Dicey catalog provides a good snapshot of the kinds of popular print made available. The catalog entices the potential consumer with a list of "old ballads"; "patters" (short songs); "garlands" (long narrative ballads often divided into not just two but as many as five multiple parts, like acts in a play); and, in a separate section at the end of the catalog, an offering of "near Two Thousand different Sorts of SLIPS, of which the New Sorts coming out almost daily render it impossible to make a Complete Catalogue."[4] Some collectors of a later generation than Pepys still determinedly sought out survivors of the much earlier heyday black-letter ornamental ballad (both in folio format and its half-folio cousin). But white letter, and especially slips, continued to dominate what was being produced by printers and thus what was available for collection, as evidenced in the mammoth assemblage of twenty-four volumes of white-letter ballads compiled by Sir Frederic Madden (1801–73), held at the University of Cambridge Library.

To capture the wide arch of their collecting and production history and so place seventeenth-century black-letter broadside ballad collectors in full perspective, we must further note that among the generations of ballad collectors and producers of the eighteenth into the nineteenth century, there emerged a significant counter-collecting/counter-producing movement. It tellingly appeared on the scene soon after the ballad lost the prominence of its eye-catching ornament, including its swirling, decorative black-letter type and also its named tune titles. Most of these print casualties were just temporary on broadside ballads other than the dominating slip songs, lasting some ten to fifteen years (c. 1690–1705)—only the ornamental black-letter typeface permanently disappeared at the end of the seventeenth century (resurfacing occasionally in the printing of just a single word or phrase in later ballads).[5] Still, as if in response to the notable diminution in the visual media of the printed ballad, many among the new generation of eighteenth-century collectors became intent on redefining the ballad not as occasional print but as "traditional" oral history, and—somewhat ironically, given their rejection of print—they folded together the practices of ballad collecting and publication. Among this new ballad sect was the anonymous but influential author/editor (perhaps Ambrose Philips) of *A Collection of Old Ballads* (3 vols., 1723–25)[6] and his slightly older contemporary, Thomas Percy (1729–1811), author of *Reliques of Ancient English Poetry* (3 vols., 1765). Their most influential generational successor, whom we've previously met, was Francis James Child (1825–96), author and editor of *The English and Scottish Ballads* (8 vols., 1857–59, with two subsequent editions, 1860 and 1866), later reissued and retitled *The English and Scottish Popular Ballads* (5 vols., 1882–98; note the author's addition of "Popular").

Both in alliance with and counter to the broadside ballad's temporary loss of illustration and tune titles, as well as its newly elevated roman typeface—carrying "classical" connotations—these collectors/scholars/editors (culminating with Child) extended their gaze far back in history to find authentication for their theory of the traditional oral ballad in Homer, who was now newly identified as a ballad singer. At the same time, as we have seen, they asserted that oral ballads expressed, before the coming of print, the "true," "pure," and "ancient" history of England—history here being characterized as "popular" in the sense of the "folk."[7] Child, as noted in Chapter 1, referred to the Pepys and Roxburghe collections of mostly black-letter ballads as "on the whole . . . *veritable dung-hills*"; he published instead scholarly editions of ballads that he declared were collected from oral renditions made by uncorrupted—that is, remotely located—country singers, and/or derived from ancient manuscripts (such as the Percy Folio).[8] However, Child's ballad editions were often collations, which he constructed according to his own personal, if never fully spelled-out, rules. With absolute conviction, he offered just 305 "true" ballad survivals. But what about the seventeenth-century collectors of the "veritable dung-hills" of printed broadside ballads, whose efforts contributed significantly to preserving an enormous number of pre-1701 ballads (approximately 12,000, according to EBBA's latest estimate)?

The collectors of mostly black-letter broadside ballads in seventeenth-century England form something of an interconnected network. I use the term "network" with deliberation, drawing, as does Manuel DeLanda, on the idea that "in network theory the emphasis is always on relations of exteriority." DeLanda explains: network theory focuses on "*the pattern of recurring links*, as well as the properties of those links . . . not the attributes of the persons [such as the properties of gender or race] occupying positions in a network" (56). A network can be stronger or weaker depending on the intensity of the connectivity among its indirect links (for example, whether friends of my friends know each other) and on its stability (whether friends of my friends are also friends), which together create a low or high degree of solidarity and thus a weaker or stronger network (56–57). The network of black-letter ballad collectors, as we shall see, reveals a moderate-to-high level of solidarity. It included prominent and recognizable figures, such as Samuel Pepys and Robert Harley, 1st Earl of Oxford, but also more historically unrecognized persons, such as the paleographer Humfrey Wanley (who was appointed Harley's librarian), the eccentric Oxfordian Anthony Wood, and the shoemaker-turned-book-entrepreneur John Bagford. Furthermore, looking closely at any one collector and his assemblages reveals not simply information about that individual but also a maze of connections with other collectors. Our focus in this chapter and the next will be on the largest collector of seventeenth-century black-letter broadside ballads who lived during that century, Pepys, and on those to whom he was linked in his ballad-assembling cause. As we shall see, many of these antiquarians knew each other or were connected through their friends, and they were apparently on good terms. To the extent their network was open to expansion, drawing in strangers, and had a scholarly and social agenda (as we also shall see more fully in the next chapter), it can, in fact, be considered a public. Lesley Cormack's thumbnail definition of publics, in her discussion of the network of chorographers of early modern England, is also a fitting characterization for ballad-collecting networks: "a loose collection of people, not all of whom have personal knowledge of one another, connected by a common interest in a particular subject and with some social or political goal in mind" ("Forms of Nationhood and Forms of Publics," 164).

As with Cormack's chorographers, the black-letter ballad collectors I track in this chapter formed a relatively small network. But, as Cormack also notes, the population of early modern England was itself relatively small (165). Furthermore, I will argue, size is not the most important determining factor here; much more salient is the level of interpersonal engagement between a network's participants in support of their shared subject or "cause," to which we must at all times stay attuned. This chapter will focus specifically on these men's common desire to collect black-letter broadside ballads and on similarities in their practices of assembling them. But in the next chapter, our investigation will take on something of a forensic tone, as we interrogate the evidence we have gathered about the collectors in order to piece together a picture of the larger cultural causes that bound them into a temporary but vibrant public. What we shall discover is that built upon—or, rather, intimately interconnected with—their fascination with the passing present of ornamental black-letter broadside ballads is an avid shared interest in documenting and understanding the role of black letter in the transitional history of calligraphy and its often vexed relationship to print.

But before addressing these larger shared interests, we need to examine more closely the collecting practices of our black-letter broadside ballad *network* within the kind of lived ballad *culture* of production, dissemination, and consumption that we have so far been pursuing. Such investigations are not for the faint of heart. The problem we immediately face is that such an examination opens up another, diachronic network, not simply from publisher to some named collector in the period but often more messily: from publisher to individual collector, perhaps through another consumer(s) or collector(s); to subsequent collectors (perhaps from a later period); and then, eventually, to libraries or museums (of even a later time), which now hold the assembled artifacts. Many historical gaps, rearrangements, and discontinuities in the collecting processes interrupt our tracing of this passage through time, just as they did in the case of the Manchester collection of black-letter ballads (as noted in the Introduction). Admittedly, it is unlikely that we will ever recover all the details about how ballads were gathered at any one time, let alone over large periods of time, and even exactly how many hands played a role (and the decisions behind such roles). Nevertheless, investigation into our black-letter ballad collectors of the seventeenth century strongly suggests that they and their helpmates were very much attuned to their own historical period. We shall also see some continuity between these earlier contemporaries' approaches to the assemblage of black-letter broadside ballads and the practices of successive collectors/owners, as if the later antiquarians were attempting to preserve something of the heyday ballad artifacts' earlier culture, not just their materiality. But, as we shall further see, such apparent continuities in collecting practices also—indeed, necessarily—evince fascinating transmutations reflecting the later collectors' own changing times.

Remembering by Dismembering: Collecting the Physical/Visual Artifact

If we focus on those collectors of roughly the same generation who not only preserved seventeenth-century broadside ballads but privileged black-letter heyday ballads—Wood, Pepys, and Bagford—we find a network of exchange that touches even the next generation, represented by Harley (who spans the seventeenth and eighteenth centuries). I have roughly sketched out this network in Figure 17. The diagram is not meant to be all-inclusive; rather, it is intended to give a working idea of the interconnections of black-letter broadside ballad collecting in seventeenth-century England. Arrows depict the direction of connectivity; solid lines indicate stronger links (passing of actual ballads); dotted lines indicate weaker links (communication about ballads or about a person collecting them); and double solid lines depict the transfer of an entire ballad collection (usually on the death of its owner). What stands out is the centrality of the key players—Pepys, but also, interestingly, Bagford—in black-letter broadside ballad collecting in the period. Their individual connections, furthermore, extend outward to embrace a significant number of parties in an intricate network. If we also examine the various collectors' characteristic assembling strategies after procuring ballads, what becomes evident are forces of fragmentation. Such fragmenting forces can be felt in the (sometimes near-obsessive) assembling and disassembling of collections in their making, both by the original collector and by subsequent owners. One caveat: since these collectors foregrounded ballads as visual artifacts, as we shall further pursue, this chapter and the next follow suit. Musical analysis thus momentarily recedes into the book's background; but it subsequently makes a strong comeback in the spirit of the early modern lived experience of broadside ballads as moving multimedia, including interrelated text, illustration, and song.

Pepys makes it clear on the title page to his collection of ballads (Figure 18), notably handwritten in black letter, that the broadside ballad format of his time was changing visually and that his collection was intended as a personal record of that transition. Under "My Collection of Ballads" and a prominent

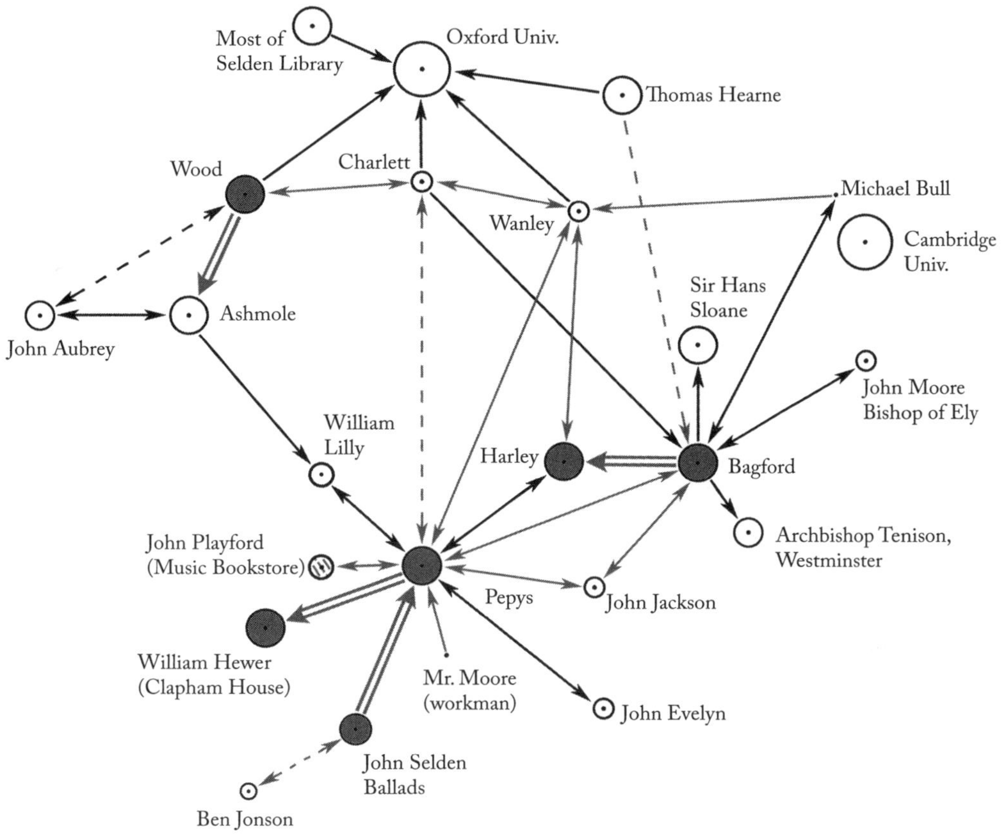

Figure 17. Sketch of the Network of Seventeenth-Century Black-Letter Broadside Ballad Collectors.

picture of himself, Pepys writes: "Begun by Mr. [John] Selden; Improved by the additions of many Pieces elder thereto in Time; and the whole continued to the year 1700. *When the Form, till then peculiar thereto, vizt. of the Black Letter with Picturs seems (for cheapness sake) wholly laid aside, for that of the White Letter without Pictures*" (EBBA 32621; my emphasis). In the handwritten table of contents to his collection (EBBA 31620, Figure 19), Pepys then multiply divides his ballad assemblage as a whole. Running down the left-hand side of the contents page, he partitions the collection into ten topics, or "Heads of Assortment," such as "Devotion and Morality" and "Marriage, Cuckoldry Etc." Along the top, though, Pepys gathers the ballads differently, by volume number and format, according to an unstated rough chronology. Volume 1, "MSS & Long Ballads antient," consists of transcriptions of four sixteenth-century printed ballads (the "MSS"), which were all hand-copied in black-letter script, with the exception of one comprised mostly of musical score.[9]

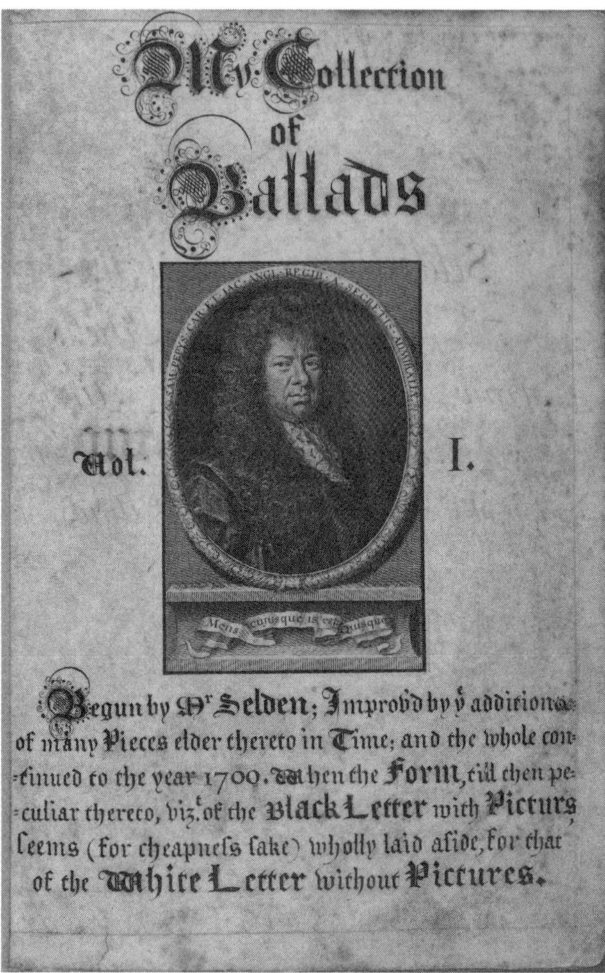

My Collection of Ballads

Vol. I.

Mens cujusque is est quisque

Begun by Mr Selden; Improv'd by y^e addition of many Pieces elder thereto in Time; and the whole con-tinued to the year 1700. When the Form, till then pe-culiar thereto, vizt of the Black Letter with Pictures, seems (for cheapness sake) wholly laid aside, for that of the White Letter without Pictures.

Figure 18. Title Page to Pepys's five-volume ballad collection, "My Collection of Ballads," EBBA 32621. Magdalene College, Cambridge, Pepys Library, Front Matter, Pepys Ballads, 1:{ix}. By permission of the Pepys Library, Magdalene College, Cambridge.

By "Long Ballads antient," which he groups with "MSS," Pepys does not mean simply old narrative stories; as a glance through the section quickly makes clear, he more specifically denotes the heyday ornamental two-part broadside ballads printed on large folio sheets (roughly 290 x 340 mm in size), consisting of black-letter typeface, many illustrations and ornaments, tune titles, and a smorgasbord of topics. Other than the four manuscript transcriptions, these are the earliest datable ballads Pepys owned and were mostly acquired on the auction of Selden's ballad collection. Pepys names his next, largest section "Common Ballads in the Black Letter" (Volumes 2–4); these appeared on the ballad scene c. 1640–50 and remained popular through the century. They resemble the earlier heyday ballad artifacts, except that the sheets are of a smaller, half-folio size (roughly 190 x 296 mm)—hence making less room for texts and eliminating the need for "parts," and, therefore, contrasting with

Contents of ye sever.ll Vol.s under ye following Heads of Assortment; viz.	MSS & Long Ballads antient		Common Ballads in the Black Letter.						Verse-Ballads in ye White Letter.	
	Vol. I.		Vol. II.		Vol. III.		Vol. IV		Vol. V.	
	From	To	From	To	From	To	From	To	From	To
	Pag.	Pag.	Pag.	Pag.	Pag.	Pag.	Pag.	Pag.	Pag.	Pag.
1 Devotion & Morality	27.	62.	1.	95.						
2 History True & Fabulous.	63.	104.	97.	130.						
3 Tragedy—viz. Murd.rs Execut. Judgm. of God	105.	149.	139.	200.					1.	28.
4 State & Times	151.	221.	201.	374.					29.	151.
5 Love—Pleasant.	223.	341.			1.	310.	1.	72.	153.	271.
6 Do Unfortunate	343.	373.			311.	390.	Do	Do	273.	357.
7 Marriage, Cuckoldry &c.	375.	415.					73.	153.		
8 Sea—Love, Gallantry, & Actions	417.	423.					155.	224.	359.	387.
9 Drinking & Good Fellowshipp	425.	447.					225.	375.	389.	436.
10 Humour, Frollicks &c mixt.	449.	467.								

Figure 19. Table of Contents to Pepys's five-volume ballad collection, "Contents of ye sever[a]ll Vol.s under ye following Heads of Assortment," EBBA 31620. Post-photographic processing by EBBA. Magdalene College, Cambridge, Pepys Library, Pepys Ballads 1.1–2. By permission of the Pepys Library, Magdalene College, Cambridge.

those ballads Pepys calls "Long." Later in the century, the "Common" black-letter ballads also typically feature a verse (printed in white letter) between the ballads' titles and their tune titles, which gives the gist of the ballad's theme or plot. Set apart from these is Pepys's last section, Volume 5, "Verse Ballads in the White Letter," which were most frequently found in the latter half of the century, becoming dominant by the century's end. These are also in half-folio size, though usually printed in portrait rather than in landscape format, without tune titles, and with little or no illustration. They covered a wide range of topics but, as noted above, favored politics.[10]

The fact that Pepys grouped together manuscript ballads and long ancient ballads in black letter is telling, and a conjunction we shall explore more fully in the next chapter. For the moment, we will focus on the extent to which he envisioned his collection as capturing a nearly past moment of decorative black-letter broadside ballads, both "Long" and "Common" (Vols. 1–4). In his title page, Pepys speaks as if the typeface and ornamentation were twinned: "Black Letter with Picturs." That is, he recognized that black-letter broadside ballads were intensely visual. The typeface was in this sense a complement to the pictorial; it evidenced, notes Stanley Morison, speaking of printing in general, an "extreme fondness for decoration" (*John Fell*, 109). Even beyond the early modern period, in the nineteenth century, black-letter typeface and ornamentation were seen as twins: take, for example, the Earl of Crawford's explanation of how he ended up amassing his huge collection of black-letter broadside ballads, which expanded to more than 1,500 items. In the preface to his printed catalog of this impressive assemblage, he states that it "has grown from modest size to considerable volume." The reason? "I bought a few at first as typographical curiosities, and to illustrate the woodcut ideas of the times; but I soon desired to acquire more."[11] Note that black-letter typeface, by the nineteenth century, was a "curiosity," but also consider that, in Crawford's ambiguous wording, it can be seen to "illustrate"—rather than to be illustrated by—the woodcuts of the earlier time. Again, black letter and ornamentality are conjoined. And, like a moth to the aesthetic flame, Crawford was increasingly drawn by both visual dimensions of black-letter broadside ballads—typeface and pictures—to expand and yet further expand his collection (and also to repeatedly bind, unbind, and then rebind the ballads as the collection grew—ultimately, keeping them unbound to make easier his addition of more ballads).

Still, as much as collectors of the seventeenth century and later historical periods valued black-letter typography and its accompanying woodcut illustrations on ballad sheets for their combined visual appeal, such aesthetics did not stop them from dismembering the treasured visual artifact. What we see are widespread practices of taking the "whole" object apart: not only tightly trimming ballad sheets by cutting off their margins but also often cutting the sheets in two and then pasting the segmented pieces down on album pages or backing papers according to what might have been a strategy but often appears more like personal fancy. Valuable component parts could also be "unplugged" from the whole (to invoke DeLanda's phrasing), as we shall further observe. Those collectors living in the seventeenth century who, like Pepys, appear to have been acutely aware of the passing present moment of "black letter with picturs" were thus at the same time actively aligned with the general practices of their contemporaries in producing, distributing, and consuming broadside ballads through assemblage, disassemblage, and reassemblage. The palpable difference is that these antiquarian collectors, in remembering through physically conserving ballads, dismembered them by *physically* taking them apart.

They did not—or did not only—do as many of their contemporaries would have done: that is, simply *mentally* and in passing select bits and pieces of the ballads they encountered, accumulating a virtual cache of piecemeal "hits." Rather, they collected caches of material data. Their personal assemblages of "hits" took tangible form as if they were drawn by a mirage-like idea: that, by collecting these artifacts, they had finally found a way to still the constant motion of broadside ballads and their constituent multimedia bits.

Recognition of the dismembering practices of contemporary printing, publishing, and reception of broadside ballads especially puts in context as more "normal" or "representative" some of the apparent oddities practiced by Pepys, our most prominent and avid collector of English seventeenth-century broadside ballads and other popular print. Pepys was without doubt an eccentric man, one who would write in cipher in his diary (although not that indecipherably, when referencing in his broken colloquial French a sexual dalliance), and who was compulsively determined to resist the forces of dispersion and transmutation that characterized the print culture of his age. Indeed, as Pepys witnessed the breakup of his contemporaries' libraries, such as that of Selden, he fought to hold his own library together. This practice of tightly controlled assemblage notably involved an emphasis on the visual look as much as on the integrity of his library. He obsessed that his books be bound alike, with his arms printed on each copy, and even made "lifts" for books, which resembled actual bindings, so that the texts would all look the same height. He also repeatedly cataloged and re-cataloged his collection as he added new items. His will testifies to his strategy to maintain an intact whole: it specifies that his library should be "closed" by his nephew John Jackson (who fittingly rounded it off, in his calculation, to exactly 3,000 volumes), names the exact place where the library should be housed (in its own special room in Magdalene College, Cambridge, or, failing that, in Trinity College), refuses any lending of the books from the library grounds, and limits visitors to no more than ten books at a time.[12] Such determination "to hold it together" won praise from Pepys's friend and fellow collector John Evelyn, who was keenly aware that dismemberment threatened the collector at every turn: "You have declared," he wrote to Pepys, "that you will endeavor to secure what with so much cost and industry you have collected, from the sad dispersions many noble libraries and cabinets have suffered in these late times: one auction, I may call it diminution, of a day or two, having scattered what has been gathering many years."[13]

As in his meticulous cataloging of his books, Pepys's collecting practices thus sought to resist fragmentation—the dreaded fate of being, in Evelyn's words, "scattered"—and strove instead to institute an integrated and enduring whole library. But one cannot escape one's cultural formations, and Pepys's very urge to wholeness itself caused dispersal. Following the drive to collect by uniform size, for instance, Pepys separated out books of like kind, even those of the same genre. He constantly reshuffled his books around in this cause, to the extent that in early arrangements of his library, he divided up his six-volume diary (1660–69), dispersing the separate volumes to four different parts of the library because all but two were different sizes.[14]

With the ballads and prints he collected, Pepys had a determined strategy to bring them into a unified aesthetic vision as well. But once again we discover, in fact, a constant and tactical (rather than merely strategic) process of in-the-moment reshuffling to meet the changing demands of his growing collection and how it should be organized. As he added to his broadside ballad volumes, Pepys repeatedly moved the ballads around—a process called "garbling." The term has a long history. According to the *Oxford English Dictionary* (*OED*), "garbling" means "to select or sort out the best in (any thing or set of things)" (*OED* 2a). Significantly, however, by 1692, "to garble" could also mean "to mutilate" (*OED* 3), and as early as 1661 "garbled" could be confused with "garbage" (*OED* 4). Pepys's garbling of his growing collection of broadside ballads involved mutilating by breaking the bindings apart, re-sorting the ballads within and between volumes, and then rebinding them into new assemblages. He garbled and regarbled many times. His individual ballads and their album pages thus often display many numbers on the sheets. Each number but the last (in red ink, probably made by John Jackson after Pepys's death) indicates a different position the ballad had at one time assumed in the ephemeral assemblage that for a time made up Pepys's stable and collective "whole"—before undergoing another garbling of disassembly and reassembly (Goldstein, "The Pepys Ballads," 286–87).

Pepys settled, near the end of his life, on a strategy of grouping the ballads into five volumes, doubly categorized in his table of contents, as described above (see Figure 19), both by the aesthetic format of the ballads in the five volumes (named along the top of the table) and by ten themes or subjects, which run through the five volumes (listed down the left side of the table). However, as a close look at the table shows, the protean nature of broadside ballads undermined any strategic "whole" or stable organization. Pepys's subject categories at times completely collapse. This is evident, for example, in the ditto marks for "Love Unfortunate" directly below the same page numbers given for "Love Pleasant" listed under Volume 4 on the contents page, and the conflation of categories 9 and 10 in Volumes 4 and 5. Further frustrating any neat assemblage, we discover a new category pop up, one not listed in the table of contents, on actually reading through Volume 1. Titled "Promiscuous

Supplement," it appears toward the end of the volume and consists of ballads that belong to the smaller-sized format and time period of "Common Ballads in the Black Letter" (Vols. 2–4). The problem Pepys apparently faced, however, was that, despite the likenesses with the common ballads in being printed on smaller sheets of paper, these ballads gathered rather haphazardly at the end in Volume 1 were frustratingly *un*common. They are, notably, all divided into two parts, like the "Long Ballads antient." On encountering these ballads, Pepys would seem to have made a tactical, on-the-fly alteration to his collection's existing arrangement (so spontaneously made that "Promiscuous Supplement" does not even make it into his table of contents). Broadside ballads are constantly aesthetically moving to the extent that, despite Pepys's determined efforts, they cannot be pinned down.[15]

Pepys's personal compulsion toward aesthetic wholeness, which we have seen in his organizing of his library, also worked against his attempts at assembling his ballads into a coherent and stable unity. Even before being confounded by his "Promiscuous Supplement" at the end of Volume 1, the reader is struck, on opening the albums, by Pepys's habit of cutting away bits of ballad sheets so that they would fit onto his identically sized album pages. He sometimes cut off parts of a ballad's text or ornament in doing so; for instance, "The Last News from Frauce [France]" is missing the top of part of its title as well as the plume to the hat of the cavalry rider represented in the third woodcut (Pepys Ballads 2.206, EBBA 20817). Most radically, Pepys typically segmented the large two-part ballads of Volume 1 that had originally been printed on a single broadsheet. He cut the sheets into two pieces, consisting of their First Part and Second Part, respectively, and then tightly trimmed their inner margins so that each half would fit pasted onto separate but facing album pages. Whole ballads were thus dismembered and reassembled out of fragments.

Other ballad collectors of the period employed similar improvisational dismembering tactics to make ballads fit whatever "big picture" or large collecting strategy they might have had in mind: Selden, Bagford, and the collectors for Harley (probably Bagford and Wanley), whose expanded collection became later known as the Roxburghe ballads, all rearranged and trimmed as well as cut apart and pasted with abandon.[16] Often the processes of fragmentation look downright haphazard. Bagford's archiving of the ballad "The Chamberlain's Tragedy" (Bagford 2.52; EBBA 36418), for instance, involves cutting the ballad into two pieces by chopping right through the last word of the ballad's main title ("Traged | y:") as well as the endings of other text in the far right column. He also cropped the lower portion of the right half of

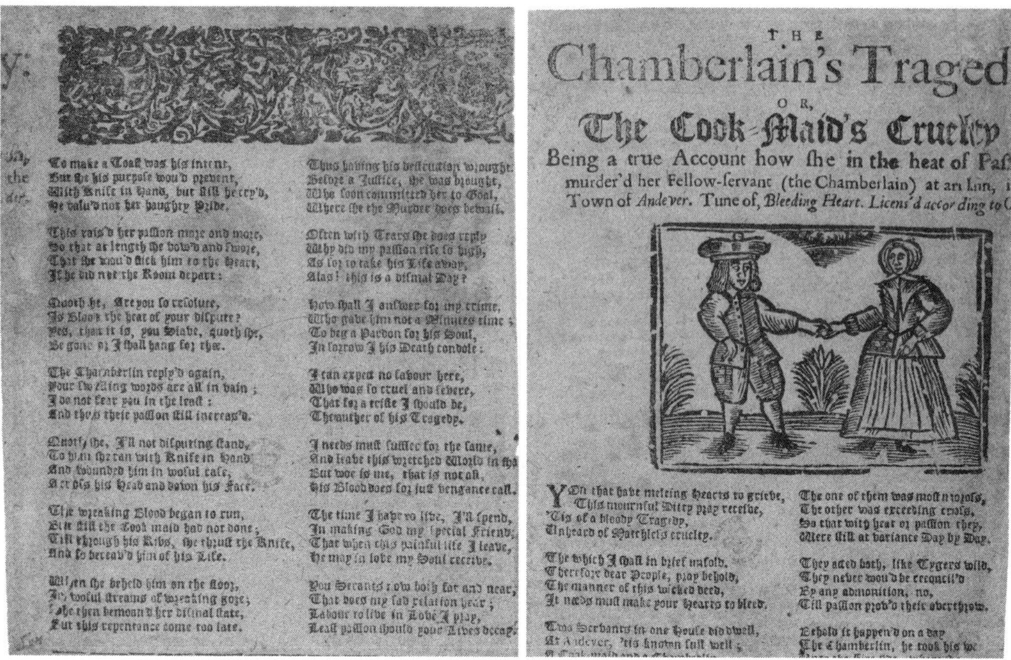

y:

To make a Toast was his intent,
But she his purpose wou'd prevent,
With Knife in hand, but still he cry'd,
He valu'd not her haughty Pride.

This rais'd her passion more and more,
So that at length she vow'd and swore,
That she wou'd stick him to the Heart,
If he did not the Room depart:

Quoth he, Are you so resolute,
Is Blood the heat of your dispute?
Yes, that it is, you Slave, quoth she,
Be gone or I shall hang for thee.

The Chamberlin reply'd again,
Your swelling words are all in vain;
I do not fear you in the least:
And thus their passion still increas'd.

Quoth she, I'll not disputing stand,
To him she ran with Knife in hand,
And wounded him in woful case,
Across his Head and down his Face.

The wreaking Blood began to run,
But still the Cook maid had not done;
Till through his Ribs, she thrust the Knife,
And so bereav'd him of his Life.

When she beheld him on the floor,
In woful streams of wreaking gore;
She then bemoan'd her dismal state,
But this repentance come too late.

Thus having his destruction wrought,
Before a Justice, she was brought,
Who soon committed her to Goal,
Where she the Murder does bewail.

Often with Tears she does reply
Why did my passion rise so high,
As for to take his Life away,
Alas! this is a dismal Day?

How shall I answer for my crime,
Who gave him not a Minutes time;
To beg a Pardon for his Soul,
In sorrow I his Death condole:

I can expect no favour here,
Who was so cruel and severe,
That for a trifle I should be,
The author of his Tragedy.

I needs must suffer for the same,
And leave this wretched World in sha
But woe is me, that is not all,
His Blood does for just vengance call.

The time I have to live, I'll spend,
In making God my special Friend;
That when this painful life I leave,
He may in love my Soul receive.

You Servants now both far and near,
That does my sad relation hear;
Labour to live in Love I pray,
Least passion should your Lives decay.

THE
Chamberlain's Traged
OR,
The Cook-Maid's Cruelty
Being a true Account how ſhe in the heat of Paſ
murder'd her Fellow-ſervant (the Chamberlain) at an Inn, i
Town of *Andever*. Tune of, *Bleeding Heart*. *Licens'd according to C*

You that have melting hearts to grieve,
This mournful Ditty pray receive,
'Tis of a bloody Tragedy,
Unheard of Matchless cruelty.

The which I shall in brief unfold,
Therefore dear People, pray behold,
The manner of this wicked deed,
It needs must make your hearts to bleed.

Two Servants in one House did dwell,
At Andever, 'tis known full well;

The one of them was most morose,
The other was exceeding cross,
So that with heat or passion they,
Were still at variance Day by Day.

They acted both, like Tygers wild,
They never wou'd be reconcil'd
By any admonition, no,
Till passion prov'd their overthrow.

Behold it happen'd on a day
The Chamberlin, he took his wa

Figure 20. Adjusted facsimile, "The Chamberlain's Tragedy: OR, The Cook-Maid's Cruelty; Being a true Account how she in the heat of Passion, murder'd her Fellow-servant (the Chamberlain) at an Inn, i[n] the Town of Andever" (c. 1670), EBBA 36418. Post-photographic processing by EBBA. British Library, Bagford 2.52*, C.40.m.10.(52*).

the sheet. Then—to add insult to injury—he (or his assistant) pasted the two sections of the ballad onto two facing pages of his album in the wrong order (the "y:" and the other bits of last letters from the far half of the ballad's text now being the first printed letters we see (on the verso page), sticking out from the rest of the text; see Figure 20).[17] And, of course, read as such from left to right, the text is meaningless.

In similar spirit, Harley, or more likely one of his assistants, made some very creative reassemblages to Volume 2 of what is now the four-volume (in five books) Roxburghe collection. We cannot definitively say that what looks like multiply re-creative bric-a-brac work was done under Harley's ownership of the ballads, given that the collection passed through at least four sets of hands from the seventeenth to the nineteenth centuries and was repeatedly added to, regarbled, and rebound. Still, at the time of his death in 1724, Harley had amassed an impressive three volumes of ballads. His successor to this assemblage, James West, president of the Royal Society, made some more additions, as did the third owner, Thomas Pearson, who also rebound the three volumes into two, with printed title pages and indexes. But Harley's acquisitions probably form the bulk of the first two volumes. The next owner after Pearson, John Ker, 3rd Duke of Roxburghe, after whom the entire collection became named, mostly increased it with the immense, now third volume (in two books, or "Parts"). Finally, Benjamin Heywood Bright contributed a fourth volume.[18]

What we see in the second volume of the Roxburghe ballads, those probably assembled under Harley's ownership, is a new re-creative strategy—at times resembling playful tactics—by which the ballads were cut apart and reassembled. The innovation? A new arrangement of the separated ballad halves or parts. In the first volume of the Roxburghe collection, as we have seen, the ballads followed the typical Pepysian collecting practice of being cut in half (usually divided by part), with each half pasted onto facing album sheets. In the innovative tactic, the cut-apart right half of the ballad was not pasted down facing but rather *below* its other half. What previously preserved the idea of the sheet, allowing us to at least visually and imaginatively cross the empty divide of the album's gutter, suffered a disorienting about-face: left and right halves became upper and lower parts. Often this practice required extremely tight trimming of the ballad sheets and of their cut-apart fragments (so that the subtitle "The Second Part, to the Same Tune," if such a subtitle were printed, might be cut off). We also regularly witness what can only be described as *cramming* the two halves vertically onto a single album page so that both would fit within the preprinted ornamental border of the album pages. Exemplary are the two ballads, "The Careless Gallant" (verso) and "Celinda's last Gasp" (recto), shown in Figure 21. In all likelihood, we begin to see this phenomenon in the second volume of the Roxburghe ballads because, as mentioned above, ballad sheets in the course of the century became smaller, half-folio in size. That was the case with the "Common" ballads Pepys collected as well. But the Roxburghe albums are taller (if also thinner) than the Pepys books, providing more space within which to pull off this new space-conserving strategy. Still, the ornamental border printed directly onto the album pages often proved to be a problem; sometimes the assembler pasted over the border because the two ballad pieces, even tightly trimmed, would otherwise simply not have fit within it (as in the case of "The Careless Gallant").

With an imaginative zest for such layered reassemblage of ballad fragments, likely the same helping hand often pasted between the layered halves some of the Roxburghe album page's border ornament that he had extracted

Figure 21. Album facsimile, "The Careless Gallant: Or, A farewel to Sorrow. Whether these Lines do please, or give offence, Or shall be damn'd as neither wit nor sence, The Poet is, for that, in no suspence, *For it is all one a hundred years hence*" (1674–79), EBBA 30270, and "Celinda's last Gasp: Or, Her Farewel to False *Coridon*" (1680), EBBA 30272. British Library, Roxburghe 2.44, C.20.f.8.44. © The British Library Board.

from extra blank pages. He thus both marked off and called attention to his self-made divisions between the cut-apart pieces of the ballad sheet. This ingenious tactic can be seen in the ballad on the left album page of Roxburghe 2.98–99 (EBBA 30564), titled "David and Bersheba" (Figure 22). By thus transferring a fragment of ornament from the album backing paper to mark the division between two sections of the ballad sheet he himself had created by cutting apart the originally whole ballad, this inventive assembler, whether consciously or not, imitated something of the technique employed by print-

Figure 22. Album facsimile showing album ornament inserted between left and right halves of the ballad "David and Bersheba" (c. 1695), EBBA 30564. British Library, Roxburghe 2.98, C.20.f.8.98. © The British Library Board.

ers in the seventeenth century. Common practice was to use dividing lines of ornament to demarcate sections of the ballad text, especially columns of verse or the body of the text from the title and woodcut illustrations (as seen in Figures 10, 12, and 14). The assembler has at the same time imitated the practice whereby these same earlier printers physically moved around bits and pieces of ballad media (whether of texts, tune titles, or ornaments) in producing "whole" broadside ballads (and, for that matter, the way consumers associatively did so when making mental hits).

The all-time winner for imaginative and—by comparison with other ballad collectors, seemingly idiosyncratic—remembering through dismembering, however, goes to a descendant of these seventeenth-century black-letter ballad collectors. Though of a later period and thus not connected to the members of the seventeenth-century network sketched in Figure 17 during their lifetimes, this collector's crafty reassembling practice is worth including here because it evokes, while at the same time outdoing, the puzzle-piece ballad making of the earlier period. I refer to the remarkable reassemblage we find in one of the many collections of James Orchard Halliwell-Phillipps, an early nineteenth-century antiquarian. Halliwell-Phillipps assembled a number of broadside ballad collections, including the 420 mostly seventeenth-century black-letter broadside ballads later purchased by William Euing in 1856, and now known by Euing's name. Probably the claim to fame (or to infamy) of re-creative reassemblage in this collection again goes more appropriately to an assistant's hand, especially since we do not see the same phenomenon in the larger Halliwell-Phillipps collection of early broadside ballads now held at Chetham's Library, Manchester.

We find in the Euing collection five broadside ballads in which the first (and often largest) woodcut illustration has at some point been cut or torn out of the ballad sheet. Clearly, the illustration was considered by the perpetrator of this extraction to be the most important part of the ballad artifact. The mutilating act resembles our common practice today of cutting out or simply tearing out a piece of a newspaper or magazine that we want to keep (whether an image, a story, an ad, a coupon, or the like), and leaving behind, or disposing of, the larger entity from which the desired fragment was taken. In the case of the five Euing ballads bereft of their most eye-catching ornamental part, we cannot know with any certainty when the extraction occurred. It could have happened as far back as the seventeenth century or later in time. But the effect, especially in those instances in which the illustration has been roughly ripped out, is to communicate the idea that there was never a perceived integral aesthetic entity worth preserving to begin with. In the mind of the culprit(s)—whether because the broadside ballad artifact was considered entirely disposable or as composed of autonomous unpluggable and repluggable parts (like the assemblages theorized by DeLanda)—leaving a hole in the whole sheet was immaterial. We find similar examples of this practice in the large Crawford collection of some 1,500 early, and mostly heyday, ballads collected about the same time (in the late eighteenth and into the nineteenth century). Though my research has not yet turned up further instances, I suspect that the custom of tearing or cutting out illustrations from broadside ballads must have been frequent and have had a very long history, extending back to the ballad heyday. But, if so, it seems that most of the later antiquarians either didn't get hold of the remaining parts (perhaps they had been promptly disposed of by their original owners) or else the collectors themselves did not consider any found bits and pieces important to preserve—just leftovers. Collectors living at, or close to, the time of the ballad's printing could also have thought that they would have ready access to an unmarred (intact) copy of the ballad from the same print run (which would have been, indeed, often the case). But the assembler of the Halliwell-Phillipps collection purchased by Euing, like Crawford, thought differently. Or maybe he was thinking along the same lines but saw the bits and pieces of the original whole artifact as an opportunity to do some creative rearranging to make another, if illusory, whole.

In the two cases I have found in which an illustration had simply been torn or ripped out of the ballad, leaving jagged edges, the assembler of the Euing collection simply preserved what was now an incomplete whole (as did the assembler of the Crawford collection). He mounted onto backing paper what remained of the broadside ballad, hole and all, as can be seen, for example, in "The Happy Husbandman" (Euing Ballads 137, EBBA 31845). However, and most fascinating, in the three instances in which the image thief, apparently wanting a clean-edged illustration, carefully cut the ballad sheet with scissors into many parts, the Euing-collection assembler creatively put the leftover fragments back together. He essentially reassembled them to make a new ballad that looked intact. In this process of putting the Humpty Dumpty ballad pieces back together again, what was once a landscape-oriented ballad became a portrait-oriented one. At the same time, the illustrations that were originally on the right side of the ballad were moved to where the extracted main picture had been—that is, just below the titles of the ballad and tune. The reassembler thus re-creatively filled in the hole left by the missing picture, as evident in "The Loves of Jockey and Jenny," Euing Ballads 173, EBBA 31928 (Figure 23). What we on first glance see here is an apparently trimmed but otherwise unmanipulated broadside ballad, pasted onto a large backing sheet (what EBBA terms an "Album Facsimile"). Other than in its orientation, the ballad looks like one of Pepys's "Common Ballads in the Black Letter," no? Yes; and no. On close inspection, and especially with the aid of a high-resolution color facsimile, one detects subtle differences in the coloring of several sections of the ballad sheet, as well as faint dividing lines. Under this closer scrutiny, it becomes clear that our apparently whole ballad in fact consists of four put-together independent fragments. Fortunately, EBBA holds a number of very

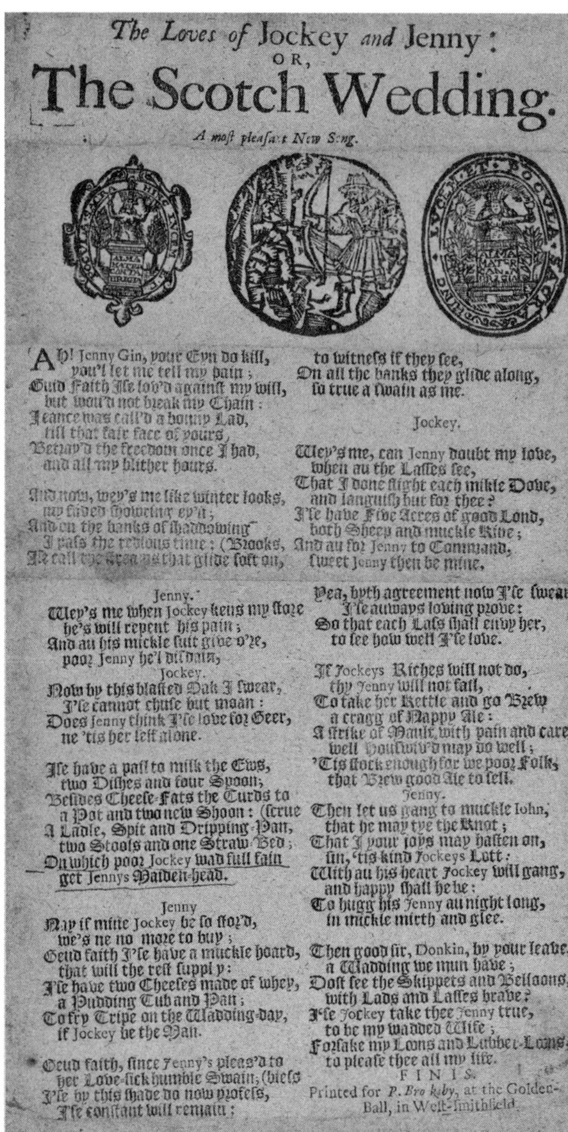

The Loves of Jockey *and* Jenny:
OR,
The Scotch Wedding.
A most pleasant New Song.

AH! Jenny Gin, your Eyn do kill,
you'l let me tell my pain;
Guid Faith Ise lov'd against my will,
but wou'd not break my Chain:
I eance was call'd a bonny Lad,
till that fair face of yours,
Betray'd the freedom once I had,
and all my blither hours.

And now, wey's me like winter looks,
my faded showering ey'n;
And on the banks of shaddowing
I pass the tedious time: (Brooks,
I'e call the Streams that glide soft on,
to witness if they see,
On all the banks they glide along,
so true a swain as me.

Jockey.

Wey's me, can Jenny doubt my love,
when au the Lasses see,
That I done slight each mikle Dove,
and languish but for thee?
I'se have Five Acres of good Lond,
both Sheep and muckle Kine;
And au for Jenny to Command,
sweet Jenny then be mine.

Jenny.
Wey's me when Jockey kens my store
he's will repent his pain;
And au his mickle suit give o're,
poor Jenny he'l disdain,
Jockey.
Now by this blasted Oak I swear,
I'se cannot chuse but moan:
Does Jenny think I'se love for Geer,
ne 'tis her self alone.

Ise have a pail to milk the Ews,
two Dishes and four Spoon;
Besides Cheese-Fats the Curds to
a Pot and two new Shoon: (scrue
A Ladle, Spit and Dripping-Pan,
two Stools and one Straw-Bed;
On which poor Jockey wad full fain
get Jennys Maiden-head.

Jenny
Nay if mine Jockey be so stor'd,
we's ne no more to buy;
Geud faith I'se have a muckle hoard,
that will the rest supply:
I'se have two Cheeses made of whey,
a Pudding Tub and Pan;
To fry Tripe on the Wadding-day,
if Jockey be the Man.

Geud faith, since Jenny's pleas'd to
her Love-sick humble Swain; (bless
I'se by this shade do now profess,
I'se constant will remain;
Yea, byth agreement now I'se swear,
I'se auways loving prove:
So that each Lass shall envy her,
to see how well I'se love.

If Jockeys Riches will not do,
thy Jenny will not fail,
To take her Kettle and go Brew
a cragg of Nappy Ale:
A strike of Mault, with pain and care,
well houswiv'd may do well;
'Tis stock enough for we poor Folk,
that Brew good Ale to sell.
Jenny.
Then let us gang to muckle Iohn,
that he may tye the Knot;
That I your joys may hasten on,
sin, 'tis kind Jockeys Lott:
With au his heart Jockey will gang,
and happy shall he be:
To hugg his Jenny au night long,
in mickle mirth and glee.

Then good sir, Donkin, by your leave,
a Wadding we mun have;
Dost see the Skippers and Bellaons,
with Lads and Lasses brave?
I'se Jockey take thee Jenny true,
to be my wadded Wife;
Forsake my Loons and Lubber-Loons,
to please thee all my life.
FINIS.
Printed for *P. Bro kaby*, at the Golden-Ball, in West-smithfield.

Figure 23. Album facsimile, "The Loves of Jockey and Jenny: Or, The Scotch Wedding" (1684–85), EBBA 31928. University of Glasgow Library, Euing Ballads 173. By permission of University of Glasgow Library, Special Collections.

close editions of the same ballad, with exact title and imprint and wording, among which is Pepys Ballads 4.110 (EBBA 21774). After consulting these "duplicates"—a word one must always use cautiously in referring to ballad sheets, which slip and slide on the press bed, are differently inked, and are corrected on the fly by the printer and/or his apprentice—we can remake an approximation of the original "Ballad Sheet Facsimile" of Figure 23. But we could show more restraint than our imaginative re-creator. That is, we could reconstruct something of the way the ballad would have looked as it had come off the press but resist overmanipulating the image, tempting though it may be to steal a "duplicate" illustration (if only in facsimile) and fill in the hole ourselves. Such a light reconstructive touch would convey an idea of the original printing while foreshadowing the ballad's later mutilation. EBBA has chosen this Janus-faced approach: we put the ballad parts back together in their approximate original placement, but we did *not* fill in the hole with an image extracted from a "like" facsimile (Figure 24).

Figures 23 and 24 demonstrate EBBA's ways of offering multiple, though differently illustrative, ballad facsimile viewings for modern users. But what can we glean about the in-between historical moment (post-heyday; pre-digital) that impelled a radical, physical reassemblage of ballad fragments into a new whole by early antiquarians? At one level, though a cut-and-paste ethos has been taken to its extremes in our Euing ballads, the practice seems much in accord with those of seventeenth-century printers and publishers, who in their shops resorted to similar tactics. As we have seen, they also reassembled bits and pieces of already printed ballads, unplugging component parts from one and plugging them into another, in the making of marketable artifacts that they then relabeled "new." But one might correctly counter that rarely did our seventeenth-century black-letter ballad collectors, to the extent evidence has survived, preserve the literal fragments or "leftovers" of already printed ballads when they had been so drastically cut apart. The most common exception is that they all kept from time to time cut-apart halves of a ballad, even if the other half was out-of-order in the collection or just plain missing. The unique exception can be found in Bagford's more radical bricolage-like collecting. But Bagford's unusual assemblages were part of a larger historical and scholarly agenda, which we will discuss in the next chapter. Early modern collectors, furthermore, may have gestured to a whole ballad through fragments when they pasted into albums the mostly intact ballad halves or parts so that they faced each other, even if the two halves were not from the same ballad (as is often the case in the Manchester Central Library two-volume collection). But seventeenth-century collectors never attempted to merge the fragments so as to effect an illusion of an integrated whole. Even when the crafty assistant to Harley inserted a strip of album-page ornament between the left side (now upper half) and right side (now lower half) of a ballad pasted onto a single album page, he called attention to his tactic through the obvious sameness of album-page ornament he pasted in and also by extending it beyond the ballad sheet on both sides so that it connects to the framing album-page ornament. This cunning fellow may have been deliberately imitating early modern

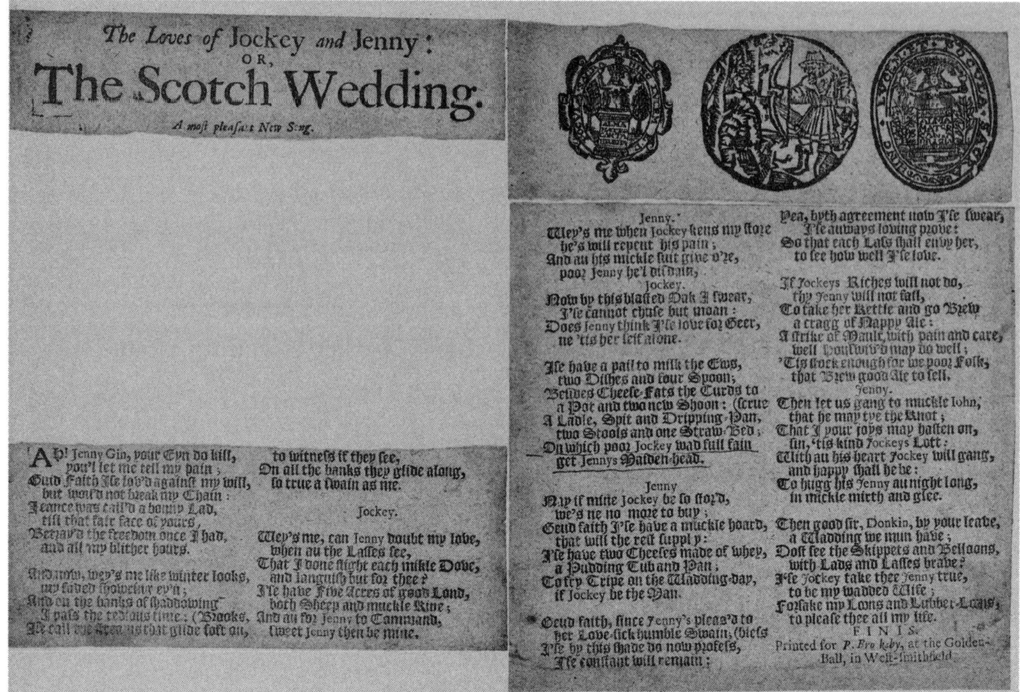

Figure 24. Ballad sheet facsimile, "The Loves of Jockey and Jenny: Or, The Scotch Wedding" (1684–85), EBBA 31928. Post-photographic processing by EBBA. University of Glasgow Library, Euing Ballads 173. By permission of University of Glasgow Library, Special Collections.

printers' own use of ornamental borders and lines to segment ballad parts; in any case, he apparently delighted in showing off his tactic of moving puzzle pieces around, remaking the ballad product.

The re-creative worker on the nineteenth-century Halliwell-Phillipps-turned-Euing collection, however, took such play to more deliberate and seemingly serious ends. His intent was clearly to create a lifelike illusion of an integral ballad whole out of what were in fact dispersed fragments of a previously intact ballad sheet. In this sense, he belongs more with those antiquarians, beginning in the mid-eighteenth century and peaking in the nineteenth century, who were fascinated with forgeries. Exemplary is James Macpherson, who fabricated and then claimed to have discovered the epic poems by the supposed ancient Ossian bard (published in 1760). Often such counterfeits, like the Ossian poems, were knavishly and ironically presented to the public as fragments. Doing so aligned the forger's "art" with the literary cause of the late eighteenth- and early nineteenth-century Romanticists. As we discussed earlier, the authors involved in this movement sought an unattainable ideal of an aesthetic whole by working through literary fragments. Though, unlike the Romantics, our nineteenth-century artful assembler of ballad fragments seems to have seriously entertained the ideal of re-creating a lasting whole, like them, he must also have recognized that his end product was but the verisimilitude of such a re-creation. A discerning eye, or simply a reader of the ballad text, would have discovered the ruse immediately. Not only do the tints of each fragment of ballad paper vary from piece to piece (since they have been taken from different parts of the whole sheet), but also the assembler's fragments, when read consecutively, never fully come together to communicate denotative sense. Reading the reconstructed text of this ballad, as an audience or a consumer would, running one's eye down the first column and then down the next, one quickly becomes aware of the hilarious transparency in the ballad puzzle: the rearranged pieces of material text make nonsense.

Cutting out fragments from prints, re-ordering them, and pasting them alongside text into something resembling a "whole," of course, has a long history, especially in the forms of Renaissance collage work we discussed in the Introduction. But most of the examples that have been studied so far by scholars, such as the Little Giddings' harmonies, resulted from concerted, careful, and laborious strategies toward creating a new "holistic" vision, or what Adam Smyth refers to as "splendid totality" ("Little Clippings," 597). Broadside ballads, in all their mass-marketed but also fragmentary moving media, were lived by contemporaries in the ephemeral, tactical moment. They were produced provisionally, in the moment, and on the fly (not with a view to a lasting "totality") by producers and ultimately disseminators, consumers, and even collectors. Marked by the piecemeal and haphazard and aimed to cater to the masses, in all their variety, these artifacts lay far afield from the restrictive number of carefully constructed books of harmonies and collage artifacts produced by and for the middling to high leisured sorts.

Our crafty assembler of disparate fragments of the Halliwell-Phillipps-turned-Euing broadside ballads appears to have had no religious and political agenda but rather an aesthetic one. Perhaps such an objective could only be executed by a nineteenth-century collector afforded the affective distance and the freedom to play at re-creating the in-the-moment experiential moving media of broadside ballads as we have seen them at work in the seventeenth century. In this sense, he was unique. Certainly, antiquarians from the eighteenth century, and most other collectors of broadside ballads who followed them, tended to treat ballad artifacts with great respect. They embraced a kind of reverence for, if at the same time a remove from, the acquired historical thing. The past was perceived at a distance and the received artifact as finished. Ballads may have come down to them tightly trimmed or otherwise mutilated, but most antiquarians of this later period then sought to preserve their integrity in whatever form they were received. This more curatorial and holistic—even revered—attitude to the handed-down ballad artifacts can be seen, for instance, in the collections of printed ballads made in the eighteenth century by Francis Douce and Richard Rawlinson; in the nineteenth century by Frederic Madden and Benjamin Heywood Bright (who added a fourth volume to the Roxburghe ballads, preserving each ballad intact, pasted sideways on its own individual recto page of his album); and even in the twentieth century, by the ephemera-obsessed John Johnson.[19]

The irony, of course, is that our black-letter broadside ballad collectors of the seventeenth century, in their own unique ways, inhabited their period's ballad culture wholly. As we have seen, they lived in a time marked by the physical dismembering of broadside ballads in the very act of their production. Printers and publishers (sometimes in cahoots with authors) at will detached parts of ballads—texts, pictures, or tunes—and inserted them into other ballads, or simply rearranged them on the ballad sheet (or rearranged smaller bits of the media, like the moved-around pieces of lines of text and even letters and punctuation in the "Mock-Beggar Hall" ballads). Experientially encountering such imaginative collage work, contemporary consumers, as we have further uncovered, would naturally have made random mental hits not only to whole ephemeral artifacts but also to their constituent bits and pieces, assembling a mental cache of associations that allowed them to play re-creatively and recreatively with connections. As for the collectors of the time, it is as if we come full circle when we see them trim, cut, and rearrange broadside ballads on their album or backing pages. It is as if they are returning to the originary physical processes of piecemeal ballad making in shops. With no deceit intended, they preserved broadside ballads fragmentarily. They remembered by dismembering. To reinvoke DeLanda, producers, consumers, and collectors explicitly or implicitly thus rejected a notion of a complete whole that was made up of parts defined by "relations of interiority," which, once in place, were conceived of as unmovable. Broadside ballads, instead, were constituted of parts determined by "relations of exteriority": the individual bits were like Lego-block pieces, often the same, often different, and as such almost infinitely moving parts. In this sense, the strategically minded Pepys—always seeking and failing to achieve a fixed and lasting structural whole for his collection, and thus forced to resort to compensatory tactics—was much more like his tactically minded early modern contemporaries than he might at first seem to be (or have himself acknowledged).

The collectors' network of black-letter ballads of the seventeenth century, then, remembered by dismembering; they preserved ballad artifacts for posterity often by fragmenting them into component, autonomous parts. The same participants also evinced distinctive ideas of what a ballad is or should be. While by no means disparaging the oral (as later folklorists would dismiss print), they shared an acute appreciation for the *visual appeal* of the black-letter typeface on the broadside, which they saw as inextricably tied, as it was for the general public, to illustrations. What we shall additionally see in the next chapter is an appreciation of black-letter print that extends to or, one might equally say, emerges from, a fascination with handwriting and its interconnectedness with the machine-printed. The nature of this interconnection, contemporaries of the time recognized, marked a crucial, if passing, moment in print history, as well as in actual or lived history, writ or printed with a small "h." In this sense, such reciprocity was intimately connected to the occasional and transitory experience of everyday living. Our black-letter ballad collectors saw, in both handwriting and print, an ephemeral moving or "passing present." This is the focus of Chapter 5.

CHAPTER 5

The Passing Present of Black Letter and Calligraphy

So far, I have not delved into the lived connections that made up the network of collectors of black-letter broadside ballads in the seventeenth century other than to roughly sketch out those relationships and show how central Pepys was to their creation. I have also, so far, only on a case-by-case basis focused on what can be seen as a cross-network of "like" practices of preserving black-letter ballads for posterity by remembering them, paradoxically, through dismembering them. In trimming, cutting apart, and rearranging with abandon in their preservationist practices, ballad collectors participated in the collage-work zeitgeist of their time. Their collecting was symptomatic of an infectious early modern fervor impelling producers, disseminators, and consumers of such popular artifacts both physically and mentally to make and remake ballad multimedia in bricolage-like fashion. The one distinction that our collectors have shown was a preoccupation with the black-letter ballad as an aesthetic versus oral artifact. Such a fascination with the visual look of these printed ballads carried over to many antiquarians of later periods, as we saw demonstrated in period-specific ways, whereby dismembering became key to aesthetic re-creation.

But there is much more that drove the preservation practices of black-letter broadside ballad collectors. We find not simply that these collectors shared methods of assembling ballads and of privileging the visual but also that they were remarkably united by a larger cause. That cause is tied to the history of print. It arises from the collectors not only recording but also simultaneously responding to the evolving *and* devolving intimacy between black letter and calligraphy. The second half of this chapter will concentrate on this agenda as a larger unifying force within our network of black-letter broadside ballad collectors—to the extent that these assemblers might even be said to constitute, at times, a recognizable public. As in Chapter 4, I begin by focusing on the central figure in our black-letter ballad collecting network, Samuel Pepys, and turn first to survey his much understudied but impressively monumental three-volume "My Calligraphical Collection." Though never published in print or online, this large folio collection by Pepys is critical to understanding print history and to historically situating the early modern cultural experience of broadside ballads.

"My Calligraphical Collection"

About the same time that Pepys seriously began work on his ballad collection (likely in the 1680s), he as diligently started his collection of calligraphy to chronicle the history of handwriting. Pepys was hurriedly striving to finish both collections in the face of failing health (he died in 1703).[1] Echoing the title to his ballad collection, "My Collection of Ballads," Pepys named his completed collection of handwriting "My Calligraphical Collection" and affirmed its completion about the same time as that of his collection of ballads: "Put together Anno Domini 1700."[2] Compiled at the same time, perhaps even side by side on nearby tables, the two collections exhibit the contemporary habit of remembering by dismembering. Indeed, if Pepys garbled and regarbled his broadside ballads as well as trimmed them throughout and cut them apart in the first volume of his ballad collection, he even more energetically garbled, cut, and pasted fragments of handwriting and print into his calligraphy collection. His bricolage work is especially foregrounded at the beginning of the first volume and at the end of the third volume of the collection, leaving one with a sense of framing dismemberment.

Toward the end of his last volume, Pepys displays what he refers to as "MSS Pieces" (leaves or parts of handwritten pages), "slipps" (thin strips of handwritten parchment or paper) and "Graven Knotts and Pieces" (samples of decorative flourishes taken mostly from engraved advertisements and trade cards of various writing masters). Toward the opening section for the first volume, he offers eight eye-catching pages that individually sport anywhere from two to five manuscript fragments (every piece individually framed, or contained, within hand-ruled lines of black ink, like a picture). Added to these bordered manuscript pieces and creating an unsettled sense of the partiality of visualized text are the annotations to these fragments. The content was provided by Humfrey Wanley. We recall that Wanley was a member of

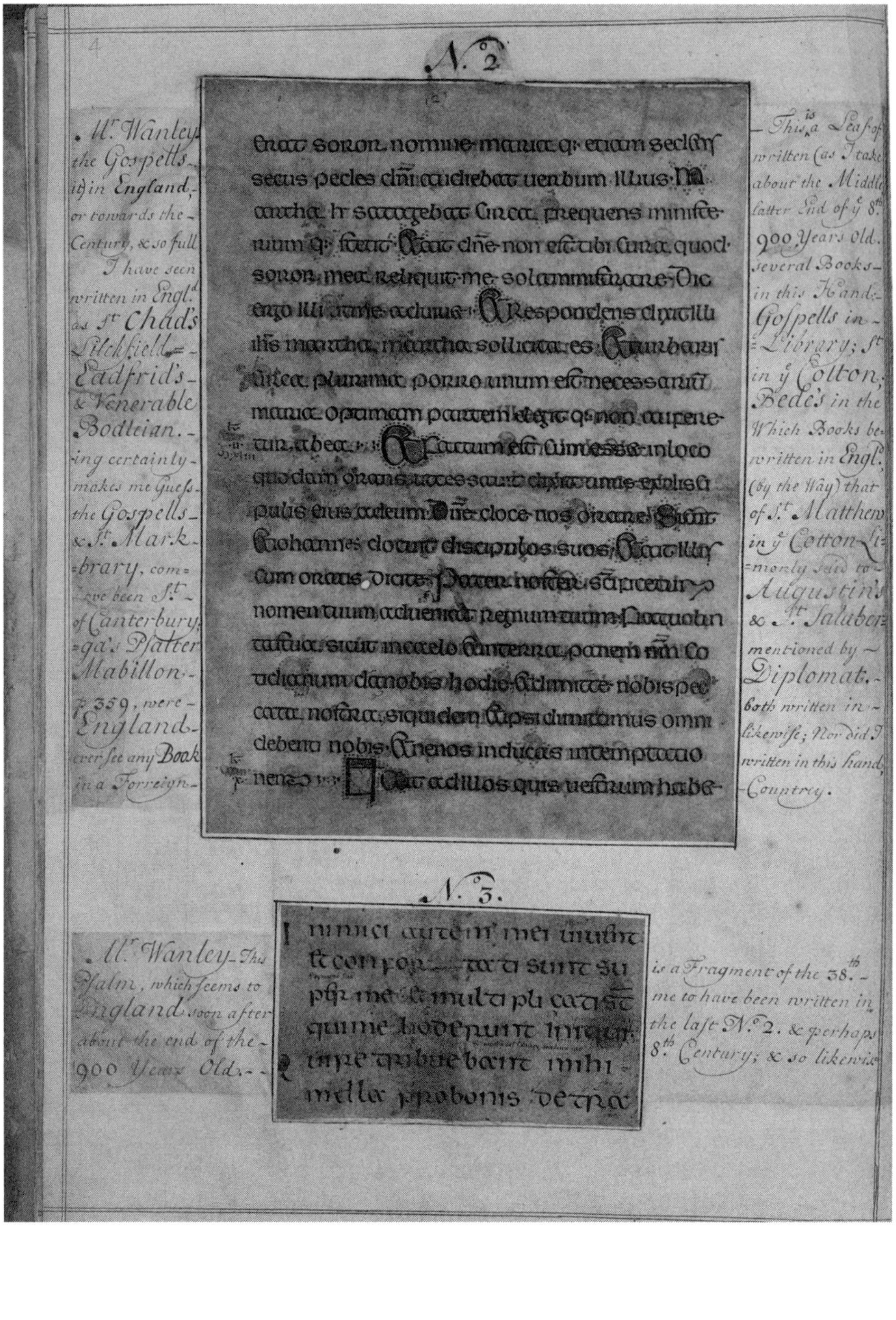

4

. Mr. Wanley
the Gospells
it) in England,
or towards the
Century, & so full
I have seen
written in Engl.d
as St. Chad's
Litchfield=
Eadfrid's
& Venerable
Bodleian.
=ing certainty
makes me Guess
the Gospells
& St. Mark
=brary, com=
=ve been St.
of Canterbury;
=ga's Psalter
Mabillon
p. 359, were
England
ever see any Book
in a Forreign

N.o 2.

erat soror nomine maria q· etiam sedens
secus pedes dn̄i audiebat uerbum illius· Ma
rtha. h satagebat circa frequens ministe-
rium q· stetit· Et ait dn̄e non est tibi cura quod
soror mea reliquit me solam ministrare· dic
ergo illi ut me adiuuet· Et Respondens dixit illi
ihs martha martha sollicita es et turbaris
erga plurima. porro unum est necessarium
maria optimam partem elegit q· non auferetur
ab ea· Et factum est cum esset in loco
quodam orans ut cessauit dixit unus ex disci
pulis eius ad eum· Dn̄e doce nos orare Sicut
et iohannes docuit discipulos suos· Et ait illis
cum oratis dicite· Pater noster sc̄ificetur
nomen tuum adueniat regnum tuum fiat uolun
tas tua sicut in caelo et in terra panem nr̄m co
tidianum da nobis hodie· Et dimitte nobis pec
cata nostra siquidem et ipsi dimittimus omni
debenti nobis· Et ne nos inducas in temptatio
nem· Et ait ad illos quis uestrum habe-

- This is a Leaf of
written (as I take
about the Middle
latter End of ye 8th.
900 Years Old.
several Books
in this Hand:
Gospells in
=Library; St.
in ye Cotton;
Bede's in the
Which Books be
written in Engl.d;
(by the Way) that
of St. Matthew
in ye Cotton Li=
=monly said to
Augustin's
& St. Salaber=
mentioned by
Diplomat.
both written in
likewise; Nor did I
written in this hand,
Country.

N.o 3.

. Mr. Wanley - This
Psalm, which seems to
England soon after
about the end of the
900 Years Old.

Inimici autem mei uiuunt
et confor-tati sunt su
per me et multi pli cati sunt
qui me oderunt inique.
Qui retribuebant mihi
mala pro bonis detra

is a Fragment of the 38th.
me to have been written in
the last N.o 2. & perhaps
8th. Century; & so likewise

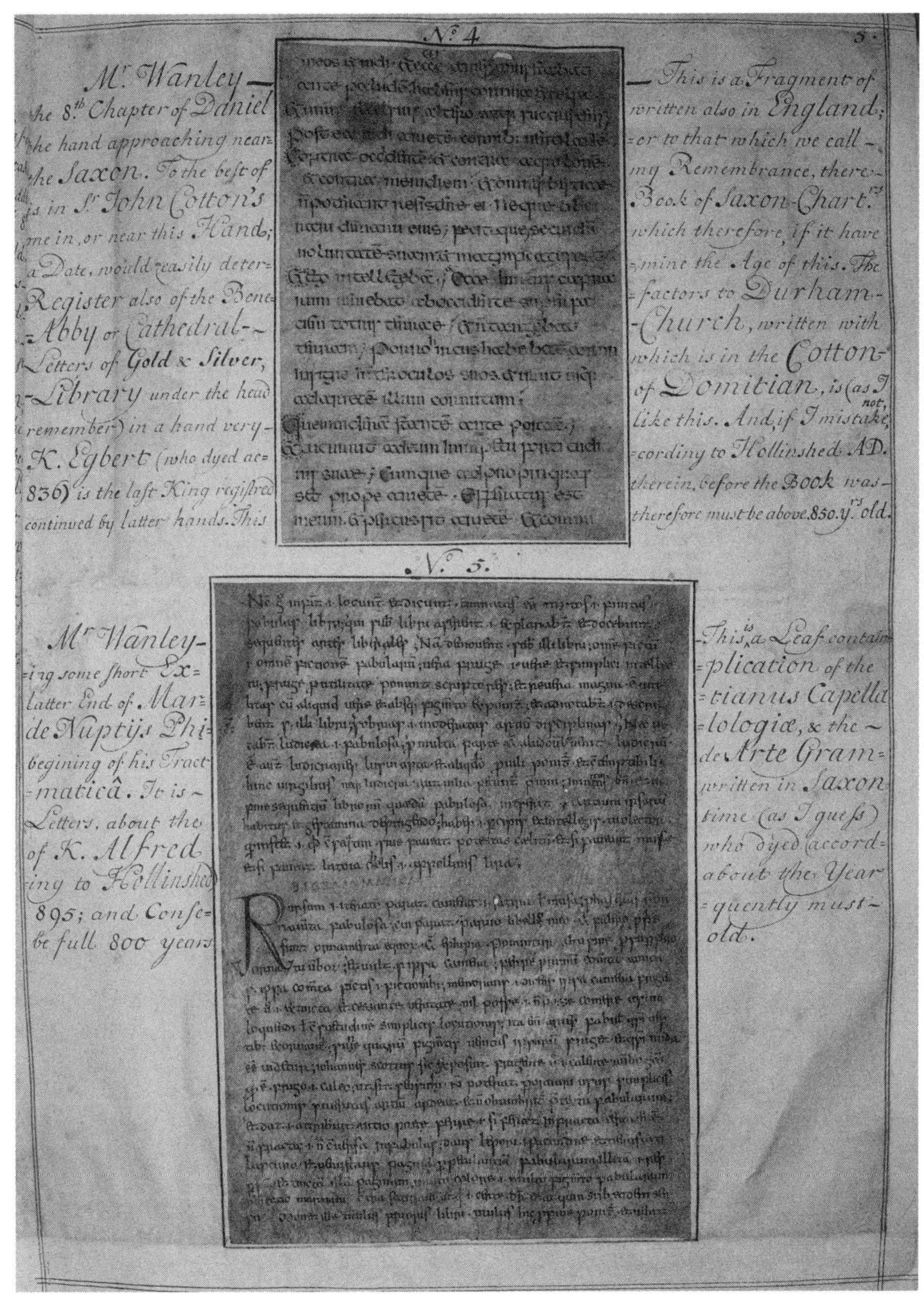

Figure 25. Sample of fragments of handwriting annotated on either side by Humfrey Wanley, in Pepys, "My Calligraphical Collection," pp. 4–5. Magdalene College, Cambridge, Pepys Library PL 2981. By permission of the Pepys Library, Magdalene College, Cambridge.

Pepys's black-letter ballad-collecting network. He was, in addition, drawn into Pepys's assemblage of his calligraphy collection when asked by one of Pepys's friends in that network, Dr. Arthur Charlett, to help Pepys identify some of his antique fragments of early handwriting (going back as early as the eighth century). But Wanley's explanatory annotations to each fragment are themselves rendered on the album page piecemeal. Rather than being inserted in their entirety on one or the other side of, or above or below, the manuscript fragments they describe, the individual annotations are split apart so that they frame the already framed (as in outlined) manuscript pieces. Written in a modern hand, each note first appears to the left side of the pasted and ruled fragment on the album page, then jumps across it, to continue the annotation's explanation on the right side of the fragment. Further highlighting the reader's resulting sense of intense segmentation—created both by extracting a piece of manuscript from its whole and by dividing the explanatory text, making it leap over the manuscript piece—are the many hyphens placed on either side of the featured fragment indicating seemingly arbitrary breaks in the text of the annotations. Each hyphen gestures across the fragment to yet another hyphen on the other side that functions to look back to the first hyphen in an attempt at connection. See, for example, pages 4–5 of Volume 1, in Figure 25. Wanley's explanation, written in modern script, is thus ironically dismembered by the black-letter script, which, as a fragment, is itself but a part of a dismembered whole.

In many ways, of course, providing supplementary annotation is common and akin to the early modern practice of inserting printed or handwritten notes, or slips (of the kind Pepys refers to above), into the margins of a book's page. But Pepys here pushes the limits of this practice, while barely remaining within it. He, or his helper, renders Wanley's annotations, as they do the text annotated, in visually piecemeal fashion. Fragmentation rules. The resultant garbled, disjunctive effect is even more extreme than that created by the famous regarbler Thomas Milles, who multiply and obsessively inserted additions upon additions, through slips and notes, both printed and handwritten, in retailoring the annotations to his self-authored publications in the period. Even once printed, his works were, in this sense, never really "finished" (Sherman and Wolfe, "Hybrid Books," 477). As in the Romantic movement, they emerge as parts of some imaginary and unattainable whole. Pepys's rendering of Wanley's annotations further stand out visually and disjunctively in his framing old script with new, ornamental with plainer handwriting, and, in each case, breaking apart visual and meaningful sense. Ironically, the foregrounded ancient handwritten fragment, doubly framed, thus appears to the eye even more aesthetic and picture-like compared with the partitioned but simpler modern writing that frames it. But with multiple framed pieces on any one page, the overall effect is of multiply moving aesthetic centers of focus.

Even the core of Pepys's three-volume "My Calligraphical Collection," which mostly consists of seventeenth-century copybooks (from England, in the first volume; from France, Spain, and Italy in the second; and from the Netherlands in the third), exhibits compulsive dismemberment. Each copybook has been cut apart. Its separated pages have then been pasted onto the album pages, again individually framed with hand-ruled black lines. Anywhere from four to six framed copybook pages are pasted onto each album page. The cutaway pages thus convey their status as parts disconnected from the whole books into which they had been previously consecutively assembled and bound. Extracted and isolated within ruled lines, each page further conveys its identity as a component part of the now only imagined whole but also—even more so—as an independent identity, along the lines pursued in DeLanda's theory. Underscoring their singularity is the way in which the individual pages, each representing a style of handwriting, are typically bordered within the cutout page by decorative lines. Such ornamental framing, made by the copybook author's drawn lines, often takes the form of remarkable swirls and circles. The encircling lines themselves can acquire an individual identity: they can morph into real and imaginary creatures—birds, angels, humans, and ornate objects—especially in the pages in Pepys's collection taken from the three copybooks of Edward Cocker. The technique Cocker and others used was known as "striking" (tracing shapes with the nib of the pen through curling strokes, without ever lifting the pen from the page).[3] The addition of this lively artistic framing of the page, when added to the independence of the page effected through its extraction from an unseeable whole and its isolation within ruled lines, functions to bring the page itself alive. It is as if the page were a singular organism generated by the hand inseparable from its human creator.[4] The overall effect is, well, striking.

The twin historical timing and similarities—the remembering by dismembering—in Pepys's collecting practices for his ballad and calligraphy albums point to a much deeper interconnection in Pepys's thinking about the two textual media he was devoted to preserving—handwriting and black-letter print—and what exactly he thought he was preserving. He notes on his handwritten calligraphy collection's title page—which features a plethora of writing styles, in which black letter most notably stands out—that his collection has been assembled to chronicle the history of handwriting within the last 1,000 years.[5] Pepys then adds to the title page (*Calligraphy*, 1) an additional motivation for creating his collection: to chronicle "the Competition for Mastery, between the Librarians [i.e., masters of penmanship] & Printers, upon the first breaking-out of the Latter." The immediately following pages are Pepys's meticulous indexes of his collection's content and then Wanley's annotated old manuscript fragments. But, fascinatingly, rather than proceeding at this point to seventeenth-century copybooks, which are the reputed focus of his collection, Pepys tactically—at least, from the reader's perspective, it feels tactical in effecting what seems like a spur-of-the-moment, yet deliberate, gesture—interrupts the strategy of his narrative structure. He unexpectedly inserts a page that returns to the point made on his title page about the "Competition for Mastery" between penmen and printers.

This point about competition is here iterated by means of Pepys's handwritten, *almost* verbatim, "Extract" from John Ayres's "To the Reader." The selected passage concludes the first part, and precedes the second part, of Ayres's recently published (from Pepys's perspective, at least) book, *A Tutor to Penmanship* (1698). In this extract, we are given the background to the "Competition for Mastery" that Pepys references on his title page. The Ayres excerpt, as transcribed by Pepys, makes the observation that the "Art of *Writing*" was performed dexterously and curiously by "The Librarians of Old (before Printing came in use)" but suffered severely with the rise of printing. In this estimation, "Printing for its *Cheapness* and Dispatch *got Esteem*, so these Ingenious Men [Masters of Penmanship] by the *loss* of their Imployment, Declined and Dwindled away." Ayres—channeled here through Pepys—sees an eventual revival in the art of handwriting in "the middle of Q. *Elizabeths* Reign," which Pepys subtly changes to "*near the End of Q. Elizabeth's*" (author's emphases). What Pepys also changes, in a more major way (and in what again feels like a spontaneous, tactical decision), is the significant part he leaves out. Pepys elides the section from Ayres's "To the Reader" where the author gives the reason for the revival of handwriting. The cause, Ayres declares in the now-deleted section of his address, is "*Engraving Writing* on Copper Plates." For Ayres, the invention of copperplate engraving, which was encouraged with the invention of the rolling press, allowed expert calligraphers to work in collaboration with press engravers to print what would look like handwriting. Such collaboration opposes the practices of letterpress printing, which left both the calligrapher and scribe totally out of the picture. Letterpress printing, of course, relies for its execution foremost on a compositor, who sets in place the movable pieces of metal type and woodcuts.[6] Ayres adds, in the excised text about writing masters working with engravers, "and it is strange to consider, what wonderful *Perfection* the way of *Writing* now used, was brought to on a sudden, by the great Masters of that Age, who furnished the World with *Curious Pieces of Art*" ("To the Reader").

Why Pepys would leave out Ayres's full explanation for the decline and revival of calligraphy at first seems puzzling, especially considering that most of Pepys's collection consists precisely of pages from *engraved* copybooks. It is fascinating that he also leaves out of his declared extract Ayres's further, and main, explanation for the competition being so stiff between penmen and printers, an explanation, according to Ayres, that goes beyond simply the cheapness and production-speed of print. The main problem, Ayres says, is that printers so expertly imitated handwriting: "Consider how these poor *Librarians* or *Writers* were put upon by the *Art of Printing*; which at first was so Critically performed, and so well Imitated the *Black Letter* (which was then Generally Written) so Nicely, that it continued near *Twenty Years* in the World, before it was *discerned* from Writing." Worse, Ayres states, not only were people fooled for twenty years by printing into thinking it was handwriting, but even once they were aware of the difference, "the *Printers* still proved too hard for them [the calligraphers], for *they* [the printers] still Imitated the Writing to such Perfection that at last the *Writers Trade* was wholly laid aside; and *Printing* prevailed so far, that *Penmanship* was in a manner lost" ("To the Reader"; author's emphases).

Given Pepys's fascination with black letter *as well as* the fact that his calligraphy collection consists mostly of engraved copybooks (disassembled as they are), it would be astonishing for Pepys either to be uninterested in or to simply forget this crucial portion of Ayers's argument. Much more likely, especially when we consider this moment of omission given the wealth of information he has elsewhere left about his habits of thought, is that Pepys engaged in a tactical forgetting or deliberate ad-libbed redirection of Ayres's words, as indicated in his adding to his extract from Ayres's preface at the end, as if it were part of Ayres's original text, the earlier point he made on his title page about "the Competition . . . between the Pen-men & Printers." What Pepys further adds to this statement is "& expressed by a Collation of Original Proofs of the Works of both, exhibited on the next Page." Rather than neglecting Ayres's comments, Pepys seems stuck on, or perhaps more accurately preoccupied with, Ayres's reference to the "competition" between the two media of handwriting and printing. Pepys knew full well that this competition was rooted in imitation by print of handwriting. However, rather than copying out Ayres's statement about this major point, Pepys, true to his fascination with the powerful appeal of the visual, *illustrates* it: "& expressed by a Collation of Original Proofs of the Works of both, exhibited on the next Page." What

miseratio societ angelicis choris
cum qui venturus est. R. Salva
domine. Hic rogite sacerdos
eo dicens. Pater nr̄. Et ne nos
inducas in iudicium cum suo tu
A porta inferi. Credo videre bo
Dominus vobiscum.
Inclina domine aurem tuam
ces nr̄as quibus misericordiam
supplices deprecamur ut anima
muli tui quam de hoc seculo m
iussisti in pacis ac lucis region
stituas et scōr tuor̄ iubeas es
sortem. p.

In paradisum deducant te an

geli in suo conventu suscipiant t

minuisti eū paulominus ab ange
lis gloria ꝛ honore coronasti eū: ꝛ con
stituisti eū super opera manuū tuarū.
Omnia subiecisti sub pedibus eius
oves et boves vniuersas: insuper et
pecora cāpi. Volucres celi et pisces
maris: qui perambulant semitas ma
ris. Domine dn̄s noster: q̄ admirabi
le est nomen tuum in vniuersa terra.
Gloria patri. An. Benedicta tu in
mulieribus ꝛ benedictus fructus ve
tris tui. An. Sicut mirra. Ps.
Celi enarrant gloriā dei: et opa
manuū eius annūciat firma
mentū. Dies diei eructat verbū: et
nox nocti indicat scientiā. Non sunt
loquele neq̄ sermones: quor̄ non au
diant voces eorū. In omnem terrā
exiuit sonus eorum: et in fines orbis
terre verba eorū. In sole posuit ta
bernaculum suū: ꝛ ipse tanq̄ sponsus
procedens de thalamo suo. Exulta

Te igitur clementissime pater p iesū christū filiū tuū dominū nostrū supplices rogamꝰ. toꝛpei clinato donec dicat ac petimus. Hic erigens se facerdo. osculet altare a dextris sacrificij dicens. Uti accepta habeas ꝛ benedicas. Hic faciat facerd. tres cruces super calicē et panē dicendo Hec do✠na Hec✠munera. Hec✠sancta sacrificia illibata. Factis signaculis super calicem: eleuet manus suas ita dicens. In primis que tibi offerimus pro et

tholica: quā pacificare: custodire adunare ꝛ regere digneris toto orbe terrarū vna cū famulo tuo papa nostro N. et antistite nr̄o N. id est pro ꝓprio epo tātū. et rege nostro N. et dr̄ noiatim. Sequatur Omnibus orthodoxis atq̄ catholice et apostolice fidei cultoribus.

Memento domine famulorum famularūq̄ tuarū. N. et N. In qua oratione ordo debet attēdi propter ordinē caritatis. Quinquies orat sacerdos Primo p seipso Secūdo p patre ꝛ ma

serenos. Inde etiā moy
si famulo tuo manda
sti dedisti: ut aaron fratrem
suum pus aqua lotum
p infusionē huiꝰ unguen

... usq̄ in seculum fiat pax
Requiem eternam ...
Anima domine animam meam
quia peccavi tibi ...
Quemadmodum ...
Desiderat ceruus ad fon
tes aquarum: ita desiderat
anima mea ad te deus. Si
tivit anima mea ad deum
fontem vivum quando ve
niam et apparebo ante faciem
dei. Fuerunt michi lacri
me mee panes die ac nocte
dum dicitur michi cotidie
ubi est deus tuus. Hec re
cordatus sum et effudi in me
animam meam: qui transi
bo in locum tabernaculi ad
mirabilis usq̄ ad domum
dei. In voce exultationis

Psalterium

Dedit q̄ eis pater suus hereditatē inter
fres eorū. Vixit aūt iob post flagella h
centū q̄draginta ānis ꝛ vidit filios suos
ꝛ filios filior̄ suor̄ usq̄ ad q̄rtam gnā
tionē ꝛ mortuꝰ est senex ꝛ plenus dierū.

Explicit liber iob. Incipit prologꝰ bea
ti Hieronymi presbyteri in Psalteriū.

Psalteriū rhome dudum
positus emēdarā ꝛ iuxta
septuaginta interpretes
licet cursim: magna tn̄ ex
parte correxeram. Qd q̄
rursū videtis o paula ꝛ eustochiū scripto
rum vitio depravatū. plusq̄ antiquum
errorem q̄ nouā emēdationē valē: me
cogitis ut veluti q̄dam nouali scissū iā
aruū exerceā ꝛ obliquis sulcis renascen
tes spinas eradicē. equū esse dicentes ut
qd crebro male pullulat crebrius succi

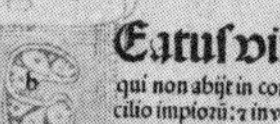

Eatus vir
qui non abijt in con
cilio impiorū: ꝛ in via
peccatorū nō stetit: et
in cathedra pestilētie
non sedit. Sed in lege dn̄i volūtas eius:
ꝛ in lege eius meditabitꝰ die ac nocte. Et
erit tanq̄ lignū qd plantatū est secꝰ de
cursus aquarū: qd fructum suū dabit in
tpe suo. Et foliū eius non defluet: ꝛ oīa
quecūq̄ faciet pspera būtꝰ. Nō sic impij
nō sic: sed tanq̄ puluis quē pijcit ventꝰ
a facie terre. Ideo nō resurgant impij in
iudicio: neq̄ peccatores in cōsilio iustor
rū. Qm̄ nouit dn̄s viam iustorū: ꝛ iter
impior̄ peribit. Psalmus dauid.
Quare fremuerūt gentes. II
ꝛ ppli meditati sūt inania. Asti
terūt reges terre ꝛ pncipes con
uenerūt in vnū: aduersus dn̄m ꝛ aduer

Quo de re putandū est fratres eū
voluisse aliquid, sed minime potuis
se quia si venerabilis viri mentem
aspicimus dubiū nō ē q̄ eandem se
renitatē in qua descenderat voluit
permanere. Sed contra hoc q̄ po
tuit in virtute omnipotentis dei ex
feminā pectore miraculū inuenit.

beati valentini martiris tui natali
cia colimus a cunctis malis immine
tibus eius intercessione liberemur. p
Valentinus venerādus ... cō
pbiter fuit quē claudius im
perator ad se adduci faciens inter
rogauit. Quid est valentine cur ami
cicia nostra nō frueris: ut deos no
stros adorans suspicionē tue absti
nas vanitatis. Cui valentinus si
graciā dei scires ista nequaq̄ dice
res ab ydolis animū reuocares, et
deū qui in celis est adorares. Tunc

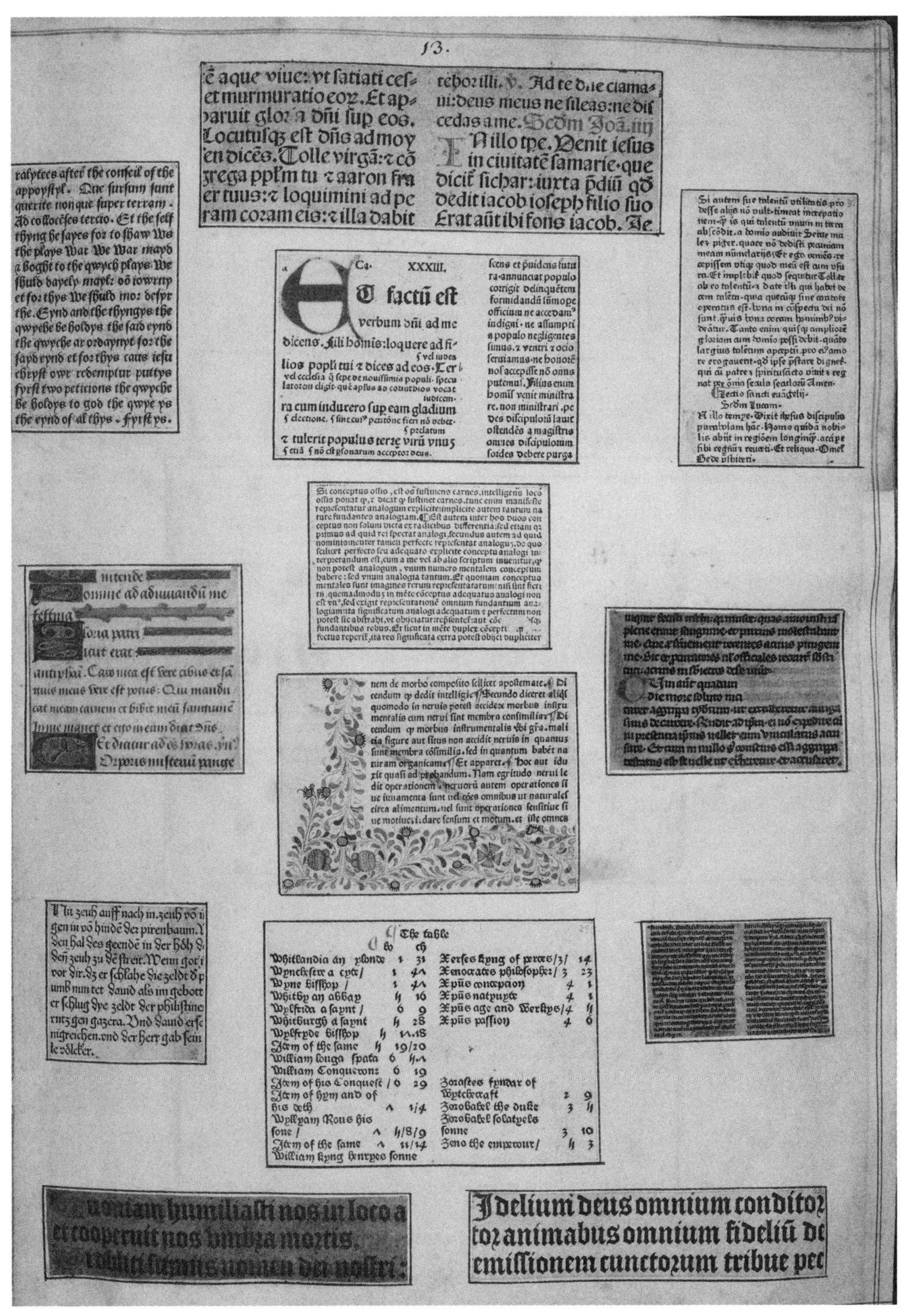

Figure 26. Fragments of handwriting and print in black letter, in Pepys, "My Calligraphical Collection," pp. 12–13. Magdalene College, Cambridge, Pepys Library PL 2981. By permission of the Pepys Library, Magdalene College, Cambridge.

follows on the next page—indeed, over four of the next pages—assembled, we must recall, by Pepys, not by Ayres, though the reader might be fooled into assuming the opposite—is visual proof of the competition between penmen and printers in the form of the imitation, or at the very least "sameness," of fragments of black-letter handwriting and print. We can thus see experientially the difficulty of discerning the difference between the two media. The array of fragments assembled here by Pepys from print and from handwriting is large. There are as many as thirteen items to an album page. See, for example, pages 12–13 of Volume 1 of his calligraphy collection in Figure 26.

What a plethora of bits and pieces where black-letter handwriting and black-letter printing lie side by side in imitation and, as Pepys underscores, "competition"! In stating this point about the competition of handwriting and print a second time and then following it on the second iteration with physical illustrations of such competitive imitation, Pepys fixates on the competition *as ongoing* (or, at the very least, as rethought by Pepys again and again), to the point that he feels compelled to illustrate it on his pages with actual, material fragments of both media. Pepys was on to something. Handwriting and print continued to imitate, influence, and compete with each other beyond the last years of Elizabeth's reign, as Harold Love astutely observes. Love traces the interrelationship between these two modes of communication well into the later Stuart era. He especially focuses on how any governmental clamping down on political print encouraged handwritten satires (*Culture and Commerce of Texts*; *English Clandestine Satire*). But factors other than political repression breathed life into script. Notably, for instance, there was a resurgence of scriptoriums in the Restoration, even when the 1662 Licensing Act for printed texts lapsed between 1679 and 1685 (Cameron, "Late Seventeenth-Century Scriptorium," 15, 31).[7] For Pepys, indeed, what handwriting "means" cannot be extracted from the meaning of print, and both modes of communication are inextricably caught up in historical change. Pepys personally experienced such changes as he assembled his calligraphy and ballad collections in the course of the turbulent and uncertain seventeenth century. Pepys knew script and print were multiply moving media, together evolving in response to their times as well as to each other, and he was most interested in capturing their interactive, if always complex, transitional history.[8]

The Imprint of the Scribal Hand in Black-Letter Typeface

The foundation for the intimate historical engagement between handwriting and print lies in the derivation of the first type fonts from scribal black letter.

The idea on the part of printers was to smooth the transition for the public from reading handwritten texts to reading the printed word. There was clearly much experimentation on this front by William Caxton upon launching the first printing press in England. As Gerald Egan summarizes, drawing on the landmark work of Daniel Berkeley Updike and Stanley Morison, early English printers quickly adopted the typeface that imitated the scribal style of *textura* lettering (angular, close-together, thick strokes—giving the impression of "blackness" of the page, which resulted in the name "black letter"). The script was widely used for formal ecclesiastical documents and also for less formal, commercial postings in the eleventh through the thirteenth centuries.[9] As this scribal style evolved, Morison notes, what was first an effect of efficiency (to take up less space on the page and write faster) turned into "a deliberately artistic" form: "the artistic fad of black-for-black's-sake" (*John Fell*, 111). The "fad" of calligraphical black-letter artistry sheds more light on why black-letter typeface would be associated with pictures by Pepys and his contemporaries. Indeed, Pepys's phrase "Black Letter with Picturs" on the title page to his ballad collection in this sense seems almost a redundancy or an equivalency. Black-letter handwriting, and its press partner black-letter print, were pictorial. Such was likely even more the case for those who could not read or who had limited literacy; this large sector of the population (in London, and, much more so, in the countryside) might well have especially admired the ornamental, printed black letter as something like art.

Another generative interconnection between aesthetic black-letter handwriting and print, which specifically pertains to the emergence of printing in England, is the fact that, as Heal points out, it was "a skillful calligrapher, one Collard Mansion, about the year 1473," who set up Caxton with a printing press at Bruges. From that press, Heal conjectures (*English Writing-Masters*, xiv), Caxton printed his first book in English, *The Recuyell*; it was not until 1477, however, that Caxton published in England. Of course, though countries across Europe influenced each other's written hands and print types, every region developed its own hybrid style, with the French and Dutch having a special influence on typefaces up to the end of the seventeenth century because they dominated the casting of type matrices and sorts.[10] Thus, though Egan is correct that black-letter typeface derived from *textura* lettering in general, it is also significant that Caxton trained on the continent (Bruges and, more important, France) and was therefore well-versed in the most fashionable, high-status hands of his own day. Caxton began his English career with a striking, hybrid typeface—often called Anglicana, but also known as "*bastarda*" (or "bâtarde") because of its mixed parentage. Even more influential than Anglicana, however, was the typeface Caxton brought to England in the

1490s: a stylish Parisian take on *textura* that closely resembled home-grown English black-letter handwriting. So closely did the English associate versions of this typeface with their own country that it quickly became seen as the national typeface and retained this reputation until the eighteenth century.[11]

The English, in fact, referred to black letter as "Old English" or "Old Tudor Black," or simply as "English" or even—for the type's largest body (i.e., point size)—"English English."[12] Thus, toward the end of the seventeenth century, when Bishop Fell, aided by his employee Thomas Marshall, wanted to create a fourth font of black-letter typeface for Oxford University Press, he eventually turned (after much searching and negotiation on the continent) to a native countryman. Giving up a search in foreign lands, Fell ordered a specially tailored English-style type from his own English punchcutter at Oxford. Fell called it "New English" (Morison, *John Fell*, 114–17).

In wanting to collect yet another black-letter typeface so late in the seventeenth century, Fell may have been thinking as much like an antiquarian as a printer. After all, as early as the late sixteenth century, roman or italic font had come to dominate most kinds of printed texts. Fell surely recognized that black-letter script and type were no longer the "*lettera moderne*" in England (to use a term coined by the Italian humanists in the fifteenth century). Rather, they were becoming something that was more distant if also paradoxically more profound, England's own "*lettera antica*" (to repurpose the humanists' term of praise for the roman styles they admired as classical). In sum, both black-letter script and type were increasingly seen as out of date.[13] The new "modern" script, slowly emerging over the course of the seventeenth century and becoming dominant by the mid-eighteenth, as noted above, was the calligraphical equivalent to roman type: a clean cursive or running round style, incipient in many of the examples provided by Ayres.

It is, indeed, against this background that we should consider Pepys's cut-up version of Ayers's own observations. Pepys was a firsthand witness to this evolution, living in the experiential thick of the humanist discourse which, by the end of his century, had dismissed all the native forms of black-letter script—not only bâtarde/Anglicana and *textura* but also their descendent, secretary script—as "barbarous" and "Gothic." He must have been attuned to the developing new interest, spurred by commercial practices, in the rounder script popular among his contemporaries—and he might well have agreed with later scholars like Heal about the "dull" and clerk-like nature of this hand (Morison, *Fell*, xxxiii).

But as Bishop Fell's interest in black letter testifies, the desire for this once-national typeface held on in England, and not only out of an antiquarian interest in the past. As other styles of script and print became available, black letter continued to be represented in the copybooks that proliferated in the seventeenth century. It also dominated two important kinds of native print up to the century's end: on the one hand, elite ecclesiastical and legal texts, and on the other hand, texts that especially targeted the masses, such as romances and all kinds of cheap print, including commercial labels, pamphlets, chapbooks, and, of course, broadside ballads. Black letter combined these elite and popular forms in yet one other medium wherein it held prominence: the proclamation, the embodied word of authority (which might be posted side by side with a printed ballad).

The question of why black letter endured in England for so long, especially in the above specified printed forms, has sparked much debate. We need briefly to revisit this dispute with fresh eyes that consider the *how* as much as the *why*. We will then be in a better position to revisit Pepys's calligraphy collection and consider its surprising conclusion, as well as to visit anew our network of black-letter broadside ballad collectors and understand a larger cultural crusade that unified them: specifically, their shared preoccupation with the interrelationship between handwriting and print and with their devotion to recording the "passing present" of black letter.

Charles Mish and Keith Thomas attribute the "hanging on" of black letter in popular print, such as broadside ballads and proclamations, to its being used in elementary texts for schoolchildren, such as hornbooks (by which children first learned to read), catechisms, psalters, and primers. "Black letter was the type for the common people," Thomas argues, requiring "a more basic skill than roman-type literacy." But Mark Bland and Zachary Lesser consider the holdover of black letter as a culturally constructed "*nostalgia* for a traditional, communal English past."[14] Among the evidence Lesser marshals in support of this argument is the fact that, from the late sixteenth century on, "virtually all black-letter books contained a roman (and italic) title page." The titles of black-letter ballads and proclamations, as he goes on to note, generally appeared in roman type. Lesser also iterates Egan's observation that black letter significantly dominated "books obviously intended not for the common reader but for a highly specialized, elite reader: almost all law books were printed in black letter."[15] For these key reasons, in addition to the others he cites, Lesser concludes that "one of the dominant meanings of black letter in this period . . . was the powerful combination of Englishness (the 'English letter') and pastness (the 'antiquated' appearance of black letter by the seventeenth century)." As a result of such "typographic nostalgia," he continues, "a large part of what modern scholars are really discovering when they perceive 'popular culture' in black letter is the construction of this nostalgia in the very texts they are reading." Lesser then appends a political twist to his argument: "Like most nostalgic myths, typographic nostalgia presents an image of unity, as shown by the use of the typeface in the *Book of Common Prayer* catechisms, and official proclamations, all texts designed to enforce conformity" (103–5, 107).[16]

At this point, I feel myself pulling back. I agree with Lesser that past scholars, like Mish and Thomas, have too often and too consistently associated black letter only with the low, the common, or the "popular"—the word Lesser favors, which, in his interpretation, implies a separation of high from low. As my preceding discussion shows, I also fully agree with his argument that black letter had strong national connotations. But I feel hard pressed to see an "enforced conformity" behind the persistence of black-letter type. For instance, the holding onto black letter in printed legal and ecclesiastical documents—where evidence of such coercion would most likely be found—can also be explained as resulting from the inherent conservatism of such genres. In this light, black letter might be seen as a communication of "*continuing* authority." Continuity is why precedence is so important in laws. It is also why "ancient" terms and phrases live on. And it is why seemingly old-fashioned aesthetics are preserved. Being printed in black letter, legal and ecclesiastical rules reached for precedence as far back as the aesthetics of medieval scribal documents written in *textura*, the main source of handwriting, as we have seen, generative of black-letter typeface.

The importance of continuity to all claims to legal authority (not necessarily involved in coercion) also makes it somewhat problematic to designate black letter as indicative of that which is lost—for it is not quite lost yet. This typeface tenaciously, if sometimes haltingly, endured in the ongoing present of the seventeenth century, ruling not only printed documents of authority but also more mass-marketed books and, especially, single-sheet broadside ballads, which reached even the low. This ongoing present practice pushes against Lesser's idea of loss. His notion of a constructed and past print community of black letter, I would go so far as to suggest, is itself constructed in a manner that anticipates, with a change of media, the imagined preprint oral community advanced by later antiquarians of the eighteenth century and onward. But, as we shall more fully see, consideration of the ongoing lived practice of learning to read in black letter by all classes *much of the time* in the seventeenth century, combined with the incorporation of black letter into copybooks, even while roman and italic were on the horizon, suggests that the continuing widespread fascination with black letter in the period occupied a charged convergence of historical past and immediate present—what I call a "passing present."

Capturing Continuity in Transition: Hornbooks

As with early modern contemporaries first learning to read, we can ascertain much about black letter by concentrating on hornbooks. I stress "much of the time" in the sentence that concludes the previous section because it is important to recognize that even hornbooks were in transition during the seventeenth century. What remained consistent throughout the period was their general format and content. They were quite small, about 5″ by 3″, excluding their handles, making them easily portable—that is, they were moving media, like broadsheets. The common hornbook was made of wood (or, in later periods, of cardboard). The handle often had a hole at the top for a string to be looped through, so they could be hung around a child's neck or waist, presumably to prevent loss. The text, printed multiple times on a single sheet of paper, which was later cut apart to fit onto the wooden board, consisted of the alphabet in uppercase, then again in lowercase, followed often by diphthongs, and, finally, the Lord's Prayer. The paper text was then covered with a thin sheet of horn to protect it and both were affixed to the board—hence, "*horn*-book." But despite many enduring features through the seventeenth century, hornbooks were undergoing a transition in the type of print they displayed. As documented by Andrew W. Tuer, by the time of Charles II, we find some hornbooks printed not in black letter but in roman typeface.[17]

The transition in hornbooks from black letter to roman type, however, was not smooth. It occurred over an extended period, during which the two typefaces overlapped—even sometimes appearing on the same page, as Lesser observes ("Typographic Nostalgia," 103), especially in post-mid-century black-letter broadside ballads. That intermixing, however, does not necessarily imply, as Lesser argues, a literacy beyond black letter. It could well be that the lower sorts who learned the alphabet and rudimentary reading in black letter (specifically, of the Lord's Prayer) would not have been able to read other typefaces but were allured by what seemed the innovative presence of roman and italic type. The latter typefaces might not have been fully comprehensible by those schooled only so far as black-letter hornbooks, but they might have been still fascinating for their very exoticism or out-of-reach "up-to-dateness." It's not only the past that appeals to the viewer. Sometimes the more fashionable present, even if not fully understandable, has just as strong, if not stronger, an attraction in the form of "novelty." Titles and title pages were designed to catch the eye, and printers often did so by switching out the typefaces as well as using multiple sorts and fonts before settling, in the main text, on readable black letter. Though intermingling with and pressured by newfangled typefaces, black letter nevertheless hung on as the primary print for the masses. It is thus not insignificant that, among the extensive volumes of single sheets and fragments of print and handwriting that John Bagford obsessively assembled, he included an uncut sheet of sixteen black-letter hornbooks, printed, by Tuer's estimation, around 1700 (310). The sheet was uncut, likely because it slipped in being run through the press, resulting in the slight blurring of the print, detectable in Figure 27 (this imperfection, making it unusable other than as waste paper, is the likely reason Bagford got hold of it). Schoolbooks showed resistance in transition toward new styles of typeface even in the next stage of textbooks students would take up, should they be allowed to advance their schooling beyond hornbooks: that is, to primers. For instance, in his 1659 *The Petty-Schoole* (1659), Charles Hoole proudly declares, "I have published a new Primar; in the first leafe, where I have set the roman Capitalls (because that Character is now most in use, and those letters the most easie to be learn't)." But by contrast, again as late as Bagford's uncut sheet of hornbooks, 1700, there appeared the anonymous *Best and Plainest English Spelling-Book Containing ALL The Different Words, Syllables, & Letters in the Old English Character* ("the Old English Character" being black letter); this schoolbook included not only a hornbook ABC but also a catechism and primer (and this is just the first part).

Complicating the development of the printed typeface by which children learned to read and write was economics. Bottom line: once a hornbook was purchased by a free school, it was unlikely to be replaced until absolutely necessary, even though the going rate for the learning tool varied from just a halfpence to a pence in the seventeenth century (about the same price as a broadside ballad). Supplies provided in free schools were, well, free for students' use, though the cost of supplies added up quickly for the institutions, making books costly to replace. This is just one way in which economics significantly drove continuity—entirely aside from such factors as reading recognition, nostalgia, or politics. Most important, when it comes to primers, which were to instruct the child beyond her or his basic ABCs, old black-letter primers would likely have been the main texts supplied in late Stuart London because there was a surplus of them in stock. R. C. Simmons notes that as late as "1676/7, '*Old* Primers' [those printed in black letter] represented 75 per cent of the total value" of the Stock of school books held by the Stationers' Company ("ABCs," 4.505; my emphasis). Faced with a backlog of black-letter "Old Primers," surely the Company would have made every effort to offload them to elementary schools before commissioning new ones.

A particularly "striking" line of continuity amid the moving transitions in education, when it came to the typeface and format of school texts, is the frontispiece to Tuer's book. It is a painting of an upper-class child, Miss Campion,

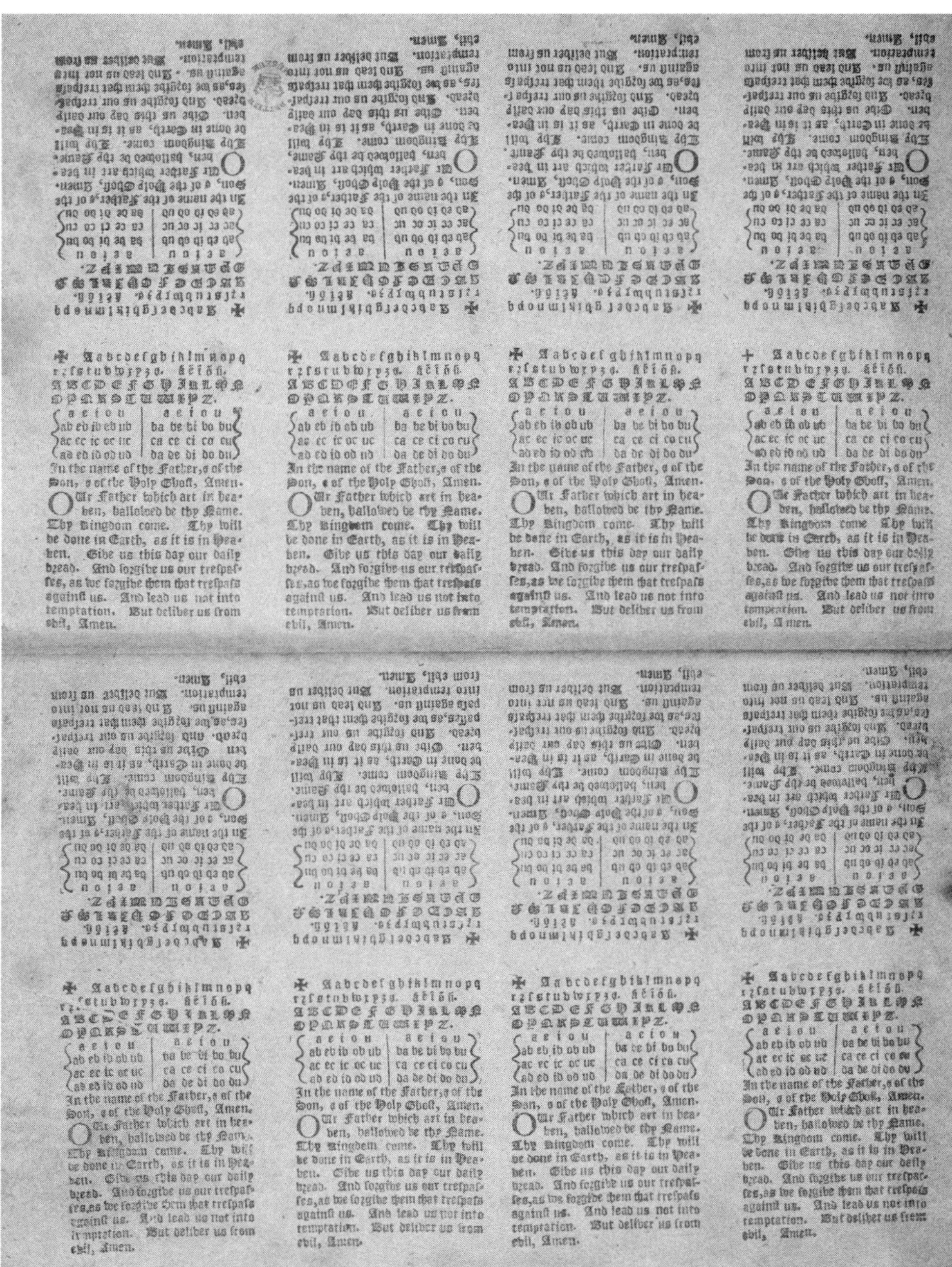

Figure 27. A sheet of uncut black-letter hornbooks collected by Bagford. British Library, Harl. MS 5943, no. 53. © The British Library Board.

aged 2, dated 1660, showing her holding a black-letter, not a roman-type, hornbook (Figure 28). This clearly staged picture could well be offered as proof of Lesser's argument that the upper as well as the lower sorts held a nostalgia for black letter as communicative of a lost age of community—one might go so far as to say of a lost age of innocence, here imaged by a child. Perhaps. But the painting could equally be said to document a realistic, if prettified, picture of a real-life girl holding her actual hornbook at the time of the painting.[18] Perhaps when the child was grown into adulthood her parents would have looked on the painting nostalgically, but not, I posit, at the time it was commissioned. As in our taking of photos of our own children posed in everyday acts, the family seems to have wanted to capture the child in a present lived experience—holding the hornbook she daily used. Like broadside ballads, hornbooks were a part of the everyday. They could have been seen everywhere in London and in the countryside, as children carried them to and from school. They were a part of the routine life of the entire spectrum of seventeenth-century society. And if actually seen and used practically in the present, would they evoke a sense of pastness? Perhaps that would have been the case to some extent, in their sporting a long-standing "old" English typeface. But, even so, given that that black letter held on precisely in mass-marketed print, even as roman type was mightily advocated by humanists to push black letter entirely out of the picture, such pastness for many in the present moment would likely have been felt something more like a "passing present."

Like broadside ballads, furthermore, hornbooks—especially in a child's hand—were much-handled in the present and turned to multiple uses, making them even more a part of the child's everyday experience. Tuer provides one illustration of boys playing shuttlecock with their hornbooks. Given the nature of children throughout history, I would suspect that hornbooks were likely also used by boys and girls for many on-the-fly purposes, including to poke and swat each other. Did children interact, as well, in a more educative way with their hornbooks, however informally? Did they trace out the black letters printed on them in these earliest stages of seeing and interacting with the print on the page? I recall my daughter at age three, before she could either read or write, copying by hand the letters she saw printed on a street sign outside a restaurant where we dined; she did so partly out of boredom and partly because she had become familiar with such signs and knew they held some importance. She thus turned her hand at imitating the letters, even though she didn't know what they were or what they spelled. Did early modern children also copy out what they saw printed on the hornbooks they so often carried around? Were they in this way experiencing what was becoming a new past as a lived present? When, later in life, contemporaries saw black letter on broad-

Figure 28. "Miss Campion" holding a hornbook, 1661. From Tuer's *History of the Horn-Book*. Image courtesy of Wikimedia Commons. https://commons.wikimedia.org. Public domain.

side ballads or elsewhere, or a child chasing a cat with a hornbook, might that moment not trigger a deep reaction at a cognitive and emotive level *in the here and now*? I am thinking of developmental psychologist Howard Gardner's theory of "multiple intelligences" or "modalities" of recognition (*Frames of Mind*). These modalities extend from the cognitive to the emotive, from the kinetic to the sensory, and from the intrapersonal to the interpersonal. Many are as pleasurably kinetic and visceral as batting a ball (or swatting a fellow child with a hornbook). They are in this way akin to other physical movements like dance, or, more subliminally, the manipulated muscles of the lungs, chords, and face in song—two media or "modalities" the broadside ballad draws on in addition to black letter.[19] Early modern contemporaries would have intensely engaged many of Gardner's modalities in their lived present, perhaps especially when lived as a passing present.

The producers of black-letter ballads, it should be further noted, themselves played with the idea that black-letter hornbooks and their lessons were multiply used on a spontaneous and day-by-day basis. For instance, they exploited the way hornbooks were intended in their creation for serious instruction but could often have been tactically redeployed by their users. In one popular woodcut illustration to a black-letter ballad titled "Rocke the cradle John" (Pepys Ballads 1.404–405, c. 1635, EBBA 20190, Figure 29), the impression shows a cuckolded husband, replete with horns, being threatened by his adulterous wife in her apparent process of schooling him. She holds a stick menacingly and directs an accusatory finger at him. She would appear to be trying sternly to teach him a lesson. He obediently holds up, and with a stylus points to, a hornbook.[20] The amusing illustration is a fitting complement to the hilarious black-letter text in which the husband, the relator tells us, foolishly makes a deal in wooing his wife that, if she will marry him, he will accept all her actions; he thus ends up being tutored unexpectedly into accepting her adultery after marriage (and her prolific birthings parented by other men). The ballad also evokes the multitude of ABC broadside ballads marketed for maids and young men, which imitated the alphabetical sequence of capital letters on a hornbook. In the case of these ballads, A through Z are ornamental letters that each individually begins the first word of a stanza, in alphabetical order. It is as if the singer were rote learning and rote teaching a hornbook about proper gender behavior. Though no actual text can be discerned on the hornbook the cuckolded husband holds up in "Rocke the cradle John," the dominance of blackness in its scrawl and overall in the woodcut impression suggests its kinship with the black-letter typeface in which the ballad has been printed. Black-letter broadside ballads, this complementary illustration and text amusingly imply, were in a broad sense educational and—just like hornbooks—could be tactically put to more than one kind of schooling. Indeed, for the consumers of broadside ballads, they offered more than one kind of educational entertainment.

A mere glance at our network of black-letter broadside ballad collectors supports our suspicions of a connection between black-letter broadside ballads and black-letter hornbooks, as well as their tactical intersection with processes of reading and writing that were both in flux. Certainly Pepys, given his interest in the history of handwriting and print, and probably as well Robert Harley, given his amassing of large volumes of historical manuscripts—both also avid collectors of old broadside ballads—must have recognized that ballads and rudimentary educational materials for teaching reading and writing were together undergoing a transition. Such a transition, as we have seen, did not follow a straight and easily traceable line any more than the popular practice of "striking" did.

There is no doubt that, by the very end of the seventeenth century—when most forms of print, including broadside ballads, favored white letter or ro-

Figure 29. Woodcut impression of a cuckold holding a hornbook, from "[Rocke the cradle Iohn, or] Children after the rate of 24 in a yeare, Thats 2 euery month as plaine doth appeare, Let no man at this strang story wonder" (c. 1635), EBBA 20190. Magdalene College, Cambridge, Pepys Library, Pepys Ballads 1.404–405. By permission of the Pepys Library, Magdalene College, Cambridge.

man typeface—black letter, whether written or printed, was in fact becoming a passed past in all forums, from high to middling to low. But the attitudes toward, and uses of, black letter in the course of the century as a whole were more unstable and uncertain than either Thomas or Lesser claims. From the streets to the courts through to the very end of the seventeenth century, we encounter multipronged, moving transitions in handwriting and print, and thus in reading; we also see, however, a remarkable and tenacious return to, or hanging onto, black letter. In the face of ongoing instability, the clear popular savoring of black letter appears to occupy a charged convergence of historical past and present.

Revisiting Pepys's "My Calligraphical Collection" and His Black-Letter Broadside Ballad Network

It is thus especially significant that Pepys concludes his "Calligraphical Collection" on the history of handwriting with examples of black-letter printing imitating black-letter handwriting imitating black-letter printing (Figure 30). In a word, we encounter a puzzle. Pepys's stated title for this last section of his work, "Conclusion," written in red, occupies a single line at the top of the album page (*Calligraphy*, 3.327 recto). On the same page, below that title, we are presented with an image and framing caption. The caption is written in an ornate but also quite rounded italic hand and is further intermixed with letters in bold black-letter script. It states: "Being a Moderne Proof, from the following Ballad, of the Imitablenesse of Printing by Hand-Writing [a ballad is shown] Equall to those of Hand-writing by Printing, exhibited at the Begining of this Collection" (referring to his earlier jumble of fragments of black-letter type imitating black-letter handwriting, which are pasted onto the album pages, as we have discussed). The image that the caption frames is that of a fragment of a "Common" black-letter ballad, with ruled border. What is unusual here is that both caption and central ballad have been *together* excerpted from another whole—they were both already partnered fragments on a sheet—and have been as a unit carefully cut out of that sheet and then pasted onto Pepys's album page as "Conclusion" to his collection. The extent to which both the caption and the image it frames have been carefully trimmed is especially evident in the ballad's bottom left and right corners, where part of the printed text juts out. Whereas in such other cases, the extending text on one or the other side would likely have been cut off in all or part, it is here fully preserved. Such multiply fragmenting but also oddly unifying practices of presentation are quite odd. Especially puzzling is the wording of the divided-up caption. One experiences a moment of confusion, even vertigo, in Pepys's statement. Isn't the ballad pictured in this "Conclusion" part of a *printed* ballad, specifically one typical of the "Common" black-letter format of the latter half of the seventeenth century, which Pepys places into Volumes 2–4 of his ballad collection? Typical of the common black-letter broadside ballad, the fragment shown on the page exhibits a title printed in mixed roman and black-letter type, just like Pepys's handwritten caption framing it, followed by a summary verse in roman italic type, a tune title in roman, and then, below a carved woodcut illustration, a portion of the ballad's main text printed in black letter. Where, then, lies the imitating handwriting within?

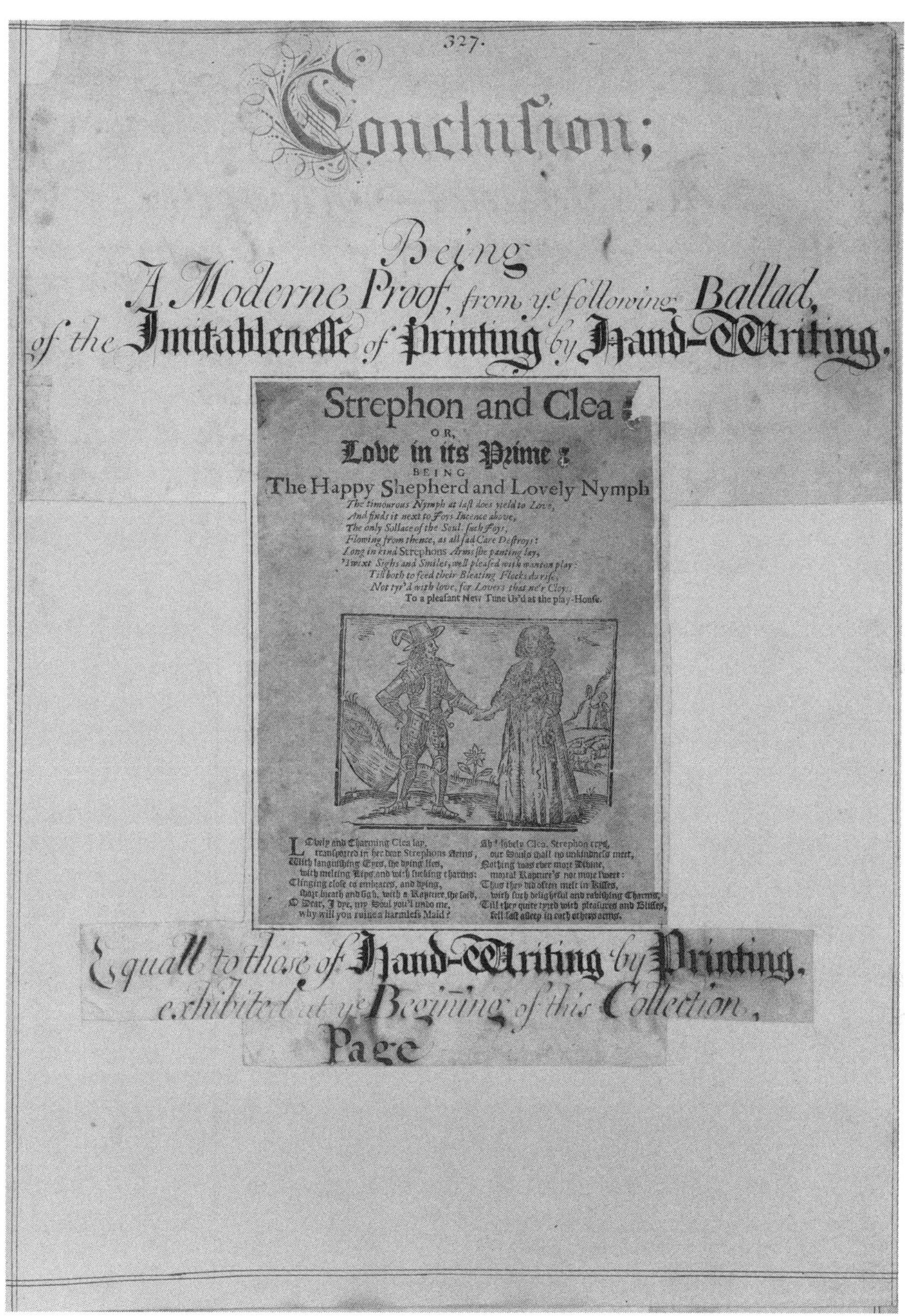

327.

Conclusion;

Being

A Moderne Proof, from ye following Ballad, of the Imitablenesse of Printing by Hand-Writing.

Strephon and Clea:

OR,

Love in its Prime:

BEING

The Happy Shepherd and Lovely Nymph

The timourous Nymph at last does yield to Love,
And finds it next to Joys Incence above,
The only Sollace of the Soul, such Joys,
Flowing from thence, as all sad Care Destroys:
Long in kind Strephons Arms she panting lay,
'Twixt Sighs and Smiles, well pleased with wanton play:
Till both to feed their Bleating Flocks do rise,
Not tyr'd with love, for Lovers that ne'r Cloys.
To a pleasant New Tune Us'd at the play-House.

Lovely and Charming Clea lay,
transported in her dear Strephons Arms,
With languishing Eyes, she dying lies,
with melting Lips and with sucking charms:
Clinging close to embraces, and dying,
short breath and sigh, with a Rapture she said,
O Dear, I dye, my Soul you'l undo me,
why will you ruine a harmless Maid?

Ah! lovely Clea, Strephon crys,
our Souls shall no unkindness meet,
Nothing was ever more Divine,
mortal Rapture's not more sweet:
Thus they did often melt in Kisses,
with such delightful and ravishing Charms,
Till they quite tyred with pleasures and Blisses,
fell fast asleep in each others arms.

Equall to those of Hand-Writing by Printing. exhibited at ye Begining of this Collection,

Page

Figure 30. "Conclusion; Being A Moderne Proof, from the following Ballad, of the Imitablenesse of Printing by Hand-Writing, Equall to those of Hand-Writing by Printing, exhibited at the Begining of this Collection," EBBA 32073. Magdalene College, Cambridge, Pepys Library, Pepys Ballads 2983(327). By permission of the Pepys Library, Magdalene College, Cambridge.

For the solution to this perplexing question, we must turn the page. In doing so, we discover, surprisingly, the flip side of Pepys's conclusion (Figure 31). There, on the album page's verso, we find a handwritten and hand-drawn remaking of the machine-printed ballad previously shown on the recto of the page. The handmade artifact, constitutive of a rewriting and redrawing of the ballad's text and main illustration, is placed slightly askew on a black background. Furthermore, as if laid atop the ballad, are two hand-drawn and hand-colored playing cards. These, also, are set awry. The effect Pepys and his co-conspirator sought to create is obviously that of trompe l'oeil: the illusion of the real. The sheet of the—at first glance—printed ballad looks even more like the real thing than the real thing. Though the top right corner has been magically repaired, the page otherwise looks more worn with age at the edges, and the top left corner curls from apparent use. Furthermore, the playing cards look as though they lie realistically atop the ballad sheet. As if continuing the "look" of the flip side of the page, this hand-drawn trompe l'oeil ballad with playing cards is framed by a handwritten caption, and again, both caption and image appear to have been extracted from another "whole" sheet, where they were already paired fragments. They again look to have been together cut out and trimmed from this sheet and then pasted into Pepys's album page, now as the definitive "Conclusion" to "My Calligraphical Collection."

The playing cards here are a "tell," pointing to some kind of game being played. The top-right card is notably a King of diamonds, perhaps suggesting the superior quality of the handiwork of the realistic handwriting-like-printing and drawing-like-woodcut-impression; but this card has been placed tipping so far forward that the king appears nearly turned upside down. The playing card and its positioning suggest that a certain unruly irony is in play, which upsets any confidence of reigning authority on any side. This unsettling sense is underscored by the second playing card placed on top of the bottom-right corner of the ballad fragment. Unlike the King of diamonds, this card is upright and more nearly vertical to the orientation of the page. But far from indicating a gesture toward resurrection of rule, the particular card shown is especially associated with trickery. It is the Jack (or Knave) of clubs. The Jack calls attention to the whole artifice of rewriting and redrawing the "original" printed broadside ballad as a knavish game.

The caption Pepys gives to this impressive artwork takes such playful trickery closer to irony, and even possibly mockery. Written now only in an ornate rounded italic script, the caption claims that no particular great skill is required to imitate by hand such a printed black-letter broadside ballad as appears on the recto of the page. The caption, as with the one framing the "real" ballad fragment, is split-titled: "The Performance of Mr. Samuel Moore, One

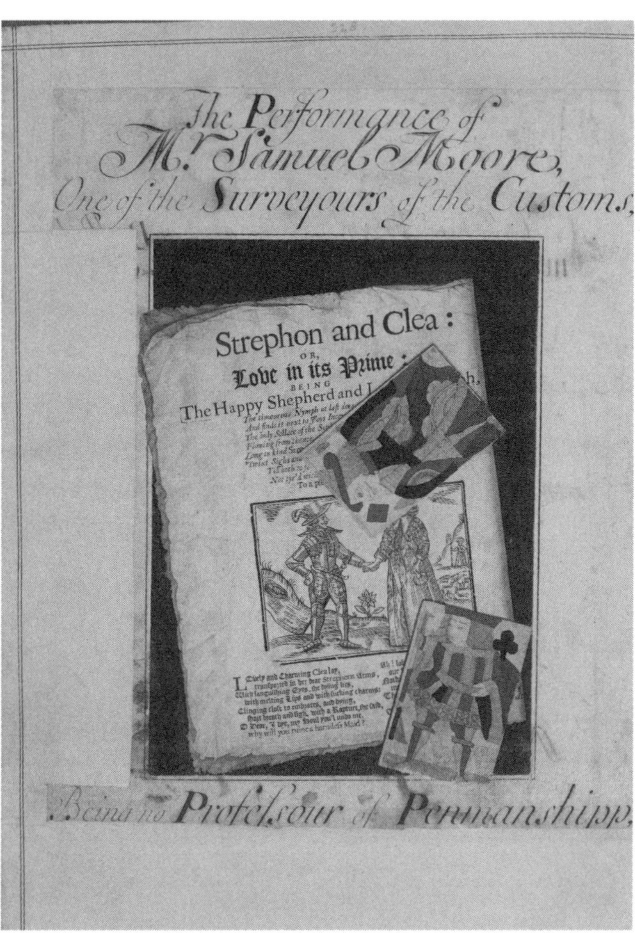

Figure 31. "The Performance of Mr. Samuel Moore, One of the Surveyours of the Customs, Being no Professour of Penmanshipp," EBBA 32074. Magdalene College, Cambridge, Pepys Library, Pepys Ballads 2983(328). On the verso of Figure 30. By permission of the Pepys Library, Magdalene College, Cambridge.

of the Surveyours of the Customs, [the ballad with playing cards atop it is here shown] *Being no Professour of Penmanship*" (implying that most anyone can do this); my emphasis. Take *that*, you printers of black letter, who for over 120 years (in Ayers's estimation) ousted the preeminence of handwriting, Pepys appears to be saying. But is he not further saying: yes, handwriting has revived in general, but, more important, *black letter* handwriting has returned—a style which is, of course, intimately akin to the black-letter typeface Pepys also here privileges? As if part of that revival, the carved figures in the woodcut impression (on the recto) and their hand-drawn imitation (on the verso) are very much of the here and now in another sense: they are fashionably dressed in present-day Caroline garb, to the extent that the armored knight has exchanged his helmet for a stylish feathered hat. At the same time, the foregrounding of a woodcut impression looks back and holds onto the vibrant past of the heyday of the ornamental, black-letter ballad. We know that ballad aesthetics were in the process of transitioning at the end of the seventeenth century, with such features as woodcuts and tune titles falling off the printed sheet to suit the new fashion for undecorated white-letter or roman ballads (without tunes, though with the occasional musical notation). In fact, Pepys laments this very fact—that "Black Letter with Pictures" is losing ground—in the title page to "My Collection of Ballads." But, as his very massive ballad collection proves, all was not yet lost, not by a long shot.

Pepys thus ends his "My Calligraphical Collection" Janus-faced. Rather than looking to a clear present, or even future, in which roman type and italic script are preeminent (though themselves, as the copybooks he spotlights foretell, destined to be succeeded by the round hand), he concludes at a point of tense juncture between handwriting and printing. The contenders all crush in at once, elbowing each other for precedence, in the forms of roman, italic, round, and black-letter typefaces and scripts. We might recall that this is exactly where Pepys began his calligraphy collection. It ain't over yet, he would seem to say of the competition between scribal and printed communication. Such ongoing rivalry is multiply conveyed: first, by the playful mockery of Pepys's surprise completion to his stated "Conclusion" on the recto page, which leaves the reader not with a sense of completion at all but rather perplexity, and impels her or him to read on—to turn the page; secondly, by the single-line affirmation in the bottom half of the caption to the handmade ballad performed by Mr. Samuel Moore that appears to deny Moore's skill in imitating the printed ballad, which artistry we've been admiring: "Being no Professour of Penmanshipp." The concluding line adds yet one more, small indicator of an ongoing rivalry that began when black-letter print imitated handwriting (and vice versa): it ends not with a period, but with a comma. This may have been an error in the handwriting, of the kind we so often see in printed ballads. Or perhaps part of the handwritten text has been trimmed away. Whatever the happenstance, the comma as a positioned pause to any "Conclusion" suggests an inconclusive process is still in play.

Pepys is not alone in his evident perception that he stands at a crossroads in the history of both handwriting and printing—a competition—and that ballads, with their black-letter print derived from medieval scribal practices, exemplify the pressure put on that historical moment. It is not coincidental that the word *manuscript* came into English as an adjective as late as 1597 and as a noun even later, in 1600. It is as if the dominance of print gave birth to the consciousness (simultaneously nostalgic and anxious) of manuscript handwriting in its many forms as itself a passing present.[21] What Pepys further points out in showing that handwriting can imitate print in his conclusion—indeed, what his entire calligraphy collection documents—is a moment in which the trace of the personal hand, which Goldberg astutely makes the focus of his book on scribal culture (*Writing Matter*), is intimately connected to print. As verso to recto, one might say, the two modes can be seen to share a page of history: scribal writing was a kind of machinery of reproduction in its heyday just as letterpress printing was a kind of manual labor (typefaces set and printed by hand). In fact, engaging such twinning is part of the goal behind the invention of engraved writing on copperplate, as represented in Pepys's pages of copybooks. But it is also often an end or side effect of black-letter print generally, which, as we have seen, originated in the effort to copy handwriting. Other collectors of primarily black-letter broadside ballads were thinking along the same lines, reinforcing the cohesion of their collecting network with an appreciation of ballad printing-handwriting in the passing present.

As part of that Janus-faced cause, John Bagford, who frequently secured printed ballads for both Pepys and Robert Harley (Ebsworth, *Bagford Ballads*, 1.v, viii–ix), also obtained for both many pieces of manuscript. It was Bagford who provided Pepys with the first nineteen and certainly oldest manuscript fragments, which Pepys placed at the forefront of his calligraphy collection. Humfrey Wanley, who had helped both Pepys and Robert Harley with their ballad collections, also had a hand in Pepys's calligraphy collection, as we have seen. Contacted by Pepys's friend Dr. Arthur Charlett to help Pepys identify the scribal fragments secured by Bagford, Wanley is given full credit by Pepys for the annotations he provided. Only twenty-three years old at the time, Wanley was already renowned as an expert paleographer.[22] Wanley had himself planned a collection of calligraphy, which, alas, was never realized.[23] A good friend of Bagford, Wanley also supported Bagford's long-in-the-works plan to write a history of print. The two of them promoted that scheme in letters addressed to Sir Hans Sloane and published in the 1706–7 issue of the Royal Society's *Philosophical Transactions*. Pepys's nephew, John Jackson (who helped Pepys assemble and catalog his library and, after Pepys's death, brought to conclusion his collections of both calligraphy and broadside ballads), subscribed to Bagford's project. So did Charlett. But the grand scheme never got off the ground. Bagford nevertheless determinedly continued to prepare for the project. He assembled huge volumes of fragments of manuscripts and print, including many title pages and, not incidentally, as we have seen, at least one still-uncut broadsheet printed with sixteen black-letter hornbook texts.[24] It is fascinating that Bagford's own collection of printed ballads begins with snippets and excerpts of manuscript and print before shifting its focus to broadside ballads (with the odd fragment of print or manuscript still inserted on a page). The collection then tracks the same historical arch as does Pepys's: from black letter to white letter.

What is now commonly known as "The Bagford Ballads" is most intriguing because it does not at first appear to have been intended as a ballad collection. The initial twenty-six pages in Volume 1 (of three volumes) encapsulate the transition from black-letter handwriting to black-letter print, as does Pepys's calligraphy collection, which then proceeds (with the odd backward glance to Ayres's discussion of black-letter handwriting and print) to focus on engraved copybooks of many different handwriting styles. But Bagford's first volume subsequently, and surprisingly (at least for a first-time reader/viewer), makes an about-face: it turns abruptly to focus almost solely on printed black-letter broadside ballads. Considered as a whole, Bagford's collection is extremely valuable not only for its placing, deliberately or not, the history of the printed ballad within that of scribal writing and print generally. Equally revelatory is its third volume, which makes another turn in its focus. Perhaps more accurately, this volume appears to lack focus. It consists of later white-letter ballads, as we would expect, but also—and this phenomenon can be seen in every named collection but that of Pepys—a mixed bag of single-sheet verse. Thinking strictly as a ballad scholar, I have to say that it's hard to fathom the rationale for Bagford's including many of the items preserved in his third album, if the two earlier volumes are to be taken as precedent. Many of the sheets of verse don't seem to be broadside ballads at all, at least not as we have come to know printed ballads in the years before, during, and immediately after their heyday. Many aren't even singable to familiar ballad tunes. I know this because I and various of my associates have tried our best to sing them (considerably problematic when sitting in the Quiet Zone of the British Library's Special Collections). We made every effort to fit the single sheets of verse into the known range of familiar ballad tunes and meters. The problematic sheets are often in iambic pentameter, which alone would not exclude them as broadside ballads (both the popular ballad tunes of "Fortune my Foe" and "Death and the Lady," for instance, can fit a five-stress poetic measure). But the single-sheet verses that prove resistant to the realm of ballad-dom are too irregular in their measure to be singable to ballad tunes. It is as if, by the third volume of his collection, Bagford had returned to his original plan to document the transition in print both before and in the "passing present" of his time.

Bagford, that is, in his third volume appears to have reverted to his apparent original goal (rooted in black-letter handwriting and black-letter print) of tracing the history of print writ large. This meant including the most current "now" of all kinds of single-sheet verse. Broadside ballads, even ballads in white letter, were no longer sufficient to capture print's passing present; additional genres had to join them, given the emergence in the seventeenth century—in a massive way—of a variety of single-page broadside verses, including many elegies, eulogies, and congratulatory poems. Some of these sheets of verse appear deliberately to gesture to their ballad ancestry, either in their aesthetic format or ballad-like wording; others, however, clearly go so much their own way as to become an entirely different entity. As if returning to his original goal, Bagford seems now more interested in tracking the transformation of the handwritten into the single printed page of verse, and then following the further transformations that occurred within this more broadly conceived genre. Such change over the course of the seventeenth century included, yes, the rise of the heyday of the ornamental, multimedia broadside ballad and its smaller-sized or, in Pepys's wording, "Common" cousin, as it can be at least partially seen in Pepys's conclusion to his calligraphy collection. But changes in seventeenth-century broadside printing also included many other types of single-sheet poetry—even those printed on both sides of the page—a seeming influence of both age-old manuscripts and of-the-moment print.

Questionable broadside ballads after about 1630 in the Bagford ballads, as noted above, include many eulogies and elegies. These single-sheet verse genres tricked me at first into believing they were ballads because in the sixteenth century it had been conventional to express eulogies and, especially, elegies in ballad form. Many elegies, for instance, are included, in the Britwell Ballads at the Huntington Library, and we find at least two instances from the late seventeenth century where broadside ballads are specifically named "An Elegy"; their status as ballads is proven by the tune title printed on each sheet.[25] But by the mid-seventeenth century, elegies of another sort proliferated as a fashion, as did their mirror single-sheet image, eulogies. Both, on the whole, seem to veer considerably off the broadside ballad's well-beaten aesthetic path, lacking the formatting, meter (both poetic and musical), and/or tune titles or other wordings we associate with broadside ballads, as this study has defined them. In sum, to the extent that Bagford included these genres, and many other new poetic single-sheet verses in his third volume, his sights would appear to have returned to what seemed to have impelled him in the first place: his planned history of print. Sadly, that long-worked-upon and much invested-in plan—not only by many in our black-letter broadside ballad network but well beyond, that is, by all those who signed up as would-be subscribers to his proposed history of print—never came to fruition. We find only traces of arrangements for Bagford's history in his multiple volumes of bits and pieces of manuscript and print. But we can trace some outlined part of his idea of such a history in his three volumes of collected "ballads."

Wanley, meanwhile, the young paleographer and aspiring publisher of a collection of calligraphy, did not simply help Pepys identify old fragments of handwriting for his own calligraphy collection, as we have seen. He provided Pepys with a handwritten copy of an older ballad than Pepys could secure in printed form—a vivid demonstration of how Pepys's "My Calligraphical Collection" intertwined with his "My Collection of Ballads." At the request of Dr. Charlett via Pepys, Wanley in 1701 secured a transcription of an early printed broadside ballad from his friend Michael Bull at Bennet (Corpus Christi) College, Cambridge. Tying this increasingly complicated black-letter, calligraphic, and print-history network more closely together, Bull, as we have seen, was another subscriber to Bagford's projected history of print. Bull's transcription for Pepys was of a mid-sixteenth-century black-letter broadside ballad celebrating Mary Tudor's ill-fated and, indeed, not real pregnancy. In a letter to Wanley that uncannily evokes the trompe l'oeil verso of Pepys's conclusion to his calligraphy collection, Bull promises that he transcribed the ballad "with all the Exactness I could," and, indeed, the ballad is carefully printed by hand in black letter. It sits near the forefront of Pepys's ballad collection, along with an excerpt from Bull's handwritten letter to Wanley testifying to such "Exactness."[26] For Pepys, a handwritten ballad was as good as a printed ballad, if it was *exactly* transcribed.

Pepys often had ballads copied out by hand—not only by Bull but also by William Hewer (who housed both Pepys and Pepys's library at Clapham late in 1701), by a Captain Allen, and by others.[27] He was discriminating, though, as instanced when an associate's servant, Will Swan, offered him a ballad to the tune of Mardike (a melody by John Playford, whose music store Pepys often frequented and which, not incidentally, stocked Playford's many editions of *The Dancing Master*, which is a gold mine of period-specific ballad tunes). Pepys was at first attracted to the ballad offered by Swan *specifically by its handwriting*. He praised it as "incomparably writ in a printed hand," and so borrowed it. But he then returned the handwritten ballad with the evaluation that "the song proved but silly [referring to the text, not the tune] and so I did not write it out" (1.41). Presented with an inscribed ballad, tantalizing specifically for its "incomparable" handwriting, Pepys in the end chooses not to copy it out with his own hand. Meanwhile, by 1701, Wanley was also working part time for Robert Harley, another acquaintance of Pepys. He had become

Harley's full-time librarian by 1708 and was a major spur to Harley's interest in manuscripts, early printed books, *and* black-letter broadside ballads. Wanley acted as Harley's intermediary in purchasing Bagford's collections on Bagford's death—this, to Thomas Hearne's ire, who believed the ballad collection was intended for him—though Harley kept his own growing ballad collection separate from Bagford's.[28]

But what about Anthony Wood? In one sense, looking at our network of black-letter broadside ballad collectors of the seventeenth century, Anthony Wood, living in Oxford and devoted to recording its history, might appear to be the odd man out. In addition to compiling information about Oxford's ancient past, Wood also compulsively gathered "heaps" (his own word) of fresh-off-the-press pamphlets, advertisements, and any other printed single sheets he could snatch up in town, including many black-letter broadside ballads. This appears his sole focus. Where, then, is the interconnection between writing and print in Wood's collecting practices? It lies in the handwritten additions Wood made to the printed texts he assembled. For Wood compulsively doodled in the margins of his collected sheets, both drawing his own pictures of persons featured in the ballad texts and woodcut illustrations, like his sketch in the margin of the sheet of the hog-faced woman already illustrated in the main woodcut on the ballad about her (see Gniady, "Hog-Faced Woman," 91–108). He also rather narcissistically—though we've all done it—repeatedly inscribed on the ballads variations on how he might publicly represent, in handwriting, his initials and name. He furthermore freely annotated the printed ballads he collected, writing on them information first and foremost about the printer, the date, and the place of printing. He then added handwritten information about the persons or incidents referenced therein (Kiessling, *Anthony Wood*, xxv, xxii–xxxiiii; also chap. 3, n16). Wood's collection of printed broadside ballads, thus fully records, indeed embodies, the personal hand in *hand*writing. It should be further noted that Dr. Charlett, who advised Pepys on his calligraphy collection, was also a good friend of Wood and acted as intermediary among Pepys, Wood, and Wanley when, in 1701, Wanley wrote to Charlett on behalf of Pepys asking Charlett if he could obtain the titles of Scotch ballads from Wood's collection, which Pepys wanted to see (Luckett, "The Collection," xvi). There is a network of ballad collecting at play here that ties together print and handwriting as well as—in a relatively small but expandable company—Pepys, Wanley, Charlett, Wood, Harley, and Bagford (and extending to include figures like Bull, Hewer, Jackson, and even lesser persons such as Mr. Moore, a workman who retrieved and returned "Ballads, old" for Pepys).[29]

Conclusion: Network or Public?

So, to end where we began, does this rhizomatic network of black-letter ballad collectors, many of whom were also working together on the historical documentation of the timely intersection between scribal and black-letter print in both the passing present and the long duration of history, form *just* "a loose network of scholars," to quote Lesley Cormack? Or could it also rise to the status of what Cormack and other members of the Making Publics project would call a public? Certainly, as with publics, this network was organic and expandable. It was open to strangers; Wanley, for example, was at first a stranger to Pepys. It also had a scholarly agenda that it tried to disseminate to a larger public, as in the projected and advertised history of print promoted by Bagford and his supporters. If not everyone in the black-letter ballad-collecting network signed on to Bagford's project, most shared his mission of not only collecting black-letter ballads but, via such ballads, capturing the momentous historical intersection between the handwritten and the printed page exemplified first and foremost in black letter.

Nor should we underestimate the extent to which the networked scholarly cause of these collectors was recognized as socially relevant to others. Like Wood, all of those interconnected through black-letter ballad collecting, however antiquarian their interests, also valued ballads as products and records of lived history—of history in the making—experienced not only by them but also by their contemporaries. At the beginning of his ballad collection, Pepys spotlights a passage he attributes to John Selden that praises ballads precisely as occasional records. The term Selden uses is "libels," which originally meant short pieces of paper, not written slanders: "Though some make slight of Libels; yet you may see by them, how the Wind sits. As take a Straw, and throw it up into the Air; you shall see by that, which way the Wind is; which you shall not do, by casting up a Stone. More Solid things do not show the Complexion of the Times so well as Ballads and Libels" (EBBA 32633; *OED*, "libel," n. 1a–b and 2). Ballads, that is, were something like the anemometers of the early modern there and then.

To be sure, our network of black-letter ballad collectors also relished many of the artifacts they assembled nostalgically: as records of a past old-style English print and of ancient English stories. On the latter front, we might think of the popular tales of Chevy Chase or Guy of Warwick or Robin Hood or of long-ago romantic love. These were the kinds of ballads later to become the focus, reimagined as oral, of the promoters, collectors, and makers of the "traditional" ballad. But our black-letter ballad collectors also savored the ballads' printed words as words in the making (whether by hand or by press) that recorded the passing here and now—recalling Selden's historical straws blowing in the wind. In addition to antique tales, they thus amassed popular ballads that addressed topical issues, such as domestic arguments and gender disputes, recent wonders, in-the-talk news, current politics, the latest fashions, and so on. Debate and answer ballads are common in their collections because such ballads circulated multiple viewpoints—the pros and cons of contemporary subjects—as if they were happening in the here and now for discussion, or, put more baldly, for mass-marketed consumption.

So, once again, is this socially aware, disseminating, sometimes publication-seeking, always preservation-seeking network of black-letter broadside ballad collectors in fact more than "just" a network? Certainly, it seems to have been considered as such by its members (whatever we might think about its size or agenda). This is especially visible at times of excited collectivity, exchange, and potential growth, as in the instance when many of the members came together on paper, if not in person, to entreat support for publication of Bagford's history of print. Their attempt to solicit enough subscribers to publish Bagford's project ultimately failed, but its very effort suggests that the participants (and others connected to them) might well have imagined themselves as forming a significant and impactful public advocating for an important cause. By my own gauge—admittedly limited by the distance of time and slimness of available evidence—what gives me some pause in definitively calling the participants a public is not so much the network's relatively small size or failure to grow substantially but rather what appears to be, for the most part, their fairly weak interpersonal relations with each other—what DeLanda would call a lack of "density." I have not found much evidence of sustained affective reciprocity within their network. And though they were certainly invested in collecting socially relevant black-letter ballads germane to the history of handwriting and print, as a group they for the most part—again, so far as I have found—appear to have been relatively uninterested in participating socially or politically in the larger forum of ballad consumerism of which they were by historical circumstance a part.

Pepys, as we shall see in Chapters 6 and 7, was the noticeable exception. It is precisely in the larger cultural forum of mass-marketed ballads and in the interactive dissemination and consumption of them, in which Pepys eagerly participated, I would argue, that we can more definitively find a ballad public in the making. For ballads were not only, or even primarily, for cutting and pasting into a collector's books, or for piling into "heaps," or for transcribing, or for documenting some impersonal history of print or handwriting. They were for gathering around, exchanging, singing, or reading out loud, and for pasting up for all (or for just a select few) to see. They were cultural artifacts that circulated in complex reflexive and nuanced ways formative of an expansive, multivalent, and organic ballad public. The interests of this broader and more interactive public cannot be as specifically pinned down as those of our black-letter ballad-collecting network. A big and dynamic ballad public is protean. In this sense, one might more accurately speak of ballad publics than *a* ballad public. But I hold to the singular because, at any point in their varied employment of ballads, most early modern participants shared a common familiarity with and an interest in popular ballad forms as well as in their potential for being multiply and tactically used—personally, socially, and politically.

If we zoom further in on Pepys and the ways he wove ballads into his day-to-day social relations, based on his *Diary* of 1660–69, we can gain a better sense of how such a vibrant, interactive, and maneuverable ballad public could work. Pepys shows us the making of tactical ballad publics in many ways. In the next two chapters, in an effort to contain my study not only of moving media but also of tactical publics, I will focus only on two of Pepys's immersive but manipulative methods: his tactical making of gendered ballad publics and his tactical making of political ballad publics.

Part III

From Networks to Publics

Samuel Pepys

CHAPTER 6

Pepys and the Making of Gendered Publics

My study of black-letter ballad collectors in the previous two chapters has uncovered a relatively small network that is unquestionably a network but questionably a public. The collectors certainly shared a similar attitude to their collecting processes—what I have dubbed "remembering through dismembering." With like mind, they often preserved the ballad artifact by unplugging and differently plugging together its component parts, as if playing with Lego blocks: trimming, cutting apart, and then pasting the ballad pieces onto album pages or backing paper. They then continually garbled and regarbled the assembled sheets, like reshuffling playing cards. As a group, they also especially admired the visual aesthetics of black-letter broadside ballads. Their fascination with black-letter print dovetailed with a keen interest in calligraphy, as both complement to and competition with that typeface. Most of our black-letter broadside ballad collectors were also acutely aware that these two interrelated modes of communication were in significant transition. They were moving media undergoing a "passing present," which further spurred the collectors' fascination with black letter as it derived from and engaged with calligraphy and the history of print more generally.

My hesitance in dubbing these collectors a ballad public, as we have seen, arises from their apparent lack of affective closeness and interaction. Samuel Pepys—a key node in our ballad network—stands out as a notable exception, as we will explore in this chapter and the next. Pepys can here be seen to enthusiastically participate in and help shape a ballad public, or at least facets of it, as he expanded upon his collecting ballad network. Pepys's ballad-making public becomes especially clear if we focus on his social interactions with his contemporaries in circulating ballads, as told in his *Diary* (1660–69). Through incidents related in Pepys's *Diary*, that is, we can extend our vision beyond the relatively small, however important, network of black-letter ballad collectors discussed in Part II to envision a much larger and more experientially intermeshed ballad public.

What makes Pepys stand out in his ballad-collecting network and at the same time renders him representative, more generally, of the culture of broadside ballads of his time is his intense investment aesthetically, socially, and politically within the larger forum of mass-marketed ballad consumerism. It is precisely in this larger ballad market, which involved a synergistic dissemination and consumption of ballads, that we find a ballad public in the making. This public is open to all levels of society, even if it is especially focused on the middling and low sorts. Ballads reached out to everyone. They did so, we have noted, in enormous quantities that spanned large spatial and temporal expanses, drew on a panoply of topics, and invited affective interaction through their multimedia, dialogue, and other formulas (such as refrains). Most, if not all, early modern contemporaries would have recognized these recurrent features of the printed ballad. Furthermore, most—even the higher sorts, despite their often publicly expressed disdain for the lowly ballad—would have appreciated that each component media or piece of a ballad was moving in many senses of the term. Through their interactive media and the tantalizing ways parts linked to other parts within and between ballads and other street ephemera, broadside ballads lent themselves to being diversely produced, voiced, viewed, and used.

Circulating in complex reflexive and nuanced modes, such cultural artifacts were formative of an expansive, multivalenced, and organic ballad public. This public may not share the same antiquarian interests as the serious collectors of black-letter scriptorial and printed ballads, whom we discussed in Chapters 4 and 5. For the most part, the masses were not likely to be scholarly invested in ballads or in their historical interaction with calligraphy, whether past, present, or future. The concerns of a large ballad public, furthermore, cannot be as specifically pinned down as can those of our black-letter ballad-collecting network. A big and dynamic ballad public is much more protean, like the broadside ballad itself. In this sense, as I stated in my conclusion to Chapter 5, one might more accurately speak of ballad publics in the plural than of *a* ballad public. But, as also noted, there is a crucial unifying singularity as well as a potentially divisive plurality to all ballad publics because most of the participants, like Pepys, shared a common familiarity with and an interest in popular ballad aesthetics, formats, and topics, as well as their potential deployment. This is how contemporaries of the period were able to tactically—that is, spontaneously and even subversively—make plural publics. Those who took part in creating and, if only temporally, sustaining any ballad public (private, social, and/or political), in other words, reflexively relied upon shared expectations about what ballads were and could be made to be. Pepys is especially absorbing as an active player in and maker of such ballad publics because he rose from the lower middling to high middling sorts. By the time he was writing his *Diary* (not published until long after his death), he was becoming a man of means and public esteem. But given his social history, especially his beginnings as an apprentice, he easily moved within the entire social spectrum from high to low. So did the kind of publics he made.

"Whassup" Publics

I propose beginning our discussion of the making of ballad publics with the point I raise above about reflexivity and shared expectations. I recall, in his simplest example of such reflexive social interplay, Michael Warner's discussion in his book *Publics and Counterpublics* (100–102) of the "talk value" built up around the many different renderings of the once widely popular catchphrase "whassup?" The modern mass marketing of this one word might seem a wild digression from our discussion about early modern ballad publics. But, like visual memes (Sisneros, "Early Modern Memes"), the mass adoption and recrafting of "whassup" in late twentieth- and twenty-first-century society in fact exposes a notable feature about the way such publics are often made throughout history. It is thus worth recalling, for some, and explaining, for others, the famed "whassup" craze.

The word *whassup* was first featured in an Anheuser-Busch Budweiser ad in the United States, launched during a televised Monday Night Football game on December 20, 1999.[1] The ad's vocabulary is minimal, at best. It opens focused on an African American man lounging on the couch in his living room watching a football game on TV and holding a bottle of Budweiser beer. The phone rings. He picks it up and says "Hello." We see on the other end of the line another African American man sprawled on his own couch watching the same game and also holding a Bud. The man who calls, a friend, says, "Hey, Ho. Whassup?" The man answers, "Nothing, Bee [likely a stand-in for "brother"]. Just watching the game. Having a Bud. Whassup with you?" Answer: "Nothing. Watching the game. Having a Bud." Response: "True . . . True." In the series of exchanges that follow, two more African American men also living in the first man's apartment join the phone conversation through extension lines; a fifth enters the conversation through the apartment's intercom, as he stands outside the building, holding a six-pack of Budweiser. Sequentially, the five bond together through an exchange of "whassups," a catchphrase that builds to a harmonic disharmony of five-part ardent and simultaneous screamings of "whassuuups!" Each friend yells the word in a different key, with variant vocal and facial expressions. By now, "whassup" has become a most meaningful nonsensical word, expressive of male, and—to the extent we always move from a neutral "hello" or, in just one instance, "yo," when the person on the line is not at first known, to an enthusiastic, racialized, and gendered "whassup?"—African American male bonding. The hilarity of the moment is emphasized by the camera flashing from face to face, as each man makes "whassup" his own but also part of a concerted cacophony in which the men vocally experience their African American friendship, even though they aren't all present in the same room.

This Budweiser ad became an instant sensation and was reissued globally in a myriad of variations on the "whassup" catchphrase that crossed not only racial and gender but also national borders. In the 2001 "Girl Invasion" version, for instance, in which the same men appear, women disturb their male bonding. The men are now all gathered physically together in the apartment watching a football game. Budweisers are either in hand or stand on the coffee table. The doorbell buzzes. In answer to the neutral query "Hello?," three African American women gathered outside the building all together yell out excitedly—their voices not only gaining volume but reaching higher notes—"Whassuuuuup?" The men look puzzled. They query each other and protest they didn't invite anyone. Finally, they look to the one African American woman in the apartment who has been until now ignored. She has been sitting on her boyfriend's knee, jiggled back and forth like a rag doll whenever the men celebrate successful game plays, her boyfriend reaching across her, as if she were not even present, for manly high-fives with his friends. She now crosses her arms and smiles smugly; her boyfriend moans, "No, no, no." The girls from outside waltz into the apartment, squealing and throwing their coats to the man who opened the door; they promptly settle in on the couch, displacing one of the men to the floor. Not really interested in the game of football, one woman goes off-game to comment on the odd look of one of the football players: "Oh, he got a big head," she says. "Look at his head. Number 94." The last words of the boyfriend are "Oh, maaannn." Cut to the Budweiser logo and, above it, the word "TRUE." The women have invaded not only the men's space but, in an enactment of de Certeau's notion of tactics, subverted them from within: they have taken over their coded language of male bonding, "whassup."[2]

Another ad, not sanctioned by Anheuser-Busch, but with the male cast of the original ad intact, although significantly older, tactically turns the now famous "whassup" catchword against the political establishment. It is eight years later, during the election campaign between John McCain and Barack Obama. A phone call imitates the first ad, but with a twist. The caller is now on deployment in Iraq, in full military gear, standing amid bombed-out buildings and yelling over swirling dust and the sound of a helicopter overhead. The friend who answers the phone now lounges in a now almost emptied-out apartment, packing boxes and debris scattered about. He holds the classified ads, clearly looking for work, while also watching President Bush on the TV telling the nation, "These are very, very difficult times . . . but our best days are ahead of us." As in the first ad, his roommate enters the picture, but he now wears a neck-brace and arm cast, and drops an open box full of packed stuff. He is told to pick up the phone's extension and, before saying "hello," complains about no access to pain killers. On recognizing his soldier-friend's voiced "whassup," he attempts to return the greeting but lets out a pained "whass—aahhh!" The other friend, working at the computer as before, is yelled at to pick up the extension; in doing so, he distractedly says "Yo," while we see on his screen the stock market plummeting. He lets out his own pained "yaaaahhh!" and tries, unsuccessfully, to hang himself. And the same man who in the original ad had rung the buzzer outside the apartment does so again, but in the midst of a global-warming-caused hurricane that provokes his own tormented "ahhhhh!" in response to a "hello." This time when all connect verbally and visually, through rapid screenshots, they express a cacophony of individually pained contortions of the "whassup" greeting that sound more like cries of despair. All then becomes quiet. The soldier-friend in Iraq, clueless to the sequence of events occurring inside and outside the apartment, again asks the familiar question to his friend, "So whassup, Bee?," and the face of his out-of-work, about-to-be evicted friend, suddenly lights up with a smile. What we see on the TV he is watching is not a football game but Barack and Michelle Obama waving to a crowd of cheering supporters. At this sight, the man softly and hopefully responds, "Change. That's what's up. Change." Cut to a black screen with the word "TRUE," then, "CHANGE," then "VOTE."[3]

"Talk value," notes Warner, referring to these popular "whassup" ads—and there are many more variations on the first ad, like variant melodies, or the same tune sung to different texts and illustrations—"allows a structured but mobile interplay between the reflexivity of publics (the talk) and the reflexivity of capital (the value)." He adds, "In contemporary mass culture, the play between these different ways of rendering the field of circulation reflexive has created countless nuances for the performance of subjectivity" (101, 102). The Budweiser ads perfectly make Warner's point.

Return to the early modern period. Mass-produced ballads, one might say, created their own market reflexivity and complex inter-articulation with conscious public appropriation of ballad "whassups." Adopted by consumers, well-known ballad catchphrases could be tactically rendered with innumerable nuances in what was—by virtue of the social circulation of ballads—a collective performativity. Pepys was a virtuoso at participating in and initiating such reflexive, if ephemeral, publics.

Pepys's "Whassup" Ballad Publics

As an instance of making a "whassup" ballad public, on April 11 and April 17, 1661, as recorded in his *Diary*, Pepys sang a bawdy ballad at a local tavern in Chatham with Captain John Allen (Clerk of the Ropeyard). Clearly much enjoying their raucous male bonding through this song, Pepys sang the same ballad with Allen soon after. The second time, Pepys says, he "did get of him [had it copied out] the song that pleased me so well there the other day" (2.78).[4] The song took the form of a medley, a very popular subgenre of broadside ballads marketed by printers and publishers in the seventeenth century, which fully exploited the Lego-block possibilities of ballad texts.[5] In addition to the word *Medley* in the titles to such ballads, there was often included the attention-getting word *New*. But—and this is the very point and attraction of medleys—all of them, even ones dubbed "new," consisted of familiar proverbs as well as catchphrases taken from parts of other popular ballads: attention-getting words or phrases in the ballads' titles, tunes, texts, refrains, and the like. Significantly, the first time Pepys refers to the medley ballad he sang with Allen, it is by the catchphrase in the last line of the song's fourth stanza, recorded in his *Diary* as "*Goe and bee hanged; that's twice god b'w'y*" (2.72). The textual context from which Pepys cites his mnemonic title is printed below, taken from the ballad's earliest extant, 1656 edition of *Wit and Drollery* (123–24), where it is named simply "Song":

> Though her disdainfulnesse my heart hath cloven [divided in two],
> Yet I am of so stately a minde,
> Nere to creep into her arse to bake in her oven
> 'Tis an old Proverbe, that cat will to kinde;
> No, I will say untill I die,
> *Farewel and be hanged, that's twice god buy [goodbye].*
> (my emphasis and gloss)

The second time Pepys sings this ballad, however, he calls it by a different catchphrase, this time remembered from the third line of the third stanza, recorded as "*Shitten come Shits, the beginning of love*" (2.78):

> What though my love as white as a Dove is?
> Yet you would say if you knew all within,
> *That shitten come shites, the beginning of Love is*;
> And for her favour I care not a pin;
> No love of mine she ere shall be.
> Sirreverence of your company.
> ["Sirreverence" = "with apologies" but also "human excrement," *OED*, 1a and 2a]
>
> (my emphasis and gloss)

That the naming of this ballad keeps changing in Pepys's mind is not a sign of early dementia but rather of the fact that the ballad itself is a composite of "whassup"-like catchphrases, any one of which, at a particular moment, and likely depending on the context of the singing or recollecting, might be the one Pepys most remembered.

In each instance of singing together this medley, Pepys and Allen "took great pleasure" (2.72) in turning what equates to popular ballad market "whassups" into a reflexive moment performative of middle-class male good fellowship, in which clearly a larger male public familiar with the early modern ballad word-hoard could also take part. The song especially boosts male egos by rechanneling frustrated sexual desire. It begins kindly, "I Prethee sweet heart grant me my desire." But in the face of sexual *denial*, it turns swiftly into a nasty misogynistic litany of filthy insults. Such literally and metaphorically shitty rallying of manhood binds tightly together what were class-wise only loosely connected middling male sorts: Allen, the ropeyard clerk, and Pepys, in his more elevated status of Clerk of the Acts to the Navy Board.

Ironically, however, Pepys later includes in his ballad collection (Pepys Ballads 3.130, EBBA 21140) not the misogynistic "man-ballad" he took such great pleasure in singing with Allen but a subversive remaking of it (see the less damaged Crawford edition of this ballad in Figure 32).[6] Titled "The Youngmans careless Wooing, And the Witty Maids Replication; All done out of old English Proverbs" (to the now lost tune "Mars and Venus"), c. 1685–88 (EBBA 32895), this version of the ballad depicts the demeaned woman verbally fighting back. Her countervoice within the context of proverbial male

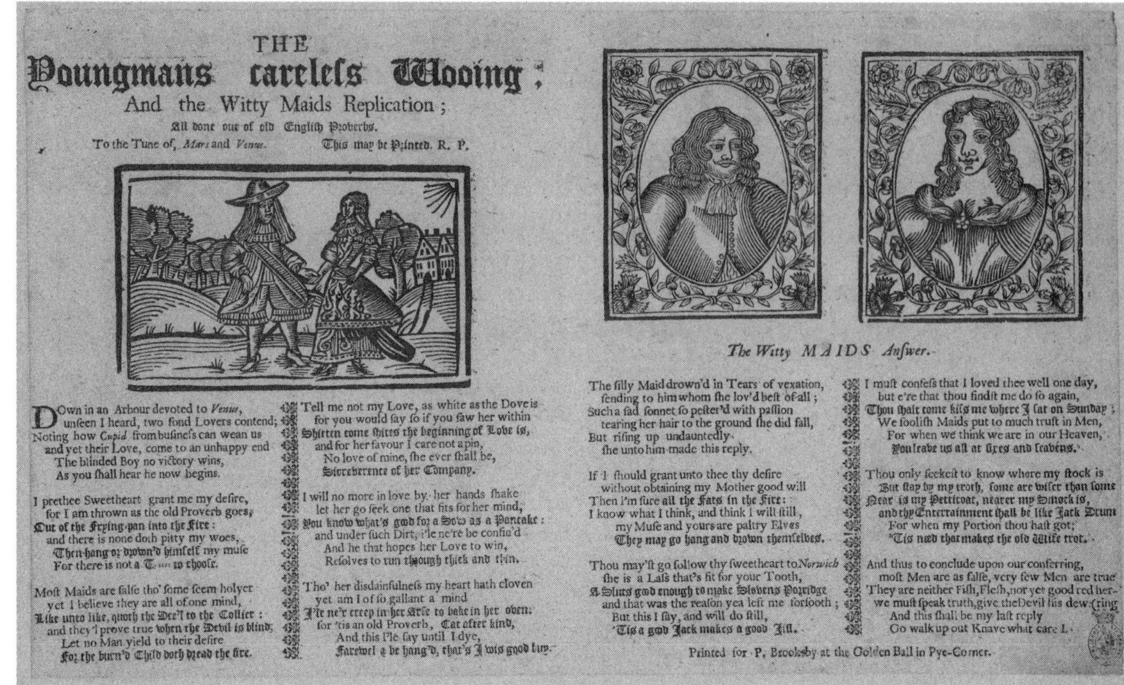

THE
Youngmans careleſs Wooing;
And the Witty Maids Replication;
All done out of old English Proverbs.
To the Tune of, *Mars* and *Venus*. This may be Printed. R. P.

DOwn in an Arbour devoted to *Venus*,
unſeen I heard, two fond Lovers contend;
Noting how *Cupid* from buſineſs can wean us
and yet their Love, come to an unhappy end
The blinded Boy no victory wins,
As you ſhall hear he now begins.

I prethee Sweetheart grant me my deſire,
for I am thrown as the old Proverb goes;
Out of the Frying-pan into the Fire:
and there is none doth pitty my woes,
Then hang or drown'd himſelf my muſe
For there is not a T.... to chooſe.

Moſt Maids are falſe tho' ſome ſeem holyer
yet I believe they are all of one mind,
Like unto like, quoth the Dee'l to the Collier:
and they'l prove true when the Devil is blind;
Let no Man yield to their deſire
For the burn'd Child doth dread the fire.

Tell me not my Love, as white as the Dove is
for you would ſay ſo if you ſaw her within
Shitten come ſhites the beginning of Love is,
and for her favour I care not a pin,
No love of mine, ſhe ever ſhall be,
Sirreverence of her Company.

I will no more in love by her hands ſhake
let her go ſeek one that fits for her mind,
You know what's good for a Sow as a Pancake:
and under ſuch Dirt, i'le ne're be confin'd
And he that hopes her Love to win,
Reſolves to run through thick and thin.

Tho' her diſdainfulneſs my heart hath cloven
yet am I of ſo gallant a mind
I'le ne'r creep in her Arſe to bake in her oven:
for 'tis an old Proverb, Cat after kind,
And this I'le ſay until I dye,
Farewel & be hang'd, that's I wis good bye.

The Witty MAIDS Anſwer.

The ſilly Maid drown'd in Tears of vexation,
ſending to him whom ſhe lov'd beſt of all;
Such a ſad ſonnet ſo peſter'd with paſſion
tearing her hair to the ground ſhe did fall,
But riſing up undauntedly.
ſhe unto him made this reply.

If I ſhould grant unto thee thy deſire
without obtaining my Mother good will
Then i'm ſure all the Fats in the Fire:
I know what I think, and think I will ſtill,
my Muſe and yours are paltry Elves
They may go hang and drown themſelves.

Thou may'ſt go follow thy ſweetheart to *Norwich*
ſhe is a Laſs that's fit for your Tooth,
A Sluts good enough to make Slovens Porridge
and that was the reaſon yea left me forſooth;
But this I ſay, and will do ſtill,
'Tis a good Jack makes a good Jill.

I muſt confeſs that I loved thee well one day,
but e're that thou findſt me do ſo again,
Thou ſhalt come kiſs me where I ſat on Sunday;
We fooliſh Maids put to much truſt in Men,
For when we think we are in our Heaven,
You leave us all at ſixes and ſevens.

Thou only ſeekeſt to know where my ſtock is
But ſtay by my troth, ſome are wiſer than ſome
Near is my Petticoat, nearer my Smock is,
and thy Entertainment ſhall be like Jack Drum
For when my Portion thou haſt got;
'Tis need that makes the old Wife trot.

And thus to conclude upon our conferring,
moſt Men are as falſe, very few Men are true
They are neither Fiſh, Fleſh, nor yet good red her-
we muſt ſpeak truth, give the Devil his dew: (ring
And this ſhall be my laſt reply
Go walk up out Knave what care I.

Printed for P. Brooksby at the Golden Ball in Pye-Corner.

Figure 32. Ballad sheet facsimile, "The Youngmans careless Wooing, And the Witty Maids Replication; All done out of old English Proverbs" (1685–88), EBBA 32895. National Library of Scotland, Crawford.EB.323. Reproduced by permission of the National Library of Scotland.

damning answers the man's insults tit for tat. In this ballad, we learn that the man has cheated on his love. But refusing to admit fault, he adopts the familiar defensive strategy of going on the attack; he vocally abuses the mistress he cheated on. Regardless of whether done consciously, his insults aimed at her further extend into an assault on all women: "Most Maids are false tho' some seem holyer [holier] / yet I believe they are all of one mind, / Like unto like, quoth the Dee'l [Devil] to the Collier" (st. 3). The lover, in sum, draws on the same demeaning gendered catchphrases of the ballad that had so delighted Pepys. In fact, the lover's attempted vindication of his cheating on the maid with another woman includes both versions of the two insulting and disgusting stanzas cited above from the previous ballad.

But the violated maid now rises to exchange insult for insult. She answers the man with just as contemptuous proverbs, accusing him of being false with a whore: "Thou may'st go follow thy sweetheart to Norwich / she is a Lass that's fit for your Tooth, / A Sluts good enough to make Slovens Porridge" (st. 9; "sloven" is "a person of vulgar or disreputable character or manners; a lout; a ruffian; a rogue"; *OED*, n. A.1). The maid concludes firmly and confidently, "And this shall be my last reply / Go walk up out Knave what care I" (st. 12). The defiled woman gets the last word—speaking, it seems, not only for herself but for all women—and insultingly rejects *the man*. Good women unite! As with Budweiser's "Girl Invasion," which reflexively plays upon the beer company's original ad of male bonding through "whassups," proverbial expressions of male bonding are here totally turned around. You can make your own "whassup" ballad public that is female in gender with the right version of the song in hand, together with a knowing and willing speaker/singer and audience.

Though the tune is not extant, the tune title alone of this feminist ballad—"Mars and Venus"—suggests union but also contestation: a war of the sexes. Broadside ballads raunchily played upon this motif in portraying the two titular gods of the tune in the act of having sex. In one version, "Mars and Venus: Or, The Amorous Combatants," c. 1681–84, owned by Pepys and Crawford, among other collectors, the amorous encounter of the two gods is told through "whassup"-type euphemisms for graphic sex.[7] Mars draws his "Weapon" to take Venus's "Castle" (st. 8), but he prematurely ejaculates in "Coney-hall, neer Navil-court" (st. 5) before penetration, and she in disgust repels him:

> . . . his Weapon got a mischance:
> And straightway it fell sick upon it,
> And in Coney-hall was forced to vomit,
>   That caus'd Venus to be angry,
> And out o'the door she did him kick. (st. 8)

In another such sexual assault on Venus, in a different ballad but one also expressed through well-known and transparent "whassup" euphemisms, Mars suffers erectile dysfunction in mid-coitus, and is again angrily (re)ejected by Venus. Ballad consumers appeared to have delighted in hearing about Mars's defeats at his own macho game of battle when trying to attack Venus's "Under Belly hill" (st. 7).[8]

The tune title of "Mars and Venus" for "The Youngmans careless Wooing" would surely have evoked for early moderns associational hits with these thinly veiled depictions of salacious, aggressive, and—funnily—ultimately unsatisfying sex by the gods of war and love. Mars, through the ballads' gendered "whassup"-ing of sex-talk, comes off particularly badly. Like Mars, the young man in his "careless Wooing" is overly confident and aggressive to no avail. He goes further in his assault (and insult) than Mars even, by trying to woo back the maid he cheated on through obscenely debasing her and, by extension, all women. Like Venus, she in turn angrily repels him, and bolsters her rebuttal with in-kind whassup debasements of *him*. Women would likely have heartily rallied around these ballads that put down the overconfident Mars and ungodly men like the young man of careless wooing, strengthening female bonds in a zestful sensual hearing and singing of them.

The illustrations to "The Youngmans careless Wooing" subtly reinforce the concluding unresolved relationship between the two "lovers," especially once seen within the context of the tune and text they decorate. As befits the latish date of the ballad's publication (1685–88), the depicted figures are dressed in Restoration garb. They are also alike finely adorned, as if belonging to the higher orders. Such attire might at first seem out of context for the gross language used in the ballad. But by virtue of the upper-class status of the figures, the illustrations imply that all social sorts can resort to crass colloquial language in a one-on-one argument, especially on the topic of sex. The image placed above the man's nasty assaults, furthermore, sets the couple in the countryside, as if to add a common, "homely" feel to their exchange of insults. But, tellingly, that same illustration ironically shows two lovers hand in hand, not at each other's throats. It appears to depict the fantasy of the young man, who thinks he can lewdly insult his way back into the maid's bed. The illustrations on the right, however, above the "The Witty Maids Answer," image a literal face-off: portraits of a man and a woman, again of the upper sorts, in which the man rather grumpily looks toward the woman, but she gazes out at the audience, in a self-satisfied manner, as if indifferent to him. One might be reminded of the smug look on the girlfriend's face in the Budweiser "Girl Invasion" version of its original "whassup" ad; there she gets her comeuppance for being ignored by her boyfriend when her girlfriends take over his man-cave, screaming *his* male-coded "whassup" catchphrase. The absolute separation of the man and woman in the portraits above the second half of "The Youngmans careless Wooing" is underscored by the fact that their busts are isolated within their own individually decorated oval frames. These two potential lovers are in no way united in love; they occupy entirely separate and independent spaces—as "men are from Mars, women are from Venus," the portraits confirm, as if looking forward in time and also echoing the tune title. The retort of the ballad, spoken by the maid—notably given equal print space with the man's—drives that point home. Recall that, like Venus, she concludes with her definitive dismissal of our would-be Marsian conquering male: "Go walk up out Knave what care I."

Neither catchphrase ballad discussed above has a refrain, not the one Pepys sings in camaraderie with Allen in the tavern, nor the one he later assembles in his ballad collection, where the woman (all women?) is given her own assertive voice in rebutting her would-be wooer's piecemeal insults poached from other ballads. But refrains to ballads could become their own "whassup" catchphrases, which could then be reflexively turned by consumers into selective bonding. They could even cross the boundary of gender in drawing on a larger public's ballad cache and expectations. As Claire Tomalin correctly observes, Pepys did not generally see women as friends, even when he "loved" them (*Samuel Pepys*, 377). But he formed a rare bond with his cousin Roger's new bride, Esther. One social occasion that exhibits and fosters this bond is when Pepys and Esther echo together, presumably with an eye-winking and knowing twist, a popular broadside ballad's catchy refrain. On February 28, 1669, Pepys travels by coach to Roger's home with Roger's daughters, Bab and Betty. Arriving, he says, "We are kindly received." But Pepys notes that his cousin Roger "is in great pain for his Man [his servant] Arthur, who he fears is now dead, having been desperately sick, and speaks so much of him, that my Cozen his wife and I did make mirth of it, and call him Arthur of Bradly" (9.460).

Arthur of Bradly (or, as his name was also spelled, Arthur of *Bradley*) is the country-bumpkin "hero" of a very popular series of ballads, datable to the early seventeenth century, and likely sung even earlier (Chappell and Ebsworth, *Roxburghe Ballads*, 7.313).[9] They include Arthur's prideful wooing of a lass he spots one day, and the subsequent gregarious, if raucous and drunken, communal wedding celebration, titled "A Merry Wedding; Or, O Brave Arthur of Bradly" (see, for example, Huth EBB65H, 2.186, in the Houghton Library, Harvard; EBBA 34628). The last part of the wedding title becomes the mainstay, with variations, of the refrain for most extant Arthur of Bradly ballads: "For the honour [sometimes "honor"] of Arthur of Bradly, / O brave Arthur of Bradly." Arthur's wooing, which survives only in a late discombobulated slip-song version in the Roxburghe ballads (3.283, c. 1700; EBBA 30998), consists of our hero coming upon an ugly maid, pridefully declaring his love for her—"for 'tis love conquers kings" (st. 2)—and then abruptly asking the maid's mother for her hand in marriage. Though the mother thinks her aesthetically challenged daughter could do better than be "a bumkins bride," Arthur boorishly interjects, "You lie, you old whore" (st. 5) and touts himself as a great catch because his father will bequeath him all his worldly possessions. This great inheritance, which Arthur proudly details, turns out to be a jumbled collection of petty items, including: "A wooden wedge and maul [hammer] . . . a dozen of wooden spoons . . . [and] an old cart-nail." To top off such measly treasures, he adds "A sweet old mustard-pot" (st. 6). In this narratively mangled slip-song, written as a barely coherent and disjointed patchwork of text-parts apparently extracted from a longer and more intelligible broadside ballad(s)—as if the slip-song were sung to match the seemingly thrown-together bits and pieces itemized as parts of Arthur's proud inheritance—Arthur pompously adds on yet other seemingly randomly associated petty objects. Not to be left out, he remembers, is "One left-hand mitten, and an old curtain ring" (st. 8). The many extant ballads that function as sequel to this pitiable wooing and bombastic self-promotion focus on the wedding celebration of Arthur and his chosen bride. Especially foregrounded is the high-kicking jig- or morris-like dancing, rather drunkenly performed but with great, if homely, good cheer by the local community. They have come together to enthusiastically contribute food, musicians, and merriment to the wedding party. Almost like clueless but familiar cartoon characters, these country folk and Arthur himself begin to grow on the reader/viewer/singer. Our growing fondness for the characters is likely due to their "silly" (as in "ignorant" but also "simple" and even "innocent"; *OED*, "silly," adj, A.2a, A3.5a) nature that embraces good ole folksy fun; as such, they become quite endearing.

Based on surviving ballads (admittedly not entirely reliable evidence of popularity, as we saw in discussing the singly extant but seemingly very popular "Anne Wallens Lamentation"), the most liked or, at least, most "kept," of the Arthur of Bradly ballads are those that focus on this wedding celebration. What stands out in versions of Arthur and his bride's grand, if lowly, country festivity is the resounding refrain "O brave Arthur of Bradly" and its most common variant, "For the honor of Arthur of Bradly." See, for example, Euing Ballads 214, c. 1660-1700; EBBA 31690 (Figure 33). As in the two other extant ballads in EBBA about Arthur's wedding (33784 and 34628), the woodcut illustrations here not only repeat from ballad to ballad but also quite oddly present to the viewer busts of a very well-to-do and fashionably dressed man and woman. Unlike the close-ups of the set-apart, isolated "lovers" in the second half of "The Youngmans careless Wooing," these figures are carved from the same block; they are *united.* They also face toward each other, suggesting a communion of sorts. Their seemingly out-of-place, high social status, however, gives one pause. Megan E. Palmer, in conversation with me, has suggested that the woodcut might well have been carved in imitation of images of the all-the-news royal wedding between Frederick Elector Palatine and Elizabeth of Bohemia in 1613.[10] For a printer to have made a deliberate connection between the most high and the most lowly of unions, in choosing

A merry Wedding
Or, O Brave *Arthur of Bradly*
To a pleasant new Tune.

See you not Peirce the Piper
His Cheeks as big as a Myter
A piping among the Swains
That dance on yonder plain,
Where Tib and Tom do trip it,
And Youths to the horn pipe nipe it
With every one his carriage
To go to yonder marriage
Not one behind would stay
But go with Arthur of Bradly
O brave Arthur of Bradly.

Why Arthur hath got him a Lass,
A bonnier never was
The chiefest Youths in the Parish
Come dancing all in a Morrice
Jumping with mickle Pride,
And each his wench by his side
With Christmas gambals flowing,
And Country wenches trouncing
They all were fine and gay
For the honor of Arthur of Bradly, &c.

And when that Arthur was married,
And his wife home had carried,
The yongsters they did wait;
To help to carry up meat
Francis carried the Frumaty,
Michael carried the Mince-Pye
Bartholomew Beef and Mustard
And Christopher carried the Custard,
Thus every one in his array,
For the honor of Arthur of Bradly, &c.

And when that dinner was ended
The maidens they were befriended
For out steps Dick the Draper
And he did strike up scraper,
Its best to be dancing a little
And then to the tavern and tipple
He called for a horn-pipe,
That went fine on the bag-pipe
Then forward Piper and play
For the honour of Arthur of Bradly, &c.

Richard he did lead it
And Margery did tread it
Francis following then
And after courteous Jane
Thus every one after another;
As if they had been sister and brother,
That it was great joy to see,
How well they did agree
And then they all did say
For the honor of Arthur of Bradly, &c.

Then Miles in his motly breeches
And he the piper beseeches
To play him Haw thorn buds
That he and his wench might trudge,
But Laurence liked not that
No more did lusty Kate
For she cry'd, canst thou not hit it
To see how fine Thomas can trip it,
For the honor of Arthur of Bradly
O brave Arthur of Bradly

Figure 33. Ballad sheet facsimile, "A merry Wedding Or, O Brave *Arthur of Bradly*" (c. 1660–1700), EBBA 31690. University of Glasgow Library, Euing Ballads 214. By permission of University of Glasgow Library, Special Collections.

such a woodcut for the Arthur of Bradly wedding celebration, might seem silly, in the sense of downright ludicrous. What could possibly justify such an association? Does the Bradly woodcut in fact vindicate the long-standing judgment that ballad illustrations were randomly chosen by printers and often disconnected to the accompanying narrative or song? The answer, and also the rebuttal, to this position lies in Arthur's own silly (ignorant, simple-minded, and yet innocent) high esteem of himself. Recall that in declaring his love for the ugly maid he passingly encounters, whom he then promptly weds, Arthur affiliates himself with royalty: he affirms, "For 'tis love conquers kings." In this delusional context, the high style of the woodcut figures, supposedly representing Arthur and his bride, might in fact go so far as to recall for some viewers the royal wedding of Frederick and Elizabeth—but not randomly. Such an associational hit tactically strikes home. It hilariously exemplifies Arthur's bombastic sense of his self-importance. As amusingly, it figures forth the quixotic high esteem in which Arthur's fellow villagers hold him, repeatedly echoed in the ballad's refrains, "O brave Arthur of Bradly" and "For the honor of Arthur of Bradly."

The variant refrains—all of which raise Arthur to noble, or at least most high, status—are so echoed within and between the Arthur of Bradly ballads that they feel like a sung chorus. Unfortunately, the "pleasant new Tune" referenced on the Arthur marriage ballad sheets is untraceable to the period, according to the authority, Simpson and EBBA's own efforts to track it down (though extant versions surface in later centuries, which Chappell references in *Popular Music*, 2.540). But even without a surviving seventeenth-century or earlier tune to draw upon for singing the Arthur ballads, their catchy refrain resounds in one's head in a way that takes on a musical as well as poetic rhythmic beat. Part of its "sticking" power is its absurdity. What has a simpleton, who asks for an ugly bumpkin's hand in marriage, and the subsequent rustic and rowdy celebration of his marriage, got to do with bravery or honor? Especially memorable is the slip-song variant (EBBA 30998), spoken in the voice of Arthur, which belabors his grandeur in a notable extension upon the now familiar refrain, "For my name it is Arthur o'Bradley O, / O *rare* Arthur o'Bradly, / O *fine* Arthur o'Bradley, O" (my emphases). Taken together, all the refrains, considered within the narrative context of the Arthur of Bradly ballads—celebrating our hero with such outlandish honorifics as "honor," "brave," "rare," and "fine"—are so outlandish that they good-humoredly mock Arthur and his community. At one level, we imagine a truly delusional, pompous, simpleminded country yokel—dubbed by Ebsworth a "swaggering royster" (*Roxburghe Ballads*, 7.313)—while at another level, we cannot but embrace Arthur's joyful and, importantly, communally sanctioned self-promotion (enthusiastically adopted by his common-folk peers). We may not be believers in Arthur's grandeur, but we can nevertheless thoroughly enjoy the rustic, good-natured, and completely oblivious ballad paeans to him in which his entire community takes part.

If we return, then, to Pepys's recounting of himself and Esther laughingly recalling Arthur of Bradly in mocking Esther's husband Roger, we might not only think of their heartless cruelty in the face of his cousin's and her husband's deep human suffering for Roger's severely ill servant but also recognize that their invocation of the Arthur of Bradly ballads, through mockery, is itself good-natured and also creates a social and, in many senses of the word, communal and "common" bond between Pepys and Esther. That social and gender-crossing bond, created through the Arthur of Bradly allusion, is especially notable because Esther is herself very plain and down-to-earth in her manners, according to Pepys. She is someone who might well fit in with the simple country folk made fun of in the Arthur of Bradly ballads. It is as if Pepys at this moment is solidifying his own earthiness as well as his acceptance of Esther, Roger's latest (and fourth!) bride, into the family circle by joining with her in invoking the Arthur of Bradly ballads.

But such ballad-made solidarity is also a destabilizing moment for us as readers, and perhaps also insidiously and thus tactically intended to be so by Pepys and even Esther. That is, we are not exactly sure whom or what is being mocked at this moment. Pepys says "my Cozen his wife [Esther] and I did make mirth of it, and call *him* Arthur of Bradly" (my emphasis). At one level, the "him" they are making fun of is clearly the servant, Arthur, who in Esther and Pepys's estimation, is being unduly raised in status by cousin Roger's overly great concern for him. But there is another, latent, and perhaps tactically subliminal suggestion in Pepys's indeterminate referent of "him" in his *Diary*—"and call *him* Arthur of Bradly"—which Roger's down-to-earth wife might well embrace along with her in-law Pepys. Could it be that, in echoing the title about the puffed-up Arthur of Bradly, the two are also making fun of Roger himself? Are they mocking him not only for overevaluating his lowly servant's importance but perhaps for himself being at times somewhat of a delusional and pompous figure, like Arthur of Bradly? Thinking along these lines, we should note that "Roger" in the period was itself one of those "whassup" names for "a male person of a particular class," specifically "manservant" (*OED*, "Roger," 2a); Roger, that is, could well stand in for his servant Arthur. In his *Diary*, Pepys often expresses a liking for his country-bred cousin Roger, whose acquired skills as a lawyer and member of Parliament Pepys depended upon for advice and news. But Pepys also refers to Roger as "ordinary" (November 19, 1664, 4.389) and "simple" (December 21, 1664, 5.351), reminiscent of Arthur of Bradly. There are also repeated hints in the *Diary* that Pepys disapproved of Roger's country-bred-turned-"sober" Puritanism that is haughtily and self-righteously critical of all things to do with the delights of the court and its cavaliers (August 4, 1661, 2.147). Such court indulgences by this point in his *Diary* were very much a part of Pepys's common experience and livelihood once he had been raised to the status of Secretary of the Admiralty. Cousin Roger, in sum, exudes an Arthur-like self-inflation but one that is in no way innocent and good-natured, especially from Pepys's perspective; by virtue of his job, Pepys had to at least partially align himself with the court that Roger so self-righteously condemns.

In a similar, though not necessarily self-consciously aligned perspective, Pepys's favorite playwright, Ben Jonson, in *Bartholomew Fair* (1614), mocks Justice Overdo's almost puritanical high-minded righteousness in attending the play's fair in disguise. Overdo's intent aligns well with cousin Roger's attitude to the Caroline court: to expose and correct all the fair's sinful "enormity." When Ursula, the lowlife pig-booth lady, asks her servant Mooncalf, "What new roarer is this?," referring to the appearance of Overdo ranting against "enormity" at her booth, Mooncalf mockingly answers, "O Lord! Do you not know him, Mistris? 'tis mad Arthur of Bradley, that makes the orations. Brave Master, old Arthur of Bradley, how do you?" (2.2). A slippage has occurred here, common to broadside ballads and performance generally. The pompous country bumpkin who thinks so highly of himself as "Brave" but also communally embraces raucous drunken dancing and the piles of food contributed by the local community to his marriage frivolity, has been turned by Jonson into a self-important condemner of just such indulgence. In the self-righteous Justice Overdo's disapproval of Bartholomew Fair's festivities, we witness again the upsetting of Arthur of Bradly's welcoming of such pleasures that we saw in Pepys's cousin Roger taking a "high" judgmental stance against what he sees as the fripperies of the Caroline court.[11]

Unlike such self-elevating types, Roger's fourth wife, Esther, as noted above, represents to Pepys what is likeable about plain, everyday, life-embracing commoners. She is akin to most of the fairgoers in Jonson's *Bartholomew Fair* and could likely easily commingle with Arthur of Bradly and his community of country yokels in the ballads that celebrate him. In Pepys's mind, Esther is "a wonderful merry, good-humoured, fat, but plain woman, but I believe a very good woman" (January 4, 1669; 9.407). Thus, when Pepys and Esther, in response to cousin Roger's somber echoing of lament over his manservant's health, evoke the many Arthur of Bradley ballads' ego-inflating double refrain—"O brave Arthur of Bradly" and "For the honor of Arthur of Bradly"—they spontaneously unite in a tactical double play. On the sly, they tactically bond in a mini-public that criticizes all pompous simpleminded sorts *not only of the lower orders but also of the socially high, especially those self-elevating sorts who are politically/religiously high-minded.* The lowly Esther and the aspiring Pepys in this moment become two unlikely comrades. United as one voice, they transcend gender conflicts, despite their opposite sexes. They conspire together, cousin and wife both good naturedly enjoying while mocking the Arthur of Bradlys of this world, and thus opening themselves up to embrace (and be embraced by) a larger lowly ballad public who would think in like mind.

Private Gendered Publics

Pepys could also self-reflexively cite conventional "whassup" ballad characters and "answer" formats tactically—to even more sly and spur-of-the-moment performative purposes. That is, he seized opportunities to use common ballad features for his own intimate ends. He did so sometimes to create a very private-public between knowing ballad aficionados. At a dinner party at Lord William Brouncker's on January 2, 1666, for instance, he meets the actress Elizabeth Knepp, who sings for the group the ballad "Barbara Allen." Unfortunately, despite its being passed down through the centuries, both before and after the early modern period, and its availability today in numerous modern variants, no verifiable seventeenth-century version of the tune has been found. No ballad by that title and to that named tune was even registered with the Stationers' Company, 1557–1709.[12] Nevertheless, many black-letter copies of the ballad survive, published as early as 1675 by the ballad partners Brooksby, Dean, Blare, and Back. It is titled, in full, "Barbara Allen's Cruelty: Or, The Young-man's Tragedy. With *Barbara Allen's* Lamentation for her Unkindness to her Lover, and her Self. To the Tune of Barbara Allen." See, for example, EBBA 35105 (Figure 34). The ballad relates the story of a young man dying from unrequited love for Barbara Allen, whose name echoes throughout each stanza, often punctuating the stanza like a refrain or "whassup" catchword. She is summoned by the rejected lover's "man," or servant, to his deathbed. But she only reluctantly attends—"So slowly, slowly . . . so slowly"—and, on arriving, heartlessly says, "Young man I think you are a dying" (st. 6). On later seeing his corpse being carried to burial, she asks that it be set down before her and cruelly "all the while she looked on, / so loudly she lay laughing" (st. 12). But, in typical ballad logic, as soon as the youth is buried, Barbara Allen is stricken with grief and regret, and dies swiftly after, crying out, "O Mother! Mother! Make my Bed / for his death hath quite undone me" (st. 13).

In the text to this ballad, women dominate, from the echoing "whassup"-ing of the name Barbara Allen in the stanzas leading up to her change of heart in the last three stanzas, to her repeated call out to her mother, marking her reversal of affect. So, too, women are prominently featured in the illustrations of the earliest and even in later extant editions of the broadside ballad.[13] Appearing atop the first two columns of stanzas are two woodcut impressions, consisting of a large picture of a huge black-draped coffin carried by three women. Beside and facing this scene, but significantly standing in a separate—that is, removed—woodcut illustration, is the figure of a woman, whom the viewer would assume is Barbara Allen. As in the narrative, she has a smile on her

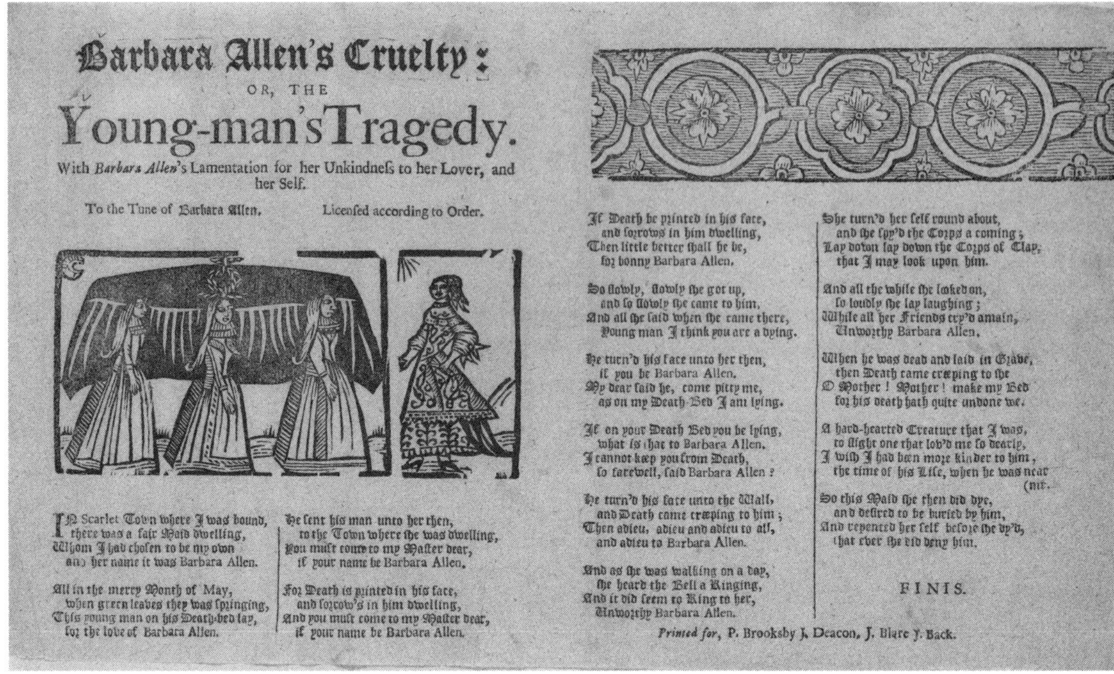

Barbara Allen's Cruelty:
OR, THE
Young-man's Tragedy.
With *Barbara Allen*'s Lamentation for her Unkindness to her Lover, and her Self.

To the Tune of Barbara Allen. Licensed according to Order.

In Scarlet Town where I was bound,
there was a fair Maid dwelling,
Whom I had chosen to be my own
and her name it was Barbara Allen.

All in the merry Month of May,
when green leaves they was springing,
This young man on his Death-bed lay,
for the love of Barbara Allen.

He sent his man unto her then,
to the Town where she was dwelling,
You must come to my Master dear,
if your name be Barbara Allen.

For Death is printed in his face,
and sorrow's in him dwelling,
And you must come to my Master dear,
if your name be Barbara Allen.

If Death be printed in his face,
and sorrows in him dwelling,
Then little better shall he be,
for bonny Barbara Allen.

So slowly, slowly she got up,
and so slowly she came to him,
And all she said when she came there,
Young man I think you are a dying.

He turn'd his face unto her then,
if you be Barbara Allen.
My dear said he, come pitty me,
as on my Death-Bed I am lying.

If on your Death Bed you be lying,
what is that to Barbara Allen.
I cannot keep you from Death,
so farewell, said Barbara Allen?

He turn'd his face unto the Wall,
and Death came creeping to him;
Then adieu, adieu and adieu to all,
and adieu to Barbara Allen.

And as she was walking on a day,
she heard the Bell a Ringing,
And it did seem to Ring to her,
Unworthy Barbara Allen.

She turn'd her self round about,
and she spy'd the Corps a coming;
Lay down lay down the Corps of Clay,
that I may look upon him.

And all the while she looked on,
so loudly she lay laughing;
While all her Friends cry'd amain,
Unworthy Barbara Allen.

When he was dead and laid in Grave,
then Death came creeping to she
O Mother! Mother! make my Bed
for his death hath quite undone me.

A hard-hearted Creature that I was,
to slight one that lov'd me so dearly,
I wish I had been more kinder to him,
the time of his Life, when he was near (me.

So this Maid she then did dye,
and desired to be buried by him,
And repented her self before she dy'd,
that ever she did deny him.

FINIS.

Printed for, P. Brooksby J. Deacon, J. Blare J. Back.

Figure 34. Ballad sheet facsimile, "Barbara Allen's Cruelty: OR, THE Young-man's Tragedy. . . . " (c. 1675–96), EBBA 35105. Houghton Library, Harvard University, EBB65H. Public domain.

face. Above the last two columns of verse is a large header ornament picturing a row of decorative flowers, traditionally perceived to be "feminine," obliquely alluding to Barbara Allen herself succumbing belatedly to love/remorse for the now dead young man.

Whether Pepys knew this ballad, either in broadside form or from oral tradition, before he heard it sung by Elizabeth Knepp, we cannot say for sure. The song gained its legendary fame in the eighteenth century, when Bishop Percy published his version of "Barbara Allen" in *Reliques of Ancient Poetry* (1765; 2.131–33), and the ballad has remained extremely popular since. But regardless of whether Pepys encountered it before he wrote about hearing the ballad sung, he declares he experienced "perfect pleasure . . . to hear her [Knepp] sing, and especially her little Scotch song" (7.1). As Chappell and Ebsworth note, the term "Scotch" had become "a polite substitution for 'rustic.'" This interchangeability of the terms likely began, they add, around the reign of Charles II. Charles was pronounced king of both England and Scotland (a title his father aspired to before him); thus ballads that had been titled "Northern" previous to Charles II's ascension, were subsequently called instead "Scotch" (*Roxburghe Ballads*, 3.433). Likely Pepys's "perfect pleasure" on hearing the ballad sung by Knepp was heightened by the ballad's down-to-earth rustic "Scottishness"—just as Pepys was drawn to the earthy Esther and the countrified "Arthur of Bradly" ballad in the incident Pepys recounts above. Pepys may well also have been attracted to the comeuppance to the brief empowerment of women, which the "Barbara Allen" ballad stresses; yes, the young maid controls the fate of the love-stricken youth (as do the women figured in the illustrations), but in the end the heroine is self-punished. Appropriately repentant for spurning the youth's love, she dies of grief and is laid in the ground beside him. But what likely most filled Pepys with "perfect pleasure" was hearing the beautiful and talented in-the-flesh actress, Mrs. Knepp, sing the ballad.

And so began an infatuation on Pepys's part that became a mutual flirtation and sexual dalliance facilitated through both Pepys and Knepp slyly adopting ballad characters. Three days after being enraptured by Knepp's singing "Barbara Allen," on January 5, 1666, Pepys traveled to Greenwich to another dinner party, hoping to "get" Mrs. Knepp, but she was busy. Her substitute? She sent Pepys "a pleasant letter, writing her [that is, signed by her] *Barbary Allen*" (*Diary*, 7.4). Given Knepp's reference to the ballad she had earlier sung in signing an alias for her real name—a ballad that reports a maid's regret on not returning the love of a smitten young man—Pepys would certainly have understood the charged meaning of Knepp's signature. The next day at a "great dinner" at Greenwich with "much company," Pepys again missed getting Knepp, and was especially frustrated because he "wrote a letter to her in the morning, calling myself *Dapper Dicky* in answer to hers of *Barb. Allen*" (7.5). "Dapper Dicky" is the title of another plaintive Scottish ballad, one in which a maid laments her lover's absence (7.5n.3).

What are Pepys and Knepp doing? They are self-consciously inhabiting a ballad public that allows them (and anyone else) to capitalize on the ballad's popular back-and-forth "answer" format and "whassup"-like catchwords, as well as the genre's formulas of echoing names and subgenre of age-old stories of forsaken love. They are also voicing ballad roles and playing with them to their own personal but still potentially public ends (since anyone seeing these letters or hearing Knepp and Pepys adopt their ballad personae would likely know exactly what the two were about). They made a ballad public of lamentable love turned to sexual courting.

Little did Pepys and Knepp know, but what was likely to them a sly tactical ploy of secretly using familiar ballads and ballad formats to flirt (to the extent that Pepys reverses his gender and adopts the role of the maid in the Dapper Dicky ballad) was not a kept secret at all. This is, of course, ironically true of Pepys's entire *Diary*, now published both in print and online, and thus globally readable by millions. He had apparently composed the *Diary* for himself privately to reread and relive his daily experiences, including his many titillating delights. It was not intended for publication or public scrutiny. But, in his drive to assemble all things, Pepys kept the volumes of the unpublished Diary in his library, which he bequeathed to the public, giving more than he expected.

Perhaps most ironic, the digitally published *Diary* has become readily available to all in an ingenious public-making blog created by Phil Gyford, www.pepysdiary.com.[14] The blog invites users to inhabit the *Diary* on an experiential day-by-day basis. It cycles through the days of the year in the *Diary*'s nearly ten years of entries, and opens up to the same month and numbered day of the *Diary* as that lived in by the modern user. So, for instance, if you visit the site on a February 22, as I did, the blog opens to Pepys's entry also for a February 22 (of whatever year in the *Diary* the blog is currently displaying in its cycle). The site also invites users to join in the events they read about and make comments (retitled by Gyford "Annotations"). The blog thus allows its public to occupy Pepys's *Diary* as if in real time and as if included in his private circle. We see a spectrum of involvement in the blog's annotations. Many comments are made by regular visitors to the site, but those notations range from the scholarly to the colloquial to the joking (evident at the simplest level in those who call Pepys, on the one end of the spectrum, by his last name and those who refer to him, on the other, as if he were a buddy—"Sam").

In one of the more scholarly annotations, made by Terry Foreman, we realize how the passing moment of bonding via familiar ballad personae as adapted by Pepys and Knepp was more momentous and enduring than either of them could ever have expected. Foreman points out to other visitors of the site that the Barbara Allen and Dapper Dicky incident was incorporated into Louis Napoleon Parker's 1916 play, *Mavourneen*. The playwright beautifully captures the "whassup" nature of circulating ballad roles. In act 3, the character Pepys emerges from the bushes having tousled with Mary Mercer (historically his wife's real-life companion with whom Pepys did in fact sexually dally). Pepys in the play hums a song for Mercer. But what the play-character Pepys does not know is that his wife has just come out of a shop and overhears them. Mercer exclaims about the song, "Lord, 'tis properly sentimental," and Pepys responds, holding Mercer's chin in his hands, "Dapper Dicky always was sentimental . . . We'll be merry, eh, chuck? [*Chucks her under the chin.*] You and Dapper Dicky." In a rage, Pepys's wife dismisses Mercer and goes on the offensive by taunting Pepys with "whassup"-like repetitions of his reference to himself as Dapper Dicky: "Ho! 'Dapper Dicky'—! . . . 'Dapper Dicky!,'" she knowingly derides. Clearly in this early twentieth-century play, which now mockingly undercuts the sentimental role-playing by Pepys of over 300 years earlier, the name alone of "Dapper Dicky" still carries reflexive collective meaning about romanticized sexual performativity; however, the original incident was supposedly meant to be a private public.[15]

Even Robert Louis Stevenson participated in the long historical reach of the public made by Pepys in playing the "romantic" role of the ballad character Dapper Dicky to Knepp's Barbara Allen. Stevenson does so in his *Familiar Studies of Men and Books*, within the context of ruminating on the nature of humans to create different roles in adapting to circumstances. His commentary merits quoting in full as conclusion to this chapter:

> We all, whether we write or speak, must somewhat drape ourselves when we address our fellows; at a given moment we apprehend our character and acts by some particular side; we are merry with one, grave with another, as befits the nature and demands of the relation. Pepys's letter to Evelyn would have little in common with that other one to Mrs. Knipp which he signed by the pseudonym of DAPPER DICKY; yet each would be suitable to the character of his correspondent. There is no untruth in this, for man, being a Protean animal, swiftly shares and changes with his company and surroundings; and these changes are the better part of his education in the world. To strike a posture once for all, and to march through life like a drum-major, is to be highly disagreeable to others and a fool for oneself into the bargain. To Evelyn and to Knipp we understand the double facing; but to whom was he posing in the Diary, and what, in the name of astonishment, was the nature of the pose?[16]

Stevenson's shrewd observation about the protean role-playing of humans well applies to ballad reception and, more generally, to ballad public adoption and making in the early modern period. For when it comes to ballads, there is a large publicly available reservoir of tunes, illustrations, and texts; from this reservoir there emerged especially popular and widespread "whassup" formats, idioms, and catchphrases that could be reflexively and tactically employed or *posed* by both producers and consumers alike.

In this chapter, we have focused on the way Pepys capitalized on such commonly accessible and popular "whassups" in his making of gendered publics.

Most of these publics are quite intimate. But they always draw on the larger ballad public in which Pepys and the masses were active and knowledgeable participants. We can never leave behind "whassup"-like ballad catchphrases that were part of the popular, if ephemeral, associative hits that early modern contemporaries could at any moment in time have made individually and as a group. Not all such publics are gendered or—in a cross-gendered way—personal in the making. In the next chapter, we will further widen our gaze from intimate circles to national spheres, and we will consider how known ballad types, formulas, and media could in fact be turned more broadly to pressing political issues that had expansive reach. At this, Pepys was also a master.

CHAPTER 7 ❧

Pepys and the Making of Political Publics

This chapter allows us not only to turn our gaze from gender to political publics but also to span differently sized publics in the making. The largest such public we will examine is accessible to us, ironically, through the perspective of Pepys while alone, ruminating on a much publicly disseminated ballad as he traveled by boat up the Thames. Of course, one can never leave gender behind, and certainly sex was almost always on Pepys's mind, even when he was attending a politically laden event. Furthermore, as Christopher Marsh has demonstrated in his masterful chapter on ballad music (*Music and Society*, 308–18 and passim), tunes associated with sex were often tactically turned to political uses, both serious and parodic. In this chapter, we will certainly see gender and sex entwine with politics, especially in the first section on making a national voice. But we will also track the serious work (and play) broadside ballads could perform in the making of political ballad publics. Worth recalling, in this light, are John Selden's words, written in the first half of the seventeenth century and transcribed by Pepys in the front matter of his ballad collection (EBBA 32622): "Though some might make slight of Libells [using the word, as previously noted, in its earliest sense: "a short treatise or writing"; *OED*, 1a]; yet you may see by them, how the Wind sits. As take a Straw, and throw it up into the Air; you shall see by that, which way the Wind is; —which you shall not do so, by casting up a Stone. More Solid things do not shew the Complexion of the Times, so well as Ballads and Libells." Broadside ballads, like straws thrown into the air, can tell us which way the political wind is blowing. Later in the seventeenth century, Andrew Fletcher expressed a similar, though more expansive observation: "if a man were permitted to make all the ballads, he need not care who should make the laws of a nation" (*Political Works*, 266).

Pepys and those with whom he interacted—even beyond his sphere of personal contact—took such sentiment very much to heart, whether in the course of assembling ballads in the print shop or consuming (and mentally reassembling) them on the streets. Fortunately, key political ballads discussed in this chapter have extant tunes; we will thus be able to examine how contemporaries reworked all the media of broadside ballads toward their engaging in and making of political ballad publics.

Political Publics: On the Wave of a National Voice

I begin by revisiting a performance of male bonding but now laden with political valence. This incident also allows us to study more deeply how tunes can play a defining part in making large ballad publics. The date is April 23, 1660, and we are on board the flagship *Naseby*, commanded by Lord Edward Montagu. Also aboard is Samuel Pepys, newly elevated from Montagu's clerk to his secretary, and Will Howe, a more junior clerk in Montagu's service. They have embarked on the momentous expedition to bring back Charles Stuart from Holland to be crowned King Charles II of England. In an evening of "extraordinary good sport" aboard the ship, Pepys reports, Montagu called for Pepys and Howe to play their treble viols, and he joins in with his own bass viol. Seemingly inspired by the music and the other festivities, Montagu then bursts into song: he "fell to singing of a song made upon the Rump, with which he pleased himself well—to the tune of *The Blacksmith*" (*Diary*, 1.114).

This ballad singing by Montagu, while one might think an inconsequential part of the shipboard "sport," marked a moment of high reflexive performativity on Montagu's part. Though singing solo, Montagu well knows he has a captive (if floating) audience; indeed, Pepys and Howe, and likely others within earshot, could well have joined Montagu in the pleasing ballad song, given the participatory nature of ballad singing and even listening. The ballad sung would certainly have been *anti*-Rump.[1] The Presbyterian Rump was first formed in 1648 when Colonel Thomas Pride, acting for the New Model Army, purged the Long Parliament of all members who resisted deposing Charles I. In the course of the subsequent Commonwealth period, the Rump became internally divided, increasingly ineffectual, and much vilified. Royalist and then more general attacks on the Rump invoked crude comparisons to buttocks productive only of smelly farts and turds. Pepys notes that "Boys do now cry 'Kiss my Parliament' instead of 'Kiss my arse,' so great and general a contempt is the Rump come to among all men, good and bad" (1.45). "Rump" had become its own multivalent "whassup" catchword reflexively used by contemporaries.

But when on October 13, 1659, the Rump was locked out of Westminster by Major General John Lambert, acting as head of an army junta, anarchy threatened. City authorities appealed to General George Monck, commander of the Republican army in Scotland, who declared in favor of the Rump and began marching South. Support for Lambert quickly dissolved and the Rump was reinstated. Still, no one knew what the final outcome would be as powerful figures maneuvered secretly in a high stakes political game. To the relief of the city, when Monck arrived in London in February 1660, he asserted his authority over the Rump and demanded free elections.[2] Inevitable to future stability, most now believed, was the restoration of the monarchy. But Montagu, like many others, kept his thoughts guarded. It wasn't until as late as March 6, 1660, that he took Pepys into his confidence. Montagu asked Pepys to be his secretary because, he said, he "needed someone he could trust" to accompany him on what he expected would be an expedition to restore the king in recognition of "the affection of the people and City" (1.77). Montagu heartily voiced such recognition in singing his anti-Rump ballad aboard the *Naseby*. The politically laden song, joining in the overwhelming contempt for the Republican Parliament, would have been deeply meaningful especially for Pepys and Montagu. Both had been active supporters of Oliver Cromwell's Commonwealth. The anti-Rump song Montagu, and very likely Pepys in camaraderie, sang belied that allegiance, replacing it with a spontaneous open voicing of cross-class, if male-gendered, and political solidarity with both "the people" *and* the monarchy.

Of particular significance in this instance of social and political bonding through song is Pepys's naming of the tune to the anti-Rump ballad that Montagu sings: "*The Blacksmith*." Tunes slipped from ballad subject to ballad subject, as we have seen, along the way changing their names (and sometimes, like men of the times, as we observe here, their loyalties). The melody of "The Blacksmith" well supports such shape-shifting. The tune was originally titled "Greensleeves." Many versions of "Greensleeves" ballads from the period are extant. The earliest English adaptation appears in an edition by Clement Robinson et al, printed by Richard Jones four years after Jones first registered the ballad in 1580 under a different title. The newly titled "Greensleeves" ballad appears in Robinson's expanded miscellany of ballads, *A Handefull of Pleasant Delites* (1584), again printed by Jones, and can be heard sung on **Track 24**.[3] Akin to "Barbara Allen," the ballad tells yet another story of spurned love but with the suggestion that the lady had returned her lover's affection before "casting him off." It seems like you can't get away from gender or sex. The jilted lover begins bemoaning that

Alas my love, ye do me wrong,
to cast me off discurteously:
And I have loved you so long,
Delighting in your companie.
[Refrain:]
Greensleeves was all my joy,
Greensleeves was my delight:
Greensleeves was my heart of gold,
And who but Ladie Greensleeves. (B2r)

It would appear from the lover's subsequent relation, especially in stanza 3, that the scornful lady has in fact been a "kept," if handsomely kept, woman. Bemoaning his spurned fate, the male lover—clearly a man of means and fashion—laments,

I bought thee kerchers [kerchiefs] to thy head,
that were wrought fine and gallantly:
I kept thee both at boord and bed,
Which cost my purse well favouredly
[Refrain follows]. (B2r and B2v)

By the early seventeenth century, the implication that the greensleeved lady was a "kept woman" rendered the term "Greensleeves" into a common metaphor for a fashionably dressed courtesan (Simpson, 271).[4]

But the ballad "Greensleeves," like a concubine, was most slippery in its allegiances. From the outset, it was two faced, registered *twice* on the same day, September 3, 1580, by two different printers under two different namings: "A newe northern Dittye of the Ladye Greene Sleves," by Richard Jones, and "The Ladie Greene Sleeves answere to Donkyn hir frende," by Edward White.[5] And so began a dizzying gold-rush grab for the "Greensleeves" title, tune, and text. Even the godly got in on the frenzy, and within twelve days of the first entry of love ballads, obtained a license for "Greene Sleves moralized." None of these earliest registered ballads survives. But we know that other early extant "Greensleeves" ballads soon turned the theme of sexual betrayal into national treachery or treason. It thus appears at first glance a truly odd slippage by which "Greensleeves" became the tune for James Smith's 1656 celebration of the trade of blacksmiths (which Pepys added to his ballad collection in a later edition, c. 1663–74). Smith's "Blacksmith" ballad became so popular that it effected a renaming of the "Greensleeves" melody, as cited by Pepys in describing Montagu's anti-Rump song—"To the tune of *The Blacksmith*." In a nutshell, as Simpson observes, "'Greensleeves' . . . appealed to a wide variety of publics" (Simpson, 273).

But what explains such a wide appeal? And what, if anything, causes the tune's particular turn to political publics, and Royalist publics at that, especially since it began as a love song? Part of the turn to politics aligned with monarchy likely had to do with the song's origins in the French court before it emigrated to England and became both naturalized and popularized there—to the point of being associated with much-loved, lowly English jigs and morris dances. The political turn to the court may have been further bolstered by the focus of the earliest registered "Greensleeves" ballad in England, or at least by Jones's 1584 printing of it, under the title, "A new *Courtly Sonet*, of the Lady Green sleeves" (my emphasis).[6] As in the ballad's being renamed a "Courtly Sonnet," the lady's would-be lover would appear to be at home at court. He certainly has considerable means to woo his lady in rich, courtly fashion. Such elite associations are not all flattering—the fashionable lady love, after all, is a kept woman. But so for a time was Anne Boleyn.[7] It is in the nature of ballad slippages to become "messy." However, we can still see how the origins of the tune in the French court and the elevated, fashionable status of wooer and lady in the earliest extant English versions of the ballad might have led cavaliers to consider it a fitting "high" melody for their Royalist cause. The slippage to songs about treason (given the beheading of Charles I) further fits that cause. But so did the apparently odd slippage to ballads about tradesmen, which followed upon James Smith's "The Blacksmith" ([J]ohn [P]hillips, et al, *Wit and Drollery*, 1656). The topic of these broadside ballads, together with the subsequent renaming of their tune as "The Blacksmith," fits not only politics but specifically political parodies of parliamentarians. That is, there is a tactically barbed allusion behind craft-specific ballads sung to "Greensleeves." The mockery lies in the fact that Oliver Cromwell was from a family of tradesmen; they were brewers. Thus, we find a host of late Commonwealth ballads attacking Oliver and particularly Richard Cromwell, his incompetent son and successor as of 1658, with such titles as "The Brewer" (1658 or 1659) and "The Protecting Brewer" (c. 1657). The "Blacksmith" ballads, it would seem, follow precisely this sly mocking vein, despite their ostensible praise of blacksmiths.

At the level of melody there is another reason for the immense popularity of the tune "Greensleeves" before it was transformed into "The Blacksmith" and turned to the political. The earliest extant notation of the tune[8] well fits the eight-line stanzas, including four lines of refrain, of the earliest extant "Greensleeves" text printed in *A Handefull of Pleasant Delites*, which we discussed above. Bell adapts that notation, in minor, to fit this text (and vice versa) in his recording of the ballad on **Track 24**. As we observed in Chapters 2 and 3, the minor can fittingly convey the lament expressed by the lover in the original "Greensleeves" ballad. Such is certainly the case to our modern ears, and was likely increasingly so to the ears of early modern contemporaries. This is by no means a rule, we have noted, especially when a ballad's text and illustrations are taken into account. But the gradual movement in the seventeenth century away from multiple modes toward today's major/minor tonality, and the accompanying association of major/minor in the period generally with upbeat/downcast affect, supports expressions of complaint, sorrow, or at least a very somber tone.

Tunes of lament can be as widely embraced and catchy as tunes of celebration—the enormous appeal of the goodnight scaffold melody "Fortune my Foe" is a case in point. But the particular composition of "Greensleeves" especially fostered its immense and long-term popularity. To begin with, "Greensleeves" is very singable. One wouldn't need to be a trained or particularly talented singer to sing it. One phrase or unit of music (like a sentence or line of verse) leads into the next phrase in an easy, flowing way. Nor are there any abrupt or unexpected shifts in the phrases from one note to another. Indeed, the range of the tune is no more than a minor thirteenth, which, as we have observed, is within a comfortable reach for an average person's voice. The one very notable leap in the melody occurs at the beginning of the first and third lines of the refrain (lines 5 and 7 of the poetic text), with the leap from a low D to the high F that lands on the music's metrically emphatic "***Green***" in "Greensleeves." This leap conveys additional phenomenal stress to the already musically as well as poetically accented title word. It is literally the high point of the lament—like a wail—in the song. Repeated twice in the refrain that concludes each stanza, the leap comes to be almost anxiously anticipated as an expression of heightened affect. Finally, there is a pleasing balance in the melody between repetition and novelty throughout, which adds to the twinning of reassurance with expectation.

What lends the melody of "Greensleeves" to trade songs and to political songs in particular—even into a host of ballad operas—is the shortened version by which it can be sung (to four lines of poetry instead of the original eight), as exemplified in Smith's "The Blacksmith" ballad. The earliest known example of this abbreviation of the tune is in the Gamble manuscript of 1659, rendered into modern notation below:

In this shortened and now Dorian version of "Greensleeves," the second and third phrases of the original music (which constitute the last half of the stanza and the first half of the refrain, respectively) are dropped. The first and last phrases are also slightly altered. The changes, as we shall see and hear, when sung to a similarly abbreviated poetic text, allow a singer to adeptly hammer home a political or satirical theme or a short ditty for the stage. Indeed, not only the four-line stanzas of the "Blacksmith" ballads but also most of the political ballads—especially anti-Rump ones—fit this shortened variant of the tune. Consider, for instance, the white-letter political broadside ballad, "The Re-Resurrection of the Rump: Or, Rebellion and Tyranny revived. *The third Edition*," 1659 (Bridgewater, HEH 133299; EBBA 32128), in Figure 35. Following upon the fame of the first trade ballad, anti-Rump ballads, such as "The Re-Resurrection of the Rump"—abbreviated as if imitating the expunged and cut-down structure of the Rump Parliament—typically renamed their melody after the tradesman ballad, "The Blacksmith." Alternatively, the tune title was named after the refrain for the first "Blacksmith" ballad—"*Which nobody (or no body) can deny*"—which can be heard in the recording of the "The Re-Resurrection of the Rump" on **Track 25**. As Dr. Charlotte Becker has noted in conversation with me, "Which nobody can deny" shuts down comebacks. There is no room for an affective soaring register of the kind expressed in the leap to "***Green-***" in "Greensleeves" at the beginning of the now-deleted second and third phrases of the longer "Greensleeves" melody. The fourth line, which is the newly dwarfed refrain, constitutes a single affirmation: "Nobody can deny." End of conversation.

We can better understand how the shortened Dorian version of "Greensleeves" can be tactically turned in its singing into political parody by addressing a notation of the recording. Consider the first stanza of "The Re-Resurrection of the Rump." It consists of three lines of four poetic and musical metric stresses, rhyming AAA, followed by the abbreviated refrain—cut

17.

THE

RE-RESURRECTION Of the RUMP:

Or, Rebellion and Tyranny revived.

The third Edition. To the Tune of the Blacksmith.

IF none be offended with the Sent,
Though I foul my Mouth, Ile be content,
To sing of the Rump of a Parliament,
Which no body can deny.

I have sometimes fed on a Rump in Sowse,
And a man may imagine the Rump of a Lowse;
But till now was ne're heard of the Rump of a House,
Which no body can deny.

There's a Rump of Beefe, and the Rump of a Goose,
And a Rump whose Neck was hang'd in a Noose;
But ours is a Rump can play fast and loose,
Which no body can deny.

A Rump had *Jane Shore*, and a Rump *Messaleen*,
And a Rump had *Antonyes* resolute Queen;
But such a Rump as ours is, never was seen,
which no body can deny.

Two short years together we English have scarce
Been rid of thy rampant Nose (Old *Mars*)
But now thou hast got a prodigious Arse,
Which no body can deny.

When the parts of the Body did all fall out,
Some votes it is like did pass for the Snout;
But that the Rump should be King was never a doubt,
Which no body can deny.

A Cat has a Rump, and a Cat has nine Lives,
Yet when her heads off, her Rump never strives;
But our Rump from the grave hath made two Retrives,
Which no body can deny.

That the Rump may all their Enemies quail,
They'l borrow the Devils Coat of Mayl,
And all to defend their Estate in Tayl,
VVhich no body can deny.

But though their Scale now seem to be the Upper,
There's no need of the charge of a Thanksgiving supper,
For if they be the Rump, the Army's their Crupper,
VVhich no body can deny.

There is a saying belongs to the Rump,
Which is good, although it be worn to the Stump,
That on the Buttocks Ile give thee a Thump
VVhich no body can deny.

There's a Proverb in which the Rump claims a part,
Which hath in it more of Sence than of Art,
That for all you can do, I care not a Fart,
VVhich no body can deny.

There's another Proverb gives the Rump for his Crest,
But Alderman *Atkins* made it a Jest,
That of all kind of Lucks, shitten Luck is the best,
VVhich no body can deny.

There is another Proverb that never will fail,
That the good the Rump will do when they prevail,
Is to give us a Flop with a Fox-tail,
Which no body can deny.

There is a Saying which is made by no Fools;
I never can hear on't but my Heart it cools,
That the Rump will spend all we have in Close-Stoo's
Which no body can deny.

There's an Observation wise and deep,
Which without an Onion will make me to weep;
That Flyes will blow Maggots in the Rump of a Sheep,
Which no body can deny.

And some that can see the Wood from the Trees,
Say this Sanctify'd Rump in time we may leese;
For the Cooks do challenge the Rumps for their Fees.
Which no body can deny.

When the Rump do sit we will make it our Moane,
That a reason be 'nacted if there be not one,
Why a Fart hath a Tongue, and a Fyest hath none?
Which no body can deny.

And whil'st within the Walls they Lurk,
To satisfy us, will be a good work;
Who hath most Religion, the Rump, or the Turk,
Which no body can deny.

A Rump's a Fag-end, like the Baulk of a Furrow,
And is to the whole like the Jayl to the Burrough;
T'is the Bran that is left, when the Meal is run thorough
which no body can deny.

Consider the World, the Heav'n is the head on't,
The Earth is the middle, and we men are fed on't;
But Hell is the Rump, and no more can be fed on't.
VVhich no body can deny.

Flectere si nequeunt superos Acheronta movebunt.

FINIS, *In English*, The RUMP.

Figure 35. Ballad sheet facsimile, "The Re-Resurrection Of the Rump: Or, Rebellion and Tyranny revived. The third Edition" (1659), EBBA 32128. The Huntington Library, Bridgewater collection, HEH 133299. Public domain.

down not only in length from the original four-line version of "Greensleeves" but further shortened in poetic stresses from the previous lines to which it is attached (as indicated by its notable indentation). A kind of resistant outlier, the refrain also ends the stanzas on an unrhymed line:

> If none be offended with the Sent,
> Though I foul my Mouth, Ile be content,
> To sing of the Rump of a Parliament,
> Which nobody can deny. (st. 1)

As with all transcriptions of sung recordings in this book, you can follow along to the notation below as rendered in a slowed-down fiddle audio (provided on **Track 26** of the Audio Companion):

This transcription shows that the singer closely followed the Gamble MS notation, though he often had to divide half notes into two quarter notes and vice versa to make the number of syllables and notes accord.

Compared with the longer, minor variant of "Greensleeves," we might at first be struck by the unexpected raised sixth scale degree (E natural or E♮) in the first measure, which marks this shortened variant of the tune as Dorian. This raised note, which is the second of two notes devoted to a single syllable, "fend"—thus stretching out the word "of-*fend*-ed—gets a small boost in its level of musical metric accent in consisting of a quarter-note beat rather than the eighth note it occupies in the longer, minor "Greensleeves." The boost is then further charged by the durational tie of the syllable over not just one but two quarter notes. It also importantly gains a greater phenomenal entrance due to the E♮ note being a whole step neighboring tone above the D from which it arises and into which the final syllable "ed" falls. In the longer, minor "Greensleeves" version, this movement is only a half-step rise and fall

(D-E♭-D). Musical metric and phenomenal emphases here—impelled by the extended, three syllables of "offended" that demand attention through song—work to bolster and extend the already strong poetic emphasis on "*fend*" and the word that syllable anchors. This cagily chosen word, "of-*fend*-ed," is thus musically and poetically foregrounded right away in the ballad, underscoring the key point of the song about the Rump Parliament: its offensiveness.

The overall effect of the recording is to turn the poetic text even more into hard-hitting satire. This phenomenon is emphasized by two metrical tactics of the music that again bolster the poetic stresses. First, the shorter Dorian variant of the melody uses fewer neighboring and passing tones, thus repeating—one might say driving home—its notes and the poetic text they intone. The effect is considerably rougher than in its longer predecessor. Second, notwithstanding the necessity of adding notes to accommodate syllables in the parodic text, the shorter, Dorian variant of "Greensleeves" relies heavily upon rhythms of half notes followed by quarter notes, as opposed to the dotted-quarter-eighth-quarter-note rhythms often used in the longer minor variant. This simpler rhythm contributes to the choppiness of the tune (as opposed, for instance, to the more regular bounciness of "Northern Nancy" in the major mode). The unfaltering—one might go so far as to say "hammering"—poetic rhyme scheme of "The Blacksmith" (A-A-A-B, C-C-C-B, etc.) contributes yet more force to its musical melodic punch.[9]

Finally, I conclude this musical analysis, as does every poetic stanza of the shorter, Dorian variant of the melody, by concentrating on the poetic and musical phenomenal emphases in its single-line refrain, "Which ***no***-bod-y *can* de-***ny***." Here "***no***" is underscored. But through emphasis and repeated long musical notes, even more so is "***ny***" in "de-***ny***." Indeed, due to the music's metric demand for four stresses in this three-stress poetic line, it is necessary to combine a dotted half and half note into a single rhythmic duration, extending "***ny***" through two beats. "Ny" is etymologically most significant as well because it is a Middle English variant of "nay(e)." That is, it is a reiteration of "***no***" (*OED*, "deny," verb). "***No***" and "***ny***" definitively close the door on any thought of an effective or affective response to the political refrain. As noted above, no comeback is allowed. These musical and poetic as well as etymological emphases, serving to shut down discussion, are further affirmed by the refrain's inclusion of only a half-hearted—just one half note, lesser stress—on the word "*can*." Even more undermining, "can" falls awry on a sharp note. A positive response—a *yes* we "*can*"—is out of the ordinary notes of the melody. "***No***-bod-y can de-***ny***" rules. *All* are "of-***fend***-ed" by the Rump.

The political satire of "The Re-Resurrection of the Rump" is likely similar to the one Montagu sang for himself and his social inferiors. To the extent the lesser sorts on board the ship engaged with Montagu's song, even if only affectively or cognitively, they became momentarily equals with him in the trade of mocking the ever-so-offensive—farty, smelly, turdy, buttocky—Rump parliament. The once tragic (or at least lamentable) love tune has perfectly mutated into a melody for the performance of male solidarity on both political and social terms. All aboard ship—commander, servants, and common seamen—who sang or simply listened to such singing became part of the fleeting making of a political public in which they were all workers in the trade of a nationalist and Royalist cause.

Private Political Publics

Politics is not always so transparent and open in the singing of ballads, however. In another, very different social occasion, at a large dinner party hosted by Lord Brouncker on January 2, 1665, Pepys turned popular knowledge of ballad content into an inside joke among the guests. For those more acutely sensitive to the historical moment, the joke could also have been interpreted as a nuanced personal and political jab. Pepys brought along to the party a broadside ballad, and was most pleased with its reception. He writes, "I occasioned much mirth with a ballet [ballad] I brought with me, made from the seamen at sea to their ladies in town—saying Sir W Penn, Sir G Ascue, and Sir J Lawson made them" (*Diary*, 6.2). More than likely, given his almost daily singing of songs after dinner, Pepys did not simply pass the ballad around but orally performed it.

It is unclear whether the "much mirth" at the party here ensued from the ballad itself or from Pepys's tongue-in-cheek naming of its authors as Sir William Penn, Sir George Ascue, and Sir John Lawson—all not writers of poetry or song but prominent naval commanders (10.312–13, 14, 229).[10] The actual author of the ballad, as most at the dinner party would have known, was Charles Sackville, later 6th Earl of Dorset, a well-known court and satiric wit. The ballad had been entered into the Stationers' Register just three days earlier under the title and tune "The Noble seamans complaint to the Ladies at Land, to ye tune of Shakerley Hay [Shackley Hay]" (6.2n1).[11] Though Sackville's copy is no longer extant as a broadside ballad, the song survives in later print and manuscript collections. The tune itself can be found in a late-sixteenth or early seventeenth-century commonplace book.[12] "Shackley Hay" was a seventeenth-century "top hit," according to Marsh (*Music and Society*, 236), and it became "legion" in the eighteenth century, under its renamed title, "To All You Ladies Now at Land" (Simpson, 650), thanks to the influence of Sackville's ballad.

You can listen to a recording of Sackville's entire ballad, sung to its tune, "Shackley Hay," on **Track 27**.

The ballad written by Sackville gently parodies the many ballads about common seamen departing from, returning to, or writing from sea to their lady loves on land. Most of these seaman/lover ballads produced in the seventeenth century are serious. But even before Sackville got his satirical hands on it, the "Shackley Hay" ballad already had parodic overtones; indeed, I suggest, the sense of spoofing seamen-returning ballads would have been an almost knee-jerk reaction by early modern contemporaries to encountering the source ballad, which was much-reprinted in the century. I refer to the broadside ballad about the ferryman Palmus and his landlubber love, the shepherdess Sheldra, cited hereafter as "Palmus and Sheldra." Significantly, Pepys owned two editions; the earlier of the two—and likely the earliest extant copy of the ballad—EBBA 20163, c. 1630, is recorded on **Track 28**.[13] The ballad was entered into the Stationers' Register in 1613. The text of the song explains the tune title: the place name of "Shackley Hay" echoes throughout the ballad. Indeed, so recurrent is "Shackley Hay" in the story that it functions like another "whassup" catchphrase. The relator sings of a lower-order seaman, a ferryman, who on returning to Shackley Hay after a "voyage" (that is, a day of rowing on the river), spurns his lady love's welcome home. What ensues is his repentance for refusing her. But in a subsequent twist, despite his repentance, she rejects *him*. She then undergoes a change of heart, but too late: he departs in his skiff from Shackley Hay. Both now twice rejected, they die from their doubly spurned love (although in the case of Palmus, with another comic twist, he in the course of dying is revived into something like a living death under the sea).

Though Chappell and Ebsworth call the story "rather romantic" (*Roxburghe Ballads*, 3.5), the frequency with which the lovers change their affection approaches the ridiculous. In addition to their almost mind-boggling number of romantic about-faces, the ferryman Palmus's imagery in attempting to woo back his love on her first rejecting him becomes absurdly inflated. He imagines that "whilst thou [Sheldra] guid'st the silken saile [remember, he's talking about his meager ferry boat!], / Ile row the silver Oares: / And as upon the streames we float, / A thousand Swans shal guide our boat" (st. 7). He further proposes to paint the shore "In golden letters" that will tell the story of "How Sapho [Sappho] lov'd a Ferriman, / being a learned Queene" (st. 8). The almost courtly sounding language, together with the dramatic flip-flopping of the characters' "love" in the song's narrative, peaks ludicrously near its end. On the apparently conclusive rejection by his "lady" (the lowly shepherdess, Sheldra), the ferryman Palmus forlornly goes to sea in his skiff, metaphorically hoping to drown himself with his overflowing tears. However, he "Threw hope away, for he, alas, / Could be no more drownd then he was" (col. 5, st. 2). But in yet one more amusing reversal, reality strikes: our ferryman's skiff encounters raging seas and is wrecked. Palmus finds himself literally drowning. But the twisty-turny, disjointed narrative does not end here. In what seems to be a truly fatuous overturning of the traditional demise of the spurned lover, Palmus is spotted sinking beneath the sea by nymphs, who happen to be sorting pearls at a feast of Neptune. They lift him up toward the surface to save him. However, yet one more mind-bending upending of the plot ensues: on lifting him aloft, the nymphs find themselves so taken by Palmus's beauty that they change course and pull him back down to live with them under the sea. The ferryman's life-in-death final fate is a somehow fitting, if very odd, conclusion to the conflicted course of affairs the entire ballad has recounted: "Thus with Nymphs he lives in the sea / That left his love at Shackley-hay" (col. 5, st. 5).

The woodcut illustration to this early "Palmus and Sheldra" ballad owned by Pepys (Figure 36) drives home the parodic elements of the ballad's narrative. The ferryman and shepherdess are here portrayed in fashionable attire and further ornamented with decorative borders on either side of the picture. Such an image of the two star-crossed lovers befits the elevated references in the ballad that one would associate with elite and courtly sorts. These include citations to the god Neptune, for example, and to other classical figures, such as Sappho and, of course, sea nymphs. Similarly lofty is the elaborate florid imagery espoused by the seaman in trying to woo back his love. But such aggrandizement in no way suits the actual lowly status of the ferryman and shepherdess nor their truly muddled—bordering on laughable—love story. The fancy dress of the woodcut figures is "off" not only in social status but also in time period. Their attire, that is, is out of date with the here-and-now of the ballad's seventeenth-century publication date. They are dressed in old-fashioned Tudor garb, not in trendy late Jacobean or Caroline style, when White was active as publisher. Text and illustration work together to bolster while they simultaneously undercut the ballad's gestures toward elevation; the ballad is just too hyperbolic, unbelievable, and disjunctive to be taken seriously as high tragic romance.

The "Shackley Hay" tune also subtly evokes but at the same time undermines any courtly or elite leanings. Below is a modern transcription of the earliest extant manuscript notation of the tune, found in the commonplace book of the Shann family of Methley, County of York, 1561–1627.[14] Notably, in this book the music notation has its own handwritten text underlay. I don't

Figure 36. Woodcut impression from "A most excellent Song of the loue of young *Palmus*, and faire *Sheldra*, with their vnfortunate loue" (c. 1630), EBBA 20163. Pepys Ballads 1.350–351. By permission of the Pepys Library, Magdalene College, Cambridge.

reproduce that underlay here because it varies from our c. 1630 ballad text and even more from Sackville's later mock-ballad; in addition, the manuscript's syllables and words do not align closely with its notes. Nevertheless, the accompaniment of text with music notation in the original manuscript proves that the tune was meant for singing (that is—to reiterate a point I made in Chapter 1—the music was not, as one might assume, notated only for an instrument). The tune's notation is as follows:[15]

Most telling—and, given our discussion to date, appropriately—the tune "Shackley Hay" is not, as notated, in the somber-sounding minor mode, nor even in the more affectively wide-ranging Dorian; rather, it is in major, here in the key of F. Though not a hard-and-fast rule, by any means, increasingly, as we have observed, the major mode was associated in the seventeenth century with an upbeat, or at least elevating, affect. In combination with the text and illustrations, major could also be used to subvert represented affect, character, and/or plotline. Based on the seeming misalignment of major mode with the topsy-turvy calamitous romance of the "Palmus and Sheldra" story, for instance, one cannot but wonder whether the tune was in fact intended to add an upbeat mockery in voicing the ballad's "tragedy."

The tune of "Shackley Hay," we note, is bit more complicated to sing than "Greensleeves"—but not by much.[16] Most challenging to sing is the whole octave jump down in the third measure (second poetic line), repeated in the seventh measure (fourth poetic line), as if diving off a cliff. Consider stanza 2, for instance, of Sackville's mocking ballad set to "Shackley Hay":

For though the Muses should prove kind,
  And *fill our* empty brain,
Yet if rough Neptune rouse the wind
  To *wave the* azure main,
Our paper, pen, and ink, and we,
Roll up and down our ships at sea—
  With a fa, la, la, la, la!
(Sackville, "To All You Ladies Now at Land," st. 2; my emphases)

The recording of this stanza can be heard on **Track 29**. The transcription of that recording is shown below, with text underlay and musical stresses indicated. The singer chose to transpose the key from F major to C major to fit his baritone voice. The fiddle audio of the transcription can be heard on **Track 30**:

In Sackville's drawing here upon the tune "Shackley Hay," which voices with tongue-in-cheek humor a confusing flurry of about-faces in love as told in the "Palmus and Sheldra" ballads, he turns the tune to more overt mockery. In his depiction, nobles, not a ferryman, complain about their absent loves (though both sets of "heroes" seem equally inept at sea). The musical octave leap downward twice, which we hear on the recording and both hear and see in the transcription of it above (also underscored in the plain text transcription further above), is exploited tactically by Sackville's choice of text to evoke a playful contradiction. The first time the octave downward leap occurs is on the words "***fill*** our," in the notes of measure 3 (near the beginning of poetic line 2); the second time, it is on "***wave*** the," in the notes to measure 7 (near the beginning of poetic line 4). In both cases, while poetic and musical stresses agree, the denotation and connotation of the words emphasized—one pointing to filling up, the other to rising up, as when the sea swells in the form of a wave—oppose the vocal dive downward. "***Fill***" and "***wave***" create expectations of an upward, not a falling, motion. How amusingly ironic is the resultant dissonance between poetic meaning and both musical meter at these key points! Sackville is tactically playing with overturning our expectations, even more so than did the anonymous author of the earlier "Palmus and Sheldra" ballads who plotted the ballad's many reversals of love.

Such poking, indeed downright satirical,[17] fun created through the striking conflict between Sackville's text and the "Shackley Hay" tune depends in large part on these moments of challenging vocal movement in the melody.

However, despite the notably ambitious leaps downward, the melody mostly has a basic, flowing rhythm. With the exception of the octave jumps downward, that is, there are no unpredictable surprises—no flats or sharps or ties. The score, furthermore, repeats a lot: the notes and arrangement of the first four measures, for instance, are duplicated almost exactly in measures 5–8 (which altogether approximately align with the singing of poetic lines 1–4).[18] And, of course, the nonsense refrain—"With a fa, la, la, la, la!"—is itself repetitive, creating a familiar and homey feel, especially with its common but still very funny, silly words. Such simple folk features easily lend the song to both singing and dancing. In fact, Marsh identifies the origins of the tune as likely in "country dance music" (*Music and Society*, 238).

Of course, in addition to the challenging octave jumps downward, the singer must make adjustments of text to the tune especially in lines 2 and 3 of the sung ballad (where the 4-3 poetic ballad measure, as we've seen happen before, runs up against the consistent 4-4 musical metric stresses); the numbers of syllables in these lines fall short. But as we can hear in the recording, singers typically adapt the text to such a divergence with the music notation by extending the last stress in the shorter poetic line. Such necessary extra emphases and elongation of the end words of these lines—falling on "brain" and "main" in the above stanza—are allowed for by the music's notation, which provides a half note instead of a quarter note at these moments.[19] More unusual is that, subsequently, in lines 5 and 6 of the extant "Palmus and Sheldra" ballads and Sackville's appropriation of their "Shackley Hay" tune, the poetic measure reverts to coincide with the four musical stresses (alternately strong and less strong) of the tune. That is, whether in the abbreviated or longer versions of the ballads to the tune (in the longer, the refrain is repeated), the poetic measure in lines 5 and 6 veers off course from the expected 4-3 poetic scansion and accords, at least syllabically, with the musical metric emphasis of 4-4. But such is not the case in the previous line, nor in line 2, nor in the refrain (whether sung singly or twice), which have only three poetic stresses. It's as if we experience poetically and musically a pull between tides or between crosswinds. The ballad momentarily, for the two lines of 5 and 6, becomes metrically tension-free. It enters smooth sailing, before encountering again the rough waters, however delightfully and mockingly received, of the refrain.

Our felt mockery of the noble seamen in experiencing Sackville's adaptation of the "Palmus and Sheldra" ballads (or, rather, his allusion to them through adopting their popular "Shackley Hay" tune) derives from the fact that his ballad is "fake-folk." It is a product of Sackville's court wit and political culture. His song on the surface feels carefully crafted to conform to the poetic and musical demands of the shorter, seven-line stanza version of ballad texts sung to the tune of "Shackley Hay," with the refrain occurring just once at the end of each stanza. In this sense, Sackville's ballad fits the times. As Simpson notes, drollery songs (satirical jest-songs especially popular in the 1670s) tended to appear in the shorter stanzaic form when written to "Shackley Hay" (648).[20] Certainly, Sackville's ballad falls into the category of a drollery. It is both more light and more parodic than its antecedents about Palmus and Sheldra (647–48), overblown as the earlier ballads are. As we have seen, Sackville now hilariously raises the lowly status of the ferryman to "nobles" (in the plural). This ironically creates a certain consonance between his story line and the "Palmus and Sheldra" woodcut illustration featuring upper sorts (Figure 36); but in addition to making these nobles out of Caroline fashion, as we have observed, Sackville portrays them as out of their supposedly elevated *intellectual* status. Despite being socially high, the seafaring nobles are even more dim-witted than our lowly ferryman. As if never having sailed on an ocean before, they complain about "How hard it is to write" (1.4) because not only do they have an "empty brain" (1.9) but also they find writing with pen and paper while on the rough seas *literally* hard.

As part of his, at this point, still playful mockery, once Sackville enters poetically and metrically smooth sailing after line 4, he takes his crafted adherence to the more regular rhythm of "Shackley Hay" to a near tedious extreme. Thus, every strongly emphasized poetic syllable in the body of stanza 2 above—with one notable exception—predictably lands on a high and musically emphasized note. But, again, Sackville tactically turns this effect to playful mockery, as in his one exception: the at first seemingly innocuous phrase—at least before sung and transcribed for all moderns to see—"***ships*** at *sea*" (measure 13; conclusion to the body of the stanza in line 6). Though "ships," in the musical meter, receives a strong stress, it is in fact divided over two relatively low notes. In contrast, the word *sea*, which in terms of the musical meter would normally receive a weaker stress, gains phenomenologically stronger musical and thus also poetic emphasis than the other secondary stresses in the stanza. This is due to its being a quarter note followed by shorter notes and also its occupying the highest and last note in an upward stepwise motion to which the singer raises the phrase "ships at sea." In sum, these lords are emphatically, the poetic and musical phenomenal movement stresses, "at ***sea***," not just "at *sea*." That is, they are literally sailing on the ocean, but also, in the early modern as well as modern sense of being "at sea," they are "at a loss" (*OED*, 2.10: "at sea"). Their brainless floating, as if aimlessly rolling on the ocean, leads naturally into the nonsense refrain that concludes the stanza and, in its meaninglessness, vocalizes the blissful ignorance of these nobles' collective "empty brain."

The music's metrical emphasis and phenomenal accent as well as the poetic meaning and meter are all in on Sackville's joke as he tactically turns these features of tune and text to mock not only the simple ballad form but, in his version, its simpleton upper-class "heroes." His newly published gem of a ballad is so lavishly silly that it could easily be interpreted by those at the dinner party, to which Pepys brought it along, as just good fun, and in no way seriously critical. But all the naval officers to whom Pepys attributes its authorship had very recently been at sea with the fleet to engage the Dutch in November 1664 (as had its nonattributed author, Charles Sackville). Their return was publicly declared a "victory." However, in his *Diary* entry early in the next month, December 3, 1664, Pepys questions how much of a victory could really be claimed, since the Dutch were at that time harbor-bound due to contrary winds (5.336; also 5.335n4).

Particularly unsettling, considering the at-the-time ongoing naval war with the Dutch, would be line 4 of stanza 5 of Sackville's ballad, shown underlined and contextualized below within the entire stanza, with musical metric stresses indicated (both strong and less strong) as can be heard in the recording of the entire ballad on **Track 29**:

Should ***fog***-gy *Op*-dam ***chance*** to *know*
Our ***sad*** and *dis*-mal ***sto***-*ry*,
The ***Dutch*** would *scorn* so ***weak*** a *foe*,
<u>And ***quit*** their *fort* at ***Gor***-*ee*;</u>
For ***what*** re-*sist*-ance ***can*** they *find*
From ***men*** who've *left* their ***hearts*** be-*hind*?-
With a ***fa***, la, *la*, la, ***la**!*
(my musical metric emphasis and syllabification)

Opdam was a Dutch admiral, and references to the Dutch are scattered throughout Sackville's ballad text.[21] But the mention of Fort Gorée is especially important and most current for January 1665, when Pepys brought Sackville's ballad to the dinner party dominated by naval officers. At this point in the song, lighthearted mockery lends itself to potentially bitter critique.

On October 24, 1664, the Dutch captured Gorée from the English and proceeded to seize all the other English holdings on the West Coast of Africa that had a year earlier been lost by the Dutch to the English. On December 22, 1664, news of the disaster on the African coast reached London. In response, Pepys wrote a letter expressing his disgust at the "cowardice" of the British fleet; despite having a major presence in the area, he observed, the British surrendered Fort Gorée with little resistance. "'Tis hard to say whether this news be received with more anger or shame," Pepys concluded, "but there is reason enough for both" (*Further Correspondence*, 1.34; see also *Diary*, 5.352–53). So Pepys's clearly made-up attribution of the ballad's authorship in bringing this particular Sackville ballad to a dinner party, filled with naval officers, in early January 1665—just eleven days after hearing of such disastrous and nationally embarrassing naval loses—could well be a veiled insult: "What are you English naval commanders doing," the ballad implies, "writing about love at sea when you are being humiliated by the Dutch?" Significantly, whereas one could sing "Gorée" as two equal quarter notes to the tune of "Shackley Hay," Bell takes advantage of the melodic structure tactically to drive home such criticism. He lengthens the first syllable, "***Gor-***" in the word, thus making more secondary the lesser stress on "*-ée*." In thus emphasizing the musical metrical stress on "***Gor-***," Bell slyly vocalizes the fact that the English cowardly "***quit***" or forsook taking up battle—and thus quit facing the literal ***gore*** of battle. But the song is so lighthearted in tone that any intended insult by the singer (in this case, likely Pepys), as if in cahoots with the author, Sackville, or any deliberate jab by Pepys in naming naval officers as the ballad's composers, though likely perceived by some with a wink and a nod, could also be most assuredly ignored or denied. In so timely bringing this satirical ballad to the naval party, Pepys has made a most subtle tactical strike.

Self-Fashioning National Publics—and Pepysian Resistance

Pepys participated on the margins, with self-reflexive resistance, in the making of an even broader ballad public, this time with serious political stakes. On March 5, 1667, Pepys records in his *Diary*, he traveled alone by water reading what he described as "a ridiculous ballad made in praise of the Duke of Albemarle, to the tune of *St. George*." He adds, "the tune being printed too" (that is, the music notation was printed on the sheet) (8.99). Given the enormous popularity of the "St. George" tune, Pepys in reading the ballad likely could not help but have heard the text sung in his head. Cognitive reflexes run deep, especially when the senses, like hearing, are involved, as Bruce R. Smith has explored (*Acoustic World*). The sole extant edition of the ballad Pepys was reading and likely mentally hearing sung is titled "An Heroical Song On the Worthy and Valiant Exploits of our Noble Lord General George Duke of Albemarle, etc. Both by Land and Sea. Made in *August*, 1666" (Figure 37; EBBA 36420, Luttrell Ballads 1.101, British Library).[22] We need to understand in

An Heroical SONG

On the Worthy and Valiant Exploits of our Noble Lord General

GEORGE Duke of ALBEMARLE, &c.

Both by LAND and SEA.

Made in *Auguſt*, 1666.

To the Tune of St. George.

King *Arthur* and his Men they valiant were and bold, the Table Round was high renown'd, twelve hardy Knights did hold; all in the dayes of old extoll'd for Chivalrie: but they long ſince are dead, and under ground do lie, to keep up *England's* Fame, our preſent Story tells, How Lord *George*, Lord *George*, in prowes now excells. *Lord* George *was born in* England, *reſtor'd his Countryes Joy, come let us ſing* Vive le Roy.

Chorus. *Lord* George *was born in* England, *reſtor'd his Countryes Joy, come let us ſing* Vive le Roy.

he *Monarchies*, all four, were purchaſed with blood;
arthage of old, and *Rome* as bold, each other long withſtood;
and many Lives were loſt in every enterprize.
rlando Furioſo, he was more raſh than wiſe:
ut never heard before, ſo well contriv'd a thing,
low Lord *George*, Lord *George*, in Peace brought home our King.
Lord George *was born in* England,
Reſtor'd his Countryes Joy,
Come let us ſing Vive le Roy.

French Maunſieur Complements his Cracks and Cringes many;
The *Spaniſh Don* his Hat keeps on, and looks as big as any;
The *Iriſh Tory* fierce; *Venetians* Courage Hot;
The *Welſhman* ſtill high born; moſt ſubtle is the *Scot*:
But yet among them all, deny it now who can,
Still Lord *George*, Lord *George* Renowned *Engliſh-man*.
Lord George, &c.

Darby and *Capel* both did Noble Martyrs die,
Their lateſt breath, unto the Death, pronouncing Loyaltie;
Good Subjects many more, did ſuffer Deaths moſt vile;
In *Scotland* brave *Montroſs* was murdered by *Argyle*:
For King and Countries ſake, all thoſe laid down their Lives;
But Lord *George*, Lord *George*, to ſerve his Prince ſurvives.
Lord *George*, &c.

Brave famous Noblemen, and others here did fight
For *Charles* His Cauſe, when 'gainſt the Lawes detained was His right:
In thoſe unhappy Wars, dy'd many Worthies good,
Did win Immortal Fame by Loſing Loyal blood:
Yet maugre all their Force, Uſurpers got the Throne;
But Lord *George*, Lord *George*, He gave the King his own.
Lord *George*, &c.

By many Battles fought, the *Turk's* a Potent Lord;
King *Philips* Son of *Macedon*, got all the World by's Sword;
Great *William* 'gain'd this Land, and all the *Danes* drave out;
Fifth *Harry* Conquer'd *France*, by force and valour ſtout:
Their Greatneſs to Encreaſe, theſe exercis'd their might;
But Lord *George*, Lord *George*, doth for his Maſter fight.
Lord *George*, &c.

Jephtha and *Gideon* by Miracle did ſtrike;
The Son of *Nun* did ſtay the Sun, no Man did do the like;
Sampſon was the ſtrongeſt begot of humane race;
Jonathan and *David* kill'd *Philiſtins* apace:
All thoſe did fight on Land, their Foes when ſlaughter'd they;
But Lord *George*, Lord *George* rides Conquerour at Sea.
Lord *George*, &c.

Of many brave Exploits do ancient Stories tell,
But Sea-fights ſuch as ours with *Dutch*, yet none could parallel:
Towards *Midſummer* the Moon works ſtrongly on their brain,
If in the Month of *June* they venture once again;
For thrice they had the worſt at that time of the year,
And Lord *George*, Lord *George* ſtill keeps them all in fear.
Lord *George*, &c.

We often read of Knights, Wilde Beaſts did overcome;
Our General, beyond them all, beats *Belgick Lyon* home;
A Beaſt of wondrous Size, ſometime did hold him play,
But he the Conqueſt gain'd, upon St. *James's* day:
The *Lyon* then was hurt, did lamentably rore,
But Lord *George*, Lord *George* ſince that did wound it more.
Lord *George*, &c.

The Victory obtain'd, was further ſtill made good,
Our *Engliſhmen*, unto their Den, the *Dutchmen* home purſu'd:
Their *Fleet* in Harbour fir'd, their Village ſack'd and burn'd,
Made *Butterboxes* ſwear the *Monck* to Devil was turn'd;
As flam'd the *Trojan* Walls, ſo did their Ships or worſe,
For Lord *George*, Lord *George* ſent in the Wooden-horſe.
Lord *George*, &c.

If daring *Frenchmen* now our Valour longs to try,
Soon as he will, we ready ſtill, his Mind to ſatisfie:
His Itch ſhall quickly Cure, when he ſhall feel our Sword
With *Dutch* not blunted yet, we'l t'other Bout afford;
And if he thinks it good, the *Dane* may likewiſe call,
For Lord *George*, Lord *George* doth hope to beat them all.
Lord *George*, &c.

Succeſs wait on his Arm, till Tryumph bring him home
To Native Soil, enrich'd with Spoil of Enemies o're-come:
Whilſt they by *Weeping-Croſs* are driven back again,
May he with Joy return to his Dear Soveraign;
And in his proper Orb, with Honour ſtill attend,
Till Lord *George*, Lord *George* 'mong Angels ſhall aſcend.
Lord George *was born in* England,
Reſtor'd his Countryes Joy,
Come let us end Vive le Roy.

[*Licens'd according to Order.*]

London, Printed by *W. Godbid* for *John Playford* at his Shop in the *Temple*. 1667.

Figure 37. Ballad sheet facsimile, "An Heroical Song On the Worthy and Valiant Exploits of our Noble Lord General George Duke of Albemarle, &c. Both by Land and Sea. Made in *August*, 1666" (1667), EBBA 36420. British Library, Luttrell Ballads 1.101, C.20.f.3.(101.).

detail this broadside ballad's appropriation of the "St. George for England" tune, and, by association as well, versions of the traditional text and image of St. George, before we can fully fathom why Pepys was so irked by the remade multimedia artifact he held in his hands. The imprint to the ballad—"Printed by W[illiam] Godbid for John Playford . . ."—might explain the presence of music notation on the sheet. We have seen that Playford was a well-known music publisher and bookseller, most famed for his multiply reprinted edition of ballad dances and tunes. Pepys regularly frequented Playford's shop.

As we have further noted, music notation—whether nonsensical (therefore apparently just ornamental) or meaningful (that is, a good fit for singing the text of the ballad)—begins appearing late in the seventeenth century on quite a few broadside ballad sheets issued across a range of publishers. Such notated ballads are usually in white-letter, or roman, font, since that typeface was coming to dominate the ballad print scene by this time. Printed music notation also coincided with the decline of more representational woodcut illustrations on broadside ballads, such as the famed and much-used woodcut of St. George slaying the dragon (see Figure 38).

The increasing appearance of music notation on ballad sheets also coincided with the rise of cheap songbooks. The genre of the songbook up to the 1660s had mostly been reserved for the more wealthy and more educated. But the music scene was noticeably changing in the latter half of the seventeenth century. The less well-to-do and less educated (even less musically erudite) demanded access to the "higher" genre of songbook in an affordable format—hence the marketing of cheap songbooks. Never to be outdone, broadside ballad printers and publishers refashioned their own artifacts, printing ballads with not just tune titles but music notation on the sheets, to compete for this opening consumer market. The notation on the "Albemarle" broadside ballad, then, depending on one's musical education, served the audience/consumer as ornament or as meaningful notation to the song, and, perhaps for many, as both (to the extent the image of a musical score stood in for what in an earlier time would have been an eye-catching woodcut illustration).[23] As we shall see, the addition of a harmonic chorus to the music notation on the "Albemarle" ballad, like the text of the ballad, could also be arousingly political.

The music printed on the "Albemarle" broadside ballad, shown in Figure 37, is our earliest extant source for the tune "St. George for England." The melody was variously titled. As in the "Albemarle" ballad, it could be named simply "St. George," or, as in other ballads, "St. George and the Dragon" or "St. George for England and the Dragon" (Simpson, 628).[24] As befits the celebratory theme of the traditional "St. George" song—a tribute to England's patron saint as the best of all heroes, whose competitors for fame (all champions of mythic proportions) are at length listed and dismissed as inferior—the tune is in the major mode, here in C major. For those moderns who might be thrown off by the music notation on the sheet showing diamond-shaped notes and flags at the end of their stems (the flags indicating that the time held on the note should be halved so that the many quarter notes become eighth notes), I provide a diplomatic transcription below. The transcription includes the text underlay as indicated on the sheet with the addition of musical metric emphases and syllabic divisions, aligning the text with notes as sung (discussed further below):[25]

Notice that the sheet music notation not only indicates how the tune, including its refrain, should be sung by one person but also provides a harmonic chorus (marked on the original sheet by a bass clef at the beginning of the shorter, fourth line directly below that part of the solo refrain above it, with which the notation harmonizes, as well as by the word on the sheet of "chorus" printed above the bass clef). According to the disposition of the singers—that is, if two or more were present—they could have sung the refrain in choric harmony.

As a lone singer, Bell resorts to an ingenious tactic to effect the harmony offered by the addition of the optional bass chorus. His trick befits the spirit of a digital archive designed to re-create something "like" a lived experience; it also captures the spirit of the tactical as defined by de Certeau and as promoted by the tactical media movement we surveyed in Chapter 1. Befitting the use of tactical media, Bell draws on at-hand affordable technology to maneuver around the demands of convention. Quite simply, he recorded the first stanza of the ballad and then recorded his own voice again to create harmony in the refrain. In an audio version of trompe l'oeil—what one might dub "trompe l'oreille"—we hear the illusion of a second person joining the song, as if united in agreement, at the end of every stanza (one can listen to this oral tactic in his singing of the first stanza of the "Albemarle" ballad on **Track 31** of the

Audio Companion). As we listen, we can begin to understand the larger intent behind the "Albemarle" ballad's alteration and elaboration upon the traditional "St. George" refrain. The multiply voiced chorus was meant to be expressive of many people linked together in harmonious song, as if the nation's masses of different voices united as one under "St. George"—or rather, more politically and pointedly in the remaking of the familiar ballad, as we shall further explore, under Lord George (that is, the Duke of Albemarle).

You can also hear the entire "Albemarle" ballad sung to "St. George" without the bass harmony, as it would have been voiced by one person, whether hawking on the streets of London, spinning by the domestic hearth, working in a shop, or milking a cow in the countryside. In this solo rendering of the tune, only the top line of the chorus (the last half of line 3 of the music notation) would have been sung (**Track 32**). Below is a transcription of the first stanza of that recording notated in the beta version of Minstrel; the slowed-down audio fiddle version of the transcription is on **Track 33**:

For comparison, and so we can see more clearly the truly sly political appropriation at work in the "Albemarle" ballad, I also provide a recording on **Track 34** of the earliest extant broadside ballad about St. George and the Dragon. It is dated 1612 and is in the Pepys collection (Pepys Ballads 1.87, EBBA 20041). The Pepys St. George and the Dragon ballad sports a significantly different text than the tricky imitation of it turned into a tribute to Lord George Albemarle. Singing this earlier version thus requires different adjustments of text to notes and notes to text than singing the "Albemarle" verse. My analysis of the musical metric stresses of the "St. George" tune, however, will focus on the latter, the remade version of the "St. George" ballad. By closely studying the "Albemarle" ballad's text as sung, one can detect a truly crafty brilliance in its tactical remaking of a national public traditionally fashioned by ballads in tribute to St. George, *not* Lord George. The Albemarle re-creation of the "St. George" ballad, as Pepys testifies, was in large part successful in whipping up large-scale enthusiastic public support for Albemarle. But all such tactical publics can only be temporary—being made as they are simultaneously being unmade—especially political ballad publics. Such publics, especially, like news, can only last in and for the historical moment.

If we now turn to focus on text and tune in the "Albemarle" ballad, which appropriates its predecessors' famous melody, we find that, like many national anthems, it is not an easy sing. The main challenge of the "St. George for England" tune is not that it has a wide range of notes but that it is unpredictable. For this reason alone, it doesn't fall into the class of traditional folk tunes as does, for instance, "Shackley Hay." The notation also requires a very quick musical wit. On listening to its singing in **Tracks 31–34**, you will notice that in order to fit text to tune, the singer must sing one line of text for every two measures. This in itself is not unusual for ballads. But in the "St. George" tune, each measure of the notation in the twelve measures that constitute the body of the stanza is filled with many short notes. Most of these notes are eighth notes as opposed to the typical quarter notes. The ballad is consequently *very* fast paced; words must trip off the tongue.

In addition to the demands of speedy dexterity for twelve measures (six lines of poetry), the singer must then unexpectedly slow down. There occurs a dramatic turn toward the end of each stanza in the third line of music notation (after the twelfth measure), where the refrain or chorus begins, "*Lord* George was *born in* England, . . ." Whereas in the body of the stanza we see that most of the notes are eighth notes, forcing the singer to speed along, in the chorus they elongate to become mostly quarter notes, moving often to half and even whole notes, especially in the final measures of the music. Time suddenly, as if on the fly, decelerates. Indeed, in the final line of the three-line chorus, if we look at Pepys's traditional version of it in the "St. George" ballad, each word is held for a very long time and thus greatly emphasized: "Sing Hony soit qui mal y panse" (literally, "Shame upon him who thinks evil upon it"). This French phrase is given such emphasis because it became the motto of England's most distinguished chivalric fraternity, the Order of the Garter, founded in 1348 and dedicated to St. George. The considerable slowing down of the ballad's pace in this chorus and the driving home of each word in voicing the Order of the Garter's motto makes the song sound almost regal. It is as if we are indeed hearing a national anthem. And, like many national anthems—certainly like the American one, as we have seen—the tune proves a major challenge for most singers.

But just as Americans have learned to sing "The Star-Spangled Banner," however much we might struggle and even falter with its wide range (a twelfth), so most early moderns—who were more familiar with a wide range of notes in ballads and with singing a broad variety of rhythms, as we have noted—would for the most part likely have managed, or strived to manage, the "St. George" tune. They might even have heartily embraced it and made a competition of doing so: racing through the song's tongue-tripping speedy delivery and then abruptly hitting the breaks, as if encountering a "Slow" sign and seeing the finish line ahead. We must remember as well that not only were the "St. George" ballad and tune extremely popular as something along the lines of England's national anthem, but they were much older than our oldest extant copy. Having likely heard the song frequently sung, passed down through generations, most contemporaries probably did not need to rely on reading the "St. George" music to know the melody (though for that very reason they might have delighted in seeing how the words lined up with the musical notes on the broadside, however tactically realigned in the rewritten text and alterations of the tune in the "Albemarle" ballad).

It is important to note that, both in the earliest extant text of the traditional ballad about St. George and the Dragon, as seen in the Pepys version, and in the later "Albemarle" revision, which provides us with the earliest extant music notation, it is neither the word "Saint" in the one nor "Lord" in the other that are given poetic and musical emphasis. The strongest accent in both versions falls on the word, repeated three times, that unites the two songs: "***George***." This triply accentuated word ties together the traditional broadside ballad and the slyly revised broadside ballad, which are both sung to the tune of "St George for England." The Albemarle ballad, that is, only subliminally suggests that Lord George, Duke of Albemarle, is saint-like. It would be a sacrilege to say so openly. But one might declare with confidence (and without fear of condemnation) that what is being celebrated in both printed versions of the tune and text is two Georges that rise above the greatest of England's heroes. If both heroes are not together openly deemed saints, they are similarly unequivocally praised as the most superior "Georges" of England.

Significant changes *are* made to the traditional refrain, however, in the Albemarle's reworking of the "St. George" ballad text (variant though the earlier editions of that text may be). St. George, as the age-old story goes, just happens to be an English knight who proves himself so superior that he is adopted as the nation's patron saint. But Albemarle, in the remade ballad, seems even more of an English national hero from the very beginning. Tactically and contemporarily privileging Lord George as a great English champion not in fighting a mythical dragon but in warring with very real enemies of England—especially the Dutch—the revised refrain in the "Albemarle" version leaves out all reference to France and cuts down the amount of French language used. Consider the full traditional refrain as seen in the first stanza of the Pepys version: "Saint George, Saint George the Dragon made to flee; / S. George for England, S. Dennis is for France, / *Sing Hony soit qui mal y pense*." The "Albemarle" refrain, by contrast, is more simply but also more craftily rewritten: "*Lord* George *was born in* England, */ Restor'd his Countryes Joy, / Come let us sing* Vive le Roy." Only a trace of the French remains: in the well-recognized—one might say naturalized—expression, "Vive le Roy" ("Long live the king"). Furthermore, in the traditional Pepys version, "***France***" is given great emphasis because of the music's metrical placement in which the word uses up an entire measure of notes and is not followed by a secondary music emphasis. But in the "Albemarle" revision, as seen above, all that metrical power is redirected to the more general celebratory word, "***Joy***." Renowned here is England's restored bliss (*as if* Lord George were a Christ-like savior—"Lord God"). The redirected emphasis in the "Albemarle" ballad on "***Joy***" also diverts potential for any interpretation of a traitorous undercutting by Lord George of the subsequent rhyming and concluding word, "***Roy***," which in the "Albemarle" ballad refers to King Charles II. The final line of the refrain, in terms of both poetic and musical emphases, instead confirms a call to celebrate—to "***sing***." In doing so, it also tactically adds, as if an afterthought, a bow to Charles in the now English-naturalized expression "***Vi***-ve‿le ***Roy***." Here "***Roy***" gets its own strong poetic and musical stress as well as its own entire musical measure; if inserted as if an afterthought and if expressed through a cliché, "***Roy***" still crowns the refrain. So the "Albemarle" ballad text and tune celebrate Lord George, Duke of Albemarle, while always making him an (as yet) uncanonized hero striving for England's (versus France's) ***Joy***, always in the service—"***Come . . . sing***"—of England's "***Roy***," or King. The ballad is a tactically brilliant tribute to Albemarle as *almost* God-like and king-like while remaining slyly under the guise of celebrating Charles II.

The tactical politics in this ballad, which so disgusted Pepys, however, are not so much in its first publication, distasteful though he would have found even that to be, as in its second publication. This is the edition he reads aboard his boat while traveling from Chatham—where Britain's naval shipyard is located—to London. The date of the ballad is slippery, however. The title declares that it was "Made in August, 1666." This month and date situate its publication during the Second Anglo-Dutch War. But the title date is only partially telling: the broadside ballad was, in fact, reissued in 1667, when Pepys records reading it. The imprint, which concludes the ballad, confirms its later republication. What political maneuvering is in play in reissuing this so very contemporary ballad? The answer lies in new troubles that arose in the naval battles with the Dutch and the much-rumored blame for them on Albemarle. In August 1666, Lord George Monck, then 1st Duke of Albemarle, was co-commander (with Prince Rupert) of England's fleet. The famously drawn-out Four Days' Battle of the war, June 1–4, 1666—at times resembling a confusing melée—ended with major English losses and accusations of "great bad management" on the part especially of the commander in chief Albemarle (*Diary*, 7.143). Pepys throughout his *Diary* is severely critical of Albemarle. Speaking of the incident in question, he notes that "it seems the Duke did give way again and again" (7.147; see also 10.115). The subsequent engagement with the Dutch, known as the St. James's Day Battle, July 25, 1666 (August 4th on the Dutch Gregorian calendar), ended more clearly in English victory. However, the English failed to decisively cripple the Dutch fleet. As a result, there was much murmuring over the poor conduct of the pursuit. It was clearly to bolster public opinion in favor of the British side that on August 6, 1666, the Crown proclaimed a day of thanksgiving for the late "victory" at sea over the Dutch. The first issuing of the laudatory ballad of Albemarle, in 1666—subtly raising the "Lord" to the status of patron "Saint" of England, equivalent to St. George—partakes of and bolsters such a national self-congratulatory celebration. The refrain is almost all in English in part to make sure it is understandable by the masses. The fact that it was also designed to be sung in harmony—to be sung by gatherings of people—is a further tactical public-making gesture, as is the invitation in the last line, "Come let us ***sing***" (the last line of the Pepys version of the "St. George" ballads, by contrast, is less invoking; it says, simply, "Sing"). Indeed, as we have seen, there is the slightest of suggestions, especially if one thinks outright or subliminally of the poetic and musical as well as the phenomenal stresses of the ballad's refrain, that singing "Vive le Roy" is as much a celebration of George Albemarle in his role of king of the navy as it is of Charles II, king of England. The ballad's refrain, in a kind of Machiavellian mode, calls out: "Everybody gather round and partake in harmonious song celebrating Lord George Albemarle, our conquering English hero on a par with England's national saint, George (and even on a par with the lord God and with the king)!" But, of course, it never declares so outright.

Most of the audience admiring the "Albemarle" ornamentation of meaningful music at the top of the broadside ballad, issued in 1666 and reissued

Figure 38. Woodcut impression of St. George slaying a dragon, from "[A m]ost excellent Ballad of S. George for England and the Kings daugh-[ter of] Aegipt, whom he delivered from death, and how he slew a mighty Dragon" (1658–64), EBBA 31774. University of Glasgow Library, Euing Ballads 92. By permission of University of Glasgow Library, Special Collections.

in 1667 (likely in March, when Pepys recorded reading it), would have made a mental associative hit with the typical woodcut picture shown on "St. George" ballads that the "Albemarle" music notation has displaced: the glorious image of St. George heroically slaying a dragon in foreign lands, as seen in Figure 38. However, in the earliest extant "St. George" broadside ballad of 1612, which Pepys owned, the image pictured on the ballad sheet is surprisingly more mundane. Represented in two adjacent woodcuts made to appear as one cut is not a dramatic battle between an unrivaled hero with a mythical ferocious monster but what seems like an everyday happenstance conversation between two seventeenth-century individuals, a knight and a gentleman.[26] The title of Pepys's version of the "St. George" ballad reflects this more quotidian woodcut impression: in full, it declares, "Saint Georges commendation to all Souldiers: or, S. Georges Alarum to all that professe

Martiall discipline, with a memoriall of the Worthies, who have been borne so high on the winges of Fame for their brave adventures, as they cannot be buried in the pit of oblivion" (title to Pepys Ballads 1.87, EBBA 20041).

The Pepys's edition, as we have noted, is in other ways like most of the "St. George and the Dragon" ballads: a "whassup" cataloging of, in Simpson's words, "Biblical, legendary, and historical adventurers, none of whom can surpass the English patron saint who slew the dragon" (628). The roll call of heroes was switched out in the various remakings of the ballad. This was apparently part of the fun and appeal of the ballad—except for the sonorous nineteenth-century editor Joseph Woodfall Ebsworth, who disliked what he saw as an unpoetic listing (*Roxburghe Ballads*, 6.726). Ebsworth so strongly expresses his distaste for the "St. George" ballad that he declares he's on the side of the dragon! He goes on to admit, if disparagingly, that the listing of "whassup" heroic figures was what made the "St. George" ballad popular: "the absurdity of the perpetual shifting of characters . . . made it the greater favourite. It became a roll-call of chivalric tales, and helped to amuse those who remembered the goodly books which are now found unreadable" (6.726). Ebsworth was, in more ways than one, clearly not of the period in which Pepys lived.

But Pepys's edition of the "St. George" ballad—a sole and earliest extant copy—itself veers off the beaten, mass-marketed path. Yes, Pepys collected a "St. George and the Dragon" ballad that played the "whassup" roll-call game Ebsworth so despised. But Pepys shows a preference for a rare edition of the "St. George" ballad that both in its woodcuts and title tactically undercuts that very "whassup" glory-mongering game. Both project the idea of everyday advice between near equals; indeed, St. George in the illustration looks like just about any contemporary knight conversing with and advising a fellow gentleman. As the title testifies, the ballad is not offered to privilege St. George over other heroes (though the text goes on conventionally to do so). On the contrary, the title declares, St. George himself commends all worthies in "a memoriall . . . [so] as they cannot be buried in the pit of oblivion." What must have especially irked Pepys about the "Albemarle" ballad was thus not so much the typical "roll-call" of chivalric heroes that maddened Ebsworth as the fact that Pepys's contemporary, Albemarle, is upheld in the ballad as the only hero, past or present, worthy of the highest praise. Further "ridiculous" in the mind of Pepys would likely have been the second column of stanzas in the "Albemarle" ballad, which remake the conventional St. George "whassup" roll call. At the top of column 2, the ballad's narrative turns instead to many references of Albemarle's supremacy in the ongoing Dutch wars: "Of many brave Exploits do ancient Stories tell, / But Sea-fights such as ours with *Dutch*, yet none could parallel."

The following list of unparalleled "brave Exploits" accomplished by Albemarle in his naval battles with the Dutch is highly inflated—in some instances, completely false. Such would certainly have raised Pepys's ire given the historical moment when the ballad was reissued, indicated in its imprint.

At the bottom right of our one surviving copy of the "Albemarle" ballad with musical notation, we noted the date of 1667, and, as we also noted, Pepys reports reading it in March of that year, not in the ballad's title year of 1666. There was good reason to reissue this ballad in celebration of Albemarle a year after its original publication. The navy at this time was under increasing scrutiny from Parliament and the city for its performance in the war with the Dutch. Investigations were still underway over reports of the cowardice of the co-commanders of the fleet (one of whom was Albemarle) when they retreated instead of pursuing the Dutch following their victory in the St. James's Day Battle of July 25, 1666. At the same time, there were widespread cries of dismay, voiced more privately by Pepys in his *Diary*, about the navy's inability to properly equip and pay its seamen. Tactically remarketing a ballad celebrating Albemarle's unparalleled successes at the time when his reputation as "hero" was in question would have been financially and nationally profitable for those on the side of Albemarle and the king, who still supported him.

Though ironically fueling the trade in aggrandizing Albemarle and his naval victories by apparently buying this broadside ballad, Pepys did not buy into the message the ballad sold. He frequently derided George Monck, raised from Lord to Duke of Albemarle, as a "heavy," "dull" man, and, put bluntly, a "blockhead." Not only did he call the ballad he read "ridiculous," but he suspected political machinations in its making: "I observe that people have some great encouragement to make ballads of him of this kind; there are so many, that hereafter will sound like *Guy of Warwicke*" (8.99)—invoking another much-beloved English hero of ballad tradition. Who exactly were "the people" making and encouraging these ballads remains unclear. But likely the Crown and Albemarle himself were behind them. Pepys was fully aware that the broadside ballad—as a single sheet easily and quickly printed for mass distribution—could speedily, when necessary, be turned tactically into political posturing. He was also more than aware that the public could have been persuaded to think about Lord George Albemarle as a national hero by exploiting the form and content of previous popular ballad texts and tunes, such as those of St. George. Most maddening, he saw people literally and metaphorically buying what the ballad sold: Lord George Monck, Duke of Albemarle, raised to the grandiose status of another patron saint of England and obliquely akin to the king of England! Pepys was canny enough to keep his skeptical thoughts to his *Diary*. But he often also expressed surprise therein at the esteem in which Albemarle was held, even in the face of concerted forces of criticism: "the blockhead Albemarle hath strange luck to be beloved," he grumbled (8.499). Ballads likely played a significant part in creating such "luck."

Conclusion: From Networks to Publics to Spheres

With this instance of large-scale marketing intended to make a ballad public that would "buy into" Albemarle's feats—as into the "Whassup?" marketing by Budweiser—we would benefit, I propose, by what might at first seem an unlikely model for conceptualizing the making of ballad publics or, more broadly, a ballad public. I propose we think of a ballad public (indeed potentially all publics) in terms of Clifford Geertz's groundbreaking vision of the Balinese cockfight ("Deep Play," 412–53). Geertz essentially envisions the cockfight of Bali in terms of encircling spheres of a culture-making public that affirmed social status. At the center of the cockfight ring are the leaders of Bali who lovingly nurture their cocks as if they were an extension of themselves, as well as their allies, who together form coalitions of bettors. Occupying the ring just outside these central figures are individuals who occasionally fight their own cocks in small matches, might make bets on the big ones, and are still very much invested in the outcome of the central "battle." Beyond these players are the petty bettors who do not fight cocks themselves but still publicly take sides at a fight. Encircled further out, on the fringe of the cockfight, are the socially marginal and poor, who are far less invested in the specific fights but take part in assorted sheer-chance gambling that occurs at encircling concession booths, as in a small fair (435; see also 432n18).

So too, with the making of a broadside ballad public, we can image a kind of Balinesian nesting of public spheres, from the more intense or strong at the center to the less invested or weak at the margins. Center stage are the important "makers." I am thinking not so much of the mostly anonymous "authors" or the occasional sponsors, like those of the "Albemarle" ballad, as the major printers and publishers or booksellers of ballads and their allies, such as prominent hawkers in the trade. Next invested are the avid purchasers of ballads, such as Pepys. Further from the center appear the minor or part-time printers and publishers and from-time-to-time buyers of ballads. And on the outskirts of the ballad public are the very occasional producers and peddlers of broadside ballads as well as the occasional listeners, viewers, readers, and singers (many of them too poor to be able to afford a ballad or too "elite" to

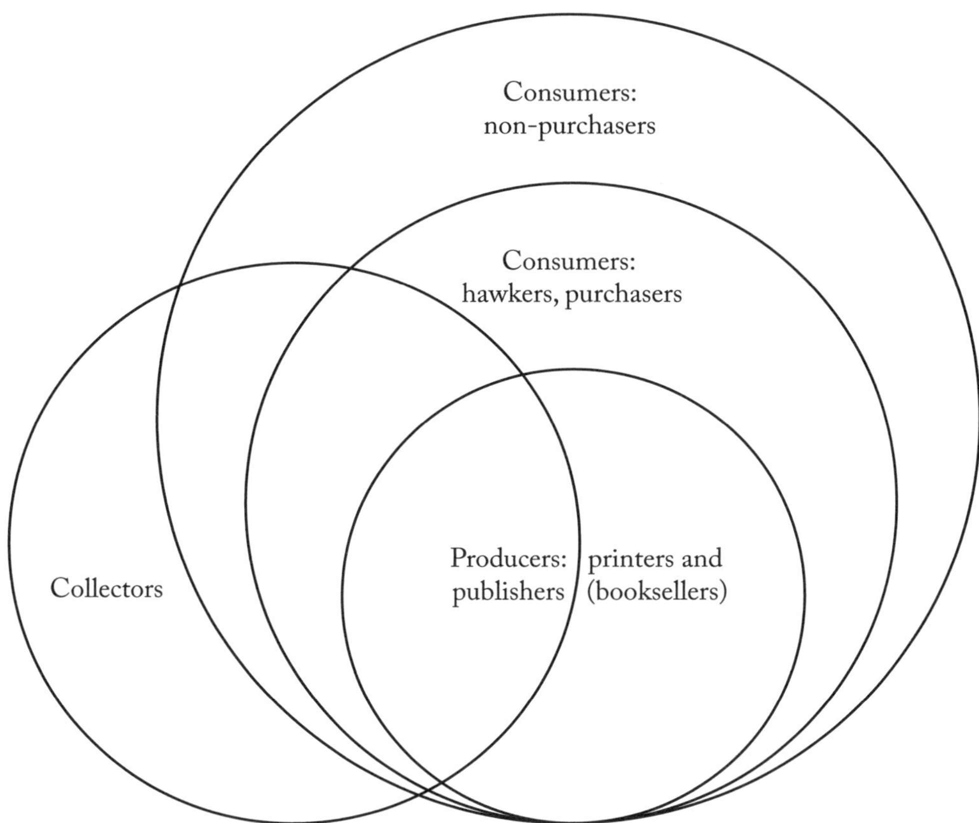

Figure 39. Ballad publics diagram. Conceived by Patricia Fumerton; executed by Eric Nebeker and Tyler Shoemaker.

lower themselves to do so). Here on the margins might also stand those who passingly reference ballads in historical or fictional texts (such as Ben Jonson in *Bartholomew Fair*).

The advantage of envisaging such a Balinesian model of the making of a ballad public is that we can clearly see that publics have a core of strength and an outside that is weaker. Of course, any group constituting all or part of an encircling sphere within the whole might become positioned slightly askew in this neat Balinesian model, if its interests become too specialized. Ballad collectors who shared Pepys's collecting priorities (Selden, Wood, Bagford, Harley, and their allies, Wanley, Charlett, etc.) can be seen to participate in and help generate a larger ballad public, but they can also be seen to have an "eccentric" agenda: documentation and preservation of black-letter script and print. Their agenda, in other words, is relatively small and outside the mass market of ballad consumerism (however much that market capitalized on a fondness for black letter). To the extent that they constituted a small network with little dissemination—though always "open" to interested outsiders—most of these collectors did not participate within a larger commercial ballad public. Our black-letter broadside ballad collectors might best be positioned slightly askew in any neat Balinesian public-sphere model, as in Figure 39. So too, one might argue, did Pepys and Knepp veer off from a larger sphere of ballad consumers in adopting their very personal "secret" game of playing Barbara Allen and Dapper Dicky.

As we have also seen in Pepys's *Diary*, hot spots can flare up at any moment and at any point in this spheric model. Certain printers or publishers could at any time become very influential, a coalition of sorts might form between collectors of ballads, or occasional makers might suddenly produce lots of ballads on a single subject, as in the mobilizing of ballads in praise of Albemarle. We see similar dramatic hot spots configure in Shakespeare's *The Winter's Tale* around Autolycus at the sheepshearing feast (4.4.220–327), and even more intensely in Jonson's *Bartholomew Fair*, where, again, layers of an onion of intensity of investment form around the ballad singer, Nightingale, and his cutpurse partner, Edgeworth (3.5.11–194). Jonson always scathingly put down ballads, as did most of the aspiring laureates of his time. But, like Pepys and so many of his contemporaries, Jonson and his cohort of playwrights also knew precisely how the ballad market worked and how it could be performatively worked on by individuals with a collective goal. They knew broadside ballads well, and further knew well how to tactically improvise the genre's reflexive "whassup" illustrations, formats, topics, and tunes to their own commercial ends. We shall explore such exploitation at work especially in the Conclusion to this book, focusing on Shakespeare's *The Winter's Tale*.

I end this chapter with a coming together, which for all the reflexivity and performativity of ballads, for all the turning of ballads to personal or political ends, was a communalization that lay at the heart of the "talk value" of ballads. I end with yet one more hot spot on the fringe of the Balinese-like sphere of an early modern English ballad public. The moment? The naval pride, as recounted in Pepys's *Diary*, turned out en masse on May 15, 1668, for the funeral of Sir Thomas Teddemen (another naval officer criticized in the Four Days' Battle; 9.200n4). Pepys was impressed by the turnout: "But Lord, to see . . . the young commanders and Thomas Killigrew and others that came" (9.200). This comment could have led to a critique by Pepys of those very "young commanders," as there was general dissent, shared by Pepys, that the navy was being stocked by Charles and his brother, York, with inexperienced courtiers rather than with seaworthy officers (7.10–22 and n1). But instead, Pepys's attention is diverted: "*how unlike a burial this was, Obrian taking out some ballets [ballads] out of his pocket, which I read and the rest came about me to hear; and there very merry we were all, they being new ballets.*" Pepys appears not to have sung these ballads—which would have been most inappropriate for him to do at a funeral—but he nevertheless read them aloud to the public gathering he had spontaneously created. At this very moment, while surrounded by many young officers he would have otherwise criticized, Pepys seems to have lost all track of time and social as well as political context. His new paragraph begins: "*By and by the Corpse went . . .*" (9.200; emphasis mine). In sum, a new commander—Obrian—violating the decorum of somberness at funerals, brings ballads in his pocket; but, instead of criticizing him, Pepys cannot help but be drawn into his circle and make his own magnetic center among them, reading the ballads out loud for the rest to gather round and hear—and "very merry we were all, they being new ballets." As if in afterthought, he notes that Teddemen's corpse passes by.

One might judge this moment severely, as a violation of ceremony, as it was. But one might also appreciate the power of the ballad to make a public, and a merry one at that, out of a group of divergently interested persons. They had come together in a moment of merrymaking that was also a moment of forgetting—forgetting not only politics but also the death that punctuated so many of the diaries of the seventeenth century, as of all time. And they ironically remind us of the life in the making through *collective* performativity of a ballad public. Broadside ballads did—and can still do—just that. In the midst of a passing historical moment, one ephemeral sheet of printed paper, as light as a mere straw, has the power to circulate and draw. Broadside ballads can momentarily create a cohesive public out of strangers, even if only in passing.

Part IV

Diachronic and Synchronic Ballad Publics

Crossing Society, History, and Space

CHAPTER 8

The Moving Violations of "The Lady and the Blackamoor"

In this part and chapter, all in one, I propose we "let the pieces fly," as in Selden's proverbial reference, cited by Pepys, of ballad straws cast into the wind. Of course, in many senses that has been the intent of all the previous chapters, to the extent that they examine the occasional, makeshift, and collage-like way in which producers and consumers of early modern Britain tactically "cast" and "caught" the protean parts of broadside ballads. But in my focusing on one particular collector and consumer of such ballads in the previous chapters—mining Samuel Pepys's many references in his *Diary* to reveal ad-hoc encounters with and uses of ballads that reflect a making of plural ballad publics—readers might want more. You might well want more than one central historical figure as representative of the public making and consuming of broadside ballads. You might well preferentially look to the larger, more woolly, reach of the opening chapters where we tracked bits and pieces of the "Mock-Beggar Hall" ballads across a range of ballads and other popular print; producers and consumers of all sorts, we saw, could assemble "like" ballad parts into a shared mental "cache." But, at the same time, you might justifiably desire a more sustained analysis not of associative hits between ballads and other popular print but of the cultural factors reflected in and refracted by a single ballad's *intra*-media. That is, you might seek revelation of more "thickness" in the historical and social contexts that shaped and were shaped by one ballad's component parts. Another desiring "more" might by this point in our study also arise: "What happens when one tracks a single broadside ballad and its potentially linked component parts across editions of that ballad and over an extended period of time?" In this part/chapter, I hope to fulfill these "wants." I propose to synchronically drill down into the potential multiple social and cultural public makings of a single meaning-filled ballad, which I have, for convenience, dubbed "The Lady and the Blackamoor," and also to diachronically track its transformations in production and meaning-making across both time and space—all the way to New World Georgia in 1789.

Belonging to the subgenre of the sensational broadside ballad, "The Lady and the Blackamoor" lends itself readily to such intensive and extensive reach. In fact, its complex and impactful facets slip out of any firm interpretative grasp. We have seen how, in their DeLandian bricolage production and dissemination, broadside ballads were always tough to pin down and control by early modern authorities and, for that matter, even by modern cultural critics. What the sensational ballad of "The Lady and the Blackamoor" vividly demonstrates is why that is so. Specifically, probing analysis of this ballad, which necessarily includes penetrating consideration of all three of its component media, clarifies the way broadside ballads as a genre tended to break apart while remaining connected both synchronically and diachronically. In a ballad's recently issued *now* and in its later reissued *afterlife*, we find that it rhizomatically disseminates meaning, sometimes in surprising and threatening ways. Context, widely defined, is critical. As we shall see, a consumer's reception of the ballad's sensational criminality could shift over time, place, and subject position; all depended on the particular assemblage of media at the time "in play" and on the social and cultural situatedness of the viewer, reader, listener, or singer. Of particular interest is the impact on consumers of the sensational crime ballad's tendency to go over the top in its emotive depictions of a dastardly deed. In what directions does such emotional excess travel? The extreme voicings and perspectives of sensational ballads would certainly be recognized as participating in horrifically major crimes, committed typically by a monstrous Other, such as an alien blackamoor. But I also posit that they might possibly secretly—and at an aesthetic remove—express more recognizable close-to-home selves of various sorts, including possibly *one's self.*

I am here expanding upon my argument in *Unsettled* that identification with an experience in a ballad is actually *more* possible when rendered at one remove metaphorically or aesthetically. Fictionalized distance allows for a negotiable and discontinuous association with characters and actions that could be couched or suppressed, even as it could also be amply dispersed and manifold. This argument dovetails nicely with Catherine Molineux's observation, which builds on the fact that the numbers of Africans and Native Americans living in or visiting Britain were small in the early modern period (up to the end of the eighteenth century, at least). Precisely because of such scarcity of such alien others in Metropolitan Britain, she argues, the early modern British experienced an affective and even a cognitive distance from the massive Atlantic slave trade on which their country thrived. However, Molineux continues, such a felt distance or perceived absence resulted not in disinterest in the Other but in "an active popular imagination of interracial relationships" that far outweighed the realities. This imaginatively active engagement *at a physical remove* led to "thousands of representations of Atlantic peoples in the seventeenth and eighteenth centuries, only some of which were based on identifiable people" (*Perfect Ebony*, 2, 5). I share Molineux's concern with the remote and thus fantasized blackamoor in early modern Britain. However, one should recognize that such stimulating fiction-making generated by actual distance from an alien Other can happen in the space of mere yards, not only thousands of miles. I here refer to Joy Wiltenburg's exploration into how laments by condemned criminals "othered" in broadside ballads paradoxically allowed audience-singers to inhabit the space of that criminal's "inner life" ("Emotional Life of Crime," 173). Extending Wiltenburg's thesis, Frances E. Dolan astutely notes that "once opened up, such a space is hard to control." Dolan adds that "whatever contemporaries made of it [the fantasized inner space of criminality] would have been unpredictable and various" ("Petty Traitor," 160). I wish to pursue in this chapter, both synchronically and diachronically, precisely the unpredictable and various "voicings" (a term I use loosely to include textual, visual, and oral representation) of sensational crime ballads, employing "The Lady and the Blackamoor" as my case study.

Georgia, North America, 1789

Let us first catch the winds of time and space and visit a news story that appeared in America in the *Georgia Gazette* of 1789. The *Georgia Gazette* was a small newspaper (typically of four pages), issued weekly and peppered mostly with short items about stolen or strayed or runaway goods, including slaves, as exemplified in the second page of the *Gazette* issued on Thursday, April 23, 1789 (Figure 40). The *Gazette* also included the occasional news story, such as the one printed at the bottom of page 3, titled "African Humanity," shown enlarged in Figure 41. The story reads, in full:

> A Moorish slave, having been severely beaten by his master, resolved on taking vengeance, which he executed in the following way: During the gentleman's absence he secured the gates (the house being in the country)

> in the strongest manner; and having fast bound his mistress and her three children, conveyed them to the roof of the house, where he sat with the greatest composure. The gentleman returning, and ringing for admittance, was surprised at seeing the slave in that situation, and threatened him with the severest punishment, if he did not open the gate immediately. The slave tauntingly replied, "He would soon make him alter his language." Then taking up two of the children, and bidding them go open the gate, he flung them over the battlements. The father, in the greatest consternation, promised him not only pardon for the two murders, but even freedom and money, if he would spare his wife and third child. "I will never believe you," exclaimed the slave, "unless you convince me you are in earnest by cutting off your nose[.]" This injunction being complied with, the villain immediately flung down the child and mother; and on hearing the piercing outcries of his master, advised him, to go hang himself, as his only resource. To complete his savage triumph, he threw himself after them, and expired without a groan.

This news story from the *Georgia Gazette* is recounted in a book that has been used for history courses at the University of California, Santa Barbara, on American immigration. The author, Michael A. Gomez, cites the entire story published in the *Georgia Gazette* as one of the most vivid examples of African antagonism to slaveholders. After reproducing the account, Gomez further concludes:

> To be sure, the preceding account is melodramatic to the point of incredulity, but whether invented, embellished, or factual, the story is clearly instructive in that it warns slaveholders of the dangers of both excessive punishment and excessive trust. That the slave would be left alone with the owner's family suggests the latter. That he was a "Moor" underscores this likelihood, given the earlier discussion of Muslims [in which Gomez shows Muslims were held in higher esteem than most other African-born]. The moral of the story is inescapable: even a privileged Muslim cannot be fully trusted, so have a care for the non privileged African-born, as they are particularly dangerous. (*Exchanging Our Country Marks*, 187–88)

Juſt Imported,

In the ſloop Harriot, Archibald Coulton, Maſter, from Philadelphia

FINE hyſon and ſouchong teas,
Superfine flour,
Ship bread,
Biſcuit in kegs,
Wrapping and writing paper,
Burlington pork and hams;
Bar iron, bliſtered ſteel, and ploughſhares;
Soft ſhelled almonds,
Mould candles,
Loaf ſugar,
Engliſh bottled porter;
Boots, mens and womens ſhoes;
New England rum,
Playing cards,
Rhode Iſland cheeſe,
A ſulkey not quite new,
Brown and white ſoap,
Aniſeed water,
Wheelbarrows, &c.

And for ſale, on the moſt reaſonable terms, for Caſh or Produce, by

D. ROBINSON,

At the ſtore lately occupied by Mr. Robert Cumming, near the Venduehouſe.

Savannah, April 23. 1789

RUN AWAY,

About ten days ago, from the ſubſcriber,

A TALL LIKELY NEGRO WENCH, named DORCAS, about 25 years of age, born and brought up in Baltimore, ſpeaks very good Engliſh, well known in Savannah. Whoever will deliver her to her owners ſhall receive FIVE GUINEAS, or, on conviction of her being harboured or carried away by any white perſon, TWENTY-FIVE GUINEAS reward.

ANDREW M'CREDIE and CO.

Savannah, April 22. 1789.

RAN AWAY,

From the ſubſcriber, ſeven days ago,

NEGRO MAN TONEY, by trade a tailor, brought from St. Croix about three years ſince, aged about 26 years, he ſpeaks plain, is ſlim made, about 5 feet 8 inches high; it is ſuppoſed he had on a coarſe brown jacket, a hair or ſhag waiſtcoat with ſtripes of green, oznab ig overalls, and check ſhirt, the collar is lined with white linen; he generally wears a handkerchief on his head. Whoever will deliver him to the ſubſcriber in Savannah, or lodge him in any gaol, ſhall receive ſix dollars reward, and all reaſonable charges.

April 23 1789 S BEECROFT

Strayed or Stolen,

From off Savannah Common, on the 11th inſtant,

A Black Horſe,

about 14 hands high, has a long tail, branded on the mounting ſhoulder NT in one, on the off thigh and under the mane with two hearts, the points joined, has a remarkable hollow in one of his jaw bones.

A Black Mare,

about 14 hands high, with a ſhort ſwitch tail, brands unknown, has ſeveral white ſpecks about her rump.

Whoever will deliver ſaid horſes to Mr. James Steuart at Auguſta, or Mr John Stacy at Midway, ſhall receive FOUR DOLLARS for each, and, if proved to be ſtolen, TEN GUINEAS on conviction of the thief, if a white perſon.

JOHN STACY.

April 20, 1789.

TAKEN UP,

A ſmall GREY HORSE,

Nearly 13 hands high, about 6 years old, paces and trots, branded I on the right thigh, has a ſwitch mane and tail. The owner may have him, by proving the property and paying charges.

JONATHAN SHAW.

Thunderbolt, April 20, 1789

TAKEN UP,

Laſt June, near Thunderbolt,

A Dark Brown Cow,

With a white ſtreak along her back, a white face, and hipſhot, no brands, one ear cropt, the other an under and upper keel. Whoever owns ſaid cow may have her, by proving her upon oath, paying charges, and applying to JOHN RENTZ jun.

Tolled before me, this 21ſt April, 1789,

JUSTUS H SCHEUBER, J. P.

GEORGIA. } By JAMES WHITEFIELD, Regiſter
(L. S.) } of Probats for the County of
J. WHITEFIELD. } Chatham, in the ſtate aforeſaid.

WHEREAS Mrs. Martha Melvin, the widow of George Melvin, late of the ſaid county, Eſquire, deceaſed, hath made application to me for letters of adminiſtration on the eſtate and effects of the ſaid deceaſed, Theſe are therefore to cite and admoniſh all and ſingular the kindred and creditors of the ſaid George Melvin, deceaſed, to be and appear before me in Savannah, on the 21ſt day of May next, to ſhew cauſe (if any they have) why letters of adminiſtration ſhould not be granted her.

Given under my hand and ſeal, at Savannah, the 20th day of April, 1789, and in the 13th year of the independence of the ſaid State

THE ſubſcribers being appointed attornies to Dr. John Irvine, during his abſence from this ſtate, requeſt all perſons indebted to him to call and diſcharge their reſpective accounts, or ſettle them by bond or note, as ſome demands againſt him require immediate liquidation

JAMES BULLOCH,
MATTHEW JOHNSTON,
JAMES ROBERTSON.

Savannah, April 17. 1789.

April 21, 1789.

MY wife Sarah having eloped from me, theſe are to warn all perſons againſt crediting her on my account, as I will not pay one farthing of any debt ſhe may contract from this date.

She has carried off part of my property, which I caution all perſons againſt purchaſing from her.

JAMES CLYATT.

Brought to the Workhouſe,

A NEGRO FELLOW, ſays his name is *Abraham*, and that he belongs to a Mr. *Alexander Frazer*, who lives on Indian Land, South Carolina; he is about five feet ſeven or eight inches high, about 24 or 25 years of age, country born.

A NEGRO WENCH, ſays her name is *Mary*, and that ſhe belongs to the ſame maſter; ſhe is about five feet two inches high, about 18 or 20 years of age, country born.

FREDERICK LONG.

Savannah, April 17, 1789.

VIENNA, December 27.

THE uneaſineſs which had ariſen from the ſteps taken by Pruſſia begin to ſubſide ſince his Pruſſian Majeſty has declared his intention to uſe all poſſible means to bring about a juſt and general accommodation; it was time that the Pruſſian Monarch ſhould explain himſelf in this manner, as otherwiſe (it is ſaid) a triple alliance would have been entered into between France, Ruſſia, and our Court.

The following is a copy of the report of Prince Gallitzin, the Ruſſian Ambaſſador at Vienna, relative to the capture of Oczakow:

" The place was taken by aſſault the 17th of December. The number of the beſiegers amounted to 14,000 men, that of the garriſon to 12,000, 7400 of whom were killed on the ſpot, excluſive of thoſe killed in the houſes. In this place they found 300 metal cannons and mortars; the grand powder magazine blew up, but they have taken a great quantity of ammunition of every kind. The number of inhabitants was 25,000, amongſt whom are 4000 very handſome women. The Ruſſians have loſt 1000 men, including 180 officers. The Bacha who commanded the fortreſs was made priſoner with the reſt of the garriſon. The Aga who commanded the troops was cut to pieces, as he would not yield."

London, January 5. Yeſterday morning died, at Caen Wood, the Right Hon. William Earl Mansfield. He is ſucceeded in his immenſe property by his nephew, Lord Viſcount Stormont; and the title goes to the noble Lord's eldeſt ſon.

The Right Hon. William Wyndham Grenville was this day elected Speaker of the Houſe of Commons. Sir Gilbert Elliot was propoſed, but on a diviſion there appeared a majority in favour of the former of 71.

15. The William Cadiz, Cowley, from Jamaica, is arrived at Waterford in diſtreſs, having had no ſuſtenance for three weeks but rum and ſugar.

20. The Mary, Cookie, from Jamaica to London, drove from her anchors in Waterford harbour, got aſhore, and it is feared will be loſt.

29. This morning died, aged 66, at his houſe in the city of Bath, Admiral Gambier. The Admiral laſt year married Miſs Necombe.

It is ſaid that the King's riches are ſeven millions in the Bank; and ſome foreigners ſay there are four millions in the Bank at Vienna.

Information has been ſent to the Admiralty Office that the ſhip Syren, Thomas Hayman, Maſter, bound from St. Ann's, Jamaica, to London, laden with ſugar, rum, pimenta, &c. was, on the 23d inſtant, driven aſhore at Beachyhead, in Suſſex, and, with the greateſt part of her cargo, totally loſt.

The Emperor's levies of money exceed thoſe of troops —at Vienna the merchants have offered him 25,000 florins, but he requires 40,000; the phyſicians have offered 10,000, but the Emperor ſays 30 000.

February 16. It has been thought that if his Majeſty ſhould really exhibit ſymptoms of returning reaſon all the meaſures relative to the Regency will be ſuſpended, and perhaps wholly revoked; but this is a miſtake, for it would be highly improper for his Majeſty to interfere in any publick buſineſs, leſt he ſhould relapſe, and it would be alſo neceſſary to eſtabliſh, in the fulleſt manner, the proofs of his ſanity. It is, however, with regret, we find that the late reports on this head are not founded upon ſuch ſubſtantial grounds as can juſtify our readers in placing much dependence on them.

The ſituation of his Majeſty is certainly, in point of health, very much improved, and ſome remarks, which have lately iſſued from him, have occaſioned a report that his intellectual powers were alſo conſiderably recovered—we are, however, aſſured, from very reſpectable authority, that, when the Prince of Wales lately viſited Kew, his Majeſty did not appear to know him. If this be a fact, and we are poſitively informed that it is, there is ſomething very baſe and ſhocking in exciting the hopes of a loyal people, with no other view than to ſerve a temporary purpoſe, and then to plunge the nation immediately after into grief, rendered more ſevere by a diſappointment of its moſt conſolatory wiſhes and cheering expectations.

20. It muſt afford our readers, and every good ſubject of theſe realms, the moſt heartfelt ſatiſfaction to be aſſured that, at a conſultation of the King's Phyſicians, his Majeſty was unanimouſly declared to have recovered the entire uſe of his reaſon; and he now appears to be advancing very faſt towards a perfect recovery of his health He has regained his appetite, ſleeps well, and awakes undiſturbed. His converſation is rational. He is ſenſible of his ſituation, and perceives his own recovery. He ſometimes enters upon particular ſubjects, and ſtops himſelf with ſaying, My head will not do for theſe things yet, but it will ſoon. On Wedneſday his Majeſty commanded his Aſtronomer to attend him in his obſervatory at Kew. He compared his time pieces with obſervations of the ſun, and computed how much each had loſt or gained in time, and went through this buſineſs as regularly and exactly as he had ever done when in the moſt perfect health; ſo that his Phyſicians are not without a ſanguine hope of ſeeing him ſoon reſume the reins of government. Every day, nay every hour, affords more favourable ſymptoms. Thirteen days have paſſed without the leaſt relapſe. He is allowed to converſe with his artiſts, gardeners, and workmen. He yeſterday aſked Dr. Willis ſome queſtions about politicks, who humbly begged of his Majeſty not to talk, or ſuffer himſelf to think, on that ſubject at preſent. The King promiſed he would not.

His Majeſty, at his own particular requeſt, is to be removed for a few days to Buckingham Houſe.

Kew Palace, February 19. His Majeſty continues to advance in recovery.

R Warren, J R. Reynolds, F. Willis.

20. His Majeſty makes daily progreſs in recovery.

G. Baker, L Pepys, F Willis.

KINGSTON, (Jamaica) March 14

ON Sunday laſt a ſmall foreign veſſel arrived in this harbour with thirty-one thouſand dollars on board. Eighteen gentlemen came paſſengers in this veſſel, to purchaſe ſlaves and dry goods.

A few weeks ago a negro wench and two children, belonging to a gentleman in the neighbourhood of Halfway Tree, ignorantly eat ſome of the root called Caſſava. The wench and children languiſhed for ſeveral days, from the pernicious effects of that poiſonous plant; one of the children very lately died, but the other and the wench it is ſuppoſed will recover.

28. A very tragical circumſtance occurred a few days ſince at Hall Head eſtate, St. Thomas in the Eaſt:— During the time of dinner a diſpute, on ſome trivial occaſion aroſe between a Mr. Biſſet (an Overſeer) and a Dr. D—e: Some friends interpoſing, the matter appeared to be ſettled, and, as the company ſat a conſiderable time after dinner, was by moſt forgot; but, when Mr B. was mounting his horſe to go home, the Doctor ruſhed on him, and with a knife ſtabbed him in the ſide.—The poor man immediately fell, dead; and the aſſaſſin, advantaging by the confuſion all preſent were thrown into, eſcaped, and has not ſince been heard of.

ST JOHN, (New Brunſwick) February 13.

EARLY this morning arrived here the Annapolis Packet, Capt. Thomas. By her we have the diſagreeable information that a fire broke out in Halifax, which conſumed 17 houſes, being the whole block belonging to Meſſrs. Cochrans of that place, and we are ſorry to add, that report ſays, very little of the effects belonging to the ſufferers were ſaved.

Philadelphia, March 11. On Saturday laſt, as the gaoler, attended by one of his turnkeys, was reconnoitring (according to his cuſtom) the eaſt wing of the gaol in this city, they were both attacked and ſeized by 22 of the moſt daring villains that ever diſgraced a priſon, in any country. With many inſulting expreſſions and biting taunts, they boaſted of their now having him in their power—and, with the moſt blaſphemous execrations, waved a large knife before his eyes and throat, threatening an inſtant revenge. After robbing him of his watch, money, and hat, and the turnkey of his coat, hat, keys, and a piſtol which he had in his pocket, theſe deliberate villains thruſt them down ſtairs, and confined them both in the dungeon for a conſiderable ſpace of time. They then clothed one Lupton, a man exactly of the ſize of the turnkey, in the hat and coat which they had robbed him of; he preceded the gang, and, as uſual with the turnkeys, rattled the keys, as a ſignal for the keeper of the outer door to come and let them out. The turnkey did not diſcover his miſtake until ſix had eſcaped, when he fortunately cloſed the grate upon the remainder.

During this time Mr. Reynolds was in "*durance vile*," and endeavouring to rouſe the officers of the houſe, by pounding againſt the door of the dungeon, when he found that the guard which they had placed over him had forſaken his poſt. His ſon, by accident, ſeeing his father's hat in the hands of ſome one of the rogues, which were ſhut in by the turnkey, ſuſpected ſomething, and ran round underneath the dungeon, and by this means whiſpered through the crack of the door to him, liberated his father and his frightened companion.

Mr. Reynolds's coolneſs and intrepidity on this occaſion only confirm the publick in their opinion, that to preſide is a dangerous office; where nightly watchfulneſs and daily penetration are ſo neceſſary requires a man of his uncommon perſeverance and aſſiduity.

We have the pleaſure to inform the publick, that, by the activity of the officers and ſervants of the gaol, &c. aided by ſome citizens, the remaining rogues were apprehended and confined in their former lodging, before eight o'clock the ſame evening.

14. We hear that the Truſtees of the Univerſity will ſome time next week deliver up to the Truſtees of the College the buildings in Fourth Street, and the other eſtates of the College, agreeably to the act of Aſſembly lately paſſed. The Univerſity will be continued in the ſame extenſive manner as heretofore, and, for this purpoſe, we underſtand, that new and elegant building known by the name of Philoſophical Hall is engaged for the reception of the ſtudents: The carpenters are buſily employed in preparing it, and expect to have it ready in ſix weeks. In the mean time the Truſtees of the Univerſity have

Figure 40. The Georgia Gazette, April 23, 1789, p. 2. By permission of NewsBank, Inc. and The American Antiquarian Society.

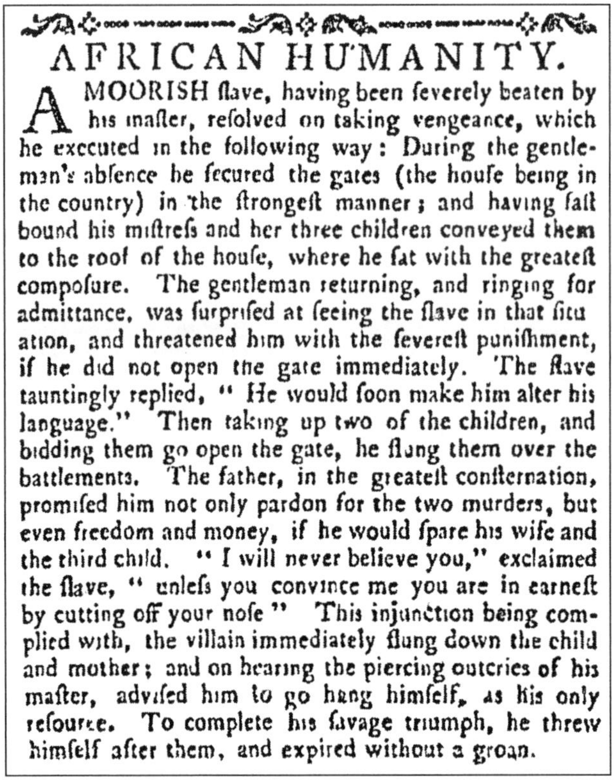

AFRICAN HUMANITY.

A MOORISH ſlave, having been ſeverely beaten by his maſter, reſolved on taking vengeance, which he executed in the following way: During the gentleman's abſence he ſecured the gates (the houſe being in the country) in the ſtrongeſt manner; and having faſt bound his miſtreſs and her three children conveyed them to the roof of the houſe, where he ſat with the greateſt compoſure. The gentleman returning, and ringing for admittance, was ſurpriſed at ſeeing the ſlave in that ſitu ation, and threatened him with the ſevereſt puniſhment, if he did not open the gate immediately. The ſlave tauntingly replied, "He would ſoon make him alter his language." Then taking up two of the children, and bidding them go open the gate, he flung them over the battlements. The father, in the greateſt conſternation, promiſed him not only pardon for the two murders, but even freedom and money, if he would ſpare his wife and the third child. "I will never believe you," exclaimed the ſlave, "unleſs you convince me you are in earneſt by cutting off your noſe" This injunction being complied with, the villain immediately flung down the child and mother; and on hearing the piercing outcries of his maſter, adviſed him to go hang himſelf, as his only reſource. To complete his ſavage triumph, he threw himſelf after them, and expired without a groan.

Figure 41. "AFRICAN HUMANITY," detail from *The Georgia Gazette*, April 23, 1789, p. 3. By permission of NewsBank, inc. and The American Antiquarian Society.

Gomez suspects the reliability of the *Georgia Gazette*'s news story, which he calls "melodramatic to the point of incredulity"; but he cannot resist using it to make a point about the distrustful and violent relationships between the African-born (whatever their social or cultural "type") and the slaveholder in America in the late 1700s.

London, England, 1569/70

What Gomez clearly does not know is that the news story recounted in the *Georgia Gazette* in 1789, which he interprets (however suspiciously) as a reflection of real-life *American* attitudes toward slaves, was actually a retelling of a popular *English* broadside ballad first registered in London more than 200 years earlier in 1569/70, re-registered under different titles twice in 1624 and again in 1675 and—apparently without registration—repeatedly reissued from 1570 to the early nineteenth century. For the period 1500–1700 alone I have so far tracked no fewer than seventeen different extant editions of the ballad (each varying in printer, tune, woodcut illustrations, and/or, more subtly, printed

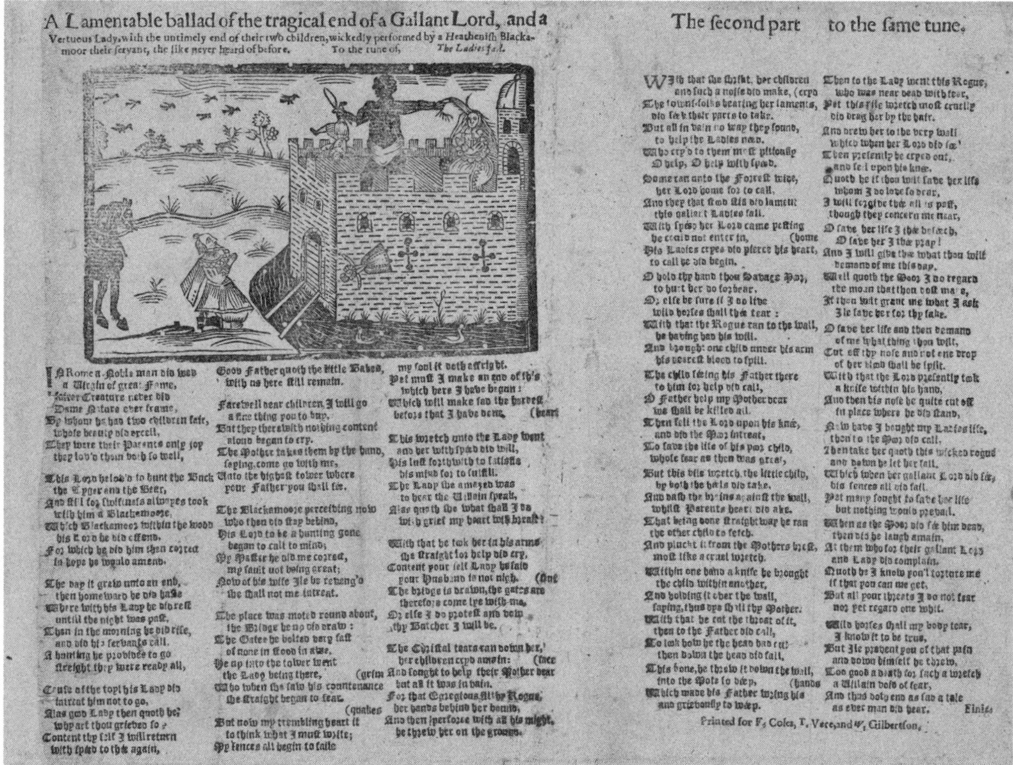

A Lamentable ballad of the tragical end of a Gallant Lord, and a Vertuous Lady, with the untimely end of their two children, wickedly performed by a Heathenish Blacka-moor their servant, the like never heard of before. To the tune of, The Ladies fall.

The second part to the same tune.

Printed for F. Coles, T. Vere, and W. Gilbertson.

Finis.

Figure 42. Ballad sheet facsimile, "A Lamentable ballad of the tragical end of a Gallant Lord, and a Vertuous Lady, with the untimely end of their two children, wickedly performed by a Heathenish Blacka-moor their servant, the like never heard of before" (c. 1658–64), EBBA 31955. University of Glasgow Library, Euing Ballads 197. By permission of University of Glasgow Library, Special Collections.

text) as well as a remarkable—considering the low survival rate of ballads—thirty-four extant copies. This was clearly an extremely popular broadside ballad. The earliest extant edition of the ballad I have found lies, together with a later edition, in William Euing's broadside ballad collection at the University of Glasgow, printed c. 1658–64 (Euing Ballads 197, EBBA 31955; Figure 42). This is the edition that I will primarily cite. The ballad most commonly appeared under subtle variations of the Euing title, "A Lamentable ballad of the tragical end of a Gallant Lord, and a Vertuous Lady, with the untimely end of their two children, wickedly performed by a Heathenish Blacka-moor their servant, the like never heard of before." For brevity, as noted above, I reference the title simply as "The Lady and the Blackamoor."[1]

The ballad story told in the extant broadside editions is longer and more detailed than that recounted in the *Georgia Gazette*. It also includes some

Figure 43. Woodcut impression from "A Lamentable ballad of the tragical end of a Gallant Lord, and a Vertuous Lady, with the untimely end of their two Children, wickedly performed by a Heathenish Blackamoor their servant, the like never heard of before" (c. 1658–64), EBBA 31955. University of Glasgow Library, Euing Ballads 197. By permission of University of Glasgow Library, Special Collections.

variations from the *Gazette* report: most notably, the ballad is set in Rome and is accompanied by a tailor-made woodcut imaging a distinctively medieval castle, replete with moat; there are only two children, not three; the lady is not only bound but raped by the blackamoor; and the lord dies on seeing his lady's fall. But the basic story line of the ballad is the same as in the *Georgia Gazette*. As in the *Gazette* news story, we hear of a blackamoor being disciplined by his lord in the woods and resolving on revenge; while the lord is away hunting, the blackamoor locks the house and follows the lady and her children up to the rooftop; when the lord returns and finds himself locked out, he threatens the blackamoor, and the blackamoor in response tosses the lord's children over the battlements; the lord begs the blackamoor to spare the lady; the blackamoor demands the lord first cut off his nose; and after the lord willingly does so, the blackamoor tosses the lady over the battlements and then throws himself after her.[2]

The woodcut accompanying the text and tune of the ballad was tailor-made for it (see detail, Figure 43). The illustration vividly captures the ballad's

Figure 44. Woodcut impression from "A Lamentable Ballad of the Tragical end of a Gallant Lord and a Vertuous Lady, with the untimely end of their two Children, wickedly performed by a Heathenish Blackamoor their servant: the like never heard of" (c. 1686–93), EBBA 30157. British Library, Roxburghe 1.220–221, C.20.f.7.220–221. © The British Library Board.

gruesome story in mid- and past action. We see, in the background, the past action in which the lord is out hunting while the blackamoor servant remains at home and terrorizes the lord's family; in the foreground, the lord, in the present, or at least in the middle of the action, and having returned from the hunt, is now addressing the ongoing threat and begging the blackamoor to spare the remainder of his family. What's missing in this woodcut impression, however, is the representation of part of the future action or end of the plot: the prone, dead, de-nosed lord.[3] This future fate of the lord can be seen restored in another extant seventeenth-century edition of the ballad, Roxburghe 1.220–221 (EBBA 30157; Figure 44). Here we can see the lord's future as well as his past and present, as he lies dead in the left middle ground, noseless (the old, worm-eaten woodcut from the Euing ballad has been entirely replaced with a block recut to restore this missing feature).

Most of the extant ballads indicate that this gruesomely illustrated story was to be sung, as if in cruel sympathy with the fate of the lord's wife, "To the tune of, *The Lady's* [or *Ladies*] *Fall.*" The tune's title reaches back to a popular

English ballad melody originally called "In Peascod Time"; Simpson gives this as the standard tune title for all subsequent renamings of the melody. Following is a notation of "In Peascod Time/The Lady's Fall" modernized from a late sixteenth-century manuscript (the original notation, typical of early music, we've observed, was unbarred). The top staff indicates the sung melody; the bottom staff, the sung or instrumental harmony:[4]

Even to the untrained musical eye, one can see that this is a very simple tune, with a tiny range of notes—a fourth. It is in the major mode (in the key of C). As we have observed, with some qualification, the major tends to be used for more upbeat songs. Indeed, this tune has a light and bouncy rhythm, similar to that of "Northern Nancy" in major when sung. James Revell Carr, in conversation with me, observed that, though it might seem odd (to the modern ear, at least) to hear a gruesome ballad sung in the major mode, such an unlikely coupling is not in fact that uncommon. The reason, he posited, is that a lighter tune provides counterpoint to, and even relief from, the extensive relation of horrible events in sensational ballads. Such relief would be called for especially given the great length of many pre-1650 two-part ballads. "The Lady and the Blackamoor" recording, available on **Track 35** of the Audio Companion, for example, runs in its entirety for almost eleven minutes! That's a lot of misery to absorb at one singing and hearing if the song were to have been sung consistently in a sorrowful or grave minor key. The more upbeat major offers some relief and even variety for the listener from the drawn-out narration of distressing events.

The tune could also perhaps be experienced as—for lack of a better word—"sweet," or what Catherine Molineux terms, describing the ballad as a whole (based on the occasional sympathetic outbursts by the narrator and townsfolk), "sentimental" (*Perfect Ebony*, 69). But I retain as more appropriate the term "sensational" and even "sensational tragedy." Indeed, it is especially hard to conjure much positive affect associated with the sentimental once the bouncy tune is made to fit the horrendous details of the text. Bell slows down the potentially uplifting melody in his singing of "The Lady and the Blackamoor" precisely to make the tune more somber and thus better suited to the gruesome story recounted. But even without employing this tactic, once text and tune are coupled, the mournful rules. A misalignment of musical and poetic stress reinforces this effect. Most notably, though the poetic meter fits the "classic" definition of ballad measure, at least as we've seen it defined in *The Princeton Encyclopedia of Poetry*—alternating lines of 4-3 poetic stresses—there is a stress-inducing tension between the music and the poetic emphases in "The Lady and the Blackamoor." The music's meter, as we have noted, demands four stresses over what roughly equates to one poetic line (the first and the third of these stresses in each poetic line are stronger than the second and fourth). But a problem arises that we have encountered before. The even lines of trimeter poetry—lines 2, 4, 6, and 8—do not contain enough poetic syllables to fit the music's prescribed metric stresses. The poetry falls short. The syllables in these lines are unable to accommodate the music's demand for an additional weaker metric stress that would normally follow the second strong stress toward the end of the poetic line. The singer typically instead subsumes the shorter repeated notes into one long note, drawing out the last syllable of the text, which poetically would already be stressed, but not more so than the previous poetic stresses of the line, to make the poetic meter fit the tune. As a consequence, this syllable receives an especially extended and strong phenomenal stress, both poetically and musically. The misalignment of media accent thus paradoxically, as if text and tune were in fact in cahoots, align in "The Lady and the Blackamoor" to effect something like a moan.

The poetic rhyme scheme further colludes with this phenomenal union of textual and musical emphasis over and above the metric stress—or, should I say, distress—even though the rhyming lines otherwise fall short. As in printed ballads generally, the rhyme scheme is not consistent throughout. But the dominant rhyming in this ballad, like its poetic meter, follows the classic ballad definition: a quatrain of abcb (here doubled to make an eight-line stanza of abcb/defe. This rhyme scheme places yet further emphasis, as if in the form of underscore, precisely at the end of the even lines where the ballad music's phenomenal stress and poetic accent collaborate to create heightened affect.

Take, for example, the second stanza of the ballad, which is the trigger for the tragic plot: the "correction" of the blackamoor in the wood. Following our previous practice of indicating the strongest two of the musical metric stresses in each poetic line with bold italics and the second strongest ones with italics, the stanza can be rendered as below:

This ***Lord*** he *lov'd* to ***hunt*** the *Buck*
  the ***Ty***ger *and* the ***Bear*** [common variant: ***Boor***],
And ***still*** for *swift*ness ***al***wayes *took*
  with ***him*** a *Black*a***moore,***
Which ***Black***a*moor* with***in*** the *wood*
  his ***Lord*** he *did* of***fend,***
For ***which*** he *did* him ***then*** cor*rect*
  in ***hope*** he *would* a***mend.*** (st. 2)

The modern notation for this stanza to "The Ladies Fall" (in later spellings, "The Lady's Fall"), which calls for the above musical metric strong and less strong stresses on the poetry, is shown below using the tool Minstrel. The notation is a transcription of Bell's interpretative singing of the stanza that necessarily makes adjustments between text and tune (**Track 36**). As always in Minstrel, the poetic text is underlaid; also, here the second half of the stanza is visually rendered below the first half and thus below the same corresponding notes because the second half repeats the first half's music notation—though variations occur and effects often differ in the singing, since the text changes.

You can hear this transcription rendered to a slowed-down fiddle audio, for ease of tracking the poetry and notation, on **Track 37**.

Observe especially the rhyming syllables in the short poetic lines: "***Bear***" (or "***Boor***"), *Black*-a-***moore***," "of-***fend***," and "a-***mend***." These heightened paired syllables chillingly encapsulate the plot of the ballad, which tracks the arresting animal-like—indeed *more* than animal-like—passion of the lord's blacka***moor*** in ***fend***ing for himself in order to ***mend***, that is, avenge, what (at least in his mind) is a misperceived offense in the woods, for which he has been unjustly punished. Again and again, despite the even poetic lines falling short of fitting the demands of the musical metric stress, these lines each move toward a mini poetic and musical climax. Their last, most musically and poetically strong syllables, gain additional phenomenal accentuation through elongation. And, again and again, these extended and thus phenomenally more emphatic musical and poetic stresses are reinforced further by the ending poetic syllables, which call out to each other through rhyme. The rhymes thus even more emphatically draw out the sensational story of the blackamoor's offense and revenge, inducing spinal chills. Other examples of such empowered rhymes: in their pleas to their lord in stanza 4 that he not desert them, the lord's wife and children entreat him not to "***go***" "***so***" (out hunting) but instead "a-***gain***" "re-***main***" with them (with the emphasis on the main gain of staying). But the lord does not listen. He leaves his family "be-***hind***," recalling the hind, buck, or hart (punning on "heart") that the lord hunts. And, as the lord goes off to hunt, so does his Moor—but within the lord's own home. Rhyming with "be-***hind***"—again evoking the hart or deer—the relator declares that, on the lord's departure, the Moor then calls to "***mind***" the lord's offense in "correcting" him on their last hunt, which discipline the Moor perceives to be "***great***." The Moor thus refuses the lady's pleas by which she did him "in-***treat***" (st. 6). The blackamoor has another horrible "great" "treat" in store for the lady and her children—and for those of us who, admittedly or not, get a thrill from the chill in reading, hearing, and seeing pictured the left-behind innocents made into victims, as if they were domestic substitutes for the lord's hunted hart/heart. Fulfilling the Moor's demand that the lord cut off his nose to save his wife, once he's been called back from hunting by the alarmed "towns-folks" (st. 12), the lord does so without hesitation. He then to the Moor did "***call***" to witness his self-maiming, but the Moor still lets the lady "***fall***" from the tower—the tune's title is, after all, "The Ladies Fall" (hereafter, "The Lady's Fall")—and throws himself after her. In sum, the lord did "***fail***" to "pre-***vail***" (st. 23), suggesting the unsuccessful low point or "***vale***" of the moat into which the Moor throws the children, the lady, and himself to their deaths. Paradoxically, the rhyming syllables of the even, trimeter lines of poetry—which notably fall short of the music's four-stress meter—in fact function, through the phenomenal musical emphasis on the poetry, to collaborate with the poetry's own strong accent and rhyme. Together poetic and musical emphases, phenomenal accents, and rhyme raise to intense heights the movingly affective narrative action. Poetically and musically—the music's strong emphasis collaborating with its phenomenal accent—an interaction of the two media emerges that enlivens the sensationalism of this tragic tale. They bring the story gruesomely *home.*

Much more is happening in the combination of poetic and musical movement throughout the ballad, which capitalizes on the limited range of the tune and the repetition of the melody of lines 1–4 by lines 5–8. These effects are admittedly—and, in a sense, given the sensational nature of the ballad, ironically—subtle because the ballad is so constrained by the melody's four-note range. But that fine range forces one's ear to attend to the smallest nuances, that is, to be on edge.

In stanza 2, for instance, the repeated nomen, "Blackamoor," is given poetic emphasis in the very fact of its being repeated twice in adjacent lines (lines 4 and 5). Our ears perk up, and with good cause. This linguistic prominence is a red flag. It is extended by the musically strong emphasis that falls on the word's last syllable, "***moore***," in the fourth line and on its first syllable "***Black***" in the fifth line. The musical metric stresses here confuse and overturn the poetry's metrical stress. Poetically, the stress would always fall on the first syllable of "Blackamoor," as can be heard in both a British and an American pronunciation of the word in the *OED.*[5] The interaction of poetic and musical meter here fails to compensate for a conflict that we saw resolved through the music's phenomenal accents and the poetry's rhymes that reinforce the otherwise falling short of the poetic meter in the even lines of the stanza. Text and tune, when it comes to the word "blackamoor," have at best a rocky relationship. In a word, "Blackamoor" is destabilizing. The effect of singing the figure's name with such difference within close-together lines enacts something like a shifting or unstable identity.

Such unsettledness continues when we look to lines 4 and 8. These lines create a subtle phenomenal accent in addition to the poetic and musical stresses. In line 4, the extended reference to "***him***"—the Lord—rises slightly, by a step, as if raising up the status of the Lord—only to fall by two notes into a "vale" of low notes lying on "a *Black*-a-***moore***" (with "***moore***," as observed above, appearing at the end of a short, rhyming line, drawn out into something like a lamenting groan). Similarly, in line 8, the word "***hope***" follows the pattern of reaching up another whole step, as if in a slight, *hope*ful rise, only to fall down a note to "he" (the blackamoor), and then into the vale of "*would* a-***mend***" (with "mend" elongated, again, into a moan). Indeed, it is as if the phenomenal musical accents combine with the poetic accents in most of this stanza to forebode just how much the blackamoor will fall short of a hoped amendment, as the even lines of the stanza, in their three poetic stresses, fall short of the four metrical stresses, forcing an extended stress on "***moore***" and "***mend***." There is no hope the blackamoor will amend but rather, in his mind, there is "more" to "mend," in terms of revenge.

Life certainly often imitates art. But the similarity in the sequence of events reported in the eighteenth-century *Georgia Gazette* to the seventeenth-century English broadside ballad, which even more affectively drives the details of the story home through its compelling intra-media of illustration, tune, and text—a ballad possibly published as early as 1569/70—is too close in too many details and too unlikely in its action to be such a case. More likely than life imitating art, what's happening in the appearance of the "news" story in the *Georgia Gazette* is that English ballad artifacts, through a much-mediated ancient history of tales and more recent broadside ballads, is being recalled and re-presented on American soil as if it actually had happened in the historical there and then. As in the telling and retelling of urban legends, the song or the actual broadside ballad or simply the mental image of the woodcut to "The Lady and the Blackamoor" likely took ship with the many emigrants from England to America in the seventeenth and eighteenth centuries, and got recollected and passed on there as "real life" news.

Of course, even if the American news story was based on ballad fiction, composed more than 200 years earlier, and even if it was "melodramatic to the point of incredulity," it nonetheless would have held resonant meaning for the residents of 1789 Georgia, specifically about master-slave relations, even to the fine point of indeed possibly prompting reflection upon master-Moor versus just plain master-African relations, as surmised by Gomez in his book of the antebellum South. Ironically, however, the visual presence of blackness, which dominates the *broadside ballads*, is mostly omitted from the *Georgia Gazette*'s retelling of their story. The early ballads are printed in eye-catching black letter, which we have come to recognize as a beloved feature of late sixteenth- and seventeenth-century heyday ballads. As such, the blackness of the text foregrounds the dominating presence of the blackamoor in the ballad. But though the basic story of the Euing broadside ballad is recollected in the *Georgia Gazette*, the ballad's multiple imaging of blackness is almost entirely and, in the American context, ironically forgotten.

The *Gazette* story most notably lacks a picture of the monstrous blackamoor, whether because of the woodcut's unavailability or because the medieval castle imaged in the cut would immediately have been recognized by its viewers as decidedly un-American and therefore unrealistic. Furthermore, the news story is printed in what contemporaries called "white letter" or, in today's terminology, "roman" font. As we have seen, white letter came to dominate all seventeenth-century publications in England by the end of that period and even earlier in political broadside ballads. Likely, given the printing of the *Georgia Gazette* in the late eighteenth century and the reliance of the colonies on imported presses and typeface from England, black letter was by that time no longer readily available or perhaps not even easily readable. Roman or white-letter type would have been the dominant typeface shipped to American printers and later reproduced in American foundries. The presence of visual blackness that characterized black letter and woodcut illustrations remains only in trace in the *Gazette* report—in the ornamental flourish that heads the story wryly titled "African Humanity."

Even more ironically, the early black-letter broadside ballads of "The Lady and the Blackamoor," which *do* showcase blackness, are not, I would argue, first and foremost about attitudes to or relationships with actual blacks in England, regardless of whether they are Moors—at least not in the story's original conception in 1569/70. Black letter served many practical, intellectual, and emotive functions in the early modern period, as we have discussed in previous chapters. One such function was a strong association made in the seventeenth century across Europe with the English nation. But black letter is not tied to the English as a race, other than in the typeface's growing deprecation in the course of the late seventeenth and into the eighteenth century as "Gothic" in the sense of "barbaric," as opposed to the classical (read "civilized") roman typeface. Furthermore, "The Lady and the Blackamoor" story goes out of its way to present itself as removed from English reality in both its sensationalism and its physical locale. The medieval-looking castle is situated in a faraway, fairy-tale-sounding land—"In Rome a Noble man did wed / a Virgin of great Fame" (st. 1)—where one might fabulously hunt not only the "Buck" and "Bear" but also the "Tyger" (st. 2). Of course, accounts of blackamoors or simply "Moors" (which generally referred to all Africans in the early reports) date back to classical, biblical, and medieval stories, as we have observed, such as the imaginative tales told in Sir John Mandeville's *Travels* composed around 1360. From the many mythological accounts of blackamoors handed down, one can extract some simple fictionalized stereotypes: blacks of Africa were heathens (the ballad's title calls the blackamoor "Heathenish"); they were naked (notice the little clothing the blackamoor wears); and they were exorbitantly sexual, the male genitalia thought to be significantly large, hence the rape of the lady in the ballad (though not, interestingly, in the *Georgia Gazette* story—crossing such a line by this point in

American history appears too horrific to even imagine). All these early folk and fantasized stories preceded the actual appearance of blacks from Africa into America and England.

Some real-life blacks from Africa, sometimes by way of America or elsewhere, certainly arrived in England by 1570. John Lok brought back "certaine black slaves" to London in 1555, and in 1562/63 John Hawkins began his first of three voyages to Africa and then on to the New World, pioneering the triangular trade route (England, Africa, New World, England) that would become the lifeline of England's Western Empire (Walvin, *Black and White*, 1, 31–35). Some Africans as slaves or perhaps free sailors likely came back on Hawkins's return voyages or on other ships arriving in English ports, especially in the major trade harbors of London and Bristol. About a decade after the blackamoor ballad's first registration, a blackamoor makes an appearance in the Bridewell Court records of 1577, and Queen Elizabeth thought the presence of blacks significant enough by the 1590s to issue proclamations ordering them deported to ease London's population growth. But the government issued similar policies about the same time against vagrants and rogues, many of whom, as I have argued in *Unsettled*, were in fact itinerant laborers, and whose numbers far outreached those of immigrant and naturalized Africans. Such proclamations are often more reflective of propaganda and displaced anxiety than reality.

Thus, despite the recent vibrant efforts by British historians to recover early resident Africans' forgotten histories, the numbers of naturalized blacks in the country remained relatively small even by the mid-seventeenth century. In 1650, only twenty blackamoors (some with Portuguese- or Spanish-sounding names, like Peter Cavandigoe, the "blackamoor") made it into Bridewell records out of approximately 40,000 recorded offenders (Griffiths, *Lost Londons*, 73–74).[6] Some African blackamoors could surely be seen exhibited as exotic curiosities in the court of Elizabeth herself (she had a black entertainer and a black page) and more so in the courts of her successors. And, by the end of the seventeenth century, blacks were a common feature not only in aristocratic but also in well-to-do middle-class households (if Pepys's patron and great uncle, Lord Montagu, had a blackamoor footboy, so Pepys in the 1670s and 1680s owned and sold two slaves, and in 1669 temporarily employed a blackamoor cookmaid as a servant; Tomalin, *Samuel Pepys*, 177). Clearly, then, the moving story of "The Lady and the Blackamoor" had the potential for racialized interpretations that would likely have acquired different, and more expansive, meanings as the ballad was reproduced in the course of the seventeenth and eighteenth and into the nineteenth centuries.

The Servants' Public

But let's return to the originary moment of the ballad's recording in the Stationers' Register in 1569/70 when so few real-life blacks would have actually been seen by the general populace of England. If we concede that the historical moment of "The Lady and the Blackamoor" at this time would have been recognized by its viewers, readers, listeners, and singers to be sensational fiction, with no grounding in any firsthand knowledge of blackamoors or any actual news event about a real-life blackamoor, especially since the story is displaced into a mythical Rome (that has tigers), one might still ask: Why isn't the blackamoor represented as a "slave"? Rome, however it might be exoticized with tigers, did have slaves in abundance, and I suspect that most early moderners knew this, just as they had received accounts of Africans who were made slaves. But, as Molineux notes, Britons mentally held a "peculiar fuzziness" about the status of blacks precisely because of the distance from America and the absence of real-life Africans even in the metropolis. Such fuzzy thinking led to a slippage in references to black slaves as servants. This slippage held true into the early eighteenth century, Molineux argues, even though by then British merchants held prominent roles in the Atlantic slave trade, because "the metropolitan market for African labor remained predominantly urban and largely luxury." After all, the British already had servants indentured under their master and mistress's rule for typically seven years. What need of slaves? Indeed, "More often than not," Molineux observes, "Britons at home referred to enslaved Africans as servants, a linguistic and visual slip that reflected the fact that bondage in Britain visually resembled other common forms of servitude" (*Perfect Ebony*, 8). Whether in its earliest incarnation our ballad blackamoor is so "fuzzily" marked or, more likely, was not associated with slaves because slaves at that time were *especially* rare entities in London, the blackamoor is denoted specifically in the ballad's title not as slave but as *servant*: "a Heathenish Blackamoor their *servant*" (my emphasis).

The fact that the blackamoor is a servant, not a slave, is reinforced by the implications that his crime in the ballad is not simply rape and murder, if that weren't enough, but "petty treason"—which slaves could not commit since they were owned by, not in service to, a master. That is, they were property. The suggestion that the blackamoor in fact commits "petty treason" is linguistically raised to high treason—rebellion against the king—in yet another slippage in which he is imagined by his lord and himself as being drawn by horses. The lord threatens the blackamoor that "wild horses shall thee tear" (col. 4, st. 3), and the blackamoor internalizes that threat as a fact in the concluding stanza: "Wild horses shall my body tear, / I know it to be true." Both master and servant are referring to the double "drawing" that was part of the punishment for high treason. The guilty party was first drawn behind a cart pulled by horses to the place of execution, and then drawn a second time; after being hanged until almost dead, he was cut down and his four limbs drawn in separate directions by horses, before he was disemboweled, then literally dismembered (his limbs that were drawn by the horses literally cut off), and finally beheaded.[7]

Viewed specifically as someone capable of committing and being punished for not only petty treason—a servant rebelling against his lord—but also high treason—a subject rebelling against his king (the lord was after all supposed to be king of his household)—the blackamoor becomes a sensationalized criminal representative of the many servants as well as apprentices, who occupied positions akin to servants, living in early modern London. Together, at the time, servants and apprentices constituted on the order of one-third to one-half of London's labor force and about one-fifth of its total population (Griffiths, *Youth and Authority*, 327). Significantly, in "The Lady and the Blackamoor," furthermore, the blackamoor is called not only a "servant" but also a "rogue." This derogatory term would trigger familiar (and, for many of the more established sorts, uneasy) associations with other servants and apprentices in the period, who were subject to arrest for vagrancy if they turned deviant and went "masterless." "Rogue" was Thomas Harman's title for the most aggressive of such vagrants, and his use of the term in his pamphlet *A Caveat for Common Cursitors*, published in 1566, twice in 1568, and again in 1573, clearly influenced its later employment in the 1572 statute against "Rogues, Vagabonds, and Sturdy Beggars."[8] The late sixteenth and early seventeenth centuries were preoccupied with the idea that youthful servants and apprentices had a "vagrant will" (Griffiths, *Youth and Authority*, 15), and could at any moment go rogue, running off at "liberty" to haunt the backstreets of London, wandering, stealing, and engaging in makeshift itinerant work to get by, including the peddling of ballads on the streets. Certainly, the number of young runaways figures hugely in the Bridewell records of the period (327). Authorities most feared that masterless servants and apprentices would band together with other vagrant rogues and cause insurrection, which, on a small scale, as in a 1595 riot, they actually did (Carroll, *Fat King*, 144).

Tellingly, servants and apprentices also had a record of banding together with poor blacks in England in the eighteenth century and with black slaves in protests and insurrections earlier in New World America, as documented by Peter Linebaugh and Marcus Rediker in *The Many-Headed Hydra*. Indeed, such banding together might well have roots in their shared bondage: many sailors and servants had been forcibly impressed or abducted—to "spirit," "barbarbos," or "trepan" someone came into common parlance by the mid-seventeenth century for such forced servitude (110–11). As if anticipating the sympatico alliances that later formed between servants/apprentices and slaves, a 1547 statute of Edward VI declared that any vagrant or runaway from his master was to be apprehended, marked with a "V" (for "Vagrant") on the breast, and made the master's slave for two years. If the servant-now-slave ran away again, he would be branded on the forehead or cheek with an "S" (for "Slave") and made a slave forever, including having rings of iron put around his neck. This statute turned out to be unenforceable and was repealed within two years, but branding, cutting off of the ends of ears and, most commonly, whipping and sending vagrants and runaways to Bridewell or into forced indenture in the Americas remained common features of subsequent laws and practice (Griffiths, *Youth and Authority*, 314, 347).

Occasionally, servants and apprentices were dragged into court for committing violent acts against their masters. But more often than not, they were themselves the victims of cruelty. Though Lawrence Stone was extreme in depicting the late sixteenth and early seventeenth centuries as a period of near sadistic flogging, at home and especially at all levels of schooling (*Family, Sex and Marriage*, 161–74), violence inflicted on children and especially on apprentices and servants was the norm. The cases that reached the courts were outrageous in their brutality. In these lawsuits we hear of masters who inflicted ferocious punishments described as "unnatural," "inhumane," "monstrous," "cruel," "strange," and "tyrannical" (Griffiths, *Youth and Authority*, 347). The specific charge most often made was of inflicting "*unreasonable*" correction for "*no cause*." So in 1630, Richard Playford filed a petition in Norwich's Quarter Sessions alleging that his master "had *unreasonably* and *without any just cause* abused and evil intreated him." The court ruled, indeed, that the master had "much abused" Playford "with *unreasonable* stripes and correction for *small or no cause*" (314; my emphases).

Such unreasonable brutality is sung about and imaged in a ballad from around 1620, "The cryes of the Dead," Pepys Ballads 1.116–117 (EBBA 20048; Figure 45). This ballad tells of a master-weaver who savagely kills two of his apprentices before being convicted for murdering a third. In each case, he is said to have beaten the child-servants "cruelly / *for no cause*" (st. 4). "Witness," the relator tells us of the second murdered child:

> Witness this harmles child
>   that he misused sore,
> Scourging him day by day,
>   *not knowing cause wherefore*,
> Unlawfull government
>   brings him unto his end,
> From such like cruelty
>   all servants God defend. (st. 9; my emphasis)

Witness also how the first woodcut illustration in this ballad echoes or prefigures that of "The Lady and the Blackamoor" (Figures 43 and 44) in which the blackamoor servant cruelly dangles his master's child by the leg. But in "The cryes of the Dead" the tables are turned: it is the *master* who victimizes, in dangling, a child/servant. This latter ballad might also provoke an associative hit for a viewer/reader/listener with "The Judgement of Salomon" (e.g., Pepys Ballads 1.30–31, c. 1630; EBBA 20143), in which a servant of Solomon dangles the child under dispute of ownership by its ankle, with sword drawn, ready to slice it into two.

Punishments enacted on youthful servants and apprentices, whether with or without cause, could be administered by either the master or the mistress of the household (Dolan, *Dangerous Familiars*). So prevalent was the practice that, as Ralph Houlbrooke observes, the clergyman Thomas Becon felt the need to preach a warning to masters not to fall out with their servants and not to "curse, and lame them, cast dishes and pots at their heads, beat them, [and] put them in danger of their lives" (*English Family*, 175). Samuel Pepys could himself be almost wantonly cruel to his servants. Finding his house "full of washing" one day and his wife angry about a visit from Pepys's associate Will, but at the same time protective of one maid he favored, Jane, Pepys instructs his wife, as if on a whim and to fulfill his own undirectable anger, "to beat at least the little girl" in their service (*Diary*, 5.13, 1664). The very next year, after hearing that his maids had let in a "rogueing Scotch woman that haunts the office, to help them wash and scour in our house," Pepys again scapegoats the child maid: "I fell mightily out, and made my wife, to the disturbance of the house and neighbours, to beat our little girle: and then we shut her down into the cellar and there she lay all the night." He adds, with no sense of remorse, "So we to bed" (*Diary*, 6.39, 1665). The cellar where their "little girle" servant was locked was where the excrement of the house was collected and must have caused a nightmarish below-ground experience for the child as

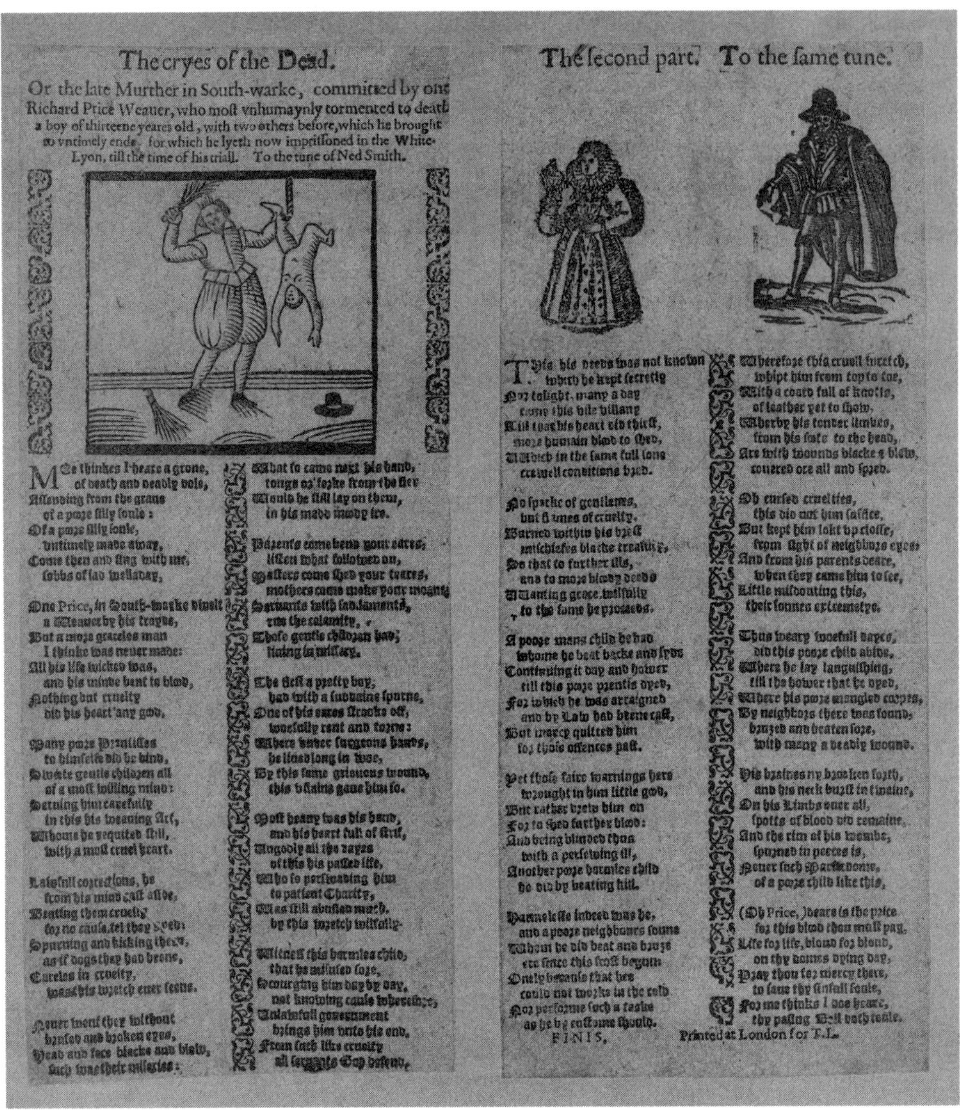

The cryes of the Dead.

Or the late Murther in South-warke, committed by one Richard Price Weauer, who most vnhumaynly tormented to death a boy of thirteene yeares old, with two others before, which he brought to vntimely ends, for which he lyeth now imprissoned in the White-Lyon, till the time of his triall. To the tune of Ned Smith.

ME thinkes I heare a grone,
of death and deadly dole,
Ascending from the graue
of a poore silly soule:
Of a poore silly soule,
vntimely made away,
Come then and sing with me,
sobbs of sad welladay,

One Price, in South-warke dwelt
a Weauer by his trade,
But a more graceles man
I thinke was neuer made:
All his life wicked was,
and his minde bent to blood,
Nothing but cruelty
did his heart any good.

Many poore Prentisses
to himselfe did he bind,
Sweete gentle children all
of a most willing mind:
Seruing him carefully
in this his weauing Art,
Whome he requited still,
with a most cruel heart.

Lawfull corrections, he
from his mind cast aside,
Beating them cruelly
for no cause, tel they dyed:
Spurning and kicking them,
as if dogs they had beene,
Careles in cruelty,
was this wretch euer seene.

Neuer went they without
brused and broken eyes,
Head and face blacke and blew,
such was their miseries:

What so came next his hand,
tongs or forke from the fire
Would he still lay on them,
in his madd moody ire.

Parents come bend your eares,
listen what followed on,
Masters come shed your teares,
mothers come make your moane,
Seruants with sad laments,
rue the calamity,
Those gentle children haue
liuing in misery.

The first a pretty boy,
had with a suddaine spurne,
One of his eares strooke off,
woefully rent and torne:
Where vnder surgeons hands,
he liued long in woe,
By this same grieuous wound,
this villaine gaue him so.

Most heauy was his hand,
and his heart full of strife,
Vngodly all the dayes
of this his passed life,
Who so perswading him
to patient Charity,
Was still abused much,
by this wretch wilfully.

Witnesse this harmles child,
that he misused sore,
Scourging him day by day,
not knowing cause wherefore,
Vnlawfull gouernment
brings him vnto his end,
From such like cruelty
all seruants God defend.

The second part. To the same tune.

THis his deeds was not knowen
which he kept secretly
For to light, many a day
came this vile villany
Till that his heart did thirst,
more humain blood to shed,
Which in the same full long
cruell conditions bred.

No sparke of gentlenes,
but sinnes of cruelty,
Burned within his brest
mischiefes blacke treasury,
So that to further ills,
and to more bloody deeds
Wanting grace, wilfully
to the same he proceeds.

A poore mans child he had
whome he beat backe and syde
Continuing it day and hower
till this poore prentis dyed,
For which he was arraigned
and by Law had beene cast,
But mercy quitted him
for those offences past.

Yet those faire warnings here
wrought in him little good,
But rather drew him on
For to shed farther blood:
And being blinded thus
with a persewing ill,
Another poore harmles child
he did by beating kill.

Harmelesse indeed was he,
and a poore neighbours sonne
Whom he did beat and bruze
ere since this frost begunn
Onely because that hee
could not worke in the cold
Nor performe such a taske
as he by custome should.

Wherefore this cruell wretch,
whipt him from top to toe,
With a coard full of knotts,
of leather yet to show,
Wherby his tender limbes,
from his foote to the head,
Are with wounds blacke & blew,
couered ore all and spred.

Oh cursed cruelties,
this did not him suffice,
But kept him lokt vp closse,
from sight of neighbors eyes:
And from his parents deare,
when they came him to see,
Little misdouting this,
their sonnes extremetye.

Thus weary woefull dayes,
did this poore child abide,
Where he lay languishing,
till the hower that he dyed,
Where his poore mangled corpes,
By neighbors there was found,
bruzed and beaten sore,
with many a deadly wound.

His braines ny broken forth,
and his neck burst in twaine,
On his Limbs euer all,
spotts of blood did remaine,
And the rim of his wombe,
spurned in peeces is,
Neuer such Martir donne,
of a poore child like this,

(Oh Price,) heare is the price
for this blood thou must pay,
Life for life, blood for blood,
on thy domes dying day,
Pray thou for mercy there,
to saue thy sinfull soule,
For me thinks I doe heare,
thy passing Bell doth towle.

FINIS.

Printed at London for T.L.

Figure 45. Ballad sheet facsimile, "The cryes of the Dead. Or the late Murther in South-warke, committed by one Richard Price Weauer, who most vnhumaynly tormented to death a boy of thirteene yeares old, with two others before, which he brought to vntimely ends[,] for which he lyeth now imprissoned in the White-Lyon, till the time of his triall" (c. 1620), EBBA 20048. Magdalene College, Cambridge, Pepys Library, Pepys Ballads 1.116–117. By permission of the Pepys Library, Magdalene College, Cambridge.

her master and mistress lay comfortably upstairs in their bed. Though Pepys identifies the maid as "our little girle," his supposedly "fatherly/masterly" correction seems to embrace, with little reflection, brutality beyond cause.

So, we might ask, how would a male or even female servant or apprentice respond on encountering the sensational violence of the broadside ballad "The Lady and the Blackamoor," perhaps belted out on the streets by a runaway apprentice or servant? We are given very little detail in the ballad as to the wrong committed by the blackamoor that provoked his master's "correction," only that the "Blackamoore within the wood / his Lord he did offend: / For which he did him then correct / in hope he would amend" (st. 2). But the blackamoor himself believes "My Master he did me correct / my fault not being great" (st. 6). How many servants and apprentices would align themselves with the blackamoor at this point? How many had only moments earlier been cursed or beaten, or locked in an excrement-filled cellar, had a pot thrown at their heads, or suffered some other violent indignity by their master or even their mistress for—in their thinking—"small or no cause"? How many would hear the blackamoor echoing other abused servants and apprentices, like Playford, when he testifies, "My Master he did me correct, / my fault not being great" (st. 6)? The ability for a servant or an apprentice to project him- or herself into the position of the "corrected" blackamoor at this moment in the ballad is especially permitted by the ballad's very vagueness about the nature of the servant's wrongdoing and his correction. The openness of the quality of the supposed wrong invites many a servant or apprentice to insert in its place remembrance of a specific injury done to him or her under which she or he might still be fuming and wishing "*if only I could get revenge*."

Listening to and seeing the extreme vengeance that the blackamoor enacts upon the lord (and maybe even upon the lady) in "The Lady and the Blackamoor" ballad might well have been pleasurable to a servant or an apprentice still hurting from his latest indignity suffered under a perceived-to-be unnaturally cruel master—who in his imagination, was just as monstrous, cruel, and inhumane as the alien figure of the blackamoor, with whom the lord in the ballad is so closely matched. She or he might have taken the opportunity in passing by to sing along, and especially voice the words of the blackamoor with more of an upbeat rhythm than a doleful one, which the tune of "The Lady's Fall" easily permits. Of course, if asked outright, the apprentice or servant would deny this—"That's a Blackamoor, not me, for goodness sake!" But this is what makes the ballad's imagined excess of violence so movingly satisfying. It allows someone to witness and subliminally partake of the outrageous act of revenge and at the same time condemn such action as the inhumane deed of an alien, fictionalized "Other," a blackamoor.

The Masters' Public

Or perhaps the ballad's explosive violence spoke subliminally to another significant sector of the population—male householders—and specifically to nervousness felt by husbands in the seventeenth century over a perceived loss of control over the domestic space of their homes to their wives. I have discussed such anxiety over the feminization of the domestic space in my article "Not Home," where I show that the alehouse run by the alewife was frequently positioned in broadside ballads in opposition to the perceived constraints of the domestic house. As I point out in that piece, we "know from the early work of Alice Clark and more recent studies by Ian Archer and others that women in the late sixteenth and especially in the seventeenth century were increasingly subject to economic and social sanctions that restricted their 'labors'—even the vagrant labors of female hawkers and fishwives—forcing their removal to the domestic sphere of the home." I conclude, "As a consequence, the domestic space became gendered female. It became 'the wife's space.' And this domination of the home by the wife, at least as expressed in the literature of the period, made men very nervous" (508). Uneasiness over the domestic space as female would explain the seeming obsession of the husband in "The Lady and the Blackamoor" with leaving home every day to go hunting—to get out of the house—despite (or perhaps because of) the extensive pleading of wife and children that he stay home. This ballad thus echoes the many alehouse ballads in which the wife begs her husband not to go out drinking and leave her alone. We are told, "This Lord he lov'd to hunt" (st. 2) and, indeed, he appears to spend little time at home, returning from the hunt at the end of the day only to set out again first thing the next morning: "Than in the morning he did rise, / and did his servants call, / A hunting he provides to go / streight they were ready all" (st. 3).

Hunting stands in here for specifically masculine activities that occur outside the home—not only drinking in homosocial alehouses but also war and even work. Hunting is a prominent motif in many of the ballads set to the tune of "The Lady's Fall" and has a long history. In the melody's earliest naming, "In Peascod Time" (recognized by Simpson as the tune's standard title for "The Lady's Fall"), the tune takes its title from the first line of an anonymous pastoral song, "The Shepheards Slumber," in *England's Helicon* (1600). The song begins "In Pescod time, when Hound to horne, / gives eare till Buck be kild."[9] Ross Duffin and Sarah F. Williams also cite another of this tune's early variant namings—"The Hunt's Up"—which further references the hunting motif prominently featured in the pastoral song's first line (Duffin, 292; Williams,

Damnable Practices, 82). Of note, looking forward in our discussion (and back to "The Lady and the Blackamoor"), this early anonymous ballad merges literal with figurative hunting: it adopts the formulaic, allegorical dream sequence wherein the shepherd's dream quickly turns to metaphorical hunting, in this case also following the formulas of Petrarchan love: the buck, also known in the period as a hart, as we have seen, becomes metaphorical for the human hearts of lovers slain en masse by a blood-bathed and exultant Cupid.

More in sympathy with later ballads to this melody, which continue in the sensational vein and the theme of strongly emphasized literal hunting (though the metaphorical is always on the horizon and available for the thinking), is the famous and age-old ballad "Chevy Chase." This wildly popular ballad was sung to a tune by the same name as the ballad's title, though Simpson also associates "Chevy Chase" with a now lost tune, "Flying Fame" (96–98). Most important to our focus on the ramifications of hunting in "The Lady and the Blackamoor," Simpson further points out the close connection between the tune of "Chevy Chase" and "In Peascod Time" (later, "The Lady's Fall"), as well as a third tune known as "The Children in the Wood." Though Simpson's language becomes dense in his discussion of the close links between these tunes, he seems to imply that the melodies are interchangeable, or that the titles for the tunes may have shifted according to audience and even generational leanings (105, 370–71). We need for a moment to pursue this idea of the interchangeability and interrelational namings of the tunes if we are to more comprehensively grasp the possible ramifications of hunting in "The Lady and the Blackamoor." In doing so, we encounter another demonstration of Manuel DeLanda's assemblage theory in which each tune—like the other component Lego pieces of a ballad—is an autonomous movable part, as if an individual, which could replace another tune, creating a new set of relations.

For the purposes of this section, focused on a master's potential assemblage of publics, we would do well now to circle back and interrogate further what motivates the master's hunting of the buck/hart in "The Lady and the Blackamoor." At the simplest level, the lord would appear to be drawn to the homosocial activity of hunting, as would seem to be the case in the other ballads where lords hunt, whatever the tune sung. We are told the lord "alwayes took / with him a Blackemoore," and he appears every morning to call together "all" his servants for the hunt, in what is clearly a companionable all-male bonding (sts. 2–3). But what is also stressed in "The Lady and the Blackamoor" is the analogy of hunting not to war—as in "Chevy Chase"—but to work and purchasing power or, to extend that analogy into a modern metaphor, to the act of "bringing home the bacon." Seen in this latter light, it is highly significant that when the children beg the father to remain with them at home, he responds, as if offering them compensation: "Farewell dear children, I will go / a fine thing you to *buy*" (st. 5.; my emphasis but also poetically and melodically emphasized and drawn out as well as given a terrifying exclamation point in the rhyming of "buy" with "cry" in line 4 of the stanza). So, too, when the lord cuts off his nose toward the end of the ballad, in an effort to save his wife after returning home from hunting, he thinks like a businessman: "Now I have *bought* my Ladies life, / then to the Moor [he] did call" (col. 4, st. 4; my emphasis).

One could argue that the lord's devotion to providing for his family encourages the listener, viewer, or reader to sympathize with him. Such sympathy could be further bolstered by the narrator's affective identification with the lord's plight. Before describing the horror of the rape of the lady and subsequent murder of the children and her, the narrator declares, "*My senses all begin to fail* / my soul it doth affright" (st. 8; my emphasis); similarly, after the lord cuts off his nose on the instructions of the blackamoor, to no avail—since the blackamoor goes back on his bargain, and does not save but rather throws the lord's wife from the tower—the narrator repeats his self-description of numbing horror, bemoaning that the lord's "*sences all did fail*" (col. 5, st. 4; my emphasis). But narrators are simply, in Dolan's term, "relators." We can share or diverge from their perspective. The distance and variety of possible perspectives that the ballad opens up are stressed by the relator of this ballad in his declaring, "I must *write*" the story (st. 8; my emphasis); this narrator describes himself as a writer, not a witness or singer of the ballad's events. Despite his declared emotion, he is thus not as experientially engaged or caught up in the ballad as he would necessarily have been were he participating in its public, or even its private, here-and-now singing of the events—which would have involved him personally voicing the words of blackamoor, lady, and children, as well as lord. Nor does he seem an immediate viewer of the ballad's striking woodcut illustration. Together with the written text, the assembled media on the sheet spark a present participatory moment that constitutes the full *sensory* ballad experience apparently beyond access to the relator/writer.

Indeed, the ballad diverges in possible perspectives much earlier in the plot than at the start of the violence by the blackamoor. We become aware of discontent at home within the family early on, despite the idealistic picture of a loving family depicted in the ballad's first stanza and the statement that the children of the lord and lady "were their Parents only joy / They lov'd them both so well." Apparently, the lord has a joy more dear to him than his children or wife: hunting. Most telling, at the heart of the familial discontent in the ballad, following upon the almost aside relation of the lord's correcting his blackamoor in the wood, who is supposed to always accompany him on the hunt, is the lord's obsession with hunting. The discord in the family arises not so much over the lord's going out hunting as over the rest of the family's pleas that he *not* do so, specifically, that he not leave them alone. This is the more specific trigger point of discontent, causing an alarming stir in the domestic relations of the household. This is also the point in the ballad's textual narrative that is most destabilizing as one progresses through the many editions of the story. In both Euing editions, we are told, "*Cause of the toyl* [or "toil"] his Lady did / intreat him not to go" (st. 4). The Wood, Crawford, and a Houghton edition offer a slight variant of this phrasing: "Cause of *his* toyl the Lady did, / intreat him not to go." In the Roxburghe, Crawford, and Douce editions, it is "*to* cause [or Cause] the toil the lady did / Intreat him not to go." In the Pepys edition, "toil" becomes seemingly oddly "tale": "To Cause the *tayl* the Lady did / intreat him not to go." But other editions return to the word *toil*, with a twist. In one Huntington edition, the phrase is ambivalently "*Because of* Toil." In another Huntington and later Johnson edition, it is more clearly "To *ease* his toil." And in a Roxburghe, Crawford, and Harding edition, it is "To *cease* his toil" (my emphases throughout).[10] The different versions fall into two camps that are radically opposite in their meanings. The musical and poetic emphases widen the gap between the two camps, though they do not always work in concert. In the Euing, Wood, Crawford and Houghton editions, first cited above, the poetic stresses at the beginning of the first line of the fourth stanza fall on "**Cause**" and "**toyl**," but the strong musical emphasis sits on the fence, falling on "***of***." In the Roxburghe, Crawford, Douce, and Pepys editions, poetic and musical emphases collude in driving home the word "***cause***." The seemingly ambivalent wording of the Huntington edition "Because of Toil," becomes less ambivalent when considered in terms of the united poetic and musical stress in this line, which also falls on "cause" in "Be-***cause***." But in the Huntington and Johnson editions, another Roxburghe and Crawford edition, and another Huntington edition, both poetic and melodic stresses fall on the words "ease" or "cease": "To ***ease***" or "to ***cease***" the "toil."

In the author's narrative of this ballad (or in the printer's accidental or deliberate typesetting of this critical moment in the narrative?), in other words, the relator's position diverges. The lady's entreating is "cause of the tale" in the singular Pepys version (though "cause" here does not get musical metric emphasis, only poetic emphasis). The implication is that her begging the lord to stay is what causes the ensuing explosion of violence—the tale of "The Lady and the Blackamoor." This interpretation is reinforced by the many versions which render the line as "to cause the toil" or, with both poetic and musical emphases, as "***cause*** of his toil." In each case, the lady's pleading the lord to stay home, followed by the pleading of her children, stirs up trouble—it evokes the

OED definition of "toil"/"toile"/"toyl" as "verbal contention, dispute, controversy, argument" (1.b)—and makes the lord even more want to resort to another *OED* definition of "toil" as "intensive labour" and "something produced or accomplished" by that labor (2.a and 2.b). That is, the lord/husband/father wants to leave the home and toil at hunting/work. There is a further complication to these interpretations, should one adopt them, in the definition, as in 1529, of "toyle" as "a net or nets forming an enclosed area into which a hunted quarry is driven" (*OED*, n.2.1). If this reading is added into the mix, the lord might well be feeling trapped by his family's contentious pleas that he stay—trammeled like the very animals he hunts! If, however, the lady's and children's entreaties for the lord to stay are meant—with both poetic and musical emphasis—"to ease his toil" or "to cease his toil"—well supported by the *OED* and as we've seen rendered by the Johnson and Harding editions—then their pleas can be understood as harmless and kindly: they are lovingly seeking to ease the lord's labors in begging him to remain with them at home.

So which is it? Are we to understand that the lady's wish that the lord stay home and stop toiling/hunting is to create ease for him, or are we to see her pleading with the lord, backed up by the nagging cries of the little babes, as the cause of trouble and precisely why the lord wants to go toiling/hunting in the first place—to get away from the confining home—and also the cause of the ensuing violent tale? The answer is as double-pronged as the question and would lie not simply in which edition of the ballad was sung but in which words were chosen to be sung by the singers, how they were sung, and their reception by certain members of their audience who might well have joined in and sung along (and, as we shall see further, what version of the image is shown). Husbands frustrated in their own domestic situations (who need not be of high status to imaginatively inhabit the lord's position as male householder) might have sympathetically adopted the latter interpretation and felt downright maddened by the so very strident and very familiar demands of the denizens of the feminized domestic space, which cause him/them to flee the home every day and toil. And they might well have felt some satisfying release of pent-up anger in the explosive dark violence that ensues.

The ballad, we recall, tells us that the lord "he lov'd" to hunt and "still for swiftnesse *alwayes* took / with him a Blackamoore" (st. 2; my emphasis). Integral to the familial disturbance is the intimate connection between blackamoor and lord that is also driven home by the musical accents. I have already noted, in our analysis of the music notation of the singing of stanza two of the ballad, on p. 280, that the word "Black-a-moor(e)" is repeated twice and very close together. In the first instance of "Black-a-moore" (as syllabically spelled), the strongest melodic emphasis falls on "***moore***" and the secondary emphasis on "*Black*"; in the second instance, the strongest emphasis falls on "***Black***" and the secondary one on "*moor*." The only other nomen repeated twice in this stanza is "***Lord***," which receives a strong melodic and poetic emphasis each time it appears (in poetic lines 1 and 5 of stanza two). In fact, extending our reading to encompass the music's phenomenal accents, we see that the first strong stress of the stanza is not only on "***Lord***" but is arrived at by the largest leap in the melody (a fourth);[11] tellingly, in the repetition of the melody in the last four lines, this same leap is occupied by "***Black***" in line 5 ("***Black***-a *moor*"), which reinforces a sympatico relationship between the two personae and the idea that the lord not only loved to hunt but "***al***-ways *tooke* / with ***him*** a *Black*-a-***moore***." Still, the title "Lord" not only gets a strong melodic emphasis in line 6 but occupies the highest note of that line. These phenomenal accents are subtle, but they get under one's skin at an almost visceral level. Together with the poetic and musical metric accents, they tell us that the lord is strongest and highest in the social structure of the ballad and also that there is an uncannily close connection between him and the blackamoor. As we have seen, the strongly accented title of "Blackamoor" is more unstable in where the emphases fall than is "Lord," suggesting an unstable identity in the servant. Equally unsettled is the blackamoor's social position. His status is at one moment as elevated as the lord's (rising to achieve the same high note at the beginning of line 5 as the lord does in line 1), but at the next moment, very much unlike the lord, the blackamoor occupies the melodic vale of being and staying down—stuck in a series of sustained low notes that even extend beyond the measure (half note/quarter note/dotted-half note)—concluding poetic lines 4 and 8: depressively flattening, respectively, the "*Black*-a-***moore***" and any hope he "*would* a-***mend***."

In terms of the plot, stanza two functions something like a fault line in the ballad marking the rupture between seeming harmony and horrifying discord. The lord, we are told, always takes with him his blackamoor, who when first introduced leaps to the same high note as the lord. But after being reprimanded on a hunt, the blackamoor, the lord's constant companion, stays behind. As a consequence, all hell breaks loose. After the lord departs, the mother takes her children by the hand saying, "come go with me, / Unto the highest tower, where / your Father you shall see" (st. 5). What they "see" in the tower instead of the father—musically stressed and drawn out—is the father's blackamoor, as if the blackamoor were standing in for the father's dark side. The uncanny connection of the lord to the blackamoor is further made visually in the woodcut through the lord's black horse (there is a long tradition of associating blacks with animals, especially horses, as we shall see in Figure 46). That connection is underscored through the lord's act of hunting in the background. Here is where the war associations of hunting in the ballad, bolstered through its possible singability to the tune of "Chevy Chase," would have especially come to mind. The lord hunts a buck, stag, or hart—accompanied by birds of offal—in the background of the woodcut while his blackamoor hunts—that is, kills—his bird-like child, which flies to its death, in the foreground. This is how hunting gets figured literally and metaphorically in "The Lady and the Blackamoor." The lord's two children of this ballad are rendered violently as if "un-borne," like the "unborne child" (st. 1) that may rue the day of the bloody hunting-turned-battle in "Chevy Chase" (c. 1625; EBBA 36103).[12]

Once again, by virtue of the blackamoor's completely alien identity—"*I've never even seen one, for goodness sake!*" the husband viewer/reader/listener/singer might protest—any such affinity with the blackamoor, any dark desire on the part of husbands to take back the domestic space of the home by killing off their constraining families, especially the wife, could have been strongly suppressed and denied. After all, the lord in the ballad asserts his love for his lady, begs for her life, and even cuts off his nose in an effort to save her. But the cutting off of the nose at this point in the ballad is as much a damning as an exculpating gesture. The action as punishment is age old. But even in Renaissance England, as Garthine Walker points out, Star Chamber punishments for false accusations included slitting of the nose, which was a synecdoche for cutting off the nose (*Crime*, 92). And if we pursue this interpretation, we could argue that the blackamoor instructs the lord to cut off his nose as testimony or proof of the lord's false accusation that the blackamoor was somehow at fault in the wood and in need of correction. But slitting and/or cutting off the nose is much more evocative of adultery. It is a punishment that euphemizes (and lessens the penalty of) male castration for adultery, as we witness enacted in the ancient Arabic folktale of "The Revenge of the Castrated Man." When Pepys's wife discovered that Pepys was having an affair with their servant Deb—that is, committing adultery—she twice threatened to slit the servant's nose (Dolan, *Marriage and Violence*, 117). Actually cutting off the nose as a punishment for adultery can be traced to biblical, Roman, Persian, and Egyptian traditions (Kitto, *Biblical Literature*, 1.78).

Sometimes it is the man, sometimes the woman, who is the target of the punishment. But in all cases the crime is adultery. So, what is the lord's crime? The lord is clearly guilty of something in this ballad. Servants and apprentices might see him as most guilty of false accusation and inhumane cruelty and thus deserving of violent punishment. Women, and perhaps secretively some men, might see him as guilty of turning his back on his domestic home—a kind of metaphoric adultery or wander*lust*—that finds fullest and darkest expression in his being party to the killing off of his wife and kids so that he can once more rule the roost and be free to come and go as he pleases. Of course, you would not have had to have been a lord to have this guilty wish and take pleasure in the violence to the family that ensues. But you would never have said it out loud. You would not likely even have acknowledged it to your conscious self. It could only have been spoken as the outrageous crime of an alien "Other" (the lord's dark side).

The Wives' Public

But let us return to the women who might encounter this ballad. So far, I've mentioned them only in passing as perhaps recognizing the domestic tension and the lord's secret guilt for the violence inflicted upon the female domestic space. But did women also have a dark side that could have been tapped by the excess of passion represented in the sensational violence of this broadside? We might here recall John Chamberlain's account in 1616 of how a woman went to witness the execution of Anne Wallen, a husband murderer, and on the way home afterward, she murdered her own child. The "desperate woman," Chamberlain observes, "coming from her [Anne's] execution, cut her child's throat, alleging no other reason for it, but that she doubted she should not have means to keep it" (cited in Dolan, "Petty Traitor," 159–60). The temporal connection alone between the two cruel events seems hardly coincidental. Close upon the woman's witnessing Wallen's barbaric execution, she inflicted a brutal execution of her own. That is, despite Wallen's public confession and repentance for murdering her husband (at least as disseminated in the sole surviving broadside ballad describing and picturing the event, in the Pepys collection, EBBA 20053) and despite the official preventative warning that burning at the stake—Wallen's punishment—was meant to convey to women about being properly submissive to male authority, something went badly wrong in the reception of the message. The mother who witnessed the execution responded to violence meant to *correct* women's possible leanings to violently taking matters into their own hands with, well, violently taking matters into her own hands—aiming her violence not at her husband but at her child.

What happened? "Anne Wallens Lamentation" (EBBA 20053) was sung to the famous execution ballad tune, also familiarly known as a "goodnight" melody, "Fortune my Foe."[13] The tune of "The Lady's Fall" was also often sung to ballads warning women against husband murder, wherein, as with Wallen, the criminalized wife, as petty traitor—the husband being the domestic equivalent of king of his household—was publicly burnt at the stake (e.g., EBBA 33911, 30366, and 35066). And yet, if Chamberlain's report is any indication, even witnessing in real life the barbarous punishment inflicted purportedly as admonishment upon husband murderers—let alone, one would think, singing of the event in the first-person voice of the condemned party—could have backfired. The grim execution of Anne Wallen did *not* act as warning but, if anything, as a prompt or trigger to similarly violent and criminal action: a woman cutting her child's throat. "When we imagine mobile identifications," Dolan summarizes, "we must also accept the possibility of messier didacticisms and less predictable effects" ("Petty Traitor," 159). Certainly, the early modern period contains many stories of women's violence against children. Infanticide, J. A. Sharpe points out, was the capital crime for which women were most often convicted (*Crime*, 158). Typically, the offender was an unmarried servant girl who killed her newborn to avoid shame and loss of position. But the crime extended across the social spectrum. In the early seventeenth century, for instance, Lady Abergavenny is reported to have "in a passion killed her own child about seven years old." The fuller details of the report are as telling as they are chilling: "She having been a great while whipping it, my Lord [her husband] being grieved to hear it cry so terribly, went into the room to plead for it, and she threw it with such force on the ground, she broke the skull; the girl lived but four hours after" (Stone, *Family, Sex and Marriage*, 169). Notice in this contemporary report that the woman's forceful dashing of the child to the ground seems to have been as much a response against the husband's intervention into her act of domestic discipline—likely perceived, as was common by women of the time, as *her* purview—as it was against the child's offense of excessive crying. Violence can have a splattershot effect.

Could the sensational violence of "The Lady and the Blackamoor"—in which one child's brains are bashed against the wall and another's throat is cut—satisfy suppressed but pent-up and potentially explosive urgings against children (and against husbands) by female viewers, readers, listeners, and singers of the ballad, even if those urgings weren't in fact acted upon? Possibly.

Perhaps even more criminally, from a feminist perspective, the excess of violence inflicted upon the lady in the ballad could have worked upon its female audience in a more self-destructive way. The over-the-top victimization of the wife—not only thrown over the castle walls into the moat by the blackamoor, but first bound and raped by him—might well reinforce a woman's view of herself in the period as needing to be violently violated to be sure of exoneration as the unwilling subject of a sexual crime. Cristine Varholy draws on Garthine Walker's work to argue that women recognized that, in cases where they are the victims of sexual assault, they are typically not believed and are instead found to be at fault and punished. As a defensive tactic, those hauled before Bridewell Court took pains to stress that the incident was an act of male violence (rather than a sexual act), that the woman's resistance was futile, that the act involved a violation of an intimate household space, and that the rape, usually euphemistically described, denoted male agency and female subjugation ("'But She Woulde not Consent,'" 56–57). So too, in the ballad of "The Lady and the Blackamoor," the lady is surprised in the remote tower of her own home by the blackamoor, who unexpectedly stayed behind instead of going out hunting with the lord, as was his wont; she is overpowered—"her hands behind her bound / and then perforce with al his might, / he threw her on the ground" (st. 11)—and the only reference to the actual sex act is the oblique parenthetical line, "he having had his will" (col. 4, st. 3). To take some satisfaction in seeing a woman thus violently made innocent and pure—"the chrystal tears ran down her face" (st. 11)—might well have been a perverse reaction by some women (and men) to this sensational ballad.

And to expand our horizon to include the racialized Other of actual blackamoors, the reality of which would have become more unavoidable and pressing with every year the ballad was issued over its 200-year history, one might argue that, to the extent, even at its early inception in 1569/70, that the ballad *is* racialized, it is racialized, as Kim Hall would argue, aesthetically and by gender. That is, in the woodcut, the fair lady (she is twice called "fair") is carefully placed alongside, if also in aesthetic contrast to, the black servant/slave (as well as to the lord, via his black horse). Visualized through such oppositional twinning in early modern representations, Hall points out, women—perhaps willingly, perhaps not—became the repositories of the symbolic boundaries of the English nation as demarcated by white masculinity. Hall provides as an example of such racialized and gendered national symbolism, the painting in which Anne of Denmark, Queen to James I, is pictured with her dark-haired horse and dark-skinned groom, as seen in Figure 46 (*Things of Darkness*, 238–39).

Striking here, as in the ballad "The Lady and the Blackamoor," is the nearly identically colored servant and horse he holds; their bodies and heads merge as one or, perhaps more accurately, we detect two heads sharing one equine body. At the same time, the black servant is aesthetically connected to James's wife

Figure 46. Paul van Somers (1576/1578–1622), *Portrait of Anne of Denmark* (1617). Oil on canvas. Hampton Court Palace. Image courtesy of Wikimedia Commons. https://commons.wikimedia.org. Public domain.

by his red livery, which is repeated in the flourishes of red ornaments decorating Anne's garb (the feather in her hat and rose and bow on her dress) as well as in the red of the rope that ties her to another figuring of the nonhuman/non-Englishman, the black-and-white dogs.

To what extent did English women (and men, for that matter), like Anne of Denmark pictured here, knowingly acquiesce in this aestheticizing of

English nationalism and imperialism whereby the self-aggrandizement of the nation is actually brutally built up on the backs of both women and racialized Others, but such violence at the same time was carefully prettified—made into art like a painting or, for the lower orders, like a broadside ballad that one could paste up as decoration on one's walls? To what extent would women of the period have self-consciously and self-sacrificingly embraced extremes of violence to further the aesthetics of British imperialism? That is one question I hesitate to answer. Perhaps there are limits to women's dark desires, if not to men's. Perhaps not.

The Child's Public

We might be tempted to neglect the little children in "The Lady and the Blackamoor" in considering possible publics. One might think they would not have been considered by authors/printers/publishers within the spectrum of their targeted market. After all, very young children, except perhaps those of the very wealthy, had no money to purchase ballads. But, as we all know from standing with a small child in a grocery store line, stocked with candy on either side of the narrow aisle, children can vocally and very insistently express their desire for consumer goods, and they often get what they want. Furthermore, though this is not the case of the blackamoor servant in "The Lady and the Blackamoor," many a servant and apprentice were in fact perceived to be (and perhaps perceived himself or herself to be) a child. Such is clearly the case in the depiction of the apprentice being dangled as victim by his master in "The cryes of the Dead" (Figure 45); he is pictured as and is called a "child." Pepys also, we recall, referred to their young female servant as "our little girle."

What reaction, then, might "The Lady and the Blackamoor" ballad have triggered in such very young children other than sheer fear of violence inflicted upon them from the servants/apprentices they lived with or even from their parents or masters/mistresses, and a consequent urge to fight back? There were, in fact, many other frights and needs that might have been activated in the minds of children by this ballad. One deep-seated anxiety, supported by other extant ballads, in addition to apprehension of physical abuse by the child's custodians or those employed by them, was, in a word, *abandonment*. Ballad producers often targeted this specific dread not by ameliorating it but by calling attention to it, as if to say, look here, young babes, this could be *you*, vulnerable to being left behind, without protection.

The most famous of such ballads concerned with a child's neglected care, expressive of both parents' and children's fears of child abandonment, is "The

Norfolk Gentleman his Last Will and Testament. . . ." (the earliest extant edition, from which I cite, is Euing Ballads 254, c. 1663–74, EBBA 31808; Figure 47). This was an extremely popular ballad; it became downright beloved in the eighteenth century when—as if zeroing in on the plight of the ballad's two children abandoned in a forest—it was retitled "The Children in the Wood." Through the "confusion" (Simpson, 370) that could swirl around associations between ballad tunes, its melody can be traced to two frequently linked tunes: "Chevy Chase" and our blackamoor ballad tune, "In Peascod Time" or "The Lady's Fall" (105, 370–71). But the tune title most often printed on editions of "The Norfolk Gentleman" in the seventeenth century is "Rogero," which will figure prominently in the conclusion to this study.

"The Norfolk Gentleman" begins by describing devoted parents who, facing death, entrust their two very young children—a boy of three and an even younger girl—as well as the children's inheritance to the care of their uncle. Big mistake. After the parents' deaths, the uncle's greed surpasses his pledged provision for his wards. He hires "two Ruffians rude" (st. 10) to take the children into the forest and kill them, as if they were animals of the hunt. But on hearing the "pretty speech" of the children (col. 4, st. 2), one of the ruffians repents the deal they had made with the uncle (col. 4, st. 2). The other rogue, however, holds firm. In the course of arguing, they break into a sword fight, in which the softer-hearted of the two slays his companion. But the plot turns ill again, with yet another instance of child abandonment: the children's new guardian, saying he is going off to find bread for them, leaves the children in the woods. He never returns. Deserted in the wild, the children wander helplessly, and the ballad moves strongly into the mode of sentimental tragedy. The babes end up, we are told, dying encircled in each other's arms, with stains of berries they had foraged besmearing their lips; a robin red-breast, as if their sole remaining caretaker, brings leaves to cover their dead bodies. As is often the case when innocents are abandoned or abused in ballads, God then viciously takes vengeance on the traitorous uncle. But one is left intensely unsatisfied with the feeling that justice has not been served, or, rather, "it is too much too late." The children, perishing alone and uncared for, seem to function as if sacrificial victims. But for what? As if providing a clue to the answer, while also adding to our unsettled affections, the tailor-made elaborate woodcut for this edition of "The Norfolk Gentleman" draws our eye (as seen in Figure 47).

This first and largest image of the broadside ballad pictures a series of key events that occur in the narrative, though they are displayed out of sequence. Centrally, in the foreground, we witness the ruffians battling one another in the woods (specifically, the critical moment when the more kindhearted of

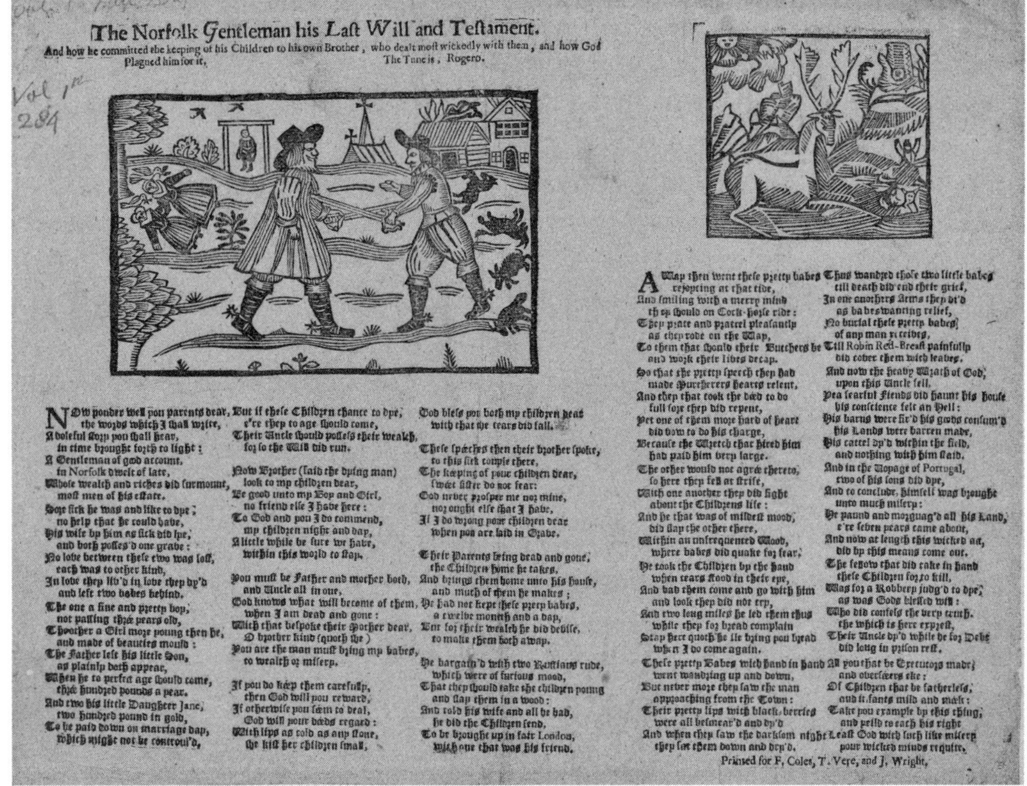

The Norfolk Gentleman his Last Will and Testament.

And how he committed the keeping of his Children to his own Brother, who dealt most wickedly with them, and how God Plagued him for it,

The Tune is, Rogero.

Now ponder well you parents dear,
the words which I shall write,
A doleful story you shall hear,
in time brought forth to light:
A Gentleman of good account,
in Norfolk dwelt of late,
Whose wealth and riches did surmount,
most men of his estate.
Sore sick he was and like to dye;
no help that he could have,
His wife by him as sick did lye,
and both possess'd one grave:
No love between these two was lost,
each was to other kind,
In love they liv'd in love they dy'd
and left two babes behind.
The one a fine and pretty boy,
not passing three years old,
The other a Girl more young then he,
and made of beauties mould:
The Father left his little Son,
as plainly doth appear,
When he to perfect age should come,
three hundred pounds a year.
And two his little Daughter Jane,
two hundred pound in gold,
To be paid down on marriage day,
which might not be controul'd,
But if these Children chance to dye,
e're they to age should come,
Their Uncle should possess their wealth,
for so the Will did run.

Now Brother (said the dying man)
look to my children dear,
Be good unto my Boy and Girl,
no friend else I have here:
To God and you I do commend,
my children night and day,
A little while be sure we have,
within this world to stay.

You must be Father and mother both,
and Uncle all in one,
God knows what will become of them,
when I am dead and gone:
With that bespoke their Mother dear,
O brother kind (quoth she)
You are the man must bring my babes,
to wealth or misery.

If you do keep them carefully,
then God will you reward,
If otherwise you seem to deal,
God will your deeds regard:
With lips as cold as any stone,
she kist her children small,
God bless you both my children dear
with that the tears did fall.

These speeches then their brother spoke,
to this sick couple there,
The keeping of your children dear,
sweet sister do not fear:
God never prosper me nor mine,
nor ought else that I have,
If I do wrong your children dear
when you are laid in Grave.

Their Parents being dead and gone,
the Children home he takes,
And brings them home unto his house,
and much of them he makes;
He had not kept these pretty babes,
a twelve month and a day,
But for their wealth he did devise,
to make them both away.

He bargain'd with two Ruffians rude,
which were of furious mood,
That they should take the children young
and slay them in a wood:
And told his wife and all he had,
he did the Children send,
To be brought up in fair London,
with one that was his friend.

Away then went these pretty babes
rejoycing at that tide,
And smiling with a merry mind
they should on Cock-horse ride:
They prate and pratel pleasantly
as they rode on the Way,
To them that should their Butchers be
and work their lives decay.
So that the pretty speech they had
made Murtherers hearts relent,
And they that took the deed to do
full sore they did repent,
Yet one of them more hard of heart
did vow to do his charge,
Because the Wretch that hired him
had paid him very large.
The other would not agree thereto,
so here they fell at strife,
With one another they did fight
about the Childrens life:
And he that was of mildest mood,
did slay the other there,
Within an unfrequented Wood,
where babes did quake for fear,
He took the Children by the hand
when tears stood in their eye,
And bad them come and go with him
and look they did not cry,
And two long miles he led them thus
while they for bread complain
Stay here quoth he ile bring you bread
when I do come again.
These pretty Babes with hand in hand
went wandring up and down,
But never more they saw the man
approaching from the Town:
Their pretty lips with black-berries
were all besmear'd and dy'd
And when they saw the darksom night
they sat them down and cry'd.
Thus wandred those two little babes
till death did end their grief,
In one anothers Arms they dy'd
as babes wanting relief,
No burial these pretty babes
of any man receives,
Till Robin Red-Breast painfully
did cover them with leaves.
And now the heavy Wrath of God,
upon this Uncle fell,
Yea fearful Fiends did haunt his house
his conscience felt an Hell:
His barns were fir'd his goods consum'd
his Lands were barren made,
His cattel dy'd within the field,
and nothing with him staid.
And in the Voyage of Portugal,
two of his sons did dye,
And to conclude, himself was brought
unto much misery:
He pawnd and morguag'd all his Land,
e're seven years came about,
And now at length this wicked act,
did by this means come out.
The fellow that did take in hand
these Children for to kill,
Was for a Robbery judg'd to dye,
as was Gods blessed will:
Who did confess the very truth,
the which is here exprest,
Their Uncle dy'd while he for Debt
did long in prison rest.
All you that be Executors made,
and overseers eke:
Of Children that be fatherless,
and infants mild and meek:
Take you example by this thing,
and yeild to each his right
Least God with such like misery
your wicked minds requite.

Printed for F, Coles, T. Vere, and J. Wright,

Figure 47. Ballad sheet facsimile, "The Norfolk Gentleman his Last Will and Testament. And how he committed the keeping of his Children to his own Brother, who dealt most wickedly with them, and how God Plagued him for it" (1663–74), EBBA 31808. University of Glasgow Library, Euing Ballads 254. By permission of University of Glasgow Library, Special Collections.

the rogues, fighting to save the children, drives a death stroke into his companion); in the left middle ground, we perceive the future of the two children, later abandoned in those same woods by the surviving ruffian, the children's supposed new guardian (the babes lie dead, arms joined, while two birds (imaging the one robin of the narrative) place leaves upon them in a semblance of a funeral ceremony); in the left background appears the future fate of that rogue, who had saved the children only to desert them in the woods; we hear late in the ballad about his execution for a different crime, a robbery (he hangs on a scaffold with carrion birds hovering above him); in the middle background, we catch sight of the top of a church, as if to signal God's hand in such punishment; on the right background, we witness yet more of God's vengeance in the images of the uncle's barns on fire and, in the right middle to foreground his farm animals killed. Perhaps meant to be comforting, in reassuring viewers that God *will* take vengeance upon evildoers, are the parallel visual spaces occupied in the illustration by the abandoned children (supposed to have been protected by their uncle and subsequently by the surviving ruffian), now lying dead in the forest, to the left of the dueling villains, and the uncle's untended domestic animals, now slaughtered and scattered on the ground to the rogues' right. But if the visual parallelism is mean to be comforting—don't worry, wrongdoing will be avenged—it is at the same time disturbing. The woodcut's middle field creates a visual plane that connects woods and fields, innocent children and guiltless creatures, killing and—if at one remove—hunting: the uncle instructs the ruffians to kill the children in the woods, as if they were animals of a hunt, and God, in his vengeance, hunts down not only the surviving ruffian but also the uncle's family (not pictured in the woodcut) and goods, including his domestic animals—the latter as devoid of wrongdoing as the children. The sacrificial slaughter of untended innocents in this ballad would seem tactically designed by its producers to feed a ballad market for those eager to experience tender, if tragic, sentiment without guilt. Parents could assuage their children and themselves (especially those adults experiencing a sweet sentimentality from the tragic deaths of children entwined together dying alone in the woods) that the ballad is a warning against evil, and especially against the evil of forsaking the vulnerable child. But, still, the double abandonment of the children in the ballad leading to their deaths in the woods, where hunting so often happens, as well as the slaughter of the domestic animals, hunted down by a divine force (however avenging of the children's neglect and demise), creates uneasy associations. Indeed, if this ballad only obliquely links child abandonment with hunting, others, like "The Lady and the Blackamoor," are more much more overt.

Perhaps the ballad that most drives home the vulnerability of children left unprotected while a parent, specifically the father, is out hunting is the popular "The Lady Isabella's Tragedy," hereafter cited as "Isabella's Tragedy" (Pepys Ballads 2.149, c. 1672–96; EBBA 20767). The ballad was to be sung, the sheet tells us, to the same named tune as in "The Lady and the Blackamoor"—"The Ladies Fall." In "Isabella's Tragedy," the child is not a "babe," like the two- or three-year-olds in "The Norfolk Gentleman" or the very young children in the blackamoor ballad. Though the child's age is not given, we are told by the relator that the girl is "belov'd" not only by her father but also "both far and near / of many a Lord and Knight," making her likely to be at least in her early teens (st. 3). But she is still clearly thought of as a child. Age is not a factor in what makes the girl vulnerable. It is her father's obsession to go hunting *every* day. Though we are told he is a loving father—as in the blackamoor ballad, we hear that the "fair" maid "was her father's only joy" (st. 4)—he obsessively leaves the home to go hunting as if avoiding the domestic, female sphere. If the lord in "The Lady and the Blackamoor," when hunting, "always takes with him his Blackamoor," the lord of "Isabella's Tragedy" always hunts with his homosocial "noble Train, / of Gentry" (st. 1). In both cases, abandoning the domestic space leaves the child or children unprotected. In "Isabella's Tragedy," hunting is a form of abandonment that makes the child victim not only to a servant but to a stepmother working in cahoots with the servant. The ballad thus falls into what we moderns might think of as a Disney tradition of the evil stepmother. But, more accurately, it belongs to an age-old folktale story line about the vulnerability of children to the violence of non-blood mothers when left unattended by their fathers.

In what by now would likely have been a shivering foreshadowing, the ballad opens with the lines, "There was a Lord of worthy fame / and a Hunting he would ride" (st. 1). Leaving the house unattended by a caring provider, who also has the ability (and, in this case, furthermore, the desire) to provide protection, inevitably bodes disaster. The lord's new wife, the stepmother, the relator tells us, has taken a distinct hatred of her "fair" stepdaughter and has long plotted the child's murder. Hunting here, as in "The Lady and the Blackamoor," moves uneasily between the literal and the metaphorical. As the father hunts in "Isabella's Tragedy," the child's stepmother deviously plots the girl's death as itself a kind of hunting, even to the extent of sharing a password drawn from the hunt with the master-cook of the house. While the father hunts the "fair" doe, that is, the stepmother sends the lord's beloved "fair" daughter home, telling the girl to instruct the cook that he should "dress to dinner straight / that *fair* and milk white *Doe.* / That in the Park doth shine so bright, / there's none so *fair* to show" (st. 8; my emphases). The ballad does not mince words, though it does mince flesh, so closely in plot to Shakespeare's *Titus Andronicus* (1593–94) that the author of the ballad, I am convinced, must have had that play in mind.[14] In *Titus*, the two sons of Tamora, a Goth newly made Queen of the Romans, while they supposedly join with others in a hunt, instead track down Titus's daughter, Lavinia, then rape and mutilate her. Reinforcing the connection to the hunt they are supposedly a part of, as in "Isabella's Tragedy," they call her a "doe": "We hunt not, we, with horse nor hound," they declare, "But hope to pluck a dainty doe to ground" (Quarto 1594; 2.2.25–26). Titus, Lavinia's father, takes his revenge upon such gruesome hunting of his daughter by serving the sons up to their mother for dinner minced in a pie. In "Isabella's Tragedy," after the innocent girl delivers the stepmother's message to the master-cook, as if in like mind to Titus, the cook promptly grabs the fair daughter and pronounces her doom, turning the literal "Doe" into a metaphorical-cum-literal one, referring to the daughter herself as the one to be slaughtered and "dressed" for dinner:

> Thou art the Doe that I must dress,
> see here behold my Knife,
> For it is pointed presently,
> to rid thee of thy life. (st. 13)

In "Isabella's Tragedy," however, not all servants turn bad. A young "Scullen boy" tries to prevent the grotesque murder and cookery of the daughter, offering himself instead as victim: "make your Pies of me" (st. 14). This sacrificial offer is rejected by the master-cook, and he threatens the servant not to divulge the sickening deed. But the servant actually does blurt out the crime, unfortunately after the fact, as the girl's father sits down before his mincedaughter pie for dinner.

The three stanzas I have focused on above from "Isabella's Tragedy" (stanzas 1, 7, and 13) can be heard on **Tracks 38–40** of the Audio Companion. They can also be seen below, notated from the recordings with text underlay (the notation, as always, is also available for following along to the sound of a fiddle, in this case on **Track 41**):

In these stanzas, we can not only hear but also see the musical metric and phenomenal emphases on "***Hunt***-ing," in stanza 1. "***Hunt***" is arrived at by a leap upward, making the musical metric stress on the syllable phenomenally even stronger. What is also musically striking is the displacement of the "Lord" in these stanzas. From the beginning, he receives a weaker musical stress: as "*Lord*," in line 1 of stanza 1, he is much less emphasized than the act of "***Hunt***-ing" that compels him. The persons who dominate in the master's stead are the stepmother whose "***I***" receives a strong musical stress as well as a secondary stress in her repeated self-referencing in stanza 7. Also emphasized is the stepmother's ally in the "***home***" (st. 7) where the stepmother dominates: not the lord as master but the servant who, in place of the lord, is the "***Mas***-ter-*Cook*." The cook asserts his own strong "***I***" in stanza 13, in a directly parallel poetic and musical metric position with that of the stepmother's in stanza 7. Driving home his importance as master-threat, the cook holds the literal and rhyming "***Knife***" that will take the metaphorically doe-like daughter's "***life***." Both poetically rhymed words receive yet further poetic and musical metric accent in being positioned at the end of the line and drawn out through extra notational length—while the Father/Lord/Master carelessly hunts doe in the park. The implication of the lord's literally hunting a "fair" doe is driven home. He is indirectly the cause of the metaphorical domestic hunt of his "fair" daughter by abandoning her—as if sacrificing her to his hunting obsession—leaving her in the abusive care of stepmother and master-cook.

The consequences for the domestic plotters of the grotesque slaughter and mincing up of the daughter into a pie in the ballad are as equally gruesome as their plot: the stepmother is burned at the stake for petty treason and the master-cook is made to stand in boiling lead (as if he himself were now being cooked). Again, the latter punishment might recall for us *Titus Andronicus* and the penalty inflicted upon that play's blackamoor, Aaron, who is buried in sand up to his neck, and left, ironically (given the serving of the queen's sons to her as mince pies) to starve. But Aaron's position in *Titus* is ambiguous and most unusual, especially in the culture of broadside ballads that address child abandonment: he is servant/companion and lover to Queen Tamora; puppet-master of all the horrid events; considering our topic of deserted children, his one striking saving grace is that he barters his life and information for the preservation of his baby parented with Tamora (who herself had ordered it destroyed). He plays every role evilly, and yet is the best protector in the play of children, or at least of his own child! As such, he is even more an anomaly than our mythically produced blackamoor in "The Lady and the Blackamoor." We might even imagine the possibility of a different ballad about the blackamoor Aaron if told from the Goths' perspective; not that far-fetched a thought, given that the successor of the Romans at the end of *Titus*, the young Lucius, aligns with the Goths and raises Aaron's bastard child. Such an alternatively imagined ballad is dizzying in its possibilities for picturing a mixed nation of Roman/classical and Goth/barbaric, as well as other intertwinings—don't forget that black-letter typeface was also considered both bastard and Gothic type by the time it was displaced by roman font. But though ballads titled "Titus Andronicus" were printed after Shakespeare's play, spoken in the first person by Titus, who summarizes from his perspective the play's plot, the alternative ballad story I propose never gets told. Perhaps it could never at this space and time have been even conceived.[15]

The scullion boy servant in "Isabella's Tragedy" is more recognizable to the everyday servant or apprentice of this time. And, surely to the delight of those youths the ballad market largely targeted, along with other social sorts, this servant survives and thrives. As if fulfilling an undercurrent fantasy in the sensational plot of "Isabella's Tragedy," the ballad offers the possibility for advancement of loyal servants who are neither alien Others nor ruthless hunters, like the stepmother and her ally, the master-cook, and like the blackamoor. The scullion boy is rewarded for his loyalty by the girl's father and made heir to all the lord's lands. There is hope in several of these ballads for some servants, at least, even if other such workers turn to black deeds of the monstrous or alien. But, once again, the young child must be abandoned of care and made hunted—turned into a sacrificial victim—for such an uplifting moral to happen.

So is that really it? Are helpless children truly only sacrificial, even disposable, in ballads, and perhaps other popular works of the period? Are they pawns doomed to serve other uplifting causes that satisfy mature consumers? Is there nothing in the ballads that would appeal to the very young child as middleman consumer? There could have been some attraction of such ballads for children, and I doubt it lay in the "comfort" that they will be avenged by God after death. They could use the ballad, on the contrary, to effect salvation *in the here-and-now*. That is, a child could point to the ballad and cry out, "Mommy! [or, more likely, *Daddy*!], please don't let that happen to me!" The children could clutch the ballad in their small hands as something to show their guardians to remind them that they are just as vulnerable children as those told about in the ballads, and thus need to be especially cared for—*more so* than those in the ballads, whose fate is always death. The problem, as seen from the child's perspective, is not that the birth-parents in all these ballads are unloving. The problem is that the actions of even loving and well-meaning guardians appear not good enough, or so the ballads imply. Children—always selfish and most attentive to their wants (and I speak here as a parent)—would have been very mindful of this fact. The ballads suggest that children, especially poor children, needed more attention and more care. The children living in the period, I posit, would likely have insisted on holding those ballads up as examples of that need.

Sadly, despite many a loving parent in the period, there were disturbing realities represented in ballads that would have furthered a child's anxious desire for yet better care and insistent pointing to ballads like "The Lady and the Blackamoor" as lessons to their parents. For the poor parent, the young child was an especial burden. Despite loving them, parents thus often reveal in ballads a repressed desire to be rid of their children. This raw fact is tactically and subtly represented in the sudden change to good fortune of the vagrant widowed mother in "A Lanthorne for Landlords" (EBBA 20064 and 30118) once she "loses" her twin children in the fields; now she can work in those same fields for a living whereas before she was whipped out of town. The further sad fact is that responsible parenting by fathers, in particular, had a weak record in the lower strata of early modern society. Abandonment was common. There is a prominent lived history of fathers deserting both their children and their wives. As I have discussed in *Unsettled* (7–9), the economic hardships of the early seventeenth century caused so many husbands to desert their families that a vagrancy statute of 1610 stipulated "That all such persons so running away, shall be taken and deemed to be incorrigible rogues." Abandoned wives often took to the roads, with or without children in tow, to seek out their irresponsible husbands and/or to beg for food, again eerily akin to the widow in "A Lanthorne for Landlords," even though that ballad veils the historical fact of desertion with the report of the father having gone off to battle and dying fighting, not willfully abandoning his family; it is the landlord who in that ballad stands in for the neglectful caregiver, evicting the wife and children.[16]

No wonder that the children in "The Lady and the Blackamoor" are instilled with an almost instinctive fear each time their daddy goes out eagerly to hunt, leaving them behind unprotected, vulnerable to themselves being hunted. Of course, at this point in the narrative, they could not possibly know what horror in fact lies in wait for them. All they, and the many children who would have listened to or viewed the broadside ballad, know at this point in the tale are the many real-life and fictional ballad stories of children in one way or another being made subject, intentionally or not, to abandonment by their guardians, and suffering irreparably from the loss of adequate protective care. At a gut level, the children in "The Lady and the Blackamoor" are sure there is trouble awaiting them when their father goes off to hunt. For no clearly stated reason, they fruitlessly cry out to their father, "Good Father quoth the little Babes, / with us here still remain" (st. 4), a plea the father completely ignores. Many a child, I would suggest, would be drawn to this ballad and identify with these children and their fears precisely out of a shared anxiety. They would have been most vocal in singing the children's cries, and in hoping the "moral" of bad guardianship might have driven home their—the children's—perspective: not alternative perspectives (which, given the single focus of children, they likely didn't even see) of servants and apprentices, or father, or mothers. Bottom line: in temporarily abandoning them for the hunt, or departing on any outing for business or pleasure, the father has left them vulnerable to being hunted; this pointed fact children could well have seen. The ballad puts its finger on a pulse of fear that all children at all times experience, but perhaps more so in the uncertain times of the early modern period, especially for those of the middling to lower orders.

Moving Publics

The threat of deadly consequences following upon abandonment experienced by the children in "The Lady and the Blackamoor" is expressed obliquely through their otherwise inexplicable cries to their father that he not leave them and go out hunting; after all, theoretically, the father's just following his daily routine of hunting from which he has in the past always come back. The ballad deflects the father's guilt of rendering his children vulnerable in leaving them unprotected onto his servant, the Moor. Indeed, the Moor functions something like a lightning rod for all the mobile and multifaceted dark fears and desires of the ballad's potential audience, who might have identified more with one or another of the victimized personae in the ballad and, in the process, made momentary assemblages of like-minded publics: assemblages of servants and apprentices, masters, wives, or even children. The blackamoor, in this sense, is not so much life-like as multiply figurative: a vehicle for the imaginative focus and expression of multifaceted moving publics.

Even if the "The Lady and the Blackamoor" *is* about a blackamoor, I thus stress, I do not want to make real-life blackamoors or other threatening aliens closer to home, such as the Spanish or Jews (Hall, *Things of Darkness*, 7; Griffiths, *Lost Londons*, 74), the smoking gun behind the horrific criminal excesses of this ballad. Or rather, if there is a smoking gun, it is a shotgun with a wide choke (meaning that the pellets are scattered over a large radius for a maximum number of hits). Bridewell Court records up to 1650 show that blackamoors living in England tended to be arrested or executed not for heinous criminal acts but for petty crimes on the same order as servants and apprentices (for "fornication," "scoffing at masters or mistresses, living vagrantly, or harming of others"); some were themselves the victims of petty crimes, such as theft, and some ended up on the parish dole. This is the more mundane tragedy of their gradual incorporation into the ordinary life of the lower orders, or poor, of English society.[17]

The ability of the broadside ballad "The Lady and the Blackamoor" to shoot off its excess of violence through the figure of the blackamoor with a wide choke, so as to scattershot hit upon other kinds of violence of the time as committed or thought by English men, youths of all ages, women, and even children—that scattershot effect counterintuitively increases rather than decreases as one progresses through the centuries in the retellings and remakings of this ballad, even as (or perhaps because) real-life blacks became more visible and more a part of everyday London.

As the ballad morphs from black-letter to white-letter, or roman, print, indeed, visual blackness in the ballad gradually dissipates, as if the typeface and, later, the woodcut illustration were also incorporated into ordinary practices, here of print shops. Evident, for example, in Figures 48 and 49 (EBBA 32501 and 31227), the absence of the thick black-letter typeface noticeably whitens the overall effect of these two mid-eighteenth-century editions of the ballad as compared with the earlier Euing or Pepys or Roxburghe black-letter editions. In one late edition of the ballad from around 1750, EBBA 34451 (Figure 50), racialized blackness is no longer prominent even in the woodcut for the ballad. The blackamoor here looks pretty much white and clothed almost in Roman garb, as if to match the humanist and classical roman typeface of the lettering that reports his tale; he looks racially the same as everyone else in the woodcut.

In another, later white-letter version of the ballad of 1780–1812, the Bodleian's Harding B 3(42) (Figure 51), there is no visual representation of the blackamoor at all—the woodcut illustration disappears—and there is not even a reference to the blackamoor in the title to the ballad. Blackness appears only in trace, minimalized into the aesthetics of the floral line that runs under the title and stands as if a place marker for the previously prominent woodcut that imaged sensationalized black violence. The effect of this ballad is similar to the aesthetic gesturing toward blackness that we saw in the *Georgia Gazette*'s retelling of "The Lady and the Blackamoor" tale in its "news" story titled "African Humanity" (see Figure 41). Furthermore, though in some later versions of "The Lady and the Blackamoor" blackness visually reemerges, it does so in its age-old

A Lamentable BALLAD of the tragical End of a gallant Lord and a virtuous Lady, and the untimely End of their two Children, wickedly perform'd by a heathenish Black-a-moor, their Servant, the like never heard of before.

To the Tune of *Flying Fame*,

IN *Rome* a noble Lord did wed,
  A Virgin of great Fame,
A fairer Creature never did,
  Dame Nature ever frame:
By whom he had two Children fair.
  Whose Beauty did excel,
They were their Parents only Joy.
  They lov'd them both so well.
This Lord he lov'd to hunt the Buck,
  The Tyger and the Bear,
And still for Swiftenefs always took,
  With him a Black-a-moor;
Which Black-a-moor in the Wood,
  His Lord he did offend.
For which he did him then correct,
  In hopes he would amend.
The Day it grew unto an End.
  Then homewards he did haste,
Where with his Lady he did rest,
  Until the Night was past.
Then in the Morning he did rise,
  And did his Servants call,
A hunting he provides to go,
  Straight they were ready all.
Because of Toil the Lady did,
  Intreat him not to go:
Alas! good Lady then, quoth he,
  Why art thou grieved so?
Content thyself, I will return,
  With Speed to thee again:
Good Father, quoth the Little Babes,
  With us here still remain.
Farewel, dear Children, I will go,
  A fine Thing for to buy.
But they therewith nothing content,
  Aloud began to cry:
Their Mother takes them by the Hand
  Saying. *Come go with me,*
Unto the highest Tower, where.
  Your Father you shall see.
The Black-a-moor perceiving now,
  Who then did stay behind,
His Lord to be a hunting gone,
  Began to call to Mind:
My Master he did me correct,
  My Fault not being great.
Now of his Wife I'll be revenged.
  She shall not me intreat.
This Place was moted round about,
  The Bridge he did undraw,
The Gates he bolted very fast,
  Of none he stood in Awe;
He up unto the Tower went,
  The Lady being there:
Who when she saw his Countenance,
  She straight began to fear.
But now my trembling Heart it quakes
  To think that I must write:
My Senses all begin to fail,
  My soul it doth affright:
Yet I must make an End of this,
  Which here I have begun,
Which will make sad the hardest heart
  Before that I have done.
This Wretch unto the Lady went,
  And her with Speed did will,
His Lust forthwith to satisfy
  His mind for to fulfil.
Then she amazed was,
  To hear the Villain speak:
Alas! quoth she what shall I do?
  With Grief my Heart will break.
With that he took her in his Arms,
  She straight for Help did cry.
Content yourself, Lady, he said,
  Your Husband is not nigh;
The Bridge is drawn, the Gates are shut,
  Therefore come lie with me;
Or else I do protest and vow,
  Thy Butcher I will be
The chrystal Tears ran down her Face,
  Her Children cry'd amain,
And sought to help their Mother dear,
  But it was all in vain,
So that egregious, filthy Rogue.
  Her Hands behind her bound,
And then by Force with all his Might
  He threw her on the Ground.
With that she shriek'd, her Childaen cry'd
  And such a Noise did make,
The Town's Folk hearing her lament,
  Did seek their Parts to take:
But all in vain, no Way was found,
  To help the Lady's Need,
Who cries to them most piteously
  O help! O help! with Speed.
Some ran unto the forest wide,
  Her Lord home for to call;
And they that stood did still lament.
  This gallant Lady's Fall.
With Speed her Lord came posting home
  He could not enter in;
His Lady's Cries did pierce his Heart,
  Her dearest Blood to spill.
Oh! hold thy Hand thou Savage Moor
  To hurt her do forbear,
Or else be sure as I do live,
  Wild horses shall the tear.
With that the Rogue ran to the Wall,
  He having got his Will,
And brought one Child under his Arm,
  To call he did begin
The Child seeing his Father there,
  To him for Help did call,
O Father help! my Mother dear,
  We shall be killed all.
Then fell the Lord upon his Knee,
  And did the Moor intreat,
To save the Life of his dear Child,
  Whose fear was then so great.
But this vile Wretch the little Child,
  By both the Heels did take,
And dash'd his Brains against the Wall,
  Whilst Parents Hearts did ake,
That being done straightway he ran,
  The other Child to fetch,
And pluck'd it from the Mother's Breast,
  Most like a cruel Wretch.
Within one Hand a Knife he brought,
  The Child within the other,
And holding it over the Wall,
  Saying thus shall die thy Mother,
With that he cut the Throat of it;
  Then to the Lord did call,
To look how he the Neck had cut,
  And down the head did fall.
Then threw the Body down the Wall,
  Into the Mote so deep;
Which made the Father wring his Hands
  And grievously to weep:
Then to the Lady went this Rogue,
  Who was near dead with Fear;
Yet this vile Wretch most cruelly,
  Did drag her by the Hair.
And drew her to the very Wall,
  Which when her Lord did see,
Then presently, he cry'd out,
  And fell upon his Knee.
Quoth he if thou wilt save her Life,
  Whom I do love so dear,
I will forgive thee all that's past.
  Though they concern me near.
O save her Life I thee beseech,
  O save her Life I thee pray,
And I will grant thee what thou wilt.
  Demand of me this Day:
Well, quoth the Moor, I do regard.
  The Moan that thou dost make;
If thou wilt grant me what I ask,
  I'll save her for thy Sake.
O save her Life and then demand,
  Of me what thing thou wilt,
Cut of thy Nose, and not one Drop,
  Of her Blood shall be spilt.
With that the Lord he presently took,
  A Knife within his Hand,
And then his Nose he quite cut off,
  In Place where he did stand.
Now I have bought the Lady's Life,
  He to the Moor did call,
Then take her, qaoth the wicked Rogue
  And down he let her fall.
Which when this gallant Lord did see,
  His Senses all did fail,
Yet many sought to save her Life,
  Yet nothing could prevail.
When as the Moor did see her dead.
  Then he did laugh amain,
At them who for their gallant Lord,
  And Lady did complain.
Quoth he, I know you'll torture me,
  If that you can me get;
But all you Threats I do not fear,
  Nor yet regard one Whit
Wild Horses shall thy Body tear,
  I know it to be true;
But I'll prevent you of that Pain.
  And down himself he threw:
Too good a Death for such a Wretch,
  A Villain void of Fear;
And thus doth end as sad a Tale,
  As ever Man did hear.

Newcastle: Printed in this present Year

A Lamentable BALLAD of the Tragical End of A Gallant LORD and Virtuous LADY

Together with the Untimely Death of their two Children,
Wickedly performed by a heathenish and blood-thirsty BLACKAMOOR, their Servant,
The like of which Cruelty and Murder was never before heard of.
To the Tune of the Lady's Fall.

Printed and Sold at the Printing-Office in Bow-Church-Yard, London.

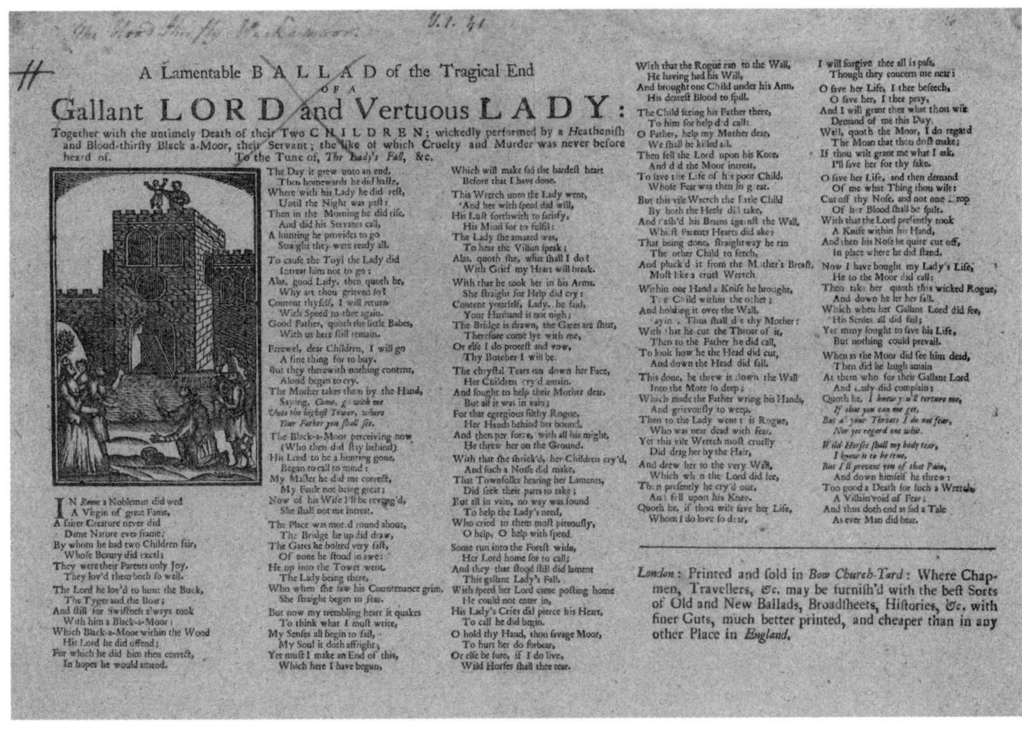

A Lamentable BALLAD of the Tragical End OF A

Gallant LORD and Vertuous LADY:

Together with the untimely Death of their Two CHILDREN; wickedly performed by a *Heatheniſh* and Blood-thirſty Black a-Moor, their Servant; the like of which Cruelty and Murder was never before heard of. To the Tune of, *The Lady's Fall*, &c.

IN *Rome* a Nobleman did wed
A Virgin of great Fame,
A fairer Creature never did
Dame Nature ever frame;
By whom he had two Children fair,
Whoſe Beauty did excel;
They were their Parents only Joy,
They lov'd them both ſo well.

The Lord he lov'd to hunt the Buck,
The Tyger and the Boar;
And ſtill for Swiftneſs always took
With him a Black-a-Moor:
Which Black-a-Moor within the Wood
His Lord he did offend;
For which he did him then correct,
In hopes he would amend.

The Day it grew unto an end,
Then homewards he did haſte,
Where with his Lady he did reſt,
Until the Night was paſt:
Then in the Morning he did riſe,
And did his Servants call,
A hunting he provides to go
Straight they were ready all.

To cauſe the Toyl the Lady did
Intreat him not to go:
Alas, good Lady, then quoth he,
Why art thou grieved ſo?
Content thyſelf, I will return
With Speed to thee again.
Good Father, quoth the little Babes,
With us here ſtill remain.

Farewel, dear Children, I will go
A fine thing for to buy.
But they therewith nothing content,
Aloud began to cry.
The Mother takes them by the Hand,
Saying, *Come, go with me
Unto the higheſt Tower, where
Your Father you ſhall ſee.*

The Black-a-Moor perceiving now
(Who then did ſtay behind)
His Lord to be a hunting gone,
Began to call to mind:
My Maſter he did me correct,
My Fault not being great;
Now of his Wife I'll be reveng'd,
She ſhall not me intreat.

The Place was mot'd round about,
The Bridge he up did draw,
The Gates he bolted very faſt,
Of none he ſtood in awe:
He up into the Tower went,
The Lady being there,
Who when ſhe ſaw his Countenance grim,
She ſtraight began to fear.

But now my trembling heart it quakes
To think what I muſt write,
My Senſes all begin to fail,
My Soul it doth affright;
Yet muſt I make an End of this,
Which here I have begun,
Which will make ſad the hardeſt heart
Before that I have done.

This Wretch unto the Lady went,
And her with ſpeed did will,
His Luſt forthwith to ſatisfy,
His Mind for to fulfil:
The Lady ſhe amazed was,
To hear the Villain ſpeak;
Alas, quoth ſhe, what ſhall I do?
With Grief my Heart will break.

With that he took her in his Arms,
She ſtraight for Help did cry:
Content yourſelf, Lady, he ſaid,
Your Huſband is not nigh;
The Bridge is drawn, the Gates are ſhut,
Therefore come lye with me,
Or elſe I do proteſt and vow,
Thy Butcher I will be.

The chryſtal Tears ran down her Face,
Her Children cry'd amain,
And ſought to help their Mother dear,
But all it was in vain;
For that egregious filthy Rogue,
Her Hands behind her bound,
And then per force, with all his might,
He threw her on the Ground.

With that ſhe ſhriek'd, her Children cry'd,
And ſuch a Noiſe did make,
That Townfolks hearing her Laments,
Did ſeek their parts to take;
But all in vain, no way was found
To help the Lady's need,
Who cried to them moſt piteouſly,
O help, O help with ſpeed.

Some run into the Foreſt wide,
Her Lord home for to call;
And they that ſtood ſtill did lament
This gallant Lady's Fall.
With ſpeed her Lord came poſting home
He could not enter in,
His Lady's Cries did pierce his Heart,
To call he did begin.

O hold thy Hand, thou ſavage Moor,
To hurt her do forbear,
Or elſe be ſure, if I do live,
Wild Horſes ſhall thee tear.
With that the Rogue ran to the Wall,
He having had his Will,
And brought one Child under his Arm,
His deareſt Blood to ſpill.

The Child ſeeing his Father there,
To him for help did call:
O Father, help my Mother dear,
We ſhall be killed all.
Then fell the Lord upon his Knee,
And did the Moor intreat,
To ſave the Life of his poor Child,
Whoſe Fear was then ſo great.

But this vile Wretch the little Child
By both the Heels did take,
And daſh'd his Brains againſt the Wall,
Whilſt Parents Hearts did ake:
That being done, ſtraightway he ran
The other Child to fetch,
And pluck'd it from the Mother's Breaſt,
Moſt like a cruel Wretch.

Within one Hand a Knife he brought,
The Child within the other;
And holding it over the Wall,
Saying, Thus ſhall die thy Mother:
With that he cut the Throat of it,
Then to the Father he did call,
To look how he the Head did cut,
And down the Head did fall.

This done, he threw it down the Wall
Into the Mote ſo deep;
Which made the Father wring his Hands,
And grievouſly to weep.
Then to the Lady went this Rogue,
Who was near dead with fear,
Yet this vile Wretch moſt cruelly
Did drag her by the Hair,

And drew her to the very Wall,
Which when the Lord did ſee,
Then preſently he cry'd out,
And fell upon his Knee.
Quoth he, if thou wilt ſave her Life,
Whom I do love ſo dear,
I will forgive thee all is paſt,
Though they concern me near:

O ſave her Life, I thee beſeech,
O ſave her, I thee pray,
And I will grant thee what thou wilt
Demand of me this Day.
Well, quoth the Moor, I do regard
The Moan that thou doſt make;
If thou wilt grant me what I aſk,
I'll ſave her for thy ſake.

O ſave her Life, and then demand
Of me what Thing thou wilt:
Cut off thy Noſe, and not one Drop
Of her Blood ſhall be ſpilt.
With that the Lord preſently took
A Knife within his Hand,
And then his Noſe he quite cut off,
In place where he did ſtand.

Now I have bought my Lady's Life,
He to the Moor did call:
Then take her, quoth this wicked Rogue,
And down he let her fall.
Which when her Gallant Lord did ſee,
His Senſes all did fail;
Yet many ſought to ſave his Life,
But nothing could prevail.

When as the Moor did ſee him dead,
Then did he laugh amain
At them who for their Gallant Lord
And Lady did complain:
Quoth he, *I know you'll torture me,
If that you can me get,
But all your Threats I do not fear,
Nor yet regard one whit.*

*Wild Horſes ſhall my body tear,
I know it to be true,
But I'll prevent you of that Pain,*
And down himſelf he threw:
Too good a Death for ſuch a Wretch,
A Villain void of Fear;
And thus doth end as ſad a Tale
As ever Man did hear.

London: Printed and ſold in *Bow Church-Yard*: Where Chapmen, Travellers, &c. may be furniſh'd with the beſt Sorts of Old and New Ballads, Broadſheets, Hiſtories, &c. with finer Cuts, much better printed, and cheaper than in any other Place in *England*.

Figure 50. Ballad sheet facsimile, "A Lamentable Ballad of the Tragical End Of A Gallant Lord and Vertuous Lady: Together with the untimely Death of their Two Children; wickedly performed by a Heathenish and Blood-thirsty Black a-Moor, their Servant; the like of which Cruelty and Murder was never before heard of" (mid-eighteenth century), EBBA 34451. Houghton Library, Harvard University, EB75 P4128C no.109. Public domain.

OPPOSITE

Figure 48. Ballad sheet facsimile, "A Lamentable Ballad of the tragical End of a gallant Lord and a virtuous Lady, and the untimely End of their two Children, wickedly perform'd by a heathenish Black-a-moor, their Servant, the like never heard of before" (c. 1730–69), EBBA 32501. The Huntington Library, HEH 289769. Public domain.

Figure 49. Ballad sheet facsimile, "A Lamentable Ballad of the Tragical End of A Gallant Lord and Virtuous Lady Together with the Untimely Death of their two Children, Wickedly performed by a heathenish and blood-thirsty Blackamoor, their Servant. The like of which Cruelty and Murder was never before heard of" (c. 1728–63), EBBA 31227. British Library, Roxburghe 3.520–521, C.20.f.9.520–521. © The British Library Board.

A Lamentable Ballad of the Tragical end of

A Gallant Lord & Virtuous Lady;

Together with the Untimely Death of their two Children.

IN Rome a nobleman did wed
A virgin of great fame,
Fairer creature never did,
Dame nature ever frame,
By whom he had too children fair,
Whom beauty did excel.
They were their parents only joy,
They lov'd them both ſo well,
The lord he lov'd to hunt the buck,
The tiger and the boar,
And ſtill for ſwiftneſs always took,
With him a blackamoor,
Which blackamoor wthiin the wood,
His lord he did offend,
For which he did him then correct,
In hopes he would amend.
The day it grew unto an end,
Then homewards he did haſte,
Where with his lady he did reſt,
Until the night was paſt,
Then in the morning he did riſe,
And did his ſervants call.
A hunting he provides to go,
And they were ready all,
To eaſe his toil the lady did,
Intreat him not to go.
Alas! good lady then quoth he,
Why art thou grieved ſo,
Content thyſelf I will return
With ſpeed to thee again.
Good father quoth the little babes,
With us here ſtill remain.
Farewell dear children I will go,
A fine thing for to buy,
But they therewith nothing content,
Aloud began to cry,
The mother takes them by the hand
Saying come go with me
Unto the higheſt tower where
Your father you ſhall ſee.
The blackamoor perceiving now
Her hen did ſtay behind,
His lord to be a hunting gone,
He then did call to mind—
My maſter he did me correct,
My fault not being great,
Now of his wife I ll be reveng'd,
She ſhall not me intreat,
The place was moated round about,
The bridge he up did draw,
The gates he bolted very faſt.
Of none he ſtood in awe,
He up into the tower went,
The lady being there,
Who when ſhe ſaw his countenance grim,
She ſtrait began to fear,
But now my trembling heart it quakes,
To think what I muſt write,
My ſenses all begin to fail,
My ſoul it doth afright;
Yet muſt I make an end of this,
Which ere I have begun,
Which will make ſad the hardeſt heart,
Before it I have done.
This wretch unto the lady went,
And her with ſpeed did will,
His luſt forthwith to ſatisfy,
His revenge to fulfill.
The lady ſhe amazed was,
To hear the villain ſpeak,
Alas! quoth ſhe, what ſhall I do,
With grief my heart will break,
With that he took her in his arms,
She ſtrait for help did cry,
Content yourſelf lady he ſaid,
Your husband is not nigh,
The bridge is drawn the gates are ſhut,
Thereforere come lie with me,
Or else I do proteſt and now
Thy butcher I will be,
The cryſtal tears ran down her face,
Her children cry'd amain,
And ſought to help their mother dear,
But all it was in vain.
For that egregious filthy rogue,
Her hands behind her bound,
And then by force with all his might
He threw her on the ground,
With that ſhe ſhrieks; her children cry'd,
And ſuch a noiſe did make,
The town ſolks hearing her lament,
Did ſeek their parrs to take,
But all in vain. no way was found,
To help this lady's need,
Who cry'd to them moſt pitiously
O help, O help, with ſpeed,
Some run into the foreſt wide,
Her lord home for to call
And they that ſtood ſtill did lament,
This gallant lady's fall,
With ſpeed her lord came poſting home,
He could not enter in,
His lady's cries did pierce his heart,
To call he did begin,
O hold thy hand thou ſavage moor,
To hurt her do forbear,
Or else be ſure if i do live,
Wild horſes ſhall thee tear.
With that the rogue run to the wall,
He having had his will,
And brought one child unto the wall,
His deareſt blood to ſpill.
The child ſeeing his father there,
To him for help did call,
O father help my mother dear,
We ſhall be killed all.
Then fell upon his knees,
And did the more intreat,
To ſave the life of his poor child,
Whoſe fear was then ſo great,
But this vile wretch the little child
By both his heels did take,
And daſh'd his brains againſt the wall,
While parents hearts did ake,
That being done away he run,
The other child to fetch,
And pluck'd it from the mother's breaſt,
Moſt like a cruel wretch.
Within one hand a knife he brought,
The child within the other,
And holding it againſt the wall,
Saying thus die ſhall thy mother,
With that he cut the throat
Then to the father he did call,
To look how he the ſame did cut,
Then down the wall her head did fall,
This done he threw it down the wall
Into the mote ſo deep,
Which made the father wring his hands,
And grievously to weep.
Who was near dead with fear.
Yet this vile wretch most cruelly,
Did drag her by the hair,
And drew her to the very wall,
Which when her lord did ſee,
Then preſently he cried out,
And fell upon his knee,
Quoth he if thou wilt ſave her life
Whom I do love ſo dear,
I will forgive thee allt hat is paſt,
Though they concern me near,
O ſave her life I thee beſeech,
O ſave her life I tee pray.
And I will grant thee what thou wilt
Demand of me this day,
Well quoth the moor, I do regard
The moan that thou doſt make
If thou wilt grant me what I aſk,
I'll ſave her for thy ſake.
O ſave her life and then demand
Of me what thing thou wilt.
Cut off thy noſe and not one drop
Of her blood ſhall be ſpilt,
With that the lord preſently took
A knife within his hand,
And then his noſe he quite cut off
In place where he did ſtand.
Now I have bought my lady's life.
Then to the Moor did call,
Then take her quoth this wicked rogue,
And dowh he let her fall,
Which when her gallant lord did ſee,
His ſenaes all did fail,
Yet many ſought to ſave his life,
Yet nothing could prevail,
When as the Moor did ſee him dead,
Then did he laugh amain,
At them who for his gallant lord
And lady did complain,
Quoth he I know you'll torture me,
If that you can me get,
But all your threats I do not fear
Nor yet regard one whit.
Wild horſes will my body tear,
I know it to be true,
But i'll prevent you of that ſport,
And down himſelf he threw,
Too good a death for such a wretch,
A villain void of fear,
And thus doth end as ſad a tale,
As ever man did hear.

Printed by J. Evans, Long-lane, London.

Figure 51. "A Lamentable Ballad of the Tragical end of A Gallant Lord & Virtuous Lady; Together with the Untimely Death of their two Children" (1780–1812). The Bodleian Library, University of Oxford, Harding B 3(42).

association with death—*memento mori*—a woodblock header centered by the skull and cross-bones that were commonplace images for mortality from very early times, well before England's firsthand encounters with Africa (Figure 52).

In perhaps the most surprising deviation from the original ballad, a version of "The Lady and the Blackamoor" tailor-made woodcut turns up on a prose broadside in the late eighteenth century that is not about slaves or blackamoors but about morally black and sensational deeds, titled "Human Monsters!! . . ." (c. 1750, EBBA 32442). The extended title to this broadside leads with an account of a man who eats live cats and was recently committed to jail for the murder of an infant, to which is added the relation of two rapes (the one we learn, in the text of the broadside, committed on an infant under nine years of age and the other, as the title states, by a boy of only sixteen). The broadside includes other bizarre as well as monstrously diabolical deeds,

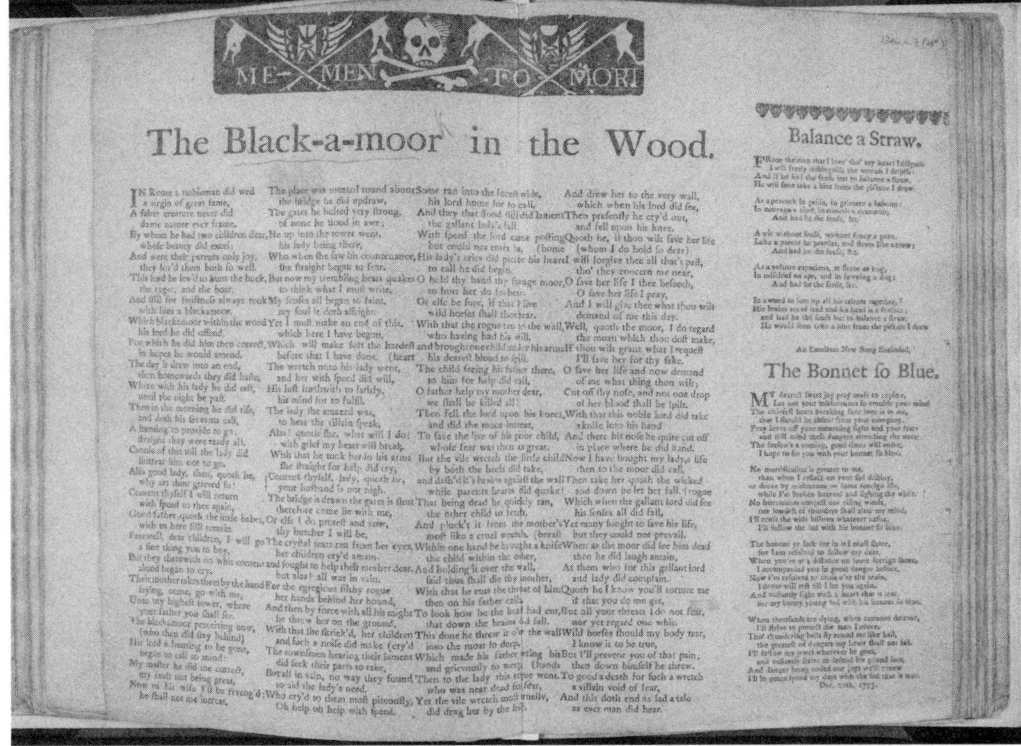
ME-MEN-TO MORI

The Black-a-moor in the Wood.

Balance a Straw.

The Bonnet so Blue.

Figure 52. "The Black-a-moor in the Wood" (1775). British Library, General Reference Collection 1346.m.7.(20.). © The British Library Board.

from (col. 2, first full paragraph) the man in Norfolk who "for a trifling wager, actually devoured two live kittens and a whole candle" to (in the next paragraph) the Scottish "story of Sandy Bane," who "conceived the most delicious repast was a human heart taken warm from the body while the blood was issuing from it, and the pulsations of life remained." All belong to what the broadside's relator calls (at the bottom of the first column) a "*black* catalogue of crimes" (my emphasis). Now blacks as well as whites might, I suppose, eat live kittens and candles, or pulsating human hearts, but this broadside determinedly points to the monstrousness in human nature generally more than to the monstrousness in blackamoors. The familiar "Lady and the Blackamoor" woodcut illustration served here as a fitting decoration to the "black catalogue of crimes" most likely because of its early association with murder and rape, not because it targeted the race of blacks.[18]

Human Monſters!!

Account of a Human Monſter, at Woodſide, near Old

Windſor, who makes a common Praiſtce of EATING LIVE CATS, &c. He was Yeſterday apprehended and committed to Goal for the MURDER of an INFANT CHILD. Alſo an account of a ſimilar Monſter at Reepham, Norfolk.

TO WHICH IS ADDED,

The Account of a RAPE committed by Mr. J. of

Broad-ſtreet St. Giles's. And an account of another Rape committed by a BOY of only Sixteen Years of Age, who is committed to Stafford Goal for Trial.

IT muſt equally be a matter of real ſurpriſe and aſtoniſhment, that ſuch depraved appetites as the following inſtances furniſhes, can exiſt in this country; or indeed that ſuch a monſtrous cannibal could diſgrace human nature. Many inſtances of brutality have of late aſtoniſhed us, and almoſt exceeded the bounds of credibility; but the following inſtances leave all others far behind them in wickedneſs.

A fellow who has long been reſident at Woodſide, near Old Windſor, who has been noted for the infamous feat of eating a cat alive, and who been in the conſtant habit of the moſt brutal and beaſtly practices, has been apprehended and committed to goal, on a charge of murdering an infant ſix years old.

That any man could be found who poſſeſſed ſo much the appetite of a cannibal as to prefer the devouring of cats and other animals alive, to the ordinary food of mankind, is almoſt beyond belief: and we certainly ſhould give it no manner of credit, was it not atteſted by an authority we could not diſpute.

But what renders this monſter, if poſſible, more completely and diabolically wicked, is, that he is charged with having added the worſt of all ſins, Murder, to the already black catalogue of crimes he has committed. Nay, ſome do not ſcruple to aſſert that it was to ſatisfy his unnatural appetite he committed this moſt horrid deed.

As a proof that the foregoing is not the only wretch of that deſcription now living, we ſhall juſt mention the following inſtance of a ſimilar depravity.—A fellow at a public-houſe at Reepham, in Norfolk, for a trifling wager, actually devoured two live kittens and a whole candle.

Theſe mens enormouſly wicked deeds remind us of the Scottiſh traditional ſtory of Sandy Bane, who, according to ſome who aſſert it on authority, uſed to devour with the moſt voracious appetite every thing while panting for life. He conceived the moſt delicious repaſt was a human heart taken warm from the body while the blood was iſſuing from it, and the pulſations of life remained.

A man was apprehended in Broad ſtreet, St. Giles's, charged with having committed a rape on the body of an infant under nine years of age; attended with ſome peculiar circumſtances we ſhall at preſent forbear to mention.

And a few days ſince, a boy of ſixteen years of age, was committed to Stafford goal, on a ſimiliar charge, and with a girl of exactly the ſame age.

Figure 53. "Human Monsters!! . . ." (c. 1750), EBBA 32442. The Huntington Library, HEH 289716. Public domain.

This isn't to say, of course, that someone looking at this broadside, or reading the many versions of "The Lady and the Blackamoor" that proliferated in England through the centuries wouldn't think about blacks in racist ways; in fact, they might even have savored the violent imaginings in the ballad of black inhumanity, heathenness, and lust. The ballad contains a hard shotgun pellet of racism, as does the broadside "Human Monsters!!" And, certainly, by the time the story of "The Lady and the Blackamoor" reaches Georgia in 1789, the scattershot possibilities of its violence have been reduced to a double-barreled rifle containing only two, both racialized, bullets, as Gomez explains: "the dangers of both excessive punishment and excessive trust" of slaves. But my point is that, in its earliest, wide-choke sensationalism that is textual, visual, and oral—its excess of violence and emotion, which aesthetically spreads associational hits broadly—the ballad has a scattershot effect that targets more than race. There is more than one place where its pellets of violence and blame might fall, especially as text, illustration, and tune move, reassemble, and morph. As is typical of multimedia ballads, there is more than one subject position capable of being voiced; and one never knows for sure where the voiced moving violations will strike home, and who will, if only spontaneously and temporarily, identify with that home as their public.

I conclude my study with something of a re-jigging of my analyses to date of the moving media and tactical publics of broadside ballads. I propose a new tactical synchronic approach not so much aimed at comprehensively exposing the mobile crisscrossing between the many assemblable and reassemblable component media and publics made viable by broadside ballads in their making and dissemination. Rather, I look beyond the protean broadside ballad as bricolage-like lived experience to its inter-involvement with other performative genres of its time, specifically drama. Consider, in this light, that ballad "jigs," sung in dialogue form, often to the accompaniment of dance and instruments, functioned as "conclusions" to plays especially in the late sixteenth and early seventeenth centuries in England. Furthermore, as Matthew J. Smith and Julia Lupton having argued, in their article "Ballads+: The Tragedy of *Romeo and Juliet* and Its After-Piece Jig," the dramatic ballad jig is in many ways an extension rather than a conclusion to the multitude of sounds, songs, and dances that are referenced throughout plays such as Shakespeare's *Romeo and Juliet*.[19] As genres, broadside ballads and drama have much in common. That said, what I propose, as concluding "jig" to my ballad study, which is *not* a dramatic study, is that there is in fact both a collaboration and a competition between ballads and stage drama that does not result in equivalence. As we shall see in *The Winter's Tale*, Shakespeare knew full well that ballads, at least in terms of their moving and participatory reach, as well as market sales, win out. That's why he so extensively invokes them in all his plays. Ballads, Shakespeare realized, like a master literary critic, can create a multimedia cross-class and fully experiential moment more extensively and intensively than can drama. But, in their very performativity, ballads might be adopted by the playwright as colonized component parts to furthering his desired dramatic experience. In *The Winter's Tale*, especially, we witness Shakespeare capitalizing on broadside ballads while at the same time addressing the limits of his (and, for that matter, all) plays.

CONCLUSION ❧

The Limits of the Shakespearean Stage

Ballading *The Winter's Tale*

The news, *Rogero*?" So asks the "First Gentleman" of the newly arrived "Second Gentleman" in act 5, scene 2 of *The Winter's Tale*, as rumors of fantastic court happenings fill the air. Autolycus, rogue and sometime balladmonger from Bohemia, now mingling as one with the unnamed and ill-informed gentlemen at Leontes' court in Sicilia, begins the questioning: "Beseech you, sir," he asks the First Gentleman, "were you present at this relation?" The First Gentleman can only provide a partial report; Autolycus "would most gladly know the issue of it."[1] What the two are trying to piece together is the story behind the sudden influx of royals and shepherds from Bohemia to the Sicilian court, and the accompanying revelations. All of this occurs behind the scenes, offstage, which makes for a fragmentary experience for both the gathered gentlemen and the larger audience watching the play. Such disconnection, I have argued in this book, is a characteristic of the piecemeal assemblage of the media that made up broadside ballads and their reception. Indeed, just two scenes earlier, broadside ballads figure prominently, sold by Autolycus in the guise of balladmonger and peddler during the sheepshearing festivities in Bohemia. But as we enter the play's end-stage in Sicilia, the bricolage makeup of a ballad relation is fractured beyond comprehension. The First Gentleman laments his "broken delivery of the business" (5.2.9). Before being dismissed along with other lords from the king's inner chamber, he caught only that the old shepherd opened a "fardel" and "methought . . . the shepherd say he found the child" (5.2.2, 5–7). He also recalls the extreme mixed emotions of the inner circle, all "staring on one another" in "dumbness," and a "notable passion of wonder" (5.2.12, 13, 15–16)—which, again, cannot but remind us of the country folk in Bohemia being struck dumb with wonder, as described by Autolycus, on listening to his broadside ballads at the sheepshearing feast. Reinforcing associations with balladry, the shepherd's fardel of trinkets would have prompted audience recollection of the pack of trifles from which Autolycus plucked his ballads. In fact, the unnamed lords of Sicilia, together ironically with Autolycus himself, who try to piece together the relation of wondrous events occurring offstage, appear as if they had themselves popped out of Autolycus's pack as "witnesses" of ballad news "more than my pack will hold" (4.4.284–85). "The news, Rogero?" seals the accumulating ballad connections that tie haphazardly together this fragmented, piecemeal witnessing.

"Rogero" is not, I posit, the name of the Second Gentleman, as one might first assume. Instead, "Rogero" is, foremost, a reference to a popular ballad tune. As such, it stands in apposition to the noun "news"[2]—once again recalling the sheepshearing feast where Autolycus flaunted what he claimed were "new" ballads and ballads of "news" or "wonders" (another word, in the singular, that echoes throughout the final act of *The Winter's Tale*, describing the near miraculous series of unfolding events). As if haltingly singing the marvelous news to the tune "Rogero," the Second Gentleman exclaims, "*such a deal of wonder is broken out within this hour, that ballad-makers cannot be able to express it*" (5.2.23–25; my emphasis).

"Ballad-makers," given the approximate dating of the play as 1610–11, undoubtedly refers to *broadside* ballad makers; the broadside ballad genre was at this time all the rage.[3] Such "ballad-makers" were the mass producers and marketers—and, as we have seen, by extension, remaking consumers—of actual artifacts: the sheets combining text, illustrations, and song of the kind Autolycus earlier sold among his other cheap wares and of the kind that have been the focus of this book. But, as we have seen, the ballad-like text or "relation" of the gentleman here is fragmented in the extreme. It pushes to near breaking point the narrative facet of the collage-like production and reception of ballad media—to such an extent that we are told that ballad makers could *not* express it. Even Autolycus, the master balladmonger and general improvisational and tactical know-it-all in Bohemia, has been left out of the loop of this wondrous Sicilian "news." And where are the illustrations and song that accompany broadside ballad sheets, other than in the brief evocation, though as if in direct address, to "Rogero"? They are present in this final act, I posit, but they are so severed and fractured in the appliqué broadside ballad conclusion of the play, so morphed from a potential whole or assemblage of relational parts, that they might not be immediately discernible without performative help. But they are there for the making, seeing, and hearing.

At this point, echoing Paulina, Leontes' own Autolycus-like improvisational and tactical artist at the Sicilian court, I ask that "You do awake your faith" (5.3.94), or in Richard C. McCoy's terms, suspend your critical disbelief (*Faith in Shakespeare*, 141). Allow me to posit a performative version of the sheepshearing feast in the concluding scenes of *The Winter's Tale* at the Sicilian court, which forms something like the second half of a two-part ballad (the Bohemian festivities being the first half). Furthermore, I ask you to consider that the play's conclusion functions at the hands of Shakespeare as a kind of deliberately dysfunctional broadside ballad that is like but also unlike—at least in its failing to sustain even momentarily—its "other half," the immediately preceding and notably extended sheepshearing scene of act 4, scene 4 of the play. Act 5 of *The Winter's Tale*, one might say, is the broadside ballad's Humpty-Dumpty who has fallen out of the larger, embracive world of Bohemia, which had openly entertained multiple media and publics, assemblable and reassemblable in improvisational ways. It allowed for a tactical media-cum-making-publics version of DeLanda's assemblage theory—most exuberantly enacted by the much-talented, if roguish, Bohemian balladmonger and singer, Autolycus. In the closed-off vision of the Sicilian court—what Emmanuel Levinas would describe negatively as an "intimate society" (cited by James Kearney, "Hospitality's Risk," 92), as we shall pursue—we simply cannot put all the Humpty-Dumpty ballad pieces back together again because the court denies the larger communal participation that such an assemblage necessarily involves. We can only watch the fractured pieces play out—text, illustration, and tune. The conclusion of *The Winter's Tale*, in sum, strives but fails to enact a full assemblage (however necessarily piecemeal) of media and publics by invoking the broadside ballad, but it remains partial in a privative way. And Shakespeare, I suspect, knew it.

My argument here involves throwing broadside ballad straws—or bits and pieces—not merely into the wind but onto the dramatic stage, where we can track associational performative hits as an extension of Chapters 1 and 2 of this book. In the process, I hope to add a new cut into the prism made up by the many genres that critics have posited go into the making of Shakespeare's fascination in his later plays with a multifaceted art—one that includes not only tragedy, comedy, romance, orality, and tales, but also, and extremely importantly, broadside ballads. The broadside ballad as a multimedia printed artifact has mostly been given short shrift by critics of *The Winter's Tale*, though many have picked up on the echoing references to the printing press in the play through such reiterated words as "copy," "print," "impression," "issue," and "sheets."[4] The more privileged genres cited as "belonging" to the sequential action of the play are canonical ones. We are typically told that the play moves from tragedy (acts 1–3) to comedy (act 4) to romance (act 5)—or simply from tragedy to romance, as Rosalie Colie argues (*Shakespeare's Living Art*, 268)—with recognizable layerings, backtrackings, and echoes of these genres. Viewing such generic mingling as both an extraordinary tactic and an authorial one, James Kearney draws on Stanley Cavell's skeptical reading of the play to argue that *The Winter's Tale* is precisely Shakespeare's exploration, even experimentation, into using multiple genres to stage the "spectacularly contingent." By this term, Kearney refers to an aesthetic of strange uncertainty imbued simultaneously with tragedy and comedy, chance and providence, luck and grace, skepticism and faith (*Shipwrecked Ethics*; see also Felperin, "Deconstruction and Presence," 3–18). I agree with Kearney; indeed, his idea of spectacular contingency allows us to venture even further into the hyper-plurality of Bolter and Grusin in our interpretation of early modern media. As we have already seen, the broadside ballad genre provided early modern contemporaries with an art that was not only at all times familiar but also always multiply participatory. It invited everyone in its orbit to become part of an aesthetic assemblage that extensively and intensively mixed media and visions. I would go so far as to argue that the broadside ballad genre is unique in its ability to encompass all the improvisational, mingled positions Kearney describes. It thus becomes an apt self-reflexive and active medium by which Shakespeare could develop and attempt to unify, even *in* fragmentation and resistance to aesthetic unity, his complex and, yes, problematized dramatic vision.

In pursuing Shakespeare's preoccupation with broadside ballads as a performative medium expressive of his late, uncertain, and motley drama, I have two other objectives in mind. First, I wish to discuss broadside ballads as performances not only similar to but also *in contrast* with theater. I thus address, perhaps in a different way than he would like, Smith's critique, expressed in his 2006 article "Shakespeare's Residuals," that the role played by both oral and printed ballads in early modern drama "has largely been forgotten" by modern theater studies. In fact, he continues, so much have ballads fallen off the performance study radar that theater scholars can no longer even find an inroad: "With scholarly argumentation and theatre history we know the nature of the evidence and what we can do with it: with ballads, we don't quite know where to begin" (216). While some scholars have since offered critical "beginnings" of such study (see, for example, the collection of essays in Fumerton, ed., *Ballads and Performance*, 2018), Smith, more than any other scholar of Shakespeare, has led the way. In "Shakespeare's Residuals" itself, he forges an inroad for integrating ballads into Shakespearean performance studies. He there particularly demonstrates how broadside ballads often tailored themselves after popular Shakespearean plays, marketing, as an afterlife, the dramatic experience of the play in the form of a single-sheet memento of the event that could be repeated as well as held onto or pasted up for display. Smith is surely correct that broadside ballad makers capitalized on Shakespeare's plays and drama in general. This is evident, for example, in the many extant ballads in EBBA with titles that include "Titus Andronicus," "King Lear," "Mad Tom of Bedlam," and the term "jig" (referring to a mixed genre closely related to the broadside ballad dialogue format, which occurred sometimes as an intermission but most often as an aftermath and, as we shall see, as an extension of and commentary upon the stage performance). But even in his brilliance, Smith, at least for the most part, makes the dangerous assumption that ballads and plays are performative allies, alike in most respects. Perhaps this might be the case when both genres are simply read or disinterestedly watched (if such "removed" reception were even possible). But multipronged and interactive engagement was the primary intent behind the making and dissemination of broadside ballads. As such, we should more questioningly ask, are printed ballads and plays really twin performative genres?

Addressing this question via broadside ballads in *The Winter's Tale*—in their *before* life, so to speak, rather than as "residuals"—will allow us to revisit many of the concerns that have been key issues of this book, for they are the same topics that Shakespeare highlights and troubles in adapting the broadside ballad to his dramatic genre. We will witness in such adaptation the same theoretical touchpoints formative of a lived ballad experience that I emphasized in Chapter 1: concepts of "moving," "assemblage," "publics," and "tactics." We will also find Shakespeare's fascination specifically with the manifold and fragmentary media of broadside ballad artifacts—text, illustration, and tune—that produced a variety of random tactical hits. We shall see not only his preoccupation with print, especially black-letter print, as it emerged from calligraphy, but also his attraction to popular ballad tunes and even eye-catching ballad illustrations. Most important, we shall recognize his awareness that, as allies *and* competitors with dramatic producers, broadside ballad makers (including manufacturers, hawkers, and also consumers), in their near-infinite and mobile performative assemblages of parts and wholes, could make possible multiple publics more deftly even than playwrights, players, and their audiences. Of course, this is not to deny the power of staged drama to, even at a remove, affectively *move* audiences. It is simply to underscore the theater's unballad-like restrictive physical sitedness (and, more relatively, that of its audiences), limiting movement and thus interaction within the place of the stage, and, furthermore, its unballad-like resistance to literal participation by its audience members in acts and speeches performed.

Shakespeare, I argue, sought to capitalize on and surpass his more *moving*, including in that context more participatory, market competitor by deploying manifold features of the broadside ballad in just about every play he wrote. But nowhere did he so extensively draw upon and anatomize the broadside ballad as genre than in *The Winter's Tale*. If not a twin, the broadside ballad was a "kin" performative genre, perfectly suited to Shakespeare's experiment in staging the "spectacularly contingent." I posit that the broadside ballad was even *more* suited to exploration of an openly uncertain performative dramatic art, given its multimedia nature. Seen as such, Shakespeare needed the hybrid broadside ballad to advance his exploratory ends. However, regardless of whether it was deliberate, his experiment ultimately failed the test of the stage. Embracing the mixed, disjunctive, and "spectacularly contingent"—all prominent facets of broadside ballads—Shakespeare pushed the outside of his dramatic genre envelope until, by the end of *The Winter's Tale*, it fell apart beyond even Pygmalion's ability to put the pieces back together.

"Enter Autolycus, Singing" (Folio, 1623)—of Moral Wonders and Belief

First, then, to the master peddler of broadside ballads in the play, Autolycus, who sings himself onto the stage in Bohemia in act 4. Most critics agree that this shape-changing trickster brings to the stage a much-needed surge of springtime festivity after the wintry tragic events that open the play in the Sicilian court. Though we soon learn it is in fact fall in Bohemia, Autolycus embodies the spirit of rebirth that spring heralds within the Bohemian world to which we have been transported from Sicilia after, Time tells us, sixteen years have passed. Autolycus enters the stage singing/celebrating just such seasonal new life: "*When daffodils begin to peer . . .*" (4.3.1). He in no way offers a return to the naïve prelapsarian ideality that King Polixenes of Bohemia had nostalgically recollected to Hermione at the Sicilian court. There, Polixenes describes himself and her husband, King Leontes, when youths, as boys like "twinn'd lambs that did frisk i' the' sun, / . . . what we chang'd / Was innocence for innocence" (1.2.67–69). Polixenes' almost wistful depiction of an Edenic state smacks of a narcissistic male homeostasis dangerous in a postlapsarian world. It raises a red flag, at which Hermione quickly swats—"by this we gather / You have tripp'd since" (1.2.75–76)—and at which Leontes, as if a raging bull, charges. Suddenly overcome with a mad certainty that his nine-months-pregnant wife has committed adultery with his best friend, Polixenes, Leontes launches a series of actions that enact fall after fall: ordering his highest adviser, Camillo, to poison Polixenes; the secret flight of Polixenes with Camillo from Leontes' court; Leontes' condemnation to abandonment in the wilds of his baby girl to whom the imprisoned Hermione gives premature birth; Hermione's public kangaroo trial for adultery and treason; the death of their son, Mamillius, from heartbreak over the accusations made against his mother; Hermione's swooning and pronounced death at the news of Mamillius's demise; and Leontes' abrupt return to sanity—all too late, alas, as his court lapses into a frozen state of sixteen wintry years of repentance; and, almost as an afterthought, the famously bizarre death of Antigonus, Paulina's husband, in Bohemia ("*Exit, pursued by a bear*," 3.3.58), after depositing the baby girl there and naming her Perdita.

Autolycus's dramatic entrance in Bohemia, cheerily singing of the seasonal rebirth of spring, contrasts not only with Polixenes' earlier imagining of an unchanging state of prelapsarian male innocence with Leontes—the two forever frisking "as twinn'd lambs"—but also with the subsequent wintry stasis into which Leontes' mad jealousy throws his court. Autolycus's public song and address to the audience also counters Leontes' solipsistic imagining of his wife's adultery, expressed in soliloquy or in private, one-on-one exchanges: self-consuming twisted vocalizations determinedly rendering women and sex as together monster-making of men. Within a single brief speech, Leontes looks upon his innocent son—soon to be sacrificed as if a lamb to his father's distorting jealousy—and in fast-forward motion mentally warps the meaning of "neat" (at first a reference to his son's cleanliness) into a preoccupation with horned animals, known also as "neat"—"steer," "heifer," and "calf" (1.2.123–25). Then, with yet another warped thought, he bends "neat" into a fixation on Mamillius as a lewd freak of hu*man*ity. He addresses him as "you wanton calf!"; that is, as a lust-filled half-boy/half-animal. His mind ever twisting, Leontes next rebounds the strangeness of this simile onto himself: "my calf?" (1.2.126–27). One cannot but think of the archetypal image of the animalized horned husband, signifying both a wife's adultery and lewd animality. A further mental association would be prominent: connection to the mythical horned half-human/half-animal satyr of unnaturally insatiable sex.

Autolycus has sex on his mind as well. But he openly sings about it as being in harmony with nature. Enthused with song, he echoes "*the sweet birds, O how they sing!*" which he imagines chanting as an accompaniment to his lusty loves: the birds trill "*summer songs for me and my aunts [doxies or whores], / While we lie tumbling in the hay*" (4.3.6, 11–12). Autolycus's tumbling with, by traditional standards, "immoral" (that is, "loose") women is carefully situated by Shakespeare: sex in Bohemia, under the aegis of Autolycus, is as natural as the urge to sing, shared by both bird and man.

As such, Leontes' earlier fall into an obsession over monstrously unnatural sex finds redemption in a more benign recognition by Autolycus that sexual desire is innate to our earthly condition and, indeed, a fact of both nature and human life. Thus, while Leontes had perversely asked Camillo why he,

Leontes, would "sully" with wild imaginings "The purity and whiteness of my sheets?" (1.2.326–27), Autolycus happily steps onto the stage singing not only of spring, songbirds, and sex but also of the rechargeable brightness of bedsheets. He revels in the quick cheat of stealing just such sheets, now literalized and cleansed through a mundane everyday activity: he snatches "*The white sheet bleaching on the hedge*" after its washing (4.3.5). It naturally follows that Autolycus lives in and for the changing moments of the day-to-day—what I have referred to previously as the "passing present." He relishes spontaneously taking advantage of unexpected occasions as well as exploiting his and others' fallen human condition. He's a rogue, yes—aren't we all after the fall?—but in relatively harmless and entertaining (if also lucrative) ways. Thus, when he spots "Clown" ("brother" to Perdita) dawdling down the road on his way to market to purchase goods for the sheepshearing feast, Autolycus tactically, that is, on the spur of the moment, devises a humorous self-referencing deceit. He describes himself as having been robbed by a person who very much resembles himself (which is technically true, since the robbery is a fiction he invented).

Given the much-needed breath of fresh, if postlapsarian, air that Autolycus infuses into the play's world, critics have generally viewed him favorably—with one important caveat: *at first*. Autolycus's many shape-shifting artistic talents have proven more controversial among critics after he throws off his assumed role of ballad peddler and faces a more elite artifice after we (and all the main characters in Bohemia) are transported back to Sicilia. This is usually where the critical tide turns. Definitively now rejected as crass and naïve is the kind of "wonder" elicited by Autolycus the balladeer. This appeal had, of course, been tactically elicited from his popular—with an emphasis on "low"—audience, keen to buy broadside ballad artifacts and other "trifles" at the Bohemian sheepshearing feast. The tide turns in Sicilia. However inspiring and invigorating the amazement Autolycus evokes from his audience in Bohemia, their wonder pales, we are told, by comparison with the elevated mystical "faith" that Paulina demands from her select aristocratic audience on witnessing a higher art at that court. After all, Paulina's miraculous sculpture of Hermione—and, by extension, many would argue, Shakespeare's preeminent aesthetic—there literally comes to life.[5]

But would the mass-marketed, and thus necessarily "low," art that Autolycus hawks be so readily dismissed at this climactic moment by Shakespeare's *historical* audience? In addressing Autolycus's talents, modern critics have mostly focused on his *literary* artistic ancestry: his self-declared Mercury bloodline revealing him to be the "artist-as-wit" portrayed in Homer and Ovid, as well as his recognizable brotherhood with the con artists sketched in Robert Greene's many cony-catching pamphlets.[6] But though both literary ancestries likely would have made associational hits in the minds of the play's early attendees, neither stereotype, I would argue, could approach the audience's everyday familiarity with and fondness for real-life hawkers of lowly broadside ballads (or, at the very least, for their wares). Disseminating the most popular artifacts of the time, base peddlers possessed their own enlivening power through the art of their hawking performances and, especially, through their invigorating multimedia wares. As we have already seen, and will pursue more fully in this conclusion, balladmongers and broadside ballads not only regularly attracted crowds of audiences of all kinds but also, in multifarious ways, brought their artifacts and audiences to life, if only in the ephemeral moment of participatory performance. Again, thinking of familiar everyday encounters of the period, we should as well reconsider the stereotypes of balladmongers as con artists peddling fakery and "mere" trifles with the ultimate goal of picking their audiences' pockets. Of course, Autolycus is in fact just such a rogue. But it seems unlikely that his audience of consumers, such as the peasants at the sheepshearing feast in *The Winter's Tale*, would have so exuberantly welcomed him in his disguise as peddler of trinkets, including most prominently broadside ballads, by eagerly gathering round to view, hear, sing, and purchase his wares if, whenever they did so, they got robbed. Word gets out. Indeed, Autolycus is more than a thieving con artist using trash to gain cash.

To be sure, wonder ballads of the kind Autolycus first draws out of his pack—the tall tales of a woman turned into a fish because she would not have sex with a man, and of the usurer's wife who gave birth to twenty money bags of gold—could be interpreted as cons. They speak of fantastical happenings while at the same time invoking a false faith in their "truth." In offering these particular fakeries as verities, the character of Autolycus allows the play to remake the earlier tragic happenings at the Sicilian court in a more lighthearted vein. The fabricated wonders he peddles might, in themselves, prompt audience recollection of Leontes' monstrous imaginings born of "nothing," and his insistence on publicizing their veracity. But a key difference presents itself to the informed audience familiar with real-life wonder ballads. Unlike Leontes' made-up fantasies, actual wonder ballads weren't all simple counterfeits. Elderton's sixteenth-century illustrated ballad of "The true fourme and shape of a monsterous Chyld," for instance (dated precisely on the sheet as 1565; EBBA 32225, Figure 54), relates "facts" of the kind exaggerated, to be sure, by Shakespeare—including also the exact day of the birth of the child, the father's name, and those present—"To witnes," writes Elderton in the prose section preceding the short three-stanza ballad, "that it is a Trouth and no

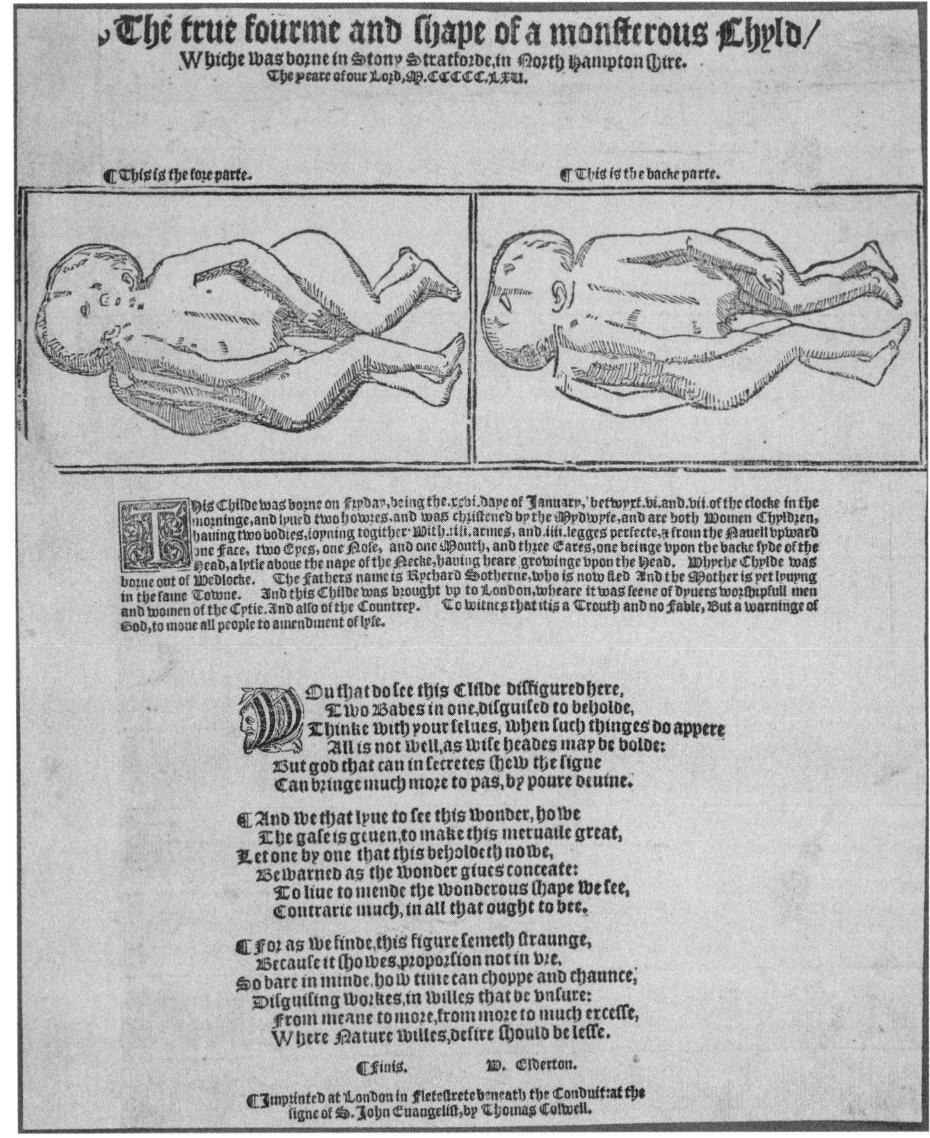

The true fourme and ſhape of a monſterous Chyld/
Whiche was borne in Stony Stratforde, in North Hampton ſhire.
The yeare of our Lord, M.CCCCC.LXV.

This is the fore parte.

This is the backe parte.

This Childe was borne on Fryday, being the .xvi. daye of January, betwyxt .vi. and .vii. of the clocke in the morninge, and lyued two howres, and was chriſtened by the Mydwyfe, and are both Women Chyldren, hauing two bodies, ioyning togither. With .iiii. armes, and .iiii. legges perfecte, & from the Nauell vpward one Face, two Eyes, one Noſe, and one Mouth, and three Eares, one beinge vpon the backe ſyde of the Head, a lytle aboue the nape of the Necke, hauing heare growinge vpon the Head. Whyche Chylde was borne out of Wedlocke. The Fathers name is Rychard Sotherne, who is now fled And the Mother is yet lyuyng in the ſame Towne. And this Childe was brought vp to London, wheare it was ſeene of dyuers worſhipfull men and women of the Cytie. And alſo of the Countrey. To witnes that it is a Trouth and no Fable, But a warninge of God, to moue all people to amendment of lyfe.

You that do ſee this Childe diſfigured here,
Two Babes in one, diſguiſed to beholde,
Thinke with your ſelues, when ſuch thinges do appere
All is not well, as wiſe heades may be bolde:
But god that can in ſecretes ſhew the ſigne
Can bringe much more to pas, by poure deuine.

And we that lyue to ſee this wonder, howe
The gaſe is geuen, to make this meruaile great,
Let one by one that this beholdeth nowe,
Be warned as the wonder giues conceate:
To liue to mende the wonderous ſhape we ſee,
Contrarie much, in all that ought to bee.

For as we finde, this figure ſemeth ſtraunge,
Becauſe it ſhowes, proporſion not in vre,
So bare in minde, how time can choppe and chaunce,
Diſguiſing workes, in willes that be vnſure:
From meane to more, from more to much exceſſe,
Where Nature willes, deſire ſhould be leſſe.

Finis. W. Elderton.

Imprinted at London in Fleteſtrete beneath the Conduit: at the ſigne of S. John Euangeliſt, by Thomas Colwell.

Figure 54. Ballad sheet facsimile, "The true fourme and shape of a monsterous Chyld Which was borne in Stony Stratforde, in North Hampton shire. The yeare of our Lord, M.CCCCC.LXV" (1565), EBBA 32225. The Huntington Library, Britwell collection, HEH 18293. Public domain.

Fable." But there is an almost eerily scientific or natural accuracy to the description and drawing on the ballad sheet of the child's features, which clearly depict real-life conjoined twins. Furthermore, whereas Leontes at first rejects any godly interjection into his monstrous jealousy—dismissing the Delphic prophecy—Elderton's ballad, like others of its kind, accepts and urges upon his audience a religious interpretation of the birth. These godly meanings take the form of warnings, but not only against sexual sins. More typically the warning is a broader admonishment: in Elderton's prose, "a warninge of God, to move all people to amendment of lyfe." The wonder can also be interpreted as illustrative, more ambiguously, of God's mysterious workings. Elderton adds, for instance, that the "straunge" "wonder" (sts. 3, 2) is evidence of both God's judgment against inordinate "willes" (st. 3) *and* His mystical powers. So, while human excesses like mad jealousy and wanton lust explain the excessive doubling of the birth, the event also proves that "god . . . can in secretes shew the signe" that reveals truth, and, indeed, that He "Can bringe much more to pas, by poure [power] devine" (st. 1). Are such mystical powers any less evocative of superlunary forces than those in the final act of *The Winter's Tale*? We might recall that the architect behind the statue's reanimation, Paulina, herself declares that just the idea of finding the "lost child," Perdita, is as "*monstrous* to our human reason" as her husband (Antigonus) coming back from the dead (5.1.40–41; my emphasis).

Similarly moralized is a monstrous-birth wonder ballad printed in the early seventeenth century, which bears much resemblance to the ballad Autolycus offers "to a very doleful tune, how a usurer's wife was brought to bed of twenty money-bags at a burden." The ballad is titled "The Lamenting Lady," to the now-familiar tune of "The Ladies Fall," regularized here to "The Lady's Fall," c. 1620 (EBBA 20210; Figure 55). Singing in the first person, a wealthy burgher's wife relates how, despite her money, she is unable to conceive a child. Subsequently, in a burst of jealousy aimed at a poor woman who comes begging at her door, holding "pretty" twin babes (st. 5), the lady lashes out, calling the woman a "Strumpt [Strumpet]" (st. 8). The beggar woman, "halfe kild with woe" (col. 3, st. 3), invokes God for revenge, concluding with the curse:

> And for these children two of mine
> heaven send thee such a number
> At once, as dayes be in the yeare,
> to make the world to wonder. (col. 3, st. 4)

God's vengeance is swift. The well-to-do lady says that she promptly "sweld so bid [big] that I appeard, / a strange and monstrous wight" (col. 3, st. 6) and—to her husband's dismay—out popped 365 babies, "In bignesse all like new bred mice" (col. 4, st. 1). The mouse-like babies are illustrated in the foreground of the second woodcut of the ballad, all packed together in a

The Lamenting Lady,

Who for the wrongs done to her by a poore woman, for hauing two children at one burthen, was by the hand of God most strangely punished, by sending her as many children at one birth, as there are daies in the yeare, in remembrance whereof, there is now a monument builded in the Citty of *Lowdon*, as many English men now liuing in *Lowdon*, can truely testifie the same and hath seene it.

To the tune of the Ladies fall.

The second part.

FINIS.

Printed at London for *Henry Gosson*, and are to be sold at his shop on London Bridge.

Figure 55. Ballad sheet facsimile, "The Lamenting Lady, Who for the wrongs done to her by a poore woman, for hauing two children at one burthen, was by the hand of God most strangely punished, by sending her as many children at one birth, as there are daies in the yeare, in re-membrance whereof, there is now a monument builded in the City of *Lowdon*, as many En-glish men now liuing in *Lowdon*, can truely testifie the same and hath seene it" (c. 1620), EBBA 20210. Magdalene College, Cambridge, Pepys Library, Pepys Ballads 1.44–45. By permission of the Pepys Library, Magdalene College, Cambridge.

single basket placed on a table to the right of the lady lying in bed. We see her praying, and beside her, her husband standing and staring at the basket, arms raised in shock. The lady, in a tactical twist on the convention of monstrous births, herself becomes a grotesque "monstrous wight" in her pregnancy and shameful "wonder" in her birthing (col. 3, st. 6). But, since she "in extremity" repents her sins, we are told that God lets the babies die out of "pitty" for her (col. 4, st. 4); they are all buried in a single grave with a monument raised to them. At this point, the ballad falls into a truly worn convention—the monument is erected as a testimonial not to be prideful above the poor.

I could cite many other broadside ballads about monstrous births and wonders that turn to God's miraculous workings in His judgment and, most important in a fallen world, to His grace; but "The Lamenting Lady" well represents the wonder genre as it had developed in the mid-sixteenth through the early seventeenth centuries.[7] To be sure, the early wonder ballads are often conventional in their morality: God always (alas, after the iniquity is done) enacts vengeance against pride, against excess, or simply in answer to a prayer from the downtrodden against an abuser. But exactly how He does so and what the moral fully means, beyond "don't be sinful," can be tactically nuanced by author and consumer alike.

Frances Dolan correctly warns, indeed, that we should not be too quick to dismiss as naïve the shepherdess Mopsa's excited belief in such wonders ("Mopsa's Method," 173–74). Hearing of the arrival of Autolycus with broadside ballads in his pack, Mopsa exclaims, "I love a ballad in print, a life, for then we are sure they are true" (4.4.261–62). But what might at first seem the enthusiasm of the ignorant, Dolan notes, is followed up by both Mopsa and Dorcas quickly questioning the truth status of the individual ballads that Autolycus offers: "Is it true, think you?"; and again, "Is it true too, think you?" (4.4.267, 283). They are interrogating the veracity of Autolycus's wonder ballads and, at the same time, I would add, recognizing that such "truth" is in crucial ways subjective: "think *you*?," they reiteratively ask. Such subjective interpretation is another condition of the fall. In other words, the outrageous marvels Autolycus peddles parody wonder ballads, to be sure—but do they, in fact, also parody the engaged lower-order and uneducated audience? Or, to put the inquiry another way: do Mopsa and Dorcas believe wholeheartedly in the truth of the ballads offered to them, or do they simply delight in the *idea* that such things might be true, an idea literally given more substance by the tangible nature of the printed sheets? How many times have you stood in the checkout line at the grocery store and picked up the *National Enquirer* to read the featured story, replete with strange illustrations, of the woman who gave birth to a martian child or of the boy born with a calf's head? Of course, we know such tales and pictures aren't *really* true. But we enjoy reading and viewing them nonetheless, precisely for their fascinating, sometimes even grotesque, details and the ridiculous testimonials they cite to support their truth status. For a passing moment, we might even be entertained by engaging with these clearly made-up stories as true wonders, just for the fun of it.

This is not some aberration of the naïve peasant, I want to emphasize. Samuel Pepys, Secretary to the Navy, as we have seen, assembled the largest collection of seventeenth-century broadside ballads in England. His emphasis was the heyday ballad (illustrated, in black letter, and naming a tune title), in all its varied subjects, including monster and wonder ballads. He also participated on numerous occasions in the making of ballad publics of all kinds, as we have further seen. Most significant for the point I am making here, Pepys took time from his busy work schedule—while he was on a political expedition to the Netherlands in 1660 to bring Charles Stuart back to England to be crowned King Charles II, no less—to visit the site in Holland where the Lamenting Lady was supposed to have given birth to her 365 mouse-sized babies. Pepys reports what he witnessed there in detail in his *Diary* (May 19, 1660).[8] Was Pepys naïve in making such a pilgrimage? Or, like Mopsa and Dorcas, did he simply enjoy the titillation of engaging in the belief and witnessing of the real-life "facts" of the wonder, however seemingly outrageous?

Nor, I stress, should such impulsive, passing, or impromptu belief in broadside ballad monstrosities or wonders be condemned as antithetical to a belief in the divine, as we have witnessed in moralized wonder ballads discussed above. Indeed, one might consider such faith, again, more embracingly: as the inverse of the skepticism expounded by modern theorists like Levinas and Derrida. Nor should we consider it a failure of "true" belief of the sort that haunted religious exponents of Protestantism in the Renaissance, such as Martin Luther. Intensely recognizing humankind's fallen nature, Luther discerned a danger in the human inability to succumb to, or accept uncritically, the wondrous gift of God's grace: that one might be led astray by doubt. Following this Lutheran vein of questioning, Kearney cites the calls on the part of Leontes and even Hermione for an explanation of "what happened?" once the statue of Hermione has come to life as threats to unconditional belief ("Hospitality's Risk," 105–6). But such questioning does not necessarily undermine belief, and certainly not as expressed via the broadside ballad for the masses. Both eager to partake in belief and yet not adverse to questioning it, Mopsa and Dorcas ask, "Is it true, think you?" In the end, belief depends on one's recognition that skepticism necessarily follows upon the fall. But so does an ongoing impulse to believe, which to a certain extent can be willfully directed; both facets of the human condition are embodied in, and capitalized upon, by Autolycus.

Performing the Aesthetic Parts: Broadside Ballads and the Making of Publics

Shakespeare puts forward and interrogates religious and secular beliefs alike—even the kind of belief in Fortune which Autolycus embraces. At the same time, he also stages how a crucial part of the delight in believing the wondrous stories told in broadside ballads (as this book has explored at length) comes from self-reflexive immersion in a multimedia, and thus multisensory, experience. He reveals a fascination with the broadside ballad's constituent parts and their implications especially when incorporated into his late dramatic experiments, most notably in *The Winter's Tale*. He further probes how, in the swirl of associative hits such piecemeal ballad media could evoke, wondrous things could happen. Publics of varied sorts could be dramatically made and unmade. The problem Shakespeare faced was how to bring to life in a staged performance (or, put more crassly, how to capitalize on for his own artistic and marketing goals) this alter-performative genre, in all its marvelous, multifaceted appeal? And, in addition, how to dramatize, as part of his artistic experimentation into different genres and beliefs, the way broadside ballads attracted and created different publics or spheres of publics?

At a performance of *The Winter's Tale*, the audience members sitting in their seats or even standing closer to the stage in the pit would have been hard put to see much detail on the ballad sheets that Autolycus pulls out of his pack and holds up for sale. However, they would probably have gotten a general impression from the sheets of a lot of blackness from the thick, curling typeface and maybe a blur of the large woodcut images running across the top and the other scattered ornaments on the pages. Even if nothing could be made out in detail, then, the early modern audience would certainly have made the connection between the printed ballads held up before them and those pictorial and sung black-letter broadside ballads they encountered daily on the streets of London and far into the countryside.

Shakespeare tactically incorporates into his drama such associations. For example, black-letter print is integrated both affectively and cognitively in seemingly unrelated voicings of his characters over bastardy. For many in the audience, I argue, following upon Kitch's groundbreaking article on the subject ("Bastards and Broadsides," 43–71), the evocation of bastardy would have triggered the connection to "*bâtarde*" or, as Englished, "bastard" print: what we saw in Chapter 5 was the originary form and name for black-letter writing and typeface (called such after local scribal styles intermingled with and blackened the look of the style of writing decreed as "rule" by Charlemagne in 780; Egan, "Black Letter"). Affectively, Shakespeare makes this connection through the "wild affection" or mad jealous rantings of King Leontes at the beginning of the play in the Sicilian court over what he claims is the bastardy of his "issue"—the as-yet-unborn child carried by his wife, Hermione. Cognitively, *bâtarde* print reappears, lurking in the philosophical debate over the morality of grafting that occurs at the sheep-shearing feast in Bohemia between that very "bastard" child—Perdita—now grown and raised as a shepherdess, and King Polixenes, earlier accused of being the adulterer and now at the feast in disguise as a shepherd or peasant to spy on his son. Perdita argues that grafting is a perversion of nature, just like bastardy. She specifically singles out "carnations and streak'd gillyvors [thought in the period to be the same flower]," dismissing them as "nature's bastards" (4.4.82–83; also Pafford note). The seeming digression and incongruity of an intellectual debate between a sixteen-year-old shepherdess and a king (in however low disguise) over bastardy, in the midst of the fun-loving festivities of a sheepshearing feast, is in fact the culmination of a repeated issue—forgive the pun—that the play addresses. Autolycus makes that issue unavoidably physically present in holding up broadside ballad sheets, printed at this time, in a black-letter version of *bâtarde*/bastard typeface for all present, at least passingly, to see, savor as the everyday, and contemplate.

Bâtarde print, Kitch argues in his article, was perceived by many as being messy, mongrel, and even "monstrous" (44 and note 16). But here is where I begin to diverge from Kitch. Those "many" who so condemned the monstrosity of black letter were primarily humanists promoting the new, sleek, classical lines of roman typeface. This was by no means the opinion held by all, as we have extensively explored in Chapter 5. Indeed, in the light of the "mongrel" nature of Shakespeare's late experiments in a "spectacularly contingent" drama—including prominently enfolding tragedy and comedy into romance—we should remember that, among dramatic works still published in black letter of the time, most prominent were romances, like those of Shakespeare's late plays. Alluding to what he clearly perceived of as the peculiarly fantastic and out-of-date nature of such romances—still much loved by the masses—Jonson derogatively called Shakespeare late *Pericles* a "mouldy tale," seemingly thinking of *The Winter's Tale* as well.[9]

Kitch further argues that Shakespeare knew full well not only that black letter was aesthetically going out of fashion with humanists, who considered it as a messy and mongrel or, more specifically, as a bastard typeface. He contends that Shakespeare exploits these negative associations to dramatize his general anxiety over print as an uncontrollable form of dissemination, or "issue," like paternity and unlike the relatively fixed or contained space of the stage. But such anxiety, we recall, belongs more to the temporarily insane Leontes; and his crazed fixation over the unconfirmable paternity or imprint of his son and unborn daughter proves radically unfounded. Shakespeare, on the contrary, reveals recognition of the aesthetic, sentimental, national, and commercial attractions of print, especially of the black-letter or *bâtarde*/bastard typeface—even as, or perhaps because, it was slowly passing out of existence. Such a strong appeal would have been felt by his audience and by himself at the most visceral level. In this context, we can understand more fully Mopsa's declaration, "I love a ballad in print, *a life*, for then we are sure they are true" (4.4.261–62; my emphasis). Mopsa does not here specify what kind of ballad she means, though she and the others gathered round are looking in that moment at Autolycus's cache of wonder ballads. She speaks generally of "a ballad in print, a life." Where does a ballad's truth lie? In part, she implies "in the print." But what is revealed in the print? "*A life*." Broadside ballads, long holding on to cherished black letter, as we have seen children's hornbooks of the time were doing, were "a life," not only because some of them told stories of real or imagined lives but also because they evoked connections with life as contemporaries lived it, experientially—unlike, for instance, some high, grand heroism often seen on stage. Printed ballads became "alive" in the artifice of the black-letter typeface impressed on the ballad sheet, in the sense that such a familiar typeface reflected the truth of the known, recognizable part of an early modern contemporary's everyday visual, affective, and cognitive life.

But black-letter typeface is just one of the multimedia that are the component parts of broadside ballads which Shakespeare exploits in his experimental dramatic art. Everywhere in the extensive sheepshearing scene are evocations, also, of the beloved woodcut illustrations and other ornaments that adorn the broadside ballad page. Most prominent are the decorative costumes of the main characters in the scene, which would have functioned as a substitute for the blur of woodcut illustrations running across the top of Autolycus's ballad sheets. I refer to the fancy clothing and disguises many of characters wear at the feast. Florizel is in shepherd disguise and Perdita dressed up so beautifully that she resembles the goddess Flora. Polixenes and his court counsellor, Camillo, willy-nilly, are part of the broadside ballads' woodcut visuals as well, in costuming themselves to look like shepherds or at least like peasants. In many pastoral broadside ballads, we have found, the illustrated lowly resemble just such lords and ladies, as evidenced in Figure 14 of "The Country Lass." Some even appear like lords or ladies in disguise as lowly peasants, as we observed in discussing the second woodcut illustration to this same ballad. Here two shepherds face each other, but the one on the right looks like an aristocrat in the *guise* of a shepherd—as Polixenes well might have appeared in his disguise at the sheepshearing feast (certainly, despite Polixenes' lowly costume, the shepherd host recognizes him as of superior status).

Further contributing to the dramatization of the visuals on the ballad sheets that Autolycus distributes are the many figurative and literal flowers scattered throughout the scene, at the hands and in the mind of Perdita. To Polixenes, she presents "rosemary, and rue" (4.4.74); to Camillo, "Hot lavender, mints, savory, marjoram," and "marigold" (4.4.104–5); and she imagines opulently decorating Florizel, if she could, with flowers of spring: "daffodils," "violets," "primroses," "oxlips," and "The crown imperial; lilies of all kinds, / The flower-de-luce being one" (4.4.118, 120, 122, 125–27). Such flowers and their foliage appear in miniature in the patterns impressed onto the sheets of broadside ballads by the many small molded metal pieces often placed in rows between woodcuts and columns of stanzas by the printer, as we can see in Figures 10, 12, 14, 33, and 45. Elaborately carved woodcut floral patterns also form the frame illustrating the two oval headpieces on the right side of the broadside ballad sheet in Figure 32. In even more complex woodcut illustrations, such detailed flowers and their foliage swirl into the carvings that make the large headers, footers, and borders on the sheets. In Figure 56, for example, the royal "flower-de-luce," with which Perdita says she would decorate Florizel if she could, is prominently centered in the woodcut header that is placed at the top of the right half of the ballad. This image is not merely decorative; it is also a heraldic woodcut, sporting a Tudor rose on the far left, and, on the right side of the fleur-de-lis, two thistles (associated with Scottish royalty since at least the fifteenth century).[10]

Noticeably in this impression invoking royalty, and in many more mundane images made from woodcuts of the period, we frequently see carnations, more often called "gillyflowers" in the period (in the header of Figure 56, for instance, the flower can be detected on the left, between the Tudor Rose and the royal flower-de-luce). Consider any listener making a visual associational hit to this woodcut header, or others like it, while attending to *King* Polixenes of Bohemia's defense of producing carnations/gillyflowers by grafting them as a natural act. His defense would extend into an assertion of the very naturalness of *Englishness*. Queen Elizabeth's famous *Rainbow Portrait*, painted around 1600, well supports this position. Her bodice features not only the English flowers of pansies, honeysuckle, and cowslips but also carnations/gillyflowers. Such flowers symbolically celebrate the queen, Roy Strong asserts, "as the bearer of the springtime *renovatio* of the golden age" of England (*Gloriana*, 160). The carnation/gillyflower thus fits naturally with the other flowers in the header of Figure 56 that pay tribute to English monarchs, as does the old English black-letter typeface of the broadside ballad the header

Figure 56. Sample of flowers on headpiece, here featuring a fleur-de-lis in the center, in a woodcut impression from "A Caveat for Young-men. Young-men Repentance do delay, And think not of their Dying day, Till Death doth come and with his Dart, Doth pierce the youngmans stubborn heart" (1680–82), EBBA 20660. Magdalene College, Cambridge, Pepys Library, Pepys Ballads 2.36. By permission of the Pepys Library, Magdalene College, Cambridge.

helps decorate. However, like Kitch and the humanists of her time condemning the black-letter/*bâtarde* typeface, Perdita imagines nature turned monstrous when she thinks of carnations/gillyflowers. She notes, we recall, that "some" call them "nature's bastards" (4.4.83). These flowers *were*, paradoxically, associated not only with Englishness but also with bastardy because they could be grown from cuttings or "slips"—"I care not / To get slips of them" out of season, Perdita affirms, to explain why she is not handing out such flowers in fall (4.4.84). But there is more at stake. As Pafford notes, the streaks in some carnations/gillyflowers further led to their association with unchaste or loose women (170). Such associational hits could also have been encouraged by broadside ballad woodcut images.

Flowers, we see, don't only constitute dividing lines and borders or headers and footers on broadside ballads; they make a showing as well in woodcut narrative scenes and portraits, either simply growing, being gestured at, or being held in a lady's hand. Often, we perceive that the flower being held is, yes, a carnation/gillyflower. The lady in the third woodcut of Figure 57, for instance, appears to be holding this very flower. Just as Perdita identifies carnations with immorality, the audience, if having seen this woodcut or another like it, might have made a similar associative hit, given that the courtly lady holding the carnation in the woodcut is bare-breasted. To display breasts was a court fashion of the time but was considered by many, and assuredly by the more simple sorts, as also a lewd fashion. Such a suggestion of salacity is bolstered in

The Merry Cuckold.
Who frolickly taking what chance doth befall,
Is very well pleaſed with Wife, Hornes and all.
To the tune of, The merry Cuckold.

YOu married men
whom Fate hath aſsign'd,
To marry with them
that are too much kind,
Learn as I do,
to beare with your wiues,
All you that doe ſo,
ſhall liue merry liues.

I haue a Wife
ſo wanton and ſo free,
That ſhe as her life,
loues one beſides me,
What if ſhe doe,
I care not a pin,
Abroad I will goe,
when my riuall comes in.

I can be merry
and drinke away care,
With Claret and Sherry
and delicate fare.
My Wife has a Trade,
that will maintain me,
What though it be ſaid,
that a Cuckold I be.

While ſhe at home
is taking her pleaſure,
Abroad I do roue,
conſuming her treaſure.
Of all that ſhe gets.
I ſhare a good ſhare,
She payes all my debts,
then for what ſhould I care.

She keepes me braue,
and gallant in cloathing.
All things I haue,
I do want for nothing.
Therefore I continue,
and winke at her faults,
And daily I ſtriue,
againſt iealous aſſaults

While for ſmall gaines:
my neighbours worke hard,
I liue (by her meanes)
and neuer regard.
The troubles and cares,
that belong to this life,
I ſpend what few dares
gramercy good Wife.

Should I be iealous,
as other men are,
My breath like to bellowes,
the fire of care
Would blow and augment,
therefore I thinke it beſt.
To be well content,
though I were Vulcans creſt.

Many a time
vpbraided I am,
Some ſay I muſt dine,
at the Bull or the Rammes:
Those that do ieere
cannot do as I may,
In Wine, Ale and Beere,
ſpend a noble a day.

The Second part. To the ſame Tune.

I By experience,
rightly do know:
That no ſtrife or variance,
(cauſes of woe)
Can make a wife
ſo bent to liue chaſt,
Thou in ſtead of ſtrife,
let patience be plac't,

If a man had
all Argus his eyes,
A wife that is bad,
will ſomething deuiſe,
To gull him to's face,
then what breeds miſtruſt,
The hornes to diſgrace,
though weare it I muſt,

Ile be content
with this my hard chance,
And in merryment
my head Ile aduance.
Wiſhing I were
but as rich as ſome men,
Whoſe wiues ſhall appeare,
yet they'l kiſſe now and then.

One trying to me,
a great comfort is,
Still quiet is ſhe,
though I do amiſſe,
She dares do no other,
becauſe ſhe knowes well,
That gently I ſmoother,
what moſt men would tell.

If I ſhould raue,
her minde would not alter
Her ſwing ſhe will haue,
though't be in a halter.
Then ſith that I get
good gaines by her vice,
I will not her let,
but take ſhare of the price.

Why ſhould I vexe,
and pine in diſpaire,
I know that her ſexe,
are all brittle ware,
And he that gets one
who conſtant abides,
Obtaines that which none,
or but few haue beſides.

Yet will I not,
accuſe my wife.
For nothing is got,
by railing, but ſtrife.
I act mine owne ſence.
intending no wrong,
No Cuckold nor Queane
will care for this ſong.

But a merry Wife,
that's honeſt I know it,
As deare as her life,
will ſure loue the Poet
And he thats no Cuckold
in Countrey or City,
Howeuer if lucke hold,
will buy this our Ditty.

Printed by the Aſsignes of Thomas ſymcock. FINIS.

Figure 57. Gillyflower, or carnation, held by a woman in the woodcut impression on the far right, from "The Merry Cuckold. Who frolickly taking what chance doth befall, Is very well pleased with Wife, Hornes and all" (c. 1619–29), EBBA 30182. British Library, Roxburghe 1.256–257, C.20.f.7.256–257. © The British Library Board.

this illustration by the significantly tall phallic flower growing up between the spread-apart legs of the gallant pictured in the second woodcut of the broadside ballad sheet, to whom the lady faces and gestures with her carnation. This phallic flower, furthermore, matches in its pointy shape the manly spurs on the gentleman's boots, all suggesting a spur to licentious sexuality.

In sum, the dramatization of flowers in the sheepshearing feast, both literally and figuratively, in being handed out and debated about, would have fortified the already strong associational hits likely made in many ways by the audience to ornamental heyday broadside ballads that Shakespeare cultivates in this scene through performative evocations of *bâtarde*/bastard/black-letter print. As with the black-letter typeface, it is as if the figures in aristocratic and pastoral guise in ballad woodcuts, and the many accompanying floral ornaments, with their potentially diverse meanings, have jumped off the ballad page and become performatively alive.

But there is more, as there must be more, as part of Shakespeare's dramatic reworking of the broadside ballad in the service of his experimental art as itself a multimedia aesthetic with mass appeal. Left to discuss are orality (song), movement—extending from the visceral to lively dancing—and the way in which assemblages of such component parts can reach out to engage communities in a plenitude of voices and stances over the subject matter(s) addressed.

To turn to this last point first, which folds into it the media of song and dance, the audience of the sheepshearing feast (like the larger audience) would certainly know from personal experience that Autolycus's wares would have been mixed and variously received, even by the low. Scholarly critics of *The Winter's Tale* have not always been so attentive to these multiplicities. Such critics focus primarily on the wonder ballads Autolycus at first promotes. But Perdita also fears that Autolycus might be carrying ballads containing "scurrilous words" (4.4.215), which fall under the umbrella term "lewd," used by Puritans and other denigrators of ballads. Perdita instructs Clown to "Forewarn" Autolycus "that he use no scurrilous words in's tunes" (4.4.215–16). Autolycus, in all likelihood, does carry many a ballad such as Perdita fears. But Clown responds tellingly: "You have of these pedlars that have more in them than you'd think, sister" (4.4.217–18). That is, there is more to the balladmonger's wares than just "scurrilous words." Clown may be a simple soul, but he knows of which he speaks. Broadside ballads, as we have observed, indeed covered all kinds of topics, many devoid of scurrility. The shepherd's servant sums up the range of ballad wares Autolycus sells: "He hath songs for man and woman, *of all sizes*" (4.4.193; my emphasis). And he apparently does.

Indeed, quickly assessing the rivalry between Mopsa and Dorcas over Clown, Autolycus tactically—that is, spontaneously but with an ulterior purpose (to sell, sell, sell, even if to sell must also mean to entertain and even instruct)—maneuvers the convention of wooing to attract all three characters. He pulls out of his pack a love ballad in three voices. It is titled, not coincidentally, "Two maids wooing a man" (4.4.290). Belying the idea that all ballads are in all ways "news," Dorcas says of the broadside ballad, "We had the tune on't a month ago" (4.4.295). The melody of this ballad, at least, is familiar, as might have been some of the often recycled woodcut illustrations and even bits and pieces of reused black-letter text, which, as we have seen, together made up a ballad artifact. But the maids are still eager to engage the ballad in singing it as if it were entirely new, which most of its text—given its fit to the passing present— probably was. In addition, in the very singing of the ballad, they make it their own and timely. Notably, Clown eagerly buys this ballad, and many more.

Imagine the two maids on the stage, as on a London street or at a country feast, closely bunching up beside Autolycus to read and sing from the same sheet he holds in his hands, creating a trio of perspectives. The two maids, as in their real play-lives, express in the song their vying for the affection of the man they desire, Clown. But on the spur-of-the-moment, Autolycus adopts Clown's role in the song, thus allowing Clown, the object of the maids' love, to be an uncommitted and entertained spectator. Autolycus opens the ballad by singing to both maids, "Get you hence, for I must go, / Where it fits not you to know." The maids repeatedly question, in response, "whither" he goeth? Further voicing their rivalry, the persona Dorcas asks to go along with him. At one point, the persona that Mopsa adopts sharpens their questioning, positing two possible destinations—"to th'grange or mill"—and Dorcas chimes in, "If to either, thou dost ill" (presumably these two places are inhabited by the two different maids, respectively; 4.4.298–305). The object of their love in the ballad dodges the questions, just as Clown dodges them by *not* joining in. But the shepherdesses, in assuming implicitly oppositional positions, take on roles close to their own—their daily vying for Clown's affection. If, however, they had individually (or even together) sung the wonder ballad of "The Lamenting Lady," they would be forced to adopt entirely different kinds of stances. That ballad is written from the perspective of a relator, rather than in dialogue form, though it often switches from one character's voicing to the other's in the middle of a line. Each maid, that is, would have had to sing the roles of two different subject voicings. Neither subject, furthermore, would have been immediately recognizable as like Dorcas's or Mopsa's own. They consist of the role of the infertile and thus resentful wealthy burgher's wife, who is monstrously but pitifully punished for insulting the beggar woman with two babes, and the role of the poor woman, who at first seems highly sympathetic to the reader/viewer/listener but then viciously invokes God's justice in wailing response to the lady's insulting her as strumpet. Instead of experiencing such nuanced chords of antipathy and sympathy in a singular voice, as "The Lamenting Lady" would require, Mopsa and Dorcas are allowed, in the song of two maids wooing a man, to maintain their oppositional personas in the play.

Despite their rivalry, the maids in singing Autolycus's offered song can be heard united not only in their vying to know "whither?" goes their would-be-lover. In the very process of singing about how they vie for the young man's love, they repeat each other's questioning words, becoming in this sense *one* voice. Dorcas recognizes a further allegiance. She berates the lover addressed in the song, affirming "If to either [th'grange or mill thou goest], thou dost ill"; she thus underscores that a choice of place (and thus, indirectly, of maid) by the Autolycus-Clown character would be an injustice to *both* maids. In their very eagerness to sing the song in the first place, the two maids appear to be as united in their love of singing love ballads, wherein they sing their rivalry, as they are in their love of broadside ballads generally. This unity, indeed, temporarily overrides their competition for Clown. As a subset of the larger peasant audience that gathers round to hear and watch them, they become their own kind of ballad public: engaged with experiencing ballad news and emotions (here of forsaken and competitive love), united in large part simply by the joy of communal song. Such a harmonious, if small, community is very different from that of the anonymous lords later gathered at the Sicilian court who try to patch together a meaningful whole out of an event from which they have been *ex*cluded. The shepherdesses' ballad song enthusiastically invites participation from a larger public; it is performed for anyone and for all.

Crafty authors, printers, and publishers, as we have seen, sought to appeal to this "all" that includes the whole spectrum, if primarily the lower half, of the population. They brought out ballads for sale not only expressive of opposite sides but also of multiple and shifting perspectives on issues—even more so than in "The Lamenting Lady"—so that contemporaries would have been exposed to a mixed bag of topics, emotions, attitudes, and subject positions, both within and between broadside ballads. "The Lady and the Blackamoor" is one such instance we studied in depth; it gives voice to a cast of dramatic characters and has a potentially scattershot public appeal. The song of the two maids wooing a man, though much simpler and shorter, gestures toward such complexity in offering a trio of perspectives wherein the maids singing (and potentially we as audience) experience both unity and conflict. In actual performance, furthermore, the ballad they sing might well have been much longer and more complicated than its printing in the Folio of 1623.

Shakespeare clearly capitalized on all facets of songs, ballads, and broadside ballads in every one of his plays, alluding to them if only through the sliver—the itty-bitty bit—of one-liners or one-phrase quotes, as we see them printed in quartos or folios. Of course, as I have argued previously, such mere snippets in print might well have been the result of the economy of print rather than the reality of performance. Why publish a whole ballad when the audience already knows it and printing out the entire song would both interrupt the reading experience and use up valuable paper? The stage event would have offered much more opportunity for extended song, likely off the cuff. A performer—especially one with singing skills, such as Robert Armin, who in 1598 replaced Will Kemp as clownish figure for Shakespeare's company, and likely played Autolycus—seeing an audience smile at a one-line/one-phrase reference to a popular broadside ballad, might well have spontaneously seized the opportunity to burst into extended song (Smith and Lupton, "Ballads+"; and Lin, *Shakespeare and Materiality*, 107–34). Stage performances, like street, public, or domestic performances of broadside ballads, were open to tactical, impromptu adjustment. This was likely even more the case when ballads were performed in significantly different venues. Consider the several movements in the staging of *The Winter's Tale* between the courtly Whitehall Palace (where elitist masques were most often performed) and the more public Globe Theater (open to the masses). Would not the singing of ballads in *The Winter's Tale* be adjusted differently in these alternating venues, due to variants in audience social make-up, staging area size, the audience's physical enclosure, or not? These are questions I cannot definitively answer, given the distance of time and the limited availability of extant evidence. Yet the questions are critical to a performance of *The Winter's Tale*, wherein broadside ballads are so integral to the play's meaningful aesthetics. One observation I am confident in making: whatever tactic adopted in the performance, even of a slightly referenced broadside ballad, what was sung would have depended not only on where the play was performed and for whom but also on the moments of rapport (or not) between actor and audiences in that particular performance, just as with parts or wholes of broadside ballads dramatically enacted by hawkers on London's streets and out in the countryside (especially at fairs).[11]

But such potentially spontaneous incorporation or, perhaps better said, "interweaving" of broadside ballads into plays of the period does not mean that the two genres of performed (let alone printed) play and broadside ballad were conjoined or even identical in their features, practice, and impact. Pursuing this query, I also question Sarah Williams's argument that ballad peddlers would have necessarily drawn on the skills of professional stage actors to *perform* their wares—an argument that privileges stage drama priority and "*action*" (*Damnable Practises*, 134–36; quote 136). There is certainly a history of performances that some hawkers would have known about, which included the dramatization of professional plays. However, that history extends far back to include nonprofessional, public performances like *Corpus Christi* plays and ceremonial processions by local guilds. None were by trained actors. Furthermore, we must recognize, professional players were confined by the place of the stage. Hawkers, however, as we have seen—whatever their performance skills—were multiply moving, almost like (and sometimes identical to because they were) vagrants: they could tactically strut about the streets and much-frequented city markets or, in their hawking, even enter alehouses and similar commonly haunted spaces. In their peddling of multimedia and hands-on artifacts, they could in consequence movingly *interact* closeup with their audience members, whether one on one or in communal groups.

Perhaps key to the distinction-in-likeness of broadside ballads and professional plays is precisely the *moving* media of the ballad. Though plays dramatize dialogue as well as soliloquies that directly address their audience, the convention of theater, at least ideally, was for the audience to be attentive but also physically and vocally at a remove from such enacted speech. Even without a proscenium arch, the physical stage functioned in this sense as something of a barrier. Audiences were meant to view and perhaps engage through feelings in the performed action but not to vocally join in, as if they were themselves one of the actors. Literally as well as emotionally sung broadside ballads, however, invited their audience to take up and momentarily inhabit the roles they vocalized, whether in dialogue or direct address, and furthermore to engage in *communal* singing of such roles, even if in partial or divisive ways.

When one also includes the personal and intimate touch in the moment of handling broadside ballads, which extends far outside the possibilities of dramatization—that is, feeling as well as seeing the cloth-made paper as well as the raised type and impressed lines of the woodcut illustrations on that paper—and when one adds in the visual appeal of most ballads' familiar images, a truly new enactive experience emerges. That dramatic broadside ballad "feel"—and I am now speaking more metaphorically—simply cannot be attained through performative drama. If this sounds like a statement of heresy, especially when discussing Shakespearean drama, I am most certainly damned. Nevertheless, despite Smith's valiant efforts to expand the reach and affect of drama phenomenologically, I would argue still that early modern contemporaries personally and socially engaged in a yet more complex, in-depth, and interactive experience in encountering broadside ballads. Crucially for those involved in the ballad's production, that experience was also more mass-marketable. Shakespeare must have recognized this fact, which would explain why he, like other playwrights of his time, worked to capitalize on broadside ballads by incorporating them into his stage aesthetics, particularly the late experimental play of *The Winter's Tale.*

As part of that experimentation, Shakespeare recognized that not everyone present at a broadside ballad performance, any more than everyone present at a stage performance (or any performance, for that matter), would have participated in the same way. The playwright turns this to his own dramatic purposes as would a hawker. *The Winter's Tal*e enacts just how differently involved audiences (creative of variant publics) would have diversely engaged both on the stage and watching the staged events of the sheepshearing scene, for instance. The model I offered for comparison to ballad publics, in my conclusion to Chapter 7, which I pursue below, is to the multiple spheres of audience participation that occurred at a Balinesian cockfight as so brilliantly outlined by Clifford Geertz. Just how much participation by characters would have taken place in a performance of *The Winter's Tale* is a theatrical production question that I cannot calculate.[12] But if we conceive of Autolycus as central balladmonger/singer and maker of the play's broadside ballad publics, which enliven the sheepshearing feast for the viewing audience of all sorts (both on and watching the stage), we can reconstruct, however roughly, different levels of involvement and belief surrounding him.

On stage, nearest the center of ballad involvement, are those assembled peasants whom, like the shepherdesses Mopsa and Dorcas, are dramatized as most invested in broadside ballads. These social sorts freely give of themselves to a communal and—in every sense—wondrously harmonious, if homely, engagement. Further out, standing back in a more detached circle, are Perdita and Florizel. Perdita is attentive to the ongoing ballad action—which by Warner's definition makes her part of the ballad public—but she is suspicious of the possibly lewd or "scurrilous words in's [Autolycus's] tunes," as we have observed. Standing at a similar distance is Florizel, who is also attentive to what's going on but dismisses the "trifles" Autolycus sells (including, presumably, his broadside ballads). However, both characters, importantly, as we have seen, are also part of the multimedia of the broadside ballad experience Shakespeare creates. Perdita hands out flowers evocative of the many floral patterns printed on ballad sheets; both illustrate the participatory moment in their fetching guises; and they further embracingly extend the ballads' physical and visceral reach by joining in dance with the shepherds. Notably, furthermore, we hear that Perdita is prone to singing like a ballad peddler! Such is the strong connotation of Florizel's lavish praise of her songs: "when you sing," he enthuses, "I'd have you buy and sell so" (4.4.137–38). Standing in an even more removed circle, although also involved and very attentive as host, is Perdita's supposed "father," the shepherd, who fears that the experientially communal festivities—which, again, he must have been attentive to in order to judge—might be pushing the outer limits of decorum. He thus moves to dismiss the next planned entertainment of peasants in dance disguised as satyrs. He worries that "too much homely foolery" might "weary" what he evidently suspects are his more elevated, however lowly dressed, visitors, King Polixenes and Camillo (4.4.333–34). These two disguised court characters stand at the farthest remove from the ballad-like festivities. Other than their added decorativeness, through their country guises, as complements to typical ballad-sheet illustrations of pastoral life, these courtly sorts are at first only able to engage in something like a broadside ballad experience through philosophical dispute:

Polixenes' long, seemingly out-of-place argument with Perdita over the ethics of grafting to make what Perdita condemns as "Nature's bastards," that is, streaked carnations/gillyflowers (which, as we have seen, point indirectly to black letter as a bastard print and to the ornamental flowers on the ballad page). This is such a dry debate that it threatens to deaden the more enlivening and engaging dialogue-in-song we have seen enacted in ballads. But the arrival of Autolycus as balladmonger/hawker jumpstarts the sense of life-giving performative balladry. In pulling actual ballad artifacts out of his pack and engaging with his country audience in a song sung in three parts—of which he plays one—Autolycus momentarily occupies the central position in our encircling sphere of ballad publics.

Not surprisingly, given the extemporaneous and mobile nature of the broadside ballad experience, characters at the feast move into and out of these loosely defined circles of publics. Though at first centrally signaling and encouraging our sense of a broadside ballad artifact turned into a lived performative experience of text, illustration, and song—extended, as was often the case with ballad tunes, into dance—Autolycus suddenly pulls back. He situates himself at the outermost edge of all the ballad-like public spheres, becoming in soliloquy a completely detached and skeptical evaluator of the happenings. Just moments earlier, Polixenes had essentially done the same thing. Realizing that the shepherd host was affirming and witnessing—thus making legal—the betrothal of his son, Florizel, to Perdita, Polixenes refuses any more to play. In a furor, he throws off his disguise, reveals himself as both king and Florizel's father, and quickly breaks up the festivities. In his extreme rage, he further threatens to disown his son, deform Perdita, and torture Perdita's shepherd family. But just before he abruptly steps far out of the broadside ballad's performative and embracive circle, Polixenes deliberately strides into the very center of its spheric action! Though he may begin the scene as an unwitting participant, he at this point eagerly draws himself into the middle of things by calling for the planned lusty dance of satyrs to proceed—contrary to his host's fear that the peasant dance would overtax him and Camillo. It would appear that Polixenes, after all, gets momentarily caught up, as if by an infectious spreading of good cheer, in the engaging ballad-like media that swirl around him throughout the scene.

The proposed dancers are described by the shepherd's servant as "three carters, three shepherds, three neat-herds [cow herders], and three swine-herds," who have made themselves "all men of hair." The servant adds, "they call themselves "Saltiers" (suggestive of both satyrs and leapers) who offer in dance "a gallimaufry of gambols . . . not the worst of the three but jumps twelve foot and a half by th' square [by the rule]" (4.4.325–29, 338–40). The dance will clearly be a form of "jig," or "jigge." The word has many meanings in the period (as we shall further explore), but I use it here in what is perhaps its most basic sense of a lively high-stepping dance to music, as discussed by Smith in his recent article on ballad dancing ("'Ball,'" 323–38). It is ironic that the shepherd host gestures to prevent this supercharged frolic considering that, when his servant first appears to announce Autolycus's arrival, he depicts his master as a fun-loving dancer himself, precisely in lively dancing to ballads: "O master!," the servant exhorts to the shepherd, once you listen to his ballads, "you would never dance again after a tabor and pipe; no, the bagpipe could not move you" (4.4.183–85). But when the shepherd host uncharacteristically moves to halt the dance, Polixenes also uncharacteristically jumps into the events in a positive, participatory way, coming to the defense of the offered jigging dance: "You weary those that refresh us," Polixenes reassures his host, "pray, let's see these four threes of herdsmen" (4.4.335–36). "Four threes," I posit, is a direct allusion to ballad measure, poetically defined, which, as we have seen, traditionally consists of alternating lines of 4-3 poetic stresses. A ballad tune that is highly adjustable to just such 4-3 poetic measure, as well as to its many variants (as we shall pursue later in this chapter), is, in fact, "Rogero." The dance of the satyrs, in sum, is yet another extension and further bringing to life of Shakespeare's already deliberate moving dramatization of texts and illustrations and tunes of the broadside ballads that Autolycus peddles.

Layers of irony (and of self-consciousness) lie in Polixenes' investment in advancing the jigging dance. It is especially ironic that this Bohemian king, even as he here engages more fully in the sheepshearing ballad-like fun, is about to bring all the festivities to an abrupt halt. But there is an even deeper irony at play. For a moment, however briefly, when Polixenes advocates for a jig of satyrs—creatures known for their lustful sexuality—he implicitly embraces a bawdiness of the kind Autolycus also frankly celebrates in his entrance song to the play. Recall that Autolycus inducts us into the world of Bohemia by singing of "tumbling in the hay" with his "aunts," or doxies. Such explicitly arousing entertainment would have been inconceivable in the opening of *The Winter's Tale*. These initial scenes take place at the sexually repressed court of Sicilia, ruled by its explosively jealous tyrant, King Leontes. There we witness Leontes' obsession over horned animals in referring repeatedly to his own son as "neat" (a calf). By contrast, if not cuckoldry, at least hearty sex, and even a fun-filled engagement with the monstrous, come to life in the gamboling dance of the half man/half goat satyrs, which are also "neat." Perhaps as ironically, it is likely that at least one of the players who assume the role of peasants dressed as satyrs had also performed in the antimasque of satyrs (where, yes, the satyrs also dance a jig) at court for Ben Jonson's masque of *Oberon* in 1611 (Pafford, note to 4.4.327–28). The shepherd's servant implies as much: "One three of them, by their own report, sir, hath danced before the king" ("king," for the masque of *Oberon*, of course, refers to James I, but in the context of the play world of *The Winter's Tale* the king is Polixenes, demonstrating the wide societal reach of ballad-like media). In Bohemia, dominated as it is by the extensive scene of the sheepshearing festivities, the satyrs fit in wonderfully with the robust features of a full-bodied ballad-like experience that includes all social sorts and the bawdy among a range of other topics.

But Polixenes cannot practice what he preaches in his theoretical argument with Perdita in favor of "bastard" (and its kinship with black letter) grafting, as illustrated in the monstrously "neat" or horned and hoofed men, whose lusty jig-like ballad dance Polixenes at first encourages—even though he has dressed up (or, more accurately, dressed down) like a figure in a pastoral ballad woodcut illustration in order to participate in the sheepshearing feast. Becoming himself something of a disruptive antimasquer to the expansive and good-natured broadside ballad events as dramatized by Shakespeare, Polixenes shuts down the entertainment which was, however briefly, open to and representative of—in text, ornament, and tune—court and commoner alike, by his refusing any more to participate.

In the rapid series of events that follows, Camillo steps in as main trickster figure, arranging the quick escape from Bohemia to Sicilia of Perdita and Florizel aboard ship, paying Autolycus to change clothes with Florizel to aid their impromptu flight, and then betraying the lovers by informing Polixenes of their actions so that the king will follow in hot pursuit and, in Camillo's plan, be reconciled with Leontes (allowing Camillo to return to his home country). When Camillo pays Autolycus to exchange clothes with Florizel, Autolycus suspects what he's up to—"I smell the trick on't," he comments in an aside (4.4.643). Nevertheless, he readily seizes the opportunity—"Sure the gods do this year connive at us, and we may do any thing extempore" (4.4.676–77). Indeed, he immediately finds another extemporaneous occasion to reap more funds by aiding the shepherd and Clown to escape Polixenes' threatened revenge; in exchange for gold, he helps them to escape onboard Florizel's ship. Repeatedly, in the spirit of balladeer, Autolycus depicts himself as seizing the moment. "Though I am not naturally honest, I am so sometimes by chance," he declares, and later reiterates the thought: "If I had a mind to be honest, I see Fortune would not suffer me: she drops booties in my mouth." He adds, having intimidated the shepherds into paying him to help them escape, "I am courted now with a double occasion—gold, and a means to do the prince, my master good; which who knows how that may turn back to my advancement?" (4.4.712–13, 832–37). In this mad rush of events, Autolycus still plays an extremely important role. Without his helping the shepherds get aboard Florizel's ship, there could be no confirmation of the final discovery scene in Sicilia. It's also significant that here, even as shape-changing opportunist, Autolycus still thinks of Florizel as his "master," whom he once served, as he says on first introducing himself: "I have served Prince Florizel, and in my time wore three-pile, but now I am out of service" (4.3.13–14). However, Autolycus's true master is Chance or Occasion, which, in the spirit of trickery, he seizes. Thus, at the Sicilian court he pretends to do service to Clown and his shepherd father, when they are newly made gentlemen there—"'tis all one to me," he says (5.2.121). This pointed comment, which is part of a long aside by Autolycus on his carefree adaptation to his new situation, belies arguments that he has undergone a reformation of character in Sicilia.[13] In fact, I argue, he remains the figure who flows with time, seizes occasions, and improvises to his benefit, like all good tricksters, balladmongers, and performers. The problem is that there is no occasion, no room, for an Autolycus figure at the center of the court of Sicilia, even when events there gesture toward new life.

Exit Pursued to Bohemia; Or, The Exclusive Court Living of High Art

In dramatically separating out and redistributing the component parts of single broadside ballad sheets in the sheepshearing festival—the visually enticing, if philosophically controversial, *bâtarde*/bastard/black-letter text, which invites diverse voicings about wonders, love disputes, and many other subjects; the even more eye-catching woodcuts of decorative figures, often supposed to be shepherds, as well as the ornamental headers, footers, borders and dividing lines in floral patterns, together with ladies pictured holding or gesturing to flowers on the sheets, including grafted carnations/gillyflowers, blooming with multipronged meaning; and the familiar, catchy songs that often lead to participatory or just toe-tapping entertaining dance (although the appropriateness of the kind of dance, as in the satyrs' gambols, could be controversial)—Shakespeare in this one extended scene dramatizes the mongrel, multisensory appeal of the ballad experience. He appropriates, too, the ballad's ability to both mix and separate out discerning publics in the service of his own tragicomic romance. His remaking of the full culture of the broadside ballad in the process serves his dramatic experiment in the "spectacularly contingent." However, such experimental making has limits of success. The broadside ballad's characteristic fragmentation is certainly familiarly present in the sheepshearing scene in the very fact that the ballad media are spread throughout the feast's performed activities. At the same time, as a local event (both temporally and spatially focused), the single scene for a time contains or "holds together" such fragmentation similar to the way such an experience is "contained" via the bits and pieces of its media assembled on the ballad sheet. Not so for the final series of scenes of the play. The concluding act becomes intensely disjunctive logically, temporally, and spatially; it is also exclusive of ballad publics. Shakespeare is deliberately here dramatizing, I propose, an *attempted* conjoined fragmentation of both play and ballad genres, wherein a single circle or even a spheric model of circles of making publics *cannot* hold. The culture of broadside ballads in the final scenes of *The Winter's Tale* thus functions like a dysfunctional media patchwork. The pieces of broadside ballads *thrown to the winds*, in Selden's imagining, nevertheless further Shakespeare's lifelong exploration into the possibilities of his dramatic medium and its message. Experimentation escalates in his late plays, where we witness often a radical convergence and divergence of tragedy and comedy, grace and chance, secular and divine, high and low, print and performance, and—within this last category—the mix of oral, aural, visual, affective, visceral, and cognitive.

With the beginning of act 5, scene 2, as we have seen, the play's narrative is exceptionally fragmentary because it is produced by relators who have been excluded from the court's happenings and are trying to piece them together. Now on the outside, not in the middle of the action, we recall, Autolycus opens the scene in Sicilia with a question to an unnamed gentleman, "Beseech you, sir, were you present at this relation [the reunion of the royal families and shepherds]?" (5.2.1). As we noted, the First Gentleman, on continuing this inconclusive conclusion, can only in answer offer a "broken delivery of the business" (5.2.9), which takes place both offstage and also behind closed doors from this character's perspective; the little he witnessed or "caught from the winds" occurred before he and the other lords present were dismissed—all significantly unnamed (as if inconsequential) lords. Now gathering together with Autolycus "on the outside," they create a momentary ballad public of courtly bricoleurs, patching together as a collective the wondrous news about the court. As in Warner's definition of the term "publics," they focus on a subject (news) and admit strangers, like Autolycus, into their critique of court happenings (*Publics and Counterpublics*).

This impromptu ballad public signals that the culture of broadside ballads remains alive in Sicilia, if undergoing somewhat of a sea change, on traveling from Bohemia. Not incidentally, in fact, the gentlemen at the Sicilian court have broadside ballads in their thoughts as they try to puzzle together something meaningful from what they hear. "Such a deal of wonder is broken out within this hour, that ballad-makers cannot be able to express it" (5.2.23–25), declares the Second Gentleman on joining the group, who seems to have gotten a handle on more news. His source of intelligence is most telling: the populace. As if grasping at straws of ballad bits and pieces thrown into the wind, the itinerant masses on the streets have caught hold of a windfall of news. By contrast, the gentlemen contained within the court only overhear information secondhand, as if passed on like a reiterated "olde tale" or "whassup" catchword (5.2.28, 62). Frustrated by their lack of access to the up-close interior court events, the second unnamed gentleman in the scene defaults to what can only be verbally conveyed, as if the courtiers were in fact overhearing stories orally passed along like an "old tale." Without more dynamically enacted media at hand, *The Winter's Tale* threatens to turn in upon itself and become, in fact, but a narrative *tale* rather than a dramatically lived, multidimensional, performed experience.[14]

Here, it is helpful to recall how Kearney draws upon Emmanuel Levinas's animosity to an "intimate society" ("Hospitality's Risk," 92–93). Though Kearney is focused on hospitality and the larger compass of the gift of grace, we might well apply Levinas's critique to any closed social circle, including those created by broadside ballad publics. The problem with such a confined society, as defined by Levinas, is that it is exclusive. "An intimate society is dual," he says, "a society of me and you. We are among ourselves. Third parties are excluded." Levinas's model for such a closed society is a couple of lovers—that is, a relation of two. Such a conflated me/you, or what he calls an "autarchy," which we have seen romanticized in literature of all ages, negates "social reality," Levinas insists. But his evocation of a "third" is unconsciously misleading, I posit. I would argue that it should be interpreted as metaphoric for more than a contained interchange of just two *or of any limited number*. Levinas, that is, clearly opposes any enclosed circle, whether made up of 2, 3, 4, or more, since all tightly interlocked intimate groups negate the possibilities, threats, and compromises that are necessary to a fully lived social, political, and economic life in this world as we know it. Such a larger societal life, in its experiential exposure to such things as chance, risk, the unexpected, and necessary mediation, can be seen in the more embracive and unruly public sphere(s) in Bohemia quintessentially embodied and often initiated by Autolycus.

Autolycus embraces an open, free-flowing lifestyle precisely because he is aware of the risks and opportunities one faces in day-to-day living and the resulting, often complicated, entanglements of social relations. That is, he does not blithely live in the moment any more than he subjects himself to undue risk (hence his avoiding highway thievery). But he seizes upon "ripe" moments when they cross his path in order tactically to reap, even in trickery, profitable social relations. This is not a one-way or closed "autarchic" street, in Levinas's negative sense. Autolycus knows full well that, to make the most for himself out of what opportunity, chance, or fortune offers him, he needs to engage in a give-and-take with others. For instance, he peddles ballads and trinkets for profit, but to do so effectively, he knows—as did the early modern producers and hawkers of broadside ballads—he has to appeal to a diverse audience.

Thus Autolycus sports at the sheepshearing feast not only wonder ballads but also ballads of all kinds, including the very popular love ballad—all to play to particular audiences. He also there interrelates with his audience in a participatory way, inviting them to join him in his song. Those most attentive to his performance, drawn closest into the center of his magnetic hawking circle, may lose their purses, but in other ways they socially profit through an immersion in communal delight, as does the larger audience of the play. In this sense, Autolycus is something of an extension of the artifacts he peddles. He is, like broadside sheets, flexibly and sometimes randomly made up of reassemblable parts (or, in Autolycus's case, "roles") of words, music, and visuals. He also tactically caters to diverse publics for financial profit. The relator in our case-study ballad, which we discussed in Chapter 1, knew only too well the potential hazards he faced in opening his ballad to more than one reading by posing a question and then tactically dodging any kind of overt, singular answer. The question "Alas poore Trades-Men, what shall we do?" is, in its very design, multiply answerable. But such a ballad, broaching opportunity and risk, would have been most unwelcome in the tightly controlled autarchic court of Leontes in Sicilia, focused as it is on its tight, intimate society of guests.

I here ask you to imagine the last events of the play from act 5, scene 2, onward, once again, as performing component parts of a broadside ballad. This time, however, rather than admiring their harmony with ballad culture, I ask you to see how these pieces have been assembled by Shakespeare in a very different way from the gathered media that make up the sheepshearing feast. In fact, now the constituent ballad parts, rather than occurring within one integrated scene, are stretched apart to near breaking point. We experience the narrative of the ballad text in act 5, scene 2, in the First Gentlemen's long, if piecemeal, relation of the wondrous discovery of Perdita's identity. But it is only after this relation is concluded, in the next scene, that we see the most eye-catching illustration to this broadside ballad-like relation of wonders: the spectacle of the (apparent) statue of Hermione. And it is only toward the end of this revelation scene that we hear the crucial ballad tune played—the music by which the artifice comes to life. The melody, until this point, had been sorely missing. Ballad text, art, and tune are present in the final act, and they are working hard to hold everything together. But they are out of order and, just as important, spread apart over more than one scene, as if they were pieces of a jigsaw puzzle that just don't fit together. They thus awkwardly and questionably form an experiential approximation of a broadside ballad whole, however much they might invoke or echo the earlier immersive dramatization of component ballad media from the sheepshearing feast.

This puzzling ballad approximation might even be read as Shakespeare's own kind of literary criticism, his active grappling with the limits of dramatic form. The play has already shown us that drama gains something from the broadside ballad: a kind of energy, immediacy, and familiarity that can bring low and high sorts into the same orbit, however momentarily. As much a sophisticated critic of the workings of genre as he is an author, Shakespeare is showing us how broadside ballads work. But he also recognizes that ballads and plays do not function in exactly the same ways, nor do they elicit the same reactions. For one thing, broadside ballads blur the distinction between producers and audiences in a way that drama cannot. With sufficient boldness, anyone can take part in a broadside ballad; very few of us, by contrast, can hope to achieve the skill and expertise of professional players, let alone jump onto the stage as actor on the spur of the moment. As moving as watching a play can be, a broadside ballad offers everyday people the experience of being *inside* the narrative, and as an actor literally participating in shaping its meaning. In this light, the ballad components of the final scene deserve renewed attention. Many scholars have noted that the play's ending is strangely dissatisfying. Despite the wondrous coming to life of Hermione's statue, which we will discuss in detail below, *The Winter's Tale* cannot quite be said to have a happy ending, for two characters remain among the unrevived dead: the bear-eaten Antigonus and, much less comically, the promising young Prince Mamillius (killed, if indirectly, by Leontes' mad jealousy). The play ends in a kind of hurried disorder, all its narrative loose ends swept quickly and smoothly out of the sight of prying eyes. Between them, Paulina and Leontes ensure that only the most intimate members of the royal circle will hear the explanation Hermione, once revived, demands. Leontes closes the play with the words, "hastily lead away." In his anxiousness to remove the unfolding of great events from a public space—even from the already limited sphere of the statue's unveiling—

to a more private one, Leontes renews Polixenes' apparent anxieties enacted in the sheepshearing scene. Just as Polixenes had called a halt to the celebration when its ballad-like, playful spirit threatened to affect the real lives of the great (via the marriage of his son to a seeming shepherdess), here Leontes asserts his power to bring an end to the revels, at least publicly. Even if the assorted lords follow the main characters offstage, Shakespeare's audience can see and hear no more of these matters. We shall return to this point shortly.

First, however, two key ballad parts of the final act deserve special attention: the visually prominent statue and the tune critical to awakening the art (discussed in its own section below). The posed statue of Hermione might well have fueled a lingering—or what Smith would call "residual"—memorial trace of the illustrations on broadside ballads. As we have seen, ballad sheets are often decorated with woodcuts of aristocratic-looking figures (even if the text is about peasants). In the sheepshearing feast we witnessed such evocations especially to pastoral broadside ballads, which were frequently illustrated in the time with figures who sported or adopted a courtly guise. Further bolstering such evocative links would have been the associational hit that might well have been made by some of Shakespeare's audience members between the statuesque figure of Hermione and the statuesque figures posed on maps as well as in a genre even more visually affiliated with the broadside ballad: popular costume books. Consider, for example, Cesare Vecellio's *Habiti Antichi, et Moderni di tutto il Mondo* (1590; revised 1598).[15] Vecellio's large volume serves as a picture book of sorts: we see page after page of woodcut illustrations of people of different classes (explicated on the facing pages). The images include many fancified women and men who look like they could have easily walked out of the costume book onto a broadside ballad, and vice versa. Figure 58 shows an upper-class Venetian bride before marriage, a pose that Hermione might well have adopted in the statue scene, given Leontes' exclamation that she looks as "when first I woo'd her!" (5.3.36). Indeed, one can easily imagine Hermione at her wedding dressed like this bride in a simple but graceful gown, with her hair falling loose onto her shoulders, as was the custom of brides. But perhaps more fitting, particularly given Leontes' previous rejection of her as his chaste wife, as if disavowing his marriage, is an image in François Despres's little *Recueil de la diversité des habits* (Paris, 1562), which illustrates an English widow showing time's toll (in Hermione's case, of sixteen years) of mourning, especially in her sunken eyes and bowed head, in Figure 59. Such popular costume books from the continent were well known in England. In fact, Jones observes, one extant edition of the cheap *Recueil* includes English transcriptions by its owner written in the margins. The route by which such a costume book might have

Figure 58. Venetian bride at wedding ("Spose Sposate"), from Cesare Vecellio's *Habiti Antichi, et Moderni di tutto il Mondo* (1590, revised 1598). Image courtesy of Wikimedia Commons. https://commons.wikimedia.org. Public domain.

traveled into the contemporary English imaginary and aligned with the broadside ballad could have been indirect but also well traveled.[16]

But such indirection does not necessarily find direction out. Even with all the component media parts of the broadside ballad active at some point in the concluding act of *The Winter's Tale*, the lively integration and openness of interrelated ballad media is missing. It's not only that text, illustration, and tune are temporally separated from each other in events surrounding the statue scene, but also that from its very beginning the final act feels centered on a Levinasian "intimate society," as noted above. Indeed, critics have expressed uncertainty over whether the unnamed lords, Autolycus, and even the shepherds would have attended the climax of the conclusion: the revelation of the stony

Figure 59. Widow ("Le dueil [deuil] de bayonne"), from François Despres, *Recueil de la diversité des habits* (Paris, 1562). Rijksmuseum, Museum of the Netherlands, Amsterdam. http://hdl.handle.net/10934/RM0001.collect.508659. Public domain.

statue as real-life Hermione. Some have asserted their firm conviction that the presence of such characters would contaminate the purity of the moment, conceived of, in their interpretation, as divinely wondrous (and, implicit in this critical position, elite). But the gentlemen "relators" certainly declare their determination to attend. The First Gentleman asserts, "Who would be thence that has benefit of access? Every wink of an eye, some new grace will be born: our absence makes us unthrifty to our knowledge. Let's along" (5.2.109–11). That such lords do gain access is stated in the 1623 Folio stage directions to the statue scene: "Enter . . . *Lords, etc.*" (my emphasis).

If the lords *are* present, I argue, even just as silent observers, the concluding scene becomes much more successful as an embracive moment. We might still wonder, however, where are the "herd" of common people for whom the broadside ballad was primarily mass marketed? The presence of middling to lowly sorts would help bring the fragmented parts of the final scenes together into a more socially inclusive ballad experience, as in the dramatization of the sheepshearing feast. Perhaps we are to think they get token representation by the shepherd father and his son, Clown, who might well follow their social superiors to the scene of the unveiling. Like the gentlemen, they certainly imply their intent to attend, significantly with Autolycus in tow: "Hark!" declares Clown to Autolycus, now in the role of the shepherds-cum-lords' one-man retinue, "the kings and the princes, our kindred, are going to see the queen's picture. Come, follow us: we'll be thy good masters" (5.2.172–75).

Still, even if these nonroyal characters—the unnamed lords, Shepherd, Clown, Autolycus—*are* present, they remain shut out of the statue scene in that they are not allowed by Shakespeare to speak; in fact, they have no speaking lines for the rest of the play after those I quote above. So, once again, where are the full-bodied sensory masses? Do they have no three-dimensional identity, mobility, and voice to allow for participation in the stage performance of a fragmented, ballad-like statue scene—no way to make the experience into more of a societal and aesthetic whole? As I mentioned above, the play ends by explicitly foreclosing the kind of publicness afforded by broadside ballads. No matter how much we might share Hermione's confusion about certain significant plot points, the members of *The Winter's Tale*'s audience are allowed only to hear the question, not its answer. By abruptly closing the play thus, Shakespeare almost implies that the larger audience has no right to ask questions—and that, in any case, the actors wouldn't answer.

Nonetheless, while theoretically silent watchers of the play and, again theoretically, not the center of attention, the audience demands consideration. Shakespeare's original audiences were comprised of all social sorts, who might remain seated or move through the stands and the pit. They might also converse with each other—even, and perhaps especially, audience members in the lowly pit, calling out to the actors in real-time response to the events on stage, as if in dialogue with the play. The audience members, among themselves and in interaction with the performers, can thus be said to create a large mass of publics, both united and divisive, silent and vocal. In these ways, they could add an interactive experiential dimension akin to that created by a ballad—the dimension Leontes seems to refuse (and fear?) in his haste to remove his own intimate circle from the public eye.

In this regard, it is important to remember the peasants at the sheepshearing feast in Bohemia, who are not unlike sectors of the audience publics in

London interacting with "hawking" players selling their show. I refer to the most lowly of the low, who would have spent as much to view the dramatic action from the street-level pit—one pence—as they would have to purchase a broadside ballad. As I previously argued, such lowly sorts would not be as naïve as literary critics have considered the entire audience of the statue scene to be (Newcomb, "Monumental Bodies," 254). The critical consensus has been that the audience would think, at least at first, that Hermione posed like a statue really was a piece of artifice that then comes to life. But given a broad-based familiarity with similar statue-like posing on broadside ballads (perhaps even seen on costume books) as well as with the conventions of the genre of popular romance—which demand resurrection of the presumed-deceased main characters at a story's end—we might question whether most of the audience wouldn't have been more suspicious. On this point, one might even argue that the low, most familiar with popular genres like these, would be the least likely to be fooled. For even as the grouped lords try to put together the bits and pieces of the wondrous discovery of Perdita, another of their class enters with news he learned from the populace celebrating on the streets, who appear already to know all. The common folk, that is, however "simple," seem to have a better grasp of what's up. Act 5, scene 2, is peppered with whassup references to "wonders," "news," and "tales"—most evocative of the kind of broadside ballads Autolycus at first pulls out of his pack at the sheepshearing feast in Bohemia. But, as I argued regarding the wonders he peddled there, the peasants are by no means naïve in accepting these tales. They question their truth status. Indeed, they would seem to know when to embrace wonder for the sheer fun of it and when, as in the conclusion of the play, to recognize wonder as another entertaining kind of artifice to be embraced for its inspiring awe but not necessarily thought of as "real."

I would further posit that, for the entire audience, regardless of whether taken by surprise, a certain uncomfortableness or disconnection might well have ruled as its members witnessed ballad-like parts—usually assembled—get dramatized in such drawn-out bits and pieces.[17] If the unnamed lords' partial relation of what is occurring behind closed doors is akin to a fractured ballad narrative, then the "picture" turned "statue" of Hermione, as noted above, looking forward to a more in-depth discussion, appears as another ballad part—the illustration—but one which is temporally and physically much separated from the earlier piecemeal relation. Furthermore, again as noted in our forward-looking gaze, the other main feature of broadside ballads—the tune—does not occur at the beginning of the news of this wonder story—where ballad tunes begin—but, rather, toward the end of the revelation scene, when Paulina instructs Leontes, "It is requir'd / You do awake your faith"

(5.3.94–95). Even this statement is somehow fractured. To reiterate Walter S. H. Lim's question, "Faith in what?"[18] The possible answers are multifariously plural.

Left on the floor in critics' pursuit of "faith," which is generally interpreted in aspiring and religious terms, is the simple Autolycan kind of faith—belief in seizing the day-to-day occasion as it presents itself and risking not knowing for sure exactly what will happen next. Such a secular notion of faith does not negate the religious version of risk: faith in grace is, after all, a divine version of surrendering oneself to good fortune. Shakespeare deliberately leaves open what kind of faith is being called upon in his embrace of all, even oppositional, positions. But whatever the faith(s) invoked, simply believing is not enough. *We clearly need music—a tune—to enliven the statue.*

Once Leontes gives the go ahead: "Proceed: / No foot shall stir"—Paulina announces, "Music, awake her: strike!" (5.3.97–98). At this point, as suggested by the word *strike*, a stringed instrument, likely a lute or viol, begins playing, and the apparent statue slowly enlivens. No dancing, no joyful song, just the melody. But the senses of the aristocratic audience on stage are now acutely awakened, and we hear allusions to vision, touch, taste, and speech from Paulina, Leontes, and Perdita in their responses: "*look* upon with marvel"; "present your *hand*"; "Lawful as *eating*"; "let her *speak* too" (4.3.100, 107, 111, 113; my emphases). The only other time in the play we have encountered such a sensory smorgasbord was when the shepherd's servant at the sheepshearing feast describes the magical effect of Autolycus's broadside ballads: Autolycus's ballads provoke lively "*dance*," the servant gushes to his master, as "he *sings* several tunes, faster than you'll *tell* [count] money," "he *utters* them as he had *eaten* ballads, and all men's *ears* grew to his tunes" (4.4.184, 185–88, my emphases).

Surely reinforced for the offstage audience by association, if only subliminally, with the earlier festive ballad experience, the music that awakens the statue provokes for all concerned a larger sensory experience than any abstract concept of faith (whether secularly and/or religiously understood). What we approach here is Gina Bloom's notion of unmediated "familiarity," which she contrasts with self-conscious "recognition." Familiarity, in this sense, is an "intense somatic experiment" (Bloom et al., "Ophelias's Intertheatricality," 171). It involves fully visual, tactile, oral, and even kinesthetic sensation (if only, in this last case, through what Smith terms the "vestigial presence" of dance; "'Ball,'" 324). As was the case with works studied earlier in this book (like Bolens's painting of the aristocratic boy, hand poised over a wobbling spinning top, ready to initiate another spin), we witness in this scene a full matrix of cognitive, affective, and visceral intelligences. They have been triggered not only by the coming to life of the statue but also by the two scenes in the final act that spark recollection of the enlivening entertainment in text, illustration, and tune (extended into dance) that we experienced in the sheep-shearing feast, as if in dramatized enactment of the multimedia of broadside ballads that Autolycus pulls from his pack.

Indeed, recollectively, we are at this moment almost within the full-bodied experience of the broadside ballad world. Almost. I ask—gesturing all the way, encouraging the fullest engagement in the awakening of Hermione and an all-embracing multidimensional belief of the kind one would experience in broadside ballads—that you once again awaken your critical faith and consider that the tune struck on Paulina's orders would have been most naturally and ideally "Rogero."

"Rogero"

"Rogero," as we have observed, was initially identified in *The Winter's Tale* by the First Gentleman, trying to piece together with Autolycus what was happening at the Sicilian court behind closed doors. When the Second Gentleman enters, the First Gentleman eagerly asks him, "The news, Rogero?" (5.2.21). The tune "Rogero" has, in a word, already been put forward as fitting for the wondrous "news" of the court.

"Rogero," indeed, perfectly encapsulates the climactic conclusion of Shakespeare's mixed and "radically contingent" experimental play. The tune invokes a multisensory awakening of affect and genre and is even mixed in its audience appeal. There is, furthermore, an aspect of the cosmopolitan at play. Like the supposed sculptor of Hermione's "statue," Julio Romano, the tune "Rogero" originated in Italian court culture. Titled "Ruggiero" there,[19] it was most often associated with a particular stanza in Ludovico Ariosto's epic romance *Orlando Furioso* (1532) in which Bradamante laments being separated from her love, Ruggiero the Saracen (XLIV, 61). The music originally consisted of a ground bass (suited to the chanting of narrative poetry), together with an overlaid melody which could be improvised upon, either via an instrument or a solo voice. As with most ballads, the melody in addition invited dancing, as we shall more fully explore below. "Ruggiero" quickly became enormously popular in Italy, spreading to the masses there even before it reached England's court. Montaigne describes how surprised he was, when on a tour of Italy in 1580–81, he encountered "peasants [in the town of Empoli, near Florence] with lute in hand, and even the pastoral poems of Ariosto on their lips," a phenomenon, Montaigne adds, that "you may see throughout Italy" (cited in Ward, "Music for 'A Handefull of pleasant delites,'" 171).

Though the tune likely traveled by way of elite circles to England, "Ruggiero" was there quickly disseminated, as well, to the populace at large. As such, it was soon thought of as a common *English*, not Italian, tune.[20] William Webbe, citing "Rogero" among other tunes with high courtly origins in his *Discourse of English Poetrie* (1586), expresses clear disgust that what he thought of as elite melodies like "Rogero" had been adopted by the low as their own, both in sung verses ("poetical ditties") and as tunes for what he considered base jig-like dances, often accompanied—to make matters worse, from Webbe's refined perspective—by the lowly fiddle: "Neither is there anie tune or stroke which may be sung or plaide on instruments which hath not some poetical ditties framed according to the numbers thereof, some to Rogero, some to Trenchmore, to downe right Squire [both ballads and dance tunes like "Rogero"], to Galliardes, to Pauines, to Yygges [Jigs], to Brawles [high-stepping, lusty dances] to all manner of tunes which everie Fidler knows better then my selfe, and therefore I will let them passe" (Ward, "Music for 'A Handefull of pleasant delites,'" 154). Not surprisingly, Marsh lists "Rogero" in the top fifty most popular ballad tunes of early modern England (*Music and Society*, 236).

The following rendering of the melody is an approximation of the way it was probably heard, sung, danced, and named on broadside ballads in England near the time of *The Winter's Tale*.[21] I must stress that this is *just one* possible rendering of a melody that held to its core harmony but shifted subtly in its notation over time; that is, the original melody had sometime earlier become unmoored from its base and thus was increasingly susceptible to extemporaneous remakings. The version offered below, then, is as if a conjectural snapshot, or, perhaps more accurately, a soundbite of what was likely heard and played in the melody's mutating history in the early seventeenth century (for ease of reading the music, the stems of the notes that constitute the melody are rendered pointing up; those of any accompaniment point down):

* - lowest note A♭/G♯ in original

The tune is in G major, with a range of a minor seventh, just one step less than an octave; its reach is from E to D. It thus easily fits within the compass of the average voice. It is also relatively easy to sing because it consists mostly of a stepwise motion. At the same time, the melody effects what can be perceived as a springiness. This sense is created by a collection of factors: the initial anacrusis (the first two pickup notes); the two pairs of repeated notes in the first measure (which would roughly match the beginnings of lines 1 and 5 of an eight-line poetic stanza)—two Bs followed by two Cs; the even number of sections of equal length; and the forward-propelling energy generated by the faster notes toward the middle. Adding the potential for yet more zest in rendering the tune, the notes include a skip from B to D in measure 2 (the second halves of these same poetic lines), and a leap upward from F# (F sharp) to B in measure 6 (corresponding to the beginnings of poetic lines 3 and 7 in an eight-line stanza).[22] One might thus easily render "Rogero" as lighthearted, skipping, leaping—that is, as a playful song.

Such potential playfulness is encouraged by the upbeat, tongue-in-cheek ballad, "A pleasant new Sonnet intituled, mine owne deare Lady brave" ("sonnet" here used in the general sense of a short verse, which this ballad is; but see also its tactical use, note 7 in Chapter 7), in Richard Johnson's *A crowne garland of goulden roses* (1612). Rather than adopting a lamentable position, as does Bradamante in *Orlando Furioso*, the would-be lover of this ballad lightly expresses his thinly veiled sexual desire for the lady he woos. He wishes to equal (and, by implication, to surpass) the intimacy of the lady's spaniel, which she holds in her lap, allows to snuggle between her breasts—even to lick them—and entertains bounding at her feet. The lover says that, like the spaniel, he wants "to please you with my skippes" and "pranking pace" (A1r–A2r). Such a "pranking pace" can be heard in Bell's upbeat singing of this playfully licentious ballad on **Track 42** of the Audio Companion. It would equally well suit the satyrs' lusty jigging dance at the sheepshearing feast in *The Winter's Tale.*

Hold on a minute, you might by now be thinking. Such cheerful skipping and leaping dance hardly fits the sober moment of the statue scene in *The Winter's Tale*, does it? If you were to state the point so flatly, you would certainly be right. But we need to fully unpack the complexity of "Rogero" as it connects to its larger cultural context and to Shakespeare's elaborate play (in many senses of the word "play"), both of which include layerings and backtrackings of meanings and genres. We cannot focus on just one isolated moment in *The Winter's Tale*, climactic and critical though that moment might be. Indeed, the play's early evocations of lusty sport, possibly through the very tune of "Rogero," at the sheepshearing feast, allow for the statue scene's mixed feelings: not a singular emotion, as expressed in Bradamante's doleful lament, but a mingling of grief *and* joy, loss *and* gain, death *and* rebirth, tragedy *and* comedy.

I will go so far, in fact, to posit that, despite "Rogero's" origins in Bradamante's lovelorn sorrow from the epic romance *Orlando Furioso*, the song as evoked in the statue scene of *The Winter's Tale*—a scene much more mixed in both affect and genre—relies upon the audience's association of "Rogero" specifically with joy and rebirth, not only mourning and loss. That is, its potentially bouncy, skipping, leaping melody, however likely more toned-down in the statue scene, as we shall see, might still potentially awaken vestigial memories for the audience of light-hearted song and high-stepping dancing—specifically, the "gallimaufry of gambols" of the kind the satyrs earlier dance.

Thus it would have been meaningfully ideal to have at least two renderings of "Rogero" in the course of Shakespeare's play so as to bring out the multidimensional affect of the awakening of the "statue" of Hermione. If "Rogero" were played to the fiddle for a skipping and leaping dance such as the satyrs' sport at the sheepshearing feast, that fact would not have been and *should not* have been wiped from the audience's memory, if the later climactic scene is to succeed, at least to the extent it *does* succeed.

The audience of Shakespeare's play would more than likely have had in mind multiple associations of "Rogero," and especially those that linked the tune to satyrs and lusty gamboling both in dramatic and extra-theatrical contexts. One especially reverberant connection is to a tune from another play of satyrs "pranking," which was often confused with "Rogero" even in Shakespeare's day. The source of the confusion arises from Robert Greene's play *History of Orlando Furioso* (published in 1594, though first performed 1591/92). In many ways, as critics have shown, Shakespeare in *The Winter's Tale* had Greene on his mind: Greene's popular fiction *Pandosto; Or, the Triumph of Time* (1588) provides the backbone of the main plotline of Shakespeare's play. But also influential are Greene's cony-catching pamphlets and his self-promoted roguish lifestyle (both are models, argues Mentz, for Shakespeare's character of Autolycus, who significantly is *not* a character in *Pandosto*; "Wearing Greene," 73–92). With such larger Greene-thinking in mind, we might recognize that *The Winter's Tale* strikingly imitates facets not only of the dark prose romance of Greene's *Pandosto* (where rebirth of the Hermione-like figure is denied) but also of Greene's *History of Orlando Furioso* (evoking in its very title the original epic romance by Ariosto and the tragic lament expressed within it of Bradamante, which became associated so strongly with the tune "Rogero"). Most striking, Orlando's madness in Greene's play is prompted by the same lunatic thinking that we see exhibited by Leontes: an insane jealousy due to the hero's falsely imagining his lover's adultery. Orlando is only cured after he twice falls asleep; each time, satyrs, as if part of a dream, emerge and dance. After the second dance of satyrs, Orlando awakens cured.

Seemingly recalling these scenes, we must note, is a broadside ballad to "Rogero," in which the tune is retitled "In Slumbring sleep I lay" (in "The poore man payes for all," EBBA 30223), wherein the relator, upon awakening, describes his dream about social injustices done to the poor. This ballad's renaming of the tune is due to a confusion and conflation in the period between "Rogero" and another melody that was actually written for Greene's satyrs' dance, titled "Orlando Sleepeth." With such slippery attributions and retitlings of related ballad melodies in mind, the audience of Shakespeare's *Winter's Tale* may well have linked the sheepshearing satyrs' gambols, which "refresh" the weary, according to Polixenes, to Greene's satyrs' dances, which also appear curative—and thought of the tune "Rogero."

There is yet one more strong link between "Rogero" and satyr-like gambols, though it is also confusing in its "mixed" associations. An apparently sincere love song, unlike the jesting lover-spaniel ballad in Johnson's collection, it occurs in an incident that George Gascoigne recounts in his *Adventures of Master F.J.* (1573). Here, the hero, Ferdinando, as related by the narrator, "taking into his hand a Lute, that lay on his Mistresse bed, did unto the note of the Venetian galliard apply the Italian dittie written by the worthie Bradament unto the noble *Rugier*, as Ariosto hath it: *Rugier qual sempre fui etc.*" (Ward, "Music for 'A Handefull of pleasant delites,'" 172). The "dittie" Ferdinando plays must have been "Rogero," given the reference to Bradamante's lament for her lost lover, Ruggiero, in Ariosto's *Orlando Furioso*. But Gascoigne in his mind mixes melodies by calling the mournful tune "the Venetian galliard," which is not only a different tune but also one conducive to yet more high-stepping, lively dance—yes, of the kind performed by satyrs—not of a bedroom love song, however lustful might be the singer's intent (Ward, 171).

The songs and ballads that we have so far discussed, deriving from a range of genres, offer a mixed bag of possible associational hits to "Rogero" for an audience of Shakespeare's *The Winter's Tale*: serious complaint of a forsaken lover at an emotional low point in a romance epic; comic, tongue-in-cheek, sexual, and bouncy wooing in a ballad songbook; more passionate bedroom love singing, which is paradoxically described as galliard-like, in a picaresque novel; wild and lusty satyrs' dancing in Greene's dark tragic-romantic play; and dream sequence of cutting social critique in a broadside ballad. Any one invocation of "Rogero" must be seen as but a fragment of this imaginary whole—a wide-ranging, sometimes conflicting and uncertain, commingling of affects, subjects, and genres.

To the extent that Shakespeare is especially focused on contingency as experienced through the genre of broadside ballads, it is notable that most associations to the tune in this genre, like that of the sleeper's dream about the exploited poor, are consistently serious in tone. But "Rogero" in broadside ballads does not always signal tragedy or even solemnity. Addressing the tune's relevance to *The Winter's Tale*, Ross W. Duffin only mentions the tragic ballad, not extant in broadside form but found in the Shirburn manuscript (compiled 1585–1616), titled "The Torment of a Jealous Mind"; in this ballad, a husband, convinced of his wife's adultery with his servant, despite her protestations to the contrary, kills both of them. Duffin argues that, due to familiarity with this ballad, the audience, on hearing the First Gentleman call out "Rogero" at the beginning of act 5, scene 2, would have been instilled with fear that the tragedy of the play's opening in Sicilia would be extended into its conclusion (*Shakespeare's Songbook*, 342–45). But, even if we exclude all the fun-loving songs and dances to "Rogero" in other genres discussed above, as well as another ballad that does not survive on a printed broadside about love that ends happily—"A Faithful vow of two constant lovers" (preserved in *A Handeful of pleasant delights*, 1584)—consider the range of extant broadside ballads to "Rogero" (at latest count, thirty-five in EBBA) that are far broader in their cognitive and affective scope.

These many extant broadside ballads to "Rogero" in EBBA include not only our awakened dreamer's song but also "The Lamentation of Follie" (by William Elderton, 32228); "A worthy Mirrour . . . of a breeding Larke" (about a mother lark's concern for the safety of her fledglings' home in the field but her self-assurance, based on a cynical assessment of human nature, which turns out to be true, that the farmer won't get help from friends or family to reap the field—only when the farmer decides to tend to the field himself does she move her fledglings out [30312, 32090, and 36305]); the popular goodnight ballad, wherein the tune is again (ironically?) renamed "In Slumbring Sleepe" after the popularity of the dream broadside ballad discussed above and Greene's play (here, a highwayman, "John Spenser," belatedly repents not only his thefts but his womanizing and thus betrayal of his "constant" and "loving wife," 20047 and 32619); "A right Godly and Christian A.B.C." (also in the Shirburn manuscript along with the jealous-husband ballad) which, pointedly for *The Winter's Tale*, begins, "Arise and *wake* from wickednesse" (30328; my emphasis), and is just one of many instructional A.B.C. ballads; yet another dreamer ballad, titled "A Comfortable new Ballad of a Dreame of a Sinner," focused on man's wickedness (20025); and the much-published "The Norfolk Gentleman" (e.g., 30201). In this last broadside ballad to the tune "Rogero" (renamed, later in the seventeenth century, "The Children in the Wood"), the relator, as we have seen, tells the story of a relative who swears to protect his dying brother's children but instead hires villains to kill them in the woods so that he can claim their inheritance—much as Leontes orders Antigonus to abandon his baby girl to die in the wilds.

Again and again, the tune "Rogero," even more than other expansive broadside ballad tunes, roams from topic to topic, often mixing within as well as between any one broadside ballad tragedy and romance, love, sex, belief, skepticism, and social critique. Like *The Winter's Tale*, these single-sheet ballads consequently also mingle cognitive affect. If members watching the play made only a partial assemblage of associations from this smorgasbord of offerings—extended to include other genres wherein the tune is referenced, including those several featuring satyrs—"Rogero" broadside ballads would significantly have reinforced Shakespeare's experiment in a mongrel genre of "radical contingency." Consider the notion of awakening, for instance. The variety of dream broadside ballads, including those associated with "Rogero's" retitling "In Slumbring Sleepe," underscore just how recurrent and slippery is the concept of sleep and awakening in Shakespeare's play, wherein skepticism (as in the awakened relator's account of his dream of rampant injustice done to the poor) and faith (as in the ballad relator's dream focused on wickedness and repentance) conjoin. Even the "A.B.C" ballad wherein no literal dreaming occurs, we recall, begins "Arise and *wake* from wickednesse."

These "Rogero" broadside ballads remind us, in our making mental "hits" to them, to be attuned to the reverberations in Shakespeare's play of the meaningfulness of dreaming and awakening. I am here looking beyond the play's obvious red flag to the dream Antigonus has wherein Hermione appears to him and tells him to deposit her baby girl in Bohemia and name her "Perdita." Dreams and awakenings are more deeply a part of the play. In firmly holding onto his sinfulness after realizing too late the innocence of Hermione, for instance, Leontes has in effect fallen into a deadly stasis like sleep, just as the revealed statue of Hermione, though aged, appears frozen in time. The notion of sleep and awakening resurfaces most tellingly when the Third Gentleman refers to the wondrous sudden happenings at court as if "credit be *asleep*" (5.2.63; my emphasis). It reaches its climax when Paulina instructs Leontes that, in order to make the statue come to life, "It is requir'd / You do *awake* your faith" (5.3.94–95; my emphasis). Wondrous miracles (which are also part of an important sub-genre of broadside ballads, we've seen) would seem to require *both* putting to sleep and awakening "credit" or "faith." At the same time, recalling the many A.B.C. ballads of the period, Leontes' dreamlike state of mourning takes the form of an extended learning lesson; Paulina acts as his most strict teacher in the ABC's of an unwavering repentance for the sin of irrationally letting fall asleep his credit or faith in Hermione's chastity.

To fill out the potential broadside ballad associations that swirl around "Rogero," we must turn to one ballad, in particular, that would especially suit those inclined to see the awakened faith Paulina requires of Leontes as a *godly* faith. It is titled "A most godly and comfortable Ballad of the glorious Resurrection of our Lord Jesus Christ"; hereafter cited as "Resurrection."[23] We have only relatively late extant copies of this much-published broadside ballad, one version of which was printed possibly as early as 1624 (Roxburghe 1.258–259, EBBA 30184). But as is the case with about 50 percent of broadside ballads, the "Resurrection" ballad was never recorded in the Stationers' Register and, even if it had been, such registration would not provide definitive proof of its pre-circulation orally or in manuscript, or indeed of its first publication. Later reissuing of ballads was common practice. Extant "Resurrection" ballads, in sum, could actually be recurrences or, if you'll excuse the pun, resurrections of an earlier publication, possibly prompted into republication by the popularity of Shakespeare's play. Certainly if *The Winter's Tale* is about the resurrection of the Christ-like Hermione from death—one interpretation the play invites—"Rogero" is the tune to be played, likely with this specific ballad in mind, if it were indeed by then in circulation. With all the above potential inspiring associational hits, "Rogero" provides hope for an enlivening remaking of some kind within the play and in the minds of the audience. Even if the dramatized component parts of a broadside ballad that make up the final act of *The Winter's Tale* cannot be held together, the tune "Rogero" could work some magic.

Lending itself to such animating readjustment and remaking is not only the tune's engaging musical meter and the wide range of subjects associated with it but also both its poetic and musical flexibility, or at least such flexibility at the voice of a tactical singer. Over the course of the sixteenth and seventeenth centuries, as observed above, the melody became separated from its ground bass. In the process, a melody that had always required extemporizing over a very regular rhythm became even more liberated. Like a masterless man or rogue, not tied to a societal foundation, it could have taken on many different variations. Given the context of Shakespeare's authorial ties with Greene as a multipronged source for his play, including the latter's rogue pamphlets and lifestyle, which likely pointed Shakespeare to the creation of the rogue/trickster/balladmonger Autolycus, one cannot but think particularly about how the tune was well-suited to that vagrant and extemporizing character. In sum, though Autolycus is sidelined as a figure in Sicilia, residual memory of his spontaneous invigorating orchestrations in Bohemia would surely have endured for the audience, especially through the play's reference to "Rogero." Such a reverberation would have been stronger if "Rogero" were the tune played for the satyrs' gamboling dance at the sheepshearing feast, where Autolycus stole the show, and then again, now more soberly, in the statue scene.[24] Even if the tune was not performed at the sheepshearing feast, contemporaries might well have made indirect associations between the satyrs' dance there and the satyrs' dance that was confused at the time with "Rogero" in Greene's play. To illustrate just how Autolycus-like or open to improvisation is the tune "Rogero," let's consider more closely its structure and the multifarious ways it might be rendered to handle the necessary adaptations in the singing of a particular text.

The term Simpson uses to describe "Rogero's" musical meter is a "loose cadence" (613). By this he means that, taking as an example a four-line poetic stanza (which would be doubled for the more typical eight-line ballad stanzas of the early seventeenth century), the "Rogero" melody could be used for singing a quatrain of traditional poetic ballad measure (4-3-4-3), of trimeter (3-3-3-3), or of poulter's measure (3-3-4-3)—the last also identified with hymnal music.[25] What Simpson has left out is that the tune also fits another poetic form of ballad measure, which does not turn up in encyclopedia definitions but is in fact common in broadside ballads, that is, tetrameter (4-4-4-4). In fact, the four stresses of musical meter (two strong and two weak), employed in theory and in practice in Shakespeare's time, most perfectly fit poetic tetrameter, as we have seen. Any poetic alteration of the tetrameter stanza presented the early modern singer not only with necessary choices but also with opportunities to improvise—no matter what tune they might be singing. In this sense, "Rogero" is not that different from other tunes, despite Simpson's championing of it as having a "loose cadence." Singing all early modern ballad texts (excepting perhaps 4-4-4-4 poetic meter) to any tune relied on a singer's tactical adjustment of text to tune and tune to text at the time of singing. But "Rogero" *does* offer more ease than many other early modern tunes for the singer to adapt differing poetic ballad measures to the tune in one important way: it offers an extra iamb at the end of each musical line that approximates the even numbered lines of verse. It is worthwhile, in our conclusion, and considering the importance of "Rogero" to *The Winter's Tale*, to tease out these options.

You can see the extra notes we are discussing in the fourth and eighth measures of "Rogero" in the transcribed original musical score on page 362. These measures each present the singer with an extra iambic foot in the case of a three-foot poetic line (the surplus notes are the two that appear directly before the two beamed notes at the end of the measure—the beamed notes are the pickup notes to be sung at the beginning of the next line of verse, in line 3, and then again in line 7 of an eight-line poetic stanza).

The singer here of "Rogero," as of other tunes, is given options in the case of a 4-3-4-3 poetic stanza, whether the pattern is repeated or not. But what would the early modern singer have done? Would she have forced the last syllable or word at the end of the short, even poetic lines to strike individually upon each of the three notes that make up the musical measure, no matter what? The notation allows the singer to easily do that should she so choose, and the text can be made to fit. Or, would she, instead, have held onto the last musical note needed for the poetic measure through the two "extra" notes, basically ignoring them except in extending the first note through two extra beats? The same question arises especially when the poetic measure is in trimeter (3-3-3-3). The decision of whether to sing the "extra" notes or hold out just the last needed note—or some combination of these tactics—in trimeter presents itself in every poetic line of the poetic text. And the singer need not have adopted the same tactical response each time! What other additions and deletions would singers have adopted when encouraged by such a "loose cadence" to make free, extemporaneous choices? Vocalists, of course, I reiterate, singing any text to tune would have always needed to make adjustments and on-the-spot alterations to conjoin poetic words or syllables with musical notes in a meaningful way (without creating a conjoined monstrosity). But the "Rogero" tune, in the context of what we have referred to as the "radical contingency" of *The Winter's Tale*, seems to encourage such extemporaneity more than most other tunes of the period.

Consider "Rogero" as it might have been sung to the "Resurrection" ballad discussed above. We notice at a glance that the ballad is in eight-line stanzas of doubled 4-3-4-3 poetic ballad measure. Now, I cannot snatch a 400-year-old singer off the streets of London to render an interpretation of this broadside ballad for us. But I can call on two experienced modern singers of early modern broadside ballads and provide you with their interpretative recordings as well as draw on Minstrel to render modern notations and fiddle audios of them. The singers' renderings of the ballad indicate independent choices in adjusting tune to text and text to tune as well as the melody's flexibility for the singers in making such choices. For ease of comparison, we will focus on just the introductory stanza of the "Resurrection" ballad:

What faithlesse froward sinfull man,
    so farre from grace is fled,

That doth not in his heart beleeve
the rising from the dead:
Or why do wicked mortall men,
their lives on earth so frame:
That being dead they do suppose,
They shall not rise again? (st. 1)

Let us turn first to Bell's recording of this stanza to "Rogero" (**Track 43**) and its transcription below according to the rules of Minstrel. As is typical in singing any music, each of the two singers' interpretations of the sung text is rendered in the key suitable to their vocal comfort zone: Bell records the ballad in C major and the second singer (Helena Harlow), as we shall hear, sings it in D flat major. But for ease of comparison Bell has rendered the transcriptions of both recordings in C major (since C major includes no sharps or flats, that's why you don't see any in the transcriptions, despite their occurrence in the source notation):

As usual, Minstrel aligns not only the underlaid syllables/words of the text to the musical notes, showing a singer's choices in singing the notation; it also clearly indicates, through its transcription of the recording, where the stronger and weaker musical stresses fall (whether in consonance or dissonance, with each line of poetic meter). In addition, you may hear the transcription of Bell's recording rendered in the Audio Companion—especially appropriately in the case of "Rogero," given Webbe's complaint about hearing the tune being both sung and played everywhere by the masses—to the sound of the fiddle (**Track 44**).

Bell has chosen in his singing to follow the original notation (see Music Notation on p. 362) relatively closely, at least for the first set of short, even lines of poetic measure (line 2, repeated in line 6), the conclusions of which roughly align with the musical measures 4 and 12. For poetic line 2, for example, as we see above, he has not simply held out the first note in the measure on which "fled" falls, but he has sung the strongly stressed word across all three notes provided from the original notation (including the extra two notes). Rather than effecting an awkwardness, the melody in Bell's choice of singing lends itself to the poetic meaning of "fled"; that is, he creates a lovely enactment of fleeing in the running of the notes. But Bell decided that it was awkward and counter-interpretative to do the same in measures 8 and 16 (poetic lines 4 and 8) when faced with three notes and the singular word/syllable, "***dead***" and "***gain***" (in "a-***gain***"). It would be especially awkward, he thought, to sing each of the available notes for the text because the notes are identical; doing so would create the effect of a series of glottal stops. Instead, Bell extends the word/syllable in these lines as if it fell on one long note. Elongating the already musical strong stress given to the singular piece of text, he creates a different kind of effect than in the trill of "fled"—more of a sense of emphatic finality. Here, a tactical alteration of the original tune to the text at hand—which the tune invites by providing three identical notes—measurably stresses the song's paradoxical theme: that the death or loss of Christ is in fact a gain.

Bell creates another paradoxically arrived-at positive effect by choosing to adhere to the middle musical measures (5 and 6 above) which make up the poetic lines 3 and 7. Doing so allows him to use the two notes allotted to the nonstressed word, "his__," in line 3 to build up momentum to the strong musical metric emphasis on "***heart__***," which is further emphasized by his extension of the word over the allotted two notes. The momentum keeps building—as does the tempo—so that the two notes that fall (literally) over "***heart__***" rush to another two-note figure, "be__." The singer extends "be__" over the two rising notes, before finding rest in completion of the syllable's other half (and the end of the poetic line): "*-leeve*." Singing this three-note movement upward, beginning with the second note devoted to "***heart__***" and extending it through the two notes devoted to "be__," Bell voices an uplifting movement that enacts a surprising fall in completion on "*-leeve*"; but at the same time, the series of notes he sings positively end in a return to where he began—on the first note devoted to "be__," which, further satisfyingly, is also the very same note on which he began the two-note "***heart__***." The effect is a charge of emotive emphasis on "heart" and "believe," which gives "be__*leeve*" more phenomenal than metrical stress: "***believe***."[26] Furthermore, "be__*leeve*" leads again into the word or words and notes of a contradiction, which is the very paradox of the resurrection, enacted in the final movement of poetic line 4.

Here, "be__*leeve*" wobbingly rises finally to a leap, creating the expectation of soaring heights on "the," beginning the line. But the notes and accompanying words then follow, instead, a slow stepwise decline, in contradiction to their poetic meaning, inviting a musically downward notation in "rise"—"***ris***-ing *from* the"—only to surprise us with the single uplifting note and word, once again drawn out, that lifts us from this downward progression (in contrast to its otherwise deflating meaning): "***dead***." Death, as in Christ's crucifixion, is not vocalized as a continuous downward spiral to oblivion but as an uplifting turn toward resurrection—for Christ and for humankind.

Bell's tactic for singing this melody, which both adheres to and subtly adjusts the melody to his interpretation of the ballad text is, however, by no means authoritative. Consider now the modern transcription (below) of the subtly variant rendering of the source notation to stanza 1 of the "Resurrection" ballad sung by Helena Harlow (available on **Track 45** and also rendered to fiddle audio on **Track 46)**:

Harlow extemporizes far more extensively, but also consistently, on our original notation than does Bell. To begin with, at the end of *every* even line, she chooses to hold the last necessary note for the poetry (for example, the first of the three notes in the fourth measure printed in the first line of music, the end of the second line of poetry), giving it additional length, rather than singing out each of the two remaining notes with a trill on the last poetic word. This tactic affords the even lines of the stanza less nuance and fluidity of meaning than in Bell's interpretation of them. However, it adds an affirmative strength to the lines' conclusions. All the poetically and musically stressed syllables ending the even lines—***fled***, ***dead***, ***frame***, ***gain***—are strongly emphasized through elongation. Harlow has chosen a clearer path, one might say, through the paradoxes evoked by these words/syllables, which the melody readily allows and the rhyme scheme reinforces. More optimistically than Bell's interpretation, Harlow's emphatic conclusions to the even lines drive home that *death has fled and life is a-gain framed.*

Further breaking with the source notation, Harlow takes a noticeable breath toward the end of the second measure in the first line of music notation (indicated by the eighth-note rest symbol between "*man*" and "so" / "*men*" and "their"), which roughly also stands at the end of the first and fifth lines of poetry, before beginning the second and sixth poetic lines. She thus cheats the beginning word of the following line—"so" and "their"—by an eighth note. To a tuned ear, this tactic effects a phenomenal accent on the already stressed next word: "***farre***" in line 2 and "***lives***" in line 6—emphasizing, at these points in the narrative, how far men's lives are from God. Following the theme of improvisation that the "Rogero" melody encourages, she has also chosen not to follow Bell in her singing as two slurred notes the "his" and "they" of lines 3 and 7, respectively. At one level, this tactic creates more emphasis on the stresses of "***heart__***" and "be-*leeve*"—especially since she decides to here increase the momentum of the second two-note figure by making it a dotted eighth plus sixteenth, repeating the same rhythm as in her swinging rendering of "***heart__***."[27] She adopts this tactic as well in her upbeat singing of the very first word of the stanza (as well as the words beginning lines 3, 5, and 7). Generally, these subtle variants in rhythm from our source notation and from Bell's rendering of the tune create an enlivening spring—a spirited vivacity—to Harlow's singing of the verse, in contrast to the points where she withdraws that effect by steadfastly holding out the final notes on the even lines. The maneuver is a tricky, Autolycus-like tactic designed to manipulate our emotions, especially the affect of those perhaps familiar with a different version of the song. Communicating the paradox of the resurrection seems not her main intent. Rather, her singing focuses more on voicing joy and hope that arise from and lead to a steadfast and heartfelt belief.

Finally, "Rogero's" flexibility—its openness to adaptation by the performer when the tune is sung to text—including variability in tempo (speed) and stylistic approach, are crucial to the aesthetic, tone, and associative hits it might provoke. Much depends on one's tactics in singing or playing the tune. If, for instance, it is sung slowly and smoothly (without changing a note or the rhythm of the source notation), which neither of our singers chose to do, the tune might not seem very suitable for cheer or dancing. Sung in this way, it *would* be suitable for gently conveying a moral message about belief, or some other serious topic, which *seems* to align with the subject matter of many of the extant broadside ballads sung (and danced) to the tune in England, as we have seen. In this more somber interpretation, the singer could manipulate any potential bounciness or swing of tune and text into a kind of up-and-down sighing or melancholic rhythm through the musical metric stresses. Both Bell and Harlow in their own ways take liberties with the source notation that has survived—and I want to underscore that I do realize "source notation" indicates only one possible version of the "received" melody. Both singers break away, especially, from the tune's ability to vocalize a bleak perspective. They recognize that even a religious ballad, such as the "Resurrection," is open to more rhythmic and affective variety. Their tactics include extended stress, acceleration or buildup of anticipation, and in the case of Harlow, even more hopeful bounce. If the singers had also chosen to sing "Rogero" more quickly and with even more spring—which many features of the melody, as we have seen, encourage or can be seized upon to foreground—the tune would have become downright jovial, even jig-like, in musical metric stress. We have observed such a version of "Rogero" in the wooing-spaniel ballad, which returns us to the whole mix of high-stepping ballads, including our "gallimaufry of gambols" of jigging satyrs in the sheepshearing feast of *The Winter's Tale* and also during Orlando's dreams in Greene's *History of Orlando Furioso*. Though we tend to think of religious tunes and love ballads as serious, I suggest that they could well have embraced such uplifting affect. Our spaniel-like wooer demonstrates great springing good cheer on the topic of love; and, similarly, a devout singer ballading the resurrection of Christ, though obviously relating a serious event, could have conveyed degrees of joyful celebration, as does Harlow.[28]

The problem is that, if the tune of "Rogero" is in fact played to awaken the statue in *The Winter's Tale*, or if another multifaceted and variously evocative ballad tune were played, or even if the audience experienced an evocation of the tune "Rogero" as it lingered vestigially and kinesthetically in their minds and bodies from other associations, the melody would evoke precisely the mixed emotions that ballads as a group tend to elicit from their audiences. That is, the tune would appeal to some listeners in one way, and to others in another. But is this a problem, or is it precisely what Shakespeare was experimenting with by mixing genres, especially through the multiple links he makes in *The Winter's Tale* to broadside ballads? There is more than one pack of possible responses to the tune "Rogero," just as there is more than one pack of reactions to the statue scene.

There are also many possible assessments of the character of Paulina who stages the statue scene. She has, for example, been linked to the biblical Paul, to old wives' tales, and to the Ovidian tradition (the last, for instance, by

Mary Ellen Lamb, in "Ovid and *The Winter's Tale*"). She is also very much an Autolycus-like rogue in her manipulating Hermione, Leontes, and her guests—for that matter, the entire audience of the play, if she succeeds in momentarily fooling us—into believing that Hermione is a statue, not a posed person. As creative puppeteer of other characters, Paulina displaces Autolycus, just as Camillo momentarily did in trickily arranging the escape of Perdita and Florizel from Bohemia. By doing so, however, she incessantly reminds us of both Autolycus's absence and his presence; that is, although the role of making and hawking wonders has now fallen into a new character's hands, it is no less visible as such. Perhaps, in fact, the work of artifice is *more* visible now, especially if the ballad singer stands on stage silently, watching. For that matter, even if we are among those who most want to believe in Paulina's wondrous faith (even if we want to believe for the sake of believing)—in a faith that can bring back to life Hermione (an event akin to Autolycus's many offered wonders), because that's what art and religion fundamentally ask us to do—we are almost sure to see that Paulina's regenerative powers are as limited as those of Autolycus. In the enlivening statue scene, we cannot forget the dead Mamillius and Antigonus (Paulina's husband), who will never be resurrected. Nor can we forget Autolycus, who may well be—and I would argue *should be*—present at this climactic moment of the play, as the instructions by the shepherd and Clown for him to follow them to the event suggest he was.

But even if Autolycus *is* present at the miraculous enlivening of Hermione's statue and raises his arm in a "right on" gesture, and even if the shepherd and Clown are also present and clap with glee, and even if the unnamed lords further attend and smile silently in appreciation, are they and the extended audience watching the play engaging in a godly moment, or a secular one, or both?[29] Whatever one's individual or group response, we must recognize the mixed bag of emotions and thoughts this final scene evokes, including the many genres still actively in play. We might call this multiplicity of commingled emotions and genres *hyper-plural*, for the same reasons I have used this term to describe the multimedia of broadside ballads. This hyperplurality undoubtedly reinforces our dissatisfaction with the play's ending-by-fragmentation. It may also, I will go so far as to suggest, constitute a tactical invitation from Shakespeare to his audience: here is space for interpretative play; indeed, here is exactly the sort of space that Polixenes and Leontes find so threatening to their authoritative power. Like a blank circle in the center of a printed page, this space—demarcated by the sights, sounds, and storytelling of Shakespeare's play—invites us to fill it up ourselves. In other words, an invitation toward interpretative criticism is at the very center of *The Winter's Tale*. It is illustrated by the many unasked and unanswerable questions with which the audience is left. If the play has a thesis, it is that circles are not the same as enclosures: a place that is too closed-off from the public, a place that cannot incorporate strangers or the varied sorts of society, is a place where nothing much is going to happen. Life stops flowing in. The place of the stage, too, is in danger of becoming too restrictive, of generating an air too refined to breathe. But this stillness is not definitive: the statue, as it were, can be brought back to life.

Recall, for a moment, that the revelation of Perdita's true identity takes place offstage—a dramatic revelation so interior that even the audience can't see it. Fortunately, we hear about her heritage all the same; but, although the news comes from the lips of a gentleman, its source is not a well-placed eavesdropping lord. Rather, as we learn in language dripping with allusions to ballad culture, the nobility only discovers what happened after the masses do—but only because the lower sorts are sharing the tale so widely. *The Winter's Tale* does not quite succeed at creating dramatic unities precisely because the play must fail in order to show how the Sicilian court fails. This is why, despite Pauline's artful miracle, some dead characters are never revived. Drama, Shakespeare seems to suggest, with self-conscious criticism, can only take its art to the edge of the stage; its work requires more supportive generic and widely disseminated performative grounds.

In the end, we cannot choose a more fruitful backdrop for Shakespeare's "spectacularly contingent," experimental drama than the broadside ballad, which by its very nature is endlessly shifting and mixed, so much so that it even lends itself to a dismembering of its own protean component parts. Shakespeare has deliberately left fragmented the ballad experience in his staged performance of his play and, if you have awakened your faith in my argument, called up a multifaceted tune to keep his ending open. Such an opening allows his audience individually and as collective publics variously to put those parts together and gather around one or another stance as in listening to or voicing a broadside ballad.

Re-Jigging Ballad and Play: Extended Assemblages and Associational Hits

But it ain't over 'til the fat lady sings or, rather, until the broadside ballad genre, and in some sense the play, returns in its transfigured form of a jig—if in fact a jig occurred on the Globe stage in 1611, which is highly likely. Certainly, a Middlesex Proclamation of 1612 indicates that jigs were alive and well in the city's theaters and perceived by the authorities to be out of control. The order declares the suppression of jigs out of fear of the "lewd and ill-disposed persons" who "do resort" specifically to the Fortune Theater (in the city) "at the end of every play," just to see the after-play jigs, as noted by Roger Clegg and Lucie Skeaping. There is no reason to think, however, as Clegg and Skeaping further posit, that the raunchy suburbs of Southwark would by this time have attracted a more orderly audience (*Singing Simpkin*, 27, 23). Certainly, Shakespeare's company performed many of its plays in the city's indoor theater of Blackfriars and at the indoor Banqueting House of Whitehall Court, both of which, unlike the Globe, were enclosed, smaller, and catered to the well-to-do. But the afterpiece of a jig might have been performed at one venue and not at the other, or performed differently at each; it could even have been an extemporaneous addition in reaction to the theatrical moment.

What exactly are we talking about when we refer to after-play jigs? We have already discussed jigs following the lines of Smith, as leaping and jumping dances ("'Ball'"), like the "gallimaufry of gambols," which the peasants dressed as satyrs perform at the sheepshearing feast in *The Winter's Tale*—a dance that, as I have argued, could well have been to the tune "Rogero." But jigs could be more than simply bouncing or—to think back to our lover-spaniel ballad—"pranking" dances to sung and/or played tunes. In EBBA, to date, no fewer than thirty-two broadside ballads sung in dialogue form between a man and a woman, often with a racy theme, have in their titles "jig" or "jigge."[30] These upbeat, usually funny, inter-exchange ballads could have been sung with or without dance and with or without instrumental accompaniment. Other jigs took the form of mini plays, usually also of a lewd or bawdy comic nature, involving not only song, dance, and instrumentation but also elements of more formal staging, including instructions of entrances, exits, and the use of stage properties; these more elaborate jigs are the focus of Clegg and Skeaping's study. One such dramatic jig, a unique survivor of the form, was collected by Samuel Pepys: "Frauncis new Iigge, betweene Frauncis a Gentleman, and Richard a Farmer," c. 1617, by George Attowell (Pepys Ballads 1.226–227, EBBA 20102); hereafter cited as "Frauncis's New Jigge."

As my after-play final request that you "do awake your faith" in reading this book, I ask you to imagine the very same instrumentalist—say, a violinist—who soulfully and gracefully might have played "Rogero" to the awakening of the apparent statue of Hermione, now returning to the stage after the final words spoken by Leontes and the exit of the players. Consider this same violinist now accompanied by the same jigging satyrs from the sheepshearing feast, together, of course, with the actor who played Autolycus (likely Robert Armin, known for his singing). Now consider the violinist turning the melody of "Rogero" from a slow, serious tune to a bouncing, jumping, and leaping melody, and the satyrs and even Autolycus dancing along in joyous and still sexually explicit gestures (for sex *is* natural), if maybe they are denuded of such flagrant trappings as flapping phalluses and the like—or not. Such two radically differently played versions of "Rogero" from our source notation, the one soulful and graceful, the other upbeat and festive, can be heard on **Tracks 47** and **48** played on the violin by Sara Bashore. Having heard both versions in the course of watching the entire *Winter's Tale*, let's posit that, as well as witnessing the after-play jig, with its gay and likely lusty dancing, the audience would have left the theater with three visions and hearings of "Rogero" and a further complication of Shakespeare's experimentation in the "radically contingent"—which extends beyond the parameters of the dramatic play itself. In the jig version, which necessarily would have reflected back on or, rather, extended the play's performance in the minds of the audience, the multisensory facets of dance, song, music, and all the senses for that matter would have been reawakened in an entirely secular, toe-tapping, and jovial way, though still reminiscent of religious connotations (for such could not have been simply forgotten). Such joyous, if sexually explicit, dancing to a high-stepping "Rogero" may have rushed onto and then off the stage in a jig focused on dancing, or it might have led into a ballad jig turned mini play, such as Pepys's "Fraunciss's New Jigge." This dramatic broadside ballad tells over again the story of imagined adultery and momentary jealousy we have just witnessed in *The Winter's Tale*. However, in the ballad jig, the wife not only remains true, as in *The Winter's Tale*, but does so comically, with no tragic results. She tells her farmer-husband of the neighboring gentleman's attempt to seduce her and of her tactical consent. Despite his brief flash of anger, she quickly assures him that she has a trick in store for her planned seducer. Her husband as quickly *believes* her. We then witness the equivalent to the bed-trick employed in *Measure for Measure* (in "Fraunciss's New Jigge" the gentleman's wife, brought into the trick, goes to bed with the gentleman in place of the farmer's wife, and all eventually have a good laugh at the gentleman and even financially profit in the end when the trick is exposed; he also promises to reform his lascivious ways). The action calls up memories from *The Winter's Tale* of suspicion, adultery, constancy, jealousy, anger, skepticism, faith, and repentance, but it does so in an entirely playful way that is meant to dispel confusion and mingled reflection over the meaning of things. It's just plain down-to-earth fun. Ballads can be that as well. You just have to pick the right one from the pack and believe in it.

Notes

INTRODUCTION

1 My own hand at the widest part of the palm and from the base of the palm to the top of the middle finger is 3.25 by 6.75 inches. Based on a random survey, I found that an adult man's hand is roughly 3.5 inches wide at the base and 7.4 inches high. See also TheAverageBody.com, which measures palm size slightly differently, www.theaveragebody.com/average_hand_size.php, accessed January 20, 2019.

2 Indeed, renumbering is the rule, rather than the exception, in manuscript archives that have gone through re-sortings over the centuries, as anyone trying to find their way through the Public Records Office can testify.

3 I am grateful to Dr. Megan E. Palmer for helping me throughout my research on this book in locating repeat impressions and dating both attire and woodcuts.

4 This is the typical positioning of the tune title on a ballad sheet: printed just below any short verse at the top of the page, which itself would have appeared under the—in this instance—cut-off ballad title. On spelling convention in this book in citing early modern type, see note in the front matter.

5 Eleven appear in EBBA (the English Broadside Ballad Archive, ebba.english.ucsb.edu); the other is preserved at the Bodleian Library (online at http://ballads.bodleian.ox.ac.uk/).

6 The online Audio Companion is available at https://repository.upenn.edu/fumerton_broadside-ballad/.

7 For a useful overview of New Textualism, including a case-study analysis of Thomas More's Utopia, see Jürgen Meyer, "Editing Textual Synergies: New Historicism and 'New Textualism,'" *Poetics Today 35*, no. 4 (2014): 591–613.

CHAPTER 1

1 For an early use of the term "intermedia," see Eric Vos, "The Eternal Network: Mail Art, Intermedia Semiotics, Interarts Studies," in *Interart Poetics*, ed. Lagerroth, Lund, and Hedling, 325. See also Rajewsky, "Intermediality, Intertextuality, and Remediation," and Scott A. Trudell, *Unwritten Poetry*, 7n24. A sign of the current critical interest in the intermedial is the seminar at the 2018 Shakespeare Association of America, titled "Intermedia Approaches to Early Modern English Song," organized by Katherine R. Larson and Sarah F. Williams.

2 Williams's study of witches and balladry admirably proposes to provide such a trifold media approach in her recent book (*Damnable Practises*), but she unfortunately falls short of extensive visual or music critique.

3 In most instances of music notation in this book, a singer's breaths and time of holding notes are not indicated; those features, however, will be prominent in the more advanced development of Minstrel for EBBA, in an effort to capture even more closely the experiential moment of singing the song.

4 Throughout this book, I use the traditional music symbols for when a note does not fall exactly in the musical scale: "♯" for "sharp," means the note should be sung or played slightly higher (by one semitone), "♭" for "flat" means it should be sung slightly lower (again, by one semitone), and "♮" for "natural" cancels previous alterations of a note for the duration of that measure.

5 Franklin, for instance, describes the phenomenon of interchangeable images in broadside ballads as an "art of collage" ("Art of Illustration," 194).

6 One can be too quick to take such expressed disparagements as absolute. As David Baker points out, for instance, Cornwallis was not completely undiscerning in his disposal of ballads as waste paper. He reserved that privilege specifically for lewd ballads; at other points in Cornwallis's remarks, Baker points out, he shows appreciation for the printed ballad as reflective of the experiential thought of the lower orders; "Against Feeling, or 'There might be thought,'" in *Ballads and Performance.* On contemporary attitudes to broadside ballads in the period, see Würzbach's foundational appendix in her *Rise of the English Street Ballad*, 253–84.

7 For emergence theory, see "Emergent Properties," *Stanford Encyclopedia of Philosophy*, first published September 24, 2002; substantive revision June 3, 2015, http://plato.stanford.edu/entries/properties-emergent/, accessed August 22, 2015. Citation from "Cellular Automata," *Stanford Encyclopedia of Philosophy*, March 26, 2012, http://plato.stanford.edu/entries/cellular-automata/, accessed August 22, 2015. Play John Conway's Game of Life at bitstorm.org/gameoflife/, accessed August 22, 2015.

8 "The Clothworkers' Company," www.clothworkers.co.uk/, accessed August 22, 2015.

9 Habermas early on, in his own contribution to Calhoun's collection, in his "Concluding Remarks," addressed the problem of homogeneity by conceding the "pluralization of the public sphere in the very process of its emergence" and "the coexistence of competing publics" in "Further Reflections," in Calhoun, ed. *Habermas and the Public Sphere*, 426. But he held firm to his historical sitedness of a fully emerged public sphere only in the eighteenth century (465).

10 Steven Mullaney, a contributor to the collective discussions of the MaPs Project, offers a similar definition of its united view of "plural" publics in his recent *Reformation of Emotions*, 149. Latent throughout this study is his allegiance to those in the MaPs collective who embraced politics as key to the formation of any public; see, for instance, his phrasing that theatrical performance allowed for "new modes of social, ideological, or political thinking" (166).

11 Paul Yachnin, "What Is a Public?," http://project.makingpublics.org/research/what-do-you-mean/ (site discontinued), accessed August 23, 2015.

12 I am grateful to Bill Brown for his help, when I was in residence with him at the Huntington Library, as I thought through the dynamics at play here. I want to add that when I use the word *printer*, I do so loosely. Watt tends to say "publisher." Many printers were also publishers, and often the relationship between the two participants in the production of a broadside ballad—especially regarding "authorial control"—is unclear. Typically, when an imprint on a ballad states "printed by" it is referring to a printer, and when it says "for," the reference is to a publisher.

13 As Rita Raley points out, advancements in media technology and opportunities for harnessing them have resulted in later proponents of the movement often engaging in quite sophisticated technology above the common person's skill set, such as data visualization; *Tactical Media*, 16.

14 The Stationers' Company maintains the Stationers' Register, where items authorized for publication (for a fee) are listed, in an early form of our notion of copyright.

15 Passed by consent of the House of Parliament and worded as an anti-papal document but also recognizing "Duty of my Allegiance" to Charles, May 1641, http://www.cornwall-opc-database.org/extra-searches/protestation-returns/protestation-oath-of-1641/, accessed August 28, 2015.

CHAPTER 2

1 As of January 1, 2015, EEBO-TCP made its first phase of transcriptions freely accessible to the public, though subscription rates still apply to future phases.

2 See, for example, Percy Bysshe Shelley's posthumous poems, *Relics of Shelley*, ed. Richard Garnett (London: Edward Moxon, 1862), "Fragments of the Adonais" and "Miscellaneous Fragments," 48–52 and 74–91. Quote from Garnett, preface, ix. Available online at https://archive.org/details/relicsofshelley00shel. For a position slightly more aligned with DeLanda, see Janowitz, "The Romantic Fragment." See also Levinson, *The Romantic Fragment Poem*, and McFarland, *Romanticism and the Forms of Ruin*. Thanks to Alan Liu for his help (drawing on his early expertise in Romanticism) in my thinking through the history of the fragment.

3 In Lev Manovich's response to Witmore's essay, "Text: A Massively Addressable Object," made on May 22, 2011 (comment #3), he disagrees with Witmore's vision of sameness across history. He notes, "The kind of addressability which is at work daily at Google computers which crawl 15 billion web pages, create massive indexes of texts and links, extract hundreds of other features from every page, etc. seems to me qualitatively different from what was done 500, 100, or 20 years ago. It is also qualitatively different from even the most daring digital humanities projects done today." Like Manovich, I see a qualitative difference, as my chapter goes on to point out, though it is not in the way Manovich had in mind.

4 The ESTC gives an estimate of 1635 for the first ballad, but there is reason to believe it could have been published slightly earlier, due to a glaring topical association it makes to a pamphlet of an earlier date, which we will discuss in the next chapter.

5 The switching out of the illustrations from ballad to ballad, which we shall examine in full, is not the most obvious evidence of different printers, as one might think. Printers inherited and loaned woodcuts, and they also actively copied each other's cuts. Also, the same printer might issue an otherwise apparently exact copy of his previous printing of a ballad but switch out all the cuts to create the illusion of a new ballad. See Stahmer, "Digital Analytical Bibliography," 267–68, 270.

6 "Jackanapes," *OED*, 2c; "Coxcombs," *OED*, 3a.

7 See Megan E. Palmer, with Charlotte Becker, *Ballad Illustration Archive Costume Book*, 2014, ebba.english.ucsb.edu/content/EBBA_Costume_Book.pdf.

8 See *Half Humankind*, ed. Henderson and McManus.

9 Malory, *Le Morte d'Arthur*, c2v. Palmer made this discovery, and the woodcut is discussed in the essay I have coauthored with her: "Lasting Impressions of the Common Woodcut," 382–99.

10 Morley discusses numerous shifts and changes in early modern music theory in Barnett, "Tonal Organization in Seventeenth-Century Music Theory." Barnett briefly discusses the decline of the idea of modes in English music theory over the first half of the seventeenth century and the gradual rise of what would eventually become the current major-minor tonality within certain influential

English music theory treatises; 436, 438–41. On changes in theories, see also Marsh, *Music and Society*, 52.

11 Butler, *Principles of Musik*, 8. Butler's seeming praise of ballads, quoted above, is qualified by a subsequent condemnation of them in his book as "corrupted . . . with dangerous immodesti, and filthy obseniti" (8). Later in his treatise he further critiques balladeers for their "obscene" and "filthy songs" and "wanton and immodest jests, or any kind of obscene scurrility" (130-31). On the Dorian mode, see also Powers, "Dorian." Though Marsh draws on a considerably more limited corpus of ballads than is available in EBBA, he is likely correct in stating that, among ballad tunes, about half are in Ionian or major keys and half are in minor, with the qualification that "a number of the latter tunes [in the minor] are clearly constructed in the Dorian mode rather than on what we would recognize as a modern minor scale" (*Music and Society*, 235). Marsh never explains the difference between minor and Dorian, however. It is not an easy task. Part of the problem is that there is more than one version of minor. The minor, closest in earlier periods to the Aeolian mode, can be effected using both the raised *and* lowered sixth and seventh scale degrees. The Dorian mode typically only raises the sixth scale degree.

12 In my analyses, I always show a specific score from a period-specific source as referent; indicate the scale used in the score and in the recordings (for example, G major); and then talk about the notes in terms of their relative alphabetical naming rather than more generally by number (for example, "the sixth scale degree"), as is practiced by music theorists. I have done this for ease of comprehension for the nonmusical. Once a note has been identified on the score, even those with little or no musical skill can figure out the names for the surrounding notes—the note on a space above a note on a line in the staff—for example, B—is named by an alphabetically higher letter—for example, C (and vice versa). An easy rule of thumb is that the notes on the lines of the staff in treble clef are EGBDF, or "Every Good Boy Drives Ferraris" and the notes on the spaces between lines spell out "FACE."

13 Of the extant notations of "Northern Nancy" given by Playford in his fourth through sixth editions of *The Dancing Master*, this is the one historically closest to our "Mock-Beggar Hall" ballads. The tune is indicated in G major. As we shall pursue in the next chapter, John Playford's son and successor switched the tune to the minor mode in the book's seventh edition of 1686 and in subsequent editions (which is itself a telling change). But for the purposes of this chapter "Northern Nancy" in major will be our focus.

14 In music theory, a "phenomenal accent" refers to accentuation not dependent on a note's place in the music's metrical hierarchy but on other contextual factors that influence the way one hears it. Lerdahl and Jackendoff define and

discuss metrical and phenomenal accent in *A Generative Theory of Tonal Music*, 17, paying particular attention to metrical accent and hierarchy in Chapter 2, 12–35. Joel Lester discusses phenomenal accent and meter, albeit using different labels, in *Tonal Music*, Chapters 2-3, 13–85.

15 The "Mixolydian" mode as modernly used is descended from the medieval Mixolydian church mode, defined by Powers and Wiering in "Mixolydian." The modern Mixolydian mode differs from the major most notably in that its seventh-scale degree is lowered by a half step. For example: in G major, the F is raised to an F♯. In G Mixolydian, the F is not sharped. A brief technical description of the modern Mixolydian and other modes can be found in Straus, *Elements of Music*, 227.

16 In this notation, the transcriber or singer has inserted an E note for "ty" in "***Cit***-y" to allow for the number of syllables needed to be sung; without that insertion he would necessarily have had to truncate "City" into one syllable and combine it with "and," creating something like "***Cit***-yand Court," which, would be more difficult to sing—though it does have the advantage of further phenomenally emphasizing the merging of the two urbane places of "City" and "Court" as negative foci of the ballad.

17 Cone first coined the term "hypermeter" to denote measures that "behave as a single beat"; *Musical Form*, 80.

18 Vocal range and flexibility were not the only necessary talents demanded of ballad singers. Despite modern textbook definitions of ballad measure as consisting of alternating lines of 4-3 stresses, rhyming ABCB or ABAB (Gahan, "Ballad Measure in Print"), we in fact see a huge variety between and even within ballads in their use of poetic and musical metric stress as well as number of lines per stanza and rhyme scheme. Textual variation required many on-the-fly adjustments to the tune as sung.

19 "Standard tune title" refers to the uber-title Simpson gives for variant namings of a tune; it is determined by tracking tune namings back through mutations to a "source," usually in an originary ballad's title, first line, or refrain.

20 The key signature implies Aeolian. But there is reason to consider the tune at least partially in Dorian because of a notable rise in notes in one musical phrase, which we shall discuss—a movement typical of the Dorian mode.

21 The single exception is the tune's first note, which is repeated for the third and fourth lines of text.

22 The transcription has been transposed up a minor-third from Playford's notation to G minor, for ease of comparison in this chapter and the next between sung and transcribed tunes with text.

23 Although this tune lies comfortably, if ambiguously, between the Aeolian (natural minor) and Dorian modes, the E-F-G motion on the words, "While

mock" is perhaps the strongest indication of the modal leaning toward Dorian in "Damask Rose."

CHAPTER 3

1 On the printing centers of Scotland that developed their ballad stock in the seventeenth century by colonization (of course through reassemblage) of London-produced broadside ballads, see Adam Fox, "Jockey and Jenny: English Broadside Ballads and the Invention of Scottishness," 201–20.

2 Marsh, *Music and Society*, 281. In his two chapters on broadside ballads, Marsh often shows an understanding of complex relations between tunes, but he more often folds the meaning of a melody into one received meaning that can then be used oppositionally.

3 On the ballad partners of 1624, see Watt, *Cheap Print*, 74–127.

4 For full transcriptions of these texts and other tracts in the controversy, see *Half Humankind*, ed. Henderson and McManus.

5 Edward Barlow, the seaman I discuss in the second half of my book *Unsettled*, was often away for years on East India voyages, and when he got paid on his return, he as often spent most of his accumulated pay on fancy clothing or the like.

6 The full title is *Hic Mulier: Or, The Man-Woman: Being a Medicine to cure the Coltish Disease of the Staggers in the Masculine-Feminine, of our Times. Expressed in a briefe Declamation*. London: 1620.

7 *Haec-Vir: Or, The Womanish-Man: Being an Answere to a late Booke intituled Hic-Mulier. Exprest in a briefe Dialogue betweene Haec-Vir the Womanish-Man, and Hic-Mulier the Man Woman*. London: 1620.

8 *Hic Mulier*, in *Half Humankind*, ed. Henderson and McManus, 272, and, as just one reference to the aristocratic fashion as "monstrous," the first paragraph of the pamphlet, 265.

9 *Hic Mulier*, in *Half Humankind*, ed. Henderson and McManus, 273.

10 Though, as we shall see, "Northern Nancy" comes to be notated in both the major and minor modes, my references here are to the tune in its major mode unless otherwise indicated.

11 Simpson points out that ballads titled "Dulcina," after which the tune was named, circulated before 1615, from which a manuscript survives with the notation for the tune, and continued in popularity beyond the Restoration (201–2).

12 Butler, *Principles of Musik*, 8. Marsh mistakenly reads Butler as saying the opposite—that most ballads are sung in the Dorian or minor key, associated

with "sobriety" and even, as it turns to the minor, Marsh says, with sadness; *Music and Society*, 235.

13 Thanks to James Revell Carr for sharing his insights about such counterpointing.

14 This metrical rhythm is called a "hemiola." The term can be summarized as the use of three equal beats in the time it takes to play two, and vice versa. For a more detailed definition of the term, see Julian Rushton, "Hemiola," *Grove Music Online*, ed. Deane Root, www.oxfordmusiconline.com, accessed October 19, 2015. It should further be noted that lines 7 and 10 of each stanza can alternatively be understood as lines 6 and 8, if we combine the half lines 5 and 6, and 8 and 9 into one line each, to make what is really a metrically eight-line, not ten-line stanza.

15 For dating, see EBBA, ebba.english.ucsb.edu/ballad/20124/citation. The other "Country Lass" ballad is Roxburghe 1.52–53 (EBBA 30039). This ballad was printed for Thomas Symcocke, likely between 1619 and 1629; the ESTC conjectures that the printer was George Purslowe.

16 On Martin Parker, see Nebeker, "Broadside Ballads," 67, 69–81; also Susan Aileen Newman, "Broadside Ballads of Martin Parker"; and Rollins, "Martin Parker, Ballad-Monger," 449–74.

17 EBBA's recording of the song clocks in at 8 minutes, 12 seconds.

18 As just one example, Edward Barlow, the son of a poor husbandman, in 1657 struck out for London at age fourteen from his north-country home in Prestwich, Lancashire, because his family could not support him (Fumerton, *Unsettled*, 63). The numbers of immigrants to London are staggering. They approached 10,000 a year in 1600 and continued to rise through the century. London's population during these years subsequently grew exponentially, from about 120,000 in 1550, to 200,000 in 1600, to 375,000 in 1650, to 490,000 in 1700 (Beier and Finlay, introduction to *London, 1600–1700*).

19 Joseph Swetnan, *The Araignment of Lewd, Idle, Froward, and vnconstant women . . .* (1615).

20 Such a complication is not just a coincidence. A long critical history has dismissed woodcut illustrations on ballads not only as crude and primitive but also as completely randomly placed on the ballad sheets with, in Simpson's words, "only the loosest regard for their appropriateness" (v). Yes, the cuts were pulled out and plugged in at the will of the printers/publishers (or in the minds of consumers in the course of making associations). But what can appear random can in fact be tactical.

21 Pepys's version of "The Country Lass," upon which we are focusing as likely the closest in time to the first "Mock-Beggar Hall" ballad (c. 1628), at first does not specifically name the tune title; or rather, it offers two tunes, the first unnamed. Under the title is stated "To a dainty new note, Which if you cannot hit / There's another tune which does as well fit. / 'That's the Mother be-

guiles the Daughter.'" It is this second tune that is later renamed "The Country Lass."

22 Simpson, 135.

23 See Pollard, "Transference of Woodcuts," in *Bibliographica*, vol. 2 (London, 1896), 343–68.

24 The Aldwell map is reproduced in *Survey of London*, ed. Sir Howard Roberts and Walter Godfrey (London: London County Council, 1950), Plate 65, facing p. 94. This map has also been digitally reproduced and enhanced, with commentary, in The Map of Early Modern London (MoEML), ed. Janelle Jensted, https://mapoflondon.uvic.ca/agas.htm?locIds=PARI1, accessed 26 April 2018.

25 Dean Stanton Barnard Jr., in the introduction to his edition of the pamphlet, *Hollands Leaguer by Nicholas Goodman: A Critical Edition* (The Hague: Mouton, 1970), 41. Hunsdon passed the manor on to Thomas Cure, the Queen's saddler, who next conveyed it in 1589 to Francis Langley, owner of the nearby Swan theater; Thomas Fairman Ordish, *Early London Theaters: In the Fields* (London, 1894), 249, 252. In 1602, it was purchased by Hugh Browker or Brooker and his son Thomas, who appear to have still owned the house at the time of the Holland incident; Barnard, *Hollands Leaguer*, 41–42. Barnard details the story of Elizabeth Holland, 33–47.

26 Noted in written correspondence with me; I am grateful to Professor Korda for allowing me to publish her insight.

27 Leba M. Goldstein, "The Pepys Ballads," 291–92. On attempts to negate concerns over William's "frostiness and sexual inadequacy" with lively songs, see Marsh, *Music and Society*, 311–15.

28 See EBBA 35353, 33670, 31959, 30825, 31954, and for the sixth by the same title as the others and thus almost definitely by the same tune, EBBA 20773.

29 *Dictionary of National Biography*, "John Playford" (1622/3–1686/7).

30 Bartel, *Musica Poetica*, 41. Though Bartel focuses on the continent, contemporary music theorists in England, as we have noted, might well also have been thinking in terms of major/minor and their respective affects, not a variety of modes.

31 Barlow, ed., *The Complete Country Dance Tunes from Playford's Dancing Master*, 10.

32 The perfect love of "Love's Solace" is out-and-out satirized in two later ballads, both published by Philip Brooksby c. 1672–96. The first of these, the very popular "The true Lovers Admonition," to the tune of "So Sweet is the Lass that Love me," the standard tune we know as "Damask Rose" (for example, in EBBA 33945), advises men that basically every woman "will take it" (a phrase repeated in the refrain of the ballad) except for black-haired women, so if you want sexual constancy, go for the black; the other, also very popular ballad,

"To her brown Beard," also to "Damask Rose" (for example, EBBA 33944), as if in answer to the first ballad, advises women against men with a range of differently colored beards as untrustworthy in love, with the safest exception, says the relator, of "him that is like to me" (st. 9), which turns out to be the man with "the brown Hair" (st. 10). This ballad ends on a repetition of the refrain that has concluded each stanza, "Ile warrant thee girl, hee'l love thee." But since this has been the refrain of all the stanzas all along, including those stanzas against men of variously colored beards, it is hardly reassuring.

33 Chartier, "Languages, Books, and Reading," 142.

34 David McKitterick, for example, argues that EBBA is "intrusively recreative" in digitally manipulating photographs of broadside ballad originals to provide multiple viewings of them as well as "alarmingly frank" in explaining its methods and goals; *Old Books, New Technologies*, 18. I address this criticism below.

35 For example, EEBO incorrectly provides only one entry for "The Languishing Young Man" (Roxburghe 2.274; EBBA 30733). But there are at least two other extant ballads with the exact same title and even imprint that EEBO posits (in square brackets): Pepys Ballads 5.312 and Crawford.EB.942 (EBBA 22149 and 33438, respectively). The EEBO editors might have thought that the Roxburghe ballad stood as representative for these other copies. But this simply is not the case. Pepys Ballads 5.312, for example, has the same title and imprint as the seemingly "same" Roxburghe ballad (as one might conclude from their identical imprints— "Printed for J. Deacon, at the Angel in Gilt-spur-street, without Newgate"), but the ballad is in other major ways, particularly in the text and (lack of) image fragments that constitute its provisional whole, an entirely different order of creature: unlike the Roxburghe ballad, the Pepys is printed in white letter (or roman typeface), without illustrations, and without a four-stanza "Answer" by the young man's lover. Clearly, one ballad facsimile image does not fit all.

CHAPTER 4

1 On Cox, see Spufford, *Small Books*, 143; the provenance of the Huth and Britwell ballads (the latter also referred to as the Heber ballads) is nicely hand diagrammed on a page accompanying the Huth collection at the Huntington Library, HEH 18262–18348 (reproduced on the EBBA website, ebba.english.ucsb.edu/page/provenance).

2 As Alexandra Franklin, project coordinator of the Centre for the Study of the Book at the Bodleian Library, noted to me in an email, one needs to be

cautious about attribution of named collections. The Ashmole ballads are, in fact, mostly political white-letter broadside ballads. However, other collectors than Ashmole were contributors to what the Bodleian today names the Ashmole collection. As the library's website observes, "Ashmole 1549–1836 and Ashmole A-H are accessions to Ashmole's original collection from the libraries of John Aubrey (1626–97), Edward Lhuyd (1660–1709), and Martin Lister (1638–1712), and from the university chemical library founded in 1683"; https://tinyurl.com/y9cds53q accessed June 9, 2020.

3 See McShane-Jones (later McShane), "'Rime and Reason,'" as well as, under McShane, her *Political Broadside Ballads*.

4 Dugaw, "Popular Market of 'Old Ballads,'" 83. The Roxburghe collection includes many such slip songs. See, for example, "The Colliers Rant" and "The Coaly Tyne," Roxburghe 3.352 (EBBA 31066) and Roxburghe 3.369 (EBBA 31079), respectively.

5 Though tune titles reappeared in many instances in the eighteenth century, they entirely fell off the ballad song sheets of the nineteenth century, which were typically larger than a slip but still small, like a large postcard.

6 Sidney Lee speculates that Philips was perhaps the compiler in his Dictionary of National Biography entry (last paragraph, after list of known works): https://en.wikisource.org/wiki/Philips_Ambrose_(DNB).

7 Ambrose, *A Collection of Old Ballads*, I: iii.

8 Cited by Brown, "Child's Ballads," 67.

9 These four manuscript ballads represent a bit of an exaggeration by Pepys, made under "My Collection of Ballads," that, in compiling his collection, he added "*many* Pieces elder thereto in Time," meaning earlier than the first half of the seventeenth century (my emphasis).

10 On ballad sheet paper and sizes, see Gerald Egan and Eric Nebeker, "Other Common Papers."

11 *Bibliotheca Lindesiana*, 1:xi.

12 See "Introduction," *Bibliotheca Pepysiana*, i–xix, which includes the two codicils Pepys made to his will, on May 12 and May 13, 1703, detailing what the finished library should look like, where it should be placed, what it should be named ("*Bibliotheca Pepysiana*"), and how it may be used (vii–x); reference to Pepys's use of lifts or "stilts" to raise books to make them even in height is on page xvi. See also "Introduction" to *Facsimile of Pepys's Catalogue*, ed. McKitterick, in *Catalogue of the Pepys Library*, 7:xi–xxxv.

13 August 12, 1689, in *Evelyn*, ed. Bray, 3:447–48.

14 Only in Pepys's last catalog of 1700 did the dismembered volumes of his life come together as a "set" on the same shelf; Pepys, *Diary of Samuel Pepys*, ed. Latham and Matthews, 1.lxviii.

15 On the problematics of Pepys's table of contents, see Fumerton, "Digitizing Ephemera and Its Discontents," 67–70.

16 The one notable exception to this seventeenth-century practice of collecting by physically dismembering or cutting apart ballads and then rearranging their constituent parts can be found in the practices of Anthony Wood. Wood preserved his broadside ballads as an assemblage of whole artifacts. Instead of cutting them apart, he folded the sheets in half and placed them in select piles with the intent of having them stitched together into volumes backed by plain cardboard (inevitable trimming of the edges of the ballads nevertheless occurred in the course of their binding). This "holistic" practice by Wood, however, likely reflects not so much a different attitude toward the ballad artifact from that of his contemporaries than Wood's lack of funds, which may well have prohibited him from purchasing additional paper onto which he could paste his ballads as well as from paying for them to be bound into albums. Certainly, in other ways, Wood contributed a collage-like character to his collecting, most notably by his inserting his own fragments into the printed artifacts, as I shall further discuss in Chapter 5. A preview: I refer to his frequently doodling on broadsides, as exemplified in his drawing the head of a hog-faced woman in the margins of the ballad he owned about just such a hog-faced "wonder," Tannakin Skinker—as if he were inserting another woodcut *and himself* into the ballad; see Gniady, "Hog-Faced Woman," 91–108. Wood also added handwritten commentaries in the margins of his ballad sheets, identifying persons, places, and events mentioned in the texts, as if personally assuming the production role of a printer providing explanatory glosses.

17 The holding library—in this instance, the British Library—at some point rebound this Bagford volume. But there is no reason to believe that the library, or other institutions that frequently bound or rebound acquisitions over time, did not observe the "original" ordering of the bound ballads as acquired, especially those belonging to a named collection. However, on rebinding this Bagford volume, a British Library conservationist *did* introduce a change in the original format, as is clear when we compare the newly bound version to an STC microfilm image of the volume before it was rebound: instead of pasting the two halves of the cut-apart ballads at the same height on facing album pages, she or he consistently positioned the ballad half on the recto page lower than the half on the verso. Also of note: the ballad whole and its ordering of cut-apart halves might not have been foremost on Bagford's mind but rather its typeface. Bagford's three-volume collection of ballads, like his collections of fragments of title pages torn from books, was part of his effort to assemble materials in preparation for writing a history of print, including

demonstrating changes in typeface and woodcuts; McC. Gatch, "John Bagford," 169. We will discuss this ultimately failed project and Bagford's collecting practices more fully in the next chapter.

18 For a detailed explanation of the provenance of the Roxburghe collection, see ebba.english.ucsb.edu/page/provenance, accessed May 6, 2018.

19 See "John Johnson Collection of Printed Ephemera," Bodleian Libraries, University of Oxford, www.bodleian.ox.ac.uk/johnson/about, accessed September 29, 2015. The exception to this rule by later collectors that I have so far encountered is a small collection of some thirty-five ballads mostly from the eighteenth century, though many boast seventeenth-century woodcut illustrations, made by the humanist artist-scholar William Hazlitt. Maddeningly, Hazlitt not only cuts two-part ballads in half but also pastes the second part of the ballad not on the facing page but on the following recto page of his album, creating the mistaken impression that each is a different ballad. But this mode of eighteenth-century collecting is the proverbial exception that proves the rule.

CHAPTER 5

1 Richard Luckett, in an interview with me, July 10, 2007.

2 Handwritten title page to Pepys's "My Calligraphical Collection," vol. 1 (of three volumes), dated 1700, in *Catalogue of the Pepys Library at Magdalene College Cambridge, Vol. IV: Music, Maps, and Calligraphy*, p. 1 of Calligraphy catalog (each catalog section of the volume is independently paginated); hereafter cited as *Calligraphy*. Note: this work is a catalogue not a reproduction of the collection, though it does reproduce some pages. For more discussion of the features of the collection, see also Heal, *English Writing-Masters*, xi–xii.

3 Morison, "Development of Hand-Writing," xxxiii.

4 And inseparable from the scriptive order of power, Goldberg would add (*Writing Matter*, 59–60).

5 Pepys's claim is only a bit of an exaggeration, since the oldest manuscript fragment is from about the eighth century. Though many of Pepys's manuscript fragments are quite old, however, his selection of copybooks is relatively recent. It consists of pages from one old wooden hand-carved book (dated by Pepys to 1590), and then ranges in order from a copybook of John Davis of Hereford, *Writing Schoolemaster* (dated in Pepys's index as 1616, but actually published 1663), to Robert More's *Writing Master's Assistant* (published 1696). The placement of the pages from More's book, appearing last in the collection, contradicts Pepys's table of contents, where he correctly lists his latest instance of copybooks as Robert Ayres's fifth copybook, *Accomplish'd*

Clerk Regraved (1700). For some reason, though, in the practical course of assembling or reassembling his collection, Pepys changed the order of the collected books and placed Ayres's 1700 edition eight slots before the last set of copybooks included in his collection—those of More—whereas it should have been placed last according to its publication date and Pepys's table of contents. Chronology, like aesthetic form, could prove a bugbear for Pepys's highly organized mind.

6 Significantly, Ayres's "To the Reader" is followed by a preface written by his engraver, John Sturt, wherein Sturt affirms "*[I] Received the greatest part of my Skill in Engraving of Letters*" from "*the Instructions which the Author afforded me*" and, furthermore, "*I cannot after all pretend to Engrave a Correct piece of Writing so well as the Original Copy.*" However, he also tactically, as if in an afterthought, inserts a subtle tribute to engravers as a separate creative body, noting that when not dealing with writing masters, "*the Engraver who understands Letters, may and does often play the Bone-setters part, when he has more skill in Writing than the Person that Imploys him.*" The relationship between "author" of the script and the "engraver" onto the copperplate was an uneasy one.

7 I am grateful to Elizabeth Heckendorn Cook for pointing out this phenomenon to me.

8 As we have seen even in broadside ballads, black-letter type morphed haltingly into white-letter or roman type in England. The pressure for change came first from the Italian humanists, who promoted the more classical look of both roman and italic. Indeed, with such humanist thinking solidly in place, by the end of the seventeenth century the native English "hands" of *batarde* (or bastard) and secretary script, as well as the typeface of black letter, were together referred to negatively as barbarous and Gothic; Dawson and Kennedy-Skipton, *Elizabethan Handwriting*, 11. Varieties of the italic hand dominate the many writing styles exhibited on the pages of the copybooks of Pepys's calligraphy collection. But the hand that would win out by the mid-eighteenth century was not "Italian" but a hybrid English, frequently referred to as the common "round" hand and most associated not with humanist arts but with English and international business or mercantilism. Note that Ayres's *Tutor to Penmanship* includes the subtitle "Shewing all the Variety of Penmanship and *Clerkship* as now practised in England" (my emphasis). In his address, "For the Lovers of Writing," prefatory to the first part of this copybook, Ayres also stresses that the book is expanded and full of varied "*Round-hands*" (my emphasis). The "winning" English round hand has raised little enthusiasm by paleologists, however: Morison, for instance, describes it as a very clean but "dull" kind of writing, especially designed for use by "clerks" in commerce and business ("Development of Hand-Writing," xxvi and throughout).

9 Egan, "Black Letter and the Broadside Ballad." Caxton's initial typefaces, while still conveying an effect of blackness on the page, more closely resembled the script "Anglicana"; but after trying out variations on this typeface, he (and other English printers following suit), post-1500, soon settled on black letter. For a comparison of the two typefaces in variant editions of the same text, see Coldiron, *Printers Without Borders*, 265 (the first passage is set in Anglicana, by Caxton c. 1477, and the second in black letter, by Wynkyn de Worde, 1510). Thanks to Leah S. Marcus for many insightful conversations about the humanist-connected emergence of these scripts/typefaces, as well as about the complicated interrelationship between and evolution of the two.

10 Lotte Hellinga conjectures more generally that "the sense of style in vernacular printing may well primarily have its roots in awareness of linguistic identity, after the Reformation mainly following the lines of the religious divide. The romance-language countries—the first among them being Italy in the 1490s, followed by France from the 1520s—adopted roman type for general use, whether Latin or vernacular. The countries with roots in the Germanic languages adopted either variations on the black-letter for their vernacular printing, or went down the route of the 'schwabacher' styles, as in the German-speaking countries"; "Printing," 3.76.

11 The typeface was also popular and long-lived in Germany (where it became known as "*fraktur*"), despite the English identifying black letter primarily with their own nation (Bain and Shaw, *Blackletter: Type and National Identity*).

12 Updike, *Printing Types*, 2.266. On "English English," see Morison, *John Fell*, 115. Another name for a specific size of black letter was "Pica English," Morison, 114.

13 Morison, "Introduction of Handwriting," xxiv note †.

14 The arguments on both sides are summarized by Egan, "Black Letter and the Broadside Ballad."

15 Lesser also observes that most grammar books (created for more advanced learning skills) tended to be "bilingual," by which he means that typically "these editions used roman (or italic) type for their Latin and black letter for their English translations and instructions"; Lesser, "Typographic Nostalgia," 104. However, in defense of Mish and Thomas, we must observe that they are not aiming as high as grammar books. Rather, they are concerned with the earliest stage of elementary education, beyond which many a child did not proceed. At this very early stage of education, children were first introduced to reading via hornbooks and primers, and both kinds of texts were typically printed in black letter up to the 1650s and even beyond.

16 Goldberg makes the same argument about handwriting, which he argues is not only expressive of subjectivity (and multiple subjectivities through copybooks) but also the grounds for literacy and, most importantly—depending on

the place, kinds, and ways script was taught—was key to limiting or advancing a subject's class and political power; in this elitist civilizing process, italic script was paramount (*Writing Matter*, esp. 41–54).

17 Most of my information on hornbooks draws on Tuer's extensive treatment of the subject, *Horn-Book*, 303. Tuer provides an excellent example of a leather hornbook, clearly made for the more well-to-do, showing Charles II on the back, with the typeface on the front in roman (Image #131, p. 304). There are other extant tailor-made ornamented hornbooks, with leather backings. Most depict the Restoration king on the back but often, instead, Saint George slaying the dragon (see, for example, Image #137, p. 313). The more simple, undecorated and thus cheaper hornbooks were less likely to survive (as with broadside ballads); both were meant for the masses.

18 Clearly the painter took the liberty of only showing the uppercase letters on the hornbook, likely because that was as much readable text that he could fit onto his rendering of such a small artifact. He thus conveys the semblance, not the actual reality, of Miss Campion's hornbook—but still a semblance that foregrounds the hornbook's black lettering and the personal, intimate connection of the artifact to the student who grasps it.

19 On the active physicality of the ballad's orality, see especially Bruce R. Smith, *Acoustic World*, 168–205. On the ballad and the bodily movements of dance, see Smith, *Acoustic World*, 133–67. Smith notes that the physicality of dancing—the muscles and neurons dancing triggered—would have remained vestigial in balladry into the seventeenth century when the visual gained prominence; see his "Putting the 'Ball' Back in Ballads."

20 Another edition of this ballad can be found in Roxburghe 3.176–177 (EBBA 30474), though the image in this instance is badly mis-inked, obscuring the husband's head. In a different ballad, the woodcut has broken in half or been deliberately cut in half, and we see only the right side of the original—the horned man pointing to the hornbook he holds up (Pepys Ballads 4.133, EBBA 21797). The cuckolded man alone appears to have been popular because we see him in an impression that is clearly a re-carving of this Pepys version: Roxburghe 2.225 (EBBA 30686). Here it should be noted, however, that the collector has so tightly trimmed the right side of the ballad that the husband's hornbook cannot be seen (so we cannot be sure if it ever made it into the re-carving). But the entire original woodcut seems also to have been popular, if also subject to change. We see its late appearance, full of wormholes, showing again the aggressive wife (with wielded stick and accusatory finger), but the husband is now missing both of his cuckold's horns—or rather, their tips—and his hornbook. The tips of the horns and the hornbook have either worn off or been cut off by the printer. Since the four extant ballads in

EBBA, which sport this old woodcut impression, are all versions of the ballad "Advice to Batchelors, Or, The Married Man's Lamentation," c. 1685 (EBBA 21767, 30108, 30884, and 35674), it would seem that the original features of a cuckold's horns and schooling indicated by a hornbook would fit the married man's lamentation. I thus posit that in this case the cutting away of the tips of the horns and the entire hornbook were likely done to trim off areas already badly degraded.

21 I am grateful to Peter Stallybrass for pointing out to me this fascinating etymology of the word *manuscript*. I share his argument that printing, in what might look like a break from manuscript culture, rather made that which was handwritten of more interest; see his "'Little Jobs.'" Of course, the English did not "invent" the naming of manuscripts; the noun "manuscriptum" was used in post-classical Latin (*OED*).

22 Luckett, "Introduction" to *Calligraphy*, v–vi. On Pepys's befriending of Wanley through Charlett and Bagford's providing Pepys with not only ballads but also manuscript and printed fragments, see Luckett, "The Collection: Origins and History," in *Catalogue of the Pepys Library, Vol. II: Ballads, Part ii: Indexes*, comp. Weinstein, xv–xvi. See also Gatch, "John Bagford as a Collector."

23 Luckett, "Introduction," *Calligraphy*, v; Wanley, as Luckett notes, mentions his calligraphic collection plan to Pepys's nephew, John Jackson, in 1701.

24 Gatch, "John Bagford, Bookseller," 153, and, for a full description of Bagford's print history scheme, 158–64. Gatch lists the subscribers to Bagford's history of print project in "John Bagford as a Collector," 99–100.

25 Both are versions of the same elegy about two faithful lovers and are to be sung, we are instructed on the sheets, to the tune "Franklin is fled away" (EBBA 20700 and 30791).

26 Gatch, "John Bagford as a Collector," 100. For a facsimile of Bull's transcription and of his letter to Pepys, see EBBA 31607 and 31608 (Pepys Ballads 1.23 and 1.24–25), respectively, with Bull's letter at the end of the latter.

27 Luckett, "The Collection," xvi. For Hewer and Allen, see *Diary of Samuel Pepys* (June 16, 1668) and II:77–78 (April 11, 1661); citations to Pepys's printed Diary will hereafter appear in the body of this chapter by volume and page, separated by a period, as is the practice in EBBA for volume and pages of broadside ballad collections.

28 Wright and Wright, eds., *Humphrey Wanley*, 1.xv. The editors attribute Wanley's interest in printing largely to his early friendship with Bagford, xvii, xxv. See also Luckett, "The Collection," xvii–xviii.

29 Luckett, "The Collection"; Tanner, *Private Correspondence*, I:167.

CHAPTER 6

1 "Whassup?" Wikipedia, https://en.wikipedia.org/wiki/Whassup%3F, accessed October 21, 2014. Budweiser 2000 Super Bowl Commercial-Whassup, www.dailymotion.com/video/xx7559_budweiser-2000-superbowl-commercial-whassup_fun, accessed November 3, 2016.

2 Budweiser True a Whassup Girl Invasion 2001, www.youtube.com/watch?v=gACEOxsSckE, accessed July 10, 2019.

3 Whassup Barack Obama 2008 Presidential Campaign-Whassup, www.youtube.com/watch?v=vRu_YLhoR4k, accessed November 4, 2014.

4 All citations to Pepys's Diary, unless otherwise indicated, will be to the published edition, *The Diary of Samuel Pepys*, ed. Latham and Matthews, 11 vols., and will appear cited hereafter as *Diary* and noted by volume and pages separated by a period (as is EBBA's practice with multivolume ballad collections). Note that Pepys used the Old-Style Julian calendar (retained in Britain until 1752) versus the New-Style Gregorian calendar, adopted by most countries in 1582. This makes his dating in the *Diary* ten days behind those of the rest of Western Europe, and us today (*Diary*, 1.cli–clii).

5 Many "Medleys" are archived in EBBA. For example, "An excellent Medley" (EBBA 31769, 30803, 33325, 35167, and 22005); "A New Merry Medley" (EBBA 22325 and 22322); "A New made Medly Compos'd out of Sundry Songs" (EBBA 22333); "An excellent new Medley" (EBBA 20031 and 30589); and "The New Compos'd Medly" (EBBA 22033).

6 I show in Figure 32 the Crawford edition of the ballad, Crawford.EB.323 (EBBA 32895), and also cite from the Crawford copy—another copy of the same edition as the Pepys—because the Pepys artifact is missing some of the left-side of its first column of verse, due to what looks like over handling combined with too tight trimming of the ballad.

7 "Mars and Venus: Or, The Amorous Combatants," c. 1681–84, EBBA 21248, Pepys Ballads 3.234; Crawford and Houghton collections, EBBA 32644 and 35324, respectively. I quote from the Crawford edition because again the Pepys copy has suffered dismemberment: in this case *both* its far left and far right columns of verse have been partly cut off through too tight trimming.

8 See "The Lovers Battle," c. 1664–88, in the Crawford, Roxburghe, and Huth collections, the last at the Houghton library; EBBA 32830, 30754, and 34469, respectively; citation from Crawford.

9 Noted by Ebsworth, who took over as editor of the last 5 of the 8 volumes of *The Roxburghe Ballads* after Chappell's death. The edited collection (which includes an abundance of later commentary by Ebsworth) is always referenced

in italics. It should not be confused with the unpublished Roxburghe ballad collection; I always cite Roxburghe ballads directly from that original source as archived in EBBA.

10 Palmer notes that the clothes worn are late Jacobean: the man's are c. 1620, somewhat later than the woman's (c. 1615). "The date clues," she observes, "are his unstarched ruff and chin-length hair, and her open-lace collar, with hair swept upward and decorated with a jewel and feather." The image of the woman, she pointedly adds, particularly resembles pictures of Elizabeth of Bohemia. For a wedding portrait of Frederick and Elizabeth, see www.pinterest.com/pin/330803535104021192/; and simply pictured as a couple, www.pinterest.com/pin/330803535104021186/, both accessed November 3, 2016.

11 Pepys never outright condemns Roger for his Puritan views, which a part of him clearly admires, but one can sometimes hear the tone of disapproval or sadness over Roger's taking such a "high" stance against court cavaliers. On June 23, 1665, Pepys three times calls Roger "high": "Roger . . . I perceive is a deadly *high* man in the parliament business, and against the Court . . . he is so *high* that he says he [speaking of Sir J. Winter, who had a timber grant that was bitterly resented by the local commoners] deserves to be hanged, and all the *high* words he could give; which I was sorry to see, though I am confident he means well" (4.193; my emphases). Affirming his self-important loftiness, cousin Roger on January 17, 1667 asks to see Charles II's mistress, Lady Castlemaine, at court, but though he "approves [her] to be very handsome," he "wonders that she cannot be as good within as she is fair without." Perhaps most disturbing is Roger's reaction to the casual cursing of Lady Castlemaine's black servant. "Her little black boy came by him; and a dog being in his way, the little boy called to the dog: 'Pox of this dog!' 'Now, says he [Roger], blessing himself, would I whip this child till the blood came if it were my child." Pepys's somewhat neutral, but also a tad critical, response: "and I believe he would" (8.32–33).

12 Rollins, *Analytical Index*. Chappell, in *Popular Music*, provides notation for the tune, 2.538. But as James Revell Carr warns, in his essay "Recording Early Broadside Ballads," though Chappell's work is extensive and thoroughly researched, he often draws on late versions of tunes and "instead of faithfully reprinting melodies from his sources, he arranged the tunes for piano, adding harmonies and altering modes to suit nineteenth-century tastes," ebba.english.ucsb.edu/page/recording-the-ballads#Simpson.

13 EBBA holds four copies of the ballad I cite, all with the same title, publishers, and rough print date of c. 1675-96 (EBBA 35105—Figure 34—30145, 33316, and 35255). It also holds two later editions, both likely from the mid-eighteenth century; each displays illustrations from different woodcuts, but those variant cuts still predominantly feature women (EBBA 31288 and 34580).

14 Unfortunately, Gyford used as his copy for his archive the flawed 1883–86 edition of the *Diary*, produced by Henry Benjamin Wheatley rather than the far superior and now authoritative one produced by Latham and Matthews first printed in 1971, which I quote throughout.

15 For the full Parker play, see www.archive.org/details/mavourneen-comedy00parkrich/page/n6/mode/2up; Blog entry or annotation by Terry Foreman, January 6, 2009, pepysdiary.com/diary/1666/01/06/#annotations.

16 The Stevenson text may be found at www.fullbooks.com/Familiar-Studies-of-Men--Books.html; the cited paragraph is from Part 4, "Chapter VIII—Samuel Pepys," and under that chapter's sub-section "The Diary." This connection to Stevenson was made in an annotation by Foreman in the Gyford blog about the same incident above, but it is dated January 7, 2009 and made visually prominent by Gyford, www.pepysdiary.com/diary/1666/01/06/#c271595.

CHAPTER 7

1 Though the exact title of the ballad is not named by Pepys, it could be any of the hundreds, if not thousands, of such anti-Rump ballads that were being disseminated in dizzying numbers, especially on the brink of and after the Restoration, 1559–1661; these politically partisan songs were printed singly as broadsides and in collections such as *The Rump* [ed. Brome] (1660).

2 Pepys chronicles the spontaneous rejoicing in London on hearing the news, declaring "it was past imagination, both the greatness and suddenness of it"; *Diary* 1.52. For a concise summary of the swiftly moving political events of October 1659 through the end of December 1659, at which point Pepys begins his *Diary*; see "Preliminary Note," *Diary*, 1.cliv. Especially attuned to the political uncertainty affecting everyone's lives at this moment in time is Tomalin, *Samuel Pepys*, 94–101.

3 *A Handefull of Pleasant Delites* was originally printed in 1566, but no copy of that edition has survived. In the 1584 version, of which only one faulty edition exists (at the British Library), Jones attributes authorship of the miscellany to Clement Robinson "and divers others." In his introduction to a modern edition of the collection, Rollins conjectures that the 1584 printing expanded upon the original 1566 text with the addition of such ballads as "Greensleeves"; see Rollins, ed., *A Handful of Pleasant Delights (1584), by Clement Robinson and Divers Others*. Each ballad in this modern edition is individually dated by Rollins in the table of contents.

4 My summary that follows of the early (and protean) history of the "Greensleeves" melody is much indebted to Simpson's extensive discussion of the tune (268–78).

5 Simpson posits that, in the ballad's first registration, "a forehanded ballad maker had anticipated public demand by writing both pieces before either was published" (269). But it could well have been the case that "Greensleeves" ballads, like so many other ballads of the period, had been for some time circulating orally and in print under the radar of the Stationers' Company, and had gathered so much momentum by 1580 that printers/publishers quickly tried to seize ownership of *their* version of the ballad through registration, even to the extent that two different publishers registered competing versions of a "Greensleeves" ballad on the very same day.

6 Though renamed a "courtly sonet" by Jones, likely in an effort to elevate the song, the printed text is in a common ballad measure of four stresses per line. See the appropriation of the newly imported sonnets of Surrey and Wyatt first by way of a more familiar ballad measure to make them more saleable in England, evident in their rewriting in *Tottel's Miscellany*; Nebeker, "Broadside Ballads," 989–1013. Once sonnets were accepted and even privileged, promoters of the lowly broadside ballad fought fire with fire by often naming ballads "sonnets"—trying to reclaim some of the fame and popularity sonnets originally stole from them.

7 Fostering the association of the earliest extant "Greensleeves" with the court is the much-cited, but unsubstantiated, theory that Henry VIII composed the ballad to woo his "kept" mistress Anne Boleyn; see, for example, www.thetudors.org.uk/greensleeves.htm, accessed December 17, 2012.

8 In William Ballet's manuscript lute book, p. 104, Trinity College, Dublin, IE TCD MS40.

9 I should add that, in both variants of the tune, high notes toward the end of the melody lend themselves to greater rhetorical strength. Also, the initial F in the second line of music in the shorter, Dorian version ("sing" in the first stanza of the recording transcribed above) has about the same amount of musical metric emphasis as it does in the longer minor variant. Furthermore, its phenomenal accent is weaker, not stronger, since the note is approached from a far shorter distance (a high D to F motion, up only a minor third in Simpson's transcription of the shorter Dorian variant; whereas the movement is a low D to a high F, a minor-tenth leap, in the longer minor variant). However, the singular use of the high note in the shorter, Dorian version, as opposed to its double-use in the longer version (where it begins both the first and third lines of that version's refrain) gives the melody greater rhetorical strength of the type suited to the kind of blunt political statements being made in "The Re-Resurrection of the Rump." By comparison, the double leap up to the high note of the original "Greensleeves" creates the sense of whining lamentation.

10 Lord William Brouncker, 2nd Viscount and host of the party, was himself Navy Commissioner (10.46–47).

11 Registered December 30, 1664; Rollins, *Analytical Index*, 170. The text I cite is from *Wit and Mirth* (London, 1714), available online at rpo.library.utoronto.ca/poems/song-written-sea, accessed December 18, 2012. The note I cite in parenthesis above to the Pepys Diary, which pointed me to Dorset as author, identifies Sackville by the honorary title received before becoming the Earl of Dorset—Lord Buckhurst; it also incorrectly substitutes "London" for "Land" in the ballad's title as it was registered.

12 The commonplace book belonged to the Shann family of Methley, County York, and is mainly in the hand of Richard Shann (1561–1627); Add MS 38599, fol. 140v, British Library.

13 The full title is "A most excellent Song of the love of young Palmus, and faire *Sheldra*, with their unfortunate Love. To the tune of Shackley-hay," Pepys Ballads 1.350–351 (c. 1630), EBBA 20163; a textually close but variant later version, also with a different woodcut is Pepys Ballads 1.478–79 (c. 1684–86), EBBA 20224. Both editions were published by I.W., likely James White I. White published yet another variant of the early Pepys copy in Roxburghe 1.436–437 (EBBA 30295), wherein the ballad's woodcut is more simply redrawn and reversed. The dating of the Roxburghe ballad cannot be narrowed down further than the dates White was active as publisher, 1602-46. But given that the woodcut of the early Pepys ballad shows signs of age—wormholes on the bottom-left of the lady's dress and worn or broken-off parts of the cut's border—White (or his printer) likely had the woodcut in Pepys's early edition roughly traced and recut for the Roxburghe edition, which places the Roxburghe ballad on the late side of White's publishing spectrum.

14 Add MS 38599, fol. 140v, British Library.

15 Like Simpson, in creating his modern transcription of the manuscript, Bell has halved the original notes for easier reading. But, unlike Simpson, he does not raise the key by a fifth, which Simpson apparently did to fit the notes more easily on the treble clef. Instead, Bell writes the tune an octave higher, while lowering the entire clef by an octave, as indicated by the number 8 written underneath each treble clef. He is thus able to preserve both original key and pitch level.

16 "Shackley Hay" has a wider range than "Greensleeves" (an octave and a fifth, or a twelfth, versus "Greensleeves's" octave and minor third, or a tenth), but this wider range is not particularly demanding.

17 Satire was well-liked by the court of Charles II and particularly characteristic of Sackville's writings.

18 There is a repeat sign, indicated by the two vertical lines together with two vertical dots in front of them, at the end of the second line of the music transcription from the original manuscript (actually placed as the first notation at the beginning of the third line). This sign indicates to the singer that he or she should repeat everything again starting with the last note of measure 8; this feature of the tune will be discussed further below.

19 Still the implications in the subtle tension here compounds the evident problem in the ballad, as we shall further pursue below: the main trouble these noblemen at sea face is that they are brain-less.

20 Depending on whether an author writes out the refrain of "fa, la la, fa, la la la la" twice in the stanza or just once, the notation above would need to be adjusted accordingly. The longer stanza also consists of ten lines, not seven, because it includes an additional two lines of poetry as well as echoing the refrain. You can hear this longer version sung by James Revell Carr on **Track 28** of the Audio Companion to the Roxburghe edition of the "Palmus and Sheldra" ballad (Pepys Ballads 1.350-351, c. 1630; EBBA 20163). Notice how Carr must observe the original notation's repeat signs, singing again the last six measures of music, with variation to accommodate the repeated refrain (lines 8–10). The Pepys refrain is also slightly different from the "Shackley Hay" shorter version: "fa, la la, fa, la la la la" is rendered more often "With a fa, la, la, la, la!"

21 Both Prior and Johnson assume the ballad was written in 1665 because of the "Foggy Opdam" reference (Lieutenant-Admiral Jacob van Wassenaer Obdam was commander of the Dutch fleet at the Battle of Lowestoft, June 13, 1665, in which action he died); see Prior, dedication, *Poems*, A3v, and Johnson, entry on Dorset in *Prefaces*, 4.4–5 (the entry for each historical figure is numbered separately in each of Johnson's volumes). But, as Ault points out, "it is now generally supposed that Dorset [that is, Sackville] wrote it [the ballad] while serving under the Duke of York in his first cruise in November 1664; when the Dutch avoided an action by retiring into port; and not, as Prior says on 'the night before the engagement' with the Dutch, in June 1665"; *Seventeenth Century Lyrics*, note entered on p. 438 for p. 335. Ault provides the earliest manuscript version of the ballad in his edition (though it is missing the refrain), 334–35.

22 There are other Luttrell collections—many duplicating other holdings—at libraries across the United States as well, such as at the Folger, Huntington, and Clark libraries. But only the British Library binds the Luttrell ballads together among the other items in Luttrell's collection and prints that volume with the title "Ballads" on the binding (Luttrell also collected many other kinds of single sheet and prose as well as many proclamations and pamphlets—all mostly political).

23 It could have been that, as in the case of the "Albemarle" ballad, where the notation actually fits the song text, such printed music functions to lure into the ballad market those higher sorts who prided themselves on being able to read music notation and, as such, could show off their skills; conversation with Erik Bell, February 25, 2016. As always, I am indebted to Bell for his musical expertise and insights.

24 Some later versions of "St. George and the Dragon" are to an alternate tune, "When Flying Fame" (often simply printed on the sheet "Flying Fame"). But "St. George for England" was the more well-known tune to the "St. George" ballads. It should also be noted that there is an entirely different "St. George" broadside ballad, with variants, that tells the story of the hero's battle with a dragon to rescue the king of Egypt's daughter and, after his victory, his marriage to her. But this ballad goes by a longer title, indicating its narrative subject—for example, "[A m]ost Excellent Ballad of St. George for England, and the Kings Daugh-[ter of] Aegypt, whom he delivered from death; and how he slew a Mighty Dragon," c. 1658–64 (Euing Ballads 222, EBBA 31713). Versions of this variant of the "St. George for England" ballads are in a different meter and sung to the tune "Queen Dido" (Simpson, 628).

25 Subtle differences exist between early modern and modern musical practice of notation, which include, for instance, the earlier composers not separating the pickup note, the first note, from the rest of the measure at the beginning of the notation. This throws off the subsequent measures of notation by a half-note beat—at least when viewed from the modern perspective. If the bars are not as significant to contemporaries of the seventeenth century in indicating phrases of music in relation to the meter or lines of the poetry, there would be no perceived problem; the notes themselves are correct for the song text. Unlike Simpson, in his modernized transcription (630), Bell here does not rebar the music to account for the pickup note at the beginning. Also, whereas Simpson effectively halves measure 13 of the original notation (immediately preceding the chorus) to better fit his own rebarring of the tune, Bell maintains the total number of note lengths in the stanza. His transcription, which is also a transcription of the sung text to the melody, as we shall further discuss, thus highlights the difference between expected and actual musical accents as well as the necessity for the singer to make tactical adjustments in fitting together text and tune.

26 The printer's tactic of making two cuts look as if they are one is a common but tricky printing practice. It's hard at first to make out that the image consists of two cuts, not one. On close inspection, the lines of grass at the bottom of each woodcut are the giveaway, in that they don't match up. In the same area, one can most clearly see the white space of a line indicating that they are separate

woodcuts simply placed very close together to look as one. In fact, I've found, the cuts often make appearances singly on other ballad sheets.

CHAPTER 8

1 The ballad registered in 1569/70 by Richard Jones, alas, is no longer extant, and, of course, we cannot thus be sure that this edition of Jones was ever printed (printers and publishers, as previously noted, would sometimes license a ballad title in order to stake a claim on the work's possible publication). The item's title also does not name the artifact specifically as a ballad. It was registered under the naming, "A strange petyfull novell [meaning new] Dyscoursynge of a noble Lorde and his lady with thayre tregicall ende of them and thayre ij cheldren executed by a blacke morryon"; Rollins, *Analytical Index*, I, entry 2542, p. 220. But Jones paid the licensing fee of four pence, which was the typical fee for registering broadsides at the time. Furthermore, Rollins, the foremost authority on broadside ballads of the early to mid-twentieth century, adds an asterisk to its title in his *Index* to indicate, he clarifies in his introduction, "that I know positively that a ballad was meant" (Rollins, "Introduction," *Analytical Index*, 2).

In addition to the extraordinary number of extant copies in broadside ballad form, there are also at least two editions in three copies of the ballad story in prose form. These were chapbooks, or cheap booklets, typically of sixteen or eight pages (our three extant blackamoor chapbooks are each eight pages).

Of important note: most extant copies of ballads are late editions. But this is by no means evidence that editions did not circulate earlier. Indeed, it was not uncommon for extant late printings to have circulated a century or more prior to other survivors, according to contemporary references. The early copies likely did not survive either because they were considered disposable and recyclable, like our modern newspaper, or because they were used up by popular demand (worn to pieces in being passed around or pasted up on walls that then were whitewashed over). Not until the fad of antiquarianism, beginning in the late seventeenth century but peaking in the eighteenth and nineteenth centuries, were these ephemera valued and preserved as records of the past.

2 Charlotte Artese tracks an old folk story, "The Revenge of the Castrated Man," in its various manifestations through the centuries, beginning with its earliest origins in Arabic, where castration is the punishment inflicted on a Moor for being caught having sex with the lord's wife. In this story, the Moor later takes revenge by threatening to throw the lord's two sons off a high tower unless the lord castrates himself, which he does, but to no avail—the children are still thrown to their death, though the lord survives. Thanks to Artese for

first calling my attention to the long history of this folk story in her paper at the 2010 Shakespeare Association of America (SAA). See her published work on this folktale in her book chapter, where she argues that it bears on Shakespeare's *Titus Andronicus (Shakespeare's Folktale Sources*, 51–78).

3 The section of the woodcut representing the prone noseless lord could have broken or worn off the woodcut, or most likely a combination of both—partly broken off and partly badly worn down—so that the printer simply cut out the remainder of the figure entirely.

4 In Drexel MS 5612, 18, written for virginal, New York Public Library; transcription from Margaret Glyn, Orlando Gibbons, 1583–1626, vol 2, p. 20, no. 11. In C major and 3/4 meter.

5 *OED*, blackamoor, n. Significantly, though the *OED* is consistent, many variations can be heard in the way the word is pronounced on the web, with emphases falling on either the first or last syllable or on both. See www.howtopronounce.com/blackamoor/, accessed April 26, 2019.

6 Griffiths's and Molineux's recent research calls into question Kathleen Chater's argument (*Untold Histories*) for the multitude of free or freed Africans and certainly a significant number of blacks of any social standing among Londoners, if not among Britons, at least up to the mid-seventeenth century; if there were such an abundance of free Africans, they would most certainly have occupied the lower ranks and thus been susceptible to arrest for vagrancy, which included those who were masterless and mobile as well as disorderly. The many calls today in Britain to recognize that Africans are a part of Britain's heritage have mostly occurred in the form of BBC productions, which often follow the life of one or only a few blacks. See Olusoga, *Black and British*, which accompanied his BBC television series; Kaufman's talks on "Black Tudors," www.mirandakaufmann.com/; and Gerzina's recent BBC4 series, "Britain's Black Past," www.bbc.co.uk/programmes/b07yvszg/episodes/player. Thanks to Sean Creighton for these references. Still, as such personal stories reveal, we are talking of in-depth research into a few individuals rather than a significant sector of the population.

7 The Treason Act of 1351 was extended to Ireland in the fifteenth century and to Scotland in the eighteenth century; it is still in force today; Acts of Parliament of England, 25 Edw. Stat. 5 c. 2; The Official Home of UK Legislation, 1267–Present, www.legislation.gov.uk/aep/Edw3Stat5/25/2/contents, accessed April 1, 2016.

8 See Pories, "Intersection of Poor Laws and Literature," 38, and Woodbridge, *Vagrancy*, 4.

9 On this anthology as being an enterprise promoted by Sir Philip Sidney's "Circle" (consisting of close-knit and like-minded poets in both their experi-

mental verse and their Protestant activism), especially in the anthology's subsequent 1614 edition, and on that Circle's engagement in vernacular pastoral satire, see O'Callaghan, "Textual Gatherings."

10 Euing Ballads 197 and 284, University of Glasgow (EBBA 31955 and 31898); Wood 401(113), Bodleian Library, University of Oxford, Broadside Ballads Online, http://ballads.bodleian.ox.ac.uk/view/sheet/712, Crawford. EB.570, National Library of Scotland or NLS (EBBA 33308), and EB75 P4128C no. 109, Houghton Library, Harvard University (EBBA 34451); Roxburghe 1.220–221, British Library and Crawford.EB.669, NLS (EBBA 30157 and 33307, respectively), and Douce 3(37B), Bodleian Library, University of Oxford, Broadside Ballads Online, ballads.bodleian.ox.ac.uk/search/?query=Douce+3%2837B%29; Pepys Ballads 1.545–547, Pepys Library (EBBA 20261); HEH 289769, Huntington Library, CA (EBBA 32501); HEH 85284, Huntington Library (EBBA 32532) and Johnson 372, Bodleian Library, University of Oxford, Broadside Ballads Online, ballads.bodleian.ox.ac.uk/view/sheet/7703; Roxburghe 3.520–521, British Library, Crawford. EB.671, NLS (EBBA 31227 and 33309, respectively) and Harding B3(40), Bodleian Library, University of Oxford, Broadside Ballads Online, ballads.bodleian.ox.ac.uk/search/?query=Johnson+372.

11 The beginning note for this leap was added by the singer who needed to accommodate the text to the tune by inserting a note at the beginning of the line; the note added, a D, is one of the potentially appropriate choices for such cases and extends the range of the tune from a fourth to a minor seventh.

12 "A memorable Song, made upon the unhappy Hunting in Chevy Chase; between the Earle *Pea[rcy]* /of England, and the Earle *Douglas* of Scotland," c. 1625, EBBA 36103, Blackletter Ballads 2.53, Manchester Central Library, Manchester, UK.

13 According to extant sources, this was the most popular tune in all of Britain and Europe up to the end of the eighteenth century, and certainly the most frequent tune "hit" in EBBA. Christopher Marsh discusses its popularity in England as well as its intertextual association with executions and other subjects, in his essay "'Fortune My Foe,'" 308–30.

14 Unfortunately, Artese, in her chapter on the folktale "The Revenge of the Castrated Man" and *Titus Andronicus*, did not know, at the time of her writing her book, of the strong link of the Titus play to "Isabella's Tragedy" (*Shakespeare's Folktale Sources*, 51–78).

15 A number of scholars have focused on the relations of the Romans and Goths in *Titus* and their intertwining historically in English culture, including Artese; Broude, "Roman and Goth," 27–34; and Royster, "White-Limed Walls," 432–55.

16 As if turning the pattern of abandonment inside out, authorities would also force the separation of poor parents, considered vagrant, from their children, making the latter apprentices with strangers (Fumerton, *Unsettled*, 9–11).

17 Other "aliens" to arrive in England, Griffiths adds, "were put back on ships as soon as possible to go back to their 'owne country,'" 74.

18 This broadside also supports Molineux's observation that there was a growing identification of blackness with political and moral corruption in the last decades of the eighteenth century, which accompanied the emergence of the black working-class Londoner in British society at this time (17). Both happenings were side effects of what I refer to as the gradual incorporation of blacks into the poor lower orders of British life.

19 See also Clegg, "'A Ballad Intituled a Pleasant Newe Jigge,'" 301–22.

CONCLUSION

1 William Shakespeare, *The Winter's Tale*, ed. J. H. P. Pafford, *The Arden Shakespeare*, 3rd ed. (London: Methuen, 1968), 5.2.21, 1 and 8, in order of citation. All future citations to this play are to this edition and will appear in the body of my text. The play was first performed on the Globe stage in 1611 (Pafford, xxi), though Shakespeare could have begun writing it in 1609 (xxiii). It was not published until its apparently hasty addition at the end of the section on "Comedies" in Shakespeare's First Folio, 1623 (xv–xviii).

2 Others have observed that "Rogero" is the title of a ballad tune; for example, Pafford's note to 5.2.21. But such critics have not drawn attention to the fact that the popular tune title is placed in apposition to "news," as if the First Gentleman were asking whether the news fit the ballad tune, "Rogero," and expecting it would (rather than addressing the Second Gentleman by his name).

3 This is not to dismiss allusions in *The Winter's Tale* to oral ballads or folktales, both of which have their own, sometimes coincident, parts to play with broadside ballads. Twice the wondrous news about the behind-the-scenes happenings is described as like an "old tale" (5.2.30, 65). In the statue scene, Paulina also self-derogatorily states that her telling those present that Hermione's statue could come alive "should be hooted at / Like an old tale" (5.3.116–17). Broadside ballads, of course, also related old tales among their expansive repertoire.

4 The most notable exception to the neglect of broadside ballads as a print genre (beyond discussion of the "fake" wonder ballads Autolycus hawks at the sheepshearing feast) is Kitch, "Bastards and Broadsides," 43–71. See also Newcomb, on the uneasy, unresolved conflict between the male impulse to fix print (what she dubs "the monumental") and the hetero impulse in the play to embrace

performativity ("the spectacular"), in "Monumental Bodies," 239–59; as well as Wittek, on news and printed ballads of the period, in *Media Players*, 27–57; and Achinstein, on the embrace of printed ballads by all classes, in "Audiences and Authors," 311–26.

5 Hale is perhaps the most unswerving in his praise of Autolycus as a force throughout the play of "unproblematic and frisky" sexuality and "comic possibility," in his "Autolycus as 'Festive' Presence," 73–74. More typical is Kaula's brief praise of Autolycus that turns into a critique in which the rogue becomes foil to Perdita, Paulina, and the aesthetic of the statue; "Autolycus' Trumpery," 287, 297–303. In the same vein, Mentz argues that "the swindle of Autolycus's ballads becomes a debased reflection of Shakespeare's dramatic art, which sells its audience an idealized 'truth' they pay to see"; "Wearing Greene," 81. Similarly, Wittek affirms that Shakespeare "purposefully sets his own art apart from (and above) balladry" and its "oafish" audience, thus deflecting accusations aligning it with the commercial theater; *Media Players*," 45.

6 Gillespie and Rhodes note that the Homer and Ovid legacy is "one half of a traditional duality," the other half being embodied in Paulina, the "artist-as-moralist"; *Shakespeare and Elizabethan Popular Culture*, 13–14. Another, older strand of literary criticism traces Autolycus's origins "to the medieval vice figure, and more precisely to the hybrid vice-clever servant of the English romantic comedies of the late half of the sixteenth century," as Knowles summarizes in "Autolycus, Cloten, Caliban & Co.," 84. Exceptions to placing Autolycus within a literary tradition mostly focus on him as a figure produced by and promoting a kind of lawless and amoral economics; see, for example, Correll, "Scene Stealers," 53–65. On Autolycus and Greene's con-artist pamphlets, including the character of the roguish Greene himself, see especially Mentz, "Wearing Greene."

7 Dolan gives the wonderful example of the wonder ballad about the woman who vomited up snakes, in "Mopsa's Method," 178–79.

8 Many other Englishmen, including John Evelyn, James Howell, and John Rawlinson, traveled to this site to witness remnants of the events told in the ballad. Pepys testifies to seeing the hill on which the lady's house, in which the children were born, stood and sunk; an inscription in the town's church that told the whole story of their wondrous birthing, in both Latin and Dutch; and two baptismal fonts (an apparently singular baptismal vessel was damaged in a fire of 1572 and replaced by the two fonts Pepys saw), one for the female babies and one for the males. The real-life lady on whom the legend is based, which Pepys accurately dates to 200 years before his time, was known as Margaret of Holland, Countess of Henneberg, and the site of her home and church was Loosduinen, Holland. For more on this fascinating legend, see https://en.wikipedia.org/wiki/Margaret_of_Holland,_Countess_of_Henneberg. Many thanks to Tassie Gniady for help in confirming this information based on her own visit to the famed site as well as to Lucie Skeaping and the Samuel Pepys Club for tracking down yet more information about it.

9 Ben Jonson, "Ode (to himself)," www.luminarium.org/sevenlit/jonson/odetohimself2.htm, accessed October 31, 2016. We have no extant quarto for *The Winter's Tale*; but if

we did, given the prominent part played by romance in this mongrel art, the play would likely also have been printed in black letter—as was Shakespeare's main source, Greene's *Pandosto*.

10 See Fox-Davies, *Complete Guide to Heraldry*, 204. As Fox-Davies notes, the thistle was first used on Scottish coinage in 1474. I am grateful to Megan E. Palmer for helping me identify the carnation on the fleur-de-lis header and in other woodcut illustrations.

11 *The Winter's Tale* was performed to a public audience at the Globe in 1611 but also to a more elite and select audience at Whitehall Banqueting House, likely in 1612, and again at court for the wedding festivities of Henrietta Maria in 1613; Pafford, xxi and xxiii-iv.

12 Few contemporary records from Shakespearean performances survive; most notable is, perhaps, Simon Forman's diary, specifically about his watching a performance of *The Winter's Tale* (cited by Pafford, xxi–ii). But many scholars have worked to reconstruct stage practices. See, for example, Gurr and Ichikawa, *Staging in Shakespeare's Theatres*; or, more recently, Van Es, *Shakespeare in Company*, whose second section is devoted to "Shakespeare as Company Man."

13 Lee Sheridan Cox, in "The Role of Autolycus in *The Winter's Tale*," goes so far as to detect evidence of Autolycus's experiencing a search for reformation in the course of the play, 291. See also Richard Knowles, "Autolycus, Cloten, Caliban & Co," 90, 93. Though Steve Mentz acknowledges Autolycus's *stated* recantation, he more rightly observes that "his repentance seems paper-thin"; "Wearing Greene," 77, 83–86.

14 Lynne Enterline and others have associated Shakespeare's preoccupation with orality in terms of an anxiousness specifically over female speech, which gains powerful, if silent, embodiment in the statue scene; "Animation in *The Winter's Tale*," 17–44. See also Wells, "Mistress Taleporter," 247–59.

15 The similarity between the images of the two printed genres, broadside ballad and costume book, was first pointed out to me by Dr. Caroline Duroselle-Melish, then assistant curator of the Department of Printing and Graphic Arts at Houghton Library, Harvard University, during my fellowship there in 2012. For digital access to Vecellio's longer, 1598, edition (wrongly identified as the 1590 edition in Google Books), see https://bit.ly/37hNK60, accessed September 7, 2018. I am grateful to Ann Rosalind Jones for her informative discussions with me about costume books of the time and for providing me with copies of representative figures illustrated. See her translation and co-edition with Margaret F. Rosenthal of costume books, Vecellio, *The Clothing of the Renaissance World*.

16 The Despres book has been translated into English by Shannon, *Various Styles of Clothing*. Jones noted to me that the Victoria & Albert Museum holds "a

copy of Despres' little book in French . . . that has occasional carefully inked-in English translations identifying the kind of person the print shows." We thus know, she continues, "some English person was reading/translating the French."

17 Kearney attributes such uncomfortableness specifically to the mixed reactions to the statue scene: "Critics often want to insist that this scene either succeeds in eliciting a kind of sublime wonder and thereby successfully figures redemption or that it fails to do so"; "Hospitality's Risk," 105. I posit that such dissonance, of which the statue scene is the climactic but component part, has been building throughout the final act in its unsettling invocation and fragmentation of broadside ballad-like parts.

18 For Lim, Shakespeare shakes the foundational ground of all belief in the play; "Knowledge and Belief in *The Winter's Tale*," 317–34.

19 Notably, Stephen Orgel, editor of the Oxford edition of *The Winter's Tale* (1996), reprints the First Folio's "Rogero" as "Ruggiero."

20 "Ruggiero" was Englished as "Rogero" in a ballad songbook by Gascoigne, *A Hundreth Sundrie Flowres* (1573).

21 MS Dd.4.23, folio 23v, Cambridge University. Helping ascertain the date of the manuscript is the fact that it stands adjacent to the lute tablature MS Dd.4.22, which is dated 1615. More definitively, the copyist of the notations, Mathew Holmes, was Chanter and "Singingman" at Westminster from 1597; he died in 1621. The years 1615–21 are, therefore, the outside dates of the "Rogero" notation. See cudl.lib.cam.ac.uk/view/ms-nn-00006-00036/1, accessed September 12, 2016.

22 The F# I here mention in measure 6 does not have a sharp sign attached to it in the notation because, by music convention, once a note is sharped or flatted in a measure (as is the first F in measure 6), that same note remains sharped or flatted throughout the rest of the measure.

23 Lupton notes that "*The Winter's Tale* was scheduled at least once for performance on Easter Tuesday, exploiting this Eucharistic theme" of resurrection; citing François Laroque in her *Afterlives of the Saints*, 216.

24 Northrup Frye also notes that when Hermione "begins to move while music plays . . . we are reminded of Autolycus and of his role as a kind of rascally Orpheus at the sheep-shearing festival," in "Recognition in *The Winter's Tale*," 245.

25 Simpson describes these measures in terms of syllables rather than feet. That is, the ballad measure, Simpson says, is 8-6-8-6, trimeter is 6-6-6-6, and poulter's measure is 6-6-8-6 (613). For the links between ballad measure, poulter's measure, and hymnal measure, see Gahan, "Ballad Measure."

26 The phenomenal effect is specifically "agogic" (from the Greek word for "leading"): a series of shorter rhythmic values (dotted-eighth, sixteenth, and

two-eighths), followed by a longer value (quarter note). Regarding tempo, when Harlow renders the text, she gradually increases the tempo to reinforce this rising affect: as she progresses through the stanza, she increases her tempo from approximately 49 bpm to approximately 55 bpm.

27 She adopts the identical tactic with the slurred notes of the first word of the stanza, "What__" and, in line 5, "Or__."

28 In her essay "Singing the Psalms," Quitslund shows that "the history of the psalms as (usually metrically versified song)"—I would add, in ballad measure—reflects "how their popular rise in the reformed Church of England reveals major crossovers not only with public worship but also with *practices of play and leisure*" (emphasis mine); *Private and Domestic Devotion*, 211–35.

29 In the end, I am inclined to agree with Knapp that the experience of believing here is of giving oneself, in a secular way like the belief we witnessed at the sheepshearing feast. That's not to discount the pack of secret Catholic idolators exhilarated by the iconic statue coming to life, or Protestant believers in a natural artifice or God's grace, or skeptics in the audience who would see merely Fortune ruling all; "Visual and Ethical Truth in *The Winter's Tale*," 253–78.

30 EBBA singers and musicians performed one such bawdy dialogue ballad at the University of California, Irvine, "A Pleasant Jigge Betwixt Jack and His Mistress," c. 1672–1702 (Crawford.EB.207, EBBA 32821), in conjunction with a lecture given there by Matthew J. Smith on the ballad-like elements within *Romeo and Juliet*. In Smith's acute argument, a bawdy and comic ballad-like jig occurring at the end of this tragic play would have been an extension, not a disruption, of the performance. This lecture has since been reworked into the coauthored piece by Smith with Lupton, "Ballads+." On the connection between ballad jigs and the dramatic jig, see also Clegg, "'Pleasant Newe Jigge,'" 301–22.

Bibliography

Primary Texts

Selected Ballads, Listed by Title

For other EBBA ballads referenced in the book, see "Citation Conventions" on p. x.

"Alas poore Trades-Men what shall we do? *Or, Londons* Complaint through badnesse of Trading, For work being scant, their substance is fadeing" (c. 1646). EBBA 36028. Blackletter Ballads, 1.38. BR f 821.04 B49. Manchester Central Library, Manchester, UK.

"Anne Wallens Lamentation, For the Murthering of her husband *Iohn Wallen* a Turner in Cow-lane neere Smith-field; done by his owne wife, on satterday the 22 of Iune. 1616. who was burnt in Smithfield the first of Iuly following" (1616). By T. Platte. EBBA 20053. Pepys Ballads 1.124–125. Pepys Library, Magdalene College, Cambridge, UK.

"*Arthur o'Bradley*" (c. 1700). EBBA 30998. Roxburghe 3.283. C.20.f.9.283. British Library, London. UK.

"Barbara Allen's Cruelty: Or, The Young-man's Tragedy. With *Barbara Allen's* Lamentation for her Unkindness to her Lover, and her Self" (c. 1675–96). EBBA 35105. EBB65H. Houghton Library, Harvard University, Cambridge, MA.

"The Black-a-moor in the Wood" (1775). General Reference Collection 1346.m.7.(20.). British Library, London. UK.

"The Careless Gallant: Or, A farewel to Sorrow. Whether these Lines do please, or give offence, Or shall be damn'd as neither wit nor sence, The Poet is, for that, in no suspence, *For it is all one a hundred years hence*" (1674–79). EBBA 30270. Roxburghe 2.44. C.20.f.8.44. British Library, London. UK.

"A Caveat for Young-men. Young-men Repentance do delay, And think not of their Dying day, Till Death doth come and with his Dart, Doth pierce the young-mans stubborn heart" (1680–82). EBBA 20660. Pepys Ballads 2.36. Pepys Library, Magdalene College, Cambridge, UK.

"Celinda's last Gasp: Or, Her Farewel to False *Coridon*" (1680). EBBA 30272. Roxburghe 2.44. C.20.f.8.44. British Library, London, UK.

"The Chamberlain's Tragedy: Or, The Cook-Maid's Cruelty; Being a true Account how she in the heat of Passion, murder'd her Fellow-servant (the Chamberlain) at an Inn, i[n] the Town of Andever" (c. 1670). EBBA 36418. Bagford 2.52*. C.40.m.10.(52*). British Library, London, UK.

"The Countrey Lasse. To a dainty new note, Which if you cannot hit, There's another tune which doth as well fit" (c. 1628). EBBA 20124. Pepys Ballads 1.268–269. Pepys Library, Magdalene College, Cambridge, UK.

"The cryes of the Dead. Or the late Murther in South-warke, committed by one Richard Price Weauer, who most vnhumaynly tormented to death a boy of thirteene yeares old, with two others before, which he brought to vntimely ends[,] for which he lyeth now imprissoned in the White-Lyon, till the time of his triall" (c. 1620). EBBA 20048. Pepys Ballads 1.116--117. Pepys Library, Magdalene College, Cambridge, UK.

"David and Bersheba" (c. 1695). EBBA 30564. Roxburghe 2.98. C.20.f.8.98. British Library, London, UK.

"An Heroical Song On the Worthy and Valiant Exploits of our Noble Lord General George Duke of Albemarle, &c. Both by Land and Sea. Made in *August*, 1666" (1667). EBBA 36420. Luttrell Ballads 1.101. C.20.f.3.(101.). British Library, London, UK.

"Newes from *Hollands* Leager: OR, *Hollands* Leager is lately up broken, This for certaine is spoken" (c. 1632). By L[awrence] P[rice]. EBBA 20283. Pepys Ballads 1.98–99. Pepys Library, Magdalene College, Cambridge, UK.

"The Lady Isabella's Tragedy. . . ." (c. 1672–96). EBBA 20767. Pepys Ballads 2.149. Pepys Library, Magdalene College, Cambridge, UK.

"A Lamentable ballad of the tragical end of a Gallant Lord, and a Vertuous Lady, with the untimely end of their two children, wickedly performed by a Heathenish Blacka-moor their servant, the like never heard of before" (c. 1658–64). EBBA 31955. Euing Ballads 197. University of Glasgow Library, Glasgow, Scotland.

"*A Lamentable Ballad of the Tragical end of a Gallant Lord and a Vertuous Lady, with the untimely end of their two Children, wickedly performed by a Heathenish Blacka-moor their servant: the like never heard of*" (c. 1686–93). EBBA 30157. Roxburghe 1.220–221. C.20.f.7.220–221. British Library, London, UK.

"A Lamentable BALLAD of the tragical End of a gallant Lord and a virtuous Lady, and the untimely End of their two Children, wickedly perform'd by a heathenish Black-a-moor, their Servant, the like never heard of before" (c. 1730–69). EBBA 32501. HEH 289769. The Huntington Library, San Marino, CA.

"A Lamentable Ballad of the Tragical End of A Gallant Lord and Virtuous Lady Together with the Untimely Death of their two Children, Wickedly performed by a heathenish and blood-thirsty Blackamoor, their Servant. The like of which

Cruelty and Murder was never before heard of" (c. 1728–63). EBBA 31227. Roxburghe 3.520–521. C.20.f.9.520–521. British Library, London, UK.

"A Lamentable Ballad of the Tragical End Of A Gallant Lord and Vertuous Lady: Together with the untimely Death of their Two Children; wickedly performed by a Heathenish and Blood-thirsty Black a-Moor, their Servant; the like of which Cruelty and Murder was never before heard of" (mid-eighteenth century). EBBA 34451. EB75 P4128C no.109. Houghton Library, Harvard University, Cambridge, MA.

"A Lamentable Ballad of the Tragical End of A Gallant Lord and Virtuous Lady Together with the Untimely Death of their two Children, Wickedly performed by a heathenish and blood-thirsty Blackamoor, their Servant. The like of which Cruelty and Murder was never before heard of" (c. 1736–63). Harding B3(40). Broadside Ballads Online. Bodleian Library, University of Oxford, Oxford, UK. http://ballads.bodleian.ox.ac.uk/search/?query=Harding+B3%2840%29.

"The Lamenting Lady, Who for the wrongs done to her by a poore woman, for hauing two children at one burthen, was by the hand of God most strangely punished, by sending her as many children at one birth, as there are daies in the yeare, in re-membrance whereof, there is now a monument builded in the City of *Lowdon*, as many English men now liuing in *Lowdon*, can truely testifie the same and hath seene it" (c. 1620). EBBA 20210. Pepys Ballads 1.44–45. Pepys Library, Magdalene College, Cambridge, UK.

"The Loves of Jockey and Jenny: Or, The Scotch Wedding" (1684–85). EBBA 31928. Euing Ballads 173. University of Glasgow Library, Glasgow, Scotland.

"Loues Solace; Or The true lovers part, & in his conclusion he shews his constant heart. He still doth praise her for her beauty rare, And sayes theres none with her that can compare." By M[artin] P[arker] (c. 1624–80). EBBA 30139. Roxburghe 1.202–203. C.20.f.7.202–203. British Library, London, UK.

"The Lovers Battle, Being a sore Combat fought between Mars and Venus, at a place called Cunney Castle, under Belly-hill. . . ." (c. 1664–88). By Thomas Robins. EBBA 32830. Crawford.EB.88. National Library of Scotland, Edinburgh, Scotland.

"The Map of Mock-begger Hall, with his scituation in the spacious Countrey, called, *Anywhere*" (c. 1633–35). EBBA 30174. Roxburghe 1.252–253. C.20.f.7.252–253. British Library, London, UK.

"Mars and Venus: Or The Amorous Combatants. . . ." (c. 1682–84). EBBA 32644. Crawford.EB.3. National Library of Scotland, Edinburgh, Scotland.

"Mars and Venus: Or The Amorous Combatants. . . ." (c. 1682–84). EBBA 21248. Pepys Ballads 3.234. Pepys Library, Magdalene College, Cambridge, UK.

"A Merry Wedding: Or, *O Brave* Arthur *of* Bradly" (c. 1693–95). EBBA 34628. Huth EBB65H, 2.186. Houghton Library, Harvard University, Cambridge, MA.

"A merry Wedding Or, O Brave *Arthur of Bradly*" (c. 1660–1700). EBBA 31690. Euing Ballads 214. University of Glasgow Library, Glasgow, Scotland.

"*Mock-Beggers Hall, with his scituation in the spacious Country, called*, Any where" (c. 1639–40). EBBA 30866. Roxburghe 3.218–219. C.20.f.9.218–219. British Library, London, UK.

"A most delicate, pleasant, amorous, new Song, made by a Gentleman that enioyes his Loue, shewing the worth and happi-nesse of Content, and the effects of loue, called, *All Louers Ioy*" (c. 1625). EBBA 20117. Pepys Ballads 1.254–255. Pepys Library, Magdalene College, Cambridge, UK.

"[A m]ost excellent Ballad of S. George for England and the Kings daugh[ter of] *AEgipt*, whom he delivered from death, and how he slew a mighty Dragon" (1658–64). EBBA 31774. Euing Ballads 92. University of Glasgow Library, Glasgow, Scotland.

"A most excellent Song of the loue of young *Palmus*, and faire *Sheldra*, with their vnfortunate loue" (c. 1630). EBBA 20163. Pepys Ballads 1.350–351. Pepys Library, Magdalene College, Cambridge, UK.

"A most excellent Song of the loue of young *Palmus*, and faire *Sheldra*, with their vnfortunate loue" (c. 1602–46; and likely pub. toward the later date). EBBA 30295. Roxburghe 1.436–437. C.20.f.7.436–437. British Library, London, UK.

"A most godly and comfortable Ballad of the glorious Resurrection of our Lord Iesus Christ, how he triumphed over death, hell, and sinne, whereby we are certainly perswaded of our rising againe from the dead" (c. 1624–80). EBBA 30184. Roxburghe 1.258–259. C.20.f.7.258–259. British Library, London, UK.

"Oh faine would I marry Yet divers occasions a while make me tarry, Before he will wedd he is thrifty to see, And set downe with Items what charge It will be" (c. 1635). EBBA 36094. Blackletter Ballads, 2.47. BR f 821.04 B49. Manchester Central Library, Manchester, UK.

"The Norfolk Gentleman his Last Will and Testament. And how he committed the keeping of his Children to his own Brother, who dealt most wickedly with them, and how God Plagued him for it" (1663–74). EBBA 31808. Euing Ballads 254. University of Glasgow Library, Glasgow, Scotland.

"A Pleasant Jigg Betwixt Jack and his Mistress: Or, The young Carman's Courage cool'd by the suddain approach, of his Master, who found him too kind to his Mistress" (c. 1672–1702). EBBA 32821. Crawford.EB.207. National Library of Scotland, Edinburgh, Scotland.

"A pleasant new Song, betwixt *The Saylor and his Loue*" (c. 1624). EBBA 20198. Pepys Ballads 1.422–423. Pepys Library, Magdalene College, Cambridge, UK.

"A pleasant new Sonnet intituled, mine owne deare Lady braue." In Richard Johnson, *A crowne garland of goulden roses Gathered out of Englands royall garden. Being the liues and strange fortunes of many great personages of this land. Set forth in many pleasant new songs and sonnets neuer before imprinted* (1612).

"The poore man payes for all. This is but a dreame which here shall insue: But the Author wishes his words were not true" (c. 1601–40). EBBA 30223. Roxburghe 1.326–327. C.20.f.7.326–327. British Library, London, UK.

"The Re-Resurrection Of the Rump: Or, Rebellion and Tyranny revived. The third Edition" (1659). EBBA 32128. Bridgewater collection. HEH 133299. The Huntington Library, San Marino, CA.

"[Rocke the cradle Iohn, or] Children after the rate of 24 in a yeare, Thats 2 euery month as plaine doth appeare, Let no man at this strang story wonder" (c. 1635). EBBA 20190. Pepys Ballads 1.404–405. Pepys Library, Magdalene College, Cambridge, UK.

"Saint Georges commendation to all Souldiers: or, S. Georges Alarum to all that professe Martiall discipline, with a memoriall of the Worthies, who haue been borne so high on the winges of Fame for their braue aduentures, as they cannot be buried in the pit of obliuion" (1612). EBBA 20041. Pepys Ballads 1.87. Pepys Library, Magdalene College, Cambridge, UK.

"The true fourme and shape of a monsterous Chyld Whiche was borne in Stony Stratforde, in North Hamptonshire. The yeare of our Lord, M.CCCCC.LXV" (1565). HEH 18293. Britwell Collection. Huntington Library, San Marino, CA.

"A well wishing to a place of pleasure" (c. 1629). EBBA 30305. Roxburghe Ballads 1.454. C.20.f.7.454. British Library, London, UK.

"The Youngmans careless Wooing, And the Witty Maids Replication; All done out of old English Proverbs" (c. 1685–88). EBBA 32895. Crawford.EB.323. National Library of Scotland, Glasgow, Scotland.

"The Youngmans careless Wooing, And the Witty Maids Replication; All done out of old English Proverbs" (c. 1685–88). EBBA 21140. Pepys Ballads 3.130. Pepys Library, Magdalene College, Cambridge, UK.

Other Primary Sources

1 Edward 6, c. 31. 1537. In *Statutes of the Realm*. 9 vols. London: The Record Commission, 1810–25.

1 James 1, c. 7. 1603. In *Statutes of the Realm*. 9 vols. London: The Record Commission, 1810–25.

The Aldwell Map. In *Survey of London*, ed. Sir Howard Roberts and Walter Godfrey. London: London County Council, 1950.

The Agas Map." In *Civitas Londinvm* (c. 1562). Digitized in *The Map of Early Modern London*, dir. Janelle Jenstad. *MoEML*, 2012. mapoflondon.uvic.ca. Accessed June 10, 2020.

Anon. *The Best and Plainest English Spelling-Book Containing ALL The Different Words, Syllables, & Letters in the Old English Character.* London: 1700.

Anon. "The Sheepheards slumber." In *Englands Helicon: Casta placent superis, pura cum veste venite, et minibus puris sumite fontis aquam.* Attributed ed. John Bodenham (fl. 1600). London: Printed by I. R[oberts] for Iohn [John] Flasket, 1600.

Ariosto, Ludovico. *Orlando Furioso.* 1532.

Ayres, John. *The Accomplish'd Clerk Regraved: A New Copy-Book Shewing the Natural Freedom of the Pen and an Improvement of ye Clerk-like Way of Writing the Hands now Most in Use.* London: 1700.

———. *A Tutor to Penmanship, or The Writing Master, a copy shewing all the variety of penmanship and clerkship as now practised in England. In II. parts.* London: 1698.

Bandello, Matteo. *Novelle.* 3 vols. Lucca, Italy: 1554; repub. Lyons, France: 1573.

Barlow, Jeremy, ed. *The Complete Country Dance Tunes from Playford's "Dancing Master" (1651–ca. 1728).* London: Faber Music, 1985.

Barnard, Dean Stanton. Introduction to *Hollands Leaguer by Nicholas Goodman: A Critical Edition.* Ed. Dean Stanton Barnard. The Hague: Mouton, 1970.

Browne, William. *Britannia's Pastorals, The Second Book.* London: 1611.

Butler, Charles. *The Principles of Musik, in Singing and Setting with the Two-fold Use Thereof, Ecclesiasticall and Civil.* London: 1626.

Chappell, William. *Popular Music of the Olden Time: A Collection of Ancient Songs, Ballads, and Dance Tunes, Illustrative of the National Music of England.* 2 vols. London: Cramer, Beale, & Chappell, 1859.

Chappell, William and Joseph Woodfall Ebsworth, eds. *The Roxburghe Ballads.* 27 parts. Hertford: Stephen Austin & Sons, 1869–99. Reprinted 9 vols. in 8 (vols. 1–3 ed. Chappell; vols. 4–8 ed. Ebsworth). New York: AMS Press, 1966.

Chardin, Jean-Baptiste-Siméon. *L'Enfant au Toton: August Gabriel Godefroy (1728–1813).* 1738. Oil on canvas. São Paulo Museum of Art.

Charles I. "The Protestation Oath of 1641." In *Cornwall Protestation Returns 1641.* From a transcript (c. 1914) by Reginald Morshead Glencross. Additional material by H. L. Douch. Ed. and pub. T. L. Stoate, 1974. *Cornwall OPC Database.* www.cornwall-opc-database.org/extra-searches/protestation-returns/protestation-oath-of-1641/. Accessed Aug. 28, 2015.

Chettle, Henry. *Kind-Heartes Dreame.* 1592. Collected with William Kemp, *Nine Daies Wonder* (1600). Ed. G. B. Harrison. New York: Barnes and Noble, 1966.

Child, Francis James. *The English and Scottish Ballads.* 8 vols. Boston, MA: Little, Brown and Co., and Cincinnati, OH: Moore, Wilstach, Keys and Co., 1857–59; Boston: Little, Brown and Co., 1860, 1866.

Child, Francis James, and George Lyman Kittredge. *The English and Scottish Popular Ballads.* 5 vols. Boston: Houghton Mifflin, 1882–98.

Coke, Sir Edward. *Les Reports de Edward Coke. . . .* 11 vols. London: 1600–15, 1658, 1659.

Davis, John, of Hereford. *The Writing Schoolemaster, or, The Anatomie of Faire Writing.* London: 1663.

Deserps [Despres], François. *Recueil de la diversité des habits.* Paris: 1562. In *A Collection of the Various Styles of Clothing which are Presently Worn in Countries of Europe, Asia, Africa, and the Savage Islands, All Realistically Depicted*, ed. and trans. Sara Shannon, intro. Carol Urness. Minneapolis: James Ford Bell Library, 2001. Dist. by the University of Minnesota Press.

Ebsworth, Joseph Woodfall, ed. *The Bagford Ballads.* 3 vols. Collected into 2 vols. Hertford: Stephen Austin and Sons, 1876–78. Reprint, New York: AMS Press, 1968.

English Short Title Catalogue (ESTC). Online database covering 1473–1800 (incorporating and updating the two *Short-Title Catalogues* (STC) by Pollard and Redgrave and by Wing, respectively. Hosted by British Library, http://estc.bl.uk/F/?func=file&file_name=login-bl-estc.

Evelyn, John. Letter, August 12, 1689. Vol. III. In *Diary and Correspondence of John Evelyn*, ed. William Bray. London: G. Routledge and Sons; New York: E. P. Dutton and Co., 1906.

Fletcher, Andrew. "Letter to the Marquis of Montrose." In *The Political Works of Andrew Fletcher, Esq., of Saltoun.* Glasgow: 1749.

Gascoigne, George. *The Adventures of Master F.J.* London: 1573.

———. *A Hundreth Sundrie Flowres Bounde vp in One Small Poesie. . . .* London: c. 1573.

The Georgia Gazette. Thursday, April 23, 1789. NewsBank, Inc. and American Antiquarian Society.

Gibbons, Orlando. *Complete Keyboard Works in Five Volumes.* Trans. and ed. Margaret H. Glyn. London: Stainer & Bell, 1924–25.

Greene, Robert. *Greene's Groats-Worth of Wit, Bought with a Million of Repentance.* London: 1592.

———. *Pandosto. Or the Triumph of Time.* London: 1588.

———. *The History of Orlando Furioso.* London: 1594.

Gyford, Phil. *The Diary of Samuel Pepys: Daily entries from the 17th century London diary.* www.pepysdiary.com. Accessed Nov. 22, 2019.

A Handeful of pleasant delites . . . by Clement Robinson and Divers Others. Published and printed by Richard Jones. London: 1584. Reprinted ed. Hyder E. Rollins, *A Handful of Pleasant Delights (1584) by Clement Robinson and Divers Others.* Cambridge, MA: Harvard University Press, 1923.

Haec-Vir: Or, The Womanish-Man: Being an Answere to a late Booke intituled "Hic-Mulier." Exprest in a briefe Dialogue between Haec-Vir the Womanish-Man, and Hic-Mulier the Man-Woman. London: 1620.

Harman, Thomas. *A Caveat for Common Cursitors.* London: 1566, 1568, 1573.

Hic Mvlier: Or, The Man-Woman: Being a Medicine to cure the Coltish Disease of the Staggers in the Masculine-Feminines, of our Times. Expressed in a briefe Declamation. London: 1620.

Hollands Leagver: Or, An Historical Discovrse of the Life and Actions of Dona Britanica Hollandia the Arch-Mistris of the wicked women of Evtopia. . . . London: 1632.

Hollyband, C[laudius]. *Campo Di Fior, or the Flovery Field of Fovr Languages. . . .* London: 1583.

Holmes, Mathew. *Mathew Holmes lute books* (c. 1605–15). Cambridge University Library. MS Nn.6.36. University of Cambridge Digital Library. cudl.lib.cam.ac.uk/view/ms-nn-00006-00036/1. Accessed Sept. 12, 2016.

Hoole, Charles. *The Petty-Schoole. . . .* London: 1659.

"Human Monsters!! . . ." (c. 1750). EBBA 32442. HEH 289716. The Huntington Library, San Marino, CA.

Johnson, Richard, comp. "A pleasant new Sonnet intituled, mine owne deare Lady braue." In *A crowne garland of goulden roses Gathered out of Englands royall garden. . . .* London: 1612.

Johnson, Samuel. *Prefaces, Biographical and Critical: To the Works of English Poets.* 10 vols. London: 1779–81.

Jonson, Ben. *Bartholomew Fair.* Ed. E. A. Horsman. London: Methuen, 1960.

———. "Ode (to himself)." In *The Oxford Book of Seventeenth Century Verse.* Ed. H. J. C. Grierson and G. Bullough, 179–80. Oxford, UK: Clarendon Press, 1934. Published online at Luminarium, June 8, 2001. https://www.poetryfoundation.org/poems/44462/an-ode-to-himself. Accessed June 10, 2020.

Jorgens, Elise Bickford, ed. *English Song, 1600–1675: Facsimiles of Twenty-Six Manuscripts and an Edition of the Texts.* 12 vols. New York: Garland Publishing, 1986–89.

"June 1643: An Ordinance for the Regulating of Printing." In *Acts and Ordinances of the Interregnum, 1642–1660.* Ed. C. H. Firth and R. S. Rait, 184–86. London: His Majesty's Stationery Office, 1911. *British History Online.* www.british-history.ac.uk/no-series/acts-ordinances-interregnum/pp184-186. Accessed Aug. 27, 2015.

Lindsay, James Ludovic, Earl of Crawford. *Bibliotheca Lindesiana: A Catalogue of a Collection of English Ballads of the XVIIth and XVIIIth Centuries, Printed for the Most Part in Black Letter.* Privately printed, 1890. Reprinted in 2 vols. New York: B. Franklin, 1961.

Malory, Sir Thomas. *Le Morte d'Arthur.* Westminster, UK: Wynkyn de Worde, 1498.

More, Robert. *The Writing Master's Assistant. . . .* London: 1696.

Morley, Thomas. *A Plain and Easy Introduction to Practical Music.* London: 1597. Reprinted and edited, Alec Harman. New York: Norton, 1963.

Painter, William. *The Palace of Pleasure.* London: 1566.

Parker, Louis Napoleon. *Mavourneen: A Comedy in Three Acts.* New York: Dodd, Mead and Company, 1916. www.archive.org/details/mavourneencomedy00parkrich.

Pepys, Samuel. "My Calligraphical Collection." 3 vols. 1700. Pepys Library, Magdalene College, Cambridge, Cambridge, UK.

———. *The Diary of Samuel Pepys.* Ed. Robert Latham and William Matthews. 11 vols. Berkeley: University of California Press, 1995.

———. *Further Correspondence of Samuel Pepys, 1662–1679, from the Family Papers in the Possession of J. Pepys Cockerell.* Ed. J. R. Tanner. 3 vols. London: G. Bell and Sons, 1929.

———. *The Pepys Ballads.* Ed. Hyder E. Rollins. 8 vols. Cambridge, MA: Harvard University Press, 1929–32.

———. *The Pepys Ballads.* Ed. W. G. Day and the Pepys Library. 5 vols. Cambridge, UK: D. S. Brewer, 1987.

———. *Private Correspondence and Miscellaneous Papers of Samuel Pepys, 1679–1703.* Ed. J. R. Tanner. 2 vols. New York: Harcourt Brace & Company, 1926.

Percy, Thomas. *Reliques of Ancient English Poetry.* 3 vols. London: 1765.

Philips, Ambrose. *A Collection of Old Ballads: Corrected from the Best and Most Ancient Copies Extant; with Introductions Historical, Critical, or Humorous.* 3 vols. London: 1723–25.

Phillips, John, E. M., and J. M., comps. "Song." In *Wit and Drollery, Joviall Poems: Corrected with much amended, with Additions.* London: 1656; reprinted, 1661.

Playford, John. *The Dancing Master.* 18 eds. London: 1651–1728.

———. *A Booke of New Lessons for the Cithern & Gittern Containing many New and Excellent tunes, Both Easie and Delightfull to the Practitioner. With plain and easie Instructions, teaching the right use of the hand, and perfect tuning of both Instruments, never before printed.* London: 1652.

Prior, Matthew. Dedication to *Poems on Several Occasions.* London: 1718.

The Rump, or A Collection of Songs and Ballads, made upon those who would be a Parliament, and were but the Rump of an House of Commons, five times dissolv'd. [Ed. Alexander Brome]. London: 1660.

The Roxburghe Ballads. Ed. Charles Hindley. 2 vols. London: Reeves and Turner, 1873–74.

The Roxburghe Ballads. Ed. William Chappell and Joseph Woodfall Ebsworth. 27 parts. Hertford: Stephen Austin & Sons, 1869–99. Reprinted 9 vols. in 8 (vols. 1–3 ed. Chappell; vols. 4–8 ed. Ebsworth). New York: AMS Press, 1966.

Sackville, Charles, Earl of Dorset. "Song, Written at Sea." In *Wit and Mirth.* London: 1714. Ed. G. G. Falle. Representative Poetry Online. University of Toronto Libraries. http://rpo.library.utoronto.ca/poems/song-written-sea. Accessed Dec. 18, 2012.

Shakespeare, William. *The Winter's Tale.* Ed. Frank Kermode. 2nd ed. New York: Penguin Group/Signet Classics, 1998.

———. *The Winter's Tale*. Ed. J. H. P. Pafford. London: Methuen, 1963.

———. *The Winter's Tale*. Ed. Stephen Orgel. Oxford, UK: Oxford University Press, 1996.

Shelley, Percy Bysshe. "Fragments of the Adonais." In *Relics of Shelley*, ed. Richard Garnett, 48–52. London: 1862. https://archive.org/details/relicsofshelley00shel.

———. "Miscellaneous Fragments." In *Relics of Shelley*, ed. Richard Garnett, 74–91. London: 1862. https://archive.org/details/relicsofshelley00shel.

Short-Title Catalogue of Books Printed in England, Scotland and Ireland, and of English Books Printed Abroad, 1475–1640 (STC). Eds. A. W. Pollard and G. R. Redgrave. London: The Bibliographical Society, 1928. Online as *English Short Title Catalogue*, covering 1473–1800 (incorporating and updating the STC by Pollard and Redgrave and its extension by Wing (next citation). http://estc.bl.uk/F/?func=file&file_name=login-bl-estc.

Short-Title Catalogue of Books Printed in England, Scotland, Ireland, Wales, and British America, and of English Books Printed in Other Countries, 1641–1700 (often cited as Wing). Ed. Donald Goddard Wing. Continuation of the *Short-Title Catalogue of Books . . . 1640*. London: The Bibliographical Society, 1945–51. Online as *English Short Title Catalogue*, covering 1473–1800 (incorporating and updating the STC by Wing and by Pollard and Redgrave (citation above). http://estc.bl.uk/F/?func=file&file_name=login-bl-estc.

Stevenson, Robert Louis. *Familiar Studies of Men & Books*. London: 1882. www.fullbooks.com/Familiar-Studies-of-Men--Books4.html.

Swetnan, Joseph. *The Araignment of Lewd, Idle, Froward, and vnconstant women: Or the vanitie of them, choose you whether. With a Commendation of wise, virtuous and honest women. Pleasant for married men, profitable for young Men, and hurtfull to none*. London: 1615.

Tottel, Richard. *Songes and Sonettes Written by the Ryght Honorable Lord Henry Howard Late Earle of Surrey, Thomas Wyatt the Elder, and Others*. London: 1557.

Vecellio, Cesare. *The Clothing of the Renaissance World (Europe, Asia, Africa, America): Cesare Vecellio's "Habiti Antichi et Moderni."* Trans. and ed. Ann Rosalind Jones and Margaret F. Rosenthal. London: Thames and Hudson, 2008.

Webbe, William. *Discourse of English Poetrie*. London: 1586.

Wright, C. E., and Ruth C. Wright, eds. *Humfrey Wanley and the History of the Harleian Library: A Reprint of the Introduction to "The Diary of Humfrey Wanley, 1715–1726."* 2 vols. London: Bibliographical Society, 1966.

Wright, Thomas, ed. *The Historical Works of Giraldus Cambrensis, containing: The Topography of Ireland, and the History of the Conquest of Ireland*. Trans. Thomas Forester. London: 1863. Reprint, New York: AMS, 1968.

Wycherley, William. *The Country Wife*. 1675. Ed. Thomas H. Fujimura. Lincoln: University of Nebraska Press, 1965.

Secondary Sources

Achinstein, Sharon. "Audiences and Authors: Ballads and the Making of English Literary Culture." *Journal of Medieval and Renaissance Studies* 22, no. 3 (1992): 311–26.

Alchin, Linda. "Greensleeves." *The Tudors Website*. www.the-tudors.org.uk/greensleeves.htm. Accessed Dec. 17, 2012.

Artese, Charlotte. *Shakespeare's Folktale Sources*. Lanham, MD: University of Delaware Press, 2015.

Atkinson, David. *The Ballad and Its Pasts: Literary Histories and the Play of Memory*. Cambridge, UK: D. S. Brewer, 2018.

———. *The English Traditional Ballad: Theory, Method, and Practice*. Aldershot, Hants: Ashgate, 2002.

Ault, Norman, ed. *Seventeenth Century Lyrics from the Original Texts*. London: Longmans, Green and Co., 1928.

Backhouse, Clare. *Fashion and Popular Print in Early Modern England: Depicting Dress in Black-Letter Ballads*. London: I. B. Tauris & Co. Ltd, 2017.

Bain, Peter, and Paul Shaw, eds. *Blackletter: Type and National Identity: A Catalogue of an Exhibition*. New York: American Printing History Association, 1999.

Banks, Kathryn, and Timothy Chesters, eds. *Movement in Renaissance Literature: Exploring Kinesic Intelligence*. Cham, Switzerland: Palgrave Macmillan, 2018.

"Barack Obama 2008 Presidential Campaign—Wassup 2008." Nov. 6, 2008. *YouTube*. www.youtube.com/watch?v=vRu_YLhoR4k.

Barbour, Judith. Email correspondence with Patricia Fumerton. 2008.

Baker, David, with Travis Alexander, Adam Engel, Katharine Landers, Mary Learner, and Ashley Werlinich. "'Dangerous Conjectures': Ophelia's Ballad Performance." In *Ballads and Performance: The Multi-Modality Theatricality of the Early Modern Stage*, ed. Patricia Fumerton. Santa Barbara, CA: EMC Imprint, 2018. http://scalar.usc.edu/works/ballads-and-performance-the-multi-modal-stage-in-early-modern-england/thinking-with-ballads-on-the-early-modern-stage----david-baker.

Barnett, Gregory. "Tonal Organization in Seventeenth-Century Music Theory." In *The Cambridge History of Western Music Theory*, ed. Thomas Christensen, 407–55. Cambridge, UK: Cambridge University Press, 2002.

Barrow, Theodore. "From 'The Easter Wedding' to 'The Frantick Lover': The Repeated Woodcut and Its Shifting Roles." In *Studies in Ephemera: Text and Image in Eighteenth-Century Print*, ed. Kevin D. Murphy and Sally O'Driscoll, 219–40. Lanham, MD: Bucknell University Press, 2013.

Bartel, Dietrich. *Musica Poetica: Musical-Rhetorical Figures in German Baroque Music.* Lincoln: University of Nebraska Press, 1997.

Baskerville, Charles Read. *The Elizabethan Jig and Related Song Drama.* New York: Dover, 1965.

Beier, A. L. *Masterless Men: The Vagrancy Problem in England, 1560–1640.* London: Methuen, 1985.

———. "Social Problems in Elizabethan London." *Journal of Interdisciplinary History* 9, no. 2 (1978): 203–21. https://doi.org/10.2307/203225.

———. and Roger Finlay. Introduction to *London 1500–1700: The Making of the Metropolis*, ed. A. L. Beier and Roger Finlay. London: Longman, 1986.

Bell, Erik. "Fitting Texts to Tunes: Separation, Reconciliation, and Melodic Malleability." In *The Making of a Broadside Ballad*, ed. Patricia Fumerton, Andrew Griffin, and Carl Stahmer. Santa Barbara, CA: EMC Imprint, 2016. http://press.emcimprint.english.ucsb.edu/the-making-of-a-broadside-ballad/erik-bell-matching-ballads-to-tunes.

Bennett, Jane. *Vibrant Matter: A Political Ecology of Things.* Durham, NC: Duke University Press, 2010.

Berto, Francesco, and Jacopo Tagliabue. "Cellular Automata." *Stanford Encyclopedia of Philosophy.* March 26, 2012. Updated Aug. 22, 2017. http://plato.stanford.edu/entries/cellular-automata/. Accessed Aug. 22, 2015.

Bialo, Caralyn. "Popular Performance, the Broadside Ballad, and Ophelia's Madness." *Studies in English Literature, 1500–1900* 53, no. 2 (2013): 293–309. https://doi.org/10.1353/sel.2013.0014.

Blagden, Cyprian. "Notes on the Ballad Market in the Second Half of the Seventeenth Century." *Studies in Bibliography* 6 (1954): 161–80. https://www.jstor.org/stable/40371127.

Bloom, Gina, Anston Bosman, and William N. West. "Ophelia's Intertheatricality, or, How Performance Is History." *Theatre Journal* 65, no. 2 (May 2013): 165–82. https://doi.org/10.1353/tj.2013.0041.

Bolens, Guillemette. *The Style of Gestures: Embodiment and Cognition in Literary Narrative.* Baltimore: Johns Hopkins University Press, 2012.

Bolter, Jay David, and Richard Grusin. *Remediation: Understanding New Media.* Boston: MIT Press, 1999.

Boyer, Allen D. "Coke, Sir Edward (1552–1634)." *Oxford Dictionary of National Biography.* Oxford, UK: Oxford University Press, 2004. Published online Sept. 23, 2004; updated Jan. 8, 2009. https://doi.org/10.1093/ref:odnb/5826. Accessed Feb. 4, 2016.

British Book Trade Index (BBTI). Bodleian Libraries, University of Oxford, Oxford, UK. http://bbti.bodleian.ox.ac.uk.

Broadside Ballads Online. The Bodleian Libraries, University of Oxford, Oxford, UK. http://ballads.bodleian.ox.ac.uk/.

Brooks, Christopher W. *Lawyers, Litigation, and English Society Since 1450.* London: Bloomsbury Academic, 1998.

Broude, Ronald. "Roman and Goth in *Titus Andronicus.*" *Shakespeare Studies* 6 (1970): 27–34.

Brown, Mary Ellen. "Child's Ballads and the Broadside Conundrum." In *Ballads and Broadsides in Britain, 1500–1800*, ed. Patricia Fumerton and Anita Guerrini, with Kris McAbee, 57–74. Farnham, Surrey, UK: Ashgate, 2010.

Buchan, David. *The Ballad and the Folk.* London: Routledge & Kegan Paul, 1972. Reprint, East Linton: Tuckwell Press, 1997.

"Budweiser 2000 Super Bowl Commercial—Wassup." *Dailymotion.* www.dailymotion.com/video/xx7559_budweiser-2000-super-bowl-commercial-wassup_fun.

"Budweiser True a Whassup Girl Invasion 2001." *YouTube.* July 7, 2009. www.youtube.com/watch?v=luF-2mKm8Lo. Accessed Nov. 4, 2019.

Burk, Tara. "'A Battleground Around the Crime': The Visuality of Execution Ephemera and Its Cultural Significances in Late Seventeenth-Century England." In *Studies in Ephemera: Text and Image in Eighteenth-Century Print*, ed. Kevin D. Murphy and Sally O'Driscoll, 195–218. Lanham, MD: Bucknell University Press, 2013.

Calhoun, Craig, ed. *Habermas and the Public Sphere.* Cambridge, MA: MIT Press, 1993. Reprinted 1996.

Cameron, W. J. "A Late Seventeenth-Century Scriptorium." *Culture, Theory, and Critique* 7, no. 1 (1963): 25–52. https://doi.org/10.1080/14735786309391446.

Carr, James Revell. "Recording Early Broadside Ballads." English Broadside Ballad Archive. 2007. ebba.english.ucsb.edu/page/recording-the-ballads#Simpson.

Carroll, William C. *Fat King, Lean Beggar: Representations of Poverty in the Age of Shakespeare.* Ithaca, NY: Cornell University Press, 1996.

"Catalogues & Finding Aids." Weston Library, Bodleian Libraries, University of Oxford, Oxford, UK. www.bodleian.ox.ac.uk/finding-resources/catalogues. Accessed Jan. 16, 2013.

Chartier, Roger. "Languages, Books, and Reading from the Printed Word to the Digital Text." Trans. Teresa Lavender Fagan. *Critical Inquiry* 31, no. 1 (Autumn 2004): 133–52. https://doi.org/10.1086/427305.

Chater, Kathleen. *Untold Histories: Black People in England and Wales During the Period of the British Slave Trade, c. 1660–1807.* Manchester, UK: Manchester University Press, 2009.

Chess, Simone. "'And I my vowe did keepe': Oath Making, Subjectivity, and Husband Murder in 'Murderous Wife' Ballads." In *Ballads and Broadsides in Britain, 1500–1800*, ed. Patricia Fumerton and Anita Guerrini, with Kris McAbee, 131–48. Farnham, Surrey, UK: Ashgate Press, 2010.

Clegg, Roger. "'A Ballad Intituled a Pleasant Newe Jigge': The Relationship between the Broadside Ballad and the Dramatic Jig." In "Living English Broadside

Ballads, 1550–1750: Song, Art, Dance, Culture," ed. Patricia Fumerton. Special issue of *Huntington Library Quarterly* 79, no. 2 (2016): 301–22. https://doi.org/10.1353/hlq.2016.0015.

Clegg, Roger, and Lucie Skeaping. *Singing Simpkin and Other Bawdy Jigs: Musical Comedy on the Shakespearean Stage: Scripts, Music and Context.* Exeter, UK: University of Exeter Press, 2014.

The Clothworkers' Company. www.clothworkers.co.uk/. Accessed Aug. 22, 2015.

Clough, Patricia Ticineto, and Jean Halley, eds. *The Affective Turn: Theorizing the Social.* Durham, NC: Duke University Press, 2007.

Coldiron, A. E. B. *Printers Without Borders: Translation and Textuality in the Renaissance.* Cambridge, UK: Cambridge University Press, 2015.

Colie, Rosalie Littell. *Shakespeare's Living Art.* Princeton, NJ: Princeton University Press, 1974.

Cone, Edward T. *Musical Form and Musical Performance.* New York: W. W. Norton, 1968.

Conway, John. *The Game of Life.* www.bitstorm.org/gameoflife/. Accessed Aug. 22, 2015.

Correll, Barbara B. "Scene Stealers: Autolycus, *The Winter's Tale* and Economic Criticism." In *Money and the Age of Shakespeare: Essays in New Economic Criticism*, ed. Linda Woodbridge, 53–65. Houndsmill, Basingstoke, UK: Palgrave Macmillan, 2003.

Cormack, Lesley B. "Forms of Nationhood and Forms of Public: Geography and Its Publics in Early Modern England." In *Forms of Association: Making Publics in Early Modern Europe*, ed. Paul Yachnin and Marlene Eberhart, 155–75. Amherst: University of Massachusetts Press, 2015.

Cox, Lee Sheridan. "The Role of Autolycus in *The Winter's Tale.*" *Studies in English Literature, 1500–1900* 9, no. 2 (1969): 283–301. https://doi.org/10.2307/449781.

Cressy, David. "Literacy in Context: Meaning and Measurement in Early Modern England." In *Consumption and the World of Goods*, ed. John Brewer and Roy Porter. 1st edition: London: Routledge, 1994, pp. 305–19. Reprinted e-book, 2013.

Curran, Kevin. "Virtual Scholarship: Navigating Early Modern Studies on the World Wide Web." *Early Modern Literary Studies* 12, no. 1 (May 2006): n.p. https://extra.shu.ac.uk/emls/12-1/currvirt.htm. Accessed Nov. 22, 2019.

Dawson, Giles E., and Laetitia Kennedy-Skipton. *Elizabethan Handwriting, 1500–1650: A Manual.* New York: Norton, 1966.

de Certeau, Michel. *The Practice of Everyday Life.* Trans. Steven Rendall. Berkeley: University of California Press, 1988.

DeLanda, Manuel. *A New Philosophy of Society: Assemblage Theory and Social Complexity.* London: Continuum, 2006.

Deleuze, Gilles, and Félix Guattari. *A Thousand Plateaus: Capitalism and Schizophrenia.* Trans. and foreword by Brian Massumi. Minneapolis: University of Minnesota Press, 1987.

Diehl, Huston. "'Strike All that Look Upon with Marvel': Theatrical and Theological Wonder in *The Winter's Tale.*" In *Rematerializing Shakespeare: Authority and Representation on the Early Modern English Stage*, ed. Bryan Reynolds and William N. West, 19–34. Basingstoke, UK: Palgrave Macmillan, 2005.

Dolan, Frances E. *Dangerous Familiars: Representations of Domestic Crime in England, 1550–1700.* Ithaca, NY: Cornell University Press, 1994.

———. *Marriage and Violence: The Early Modern Legacy.* Philadelphia: University of Pennsylvania Press, 2008.

———. "Mopsa's Method: Truth Claims, Ballads, and Print." In "Living English Broadside Ballads, 1550–1750: Song, Art, Dance, Culture," ed. Patricia Fumerton. Special issue of *Huntington Library Quarterly* 79, no. 2 (2016): 173–85. https://doi.org/10.1353/hlq.2016.0014.

———. "Tracking the Petty Traitor Across Genres." In *Ballads and Broadsides in Britain, 1500–1800*, ed. Patricia Fumerton and Anita Guerrini, with Kris McAbee, 149–72. Farnham, Surrey, UK: Ashgate Press, 2010.

———. *True Relations: Reading, Literature, and Evidence in Seventeenth-Century England.* Philadelphia: University of Pennsylvania Press, 2013.

Doty, Jeffrey S. "What Is a Public?" Making Publics, 1500–1700: Media, Markets, and Association in Early Modern Europe (MaPs). http://project.makingpublics.org/research/what-do-you-mean/ (site discontinued). Accessed Aug. 23, 2015.

Drabkin, William. "Motif [motive]." *Oxford Music Online: Grove Music Online.* Oxford, UK: Oxford University Press, 2001. Published online 2001. https://www.oxfordmusiconline.com/search?q=motif&searchBtn=Search&isQuickSearch=true.

Duffin, Ross W. *Shakespeare's Songbook.* Foreword by Stephen Orgel. New York: W. W. Norton, 2004.

———. *Some Other Note: The Lost Songs in English Renaissance Comedy.* Foreword by Tiffany Stern. New York: Oxford University Press, 2018.

Dugaw, Dianne. "The Popular Marketing of 'Old Ballads': The Revival and Eighteenth-Century Antiquarianism Reconsidered." *Eighteenth-Century Studies* 21, no. 1 (1987): 71–90. www.doi.org/10.2307/2739027.

———. *Warrior Women and Popular Balladry, 1650–1850.* Cambridge, UK: Cambridge University Press, 1989.

Duranti, Luciana. "Archives as a Place. [Paper presented at a half-day seminar in Sydney on Oct. 19, 1995.]" *Archives and Manuscripts* 24, no. 2 (Nov. 1996): 242–55.

Early English Books Online (EEBO). ProQuest LLC. Updated June 10, 2020. proquest.com/go/eebo.

Early English Books Online-Text Creation Partnership (EEBO-TCP). https://quod.lib.umich.edu/e/eebogroup/.

Egan, Gerald, and Eric Nebeker. "Other Common Papers: Papermaking and Ballad Sheet Sizes." English Broadside Ballad Archive. 2007. ebba.english.ucsb.edu/page/papermaking. Accessed Nov. 5, 2015.

Eighteenth Century Collections Online (ECCO). Gale. www.gale.com/primary-sources/eighteenth-century-collections-online.

English Broadside Ballad Archive (EBBA). Dir. Patricia Fumerton. University of California, Santa Barbara. ebba.english.ucsb.edu.

Egan, Gerald. "Black Letter and the Broadside Ballad." ebba.english.ucsb.edu/page/black-letter. Accessed November 3, 2019.

Enterline, Lynn. "'You Speak a Language that I Understand Not': The Rhetoric of Animation in *The Winter's Tale*." *Shakespeare Quarterly* 48, no. 1 (1997): 17–44. https://doi.org/10.2307/2871399.

Felperin, Howard. "'Tongue-tied our queen?': The Deconstruction of Presence in *The Winter's Tale*." In *Shakespeare and the Question of Theory*, ed. Patricia A. Parker and Geoffrey H. Hartman, 3–18. New York: Methuen, 1985.

Fischlin, Daniel. *OuterSpeares: Shakespeare, Intermedia, and the Limits of Adaptation*. Toronto: University of Toronto Press, 2014.

Fleming, Juliet. "The Renaissance Collage: Signcutting and Signsewing." In *The Renaissance Collage: Toward a New History of Reading*, ed. Juliet Fleming, William Sherman, and Adam Smyth. Special issue of *Journal of Medieval and Early Modern Studies* 45, no. 3 (September 2015): 443–56. https://doi.org/10.1215/10829636-3149095.

Fleming, Juliet, William Sherman, and Adam Smyth, eds. *The Renaissance Collage: Toward a New History of Reading*. Special issue of *Journal of Medieval and Early Modern Studies* 45, no. 3 (Sept. 2015): 443–641.

Foreman, Terry. Blog entries ("Annotations") to "Saturday 6 January 1665/66." *The Diary of Samuel Pepys: Daily entries from the 17th century London diary*. www.pepysdiary.com/diary/1666/01/06/#annotations. Accessed Jan. 6, 2009.

Fox, Adam. "Jockey and Jenny: English Broadside Ballads and the Invention of Scottishness." In "Living English Broadside Ballads, 1550–1750: Song, Art, Dance, Culture," ed. Patricia Fumerton. Special issue of *Huntington Library Quarterly* 79, no. 2 (2016): 201–20. https://doi.org/10.1353/hlq.2016.0007.

———. *Oral and Literate Culture in England, 1500–1700*. Oxford Studies in Social History. Oxford, UK: Oxford University Press, 2000.

Fox-Davies, A. C. *A Complete Guide to Heraldry*. New York: Bonanza Books, 1985.

Franklin, Alexandra. "The Art of Illustration in Bodleian Broadside Ballads Before 1820." *Bodleian Library Record* 17, no. 5 (2002): 327–52.

———. "Making Sense of Broadside Ballad Illustrations in the Seventeenth and Eighteenth Centuries." In *Studies in Ephemera: Text and Image in Eighteenth-*

Century Print, ed. Kevin D. Murphy and Sally O'Driscoll, 169–94. Lanham, MD: Bucknell University Press, 2013.

Fraser, Nancy. "Rethinking the Public Sphere: A Contribution to the Critique of Actually Existing Democracy." In *Habermas and the Public Sphere*, ed. Craig Calhoun, 109–42. Cambridge, MA: MIT Press, 1993. Reprinted 1996.

Friedman, Albert B. *The Ballad Revival: Studies in the Influence of Popular on Sophisticated Poetry*. Chicago: University of Chicago Press, 1961.

Frye, Northrop. "Recognition in *The Winter's Tale*." In *Essays on Shakespeare and Elizabethan Drama in Honor of Hardin Craig*, ed. Richard Hosley. Columbia: University of Missouri Press, 1962.

Fumerton, Patricia, ed. *Broadside Ballads from the Pepys Collection: A Selection of Texts, Approaches, and Recordings*. Tempe: Arizona Center for Medieval and Renaissance Studies, 2012.

———. *Cultural Aesthetics: Renaissance Literature and the Practice of Social Ornament*. Chicago: University of Chicago Press, 1991. Repub. in Japanese with a new Author's Preface, trans. Shogo Ikuta, Osamu Yagawa, and Akira Inoue. Tokyo: Shohakusha Press, 1996.

———. "Digging into 'Veritable Dunghills': Re-appreciating Renaissance Broadside Ballads." In *A Companion to Renaissance Poetry*, ed. Catherine Bates, 414–31. Hoboken, NJ: Wiley-Blackwell, 2018.

———. "Digitizing Ephemera and Its Discontents: EBBA's Quest to Capture the Protean Broadside Ballad." In *Studies in Ephemera: Text and Image in Eighteenth-Century Print*, ed. Kevin D. Murphy and Sally O'Driscoll, 55–98. Lanham, MD: Bucknell University Press, 2013.

———, dir. English Broadside Ballad Archive (EBBA). University of California, Santa Barbara. ebba.english.ucsb.edu.

———. "Making Printing Publics." Introduction to *Printing Publics: A Special Issue Dedicated to the Memory of Richard Helgerson*, ed. Patricia Fumerton. Special issue of *Early Modern Culture: An Electronic Seminar* 8 (September 2010).

———. "Mocking Aristocratic Place: The Perspective of the Streets." In *Vagrant Subjects*, ed. Linda Woodbridge and Craig Dionne. Special issue of *Early Modern Culture: An Electronic Seminar* 7 (2008).

———. "Not Home: Alehouses, Ballads, and the Vagrant Husband in Early Modern England." *Journal of Medieval and Early Modern Studies* 32, no. 3 (2002): 493–518.

———. "Remembering by Dismembering: Databases, Archiving, and the Recollection of Seventeenth-Century Broadside Ballads." In *Early Modern Literary Studies* 14, no. 2, Special Issue 17 (September, 2008), https://extra.shu.ac.uk/emls/14-2/Fumerrem.html. Reprinted in *Ballads and Broadsides in Britain, 1500–1800*, ed. Patricia Fumerton and Anita Guerrini, with Kris McAbee, 13–34. Farnham, Surrey, UK: Ashgate Press, 2010.

———. *Unsettled: The Culture of Mobility and the Working Poor in Early Modern England.* Chicago: University of Chicago Press, 2006.

Fumerton, Patricia, Andrew Griffin, and Carl Stahmer, eds. *The Making of a Broadside Ballad.* Santa Barbara, CA: EMC Imprint, 2016. http://press.emcimprint.english.ucsb.edu/the-making-of-a-broadside-ballad/index.

Fumerton, Patricia, and Anita Guerrini, eds., with Kris McAbee. *Ballads and Broadsides in Britain, 1500–1800.* Farnham, Surrey, UK: Ashgate Press, 2010.

Fumerton, Patricia, and Megan E. Palmer, with William Palmer. "Lasting Impressions of the Common Woodcut." In *The Routledge Handbook of Material Culture in Early Modern Europe*, ed. Catherine Richardson, Tara Hamling, and David Gaimster, 383–99. New York: Routledge, 2017.

Gahan, Bill. "Ballad Measure in Print." English Broadside Ballad Archive. 2007. ebba.english.ucsb.edu/page/ballad-measure-in-print. Accessed March 23, 2018.

Garcia, David, and Geert Lovink. "The ABC of Tactical Media." *Nettime-l.* May 16, 1997. www.nettime.org/Lists-Archives/nettime-l-9705/msg00096.html. Accessed Aug. 14, 2015.

Gardner, Howard. *Frames of Mind: The Theory of Multiple Intelligences.* New York: Basic Books, 1983. Reprinted 2011.

Gatch, Milton McC. "John Bagford as a Collector and Disseminator of Manuscript Fragments." *The Library* s6-VII, no. 2 (June 1985): 95–114. https://doi.org/10.1093/library/s6-VII.2.95.

———. "John Bagford, Bookseller and Antiquary." *The British Library Journal* 12, no. 2 (1986): 150–71. https://www.jstor.org/stable/42554242.

Geertz, Clifford. "Deep Play: Notes on the Balinese Cockfight." In Geertz, *The Interpretation of Cultures: Selected Essays*, 412–53. New York: Basic Books, 1973.

Gerzina, Gretchen. "Britain's Black Past." *BBC 4 Radio.* www.bbc.co.uk/programmes/b07yvszg/episodes/player.

Gillespie, Stuart, and Neil Rhodes, eds. *Shakespeare and Elizabethan Popular Culture.* New York: Arden Shakespeare, 2006.

Gniady, Tassie. "Do You Take This Hog-Faced Woman to Be Your Wedded Wife?" In *Ballads and Broadsides in Britain, 1500–1800*, ed. Patricia Fumerton and Anita Guerrini, with Kris McAbee, 91–108. Farnham, Surrey, UK: Ashgate Press, 2010.

Goldberg, Jonathan. *Writing Matter: From the Hands of the English Renaissance.* Stanford, CA: Stanford University Press, 1990.

Goldstein, Leba M. "The Pepys Ballads." *The Library* s5-XXI no. 4 (1966): 282–92. https://doi.org/10.1093/library/s5-XXI.4.282.

Gomez, Michael A. *Exchanging Our Country Marks: The Transformation of African Identities in the Colonial and Antebellum South.* Chapel Hill: University of North Carolina Press, 1998.

Greenblatt, Stephen. *Renaissance Self-Fashioning: From More to Shakespeare*. Chicago: University of Chicago Press, 2005.

Gregg, Melissa, and Gregory J. Seigworth. *The Affect Theory Reader*. Durham, NC: Duke University Press, 2010.

Griffiths, Paul. *Lost Londons: Change, Crime and Control in the Capital City, 1550–1660*. Cambridge, UK: Cambridge University Press, 2008.

———. *Youth and Authority: Formative Experiences in England, 1560–1640*. Oxford: Clarendon Press, 1996.

Gurr, Andre, and Mariko Ichikawa. *Staging in Shakespeare's Theatres*. Oxford, UK: Oxford University Press, 2000.

Habermas, Jürgen. *The Structural Transformation of the Public Sphere: An Inquiry into a Category of Bourgeois Society*, trans. Thomas Burger, with the assistance of Frederick Lawrence. Cambridge, MA: MIT Press, 1989.

Hailwood, Mark. *Alehouses and Good Fellowship in Early Modern England*. Woodbridge, Suffolk, UK: Boydell Press, 2014.

Halasz, Alexandra. *The Marketplace of Print: Pamphlets and the Public Sphere in Early Modern England*. Cambridge, UK: Cambridge University Press, 1997.

Hale, John J. K. "Autolycus as 'Festive' Presence in *The Winter's Tale*." *Shakespeare Newsletter* 46, no. 3 (1996): 73–74.

Half Humankind: Contexts and Texts of the Controversy About Women in England, 1540–1640, ed. Katherine Usher Henderson and Barbara F. McManus. Urbana: University of Illinois Press, 1985.

Hall, Kim F. *Things of Darkness: Economies of Race and Gender in Early Modern England*. Ithaca, NY: Cornell University Press, 1995.

Heal, Ambrose. *The English Writing-Masters and Their Copybooks, 1570–1800: A Biographical Dictionary & a Bibliography*. Introduction by Stanley Morison. Cambridge, UK: Cambridge University Press, 1931.

Hellinga, Lotte. "Printing." In *The Cambridge History of the Book in Britain, Volume III, 1400–1557*, ed. Lotte Hellinga and J. B. Trapp, 65–108. Cambridge, UK: Cambridge University Press, 1999.

Henderson, Cinque. "Anthem of Freedom: How Whitney Houston Remade 'The Star-Spangled Banner.'" *New Yorker*, Jan. 27, 2016. www.newyorker.com/culture/cultural-comment/anthem-of-freedom-how-whitney-houston-remade-the-star-spangled-banner. Accessed July 29, 2017.

Houlbrooke, Ralph A. *The English Family, 1450–1700*. London: Longman, 1984.

Hyde, Jenni. *Singing the News: Ballads in Mid-Tudor England*. New York: Routledge, 2018.

Iconclass: A Multilingual Classification System for Cultural Content. http://www.iconclass.org/. Accessed Aug. 10, 2010.

Interart Poetics: Essays on the Interrelations of the Arts and Media. Ed. Ulla Britta Lagerroth, Hans Lund, and Erik Hedling. Atlanta, GA: Rodopi, 1997.

Janowitz, Anne. "The Romantic Fragment." In *A Companion to Romanticism*, ed. Duncan Wu, 442–51. Oxford, UK: Blackwell Publishers, 1999. Available in Blackwell Reference Online. Sept. 16, 2015. https://onlinelibrary.wiley.com/doi/abs/10.1002/9781405165396.ch44. Accessed June 10, 2020.

Jenstad, Janelle, dir. *Map of Early Modern London (MoEML)*. Victoria: University of Victoria. http://mapoflondon.uvic.ca. Accessed Apr. 26, 2018.

"John Johnson Collection of Printed Ephemera." Bodleian Libraries, University of Oxford. http://www.bodleian.ox.ac.uk/johnson/about. Accessed Sept. 29, 2015.

Johns, Adrian. *The Nature of the Book: Print and Knowledge in the Making.* Chicago: University of Chicago Press, 1998.

Kaufmann, Miranda. *Miranda Kaufmann: Historian, Journalist, Raconteuse.* http://www.mirandakaufmann.com/. Accessed Aug. 8, 2015.

Kaula, David. "Autolycus' Trumpery." *Studies in English Literature 1500–1900* 16, no. 2 (1976): 287–303. https://doi.org/10.2307/449769.

Kearney, James. "Hospitality's Risk, Grace's Bargain: Uncertain Economies in *The Winter's Tale*." In *Shakespeare and Hospitality: Ethics, Politics, and Exchange*, ed. David B. Goldstein and Julia Reinhard Lupton, 89–111. New York: Routledge, 2016.

———. *Shipwrecked Ethics: Mixed Action and the Experience of Moral Luck.* Forthcoming.

Kiessling, Nicolas K. *The Library of Anthony Wood.* Oxford, UK: Oxford Bibliographical Society, 2002.

Kitch, Aaron. "Bastards and Broadsides in *The Winter's Tale*." *Renaissance Drama* 30 (1999/2001): 43–71. https://doi.org/10.1086/rd.30.41917355.

Kitto, John, ed. *The Encyclopedia of Biblical Literature.* 2 vols. New York: Mark Newman & Co., 1851.

Knapp, James A. "The Bastard Art: Woodcut Illustration in Sixteenth-Century England." In *Printing and Parenting in Early Modern England*, ed. Douglas A. Brooks, 151–72. Aldershot, Hampshire, UK: Ashgate, 2005.

———. "Visual and Ethical Truth in *The Winter's Tale*." *Shakespeare Quarterly* 55, no. 3 (2004): 253–78.

Knight, Jeffrey Todd. *Bound to Read: Compilations, Collections, and the Making of Renaissance Literature.* Philadelphia: University of Pennsylvania Press, 2013.

———. "Needles and Pens: Sewing in Early English Books." In *The Renaissance Collage: Toward a New History of Reading*, ed. Juliet Fleming, William Sherman, and Adam Smyth. Special issue of *Journal of Medieval and Early Modern Studies* 45, no. 3 (September 2015): 523–42. https://doi.org/10.1215/10829636-3149143.

Knowles, Richard. "Autolycus, Cloten, Caliban & Co.: 'Comic' Figures and Audience Response in Shakespeare's Last Plays." *Upstart Crow* 9 (1989): 77–95.

Lake, Peter. *How Shakespeare Put Politics on the Stage: Power and Succession in the History Plays.* New Haven, CT: Yale University Press, 2017.

Lake, Peter, and Steven Pincus. "Rethinking the Public Sphere in Early Modern England." In *The Politics of the Public Sphere in Early Modern England*, ed. Peter Lake and Steven Pincus, 1–30. Manchester, UK: Manchester University Press, 2007.

Lamb, Mary Ellen. "Ovid and *The Winter's Tale*: Conflicting Views Toward Art." In *Shakespeare and Dramatic Tradition: Essays in Honor of S. F. Johnson*. Ed. W. R. Elton and William B. Long. Newark: University of Delaware Press, 1989.

Latham, Robert, ed. *Catalogue of the Pepys Library at Magdalene College Cambridge, Vol. IV: Music, Maps, and Calligraphy*. Cambridge, UK: D. S. Brewer, 1989.

———. "The Collection: Origins and History." In *Catalogue of the Pepys Library at Magdalene College Cambridge, Vol. II: Ballads, Part ii: Indexes*, comp. Helen Weinstein. Cambridge, UK: D. S. Brewer, 1994.

———. Introduction. *Catalogue of the Pepys Library at Magdalene College Cambridge, Vol. IV: Music, Maps, and Calligraphy*, ed. Robert Latham. Cambridge, UK: D. S. Brewer, 1989.

Lerdahl, Fred, and Ray S. Jackendoff. *A Generative Theory of Tonal Music*. Cambridge, MA: MIT Press, 1983.

Lesser, Zachary. "Typographic Nostalgia: Play-Reading, Popularity, and the Meanings of Black Letter." In *The Book of the Play: Playwrights, Stationers, and Readers in Early Modern England*, ed. Marta Straznicky, 99–126. Amherst: University of Massachusetts Press, 2006.

Lester, Joel. *The Rhythms of Tonal Music*. Carbondale: Southern Illinois University Press, 1986.

Levinson, Marjorie. *The Romantic Fragment Poem: A Critique of a Form*. Chapel Hill: University of North Carolina Press, 1986.

Library of Congress Training for RDA: Resource Description & Access. *FRBR: FRBR, RDA, and Marc*. Cooperative and Instructional Programs Division, Library of Congress. September 2012. tinyurl.com/oe7dro9. Accessed Aug. 13, 2015.

Lim, Walter S. H. "Knowledge and Belief in *The Winter's Tale*." *Studies in English Literature, 1500–1900* 41, no. 2 (2001): 317–34. https://doi.org/10.2307/1556191.

Lin, Erika T. *Shakespeare and the Materiality of Performance*. New York: Palgrave Macmillan, 2012.

Linebaugh, Peter, and Marcus Rediker. *The Many-Headed Hydra: Sailors, Slaves, and Commoners, and the Hidden History of the Revolutionary Atlantic*. Boston: Beacon Press, 2000.

Littleton, Charles. "The 'warming-pan baby': James Edward Francis Stuart." July 26, 2013. *The History of Parliament*. Blog. http://thehistoryofparliament.wordpress.com/2013/07/26/the-warming-pan-baby-james-edward-francis-stuart/. Accessed Feb. 21, 2016.

Love, Harold. *The Culture and Commerce of Texts: Scribal Publication in Seventeenth-Century England.* Oxford, UK: Clarendon Press of Oxford University Press, 1993. Reprint, Amherst: University of Massachusetts Press, 1998.

———. *English Clandestine Satire, 1660–1702.* Oxford, Uk: Oxford University Press, 2004.

Lovink, Geert. *Institute of Network Cultures.* 2004. http://networkcultures.org. Accessed Aug. 20, 2015.

———. "Tactical Media, the Second Decade." Preface to *Brazilian Submidialogia.* Oct. 19, 2005. web.archive.org/web/20171022145539/http://geertlovink.org/texts/tactical-media-the-second-decade/. Accessed Aug. 3, 2015.

Luckett, Richard. Interview with Patricia Fumerton. July 10, 2007.

———. "The Collection: Origins and History," in *Catalogue of the Pepys Library, Vol. II:ii: Ballads, Indexes*, comp. Helen Weinstein. Woodbridge, UK: D. S. Brewer, 1994.

———. "Introduction" to *Catalogue of the Pepys Library at Magdalene College Cambridge, Vol. IV: II.i. Ballads, Catalogue*, ed. John Rosamond Stevens, Sarah Tyack, and David McKitterick. Woodbridge, UK: D. S. Brewer, 1989.

Lupton, Julia Reinhard. *Afterlives of the Saints: Hagiography, Typology, and Renaissance Literature.* Stanford, CA: Stanford University Press, 1996.

———. "Judging Forgiveness: Hannah Arendt, W. H. Auden, and *The Winter's Tale.*" *New Literary History* 45, no. 4 (Autumn 2014): 641–63. https://muse.jhu.edu/article/567297. Accessed June 10, 2020.

Macko-Hardy, Katie (formerly Macko, Mary Kathryn [Katie]). "Why Is the National Anthem so Hard to Sing?" *O Say Can You See? Stories from the National Museum of American History.* Blog. May 14, 2014. Smithsonian: National Museum of American History, Kenneth E. Behring Center. http://americanhistory.si.edu/blog/2014/05/why-is-the-national-anthem-so-hard-to-sing.html. Accessed July 29, 2017.

"Margaret of Holland, Countess of Henneberg." *Wikipedia.* Updated Apr. 13, 2018. https://en.wikipedia.org/wiki/Margaret_of_Holland,_Countess_of_Henneberg.

Marsh, Christopher. "'Fortune My Foe': The Circulation of an English Super-Tune." In *Identity, Intertextuality, and Performance in Early Modern Song Culture*, ed. Dieuwke van der Poel, Louis Peter Grijp, and Wim van Anrooij, 308–30. Special issue of *Intersections: Interdisciplinary Studies in Early Modern Culture.* Amsterdam: Brill, 2016.

———. "A Woodcut and Its Wanderings in Seventeenth-Century England." In "Living English Broadside Ballads, 1550–1750: Song, Art, Dance, Culture," ed. Patricia Fumerton. Special issue of *Huntington Library Quarterly* 79, no. 2 (2016): 245–66. https://doi.org/10.1353/hlq.2016.0010.

———. *Music and Society in Early Modern England.* New York: Cambridge University Press, 2010.

Massumi, Brian. *Parables for the Virtual: Movement, Affect, Sensation.* Durham, NC: Duke University Press, 2002.

May, Steven W., and Arthur F. Marotti, eds. *Ink, Stink, Bait, Revenge, and Queen Elizabeth: A Yorkshire Yeoman's Household Book.* Ithaca, NY: Cornell University Press, 2014.

McCoy, Richard C. *Faith in Shakespeare.* Oxford, UK: Oxford University Press, 2013.

McDowell, Paula. "'The Art of Printing was Fatal': Print Commerce and the Idea of Oral Tradition in Long Eighteenth-Century Ballad Discourse." In *Ballads and Broadsides in Britain, 1500–1800*, ed. Patricia Fumerton and Anita Guerrini, with Kris McAbee, 35–56. Farnham, Surrey, UK: Ashgate Press, 2010.

McFarland, Thomas. *Romanticism and the Forms of Ruin: Wordsworth, Coleridge, and Modalities of Fragmentation.* Princeton, NJ: Princeton University Press, 1981.

McIlvenna, Una. "The Rich Merchant Man, or What the Punishment of Greed Sounded Like in Early Modern English Ballads." In "Living English Broadside Ballads, 1550–1750: Song, Art, Dance, Culture," ed. Patricia Fumerton. Special issue of *Huntington Library Quarterly* 79, no. 2 (2016): 279–99. https://doi.org/10.1353/hlq.2016.0013.

McKitterick, David. Introduction to *Catalogue of the Pepys Library at Magdalene College Cambridge, Vol. VII: Facsimile of Pepys's Catalogue, Parts i and ii*, ed. David McKitterick, Gerry Bye, Robert Latham, and the Pepys Library. Woodbridge, UK: D. S. Brewer, 1991.

———. *Old Books, New Technologies: The Representation, Conservation and Transformation of Books Since 1700.* Cambridge, UK: Cambridge University Press, 2013.

McShane, Angela (formerly McShane-Jones). "Digital Broadsides: The Upsides and the Downsides." *Journal of Media History* 23, no. 2 (2017): 281–302. https://doi.org/10.1080/13688804.2017.1307099.

———. "'Rime and Reason': The Political World of the English Broadside Ballad, 1640–1689." Ph.D. diss., Department of History, University of Warwick, 2004.

———. *Political Broadside Ballads of Seventeenth-Century England: A Critical Bibliography.* London: Pickering & Chatto, 2011.

Mentz, Steven R. "Wearing Greene: Autolycus, Robert Greene, and the Structure of Romance in *The Winter's Tale.*" *Renaissance Drama* 30 (1999–2001): 73–92. https://doi.org/10.1086/rd.30.41917356.

Meyer, Jürgen. "Editing Textual Synergies: New Historicism and 'New Textualism.'" *Poetics Today* 35, no. 4 (2014): 591–613.

Molineux, Catherine. *Faces of Perfect Ebony: Encountering Atlantic Slavery in Imperial Britain.* Cambridge, MA: Harvard University Press, 2012.

Morison, Stanley. "The Development of Hand-Writing: An Outline." In *The English Writing-Masters and their Copybooks, 1570–1800: A Biographical Dictionary & a Bibliography*, by Ambrose Heal. Cambridge, UK: Cambridge University Press, 1931.

———. "Introduction of Handwriting." In *The English Writing-Masters and their Copybooks, 1570–1800: A Biographical Dictionary & a Bibliography*, by Ambrose Heal. Cambridge, UK: Cambridge University Press, 1931.

Morison, Stanley, with the assistance of Harry Graham Carter. *John Fell, The University Press and the "Fell" Types. . . .* Oxford, UK: Clarendon Press, 1967.

Mullaney, Steven. *The Reformation of Emotions in the Age of Shakespeare*. Chicago: University of Chicago Press, 2015.

Murphy, Kevin D., and Sally O'Driscoll, eds. *Studies in Ephemera: Text and Image in Eighteenth-Century Print*. Lanham, MD: Bucknell University Press, 2013.

Nebeker, Eric. "Ballad Sheet Sizes." http://ebba.english.ucsb.edu/page/sheet-sizes. Accessed Feb. 16, 2019.

———. "The Broadside Ballad and English Literary History, 1540–1700." Ph.D. diss., University of California, Santa Barbara, 2009.

———. "Broadside Ballads, Miscellanies, and the Lyric in Print." *ELH* 76, no. 4 (2009): 989–1013.

Newcomb, Lori. "'If that which is lost be not found': Monumental Bodies, Spectacular Bodies in *The Winter's Tale*." In *Ovid and the Renaissance Body*, ed. Goran Stanivukovic, 239–59. Toronto: University of Toronto Press, 2001.

Newman, Steve. *Ballad Collection, Lyric, and the Canon: The Call of the Popular from the Restoration to the New Criticism*. Philadelphia: University of Pennsylvania Press, 2007.

Newman, Susan Aileen. "The Broadside Ballads of Martin Parker: A Bibliographical and Critical Study." Ph.D. diss., University of Birmingham, 1976.

O'Callaghan, Michelle. "Textual Gatherings: Print, Community and Verse Miscellanies in Early Modern England." In *Printing Publics: A Special Issue Dedicated to the Memory of Richard Helgerson*, ed. Patricia Fumerton. Special issue of *Early Modern Culture: An Electronic Seminar* 8 (September 2010).

O'Connor, Timothy, and Hong Yu Wong. "Emergent Properties." *Stanford Encyclopedia of Philosophy*. Sept. 24, 2002. Substantive revision June 3, 2015. plato.stanford .edu/archives/sum2015/entries/properties-emergent/. Accessed Aug. 22, 2015.

OED. Abbreviation for *Oxford English Dictionary: The definitive record of the English language*. https://www.oed.com/.

Olusoga, David. *Black and British: A Forgotten History*. London: Macmillan, 2016.

O'Neill, Edward. "FRBR: Application of the Entity-Relationship Model to Humphry Clinker." Transcribed by Judith Hopkins. ALCTS/CCS/Cataloging and Classification Research Discussion Group. June 15, 2002, Atlanta, GA. http://www .acsu.buffalo.edu/~ulcjh/FRBRoneill.html. Accessed June 10, 2020.

Ong, Walter J. *Orality and Literacy: The Technologizing of the Word*. London: Methuen, 1982.

Ordish, Thomas Fairman. *Early London Theatres: In the Fields*. London: E. Stock, 1894.

Oxford English Dictionary: The definitive record of the English language (*OED*). https://www.oed.com/.

Palmer, Megan E., and Charlotte Becker. *Ballad Illustration Archive Costume Book.* 2014. English Broadside Ballad Archive. ebba.english.ucsb.edu/content/EBBA_Costume_Book.pdf.

———. "Cutting Through the Wormhole: Early Modern Time, Craft, & Media." In *The Making of a Broadside Ballad*, ed. Patricia Fumerton, Andrew Griffin, and Carl Stahmer. Santa Barbara, CA: EMC Imprint, 2016. press.emcimprint.english.ucsb.edu/the-making-of-a-broadside-ballad/cutting-through-the-wormhole-early-modern-time-craft-amp-media-1.

———. "Picturing Song Across Species: Broadside Ballads in Image and Word." In "Living English Broadside Ballads, 1550–1750: Song, Art, Dance, Culture," ed. Patricia Fumerton. Special issue of *Huntington Library Quarterly* 79, no. 2 (2016): 221–44. https://doi.org/10.1353/hlq.2016.0009.

Plomer, H. R. "The Eliot's Court Printing House, 1584–1674." *The Library*, s4-II, no. 3 (1921): 175–84. https://doi.org/10.1093/library/s4-II.3.175.

Pollard, Alfred W. "The Transference of Woodcuts in the Fifteenth and Sixteenth Centuries." In *Bibliographica*, ed. Alfred W. Pollard. Vol. 2. London: K. Paul, Trench, Trübner and Co., 1896.

Pories, Kathleen. "The Intersection of Poor Laws and Literature in the Sixteenth Century: Fictional and Factual Categories." In *Framing Elizabethan Fictions: Contemporary Approaches to Early Modern Narrative Prose*, ed. Constance C. Relihan. Kent, OH: Kent State University Press, 1996.

Poulton, Diana. "The Black-Letter Broadside Ballad and Its Music." *Early Music* 9, no. 4 (Oct. 1981): 427–37. https://doi.org/10.1093/earlyj/9.4.427.

Powers, Harold S. "Dorian." *Oxford Music Online: Grove Music Online.* Oxford, UK: Oxford University Press, 2001. Published online 2001. https://doi.org/10.1093/gmo/9781561592630.article.08032.

Powers, Harold S., and Frans Wiering. "Mixolydian." *Oxford Music Online: Grove Music Online.* Oxford, UK: Oxford University Press, 2001. Published online 2001. https://doi.org/10.1093/gmo/9781561592630.article.18807. Accessed Oct. 12, 2015.

The Princeton Encyclopedia of Poetry and Poetics, ed. Alex Preminger, Frank J. Warnke, and O. B. Hardison Jr. Princeton, NJ: Princeton University Press, 1974.

"Provenance of the Huntington Collections." English Broadside Ballad Archive. ebba.english.ucsb.edu/page/provenance2.

Quitslund, Beth. "Singing the Psalms for Fun and Profit." In *Private and Domestic Devotion in Early Modern Britain*, ed. Jessica Martin and Alec Ryrie, 237–58. Farnham, Surrey, UK: Ashgate, 2012.

Rajewsky, Irina O. "Intermediality, Intertextuality, and Remediation: A Literary Perspective on Intermediality." *Intermédialités* 6 (2005): 43–64. https://www

.erudit.org/fr/revues/im/2005-n6-im1814727/1005505ar.pdf. Accessed June 10, 2020.

Raley, Rita. *Tactical Media.* Minneapolis: University of Minnesota Press, 2009.

Rhodes, Neil, and Jonathan Sawday, eds. *The Renaissance Computer: Knowledge Technology in the First Age of Print.* New York: Routledge, 2000.

Rollins, Hyder E. *An Analytical Index to the Ballad-Entries (1557–1709) in the Registers of the Company of Stationers of London.* Chapel Hill: University of North Carolina Press, 1924. Reprint, Hatboro, PA: Tradition Press, 1967.

———. "The Black-Letter Broadside Ballad." *PMLA* 34, no. 2 (1919): 258–339. https://www.doi.org/10.2307/457063.

———. "Martin Parker, Ballad-Monger." *Modern Philology* 16, no. 9 (1919): 449–74.

———. *The Pepys Ballads.* 8 vols. Cambridge, MA: Harvard University Press, 1929–32.

Royster, Francesca T. "White-Limed Walls: Whiteness and Gothic Extremism in Shakespeare's *Titus Andronicus.*" *Shakespeare Quarterly* 51, no. 4 (2000): 432–55. https://doi.org/10.2307/2902338.

Rushton, Julian. "Hemiola." *Oxford Music Online: Grove Music Online.* Oxford, UK: Oxford University Press, 2001. Published online 2001. https://doi.org/10.1093/gmo/9781561592630.article.12768. Accessed Oct. 19, 2015.

Sharpe, J. A. *Crime in Early Modern England, 1550–1750.* 2nd ed. London: Longman, 1999.

Shepard, Leslie. *The Broadside Ballad: A Study in Origins and Meaning.* London: Herbert Jenkins, 1962. Reprint, Hatboro, PA: Legacy Books, 1978.

Sherman, William, and Heather Wolfe. "The Department of Hybrid Books: Thomas Milles Between Manuscript and Print." In *The Renaissance Collage: Toward a New History of Reading,* ed. Juliet Fleming, William Sherman, and Adam Smyth. Special issue of *Journal of Medieval and Early Modern Studies* 45, no. 3 (September 2015): 457–85. https://doi.org/10.1215/10829636-3149107.

Sidgwick, F. Introduction to *Bibliotheca Pepysiana: A Descriptive Catalogue of the Library of Samuel Pepys,* ed. F. Sidgwick. London: Sidgwick & Jackson, Ltd., 1914.

Simmons, R. C. "ABCs, Almanacs, Ballads, Chapbooks, Popular Piety and Textbooks." In *The Cambridge History of the Book in Britain, Volume IV: 1557–1695,* ed. John Barnard and D. F. McKenzie, 504–13. Cambridge, UK: Cambridge University Press, 2002.

Simpson, Claude M. *The British Broadside Ballad and Its Music.* New Brunswick, NJ: Rutgers University Press, 1966.

Sisneros, Katie. "Early Modern Memes: The Reuse and Recycling of Woodcuts in 17th-Century English Popular Print." *The Public Domain Review.* June 7, 2018. https://publicdomainreview.org/2018/06/06/early-modern-memes-the-reuse-and-recycling-of-woodcuts-in-17th-century-english-popular-print/. Accessed June 9, 2018.

Skeaping, Lucie. *Broadside Ballads: Songs from the Streets, Taverns, Theatres, and Countryside of 17th-Century England.* London: Faber Music, 2005.

Smith, Bruce R. *The Acoustic World of Early Modern England: Attending to the O-Factor.* Chicago: University of Chicago Press, 1999.

———. *Phenomenal Shakespeare.* Chichester, UK: Wiley-Blackwell, 2010.

———. "Putting the 'Ball' Back in Ballads." In "Living English Broadside Ballads, 1550–1750: Song, Art, Dance, Culture," ed. Patricia Fumerton. Special issue of *Huntington Library Quarterly* 79, no. 2 (2016): 323–38. https://doi.org/10.1353/hlq.2016.0017.

———. *Shakespeare|Cut: Rethinking Cutwork in an Age of Distraction.* Oxford, UK: Oxford University Press, 2016.

———. "Shakespeare's Residuals: The Circulation of Ballads in Cultural Memory." In *Shakespeare and Elizabethan Popular Culture*, ed. Stuart Gillespie and Neil Rhodes, 193–218. London: Bloomsbury Methuen Drama, 2006.

Smith, Matthew J., and Julia Lupton. "Ballads+: The Tragedy of *Romeo and Juliet* and Its After-Piece Jig." In *Ballads and Performance: The Multi-Modality Theatricality of the Early Modern Stage*, ed. Patricia Fumerton. Santa Barbara, CA: EMC Imprint, 2018. http://scalar.usc.edu/works/ballads-and-performance-the-multi-modal-stage-in-early-modern-england/ballads-staging-the-jig-inromeo-and-juliet----julia-reinhardt-lupton-and-matthew-smith.

Smyth, Adam. "Little Clippings: Cutting and Pasting Bibles in the 1630s." In *The Renaissance Collage: Toward a New History of Reading*, ed. Juliet Fleming, William Sherman, and Adam Smyth. Special issue of *Journal of Medieval and Early Modern Studies* 45, no. 3 (September 2015): 595–613. https://doi.org/10.1215/10829636-3149191.

Spufford, Margaret. *Small Books and Pleasant Histories: Popular Fiction and Its Readership in Seventeenth-Century England.* Cambridge, UK: University of Cambridge Press, 1981.

St. Clair, William. *The Reading Nation in the Romantic Period.* Cambridge, UK: Cambridge University Press, 2004.

Stahmer, Carl. "Digital Analytical Bibliography: Ballad Sheet Forensics, Preservation, and the Digital Archive." In "Living English Broadside Ballads, 1550–1750: Song, Art, Dance, Culture," ed. Patricia Fumerton. Special issue of *Huntington Library Quarterly* 79, no. 2 (2016): 263–78. https://doi.org/10.1353/hlq.2016.0011.

Stallybrass, Peter. "'Little Jobs': Broadsides and the Printing Revolution.'" In *Agent of Change: Print Culture Studies after Elizabeth L. Eisenstein*, ed. Sabrina Alcorn Baron, Eric N. Lindquist, and Eleanor F. Shevlin, 315–41. Amherst: University of Massachusetts Press, 2007.

Steggle, Matthew. "'Knowledge will be multiplied': Digital Literary Studies and Early Modern Literature." In *A Companion to Digital Literary Studies*, ed. Susan

Schreibman and Ray Siemens, 82–108. Malden, MA: Blackwell, 2008. tinyurl.com/v6853v2. Accessed Nov. 2, 2008.

Stone, Lawrence. *The Family, Sex and Marriage in England, 1500–1800.* New York: Harper & Row, 1977.

Straus, Joseph N. *Elements of Music.* 3rd ed. Boston: Pearson, 2012.

Strong, Roy C. *Gloriana: The Portraits of Queen Elizabeth I.* New York: Thames and Hudson, 1987.

Symonds, Deborah A. *Weep Not for Me: Women, Ballads, and Infanticide in Early Modern Scotland.* University Park: Pennsylvania State University Press, 1997.

Theimer, Kate. "Archives in Context and as Context." *Journal of Digital Humanities* 1, no. 2 (2012). journalofdigitalhumanities.org/1-2/archives-in-context-and-as-context-by-kate-theimer/. Accessed Aug. 29, 2015.

Thompson, Robert. "Playford, John. (1622/3–1686/7)." *Oxford Dictionary of National Biography.* Oxford, UK: Oxford University Press, 2004. Published online Sept. 23, 2004; updated Jan. 3, 2008. https://doi.org/10.1093/ref:odnb/22374.

Thomson, Peter. "The Comic Actor and Shakespeare." In *The Cambridge Companion to Shakespeare on Stage*, ed. Stanley Wells and Sarah Stanton, 137–54. Cambridge, UK: Cambridge University Press, 2002.

Thomson, Robert S. "The Development of the Broadside Ballad Trade and Its Influence upon the Transmission of English Folksongs," Ph.D. diss., University of Cambridge, 1974.

Tillett, Barbara. "What Is FRBR? A Conceptual Model for the Bibliographic Universe." *Australian Library Journal* 54, no. 1 (2005): 24–30. https://doi.org/10.1080/00049670.2005.10721710. Published online, Library of Congress Cataloging Distribution Service. www.loc.gov/cds/downloads/FRBR.PDF. Accessed Aug. 12, 2015.

Tomalin, Claire. *Samuel Pepys: The Unequalled Self.* New York: Alfred A. Knopf, 2002. Reprint, Vintage Books, 2003.

Treason Act 1351. 1351, Chapter 2, 25 Edw. 3 Stat. 5. Legislation.gov.uk: The Official Home of UK Legislation, 1267–Present. Delivered by The National Archives. www.legislation.gov.uk/aep/Edw3Stat5/25/2/contents. Accessed April 1, 2016.

Tribble, Evelyn B. *Cognition in the Globe: Attention and Memory in Shakespeare's Theatre.* New York: Palgrave Macmillan, 2011.

Trudell, Scott A. *Unwritten Poetry: Song, Performance, and Media in Early Modern England.* Oxford, UK: Oxford University Press, 2019.

Tuer, Andrew White. *History of the Horn-Book.* 2 vols. New York: Charles Scribner's Sons, 1896. Reprinted in 1 vol., New York: Arno Press, 1979.

Updike, Daniel Berkeley. *Printing Types: Their History, Forms, and Use. A Study in Survivals.* 2 vols. London: Oxford University Press, 1962.

Van Es, Bart. *Shakespeare in Company*. Oxford, UK: Oxford University Press, 2013.

Varholy, Cristine M. "'But She Woulde Not Consent': Women's Narratives of Sexual Assault and Compulsion in Early Modern London." In *Violence, Politics, and Gender in Early Modern England*, ed. Joseph P. Ward, 41–66. New York: Palgrave Macmillan, 2008.

Vos, Eric. "The Eternal Network: Mail Art, Intermedia Semiotics, Interarts Studies." In *Interart Poetics: Essays on the Interrelations of the Arts and Media*, ed. Ulla Britta Lagerroth, Hans Lund, and Erik Hedling. Atlanta, GA: Rodopi, 1997.

Walker, Garthine. *Crime, Gender, and Social Order in Early Modern England.* New York: Cambridge University Press, 2003.

Walvin, James. *Black and White: The Negro and English Society, 1555–1945.* London: Allen Lane, Penguin Press, 1973.

Ward, John. "Music for 'A Handefull of pleasant delites.'" *Journal of the American Musicological Society* 10, no. 3 (1957): 151–80.

Warner, Michael. *Publics and Counterpublics.* New York: Zone Books, 2002.

Watt, Tessa. *Cheap Print and Popular Piety, 1550–1640.* Cambridge, UK: Cambridge University Press, 1991.

Wells, Marion. "Mistress Taleporter and the Triumph of Time: Slander and Old Wives' Tales in *The Winter's Tale.*" In *Shakespeare and the Low Countries*, ed. Douglas A. Brooks. *Shakespeare Yearbook* (Book 15), pp. 247–59. Lewiston, NY: Edwin Mellen Press, 2005.

Williams, Sarah F. *Damnable Practises: Witches, Dangerous Women, and Music in Seventeenth-Century English Broadside Ballads.* Farnham, Surrey, UK: Ashgate, 2015.

Wiltenburg, Joy. "Ballads and the Emotional Life of Crime." In *Ballads and Broadsides in Britain, 1500–1800*, ed. Patricia Fumerton and Anita Guerrini, with Kris McAbee, 173–88. Farnham, Surrey, UK: Ashgate, 2010.

———. *Disorderly Women and Female Power in the Street Literature of Early Modern England and Germany.* Charlottesville: University Press of Virginia, 1992.

Witmore, Michael. "Text: A Massively Addressable Object." *Wine Dark Sea: Literary and Cultural History at the Level of the Sentence.* Dec. 31, 2010. http://winedarksea.org/?p=926. Accessed Sept. 13, 2015.

Wittek, Stephen. *The Media Players: Shakespeare, Middleton, Jonson, and the Idea of News.* Ann Arbor: University of Michigan Press, 2015.

Woodbridge, Linda. "Patchwork: Piecing the Early Modern Mind in England's First Century of Print Culture." *English Literary Renaissance* 23, no. 1 (Dec. 1993): 5–45. https://doi.org/10.1111/j.1475-6757.1993.tb01050.x.

———. *Vagrancy, Homelessness, and English Renaissance Literature.* Urbana: University of Illinois Press, 2001.

Würzbach, Natascha. *The Rise of the English Street Ballad, 1550–1650.* Trans. Gayna Walls. Cambridge, UK: Cambridge University Press, 1990.

Yachnin, Paul, dir. Making Publics, 1500–1700: Media, Markets, and Association in Early Modern Europe (MaPs). McGill University. 2005–2010. http://project.makingpublics.org (site discontinued). Accessed Aug. 23, 2015.

———. "What Is a Public?" Making Publics, 1500–1700: Media, Markets, and Association in Early Modern Europe (MaPs). http://project.makingpublics.org/research/what-do-you-mean/ (site discontinued). Accessed Aug. 23, 2015.

Zumthor, Paul. "Intertextualité et mouvance." *Littérature* 41 (1981): 8–16.

———. *Toward a Medieval Poetics.* Trans. Philip Bennett. Minneapolis: University of Minnesota Press, 1992.

Sources for Music Notations

NOTE: All notational transcriptions of recordings with text overlay are created by Erik Bell. They observe traditional vocal notation rules and favor rhythmic changes (over Simpson's or Playford's abstracted notations), in order to show how singers adjusted tunes to specific texts, and vice versa. The English Broadside Ballad Archive (EBBA), ebba.english.ucsb.edu, fully catalogs and provides audio recordings as well as multiple image facsimiles of all EBBA ballads cited below. Search by the EBBA number provided. For other ballad texts and for all original tunes, source information is provided.

1. Page 30. "Drive the Cold Winter Away," in minor, from John Playford, *The Dancing Master*, 1651, p. 39, British Library.
2. Page 31. Modern transcription of recording of stanza 1, lines 1–4 of "Oh faine would I marry," EBBA 36094; sung to the tune "Drive the Cold Winter Away," in minor, by Erik Bell.
3. Page 86. Modernization of "Northern Nancy," in major, from John Playford, *The Dancing Master*, 1670, p. 146, British Library.
4. Page 89 Modern transcription of recording of stanza 2, lines 5–8, of first "Mock-Beggar Hall" ballad, EBBA 30174; sung to "Northern Nancy," in major, by Erik Bell.
5. Page 93. Modernization of "Damask Rose" (alternatively titled "Omnia Vincit Amor"), in the Skene MS, notated in Dorian, National Library of Scotland; source for John Playford's *The Dancing Master*, 4th–6th editions, 1660–79.
6. Page 93. Modern transcription of recording of stanza 2, lines 5–8, of first "Mock-Beggar Hall" ballad, EBBA 30174; sung to "Damask Rose," in Dorian, by Erik Bell.
7. Page 111. Modern transcription of "Dulcina," 1615, in Ionian (equivalent to modern major), MS 24665, fol. 35v, British Library.
8. Page 120. Modern transcription of tune "That's the Mother beguiles the Daughter" (later retitled "The Country Lass"), in major. Notation from a cittern set in

John Playford, *A booke of New Lessons*, 1652, no. 15, p. 7, Glasgow Library. Initial notes have been added to the first and last phrases to accommodate iambic meter.

9. Page 122. Modern transcription of recording of refrain (lines 9–12) of stanza 1 of the ballad "The Country Lass," EBBA 20124; sung to "That's the Mother beguiles the Daughter" (later retitled "The Country Lass"), in major, by Rachel Short.
10. Page 132. "Northern Nancy" in minor, John Playford, *The Dancing Master*, 1686, 7th edition, p. 146 British Library.
11. Page 133. Modern transcription of recording of stanza 2, lines 5–8, of first "Mock-Beggar Hall" ballad, EBBA 30174; sung to "Northern Nancy," in minor, by Erik Bell.
12. Page 136. Modern transcription of recording of penultimate stanza, lines 5–8, of "Love's Solace," c. 1632, EBBA 30139; sung in minor, by Helena Harlow.
13. Page 237 Modern transcription of "The Blacksmith," in Dorian, Drexel MS 4257, "entitled 'Of all the sciences under the sunn'"; from John Gamble MSS, "His booke, amen 1659," in Jorgens, *English Song, 1600–1675*, vol. 10, 121.
14. Page 239. Modern transcription of the recording of stanza one of "The Re-Resurrection of the Rump," 1659, EBBA 32128; sung to the tune "Which no body (or nobody) can deny" (retitling of "The Blacksmith"), in Dorian, by Erik Bell.
15. Page 245. Modern transcription of "Shackley Hay," from the commonplace book of the Shann family of Methley, County York, mainly in the hand of Richard Shann (1561–1627), Add MS 38599, fol. 140v, British Library.
16. Page 246. Modern transcription of recording of Charles Sackville, "To All You Ladies Now at Land," stanza 2; sung to the tune "Shackley Hay," in major, by Erik Bell.
17. Page 253. Modern transcription of music notation as it appears printed on broadside ballad, "[An Heroical Song] On the Worthy and Valiant Exploits of our Noble Lord General George Duke of Albemarle, etc. Both by Land and Sea. Made in *August*, 1666. *To the tune of St. George*" EBBBA 36420. In major, Luttrell Ballads, 1.101, British Library. Facsimile provided in Figure 37.
18. Page 254. Modern transcription of solo recording of "[An Heroical Song] On . . . our Noble Lord General George Duke of Albemarle, etc. . . ." EBBA, 26520. Luttrell Ballads, 1.101, British Library; sung to the tune "St. George," in major, by Erik Bell.
19. Page 278. Modern transcription of "In Peascod Time," later named "The Lady's [or Ladies] Fall." In Drexel MS 5612, 18, written for virginal, New York Public Library; transcription from Margaret Glyn, *Orlando Gibbons*,

1583–1626, vol. 2, p. 20, no. 11. Top staff melody; bottom staff harmony. In C major and 3/4 meter.

20. Page 280. Modern transcription of recording of second stanza of "The Lady and the Blackamoor" ballad, EBBA 31955, to the tune of "The Ladies Fall" (standard title "In Peascod Time"). In adjusting tune to his unique voice and the demands of the text, the singer chose to record it in G major and 6/4 meter.
21. Page 308. "The Lady Isabella's Tragedy," EBBA 31937, stanzas 1, 7, and 13; sung to "The Ladies [or Lady's] Fall" (standard tune title "In Peascod Time"), in major, by Erik Bell.
22. Page 362. Modern transcription of tune "Rogero," in major; from MS Dd.4.23, fol. 23v, Cambridge University.
23. Page 371. Modern transcription of recording of the "Resurrection" ballad, EBBA 30184; sung to the tune "Rogero," in major, by Erik Bell.
24. Page 373. Modern transcription of recording of the "Resurrection" ballad, EBBA 30184; sung to the tune "Rogero," in major, by Helena Harlow.

Index

Page numbers in italics refer to diagrams, figures, and musical notations. Ballad titles are abbreviated and modernized as indicated in the text.

Acknowledgments

A cornucopia of people deserve thanks for their support and often—most helpful when one gets lost in the weeds of a monster project—for gently knocking good sense into me and steering me back onto the right path as I worked on this book.

First and foremost, I extend my gratitude to all the UCSB team members of the online English Broadside Ballad Archive (EBBA), who have grown in number to an army of some 400 persons since I founded the project in 2003. Every one of them—many of whom participated in classes I taught on English broadside ballads—has in some way helped shape my thinking about the gnarly and protean genre of the printed ballad. They have also kept me laughing even in the face of feeling sometimes overwhelmed. I owe special thanks among my EBBA team to Erik Bell (EBBA's and my book's music specialist, who was an invaluable guide in my ventures into "the last frontier" of cultural studies—music), Katie Adkison (not only one of the smartest but nicest persons I've worked with), Caroline Bennet, Kristy McCants Forbes (who, in addition to her many shrewd insights, successfully tackled obtaining the multitude of additional images and all the permissions I needed for the book), Eric Nebeker, Megan E. Palmer (who may have memorized every woodcut in EBBA, which proved instrumental to my study of the ballad's visual media, and who also superbly edited much of my prose), Tyler Shoemaker (for his wisecracking wisdom as well as for professionally upgrading in Photoshop my awkwardly hand-drawn charts and ensuring that my many illustrations were done right), and, finally, Carl Stahmer, now at UC Davis but still a member of EBBA's team (digital guru and straight shooter of advice). Among my UCSB Early Modern Center faculty colleagues, I owe special thanks to Andrew Griffin (who soldiered through reading many drafts of the book's early sections and always provided on-the-mark commentary).

I am also indebted to UCSB librarian Jane Faulkner, who above and beyond the call of duty ensured I had microfilm and hard-copy access to materials I needed for my research. The marvelous staff members of the South

Hall Administrative Support Center (SASC) at UCSB were also crucial in making travel and technology available to me when I needed it. I thank, in particular, Brian Reynolds, the English Department's now former (alas) IT genius, deservedly promoted to higher and farther heights, but who, during my long time working on this book and EBBA, provided unfailing technology support; he was my knight in shining armor, riding to the rescue when servers failed or when I accidentally deleted documents.

I have presented parts of this book as talks at too many conferences and invited lectures to mention, but among those participants or audience members from whom I received wonderful feedback are Heidi Brayman, Fran Dolan, Andrew Gordon, Tim Hitchcock, Heather James, Christopher Marsh (who also generously critiqued two long chapters), Una McIlvenna, Leanna McLaughlin, Catherine Molineux, Bruce Smith, Richard Strier (whose comments took the form of mostly resistant but still useful queries, in a University of Chicago graduate seminar on my blackamoor chapter), and Susan Wiseman.

Those involved in the Making Publics project at McGill University (2005–10) are also too many to thank individually, though I must single out the director of the project, Paul Yachnin, and his then assistant, Marlene Eberhart. I have also benefited from the perceptiveness of the many scholars I encountered in various in-residence fellowships I have been fortunate to be awarded: fellows at the Huntington Library (especially Bill Brown, the late Chris Brooks, Mark Hailwood, Cynthia Nazarian, and Peter Stallybrass); the Huntington curators Mary Robertson and Steve Tabor; and the library's research director, Steve Hindle; the curators at the Houghton Library, Harvard University (especially the then print specialist there, Caroline Duroselle-Melish, now at the Folger); fellow in-residence scholars at the Australian National University, Canberra—who prompted profitable side excursions to the University of Sydney and to Perth; those at the University of Canterbury, New Zealand, during my brief residency there, especially musicologist Francis Yapp, who graciously read and provided insightful feedback on key music chapters; and the fellow seminarians at The Robert Penn Warren Center for the Humanities at Vanderbilt University (where I most benefited from the master of ephemera as well as generally smart and good person Kevin Murphy). Vanderbilt emerita Leah Marcus, long-time friend and colleague, had not only the grace but also the stamina to read the entire manuscript in one of its last re-creations and, as always, offered unfalteringly sharp commentary.

Many thanks as well to Jerry Singerman, Senior Editor at the University of Pennsylvania Press, for having the gumption to take on such a large multimedia project, and to his wonderful staff in production and editing, especially managing editor Noreen O'Connor-Abel, who has always been sharp, reasonable, and quick to answer any question. Also, I am most grateful to the anonymous, extraordinarily shrewd readers of the original manuscript I submitted to the press.

Absolutely critical to my digital archive and this book has been the National Endowment for the Humanities (NEH), which has sustained EBBA through to-date eight grants and my book through two, and, in particular, to the NEH's extraordinarily supportive team of project managers. How might I (academically) have completed my research without you? I have been additional funded by many a UCSB Faculty Research Senate Grant and the unfailing financial and intellectual backing of my university's upper administration.

Finally, and not incidentally, is the enormous gratitude I owe for the life support provided by my workaholic, brilliant, funny, and thoughtful husband, Alan Liu, who sees where no man or woman has gone before, and by my daughter, Lian Fumerton-Liu, cause of much distraction from my work, but without whom this book has no meaning. To her it is dedicated.